WE KEEP THE DEAD CLOSE

WE KEEP THE DEAD CLOSE

A MURDER AT HARVARD AND
A HALF CENTURY OF SILENCE

BECKY COOPER

GRAND CENTRAL
PUBLISHING

NEW YORK   BOSTON

Grand Central Publishing
Hachette Book Group
1290 Avenue of the Americas, New York, NY 10104
grandcentralpublishing.com
twitter.com/grandcentralpub

First Edition: November 2020

Grand Central Publishing is a division of Hachette Book Group, Inc. The Grand Central Publishing name and logo is a trademark of Hachette Book Group, Inc.

The publisher is not responsible for websites (or their content) that are not owned by the publisher.

The Hachette Speakers Bureau provides a wide range of authors for speaking events. To find out more, go to www.hachettespeakersbureau.com or call (866) 376-6591.

Print book interior design by Abby Reilly.

Library of Congress Cataloging-in-Publication Data has been applied for.

ISBNs: 978-1-5387-4683-7 (hardcover), 978-1-5387-4684-4 (ebook)

Printed in the United States of America

LSC-C

10 9 8 7 6 5 4 3 2 1

For my parents

CONTENTS

For we live in several worlds, each truer than the one it encloses, and itself false in relation to the one which encompasses it. [. . .] Truth lies in a progressive dilating of the meaning [. . .] up to the point at which it explodes.

—Claude Lévi-Strauss, *Tristes Tropiques*

The primary characteristic of the deepest reaches of the past, especially for the sort of observer whose paramount concerns are those of the present, is the accommodating silence found there. The quieter an epoch on its own terms, the more loudly it can be made to speak, in the way of a ventriloquist's dummy, for ours.

—Gideon Lewis-Kraus, "Is Ancient DNA Research Revealing New Truths— or Falling into Old Traps," *New York Times Magazine*

Part One

THE STORY

MORNING OF GENERALS

IT WAS THE WARMEST IT had been in more than a week, but Bostonians turning on their morning radio broadcast woke up to gale warnings along the coast. In Cambridge, across the Charles River, the day was equally grim. A wintry mix of fog and rain and snow hung over the city, and the streets of Harvard Square were quiet.

A delivery person piled stacks of that day's *Harvard Crimson* inside the undergraduate houses. The front page was a black-and-white picture of a girl curled up in fetal position on the floor of one of the campus libraries. Her head was propped on a book. Her feet were bare. She had on jeans and a sweater and looked more like a body than a person. The caption read, "There was the girl who fell asleep on her book and dreamed, and there was the boy who dreamed of the girl asleep on her book, and...Don't let the times get you down."

January 7, 1969, was the second day of reading period. For most students, with eleven anxious, prolonged days to study before finals, those first mornings were for sleeping. But for a subset of the anthropology doctoral students, that morning was the most nerve-racking one all year.

By 9 a.m., they were packed into a lecture hall at the top of the Peabody Museum. The five-story red-brick building with its grand European-style black doors served as home base for the university's Anthropology department. Founded in 1866, the museum's history as an institution, its docents proudly remind visitors, *is* the history of American anthropology.

The students were there to take the first of three parts of their general exams. They had been studying for months, and the stakes were high. If they failed, they risked getting moved off the PhD track into a "terminal" master's, a gloved way of saying "kicked out."

The museum sometimes smelled like the mummies casually stored on its fourth floor: spicy and musty, though not altogether revolting. But that winter morning, all the smells had stilled. Now it was just elbows propped on desks, hands moving across blue books, pens filling in short-answer essays. Between the nerves and the number of students, only a few people noticed that one student had failed to show up: Jane Britton.

2018: APTHORP HOUSE

MY ROOM IS ON THE third floor of a mansion called Apthorp House, a part of Harvard's Adams House dorms. Apthorp, shaped like a wedding cake, is *jonquil*, that distinctly New England shade of daffodils and buttercream. My bedroom is a cross between a bunker and a tree house, and the ceilings are so low I regularly hit my overhead lamp when I throw my hands up excitedly. From the front door, I can see the room I lived in my sophomore year, as well as the fire escape I used to climb when I locked myself out of that room. It's the same rickety ladder a crush surprised me by scaling that fall. The same landing I sat out on and listened to sad Bob Dylan and wished I smoked when things ended a month later. Some days I catch myself forgetting that ten years have gone by.

Apthorp, everyone agrees, is haunted, and we're pretty sure the ghost is General Burgoyne, a British officer who was held captive in the house during the Revolutionary War. We have, inexplicably, a life-size cutout of him in the basement. I can't decide whether it's a joke or an educational tool—*And here you have the boots that make those clomping sounds*—but there's a touch of cruelty in his continued entrapment.

I share Apthorp with the faculty deans of Adams House who are in charge of house life—dances, the housing lottery, the annual Winnie-the-Pooh Christmas read—as well as three recent Harvard graduates. The four of us are called Elves, which means we get room and board in exchange for baking cookies for the undergraduates' monthly teas. It makes about as much sense to me as it does to you, but it's one of those quirks you get used to at Harvard. Like Norm the French translator with a cotton-candy puff of hair who graduated from Harvard in 1951 and never really left Adams House; or Father George, a fixture in the dining hall for reasons I don't quite understand, who seems to have as many degrees in the hard sciences as he has jokes. *Of course*, you quickly learn you have to say.

Elves are usually students straight out of graduation. So when Lulu, one of the other Elves, heard I was turning thirty this year, she looked at me like a messenger from the other side. "Is it true," she started in her super-earnest tone, "that when you turn thirty, all your friends leave you because they get married, and your body falls apart?" I hugged my knees, bandaged from a fall that afternoon, to my chest. "Mhmm," I nodded to Lulu.

Boston, especially Harvard Square, is a transient place, remade every fall when a new wave of people washes through. The heavy brick of the buildings only emphasizes the impermanence of everything here but the institution itself. When I told friends in Brooklyn that I was moving back to Boston, one quipped, "Does anyone do that *voluntarily?*"

I hadn't. When the undergraduates ask, I tell them that I'm here writing a book about archaeology in the 1960s. "Anything in particular," they ask, eager to make some kind of connection. "Not really," I say. "Oh, cool," they say, meaning, *You left your job for this?*

I don't tell them what I'm working on because I'm unwilling to turn it into small talk. It's too weird, too obsessive, too personal. I don't tell them about the bulletin boards in my tree-house room with theories and photos, a map of Iran, a blueprint of an apartment building, all stuck to my cork boards with dissection needles. I don't mention my shelf topped with talismans—a sherd of milky Ramah chert; Kodachrome slides of a farm out in Bolton; a profile gauge for drawing pottery. I try to laugh off the ribbed metal baton on my key chain when it clunks on the dining-hall table. I definitely don't mention that a Harvard police officer gave it to me and taught me how to wrap my fingers around it and lift it over my shoulder, ready to jam down in the soft triangle of flesh between someone's clavicle and shoulder blade, like an ice pick.

I'm here because, for the past ten years, I have been haunted by a murder that took place a few steps away. It was told to me my junior year of college like a ghost story: A young woman, a Harvard graduate student of archaeology, was bludgeoned to death in her off-campus apartment in January 1969. Her body was covered with fur blankets and the killer threw red ochre on her body, a perfect re-creation of a burial ritual. No one heard any screams; nothing was stolen. Decades passed, and her case remained unsolved.

Unsolved, that is, until yesterday.

THE FABLE

WHEN I FIRST HEARD THE story, the body was nameless. It was 2009, the spring semester of my junior year, and one of those first warm days in Cambridge that almost erased how long the winter had been. I had just turned twenty-one. My fears that Harvard would be an ugly, mean place had been buried under the awe of getting to know my fellow undergraduates. For every new classmate I met, I tried to come up with a backstory that was more interesting than the truth. I invariably lost. Isaac turned out to be a unicycle-riding astrophysicist; Sandy was a violinist for Cirque du Soleil; my roommate Svetlana was leading a tuberculosis study in Siberia. For the most part, we were all just a bunch of driven weirdos, convinced we could work hard enough to change some corner of the world.

It still occasionally felt surreal that this institution had welcomed me in. I had grown up in a tiny apartment in Jamaica, Queens, in a family where ordering a drink with dinner was considered an unnecessary indulgence. My parents loved me fiercely, but it had been a lonely journey finding my way into a world that was bigger than they could imagine.

At Harvard, I could talk about philosophical pragmatism over breakfast and spend hours picking apart David Foster Wallace with my tutorial leader. I learned, while trying not to let on that I was learning, that I was supposed to choose courses based on professors as much as on the course content; that professors who were leaders in their field were called superstars; that I should say my first and last name when introducing myself at the Hasty Pudding social club. I had almost gotten used to my teachers breezily refer-encing, by first name, the people we were reading about in the textbooks. I was on full financial aid, but no one cared about my past. Instead, I ate baked Brie and drank sherry and was courted by a boy whose family practically owned a palace in London. Everything felt abundant, and everything felt within reach. It was exhilarating and seductive. By the time I heard the story about the murdered student, I felt, for the moment, that I had left Queens far behind.

That afternoon, my friend Lily was propped on her picnic blanket, her long blond hair almost blowing into the sweet potato sandwiches we had taken to go. We were in John F. Kennedy Park, a stretch of grass near the Charles River, across the street from one of the dorms. The University Road building that would come to shape my next decade lurked, unnoticed, just a block away. Lily and I had been friends since the beginning of sophomore year, but she had the tendency to fall in love dramatically, and in those phases, I would lose her to whoever was on the other end of her breathless love letters. This was the first time I had gotten her alone since she and Morgan had started dating that winter.

Morgan Potts had already graduated, but he had quit his job and moved back to Cambridge for Lily. We had mutual friends, so I knew two things about him: that he was a great storyteller and that he was in the Porcellian Club. The PC, as everyone called it, was considered the most elite of the all-male final clubs—our version of a fraternity. I had a complicated relationship with these clubs. On the one hand, the power dynamic made me uncomfortable. They controlled the parties and the alcohol and the invitations; it was common to see hired bouncers name-check lines of girls standing outside the front doors on Friday nights. But I had to admit there was a security in knowing my name was on the list. And I had been pleasantly surprised to find that the PC guys were more eccentric than snotty. Back then, I was blind to the idea that an institution could still be destructive even if its members were good people.

Halfway into our lunch, Morgan entered the park. Lily shrugged apologetically. We scooted on our blankets, and he sat down. I understood what Lily saw in him: He had green eyes and an Australian accent and a brain that could simultaneously retain the most specific of historical facts and spit them out with a romantic spin. If he was going to interrupt our lunch, he could at least share a classic Morgan tale in exchange. I tried to bait him with a ghost story, some half-remembered lore involving an old fire truck that stood guard in Harvard Yard near the turn of the century.

"You want to hear a really crazy Harvard story?" he asked and launched into his version of a macabre legend like a well-worn fairy tale.

In the late 1960s, a beautiful young graduate student in archaeology was found murdered, bludgeoned to death. The rumor was she'd been having an affair with her professor. It started on the dig they were on together in Iran, and when they got back, she wouldn't give it up. The professor couldn't have the university find out about their affair, and he went to her apartment one night. They talked, and he struck her with an archaeological stone tool he had taken from the Peabody Museum. Neighbors heard nothing.

He picked up her body and hid her under his coat. He walked ten blocks back to his office in the Peabody Museum, and lay her on his desk. He stripped her naked and lay three necklaces that they had found together in Iran on her. He transformed her into the princess of their dig site, the one that they had uncovered months before. He sprinkled red ochre powder over her.

Police found her the next day and questioned the professor. The school forced the Crimson to change its article about the murder. They couldn't have it point to one of their own. A version ran that morning, and by that afternoon, there was no record of it. Suddenly, everything was hushed up. The press stopped writing, the family never investigated, and the police never arrested anyone.

Morgan stopped. You'd think I would have memorized his face, or Lily's, or created some trace that I could follow to how I felt at the time. But all I remember is that I heard the story, and it was sunny, and she was nameless.

"But the detail that really gets me," Morgan added, "is that when police found her body, they found cigarette butts burned into her stomach. In some sort of ritualistic pattern that also had meaning at the site. Think about it," he emphasized, "he'd have to have stayed and smoked all those cigarettes in order to do what he did. A hundred cigarettes, they said. How do you do that? How do you sit calmly and do that?"

JAMES AND IVA

FROM THE MOMENT I HEARD the story about the murder, so much about it barbed me. It wasn't because I believed it—it seemed outlandish and obviously embroidered—but because I *could* believe it. The very things that made me love Harvard—its seductiveness, its limitlessness—also made it a very convincing villain. Harvard felt omnipotent.

That omnipotence, on most days, was an amazing thing: It manifested as a sense that anything was possible. As an undergrad, I felt like I got three wishes. I had to do my own work, and find my own hidden opportunities, but there was a sense that if I dreamed it, nothing was too big an ask. There was always an expert coming through town, or a professor who was friends with your heroes, or some dream research opportunity that a friend happened to mention.

The power also manifested as benign glimpses of Harvard's ability to skirt the rules. Sure, there were drinking laws in Massachusetts, but on Thursday night "Stein Clubs" at the houses, you didn't necessarily need to be twenty-one. Harvard had its own police force with its own amnesty policy. If you were from a country for which the US had strict visa requirements, Harvard could write you a letter.

So imagining that power having a dark side—one that could silence an unflattering story, control the press, guide the police—wasn't too hard. My freshman seminar professor had warned our class that Harvard was an institution on a scale we could not imagine: "Harvard will change you by the end of your four years, but don't expect to change it." It wouldn't be surprising if an institution that prided itself on being older than the US government might have behaved as though it were accountable only to itself.

But the story lived, filed in my head, as a fable.

Until it came up again.

It was the summer of 2010, more than a year after that picnic conversation, and I was early for a guidance chat with my adviser, James Ronan.[1] James was a doctoral candidate in archaeology, and he had been my resident tutor. He often left his door open, and our chats—about his archaeological digs, or psychogeographic maps, or microbreweries—always made me feel better when Harvard got to be too much.

The meeting was in the Laboratory for Integrated Science and Engineering, a shiny building in the part of campus I never went to—a little glass-and-steel enclave between the brick of the Yard and the brick of the Peabody and the Geological Museums. It was largely for engineers and biochemists, but it had a nice café in the lobby, which was pin-drop quiet. People didn't leave their labs very much.

James saw me loitering awkwardly near the front of the café trying to kill

---

1 Pseudonym.

time and waved me over. He was in the middle of a meeting with someone I had seen around campus. I didn't know her name, but I knew her big, wavy hair and contagious laugh from the dining hall.

"Becky, Iva;[2] Iva, Becky," James said.

There were only two seats at their table, so I stood in front of them as they wrapped up their discussion, unsure whether they really wanted me to listen in. Near the end of their chat, I heard enough to piece together that they had moved on to lighthearted speculation about Indiana Jones. Legend at the school was that the character was based on Samuel Lothrop, a former Peabody Museum curator who had doubled as a spy for the US government. "It wasn't rare for archaeologists to be spies," they said, turning to include me. For decades, they explained, archaeology provided one of the most convenient covers for espionage, especially during the First and Second World Wars.

Intrigue, secrets, double identities. I couldn't help myself. For the first time since Morgan told me the story of the murdered archaeology student, I began to retell it. By the time I got to the implausible dragging of the body back to the museum—*How could no one see the body?*—I already regretted starting the tale. But I finished anyway. "And nothing happened to the professor."

They stared at me.

"I think," I backtracked. "I mean. It's just a story I heard."

Finally James said something: "It was in her apartment, not the Peabody."

"And he's still here," Iva said.

THE BODY

THE GENERAL EXAMS FINISHED JUST after noon. As the students packed their bags, a few speculated on where Jane Britton might be. Jane was known for her morbid humor and for her disappearing spells—the kind of girl to blurt out in the middle of a perfectly happy get-together, "Christ, the only reason I

---

2   Pseudonym.

get up in the morning is because I hope a truck will run over me." She seemed to enjoy getting a rise out of people. Like the other time when, after an unexplained absence, she appeared in the Peabody smoking room and announced to those present: "The rumors of my death have been greatly exaggerated." People knew she was fundamentally a good student, one of the few who had gone directly from Radcliffe, Harvard's sister school, into Harvard's PhD program. Missing Generals would have been out of the question.

Jane's boyfriend, Jim Humphries, had called her twice that morning before he left for the Peabody Museum. He was taking the exam that day, too. Jim, twenty-seven, was a few years older than Jane. Canadian and six foot seven, with sandy-blond hair, parted to the side, and horn-rimmed glasses, Jim looked more like an engineer or architect than the archaeologist he was training to be. He was a quiet person, reserved to the point of brooding, whose face wasn't expressive even at the best of times. He was known around the Peabody as The Gentleman, for doing old-fashioned, courtly things like helping girls with their coats and writing thank-you notes for dinner parties.

Jane and Jim had met in the spring of 1968, during a seminar to prepare for a summer expedition in Iran. The site was called Tepe Yahya, and the dig was led by a young Harvard professor named Clifford Charles Lamberg-Karlovsky. Graduate students called him Karl or CCLK, or, more covertly, Count Dracula, due to his rumored Eastern European aristocratic background and air of mystery. The young professor was a rising star in the department and an emerging leader in Near Eastern archaeology. The success of the '68 season only enhanced this reputation. Not long after the expedition crew returned to the States, the *Boston Globe* hailed Lamberg-Karlovsky as the discoverer of what appeared to be Alexander the Great's lost city of Carmania.

It was on this dig in southeastern Iran that Jane and Jim's relationship blossomed. "They had a chance to feel for each other's loneliness," a fellow digger would later tell reporters. Recently, Jane had talked to her friends about the possibility of marriage. She liked to joke that it would be held at the Church of the Unwarranted Assumption.

Jane hadn't answered either call, which Jim thought was odd, but he assumed she couldn't sleep and had gone over to her neighbors' place for breakfast. He had seen her the night before and, other than being nervous about the test, she had seemed fine. But when she wasn't in the exam, either, he knew something had gone wrong—she was sick or had slept in. He didn't let himself consider worse.

After turning in their tests, a group of graduate students headed for lunch, and they invited him along. Jim politely declined and went outside and across the road to call Jane one more time. He didn't want to use the telephone in the museum because he knew everyone would be listening. Again, Jane didn't answer.

Jim started the fifteen-minute walk from the museum to Jane's apartment, a four-story walk-up, a short block past the Square, on a side street that connected Mount Auburn Street to the Charles River (where John F. Kennedy Park would eventually sit). Her address—6 University Road—was one of five entrances to a red-brick-and-limestone building known as The Craigie. It took up a full square block and was commissioned by Harvard in the late 1890s to provide a less expensive housing option for students.

The suites were small, but the building was full of lovely touches—natural wood trim, a large courtyard, and corner bay windows. Over the years, however, particularly as Harvard's housing system developed and provided undergraduates with on-campus accommodations, the building had fallen into disrepair.

The surrounding area had also deteriorated. It became a kind of no-man's-land of Harvard Square, home to parking lots, a trolley yard, and an alley that led to the river. Before developers turned those lots into the upscale Charles Hotel in the '80s, the only reason to walk to that part of town was the Mount Auburn post office across the street and Cronin's, a watering hole with a small TV screen and cheap beers.

But the rents were low—Jane's was $75 a month—and the building was centrally located, so it was still real estate coveted by graduate students, particularly in the Anthropology department, where units were passed down from one generation to the next. Jane had secured her apartment thanks to her now next-door neighbors, Don and Jill Mitchell, who were students specializing in Pacific Island anthropology.

Besides, Jane wasn't bothered by the building's shabbiness. While the Mitchells always used their dead bolt, Jane almost never locked her door. She seemed to live with a sense of invulnerability.

Jim reached University Road around 12:30 p.m. He pushed in the front door and walked up the stairs, flooded by the gray winter sun from the skylight. The stairwell dead-ended at the fourth-floor landing. The hallway walls were apple green and peeling. Jim walked past the Mitchells' place. Jane's, the smallest of the three apartments on this floor, was at the end of an alcove. It was unmistakable. Blue, green, and yellow polka dots decorated the left side of her hallway, and on her front door, which she had painted gold, was a piece of typewriter paper with a quote she had found amusing. Police would later remove the paper as evidence:

"Maybe," said Mrs. Kylie, "(she's) an archaeologist because (she) didn't have a sandbox when (she) was little." September, 1968.

Jim knocked on Jane's door, even though he knew better than anyone that it would be unlocked, especially in the winter when the radiator heat made the wood swell and the lock finicky.

Don and Jill Mitchell heard the noise and thought it might be Jane coming home from her exam. Don, whose thick mustache made him look much older than his twenty-five years, walked into the hallway.

"Is Jane home?" Jim asked.

"I guess so."

"Well, she didn't take her quiz."

Don's face changed. He encouraged Jim to go in and check, so Jim knocked on Jane's door again. No answer. This time Jim reached for the handle and gave it a shove, and it opened.

"Can I come in?" Jim called out. Don waited by the door. Again no answer. Jim felt a cold gust of air coming from the kitchen and saw that the window was wide open. He was certain it hadn't been open the night before. Jim reached his head back to look into the kitchen. There was no one there except Jane's pet Angora cat, Fuzzwort. Jane sometimes left the window open because she thought there was a gas leak in her kitchen, but she'd only do that when the Mitchells were looking after her cat; the screen had long ago rotted off, and Fuzzwort liked to run out onto the fire escape.

Jane's room was its usual homey mess. Books. Ashtrays. Manuscripts. Cups and cigarette butts. A turtle tank, soupy with algae, rested on her dresser. Shards of light glittered through the wine and brandy bottles she had arranged in her windows to catch the sun—a Dionysian pane of stained glass. Ceramic owls and artifacts from Jane's travels lined the shelves. Paintings, some of which Jane had done herself, hung in their frames. The walls were white, and on the one by the kitchen, she had painted cats, giraffes, and owls, capricious and dreamy. Their eyes filled the room.

It was not until he fully walked into the apartment that he could see her. Jane's right leg hung over the side of her bed, which was a mattress on top of a simple box spring, placed directly on the floor. Her blue flannel nightgown was pulled up to her waist. He didn't try to shake her awake. He walked out of the room and asked Don to get Jill because he didn't think anything was seriously wrong, and Jane's state of undress made it seem more like "a woman's job." Jill left her apartment, walked into Jane's, and came back out almost immediately. She needed to lie on her bed. She felt sick.

Don walked in this time. He approached the bed and noticed, with a bolt of guilt, that Jane wasn't wearing underwear. Above her waist was a pile of long-haired sheepskin rugs and her fur coat. She was buried facedown underneath. He walked closer and pulled back the coat until he could see the back of her head. There was blood on the sheets. And the pillows. And on the rugs. And around her neck. He didn't turn her over. There was no question: She was dead.

IT BEGINS

I ASKED IVA AND JAMES to tell me everything they knew. They looked uncomfortable, whispering despite the fact that there wasn't really anyone there but the barista.

The professor's name was Karl Lamberg-Karlovsky, they said, and the story James had heard, like the one Morgan told me, was that this Harvard professor—tenured, and still on faculty—had an affair with his student and killed her when she wouldn't end the liaison and threatened to tell either his wife or the university, he couldn't remember which. His version also involved red ochre, but none of the cigarette butts. Red ochre, they explained, was used in many ancient burial rituals, either to preserve the dead or to honor them on their way to the afterlife. Its use seemed to limit the circle of suspects to someone with intimate knowledge of anthropology. Everyone in the department at Harvard, they said, knew the story. They had heard that another Harvard archaeology professor got too drunk at a recent faculty dinner and spilled the sordid tale to his students. In fact, they wouldn't be surprised if most people in the field of archaeology knew and whispered about that particular professor.

I couldn't understand how such a huge scandal, if any of it was true, could stay so quiet.

Iva and James explained that archaeology is a small and venal world. Everyone knows everyone's business, but the rumors stay within the walls of the discipline. To figure out this murder, they implied, I would have to understand the world of academic archaeology.

———

From my dorm room that night, I Googled everything I could about the case, starting with "red ochre Harvard," since I still hadn't learned the victim's name. While some of the more salacious aspects of Morgan's original version turned out to be exaggerations, so much of it was there: the ochre, the Iranian dig, and reports of "hostilities" on the expedition. There was even mention of a cigarette butt that figured prominently in the crime scene. Gone was the jewelry on her neck and the ritual burns, but what my research turned up was stranger still. Jane's father was the vice president of administration at Radcliffe College at the time of her death. If anyone had the power and clout to investigate, he did. But, it seemed, he never pursued it; in the articles, there was just a single mention of a grand jury hearing, and nothing about its outcome. Her death quietly faded into rumor. The lack of answers didn't make sense.

And there was Professor Lamberg-Karlovsky—the one still on faculty— at the Cambridge Police precinct house on the day her body was found. "I came here to be of whatever assistance I can be to police," he had told the *Boston Globe*. "I knew Jane both as an undergraduate student and a graduate student. She was an extraordinarily capable and talented girl [...] This doesn't seem possible, her dying. I saw her just three days ago."

And there he was again, in the *New York Times*: Professor Lamberg-Karlovsky pacing in the office of Stephen Williams, the director of the Peabody Museum and the head of the Anthropology department. "Both men have been stung by the impact of the sensational national publicity that has engulfed them," Robert Reinhold, the *Times*'s Boston correspondent, wrote.

The articles described Jane as brilliant, talented, attractive, good at many languages, great at drawing, a lover of Bach, and an accomplished horseback rider. She had grown up in Needham, Massachusetts, a quiet suburb on the outskirts of Boston, and her childhood, as one article put it, was "as American as Plymouth Rock." She was a Girl Scout, a regular worshipper at Christ Episcopal Church, and she had excelled at Dana Hall, the prestigious all-girls boarding school in Wellesley she attended before Radcliffe. She loved Kurt Vonnegut and often quoted him. "Peculiar travel suggestions are like dancing lessons from God," she would say, perhaps dreaming of digs in distant countries, though her favorite was from *The Sirens of Titan*: "I was a victim of a series of accidents, as are we all."

A darkness crept around her edges as well. Jane had a reputation for her devastating wit, and if she wasn't careful, her remarks pushed past clever to downright mean. According to Ingrid Kirsch, a friend from Radcliffe, Jane "had a kind of insight into people that was disconcerting. She could stop a conversation by coming out with a single sentence." One of Jane's favorite sayings was, "If justice be cruel and dishonesty be kind, then I prefer to be cruel."

Despite this unflinching frankness, Jane was also portrayed as a "vulnerable person." A former college friend questioned Jane's friendliness to "hangers-on and acid heads who you would not call young wholesome Harvard and Radcliffe types." There was talk of a secret abortion, and affairs with at least one professor.

If anything, Jane's defining characteristic seemed to be her ability to evade straightforward description. As her neighbor Don Mitchell told the *Times* reporter: "It is not possible to characterize her lifestyle because she changed it so often. She was never taken in by any ethos, but she went through a period of painting on her wall and then she would not do that, then it was music and she would not do that."

I recognized that mix of verve and self-doubt. That drive, that zest, and that vulnerability. I understood—or at least believed that I did—that at the center of this brilliant, vivacious woman was a loneliness and a fundamental need to find somewhere to belong that I knew all too well. I felt connected to her with a certainty more alchemical than rational.

I wanted to see her face.

None of the online versions of the articles came with any picture, so I kept searching—combinations of her name, the professor's name, the dig they went on, the name of her hometown—until finally, in one of the Iranian expedition monographs, I hit upon a black-and-white image from the 1968 season. It was a photograph of the eight-person crew that summer—plus Karl's wife, the government's antiquities representative, the cook, and a few local villagers—set against the background of the expedition Land Rover and the mountains. It read like a primer to the suspects in an Agatha Christie novel. Karl leaned against the Land Rover tall and handsome, while his wife, Martha, in a prim shift dress, positioned herself close enough that her arms brushed against his. Jim Humphries, Jane's boyfriend, stood by himself in the back row, arms crossed, a head above everyone else, while four students whose names I did not yet know—Arthur and Andrea Bankoff, Phil Kohl, and Peter Dane—scattered themselves around the vehicle. Finally, lying on the ground at everyone's feet, in a tight-fitting long-sleeved shirt with slacks and sneakers, her head propped on one elbow, her dark hair cascading down her arm, a cigarette in her other hand, was Jane. Her downward gaze was coy and irreverent, and her body zigzagged around the crew. She was six months shy of her end.

The first season of Tepe Yahya, 1968. (Fig F.6 on page XXXI, from D. T. Potts, Excavations at Tepe Yahya, Iran, 1967–1975: The Third Millennium, *American School of Prehistoric Research, Bulletin 45. © 2001 by the President and Fellows of Harvard College, courtesy of the Peabody Museum of Archaeology and Ethnology, Harvard University, by permission from Richard Meadow.)*

SECRETS

THAT NIGHT, AFTER READING ALL the articles I could find about Jane, I lay there unable to sleep. Some of what I was feeling was exhilaration. A lot of it was fear. The story, after all, appeared to have been effectively silenced; it seemed possible that Harvard had systems in place to ensure that it maintained control of the narrative. Would they kick me out of the school? Would I be disappeared by morning? Would someone come into my dorm and bash my head in? My conjectures were decreasingly tethered to reality. Still, I couldn't be sure the lengths to which Harvard might go to make sure this story stayed buried.

But most of what was keeping me up was an incredulity verging on anger. Seeing Karl's name in the articles had made the rumors about him feel plausible. If the story was true, why was no one listening or investigating? I couldn't accept the possibility that this was just an open secret I would file away and move on from. The way I saw it, either Harvard had covered up a murder and was allowing a killer to remain on faculty, or we were imprisoning an innocent man with our stories. I wondered if I could be the one to take this rumor seriously.

The impulse to solve Jane's case was a familiar one. As a child, I was obsessed with crime, with secrets, and with puzzles. One of my earliest memories is of being fixated on some graffiti underneath a piece of kindergarten playground equipment that said: JESSE JAMES WAS HERE. I became convinced that Jesse James was a fugitive who had left a net-work of clues on all the playgrounds in Queens. Every time I went to a playground, I always checked underneath the slides and under the dirty wooden slats. A wad of gum would turn into a signal to his bandit girl-friend that he had been there and was on the run, but still okay. Graffiti in the same pen but a different handwriting meant that someone was close on his tail.

In middle school, my drive to investigate fed my affinity for being an observer, and I became a watcher, a chameleon of social habits. I tried to conceal the fact that I almost always felt like an outsider by scrutinizing the way people talked, the way people ate, and then adopting the patterns of those around me.

Later, I dreamed of becoming a forensic analyst, a cryptographer, a neuroscientist with a focus on abnormal psychology—anything that let me be the one to solve mysteries. I ultimately chose writing because I felt I could, through narrative, get into the mind of my character in a way that was more real, if less scalably objective, than by scrutinizing calcium and potassium channels.

Over the years, I never lost my sense that there was more under the surface or my desire to get inside the dark. But lying there that night, I was also old enough to recognize that my belief that I could solve a murder on my own that had eluded cops for over forty years might be as naive as the thought that I could find the whereabouts of Jesse James.

THE COPS ARRIVE

DETECTIVES WILLIAM DURETTE, MICHAEL GIACOPPO, and Fred Centrella arrived not long after Don Mitchell's call to the Cambridge Police, and when they entered Jane's room, her cat skittered out from his hiding place. The detectives took stock of the scene. Valuables—money, jewelry—lay untouched, in plain sight. There were no signs of a struggle in the apartment, except for the bloodstained bed. Two of Jane's windows were open, despite the freezing Cambridge winter: one in the bedroom, which looked out on the Bennett Street parking lot; and the other in the kitchen, which led out to a fire escape and overlooked the courtyard.

Detective Lieutenant Leo Davenport, the head of the department's eighteen-man Bureau of Criminal Investigations and acting chief of the homicide division, would later publicly dismiss the significance of these open windows. The heat in the building was "oppressive," and it wasn't unusual for residents to have their windows open all winter, he told the press.

Detective Lieutenant Leo Davenport.

Davenport, a petite man whose hair looked like it was blackened with shoe polish, had been with the Cambridge Police for a dozen years. He graduated with the first class of the Cambridge Police Academy in 1947, known as the "class of brass" for how many of them advanced through the ranks. Davenport was already familiar with Jane's building because of its history of violent crime. In 1961, Jean Kessler, who had moved to the area for a job in Harvard's Music department, survived a hammer attack in her home. One report said it was her curlers that saved her. And Davenport himself had been assigned to the 1963 stabbing case of Beverly Samans, which happened just a few units over from Jane's. Albert DeSalvo, the apparent Boston Strangler, confessed to the crime, but some doubted his story. The case remains open.

Police invited Jane's parents, who had arrived shortly after the detectives and were sitting in the Mitchells' apartment, to enter Jane's room. Jane's father, J. Boyd Britton, was still in the suit and tie he had worn to work. He surveyed the room at the police's request to note if anything was missing. Nothing obvious, he concluded. Jane's mother, Ruth, approached her daughter, who was still lying on her bed.

Ruth burst into tears at the sight. "She was a good girl. I can't understand why something like this should happen to her."

Detective Giacoppo, thirty-seven, dusted the apartment for fingerprints and pulled a number for further analysis. He had long been driven by a sense of adventure and duty, lying about his age to fight in World War II. He took a few items from Jane's room as evidence and collected some samples for chemical analysis, but he planned to do the bulk of the processing and crime scene photographing the next day. He did not find a weapon.

While Giacoppo studied the crime scene, other detectives interviewed the neighbors. The building superintendent's seven-year-old daughter reported having heard strange noises on the fire escape that led to Jane's apartment from the courtyard around 9 p.m. But detectives dismissed this observation because Don said that he had entered Jane's apartment after that time to get a beer from her fridge and found nothing amiss. Another woman who lived in the building said she returned home at 12:15 a.m. and heard nothing. Stephen and Carol Presser, who lived in the only other apartment on Jane's floor, told a reporter that they didn't know her well, but they had been at a party with her on Saturday where she seemed to enjoy herself. Stephen, a Harvard law school student, said that he and Carol had been home and awake until two in the morning the night before. They heard nothing unusual, but the building did a good job at muffling sounds. They once ran a test where they turned on a stereo as high as it could go and listened from the next apartment. "We couldn't hear a thing," Stephen said. Old plans for the building revealed that the maple floors had been built specifically to be soundproof.

The only unusual thing, Carol said, was that their cat, Oliver Wendell Holmes, had been behaving strangely all night. From 8 p.m. until they went to sleep, "he was acting wild and making noises—like screams [...] He has never been like that before."

Neither of the Cambridge police patrolmen reported seeing anything unusual in the University Road area between 1 a.m. and 7 a.m. the previous night. A transit worker said he saw a man—170 pounds, about six feet— running from the building around 1:30 in the morning, but given the heavy downpour, it didn't strike him as unusual.

The closest thing that police had to an eyewitness was Ravi Rikhye, twenty-two, a former Harvard student, who had been rooming with the tenants of 5B. Ravi said that around 12:30 a.m. the previous night, he had heard the shuffling of feet on the icy sidewalk, and then a man shouting, "Get to the car, get to the car!" He looked out the window and saw two men—both with long, swept-back hair—running to an idling vehicle. But the tenants of 5B could not corroborate Ravi's account.

By late afternoon, word had reached the press, and reporters and photographers craned on the stairway to try to catch a glimpse of the crime scene. Officer Benjamin Capello stood outside Jane's door to prevent them from entering. But he couldn't stop them from lining up in front of the Bennett Street garage. They were there, ready, when detectives carried Jane's body out of the building on a stretcher.

———

A ten-minute drive away, the art deco headquarters of the Cambridge Police was busy with comings and goings. Jane's parents were among the first interviewed. They explained that Jane had been home for the holidays and gave no indication that anything was wrong. She had returned to Cambridge early because she said she wanted to get in some studying before Generals. "I talked with her on the phone Monday night," Jane's father said. "She said she had plenty of money and needed nothing." She was in an especially good mood because Jim had just come back from Canada.

J. Boyd Britton held his hat in one hand and gripped Ruth's arm with the other as they left the building. They bowed their heads toward reporters as they exited, hiding their faces. Jane's mother clutched her gloves so tightly in her right hand that her fingers looked more like a claw.

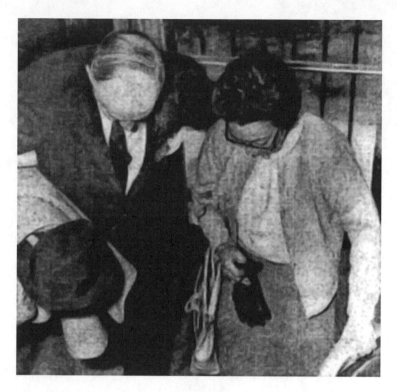

Jane Britton's parents leave Cambridge Police headquarters.

Cops questioned Don and Jill Mitchell for hours without the presence of an attorney, but the tone, at least initially, was more inquisitive than aggressive. The dynamic changed after an examiner tested Don's and Jill's hands for the presence of blood. Don's hands tested slightly positive, which was to be expected since he had touched Jane's body that afternoon. But the cotton ball that swabbed Jill's hands turned an intense blue: the result for a significant presence of blood.

"I—" Jill started. Her voice quivered. "I—I was cutting up some meat," she said. A London broil. She told cops that she also had her period.

The press were still swarming in front of the precinct house when Don and Jill were finally allowed to leave the building. Flashbulbs popped, and guys with film cameras elbowed each other for the best view. Jill walked in front of Don, staring dead into the cameras, her eyebrows furrowed into two dark streaks across her forehead.

Jill and Don Mitchell head home after speaking to detectives.

DEPARTURES

THE WORLD HARVARD OFFERED WASN'T mine to keep. After graduating in late 2010 in an unmajestic off-cycle ceremony, I walked away from Jane's story for almost two years.

I wanted to work in an office and to make a home for myself that fit better than Queens ever had. I moved away as far as I could, hoping that the sense of dislocation I had felt since I was a child could be relieved by something as simple as moving to the right city. But as much as a part of me ached to make this new city home, another part of me refused to let it become comfortable. I would go out on the weekends with a mission to buy pillows, and each time I'd come home with something more uncomfortable than the last: Glass Tupperware. A set of knives. It was as if I was playing a game with myself: unable to admit that this wasn't the right place or the right time, I instead did everything I could to kick myself out. It worked.

Six months later, I moved back in with my parents, into the apartment that I'd promised myself before that first day of college that I would never live in again. And it was there—free of the constraints of what I *should* do, contemplating instead notions of connection and lostness—that I turned back to Jane.

It wasn't heroic. There was no sense of embarking on a grand quest. It was just that I had no idea how to move on or to move out, and Jane's story seemed as good a direction as any.

It seems obvious in retrospect that Jane was still waiting there for me. In the intervening time, I had silently gotten older than her without realizing it. I was now twenty-four, and she, as she always would be, was twenty-three. I didn't know how far I would get with her story, but I knew I had to try.

I resumed my online sleuthing. Within a few months—by late summer 2012—I had learned that Jill and Don Mitchell had been anthropology professors at Buffalo State, Jane's parents had both passed away, and Jim Humphries, the boyfriend, had withdrawn from Harvard a few years after Jane's death. Now he was nowhere to be found. From Harvard's online course catalog, to which my old Harvard ID still gave me access, I learned that Professor Karl Lamberg-Karlovsky would be teaching a class that fall: Anthropology 1065: The Ancient Near East. Tuesdays and Thursdays at 10 a.m. in the Peabody Museum Room 57-E, the listing said. I knew that almost anyone could sit in on a class during Shopping Week—the first week of classes when students are still deciding what to take, and professors have no sense of who's supposed to be there—so I could slip in unnoticed. It was a few weeks away. If I really was going to do it, this was my chance.

INITIAL QUESTIONING

As NIGHT FELL ON THE day that Jane's body was found, much of Cambridge didn't yet know enough to be scared. The major papers wouldn't pick up the story until the morning, and by all appearances, Jane's University Road building had returned to normalcy. Police had left for the day, and reporters had gone home. There was no caution tape, no barriers. You could just push in the front door and climb the stairs right to Jane's hallway.

But inside the University Road apartment, the air was tense. Many residents of Jane's apartment building huddled for safety. "All the single girls, and some of the married couples have banded together for the night. We're afraid to sleep alone. We're afraid of who might come in," Jessie Gill, the chairman of the apartment's tenant union, told a *Boston Herald Traveler* reporter on the phone. "One murder is a freak thing and you can accept it for what it is. But when you get another, there is panic," she said, referring to the murder of Beverly Samans six years before.

According to Gill, she had been warning Harvard for nearly two years about the building's safety issues. It lacked automatic locks on the front doors; vagrants lived in the basement; rooms could be accessed from the fire escapes. "We have constantly asked for improvements but the only answer we get is that they will investigate. At least half of the tenants in this block are single girls. What good will an investigation do now?"

Jessie Gill opens the door to 2 University Road.

———

Police headquarters was also buzzing with activity.

Jim Humphries, who had been at the station all afternoon, was still in the middle of his interrogation. They found him forthcoming, even anxious to assist authorities. Like the Mitchells, he had agreed to speak without the presence of an attorney. But he talked about Jane with an emotional remoteness that seemed odd for someone so close to the deceased. "I suppose you'd say I was her boyfriend," he demurred.

Jim told the cops he had been away most of the fall semester. He'd gotten very sick in Iran and had stayed home in Canada to recuperate and to study for his Generals. But he had visited Cambridge a few times.

Sergeant Petersen pointed out that Jim's extended absences left a lot of Jane's time unaccounted for. "You wouldn't have any knowledge whether she had boyfriends or not, would you?" Petersen said. "You haven't seen her much."

"No. I suppose not, but we've been writing letters and talking on the telephone the odd time. She didn't strike me as the sort of girl that would, you know, play both ends against the middle."

He was in touch with Jane enough to know that her worries about the exam were because her return to Iran was contingent on her performance, and she needed to go to Iran to get material for her dissertation. Plus, Jane had failed the exams the previous year, "and in this department," Jim told the cops, if you miss the second time around, "you're finished." Jim mentioned something about Jane feeling like she had been graded unfairly the year before, but he didn't know the full story, he said, and changed the subject.

The sergeant asked about brands of cigarettes he and Jane smoked (True and Camel), whether Jane kept sharp stone tools in her apartment (he couldn't remember), and what fights he and Jane had had (only two). Jim said that they were both his fault: "Once, because I let her drive the car and I didn't realize it was a very bad road, and the other because I was pushing her too fast when we were skating." They wanted to know if he had seen a big reddish stain in the middle of the floor—other than a coffee cup he had kicked over two weeks before in the corner of the room, no. The questioning went on so long, they even made him pause in the middle of the interrogation to get them all coffee.

When Jim returned, Petersen tried to establish if he and Jane had had sex before he left that night. "You had an occasion to touch her where you had a little petting party on the couch there before you left. Right?" the sergeant asked.

Jim was adamant they hadn't. "No petting party—I just kissed her."

And then Petersen asked about a knock on Jane's door at nine o'clock that morning. According to Don Mitchell, Jim had said that it was him.

"No. I couldn't have said that," Jim said.

"They heard somebody rapping at the door around nine o'clock," Petersen insisted.

"No. I'm sure it wasn't. Whatever I said, I wasn't there. I couldn't have been. I must have said that I called her or something, but I sure wasn't there."

———

Shortly before midnight, Detective Lieutenant Leo Davenport gave the day's final update to reporters. There was no evidence of any connection to the Beverly Samans stabbing that had taken place in the same apartment complex a few years prior. He confirmed what police had determined earlier: that there was no evidence of a struggle in the apartment and that nothing appeared stolen. There was no visible blood except on the mattress and pillows.

"Time of death was estimated at between 10 and 12 hours prior to the finding of the body," Davenport said, placing the window of murder between 12:30 a.m. and 2:30 a.m. Citing the preliminary autopsy report that the coroner, Dr. Arthur McGovern, had just completed, Davenport announced that Jane had died of contusions and lacerations of the brain.

Not included in the official document, but told to reporters, was that McGovern had found two superficial gashes on Jane's forehead—a four-inch slash across her hairline and an inch-long wound just above the bridge of her nose. McGovern concluded that Jane had been facing her attacker when struck. She also had two deeper wounds on the right side of her head. But the fatal hit, he determined, was a massive blow on the left side of the head behind her ear. It had been forceful enough to crack her skull. "She had been hit from all angles," the detective lieutenant said.

Davenport quoted McGovern as saying that the weapon was both blunt and sharp, and he relayed the coroner's speculation that it could have been a sharp rock, a hatchet, or a cleaver. Davenport personally suspected the murder weapon was a ball peen hammer—commonly used for metalworking and similar to its domestic cousin except with one spherical side and one flat surface instead of a nail claw—but he did not specify what led him to that hypothesis.

McGovern had not found any clear evidence of sexual assault, but the final determination was pending a more in-depth autopsy by Dr. George Katsas, one of the state's top forensic pathologists, who was often called in for especially difficult criminal cases. He had performed the autopsies of two of the Boston Strangler victims and had a reputation for being compulsively thorough. Results would not be in for at least a week.

"We have no firm suspects at this time," Davenport said, emphasizing that Jim Humphries had come voluntarily to the police station. He had been very cooperative, and he wasn't a suspect. There was only one thing Davenport felt sure of, it seemed: "It was someone she knew."

KARL

I ARRIVED IN CAMBRIDGE THE night before the first day of fall semester. I had dragged my bag from the train station to a two-story house in Central Square, where Svetlana, my college roommate, had lived since graduation. She greeted me at the door, settled me in her spare bedroom, and told me not to worry about how long I would be in Cambridge. She had somehow convinced her housemates that letting me stay indefinitely was a good idea.

The next morning, I was up before my alarm could sound. I'd picked out my outfit the night before and looked in the mirror as I put on my backpack. *Good enough*, I thought, hoping it would let me pass for an undergraduate.

It was a fifteen-minute walk to the Peabody Museum. It had rained heavily, and the ground was wet. Cambridge was still warm, like a summer hangover, and the leaves were all green. I braced myself as I pushed through the heavy doors of the Peabody Museum and walked past the receptionist who, I prayed, wouldn't shout, *Hey, what do you think you're doing?*

I climbed to the fifth floor and headed down the long corridor past the DENTAL HARD TISSUE LAB and the COMPARATIVE LACTATION LAB. Karl Lamberg-Karlovsky's office was at the end of the hallway. His name was stenciled on the speckled glass of the door. A blue blazer pressed up against it from the other side. I didn't want to call attention to myself by lingering too long, so I continued on, turning left. In that hallway were a series of color photos of Tepe Yahya from the '70s. In one, Karl was on horseback, the impressive mound of Tepe Yahya in the distance, carved out with the steppes of their excavation. In another, Karl was leaning over a surveying tool, his white T-shirt sleeves rolled up and his long brown hair flopped over his face. A female colleague kneeled behind him, stretching a string to help him mark the outline of the trench to be excavated. He was exactly what you wanted all archaeologists to be: sexy, tan, dusty. Cowboy scholars. *I can't blame you, Jane*, I thought.

Almost everything I knew about him at that point, I had learned from

James Ronan, my adviser. He had been reluctant to speculate, worried about being seen as a gossip and afraid of the retaliation that might come from bad-mouthing someone powerful in his field. The Harvard graduate students, whose insider positions might have enabled them to investigate, felt unable to do anything because their careers were too enmeshed with the very system they were questioning. In me, I guessed, James saw someone to do the investigation he never could.

Karl had been on the faculty at Harvard since 1965. James was almost positive that Karl had already been tenured when Jane died in 1969, which meant he would only have been in his early thirties when he was promoted to full professor. James attributed this achievement largely to Karl's work on Tepe Yahya. Though early newspaper reports that Yahya was Alexander the Great's lost city of Carmania turned out not to be true, pottery artifacts pointed to this settlement being a key trading stop. It also yielded slabs with Proto-Elamite texts on them from only slightly later than the famous cuneiform tablets in Mesopotamia.

And then Karl's career in field archaeology kind of plateaued. He went on to do other things post-Yahya like directing archaeological surveys in Saudi Arabia and co-chairing the first archaeological exchange between the US and the USSR. He published widely and was the director of the Peabody Museum for thirteen years. But, according to James, nothing ever surpassed Yahya.

Over the years, as his academic reputation arguably faded, his personal reputation grew wilder and more legendary. As if to encourage this, Karl stalked the halls of the Peabody Museum in a cape—at least according to graduate student lore. To these students, he seemed to play up to a caricature of the villainous professor.

Students felt they had no choice but to take him seriously. He still wielded a lot of power in the department. He was the director of the American School of Prehistoric Research, which had money, and while Karl couldn't dictate the use of funds, he had a major say. Karl was also known as a bully, which James had experienced firsthand. Once when Karl wanted to remind James of his place in the department, he cornered James in the hallway, his imposing frame a stark, physical reminder not to cross him.

James continued: "I was talking to a graduate student who finished his degree maybe around 2000 who said, 'I never had trouble with Karl because his behavior is relatively predictable.'" It was essentially Machiavellian: "'You can always count on him to do whatever is necessary to survive and advance his own interests and as a result you kind of know what you're dealing with.'"

The whispers that followed Karl seemed, perversely, to give him more power. The story, while never proven, was never dispelled, and it lurked in the background of his interactions: *This man might have killed somebody.* No one knew how much was true, but, as James told me, "Anybody who's been in the industry for a while has heard the story, and the sick thing is that it's probably enhanced his prestige or at least this dark aura that hovers around him."

James was quick to point out that everything he knew about the crime was speculation or hearsay. He tried to reassure me: Karl was a performer whose "threats are smoke and mirrors." The myth of this man was bigger and scarier and *separate* from who he actually was. He was still married to the same woman he was during the 1968 dig in Iran, and in recent years he had devoted himself to her care. "I wouldn't worry too much, but I'd be careful, too. I think you're right to sort of tiptoe around the sides of it and pick up little bits here and there."

I was about to enter Karl's classroom, at the end of the hallway with the photos, when the most chilling story I had heard about the professor came back to me in a rush. The graduate students in the department, James said, had been secretly collecting a file on the murder through the years. He told me that the folder supposedly had information about Karl's involvement in Jane's death. It had been passed from one student to another, and he knew a couple of people who had seen it. "My hunch is that it wouldn't be anything that you didn't already have access to. Nobody really got in deep...But it was a huge part of the student lore." He didn't know who had the file now because the last person who'd possessed it had died in a hiking accident a number of years before.

That story about the file sounded like something else straight out of a folktale. The kind of fable that children told each other about avoiding the house of the witch who lived at the end of the road and the danger that befell the one who didn't listen.

The person who had died was Stine Rossel, James said. Stine had been out hiking with her husband in the White Mountains of New Hampshire when the tree trunk they were sitting on rolled down and took her with it. I realized, with a shudder, that I already knew that story. That husband had been my teaching assistant in biology; it happened the year I was in his class. I remembered reading the *Crimson* article about it. Remembered having to craft an awful email to retrieve my graphing calculator from him. How do you say, *I'm sorry for your overwhelming grief, but is my TI-83 in one of your boxes?*

The brief feeling of a long-remembered folktale vanished in the stark reality that not only had someone killed Jane, but now two people were dead. Even as I chastised myself for being superstitious, I couldn't help but feel that the story was somehow cursed.

RED OCHRE

By THE MORNING OF JANUARY 8, 1969, it was nearly impossible to pick up a newspaper in the US that didn't feature a story about Jane's murder. It made the front page of all the Boston papers, and the New York tabloids exploded with coverage. Jane's story towered over reporting on Sirhan Sirhan's trial for the assassination of RFK. QUIZ HARVARD MEN IN COED SLAYING spread over two lines of the front page of the *New York Post*.

Articles about Jane's murder ran in small papers across the country, too. They reprinted the AP and UPI wire stories and gussied them up with headlines, one more sensational than the next. DAUGHTER OF RADCLIFFE OFFICIAL BRUTALLY SLAIN (*Boston Record-American*); COLLEGE GIRL AXED TO DEATH IN BLOOD-COVERED APARTMENT (Texas's *Valley Morning Star*); POLICE SEEKING MASSACHUSETTS AXE MURDERER (*Pittsburgh Press*); SEEK WEAPON USED TO BUTCHER COED (Michigan's *Ironwood Daily*). Many articles got her age wrong, but almost none failed to mention that she was "a pretty brunette," "petite," "attractive," a "nice girl." Some ran it in the headline: PRETTY GRADUATE STUDENT FOUND SLAIN IN APARTMENT (Connecticut's *The Day*). Eventually, even *Newsweek* magazine picked up the story, and made much of Jane's cat Fuzzwort being the crime's only witness.

Brenda Bass, Jane's high school roommate, was at home in Colorado that day, with the television on. "I heard Radcliffe, and I turned around and they were talking about Jane, *in Denver!*" She amassed all the newspaper articles she could find about Jane's death and ended up with a mountain of them.

"It wasn't like her father was JFK. He wasn't a public figure. She wasn't. I mean it wasn't even that interesting: A girl gets murdered in her apartment. How many girls get murdered in their apartments every day across the country?"

Front page of the Boston Record-American *on January 8, 1969.*

Reporters and TV crews showed no signs of letting up. The *Daily News* had four reporters in town and ferried photographs back to New York via private plane. Members of the press crowded the second-floor corridor of police headquarters, poised for the next break or the next set of Jane's friends or family to pass by.

Detective Lieutenant Leo Davenport told reporters that two men were being sought for questioning in connection with the case: an ex-boyfriend who had recently dropped out of the Anthropology department and was supposed to be in Peru, but was reported to have been seen in Cambridge in recent weeks, and another man believed to have been turned down by Jane. By some accounts, this man was a faculty member.

Davenport said that, as of that morning, the murder weapon had still not been recovered, but he had learned that an archaeological tool known to have been in Jane's room before the crime was unaccounted for. He described it as a sharp stone, six inches long and four inches wide, and the papers reported that it was a gift from Don and Jill Mitchell. He had sent men to look for the tool in the trolley and subway car yards behind the University Road building.

The Mitchells and Jim Humphries had been called in for a second round of questioning to clear up "minor inconsistencies," but Davenport claimed not to be too bothered by the small contradictions in their stories. "When people are nervous, they are sometimes prone to mix up recollections. Even two police officers who view the same event wind up giving contradictory testimony sometimes." There was still no official suspect.

That afternoon, a cloud of unease hung over Harvard Square. Laurie Godfrey, a biological anthropology student in Jane's year, later described walking down the streets of Cambridge after she heard the news: It felt not so much like a dream to her as a different world, "peculiar and sinister, with a root that no one seemed to know."

The Anthropology department's ordinary business came to a halt. Stephen Williams postponed the remaining two days of Generals. In place of the usual din, the halls of the Peabody, a student remembered, filled with murmurs of a "swirling horror of interest and speculation." But what the department secretaries found most disturbing was how forbidden this speculation felt among faculty. Nobody was asking, *What can we do?* or *How did this happen?* Instead, professors were behaving as if nothing had happened.

The secretaries' fifth-floor office in the Peabody Museum.

Early suspicion among some of the graduate students was that it was a random attacker. "There was a considerable amount of crime in those years in Cambridge as well as in New York. There was the possibility that somebody had just broken in and killed her," Francesco Pellizzi, a graduate student a few years older than Jane, would later remember. Anthropology student Mel Konner had a similar memory: "I think everyone had a heightened sense of the dangers of the Cambridge streets and Harvard Square." Speaking at the time, Ingrid Kirsch, who knew Jane from Radcliffe and described her as "my closest and very best friend," told reporters, "I don't believe anyone who knew her could have done this."

———

But then, late that evening, Detective Sergeant John Galligan leaked the clue that threatened to force everything out into the light.

Galligan, a square-faced man with a button nose, was a veteran of the Cambridge PD Bureau of Criminal Investigations. He gathered the press for an informal conference. Press and police alike were weary, having worked nonstop since Jane's body was found the day before. Some of the information he relayed was routine enough. He assured reporters that "we are leaving no stone unturned in our investigation." Twenty-three people had already been questioned in connection with the case, he said. Police had scheduled lie detector tests for the following day for Jim Humphries, Don and Jill Mitchell, and a fourth person whom he refused to name.

And then a chilling detail.

Powder had been found at the scene of the crime, he said. Red powder. Powder the color of burnt brick. What some know as iron oxide, and others call jeweler's rouge, but what archaeologists know, unmistakably, as red ochre. It's what colors the rusty mountains of the Southwest, and what tints the bloody bison in the cave paintings of Lascaux. It appeared to have been thrown on the bed where Jane's body lay. It fell across her shoulders and hit the ceiling and the wall where a headboard might have been.

"It was described to me as an ancient symbolic method of purifying the body to get it into paradise," Detective Galligan said.

The theory was that the perpetrator killed Jane, then stood over her body to toss the red powder, as part of a re-creation of a burial ritual. It limited the field of suspects to those who knew about the rite, likely someone with an intimate knowledge of anthropology.

"We are dealing with a sick man," Detective Galligan said.

FIRST CONTACT

I WAS THE FIRST ONE in the classroom. Sitting down, I was disheartened by how much smaller it was than I had imagined. It was more of a seminar room than a lecture hall. *I won't be invisible.* It had a long rectangular table, with a map of the world on one side and a raised topographic map of South America on the other. Two rows of chairs circled the table. I chose one in the second row, across from the dry-erase board, and as I took my seat, I saw that some kind stranger had written GOOD LUCK! on the board in black marker. I let myself take it as a sign.

Four students entered in quick succession—two male and two female.

I jotted down observations about them in my notebook, pretending to be prepping for the class. One of the male students was muscular, with brown hair and a turquoise polo shirt. The other was shorter, bearded, and his hair was pulled back in a ponytail. They started the nonsense banter of students seeing each other for the first time after the summer even though they must have known the whole room was listening to their conversation.

The room continued to fill up. I felt myself getting more anxious by the minute.

"We don't need to segregate ourselves, gender-wise," the taller of the two male graduate students said, opening the conversation for the first time to the rest of the class. For all of my note-taking, I hadn't noticed. He was right: All of the women were clustered on my side of the table.

People laughed awkwardly, but no one moved.

"I feel like I'm not even in the right place?" a girl said. She hadn't yet learned to stop wearing the lanyard the admissions office gives freshmen.

"Where do you think you're supposed to be?" the tall guy asked.

"Archaeology."

"Yeah, you're in the right place."

Another student on my side piped up, maybe trying to make the freshman feel better. She was a brunette with a long braid. "I'm a grad student but I'm a first-year, so I'm basically a freshman."

"In what department?" the tall one asked.

"Archaeology. There are two of us."

The tall guy whistled, as if to say, *How small!* "This guy is an archaeologist, right here." He clapped his friend on the shoulders.

"What do you specialize in?" the one with the ponytail asked.

"Food, which sounds silly, but I work in Peru and Jordan," she said.

"You're supposed to say alimentary studies," the tall one corrected.

"Yeah...Alimentary studies."

Another girl walked into the room. She sat down on my side.

"Oop, well, I guess we're still segregating ourselves," the tall guy said.

And then I heard the door open from down the hallway.

COLONIALISM'S HANDMAIDEN

WHEN I SAW PROFESSOR LAMBERG-Karlovsky for the first time, he looked past me. He walked to the far end of the room and sat at the head of the table, so that the windows backlit him. He was one chair away from me. Everyone stopped talking.

He set down an inch-thick, unlabeled manila folder. Rumpled yellow loose-leaf papers—lecture notes—poked out the top and sides. They were so old they look chewed, but he didn't touch them once during class. For close to an hour, he spoke entirely from memory.

"Welcome!" he said. His voice was strong and resonant, the accent vaguely Continental. "There's no textbook available to cover the area that I intend to cover." There was one, once—"but it's out of date. It's something that I did a long time ago." *He's been here for forty-seven years*, I reminded myself. When he got tenure, Jane was still alive, I thought. He *is* the textbook.

"We'll talk about Egypt, Mesopotamia, Central Asia, up to the Indus Valley, the major civilizations, cultural complexities in each area. Our approach will be to try and see similarities and differences in the emergence of these civilizations. What is similar in the evolution of, quote, 'urbanization, civilization, literate communities'?"

I compared the man in front of me to that picture of him from the '68 season of Tepe Yahya. At nearly seventy-five, he was barely diminished by age. His frame was still imposing. His nose had grown bulbous, and his stomach had given way to a comfortable paunch, but his white hair was still thick, puffing around his ears. His brow ridge had become the most remarkable part of his face. It extended down over his eyes, carpeted by thick eyebrows that stretched up to his forehead. His nose was almost aristocratic in its excess.

"We will see throughout the semester that archaeology, unlike when I first became an archaeologist, today archaeology stands with political issues. It advocates certain aspects." For example, Saddam Hussein used to say about Iraqis that "we invented writing." "True," Karl said. It was invented in Iraq. But, of course, there was no Iraq five thousand years ago. "Archaeology has a remarkable penchant for modern political purposes," Karl said. "It's used."

No one else was taking notes. They were all just listening. I tried to take mine more discreetly.

Archaeology is an investigation, he explained, but it can also be an act of power—of finding the data and then controlling the story. "Every nation-state wants an important past," Karl said. So, often, the ruling parties will commission archaeologists. But sometimes the past that archaeologists find is not what the powers want them to find.

His hands, I noticed, shook slightly, and he wasn't wearing a wedding ring. He did have a gold signet ring on his pinkie, but I couldn't make out the image on the crest. His nails—I chastised myself for being a little creeped out—were long and very clean.

Karl segued into the history of archaeology. He explained that the importance of the past to the present comes in waves—pulses, he called them—and that we were in a moment when the past was seen as very significant to the present.

He described the long period of time between the Romans' interest in antiquity and the Renaissance's renewed interest. "It was a thousand-year night." Then, gathering steam, he delivered the rest of his lecture almost like a sermon, pressing his finger pads together to emphasize his points. Archaeology started less as a science than with travelers, adventurers—people who went to the Near East with the Bible to see whether or not there was ever a Jericho—and colonizers. "That's why you go to the Louvre in Paris, or to the British Museum, or to the Pergamon in Berlin, or to the Egyptian Museum in Turin: to see some of the great antiquities of the nation-states of the Near East.

"The colonial aspect is still very much with us," Karl continued, bringing us up to the present. His enunciation underlined his words: These rich nations—England, France, Germany—went in and plundered other nations, *collecting* their past and *controlling* it, by being the ones to *interpret* it, *to give it significance and meaning.* "Archaeology is the handmaiden of colonialism.

"Now I will say one personal aspect of the Near East. I have spent a goodly number of decades working in the Near East, but the Near East is a tough neighborhood today...I worked. I had worked. I worked for over ten years in Iran." It was his first stumble, and it seemed interesting that it coincided with the site that he, Jim, and Jane had excavated together.

He continued: "Nation-states, *now*, are terribly invested in archaeology. They want to know their pasts—not through the filter of a Soviet interpretation of what their past was, but on their own terms."

And here again, as I had during the whole class, I felt seen. I was struck by the parallels between Karl's lecture and the experience of pursuing Jane's story. But I was also hesitant to trust that these echoes existed outside of the fact that I was listening so hard for them.

"Thursday we start at 9000 BC," he said.

I put my pencil away and ran down the stairs. Of course I would be back Thursday.

THE RITUAL

THE STORY OF THE RED ochre monopolized the front page of newspapers for the next two days. STRANGE CLUE IN COED CASE read the front page of the *New York Post*. The paper described the red ochre as part of an ancient Near Eastern burial ritual, "conducted in Persia as long ago as 5000 BC," intended to "drive out evil spirits." The *Boston Record-American* published COED'S SLAYER WENT THROUGH ANCIENT RITUAL. The *Boston Globe*'s slightly more sober POLICE EXAMINE OCHRE FOUND NEAR SLAYING VICTIM was perhaps due to the Britton family friendship with the Taylors, the publishers of the *Globe*.

Front page of the Daily News *on January 10, 1969.*

For some outside Harvard's anthropology circle, the presence of red ochre at the murder scene was a small relief; it seemed less likely that Jane had been the victim of a random attack. The specificity of the crime, and "the fact that apparently Miss Britton was neither robbed nor assaulted, has enabled many students in the area to view the incident with less fright than a crime of this nature usually engenders," the MIT college paper reported.

Inside the Anthropology department, the news heightened the tension. To many, the red ochre clue signaled that the murderer had to have been one of them. Francesco Pellizzi later recalled how it made his previous theory, that a random intruder was responsible, seem suddenly implausible. Paul Shankman, a Pacific Island anthropologist who had been in the general exam room on Tuesday when Jane failed to show up, agreed: "I mean, who knows about red ochre or would, you know, have the ability to obtain red ochre?"

Other classmates were less quick to jump to conclusions about the mysterious substance given that little of the information about it was stable. Of the students, only Don and Jill Mitchell and Jim Humphries had seen the crime scene firsthand, and the newspapers gave conflicting accounts. One described it as a liquid daubed on Jane's body; others talked about it as a powder that had been strewn. It was red or mahogany or cocoa-colored. While some articles called it ochre, which is iron oxide, others called it iodine oxide—an identification, according to the *Boston Globe,* supported by laboratory technicians for the state police. Except this red powder couldn't have been iodine oxide: The only stable oxide of iodine at room temperature is clear. Jane's friend Arthur Bankoff, who had been to Iran with her and Jim but was in Italy at the time of her death, was skeptical of whether red ochre was found at the scene at all. He would later reflect: "People who said so might have heard it from someone else who might have misconstrued it [...] What does it tell you if it was a recreation? That some archaeologist did it? Maybe. But I think it was a little far-fetched. I'm going to hide behind that."

What few realized, though, was that cops had been able to keep one key detail relatively secret: Red ochre wasn't the only burial ritual element at the crime scene. At the top of Jane's bed, resting on a bloody pillow, police had found a portion of a colonial gravestone etched with a winged skull.

And fewer still knew that the Cambridge Police's source for information on red ochre came from within the Peabody Museum itself: the chairman of the department and the acting director of the museum, Stephen Williams.

STEPHEN WILLIAMS AND
DETECTIVE HALLIDAY

Detective Halliday: We are now in the Cambridge Police headquarters on the second floor at number 5 Western Avenue. The time is exactly 11:37 a.m. The date being January 7th—

Unidentified Male: Correction, the 9th.

Detective Halliday: —correction, the 9th. Present at this time is Lieutenant Donnie from the State Police, Detective Herbert E. Halliday, Cambridge Police, and your name, Professor?

Professor Williams: Stephen Williams, 103 Old Colony Road, Wellesley Hills, Massachusetts.

Detective Halliday: Now, Professor, we are going to talk about the murder of Jane Britton, and in my hand I hold some photos of the scene when our officers arrived. This is picture number one: a sheet that we can visibly see, a blanket, an afghan type of a bedspread, and a fur coat. Here is picture number two. Some of the material has been taken off of her at this particular time. We notice a blood-stained sheet, part of a fur coat, and the other paraphernalia has been put to the side. Now I show you this number three photo, which is very particular. As you notice, up at the head and to the left, there's a headstone and the picture of a skull. Can you observe the skull on that headstone?

Professor Williams: Yes, I do. I see the headstone. Yes.

Detective Halliday: Now, I bring your attention back to picture number one.

Professor Williams: Oh, yeah. Here's the—

Detective Halliday: You see the powder—

Professor Williams: Yeah.

Detective Halliday: —as it goes across?

Professor Williams: Yeah.

Detective Halliday: Now what significant thing have you observed thus far, Professor, in anthropology or archaeology in regards to these particular pictures?

Professor Williams: Well, it seems to me she's been carefully laid out in some kind of a ceremony. This certainly just didn't happen that she was laid out this way. It almost looks like someone had in mind some kind of—of ritual.

It would certainly seem that in this case the person was laid out on—rather carefully with the head between the pillows, then sprinkled with this substance, and then—then—and this—this—I don't know what it—whether this headstone was regularly here or not. It certainly again looks like a marker on a—on a grave of some sort. And certainly this—them laying these other garments over, trying—in a sense trying to—to bury her under all these things, I mean, someone certainly had in mind some kind of a burial ritual.

Detective Halliday: Ritual.

Lieutenant Donahue: Does this recall anything to you as an archaeology professor?

Professor Williams: It is quite true that red powder is usually red ochre.

Lieutenant Donahue: Can you spell that for us please?

Professor Williams: O-C-H-R-E. This is merely very high-grade iron ore, like hematite. This has been used by primitive peoples for tens of thousands of years. We can go to Maine at 3,000 BC and dig up Indian burials and find them covered with red ochre. We can go to Wisconsin and find red ochre buried. We can go to west California and find it. We can go to France, for example, and find red ochre being put in burials as much as 20,000 years ago.

Lieutenant Donahue: What would be the purpose of using the red ochre in a burial rite?

Professor Williams: Well, it varies from one place in the world to another. I mean—

Lieutenant Donahue: What are some of them? Could you give us some of them?

Professor Williams: Well, many times, for instance, in Maine, we can't ask the people of 3,000 BC why they did it. We know they were doing something extra. And that's all we can say. When you're dealing with a dead civilization, we have to interpret what these people might have had in their minds. We find the burial, it has a lot of red ochre in it, and all we can say is, "Well, they thought it was important. They took the trouble to add this to their burial ritual."

I mean, a general answer to your question, I would say that whenever we see particular care given to a burial, yes, we generally say they've thought enough of the deceased person to do this extra thing. Someone took the time to do this, didn't just kill, say, "My god, what have I done?" and run out. But we have no indications of saying that red signified good or bad in a culture.

Lieutenant Donahue: Uh-huh.

Detective Halliday: Would this be a layman's information or a person that's well read in archaeology?

Professor Williams: It seems to me like it could have been done by people from three different groups. Either someone who does have knowledge of archaeology and has read enough about burials. The second, and maybe this is just defense because that would mean that we're dealing with one of my students, is a hippie who is involved in some kind of— seen enough about rituals. And the third thing is someone who is really just psychotic, a real psychotic person who we may be interpreting some of these things—reading more into it than what's there. Now I think the last one is probably the least likely.

Red ochre is, as I say, such a general thing that it isn't the sort of special kind of information that I would think only an archaeologist might have. On the other hand, this whole burial ritual is certainly nothing that I know anything the hippies are working with or dealing with. So it does look to me, I must confess, like someone had done something rather special and had—as I said, used the term *ritual*, and I would stick with it.

Detective Halliday: Now, could this red ochre, Professor, be obtained in classrooms at Harvard?

Professor Williams: Well, I mean, Dr. Lamberg-Karlovsky has some in his office. Students are in and out of his office all the time.

KEEP THE DEAD CLOSE

I CONTINUED AUDITING KARL'S CLASS, always leaving a few seats between me and him. I tried not to find it too loaded when he said something like, "Could we just kill the lights?" The third class began with a presentation on the history of agriculture. *Click.* He changed the slide. *Click.* He showed a picture of a twelve-thousand-year-old site in Israel called Ain Mallaha. It was unique, Karl explained, because people settled there permanently *before* the invention of agriculture in the Levant. In other words, it wasn't the need to tend crops and to raise animals that led these people to give up their nomadic ways. It was complex ritual beliefs, he said, as exhibited by one particular pattern of behavior: They buried the dead under their houses. A lot of attention was paid to that dead individual, he went on. "By attention, I mean you embellish it with jewelry, with items of significance."

It struck me then that the way we relate to our dead is the oldest mark of our humanity.

"The dead are kept close to you," he said.

I circled it in my notebook.

THE PEABODY

However enigmatic red ochre was as a symbol—it could be hubris, a red herring, an act of remorse, a sign of psychosis—much of the attention within the Peabody community focused on one man who stood out from the rest of the museum: Professor Karl Lamberg-Karlovsky.

Karl's first day as an assistant professor at Harvard was in the fall of 1965. Just shy of his twenty-eighth birthday, Karl was about the same age as many of the older students in Harvard's anthropology program, having just finished his PhD at UPenn that spring. He was tall and lean, with hair down to his shoulders. He wore a leather jacket and drove a motorcycle.

By the time Karl arrived, Harvard's Anthropology department was one of the best in the world, and its center was the Peabody, which was celebrating its ninety-ninth birthday. When the Peabody was founded, anthropology was just coming into its own in the United States. The Smithsonian Institution's Castle was only ten years old; the American Museum of Natural History wouldn't be founded for another four years. The Peabody slowly changed that. What had started as a collection of artifacts became home to a codified program of teaching and research in all fields of anthropology, including archaeology.

Over the decades, the museum became cramped, split haphazardly among exhibitions for the public, office space for members of the Anthropology department and museum staff, labs, and classrooms. But it still bore the traces of its founding, when anthropology was tied to the collectors' instinct. The red brick of the building held countless dusty treasures. Barbara Allen, a former registrar of the museum, said that when you held these objects, it was impossible to ignore the feeling that they "were made to hold powerful magic." The museum's storage units overflowed with golden artifacts from Mexico's sacred cenotes. The rafters in the attic were filled with feathers and spirit masks and saliva samples from the long dead. It was disorganized enough that finding materials in the collection could feel like conducting an expedition. An unsuspecting student rooting around in the hall of New

Guinea artifacts could stumble across P. T. Barnum's mermaid casually tossed in a cabinet.

Stephen Williams in the Peabody Museum's attic storage. The photo's original caption: "Archaeological material consigned to the attic is almost as inaccessible as it was when it was in the ground." (Museum Collection © President and Fellows of Harvard College, Peabody Museum of Archaeology and Ethnology, PM2015.1.23.2)

The building itself had its own mysterious allure. A network of secret passages ran under the Peabody Museum and connected it to the neighboring Harvard University Herbaria. The basement doors that provided access were locked, but there were ways to press on their molding that would unlock them. The buttons might have been designed for housekeeping and repairmen to get around the buildings, but graduate students held it as a point of insider pride to know these entry points. During the '70s, a researcher named Andrew was often to be found hanging on his hammock in one of these tunnels, surrounded by giant jars cultivating every kind of hallucinogen. "He was perfectly happy if you wanted to go by and get a supply," a graduate student would later remember.

The community that gravitated to the Peabody was fittingly eccentric. There was Joe Johns, a Creek Indian wood carver, turned navy sniper, turned

Harvard police officer, turned Peabody Museum building manager. And Ian Graham, a Maya scholar descended from the Duke of Montrose. And of course, there was the underworld of smokers in the Peabody basement, particularly Tatiana Proskouriakoff, another preeminent Maya scholar, who smoked like a chimney and carried her own ashtray—a tiny one that flipped open, with a fan. She was meticulous about her ash. Harvard never gave her an official position in the department, not to mention a proper office, so she was always in the smoking room, drawing hieroglyphics and chatting with the graduate students who had also come down for a break. By the late '60s, it was the only place to smoke in the building, and the air was so dense it was almost blue.

The era when Karl began at Harvard was defined by the confrontations between these vestiges of the past and the demands of the present. There was still the Old Guard who had started in the era of gentlemen archaeologists. Many were known as dollar-a-year men—they came from such wealth that they only needed to be paid a token salary by the university. The head of the museum, the dapper but academically uninspiring Stephen Williams, was responsible as much for pleasing the museum's Boston Brahmin donors as for maintaining the collections. Professors wore suits and ties and ate lunch every day in the stuffy all-male faculty club. They hardly talked about work, preferring, instead, to discuss the West End duck hunting club. The one tenured female professor in the department, the cultural anthropologist Cora Du Bois, was, for some years at the beginning of her time at Harvard, the only tenured woman. When she walked through the halls, other professors literally turned away from her.

The scholars of this generation were better scientists than their predecessors—embracing such techniques as stratigraphy and radiocarbon dating—but in their way they, too, had become relics of the past. No one embodied the Old Guard more than Hallam Movius, Jane Britton's undergraduate adviser. A specialist in the European Paleolithic, Movius was straight out of the 1930s, with his hair parted in the middle and Brylcreemed. He was an old Harvard man and had been a lieutenant colonel in World War II. He ran his expeditions like an army platoon, with an egg timer to make sure conversation during the twelve-minute break never ran over.

Though Movius, unlike many of his colleagues, accepted women on his excavations, his acceptance came with certain unspoken expectations. When he found out one of his female graduate students was getting married, he tried to get her National Science Foundation funding revoked. And misogyny was far from the only prejudice he harbored. For a time he had a young woman named Adrienne Cohen as his lab technician. When she got married and became Adrienne *Hamilton*, he said, "Hamilton, that's a much better name." Adrienne knew better than to tell him that her husband was Black.

Then there was the New Guard. They were in their thirties, ambitious, hungry, from backgrounds that weren't just the upper class. But it wasn't just the demographic that was changing. Archaeologists of the younger generation were starting to rethink the discipline. They put great emphasis on the interpretative aspects of historical reconstruction and the ultimate subjectivity of all archaeologists' work. Karl summed up this new stance well in his foreword to one of the Tepe Yahya monographs: "All archaeology is the re-enactment of past thought in the archaeologist's own mind." Scholars of history don't uncover the past; they create it.

Students found themselves in the middle: caught between tenured professors whose approach to archaeology felt increasingly dated and younger professors who wielded less power in the department.

Karl was a unique bridge. He embodied the youth and rebellion of the unapologetic New Guard, but, as a descendant of Austrian nobles, the Lambergs, he was fluent in the etiquette and mannerisms of the older professors. While people made fun of Assistant Professor Tom Patterson for wearing the wrong ties to faculty club lunches, Karl prided himself on his black-tie parties. When Karl flouted the dress code—he rarely wore jackets outside formal occasions—he did so not because he didn't know the game, but because he didn't have to play it.

As Karl settled in, he seemed to become even more untouchable. Peabody rules be damned, when Karl wanted a smoke, he would close his office door and puff out the window. One time, he heard a knock on his door. It was Hallam Movius. Movius was horrified. Being a scholar to Movius meant being a gentleman. He took two steps into Karl's office. "You've been smoking!" Movius exclaimed. "I'm working!" Karl replied, unapologetic. "He was the most judicious and correct person," Karl would later say. "I wasn't."

This aura made a big impression on David Freidel, a Near Eastern archaeology undergraduate student at the time. "I mean the first time I saw him I thought, *This man's Count Dracula. He's the real deal.*" Karl even looked like him. "Tall, black hair, handsome, widow's peak, big smile . . . That was not an off-putting thing, you know? It was attractive that he was so edgy."

Karl Lamberg-Karlovsky in the window of the Peabody. (Museum Collection © President and Fellows of Harvard College, Peabody Museum of Archaeology and Ethnology, PM2004.24.29514.12)

———

Karl wouldn't have Jane in his class till the spring of 1967—the same semester he also served on the committee for her undergraduate thesis—but she had made an impression on him the year before. During her junior year, Karl had dangled in front of her the possibility of joining him on his next Mideast expedition. But out of loyalty or obligation, Jane returned to Movius's dig in Les Eyzies, France, for the third straight summer. She fantasized about putting Movius, "a pigheaded old bastard," in his place, but she knew she would have to bite her tongue. Since he was the one who had supported her application for grad school, Movius was going to be her adviser for at least another five years. "The only thing I can do is keep playing this part— even until I'm 36 or so—until I know more than he does, and then watch the fur fly."

When Karl returned from his survey of southeastern Iran in the fall of 1967, the rumor was that there was space opening up in the department for at least one more faculty member. Tepe Yahya seemed like exactly the kind of site a young professor could stake his reputation on, and the Peabody gossip was that Karl stood a very good chance of being the first person in the New Guard to be elevated to the ranks of tenured faculty member. They weren't wrong.

Around the same time, Movius suddenly announced that he would be relocating full-time to Les Eyzies and was no longer able to supervise Jane's dissertation. What was abandonment by another name became Jane's chance to free herself. The charismatic young superstar must have seemed like an escape.

———

Decades later, Francesco Pellizzi, a former student in the department, and I would talk about the rampant speculation that cropped up around Karl after Jane's death and the mystery of the red ochre. Pellizzi, who told me he was grateful to Karl despite "all his quirks," would say, "I think he's the last person who would have made that kind of mise-en-scène." I replied that it was a funny way of exonerating someone: not that *he isn't capable of murder*, but that *he's too smart to have done it that way*. Francesco laughed. "Yes, exactly."

SPEAKING OF SILENCES

I INTRODUCED MYSELF TO KARL after the third class—as someone thinking of applying to graduate school for ethnographic studies, which was true, if only a fraction of the story. "You don't need much background to be a superstar in anthropology," he told me. We bantered for a bit about what it takes to be a great ethnographer—give people time to open up and be reasonable—before I asked permission to audit his class for the semester. "Sure," he said, "if you want that kind of punishment."

After Karl's fourth class, I noticed a poster in the hallway for "Social Anthropology Day." Though social anthro was housed in the same department as archaeology, I had already come to learn that archaeology and social anthropology could not be further from each other. There was almost an animosity that came from being forced to inhabit the same department despite all the obvious differences. But, I reasoned, since it was being billed in part as an introduction to the department for prospective students, important characters in anthropology—and therefore in Jane's story—might be there.

In particular, I hoped to run into someone named Richard Meadow. Richard lurked everywhere in the periphery of Jane's story. He took that 1968 expedition photograph in Iran. He had been Jim Humphries's roommate at the time of Jane's death. Karl had been his dissertation adviser. And, like Karl, he had stayed at Harvard all these years; Richard had been the director of the Peabody's Zooarchaeology Laboratory and a senior lecturer in the department for decades now.

James Ronan, the first person who advised me to speak with Richard, warned me that getting him to talk wouldn't be easy. He was a diligent scholar and notoriously tight-lipped. But James suspected Richard just might dislike Karl enough to make an exception. "They just kind of avoided each other. Even as recently as a few years ago." The rumor was the rift had started because Richard was the one who had told police that Karl had been having an extramarital affair with Jane—a line of questioning to which Karl reportedly responded, evoking Paul Newman: "Why would I have a hamburger when I have steak at home?"

———

It was a packed house in William James Hall. People were sitting on the floor. I scanned the room, eventually spotting someone who looked similar enough to a 1970s picture of Richard Meadow to plausibly be him: glasses, mustache, sloped shoulders. I spent most of that afternoon's lecture watching him.

Gary Urton, the head of the Anthropology department, whose limp mop of hair resembled the knotted cords he studied, was up on the stage, introducing the five lecturers. The first speaker talked about her archaeological work in Mexico. The second discussed his work in Kyrgyzstan studying human settlement patterns. He said that the Kyrgyzstani regional government was extremely helpful to his expedition. "They're under the illusion— which I'm not going to dispel—that there's only one university in the United States, and that is Harvard." It got a big laugh.

And then it was Kimberly Theidon's turn. "She's just returning to us after a year at the Institute for Advanced Study at Princeton, and she's teaching this semester—memory politics...Her talk today is 'Speaking of Silences: Gender, Violence and Redress in Peru,'" Professor Urton said, and ceded the floor to her.

She was astonishing to watch, wrapped in a purple scarf, sinewy, her neck muscles like the sides of a rope ladder climbing up her throat.

"Thank you. It's actually nice to be back in certain ways." The room tittered with nervous laughter. "I say that with sincerity. I look you in the eyes when I say that. Anyway, thanks and thanks to all of you for being here. So let me begin."

Kimberly's work had brought her down to Peru to follow a truth commission in its effort to collect women's stories about violence suffered during the armed conflict in the 1980s and '90s. Kimberly began her lecture by discussing a death that happened before her arrival.

"There are two versions people tell of how this young woman died," Kimberly said. "Some told she had fallen, and some said she killed herself."

Kimberly learned that the woman was mute, and that she lived in a hillside village. At night, the soldiers who lived at the nearby base would come into the house she shared with her grandmother. "The women in the village could hear her at night. Muffled guttural sounds." These women would later confess, "'We knew by the sound. We knew what the soldiers were doing, but we couldn't say anything.'"

Kimberly broke into the present tense: "It's impossible to erase the image of this young woman screaming with all her might, but unable to say anything."

Silence, Kimberly explained, plays a huge role in her work on gender violence. "What do you do with these silences?" she asked. "How do you listen to them? How do you interpret them? When are they oppressive? And when might they constitute a form of agency? How do you understand silences as they enter and contour the archives?"

———

By the end of the last talk, the Richard Meadow–like man had fallen asleep. He nodded awake and chewed on the back of his hand as if to help himself stay alert. Gary Urton walked on stage one last time. He thanked the speakers for being indicative of the variety and quality of the teaching in the Harvard Anthropology department and invited everyone to a reception upstairs.

The fifteenth floor of William James Hall was laden with catered food. Sushi. Shrimp and cocktail sauce. Ribs. Artichoke hearts, a cheese plate, and an open bar. I had forgotten how free food abounded at Harvard events.

I headed to the wine table first. The man I was pretty sure was Richard Meadow was there, and so was the food archaeology grad student in Karl's class. I thought about approaching the professor, but it felt too soon to talk to someone so close to the center of the story. I didn't yet understand the dynamics within the department, and I worried about the conversation getting repeated and not being able to control to whom.

When maybe-Richard left, I introduced myself to the grad student. Her name was Sadie Weber. I learned she was also auditing Karl's class. She needed to prepare for next year's Generals. Sadie told me Karl had been wrong a couple of times in class, and she disagreed with his theory of agricultural development.

"You should correct him," I said.

"I don't know. I'm just a first-year. He's so much older than me."

I played dumb: "How long has he been teaching here?"

"Ha. I don't know. Like, forever. He must've started in the '60s. Like that guy"—she pointed to maybe-Richard—"was one of his students."

BLACKOUT

IT DIDN'T TAKE LONG FOR the rumors to reach Professor Lamberg-Karlovsky in those first days after Jane's murder. He found them deeply upsetting. Infuriating and misinformed—nasty even. When he spoke to the press to set the record straight, he minimized reports of hostility on the Iranian dig: "There were complaints about too much tuna fish." He dismissed the Persian ritual theory as "completely ridiculous." Karl said there was absolutely no archaeological evidence to support that red ochre was characteristic of burials in the Near East. "There are relics [in Iran] which show that the bones of decomposed bodies were coated with a red material, but we have never found a composed body or a literary text to show that any type of powder was spread over a body in a burial ceremony." Though he obliged when authorities asked him to supply a sample of the red ochre he kept in his office, Karl called it a "total fabrication to assume that because a body has paint on it that it has anything to do with a Middle Eastern ritual." He blamed "so-called Harvard scientists with little knowledge of anthropology" for spreading the rumor.

Publicly, Stephen Williams, the museum's director, also distanced himself from the red ochre rumors. "I want to underline that...information about its uses is not restricted to people with an expertise in any one field." He offered the theory that since Jane was a painter, the red might just be one of her pigments.

Later, in the privacy of the Peabody Museum, Karl cornered a graduate student who he thought was responsible for spreading the rumor. The two were alone in the museum elevator, and, with the doors closed, Karl warned him: "If you ever do or say this again...and we find ourselves in this elevator, you're not getting out of this effing elevator unless you're going to be going directly to the hospital."

―――――

At state police headquarters, 1010 Commonwealth Avenue, the Mitchells took lie detector tests. It had been two days since they found Jane's body. Their tests each lasted about an hour, and on the way out, Don spoke to reporters and complained that police had made little progress in their investigation. There was still no clear suspect, no murder weapon, no well-defined motive.

Jim Humphries arrived later that day, dressed as if he were ready to give a college lecture, in a starched white button-down, with a tie and a houndstooth blazer. He had agreed to the test the day before, but that afternoon, he informed police that he had changed his mind. He wouldn't take the test without the presence of an attorney. He walked out of headquarters, and COED'S FRIEND NIXES LIE TEST splashed across the front page of the *Daily News* that evening.

Jim Humphries on the day of the lie detector tests.

At Cambridge Police headquarters, cops leaked another major clue from the crime scene. Physical evidence, they said, suggested that Jane's killer had lingered for a time after the murder. An unstained cigarette butt had been found in an otherwise blood-splattered ashtray, indicating that the murderer had smoked a cigarette slowly enough to give the blood time to dry.

Jane's Radcliffe friend Ingrid Kirsch was also interrogated. As she left the precinct house after an hour of questioning, she complained of a lack of coordination in the police investigation. "If it wasn't as serious a case as this, it would be laughable."

———

Late that afternoon, Police Chief James F. Reagan summoned reporters to his office for the first time since the investigation began, and the press gathered, eager to hear the latest developments.

Reagan was a tall man in his early fifties, whose police hat covered his thinning white hair. Though he had only been chief of Cambridge Police since last summer, he had already overseen a handful of murders and had established a cordial relationship with reporters. But this meeting was curt and cryptic:

"There will be no statements unless they are cleared through my office," Reagan began. "The reason for this is to provide some accuracy. As I go over the papers, I find some of the statements attributed to various officers are not true."

And just like that, the meeting was over. He dismissed everyone.

Newsmen were stunned. "Suddenly the chief went from doing his job— telling us, when he could, what was going on—to an absolute freeze-out," remembered Michael McGovern, a reporter for the *Daily News*. "It was freezing cold. Nobody wanted to talk."

To Joe Modzelewski, another *Daily News* reporter, the blackout felt like a cover-up. He suspected that someone from Harvard had pressured the cops into silence. It hadn't, after all, been many years since cub reporters on the Boston beat would be warned by veteran colleagues: "Around here, Harvard is thicker than water."

"We couldn't get anybody in the administration—not even a spokesperson— to comment," Joe remembered. He had to lie and say he was from the *New York Times* in order to get anyone from Harvard to talk to him. "They just wanted to sweep it under the rug," he said, and "pretend like it didn't happen."

Reporters caught Reagan as he was leaving the office for the day. He offered no comment about the press blackout, but he said that the sharp-edged stone tool that had been missing from Miss Britton's apartment had been located. Without adding any further details, he drove away.

DANCING WITH GHOSTS

I AUDITED A FEW MORE of Karl's classes, but I was starting to feel like I had learned everything I could from his presence alone. Karl was certainly charismatic enough to support the kind of legend that students would tell and retell for four decades, but whether or not he was responsible for Jane's murder was a question I was no closer to answering than when I arrived in Cambridge.

I returned to New York where I slinked around the periphery of the story. I approached a handful of recent graduate students in archaeology to see if they had heard the same things that James and Iva had. The convergence of their stories was unmistakable. In every version, three facts stayed the same: A young woman was murdered. She had had an affair with her professor. He sprinkled red ochre on her.

I had initiated those conversations carefully. Over the months, the threads that connected generations of people in the Anthropology department had become more visible. I realized that even Morgan Potts, the person from whom I first heard the story, was at the heart of that web; when I emailed him to make sure I had remembered all the details of the story correctly, his address populated the field: danielmpotts—Dan Potts. I knew that name. It was the name of the editor who had assembled the third Tepe Yahya monograph—the one with that photo of Jane lying at everyone's feet. Morgan, it turned out, was his middle name; he was the *son* of that disciple of Lamberg-Karlovsky's. The world of archaeology felt claustrophobically small.

For the same reason, the graduate students were as skittish to talk to me as I had been to reach out to them. Two recent alumni only agreed to speak on the condition of total anonymity. One of them said: "I don't have any direct information on the whole story myself," but the fact that both he and James were "holding on to the story tells you something about its importance inside the institution."

Jane's case itself was also riddled with rabbit holes. I learned from a *Harvard Crimson* article that a year after Jane's death, Ravi Rikhye, the apparent witness to two men running to an idling vehicle, was arrested for international drug smuggling. Jessie Gill, the head of the tenant union, who led the charge against Harvard for being a neglectful landlord of the University Road building, was reportedly an FBI informant on radical activity by the Students for a Democratic Society (SDS).

And I learned that another murder occurred in Cambridge less than a month after Jane's, on Linnaean Street near Radcliffe Yard. The similarities were striking: Ada Bean lived alone and had been bludgeoned to death with a heavy, blunt instrument. She was naked from the waist down and her head and chest had been covered with a blanket. She was fifty, but she looked much younger, and she, like Jane, had dark hair and hazel eyes. Of the four murders in Cambridge in 1969, only two remained unsolved forty-five years later: Jane's and Ada's. I feared that Jane's death was not an isolated incident.

When I asked an old mentor, a professor of investigative journalism, how to keep myself safe while doing this research, he replied: "Don't do it."

———

I moved out of my parents' place and into my first apartment in Brooklyn. I started working at a café down the block because I told myself that this way I would have time for Jane: I would make terrible cappuccinos by day, and at night, I would work on the story. But in reality, for more than a year, I dragged my heels and hid from it. I had deluded myself into thinking that I had some choice in whether or not to pursue her story, not realizing that the truth was that she had already started to seep into the borders of me.

By December 2013, I had been dating Jay, a café regular, for five months, though I still spilled cups anytime my ex Bobby walked into the store. Jay worked in intelligence and wrote music on the side. I had never been in a serious relationship before. Though I had been skeptical of Jay at the beginning—he was too eager to impress, too insecure in himself—over the months, we had built a relationship on holding each other away from the darkness. (When we met, Jay had just called off his engagement. He had found out shortly before the wedding that his fiancée was in love with someone else.) He was broken; I feared that I was; and we were both afraid we were fundamentally unlovable in some way. Our bond felt like the one in *High Fidelity*: "Only people of a certain disposition are frightened of being alone for the rest of their lives at twenty-six; we were of that disposition."

One night, Jay and I walked to the Mountain Cabin restaurant in our neighborhood. We were having wine, and I was facing the door when Bobby walked in with a date. The hostess escorted them to the empty table in front of us. I had to look at him the whole time. I could hear him laugh. Jay and I hurried to finish our wine, and we got up to leave. Bobby stood up, maybe to go to the bathroom, I thought, and then he hugged me.

When Jay and I got to his place, he could see that I was still shaken. He had heard about Bobby and knew the thorns were still there. He poured Negronis and put on the record player. We pulled the chairs to the perimeter of his living room and started slow dancing. I don't think we'd said anything to each other since we walked in. I was holding his shoulder, but it felt like clutching a shield. The next song started. "You've changed / The sparkle in your eyes is gone / Your smile is just a careless yawn / You're breaking my heart." We held each other tight against the encroaching lyrics. But the song wasn't really about us. It was about Bobby. It was about Jay's ex-fiancée. It was about our relationship stopping our skid down into the dark. And suddenly, I realized, we weren't alone in the room. The reason we were together, the reason we were clinging to each other, was because of the people we carried. The people who let us believe for a moment that we weren't truly alone and then pulled the promises away. I could feel that as we circled the room, we were trying to protect each other from all that haunted us, the invisible burdens that laced our every interaction. We didn't say anything. We didn't have to.

I couldn't tell you at the time, but that was the moment that I gave in to Jane's story. I thought that despite the decades that separated us, I had found a companion in my loneliness in her. I couldn't help but imagine time collapse. I saw her doing the exact same choreography, fending off her shadows in the arms of Jim Humphries. My dance with Jay and her dance with Jim overlaid perfectly. It was an imagined scene, I knew, but the line between her and me had started to blur irrevocably. Here I was thinking that I was bearing witness to her story, while the truth was, she was watching over mine. Shaping it. Guiding me, like we were dancing.

Part Two

THE GIRL

2018: WHO WOULD YOU RATHER HAVE IT BE?

It's late afternoon on a July Wednesday in Boston that's so humid, it feels like I'm walking in a sponge. I've just come back to my phone after taking a friend to his car to find a text from Don Mitchell, Jane's old neighbor, the one who found the body. "You there?" it reads. It's stiff, formal. Strange.

After a very rocky start, Don and I now speak often. I know him well enough to know the rhythms of his communication. He happily emails long paragraphs about his garden, or his radiation treatment, or about his consulting work on the collective identity of Mauna Kea. He rarely calls and texting means news, like the time Sergeant Peter Sennott, the Massachusetts State Police detective assigned to Jane's case, contacted him for the first time. They've been in touch since, so I wonder if Sennott might again be behind this message.

My body goes back into reporting mode where everything feels more intense, where my senses strain to register things twice—once in real time, and once to engrave it into memory. He had sent the text at 4:08. It's 4:12 now.

But before I can start responding, I see Don's dot dot dots.

"Ok. While I was waiting for my radiation, Sennott called. I didn't answer, but after I was done (and waiting for the dr. consult), I texted back."

He tells me he's about to call Sennott.

I wait in the absence of dot dot dots. I'm five thousand miles away from him. Silence.

And then, four minutes later: dot dot dot.

"Well, something's about to happen. He's going to call me on Monday. He's been looking for Boyd"—Jane's brother.

To me, this can mean only one thing. They have someone. I've thought about it so many times, anticipating an outcome that I never quite believed would come to pass.

I'm too excited to keep texting. Don picks up immediately. He tells me the reception on the call with Sennott was terrible—Sennott joked that he had to climb up on a rock in his backyard—and Don needed him to repeat things multiple times before he finally understood: *You remember when I came to Hawaii, you said you really didn't trust me because you didn't think we were investigating?* Don said of course. *Well, we were,* Sennott said.

"So they've got something," Don says to me.

"Wow."

"I don't know what it is."

"Wow."

"Oh god," he says. "Who would you rather have it be?"

FUNERAL

THE MORNING OF FRIDAY, JANUARY 10, 1969, was cold and gusty, and Cambridge Police headquarters was quiet. Since Chief Reagan issued the blackout the night before, detectives had begun to treat reporters like they had the plague, and the press, in desperation, resorted to other means to get the story. William Woodward of the *New York Post* knew that Jane's funeral was scheduled for later that morning. He banged on Ingrid Kirsch's door. "I'm going with you," he demanded. "Go to hell," she said. Undeterred, he moved on to University Road and knocked on the Mitchells' door. "You're taking me to the funeral," he insisted. Don slammed the door in his face. "It's a wonder that Mitchell hasn't moved his nose over a couple of feet," Ingrid told cops.

———

Half an hour away, in Needham, Massachusetts, the first guests were already arriving at Christ Episcopal Church, a modest gray-stone building, close enough to Jane's childhood home that it had been her church.

Everyone was eyeing everyone else. Reporters studied the plainclothes officers while the detectives examined the press, and everyone took pictures of the guests as they filed into the church. Despite the subfreezing temperature, Officer Michael Giacoppo clutched his movie camera without gloves so he could better feel for the finicky adjustment knobs. He strategically positioned himself between the parking lot and the stairs where each of the 250 attendees needed to pass in order to enter. When Don Mitchell arrived, Giacoppo asked him to tell him who to film. Together, they scrutinized the crowd.

Cambridge Police Detective Michael Giacoppo holds the camera as Don Mitchell helps direct his attention.

They saw Jim Humphries walk in, accompanied by his brother who had come down from Toronto with the mission to cheer him up or, at the very least, distract him. Jim had returned to state police headquarters the day before with a fancy lawyer that Richard Meadow's father, a dean at Harvard med school, had set him up with. Jim looked paler and more sleep-deprived than usual. But as always, his expression was inscrutable.

Jill Mitchell concealed her eyes with an oversize pair of sunglasses.

Jane's mother stooped over, like her muscles no longer wanted to carry her. She hadn't bothered covering her head to fight the chill. Jane's father, who stood a step behind, looked only at his wife, as if his eyes could steady her.

Jane's parents at her funeral.

The Lamberg-Karlovskys and Stephen Williams made their way from the parking lot with Phil Kohl, the only non-Harvard person on the Tepe Yahya dig that summer, who had come up from Columbia for the funeral. Martie, Karl's wife, wore sunglasses and shrouded her head in a silk scarf, but none of the four of them made any attempt to hide their faces from the cameras. A Needham police officer held up traffic as they crossed the street. Jane's family was prominent enough in town—her father was considered its unofficial mayor—that the local police had shown up to help as a courtesy.

JAN 10 1969

Identification Bureau
Police Dept. Cambridge, Mass.

Cambridge Police photo of Phil Kohl, Stephen Williams, and the Lamberg-Karlovskys on their way to the service.

Richard Meadow walked alone, wrapped in a striped scarf, his hair flopped in front of his eyes, while other graduate students walked in packs. No one carried flowers. Jane's parents had asked, instead, for donations to be made in Jane's memory to the Peabody Museum. Mary Bunting, the president of Radcliffe, managed to slip in unphotographed, but not for J. O. Brew, the former director of the Peabody, or the secretaries who were still troubled by the department's silence.

Even William Woodward, the pushy reporter, managed to find his way into the ceremony. "My god. Has he got balls," Ingrid's husband said when he saw Woodward with Jane's neighbors, the Pressers.

———

Inside the church, wooden beams arched over a narrow nave. The walls were modest and white. A stained-glass cross glittered at the front of the altar, striking for its color in a room otherwise plain. The church was filled to near capacity. Jim Humphries sat in front with Jane's parents, her brother Boyd, and other relatives. Police scattered themselves among the mourners.

Jane's coffin lay near the altar. White roses draped her casket. Soft organ music filled the church. The Reverend Harold Chase read a few prayers and asked that Miss Britton be at "peace now and forever." There was no eulogy.

Mel Konner, an anthropology student, was struck by the decorum of the service. "I remember being there and just listening to these abstractions about heaven and being in this beautiful place and nothing being said about this horrific murder that ended this wonderful young life." It was very different from the Jewish funerals he was used to. The high, almost impersonal nature of the service felt radically disconnected from the grief and pain of her death.

A few people dabbed their eyes with handkerchiefs, but only a single sob pierced the crowd.

And then, less than thirty minutes after the prayer service started, it was over. As mourners left the church, the police resumed their filming. Don Mitchell pointed at a few of Jane's friends and told policemen, "Get him. Get a shot of him. Don't miss him."

Jim Humphries and Jane's family slipped out a side door of the church, skirting the crowd of reporters who had gathered.

TRUE CRIMSON

THE BEST PLACE TO START, I figured, was with the red ochre. If it really was the clue on which the link to the Anthropology department depended, I needed to know as much as I could about the ritual. But the trouble with the red ochre was twofold. First, I didn't know the specifics of the crime scene, because the only thing I had to go on were newspaper reports, which were sensational and often contradictory. The second problem was that the more I looked for red ochre, the more I found it everywhere. Red ochre was in the Levant, across Africa, in Neolithic burials in Europe. It was associated with the oldest known burial in the world—the forty-thousand-year-old interment of "Mungo Man and Mungo Lady" in Australia. It was a key feature of the Moorehead burial complex in Canada, a hallmark of the ritual stone coffin burials in southern Russia, and present in the Shanidar Cave in Iraq, a Neanderthal cemetery of sorts. Many countries celebrated the burial sites of their "Red Ladies": the thousand-year-old Red Queen of Palenque; the nineteen-thousand-year-old Red Lady of El Mirón in Spain; and the thirty-three-thousand-year-old Red Lady of Paviland in Britain (who turned out to be a young man). In fact, some have argued that the use of red ochre in burials may be the earliest example of symbolic thought.

Archaeologists speculated that red ochre was so widespread because the red of the iron ore was reminiscent of blood. Its very name—*hematite*—derives from the Greek for "blood-like." Reading about it, I was reminded of the history of Harvard's school color. What started as an accident—red-hued handkerchiefs bought, impromptu, for the crew team the morning of a race day, had turned crimson when drenched in sweat—became the official color of the school. "Arterial red," Harvard president Lowell had called it. As the late Reverend Gomes who taught the definitive course on Harvard history once explained: "The color of blood is true crimson."

It seemed like the only place I couldn't find red ochre associated with burials was in the one place I wanted to: ancient Iran. There were a few mentions in a couple of Neolithic sites, but those instances stood in relative isolation. And when Zoroastrianism became widespread, authorities in the area forbade cremation and burials. The purity of the earth was sacred, and the burial of a dead body, an act of pollution, so corpses were hoisted onto platforms where they would decompose in the sun and be eaten by predatory birds.

The perfect clue had turned into a perfect cipher: Red ochre was both tantalizingly specific and impossibly vague. It started to look like the ochre meant exactly nothing except perhaps that the killer knew Jane well enough to know she was an archaeologist.

The only place to start, then, was with Jane herself.

——

I constructed a list of people in Radcliffe's class of 1967 using the Freshman Register. It was a blue tome with ads for Harvard Laundry Services and Schoenhof's foreign-languages bookstore and Hickox Secretarial School, with dozens of black-and-white photos of the incoming girls. All three hundred of them. They must have been eighteen in the photos, but everyone looked older than me, hair in perfect curls. I was lucky if my bangs didn't stick to my face when I woke up.

Jane was the very last girl on the second page of pictures. Her lips were pressed together, her chin held nobly—the kind of pose I would expect more from a statue than from a yearbook shot. She looked beautiful and timeless and distant. Beneath her photo was her dorm assignment: Cabot House.

I didn't know very much about Radcliffe. By the time I got to college, it had long ago merged with Harvard, and there were very few traces of it left on campus; it existed only in the names of a few clubs, like the women's crew team or the Harvard-Radcliffe Orchestra, clinging on like an atavistic tailbone. I knew that the old Radcliffe library was now known as the cookbook library, or, more formally, as "The Schlesinger," which I didn't know how to pronounce, so I just slurred inaudibly. I also knew where Radcliffe girls had lived: the far dorms now known as the Quad that you hoped you wouldn't get lotteried into as a freshman on housing day.

And I remember being shocked when I learned from a few Radcliffe alumnae that women's Harvard diplomas were different until 2000. *Two thousand?* I knew Harvard was an all-male college for far too long, but I had no idea women graduates were still being categorized differently less than ten years before I arrived.

I went down the list of the forty-five girls who lived in Cabot with Jane in 1963. I called Suzanne Bloom. No response. I left a voicemail. Judith Pleasure. No response. Voicemail. Katharine Weston, same. Susan Talbot.

"Hello?" she said, skeptically.

At that point I almost didn't believe that there would ever be someone on the other side of the line.

I introduced myself and hedged—I said I was writing a book about Radcliffe and Harvard's merger.

"What kinds of questions are you asking the people you're talking to?" she asked.

"I'm specifically interested in tracking down friends of a girl, Radcliffe '67, named Jane Britton," I said, and squinted as if she could see me.

"Oh yeah!" she said. The hesitation had slipped from her tone.

"She was in your freshman dorm, right?"

"Yes!" Susan said. "And I was on the same floor with her. We were on dorm council together. Yes. She was a tremendous girl. Has she passed away?"

And, just as quickly as it appeared, I watched my hope deflate.

Jane had been murdered decades ago and the crime was still unsolved, I explained.

"No," Susan said, her voice softer.

"It happened in 1969. And I'm trying to unravel—"

"Oh. Jane *Britton*," she said. "Yes, I knew Jane Britton! And I knew she had died tragically. I remember walking through Harvard Square when it was still two ways and seeing the newspaper at the kiosk." The Out of Town newsstand by the Harvard Square T stop. I knew it; it was still there.

"I remember being in full stride through Harvard Square," she said, and "trying to cross the street and seeing this headline and just—stopping in my tracks, being horrified. But somehow, the bizarreness of it matched how bizarre her life was."

Hmm?

"She really was living on the edge, I thought."

Jane wasn't like any of the other girls in the dorm, Susan explained. Whereas the other girls waited around on Saturday nights for the consolation prize milk and cookies that the dorms provided for girls without dates, Jane was never there. Jane never sat around the fireplace when they locked up the dorms at night. She was never in the kitchenette at five in the morning, struggling to type the third draft of her paper. Jane threw in for pizza when the other girls didn't have enough money—but she never stuck around.

It seemed to Susan that Jane was at the crossroads of two very different lives: "She could either be the daughter that was expected by her father, and by the administration—everything by the book, this paragon of virtue. Or she could listen to the artistic, free-spirit stuff that was in her." Jane hadn't yet chosen.

She was a very good student, but it was Jane's paintings that Susan remembered most about her. "They were extremely disturbing." One was a two-by-three-foot composition about hell. It struck Susan as Jane's version of *Paradise Lost*—haunting, and completely mesmerizing. "They were all solid red," she said, unaware that her memory resonated with the theory that the red ochre was really just Jane's red paint.

"I just felt brutalized when I saw the headline about what happened to her. Totally brutalized," Susan said. "I had the feeling that she must have angered someone very immature."

Susan suggested I find Jane's freshman roommate, Elisabeth Handler, a tall, skinny girl with a mass of curly hair. She and Jane were inseparable. "They sort of looked like they were cast in *The Addams Family*."

I said thank you and was surprised that she sounded equally grateful: "Well, you have in one phone call swirled me back, what, fifty years."

"Maybe Jane will come to us in a dream," she said before hanging up.

JANE

BEHIND THE CURTAIN OF THE blackout, police struggled to make sense of the evidence. Even when the chemist's analysis came in, it didn't offer much clarity. Jane's nightgown was stained with a mixture of blood and urine, and the top rear of it was sprinkled with ochre. It had one small black smear that was similar in appearance to the black material that was also found on Jane's right hand. The analyst couldn't determine whether this was grease or soil, though one of the two frying pans in her kitchen was heavily coated with grease and carbon and contained trace bloodstains. The candelabrum on the radiator near the head of the bed held the stubs of candles. And a benzidine test revealed that the center portion of it was positive for blood. The pillow underneath Jane's bottom was heavily stained with blood and urine and semen, and those sperm cells were intact, which limited the window of sexual activity to close to her death. Officer Giacoppo also found women's underwear in Jane's bathroom, the crotch of which tested positive for semen stains but not for intact sperm cells. But Dr. Katsas's in-depth autopsy did not comment on whether Jane had been sexually assaulted. Jane's injuries weren't conclusive evidence of a struggle: Except for her head wounds, there was just one small contusion on her right arm, and a small twist of multicolor wool fibers in her left hand. Only Jane's type O blood was found in the apartment.

Detective Lieutenant Davenport joked in one of his interrogations that he and the other officers were so at sea in their investigation, they were about ready to enroll in Professor Williams's class. At least then they could learn about the ritual element of the crime scene.

The unanswered questions left police little choice but to question and re-question Jane's friends, searching for some detail they had missed the first time through. They got the names and addresses of people close to Jane. They obtained a directory of all the students in Harvard's Anthropology PhD program. They checked her recent phone calls. They scoured her phone book and diary. They studied three statements that arrived at Cambridge Police headquarters from the US embassy in Rome. They were from Arthur Bankoff, a student in the department, and Andrea, his wife, in response to questions that Don and Jill had relayed from the Cambridge Police. Though they had been abroad when Jane was killed, the Bankoffs were important friends of Jane's—they had been on the dig in Iran with Jim and Jane, and they had been neighbors for a year before that.

From the statements, police learned that Jane did not ever entertain anyone in a nightgown, and was a sound sleeper, so the circumstantial evidence didn't necessarily point to Jane knowing her killer. But the idea that she wouldn't kick the shit out of an intruder didn't quite compute. As Karl Lamberg-Karlovsky later told reporters, "Jane was not the type to let a stranger in without picking up the refrigerator and throwing it at him." Ingrid also assured cops that if Jane was aware of her attacker, she would have fought like hell. "I think she'd kick him in the balls probably," she said. "Janie's one of the most fearless human beings that I've ever met."

Jill Mitchell told cops that Jane had been attacked when she was a sophomore in college, and she had fought back. Around two in the morning, after babysitting near the Radcliffe quad, Jane was walking the short distance to her car when a man grabbed her. "She thought he was a high school kid," Jill told police. Jane pulled out the knife that she always kept in her bag for paring apples and stabbed at him. She didn't manage to cut him, but she ripped his nylon jacket, and the guy fled. "She was a fighter," Jill said. "She wouldn't just not put up a struggle. She wouldn't freeze, either. She would do something."

But then Jill remembered something else. For all the ferocity she had shown, "she never thought to scream."

———

The more the cops learned about Jane, the more confused they were about why exactly a woman so dynamic was with a man as withdrawn as Jim Humphries. Jim was as careful, stiff, and meticulous in his social interactions as he was in the field. Friends described him as a "gentleman to the point where it's almost disconcerting." He was more likely to run away from a difficult situation than to confront it head-on. And Jim's interest didn't make much sense, either: According to Ingrid, Jane's intensity would have been intimidating for anyone, but especially someone like Jim: "I should think that if I were a guy involved with Janie, I'd be scared shitless, frankly, because she came on like a ton of bricks."

The idea that cops were missing something was not helped by the fact that the chemist's analysis revealed trace bloodstains on the maroon rugby sweater that Jim was wearing that night. And traces of bloodstains over the blades of his hockey skates that he had worn ice skating.

"What was the attraction?" Detective Lieutenant Davenport asked Ingrid.

"Mystery," she said. "The fact that he was enigmatic a lot. Girls are turned on by that."

And then Ingrid added: "She fretted out in him some psychological imbalance that fascinated her—of the same sort that she had—of tremendous insecurity, a feeling of not being adequately loved."

DO YOU FOLLOW ME

TWO WEEKS LATER, JAY AND I had dinner in Brooklyn. It was a candlelit pizza place, with a garden and vintage advertising signs tucked between the foliage. I decided it would be the night I would tell him about Jane. He knew I was working on something to do with Harvard in the '60s, but he would let me leave it at that. I didn't feel like Jane was someone I could just bring up casually at a party, to leverage her like an anecdote meant to impress. But I hated living in this world alone.

Jay listened patiently. I told him how scared the Stine hiking tragedy made me. That I was worried I was getting myself in deep with something I could only see the tip of. That I found it all too easy to imagine there really was a conspiracy to keep Jane's story quiet. That even the most far-fetched of my speculations—that the dig at Tepe Yahya offered the US government an ear to the ground the decade before the Iranian Revolution—could not be immediately dismissed. Karl would later refute the idea of a Tepe Yahya government connection, and add, "I never worked for the US government."

But the CIA was the only agency that, in response to my Freedom of Information Act requests, refused to either confirm or deny the existence of records related to either Jane Britton or Tepe Yahya.

Jay wasn't convinced by my line of thinking, but he could see how real it had become for me. He held my hand and, with the other, picked up his pizza knife and molded my palm around it. Then, moving me by the wrist, he showed me how best to stab someone, as he had learned in the tactical training for his intelligence work.

Stabbing the air, scanning for exits, discussing the contents of a go-bag, agreeing on code words: I was stunned by how right it felt for us to have fallen into the role of co-conspirators. It was less lonely inside Jane's story with Jay for company. What surprised me, though, was how being enveloped together within her story also made me feel less lonely with him.

JANE AND JIM

THE SPRING BEFORE THEY LEFT for Tepe Yahya, Jane and Jim were sitting in Harkness, the student commons, with a few other graduate students. Sarah Lee Irwin, who had recently gotten divorced from a faculty member in the Anthropology department, was there too. Sarah Lee wasn't holding back in making her desire for Jim known.

After lunch, Jim left Harkness. Jane followed. She knew where he lived—in Child Hall, one of the graduate school dorms. She knocked on the door, and Jim invited her in.

"Look, I just thought I'd tell you that you're being chased," Jane said.

"Oh, by whom?"

"Well, Christ. It should be obvious you're being followed by Irwin."

Jim leaned back and gave her one of his looks, wry and confident. "Well, you know, doesn't your telling me this constitute chasing on your part?"

"Damn straight," Jane said. She turned around and walked out.

RADCLIFFE MEMORIES

ELISABETH HANDLER DIDN'T PROVE HARD to find. Her LinkedIn page came up easily enough. A tasteful chin-length cut had replaced the mass of curls of her Freshman Register photo, but she had the same round face and mischievous smile. I found her email on the website of her PR company in California, and wrote to her, with the anodyne subject line "Radcliffe Memories."

As I waited to hear back, I set my aims on tracking down the writer of the original *Harvard Crimson* article about the murder. I wanted to know if there was any truth to Morgan's story about the *Crimson* being forced to change its report.

The byline on the article belonged to someone named Anne de Saint Phalle. I found Anne in the Harvard Alumni Directory, but the listing offered no contact information, and it showed that she changed her name to Anne Khalsa. Eventually, via a French genealogy website and a *New York Times* obituary, I learned she now went by "Sat Siri Khalsa," and she was a part-time Vedic astrologer and part-time financial trader in New Mexico. She was eager to help, but when she heard what I was writing about, she said she remembered nothing about the Jane Britton case.

I emailed her a link to her *Crimson* article to see if it jogged any memories. Nothing, she replied. "Very strange. Even as if I didn't write it."

REAL ESTATE

"DOES IT TAKE A MURDER to make Harvard obey the law?" Jessie Gill, the University Road tenant union leader, asked at the Cambridge City Council meeting following Jane's murder.

Harvard was the landlord of Jane's University Road apartment building. It had bought the place in 1967 with the plan to convert it into a new university-related building. But residents had complained. They didn't want to lose their rent-stabilized apartment for yet another Harvard building. Not wanting to inflame tension with the town of Cambridge, the university had acquiesced. But it made clear that the compromise also meant that residents should not expect renovations or repairs. In exchange for getting to stay and having rents kept low, residents would have to make do with the building, as is.

Jessie Gill accused Harvard of deliberate negligence. She alleged that they had been aware for two years that the building lacked functioning locks on its main doors—a violation of Cambridge building code—and faulted Harvard for putting the bottom line above the safety of its residents. "We tried to request the locks from Henry H. Cutler, Harvard's manager for taxes, insurance, and real estate, but he told me with a smirk that 'we can't make improvements if we don't get more money out of you people.'"

Jane's murder cast an unwelcome spotlight on Harvard's real estate policies, and it was coming at a time when Harvard was in the middle of a $48.7 million fundraising drive. The faulty locks were threatening to turn into a scandal. At a news conference, a young reporter pressed Harvard's then president Nathan Pusey to answer for Harvard's negligence at the University Road building. Pusey was so outraged by this line of questioning that he had his top aide call the *Globe* management to lodge a complaint about its obnoxious reporter.

Councilwoman Barbara Ackermann said, "With all the problems that Harvard brings to this community, it is the least they can do to be law-abiding landlords. A girl is dead, and I do not say she would be alive today if there had been a lock on her door, but there is strong reason to believe that."

In the swirl of this press, University Road residents received a note from the real estate company that managed the property for Harvard: "Due to the recent happenings at 6 University Rd., the City of Cambridge has required us to install automatic locking devices on all vestibule doors, and remove all debris from the front and back halls and basement areas, and remove motorcycles from the basement."

On the day of Jane's funeral—while all eyes were on Needham—the real estate management company, on behalf of Harvard, began quietly installing locks on the doors at University Road. It had been done in such haste that no one had thought to give residents the keys to the new locks.

The *Daily News*'s Joe Modzelewski was left with the impression that neither Harvard's administration nor the police seemed too interested in finding Jane's killer. "They just wanted it to die down, bury her, and move along with life as usual at Harvard."

———

At almost exactly the same time, six miles away from Harvard Square, the gravediggers in Needham Cemetery were working hard to dig a hole for Jane's casket in the frozen winter soil. A cloudless sky hung over the small group of friends and family members who soon gathered around the Reverend Harold Chase as he performed a brief graveside ceremony. Jim stood near the back.

The Brittons were exceptionally private, and this day was no exception. The only time Jane's father showed emotion was when a photographer came close to the grave. Jane's brother Boyd rushed over to keep him from doing anything rash. A Needham Police officer also noticed and ran the photographer off.

Jane's coffin was slowly lowered into the sloping hill. Friends and family moved off the plot, and the two workmen got to work on closing her grave.

Family and close friends gather during Jane's burial service. Jane's parents and her brother, Boyd, are on the right.

ELISABETH

AT THE TWO-WEEK MARK of emailing Elisabeth under the guise of trying to plumb "Radcliffe Memories," I dared myself to call her. It was a Thursday, and I reached her at work. I introduced myself. "Yes, I know who you are. I've been ducking you," she said. I apologized for having been so persistent. She laughed and invited me to call her back on Saturday.

When she picked up the phone two days later, Elisabeth's voice was warm and buoyant. For almost half an hour we talked about her experience at Radcliffe without any mention of Jane. Elisabeth, the daughter of a *New York Times* foreign correspondent, had grown up abroad. When she got to Radcliffe, "I was a complete alien who nobody knew was an alien. I spoke the language, enough. And I didn't let on."

Blend in, she scolded herself. But it didn't help the isolation. Radcliffe felt more like living in a hotel than in a community. "It was just so demeaning to me if you compared the women's housing to the men's." The girls had curfews and "parietal" rules like "three feet on the ground at all times" when men were over. Class was a fifteen-minute walk to campus in mandatory skirts and stockings that were barely a shield against the cold. It wasn't until 1973, after the houses went co-ed and men started living in the Radcliffe quad, that Harvard committed to the shuttle service that I knew.

But I recognized more of my experience than I expected. The ambition and grit of the undergraduates. The true nature of a Harvard education: learning how to get around red tape, excelling at the game of opportunity-making, deciphering academic double-speak. And most of all, the sink-or-swim nature of its advising: "You can't cry at Harvard," Elisabeth was told her freshman year, after a Kafkaesque battle over paperwork had kept her shuttling back and forth between administrative offices. At least, Elisabeth said, she enjoyed the food at Radcliffe. The food at her British boarding school had been "the liver of ancient cows that died of scurvy; cabbage boiled down to a puddle."

But before I could ask about Jane, Elisabeth brought up her roommate: a young woman from Washington State who, she said, "was a perfectly nice person, but we didn't really have a lot in common."

As sure as I was that Jane was from Massachusetts, I was more sure that no one would dare describe her as "perfectly nice." I worried Susan Talbot had gotten everything mixed up.

Elisabeth continued: "My best friend was a couple of doors down. She had been from early teens interested in anthropology." This girl, Elisabeth explained, encouraged her to attend her first anthro class. "She got me smoking. She was the one who encouraged me to drink. All the wonderful gateways were opened by her." Compared to her roommate, "Jane—the girl I became good friends with—was very much more worldly and also a hoot."

Jane.

"To be totally honest with you," I said, "one of my main interests in this era, is..." I stumbled. "I heard about what happened to her—" I trailed off.

"Yeah," Elisabeth said, which gave me just enough courage to continue.

"—Or the rumors of what happened," I said, "and I'm interested in finding out what exactly did."

Her voice didn't falter. "Boy, I would be happy to help you with that," she said. I could feel relief pour through me like a tourniquet had been removed. "It was just horrifying."

JANE AT RADCLIFFE

THAT FIRST WEEK OF FRESHMAN year, 1963, everyone in Cabot House moved as one. It wasn't just that they all ate together. All forty-five girls, it seemed to Elisabeth Handler, were under the impression they could fit at the same round table.

At one of those group lunches, Elisabeth looked around the room. Compared with her, the other girls carried themselves like they had been groomed for Radcliffe since preschool. Julie Spring, her roommate, was the daughter of a Unitarian minister. She wore wraparound skirts and round-collared blouses. Julie's biggest worry about coming to college was whether she could learn to shave in the shower rather than in the tub. Elisabeth wasn't sure if she had ever been so young.

But she also felt bad for being annoyed by Julie's enthusiasm. To be at Radcliffe really was something to celebrate. It was the most prestigious of all the women's colleges, and, at a quarter the size of Harvard, it was the more difficult of the two to get into. "I didn't want to be the one bad apple in the bunch, where everybody else has this wonderful experience, and then this little grump in the corner is bitter about an education most people would kill for," Elisabeth would later remember.

Just then another first-year came bounding into the dining hall. "I did it!" she announced to the room. "I got into a graduate seminar!"

Elisabeth didn't even know what a graduate seminar was. *How did an eighteen-year-old manage to weasel her way into—*

"I need to do that!" Julie gasped. Elisabeth tried not to roll her eyes.

"OH FUCK," a voice said, across the table.

Elisabeth looked up. The girl was striking. Her eyes were green and widely spaced. Her skin was a pale ivory. Her hair was so black it was almost blue.

———

Jane was "a kick in the pants," Elisabeth remembered. "She was sort of like a combination of Groucho Marx and Dorothy Parker. Just without the mustache." Jane wasn't conventionally beautiful—she liked to say she was built like a brick shithouse—but she was magnetic. She smoked and eschewed hair-sprayed updos. She had a low voice and a deep laugh that erupted spontaneously, and when she was being particularly wicked, she would cock her thin eyebrows like a bow ready to spring. Jane's room, it turned out, was right down the hall from Elisabeth's, and the two quickly became inseparable.

Life in Cabot took some getting used to for both of them. First there were the spartan rooms with two wooden dressers, two small desks with a wooden chair each, and bunk beds. Jane slept on the lower bunk. There were no lamps, no curtains, no rugs. Jane's room, at least, had a window that looked out onto the quad.

The girls shared a communal bathroom, and each floor came with its own ironing board and iron. In the basement, there were laundry machines (twenty-five cents per load) and hair dryers (ten cents per fifteen minutes). Telephones were shared one for every twenty-five, but the incoming calls were routed through the student on bell desk duty, which meant their social lives were on display. Everyone could tell how popular a girl was by the thickness of her stack of pink slips of missed calls. The sign-out books— in which girls wrote where they were headed and with whom—were open for all to see.

Then there were the rules. Radcliffe distributed a handbook that the girls were expected to memorize. They were required to do five hours a week of housework: bell duty, waiting on the cafeteria tables, and light pantry work. The handbook asked that students "be discreet when sunbathing" and specified that "good taste demands that discretion shall be shown in displays of affection on Radcliffe property and in all public places." Smoking was allowed everywhere (except in bed), but alcohol was forbidden. Occasional exceptions were made for sherry.

And there were the social rules: as freshmen, they were allowed to sign out until 11:15 any night and were allotted thirty 1 a.m. sign outs per semester. But men weren't allowed except during parietal hours, the time when members of the opposite sex could be in the dorm. All men needed to be signed in and out by their hostesses, and the girl was expected to shout "Man on!" to alert people in the hall.

———

Radcliffe had started as the Harvard Annex in 1879, but women had only been allowed into Harvard classes since 1943. And that milestone was less about equality than convenience: Professors resented having to give the same class twice when their Harvard classes were empty because of the war. On the ten-year anniversary of joint instruction, the *Crimson* published an article about the Harvard instructors' experience of teaching co-ed classes. One instructor said the women in his class wore curlers and no makeup so "it was something of a shock to see a girl in your section at a House dance and discover she actually had a face after all." Another instructor said he liked dating Radcliffe students because "Wellesley girls are prettier, but that Radcliffe is more convenient." Elliott Perkins, a history lecturer and the master of Lowell House, was nostalgic for the old days. Though he "really [couldn't] tell the difference intellectually," he felt that "the Yard looked better before, with just Harvard men."

By the time Jane and Elisabeth were freshmen, Radcliffe girls were judged side by side with Harvard students: the same classes, the same professors, the same exams. Radcliffe diplomas had started also saying Harvard on them the June before Jane arrived. Nevertheless, they felt like second-class citizens. Cliffies didn't have access to the same scholarship money and financial aid. They weren't allowed to enter Lamont, the undergraduate library. They were required to have escorts walk them home from extracurriculars if they were to be out past 11 p.m. There were only nine women's bathrooms on campus, and finding somewhere to eat in the Yard to avoid trekking all the way back to the Quad between classes wasn't much easier. A freshman boy could invite a girl to eat in the all-male Freshman Union, but it was widely known that it was tradition for the men to clink their glasses with their forks when a girl walked into the dining hall—the evident goal being to make the women as uncomfortable as possible.

When classes started a week later, Jane convinced Elisabeth to try Anthropology 1a with her. The class met three times a week at 10 a.m. and was taught by Professors William Howells and Stephen Williams. Jane and Elisabeth sat together near the back of class. They would always giggle when the same boy screeched into class late and nearly fell into his seat.

They were entranced almost immediately by the world of anthropology. "I mean, *hello*," Elisabeth would later say. At Radcliffe, "I might as well have been popped out in the middle of the deepest Amazon. So this idea of 'here we will study culture, we will pick out things that will make it interesting and different, and we will not interfere, we will blend into the background with our notebook and pith helmet and everybody will be that much wiser about the subject?' It makes perfect sense that that's what I gravitated to." There was an old joke that people who went into psychiatry were unhappy with themselves. Psychologists were unhappy with society. And anthropologists were people who were unhappy with their culture.

Early that semester, one of the teaching fellows for Anthro 1a threw a party at his house and invited some members of the class. Elisabeth went, and the boy who was always late to class was there, too. Elisabeth introduced herself. She confessed that she and Jane had in fact been sticking their legs out to trip him and apologized. The boy just laughed. He said he was so tired that he didn't realize he was stumbling over anything but his own feet.

"Peter Panchy," the boy said.

Elisabeth and Peter kept talking and drinking the punch—red wine with cloves floating in it. By the end of the party, Elisabeth was drunk for the first time in her life. She threw up on Peter's shoes. He didn't mind.

Soon, Jane, Elisabeth, and Peter became a pack. They would do silly things in the back of the classroom. Sometimes Ingrid Kirsch would join them. Sometimes one or the other of them would be depressed, and Peter would bring some hideous alcohol, and they would sit out on the steps of the school across the street from the Radcliffe dorms, in the Cambridge winter, and get hammered. They bonded over the fact that they each felt alien: Elisabeth because of where she grew up; Jane because she always felt on the outside of things; and Peter because he wasn't born into the same privilege as so many of his classmates. Peter's father was an Albanian immigrant who had to quit Harvard halfway through because his family's grocery store was on the verge of bankruptcy. "Just because you've been invited, doesn't mean you belong," Peter would later remember about his time at Harvard.

———

The class of 1967 felt caught between the 1950s and '60s. There was a mandatory abstinence lecture in Cabot House for these freshmen. The girls gathered in their nightgowns and bathrobes and PJs to listen to an older student fall apart in front of them. She told them that she had been in love with an upperclassman, had dated him for two years, had a "full sexual affair" with him, and then he left her for somebody else. Susan Talbot recalled, "She was weeping and telling us to go ahead and do our dating, but don't lose your virginity to a man who's going to walk out."

In October 1963, a scandal hit. Students had been complaining about parietals, arguing that they "reinforce the idea that women are objects for sex, rather than friends or companions in love" and the only thing that they prevent is not premarital sex but "the less explicitly sexual aspects of romance: joking over breakfast, talking comfortably in the early afternoon." The administration had had enough. Two Harvard deans pushed back, expressing deep distress over what they saw as a "loose moral situation" on campus. They vowed to make the rules governing parietal hours even stricter: "It's our positive duty to deal with fornication just as we do with thievery, lying and cheating."

But not even Radcliffe and Harvard could be kept in their bubble for long. In November, President Kennedy was shot. The house administrators brought a television into the Cabot common room and the girls gathered to watch. The bell of Memorial Church, which normally rang on the hour, tolled every fifteen minutes for him. It echoed eerily through campus.

———

Sophomore year, Jane and Elisabeth moved into Coggeshall, an old frame house affiliated with Cabot, a few blocks away on Walker Street. It was homey, with 1950s living room furniture, and fewer than a dozen girls. Jane and Elisabeth were much happier there—each girl had her own bedroom, they could cook in the kitchen and invite friends over—and stayed in the house until graduation. Jane was particularly fond of the head resident's cat, Edward, a big orange fluffy creature. When poor Edward had surgery to remove his balls, his testicular misfortune was an endless source of comedic delight for Jane.

Karen Black, the head resident, was struck by Jane's charisma. Jane would "get to talking about things and you'd just sit and listen to her." She told stories about her expeditions: the caves in Abri Pataud she'd come back from digging in the previous summer, the trains in Greece, the bazaars of Athens. They were so vivid, it felt like she resurrected the past:

> Here we were, smelling like a stable, dirty, scarcely combed. Here is the Mediterranean, all plush and marble. Here are the astonished bellboys wondering whether to kick us out or not. Here is Britton, ready to do some fast talking.

"She had this terrific attachment to things of the dim past," Karen remembered.

The divide between the class years began to feel as wide as generational gaps. Drugs hit campus that year, the Supreme Court case *Griswold v. Connecticut* legalized access to birth control for married couples, and the beginnings of the civil rights and antiwar movements took hold, though initial support was small. Vietnam protesters had to dodge water balloons hurled from the freshman dorms. Harvard and Radcliffe had started actively recruiting Black candidates, but numbers wouldn't rise significantly until 1969. (In the decade prior to 1964, there were rarely more than three Black students in any of Radcliffe's graduating classes.) Susan Talbot only became aware of the political groundswell when she lost track of one of the freshmen she was in charge of. When the young student's friends reluctantly admitted that she was at a teach-in, Susan responded, fully serious, "I didn't know there was a new Chinese restaurant in the Square."

Carol Sternhell, class of '71 and one of the first students to participate in Harvard's co-ed housing experiment in the spring of 1970, would later remember the electricity of this moment: College is a time when you test the boundaries of your world—sex, drugs, experiences—anyway. To have the world's mores shatter at the same time was extraordinary.

As the present day continued to encroach on Harvard, Jane became increasingly invested in the Anthropology department. She started illustrating artifacts for Professor Movius as a side gig. Almost every afternoon, after the Peabody Library closed at 5 p.m., she would go to the Hayes-Bickford, the cafeteria on Mass Avenue, with graduate students and teaching fellows for beer and coffee and gossip. They called themselves the hunter-gatherers.

Jane would relay the scuttlebutt to Elisabeth. "It was all kind of soap-opera-y and intrigue-y and it felt really political." The way Jane talked about people in the department, it seemed like she was sleeping with everybody. "I didn't feel like I had any grounds to say, *Now, Jane, no, you shouldn't be involved in this sort of way, this isn't good for you,*" Elisabeth recalled. Sensing a certain fragility in Jane, she didn't even feel like she could ask how much was true, and, to be honest, she didn't want to know.

Jane tended toward extremes in her life as well as in her stories. She was always on some fad diet—eating too many bananas or fasting for seventy-two hours one moment, and then off to the Brigham's for a chocolate shake the next. Jane came alive at night. She worked erratically. When she focused, she blazed through her work with a vitality that had its own glow. Other times, she'd disappear into her room for days on end, only emerging for scurrying trips to the kitchen next to her room.

But those same traits—the intensity, the obstinance, the wildness—made Jane a terrific friend. She had her own gravitational pull. She may have padded herself with a wad of cynicism and pessimism but she was "a cockeyed optimist" underneath, Elisabeth remembers.

When Jane or Elisabeth got depressed or angry or sad or bored in college, they drove. Jane had access to a 1962 white convertible with red leather seats. Even in the winter, they kept the top down. They'd head to Gloucester, or to Providence, or to Revere Beach, late at night, the wind in their faces. The looming deadlines would disappear. Or when it really all got to be too much, they would treat themselves to a fancy meal at Chez Jean, a sweet French bistro on Shepard Street. At Chez Jean, "I could let my hair down with her and talk about my experiences and my past and be a little more comfortable because I sort of felt like she knew me. It wasn't . . . I didn't have to explain everything."

One such evening, there was a young couple at a table behind Elisabeth that caught Jane's attention. The guy was loudly insisting on ordering frog legs for his date, and his date kept saying, "No, I couldn't possibly." Eventually she relented. When the waiter brought the dish to the table, Jane smirked, watching the exchange happen. The girl picked up her first bite. She brought it to her lips.

Plenty loud enough for the whole restaurant to hear, Jane leaned over and let out a voluble RRRRRRIBBBITT!

BACK WITH ELISABETH

"AND THE REAL, HEARTBREAKING PART of the story—" Elisabeth said, back on that first phone call together. "Well it's all heartbreaking, but the part that just adds an extra edge of horror to it is that she had really found a good guy."

Elisabeth was talking about Jim Humphries. When Jane was the maid of honor at Elisabeth's wedding in the spring of 1968, she spent much of it gushing about some tall Canadian she had just met. "She was really, *really* happy for the first time."

———

In early January 1969, Elisabeth had gotten a call from Peter Panchy, their friend from Anthropology 1a who was by then married and living in Somerville, just east of Cambridge. He had seen Jane before Christmas, by accident. They had run into each other in the Square, and she invited him over for tea. He and Jane spent about half an hour together. She said she was really getting into ice skating, and they promised to be in touch after the holidays. When Peter and his family got back to Somerville after their holiday travels, Peter carried his daughter up to bed, put her to sleep, and turned on the evening news. Jane's face was on television.

Jane is dead, Peter told Elisabeth.

Elisabeth couldn't bring herself to go to Jane's funeral. "I felt so guilty just for being alive."

As shocking as Jane's murder was to Elisabeth, so, too, was the silence and the stalling of the investigation in the weeks that followed. "The curtains really came down in the Cambridge Police Department," Elisabeth told me. "There was a very strong sense that the fix was in."

Even years later, it seemed to her that something stood in the way of the investigation. She told me that Jane's brother, Boyd, went to Cambridge in the mid-'90s to try to see the police files. But they gave him the runaround. They wouldn't let him see a single thing. "I can't imagine what it is," Elisabeth told me. "I mean Jane's father was a very prominent man. He was a vice president at Radcliffe...He was a very big-deal businessman. Very wealthy. Very well connected. It would seem that if anyone could pull strings to solve his daughter's murder, it would be him."

I ran the married professor affair angle by her.

"You know, I wouldn't dismiss it out of hand, but I don't think it would have been going on at this point. You know—"

"Because her boyfriend at the time was James Humphries," I said.

"Right."

"And she was happy with him."

"As far as I know, yeah."

I asked Elisabeth if she had a theory of what happened then.

"I had fingered a suspect. The fact that he was in Peru at the time seemed to me just to be a minor detail. He was one of the guys that she had gotten involved with who was just bad news."

"Was his name Ed Franquemont?" I asked, pulling a half-remembered name from an old conversation with James Ronan. Years before, James had said that Ed was Jane's last boyfriend. When I had pointed out that all the newspaper reports said it was Jim Humphries, James thought he was probably just confused.

"Yes!" she said, surprised that it wasn't just her own private theory. "He was horrible to her in front of me. Just kind of abusive and rude."

Ed Franquemont had been a Harvard anthropology student, class of '67, and, like Jane, he moved straight into the PhD program before dropping out sometime before Jane's death. He and Jane dated for less than a year starting the spring of their senior year. "I was absolutely sure it was *Ed Franquemont*," Elisabeth said, practically growling his name.

And then she remembered something else. It was Jane's junior year. She could still picture the two of them sitting on the floor of Jane's room in Coggeshall. Jane was shaken. She said she had met a guy, Jerry Roth, the son of the writer Philip Roth, and they had been sleeping together "without much discussion or talk or fellowship." Jane had been haunted by a feeling that something was very wrong, so when he left her alone in his room one time, she snooped around his apartment until she found his diary.

The entries contained Jane's worst fears: descriptions of what she looked like while they were having sex. How unattractive she was. That she was "cold as a slab of china." She was so hurt and so horrified and so offended that the next time she saw him, she broke up with him on the spot. But "she was terribly, terribly distraught. I mean, she was a wreck," Elisabeth remembered, which was unusual for Jane, who always brushed things off with a joke. "It was off to the French restaurant on the spot on that one." For decades, Elisabeth, in solidarity, refused to read any Philip Roth books.

But much later, during a spate of coverage about him for his eightieth birthday, Elisabeth learned that Philip Roth never had any children. There was no son.

"So I was like, WHO THE HELL WAS THAT?"

I wondered out loud what would be so bad that she would lie about it to her best friend. Elisabeth didn't know. Neither of us, I'm ashamed to say, considered the possibility that the man was the one who had lied to Jane.

"I just took it on faith," Elisabeth said. "There was no question about it in my mind that she had been hurt by somebody and hurt quite badly," she reflected. But, "you know, obviously, she hid somebody from me. She would tell me about the events and the hurt and the insult and the sadness about it, but she hid who he was."

EVERY BAD THING YOU KNOW

ABOUT HER

THE COPS HAD HEARD ENOUGH stories about Jane's wit and bravado. Impatient, one said to Don Mitchell: "She wasn't murdered because she was wonderful.

She was murdered because she made someone angry enough to kill her, and we need to know every bad thing you know about her."

The Mitchells racked their brains, but they came up blank. And then, they realized, that blank might be exactly the answer the cops were looking for.

"Now that I think about it," Jill told Detective Lieutenant Davenport, "She could have gone out an awful lot that we didn't know about." Jill admitted that Jane's odd sleeping hours had given her pause. "Sometimes I wondered because she would sleep until noon sometimes for days on end and I'd think…she must be awake at night doing something. But I never really thought to ask her about it. [I] figured it was her own business if she wanted to sleep until noon."

The detective asked if Jane would have confided in the Mitchells. About some things, sure. "Other things I had a feeling there was a wall up."

Ingrid echoed the Mitchells' admission that large chunks of Jane's life were a mystery to her, especially that final semester. "I worried about this a lot this fall. I tried to get through to Jane, and I couldn't really, because for one reason or another, Jim was sort of sacred to her. And he didn't want to be known. He didn't want to be figured out. And she respected his desire not to be figured out, so she didn't help any of us with it."

Jim was a total mystery to the Mitchells, too. They had been in the same department for more than two years, but their first real conversation wasn't until late the previous year. Even after he and Jane became serious, they didn't interact very much. Don only saw Jim at Jane's a handful of times, and, as far as he knew, Jim only stayed the night once. "And that wasn't even because he wanted to. Humphries was very strange about that, I think."

Other people who might have known what was going on with Jane were away that semester. The Bankoffs were in Europe. Boyd had been deployed to Vietnam, and Elisabeth had moved to Norfolk, Virginia, and was busy with her first year of marriage. The cops never interviewed Elisabeth, but even if they had, she would have just underlined the mystery of Jane's final six months: "It's a question mark," she'd say decades later. "Who was she with? What was she doing? Where did she go?"

Cops pushed Ingrid to remember if Jane might have been seeing anyone else in the fall while Jim was home in Toronto for the semester. Categorically no, Ingrid said. She may not have agreed with Jane's taste in men, but Jane was a "one-man dog." Jane was committed to Jim, and "knowing Jane as well as I did, if she had violated that commitment in any overt way, then I think she would have let me know."

"Right," Detective Davenport said.

"Unless she felt guilty," Ingrid said. "In which case, she wouldn't have."

———

Growing up in Needham, Jane cultivated her own secret world. On the surface, she was playful, outgoing, charming. In grade school, she made up a "Be Kind to Garbagemen Club." But she wasn't only a sweet, smiley girl. Her temper flared occasionally, like when a neighborhood boy hit her with a snowball with a rock in it, and she let rip.

Jane, about five years old.

Jane spent a lot of her time with her neighbor, Karen John, whom she'd been friends with since nursery school. Karen was impressed by how much independence Jane's family allowed her. Jane's father was often away, and her mother never hovered. After Jane whipped through her homework, she could do whatever she wanted. Karen would often come over and they'd draw or hop around the tiny playhouse in her backyard. Sometimes they would play in the basement, and, on very special occasions, they'd go upstairs, where the additional bedroom felt like a half-hidden secret, and they would watch cowboy movies and play hide-and-seek.

It felt like Jane belonged to another world, Emily Woodbury, another childhood friend, would later remember. Everything came out of Jane a little slant. Her humor was wry, and her language, playfully off. "Let's went!" she'd shout instead of "Let's go." "Fit hit the Shan." Her childhood drawings were little monsters that illustrated idioms—a dragon with a big belly was a "pregnant pause."

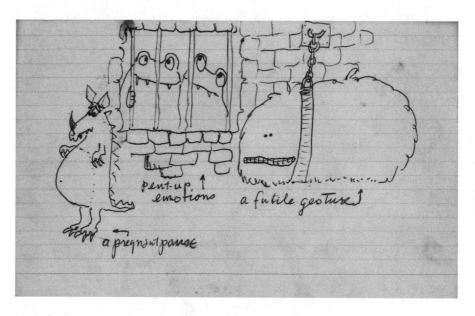

Jane's sketches.

Starting in third grade, Karen and Jane were allowed to walk around alone, and they often expanded beyond the limits of their small neighborhood. They'd walk up the hill, behind Redington Road and around the crescent of Laurel Drive, where there was a small estate, full of pine trees, closed in by a low stone wall that the girls would walk on, balancing like tightrope walkers. It felt like all hundred acres that stretched from South Street down to the Charles River were theirs. Sometimes they kept walking into what they called the Big Woods. They spent hours there, with the animals, building nests, and once, they went as far as the water in the middle of the trees, called Farley Pond, where their parents had taken them ice skating.

In elementary school, Karen and Jane took horseback riding lessons at Powers Stable in Dover. Jane fell in love with the sport and spent a summer riding on the Cape at Camp Roanna. During the school year, neighbors sometimes invited Jane on their foxhunt simulations, and she'd lose herself to the Big Woods, riding to the hounds.

"We both had a deep sense of magic," Karen remembers.

But Karen and Jane never talked about their love of the woods. They didn't have to. They didn't make up elaborate stories or games of make-believe. "She was so removed in a way from everything that she didn't have to invent stories to be kind of, you know, separate. She was already kind of in another..." Karen stopped before she finished her sentence. Perhaps it felt too obvious.

———

The gaps in Jane's timeline increased in the weeks leading up to her death. Don and Jill were used to seeing Jane every day, but when she'd started studying for her exams, Jane would disappear at eight in the morning and often wouldn't return until late at night. They could go for days without crossing paths.

Jill had hosted a party for her sister the Saturday before Jane's death. Jane left in a rush at 10 p.m., saying, "I've got to go study." But an hour or so later, when Don went over to her apartment to grab some alcohol they were storing there, he realized she wasn't home. Jill thought it was possible that Jane was out studying with friends, but Don had his doubts, which Jill later relayed to police: "If she really had a date with Jim or something like that, she could have just said that instead of saying she had to go study."

Detective Davenport pursued the clandestine affairs angle with Sarah Lee Irwin, too.

"Do you know of anyone else in the class that she was attracted to, that she tried to make out with?"

"Over a period of years?" Sarah Lee said. "Almost anyone."

WHAT'RE YOU SO AFRAID OF?

DRAFTS OF A LETTER JANE wrote to Jim Humphries, found undated and unsigned by police among her belongings:

DRAFT ONE

Thoughts after reading your letters:

T. E. Lawrence was neither independent nor free but he had passion which is an adequate substitute for both.

If I'm free and you're free, the combination of the two does not seem to me to be loss of freedom but a possibility of learning about other kinds of it. Just because you assume the risk of me and I assume the risk of you, does not mean that we put each other in a cage to insure the status quo—I mean face it kid, we'd both of us be mucking about with the same things and demons we muck about with now, mucked about with before we happened to each other... in many ways they're the same things and demons so why not derive the benefit of another point of view—we're both of us too chickenshit to dare to actually try and do something so you know the same damn demons will probably hound us all our days. We're both of us, this I knew by ESP, all ready to fail.

DRAFT TWO

Thoughts after reading your letters:

T. E. Lawrence was neither independent nor free but he had passion which is an adequate substitute for both.

It is ridiculous for you to think that I want your love on my terms; if you can't love me on your terms but have to use my terms then all I'm getting is a perverted mirror-image of myself, which I can get from my own head any time I choose, thank you very much. (My wishes in the matter are quite simple: I just want to continue being your own personal marmot and do whatever it is I do that keeps you cheerful for the rest of my days. I didn't think I was doing too badly but then I'm often misguided).

What're you so afraid of? If you'll pardon the Polonius-type tone, you simply have to learn that pain is not a necessary feature of living but merely an adjunct of having to plow through a lot of chatchka.

BOYD

AT THE END OF THE call, Elisabeth promised to put me in touch with Jane's brother, Boyd. He was now an ordained minister out in California, after a "very dissolute life of being a radio DJ and god knows what." I heard from her the next day by email. "As he says," she wrote, "this is about all he can offer." She pasted two replies from Boyd into the body of her message.

Boyd's first response:

My trip to Cambridge [...] was stonewalled by guilty cops who botched the case. I have 2 suspects: Jim [Humphries], who seems to be clean, and my old poet-piano-poseur pal Peter Ganick from Needham. Jane had the hots for him, he sold her pot. [...] It would take rendition and waterboarding, assuming he still lives, so no case is ever likely. You can give this woman my e-mail but I have nothing further.

Boyd's second response, after Elisabeth prompted him to recall an affair with a married professor:

I think the "affair" was one of (?) several, you may know of some.

He added:

She liked tall guys, and mutual manipulation. Poor brilliant, unhappy woman! Maybe more time might've made it even worse? Send this along, too . . .

I was caught off guard by the whole package: the gruffness, the density of the language, how forthcoming he was without any accompanying warmth. Boyd's stance felt so exaggerated in parts that I wondered if it was self-protection that had crystallized into something bordering on callousness.

Before I could reply, Boyd wrote again, an hour later, this time cc'ing me directly.

Don't forget her neighbors Don and Jill (Nash) Mitchell—and Arthur and Andrea Bankoff, who'd been with her on the Iran dig. Two strands there...that the voluptuous but foulmouthed Andie enraged MRS Lemberg-Karlovski [sic], wife of dig leader Karl, and Jane took Andie's side. Bad vibes but unlikely motive—or the notion L-K hyped the results of a pretty lame dig and Janie blabbed. [...]

Has this Ms. Cooper seen the "murder book"? [...] I could not, even to get it on a Boston TV coldcase show. Wonder why?

That was the first I'd seen of the theory that Jane had maybe threatened to undermine Karl's claims about Tepe Yahya. I'd also never heard of a "murder book," and asked him what it was.

He didn't bother cc'ing Elisabeth this time: "Perhaps I watch too many detective shows—by 'murder book' I meant the Cambridge Police files on the case." He told me he'd been in touch with another writer, who, unlike him, had allegedly been allowed to see the police files twenty years ago. Boyd said that the files indicated that Jane had had sex within hours of her death, and that Jim Humphries apparently satisfied a polygraph that it wasn't him. The email continued. Boyd told a convoluted tale about a suicide, a poison pen letter, and fingerprints on a horse-riding trophy. The story involved someone named Frank Powers, the veterinarian who had a connection with Jane's horse camp on Cape Cod, but I found it very hard to follow, and since the gist was that this guy had nothing to do with Jane's death, I didn't worry too much about it. There was still more to read:

I am a newsperson (CBS Radio's KROQ in L.A.). I am also an ordained Christian minister. My job is not to prosecute, but perhaps to find out and definitely to forgive. [...] You may call to arrange a voice interview, but I have nothing left except to say I think the faculty-affair line won't pay off. There was at least one, maybe more. She was, as I said, both manipulative AND victim of men. [...]

Good hunting...
Boyd Britton+

Boyd had included his phone number at the bottom of his message, and I called him the following week.

FRAGMENTS OF JANE

A YOUNG BOYD DRIPPED WATER onto the pool deck after having chugged along in his life jacket and paddled his way down the length of the country-club swimming pool when no one was looking. He was proud of his accomplishment, until Jane quipped: "Pretty good for a *baby*."

———

In fourth grade, Jane sat uncomfortably at her school desk. She needed to go to the bathroom, but the teacher refused to let her leave. Jane asked again. The teacher refused. A puddle slowly started to form under Jane's desk. The other kids noticed but, mercifully, said nothing. Jane didn't cry. She stood up and walked to the front of the class and asked the teacher again if she could go to the bathroom. "Well, yes, I guess you better had." When Jane came back, she pulled out large sheets of manila drawing paper from her desk. They were filled with her sketches of horses and, still silent, she lay them on the floor to sop up the urine.

———

Jane and Boyd wandered into their parents' room when their father wasn't home and their mother wasn't looking. They flipped through Theodoor van de Velde's euphemistically titled sex manual *Ideal Marriage*, mesmerized.

———

In boarding school at Dana Hall, Jane and her roommate knit a scarf for their Chinese evergreen tree. The scarf had the tree's name on it: Arthur. They draped it around his pot and joked about him having "Arthur-itis" and "roommate-ism."

In the school production of *Oklahoma!*, Jane was cast as Jud, the stocky male villain.

Sometimes at night, in the main building of Dana Hall, Jane's friends would catch her playing Cole Porter on the grand piano in the living room by herself.

———

The summer before Radcliffe, Jane told her friend Cathy about her plans to become a pilot. Jane said all kinds of knowledge and skills would be needed if there was a terrible war or some other disaster affecting the world, and she wanted to be ready.

———

She once tried to explain to Jill Mitchell her belief that God was more like a kind of electric force controlling people's lives.

———

Jane called Karl, who was born in Prague, the "Canceled Czech" and Martha Lamberg-Karlovsky a "Porcelain Ass."

———

In the fall of 1968, graduate student John Terrell and Jane crossed the street from William James Hall to the Peabody Museum. In what would turn out to be the last time John and Jane ever spoke, Jane turned to him and said, apropos of nothing: "I have dreams of waking up dead in that apartment."

FIRST TALK WITH BOYD

IN LOS ANGELES, WHERE BOYD had lived on and off since the '70s, he was better known as Doc on the Roq, a morning news anchor on KROQ's *Kevin & Bean* show. For a time Jimmy Kimmel was his sports announcer, and Jimmy made up a song called "What's in Doc's Butt?" It was a calypso: "I wonder what is hiding in there? / Is it a puppy or a polar bear?" I'd never heard his program, but when Boyd picked up the phone and his voice, deep and resonant, boomed on the other side, I knew it couldn't have been anyone but him. Elisabeth had said that Jane and Boyd were both the kind of people to take the oxygen out of the room, and I could see what she meant.

"So how goes your quest, and to what end?" he asked me.

I started to offer pleasantries, but he plowed right through them. He'd clearly already decided where he would take the conversation.

"There were twelve years in which I believe she was not necessarily frequently, but very possibly, sexually active." I quickly did the math; it would mean Jane started having sex when she was eleven.

"With whom?" he continued, as if in answer to my unspoken question of whom she'd lost her virginity to. "That would be hard to say except I'm sure that there was an affair with her music teacher when she attended Dana Hall. I also believe that boys' attentions to her, as well as her own strong intellectual abilities, led my parents to take her out of the public schools in Needham, and put her in Dana Hall, which was all girls...I think she also may have had something going on with the purser of the motor vessel *Augustus* during our 1960 trip to Europe. Not sure. But she had a crush, at least, on a guy in Portugal."

He told me that even when she was supposedly so happy with Jim, she'd asked Boyd if he had any suggestions for aphrodisiacs, because he "lacked sufficient ardor." A few days before her death, his friend Peter Ganick ("my old poet-piano-poseur pal") had been over to her apartment.

I tried to interrupt to ask a question, but he was already on his next thought.

"What happened to her in college was that she was more independent and that she was more sure of herself. She was a pretty woman and very voluptuously built and very intelligent. Also a little threateningly so. She did not suffer fools gladly. But at the same time, she was on an overachiever's path, trying to do as many things as possible. I think that was part of the influence of my parents."

I squeezed in a question about Jane's relationship to their parents, racing to catch up to him.

"I was more concerned about my own damn relationship with them, thank you."

I giggled nervously. I didn't want him to hang up.

"But anyway, Janie clearly was trying to gain control and approval in an area where it was prized and often withheld. So when she got off to school, I think she also sought sexual independence—it was the '60s—and I think she sought control over men."

Boyd was unafraid to tell me about the affairs that Jane had had with people in the Anthropology department. Several of her section men, he said, some of whom Jane told him about, and another he caught with Jane at their childhood home. They were fully dressed, but the upstairs bedroom, Boyd said, "had been pretty well used." Still, "of all the people she knew, none of the academic people make any sense at all," he said. "I don't see Karl Lamberg-Karlovsky or his wife pissed off at her, coming over to argue late at night, bashing her head in. None of that seems to print for me."

I asked if that meant he knew she'd had an affair with Karl.

Boyd said he had no memory of it. If anything, there was animosity between the two of them, he said. Jane didn't respect him as an archaeologist, and she made no secret of the fact that she thought his claim about having discovered Alexander the Great's lost city of Carmania was exaggerated.

It was a blow to the central tenet of Jane's story. It wasn't that the story of an affair had ever been a convincing enough motive on its own, but if that part of the story wasn't true, then neither was the certainty with which history pinned the story on Karl. The sudden enormity of the question of who had killed Jane was nauseating.

"So I'm left with either the stranger, or, since she liked them tall, the tall lover," he said.

Boyd said he had also heard about Jane's "Jerry Roth" and didn't know who it was a cover for. Jane had told Boyd that Jerry's diary called her a dreary, pretentious bitch, which Boyd said was true: "Jane *could* be dreary and pretentious and a bitch." I again had no idea what to do with a brother who was talking about his dead sister like that.

Instead, I tried to stay focused on "Jerry." I asked if he was the prime suspect during the grand jury hearing.

"I didn't know there was a grand jury hearing," Boyd said, a fact I found hard to believe.

"Did your parents ever try to reopen the case?" I asked.

"No, they did not," Boyd said. "The gossip really shocked my mother."

"Did you—" I started to ask.

"I'm sorry, go ahead," Boyd said, after interrupting me. It was an improvement, at least, from the unabated monologue at the beginning of our conversation.

"Oh, I was just going to ask whether you and your father ever talked about what happened with Jane."

"No, not the murder," he said. Well, just once. After that time the Cambridge cops refused to show Boyd the files, he flew to Florida where his father was living in a retirement community. "A grand hotel for the aging," Boyd called it. He told his father that he felt the Cambridge cops had stiffed him, and his father just shook his head. "'I don't know anything about that,'" Boyd said, imitating his father. His voice became softer and breathy. "I think he pretty much blocked it, if he knew. Again, I don't really know what people knew."

He was back to booming. "Murder cases are never closed technically within the law, but the cops don't want to reopen this one because it makes them look terrible."

I asked why, and he said, "The police misconduct. It's that simple."

"And the misconduct was what, exactly?"

"With the Frank Powers false lead," he said, speaking slowly and enunciating, as if to get it in my head, finally. It was the same horse trophy story that he'd tried to explain in the email. "They went down that track so far and this cop said he raced to the crematorium to get prints off Powers, and he matched one off a trophy from the horse-riding summer camp from four or five years before, and they thought they had a slam dunk with a dead suspect so they could close the case. Wrong. He wasn't in the country. And at that point, we never heard anything else. I was never brought in for a follow-up."

Boyd changed the subject in a flash again, unwilling to go any deeper into that trough.

"Fifty years now on the radio. Never done anything else. And in the last, we'll see, it would be at least eighteen years now, my revived Episcopalian faith led me to an offshoot of the Anglican church where I'm now an ordained preacher. So that makes my journey pretty bizarre. Because, you know, I used to hang out with Tim Leary, for Christ's sake." He laughed. "So it's been a long strange trip."

He paused for a moment to let the pun sink in.

"What would Jane have done had she lived?" he asked himself. "God only knows. I have a feeling that, were she alive today, she'd have been divorced a couple of times, with or without children. She might or might not have had tenure at a university. She might or might not have had a successful career in archaeology. I doubt very much that she would have been happy. Just have that feeling. She was always upset about something, it seemed to me. Often a cheating boyfriend"—he laughed strangely—"or worried about something. She was a great worrier. Me, in those days? I didn't give a shit. It was the easiest way to treat things." He laughed again.

"Listen," he said, an hour into the phone call, "I'm burning out this cell phone. If you have a follow-up, let's just do them by email, okay?"

There was so much more I wanted to know. His feelings about her death. Why his parents didn't force their own investigation. But I knew I only had time for one question.

"You don't know where Jim Humphries is?" I slipped in as quickly as I could.

"No, I don't. You might check Canadian academic directories. Okay, Becky, well, good luck with wherever you're going to go with this. It's a fascinating story of course, and it's a reflection of a particular time as well, and it's a cold case, unsolved. It's got all the elements. But we're all getting too old. The people who know may already be . . . You know, whoever the perp was—whether it was a street person or somebody with a PhD—is probably dead by now. So, maybe they left something. I don't know. But good luck to you."

We hung up.

I felt deeply uneasy. Finding a way into the conversation with Boyd felt like trying to run up a wall—every time I nearly found my footing, I slipped back, confused and disoriented and just a little bit hurt.

VIETNAM

ON THE NIGHT OF JANUARY 7, 1969, Boyd Britton was on the roof of a building in Tan An, a quiet town in the upper end of the Mekong Delta, one of the few facilities in the country that still had running water, having sex with a Vietnamese prostitute. He was twenty-one years old, and though he'd been in Vietnam for only a month, he had already been promoted to senior broadcast specialist. Boyd was in the 16th Public Information Detachment, part of the II Field Force in Vietnam. Or as he called it: "Three three-star generals, starched jungle fatigues, and no dope." His unit was stationed at a place called the Long Binh plantation off Highway 1.

Boyd's job was to go around conducting what the army called Hometown Interviews, asking GIs how they liked their work, so the tapes could be sent out to radio stations across the States. Before he set off on this road trip around the country, his commanding officer lent Boyd his .45, which he lugged around with his Nagra tape deck and batteries. Asking soldiers questions like that in Vietnam could get you killed.

The morning of January 8, he hitched a ride to Saigon. Boyd, like many of the people on his unit, had a radio broadcast specialty, and he wanted to get on the Armed Forces Vietnam Network. His plan was to stop off at AFVN in Saigon and investigate job prospects before continuing on to his base. But before he could check out the radio station, he ran into some guys from his unit who told Boyd they'd been looking for him. "You've got to come back now," one of them said. Boyd said he'd be heading there shortly. "No, now," the guy said. They drove him back to base.

Boyd's sergeant, a gray-haired National Guard volunteer from Pennsylvania, told Boyd that there was a message for him at Red Cross. Boyd's first thought was that one of his parents had died. At Red Cross, he was handed emergency orders to return Stateside. "Your sister Jane killed in Cambridge, Massachusetts," it said. He still didn't understand. *A traffic accident?* he wondered. *A fall from her apartment window?* He was about to get up to gather his things from his locker when they handed him a telegram from his parents. "Don't come on our account," it said.

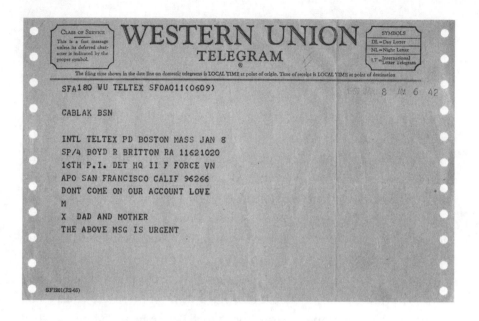

The tight-lipped, emotional disengagement of that telegram was for Boyd a crisp reminder of growing up in Needham with a family that insisted on perfection. On the surface, they really were an ideal family. "Visiting her parents," Elisabeth Handler said, "would be like going into an F. Scott Fitzgerald scenario. You heard little inside jokes about people named Muffy, or about who had drunk too much at the country club, all with sly little winks." There were never any raised voices. "We had everything we needed and almost everything we wanted," Boyd would remember.

Needham, a wealthy suburb to the southwest of Boston, was more notable for being bound on three sides by the Charles River than for much else. Jane wryly referred to the town as "gay exotic Needham." It was built on a hill. At the very top were people who owned businesses—an egg farm, an air-conditioner company. In the middle were the CEOs. And down at the bottom, in the sprawling land that spilled into the Charles River, were the people who didn't have to work for their money. "The horsey set" as Boyd liked to refer to them.

The Brittons were in the middle of the hill—on the edge of the upper crust—but it was well known that Mr. J. Boyd Britton basically ran that town. He was on Needham's finance committee, and he was the vice president of Cabot Corporation, a major defense contractor that made synthetic rubber. In Boston, where, it's said, *The Lowells speak only to Cabots and the Cabots speak only to God*, that really meant something. Their mother, Ruth, was known as Mrs. Perfect. She had her hands in everything—she was president of the PTA, Girl Scout Council chairwoman, active member of the garden club and the country club, and a Cordon Bleu–certified cook. Many knew Jane and her younger brother, Boyd, as the "smartest kids in town." The family traveled the world long before the first Boeing 767 put international travel within reach for the average person. Trips included frequent stays at the Plaza Hotel in New York, a long cruise to Venezuela, and a grand European tour, from Pompeii to England, to see Queen Elizabeth and Philip ride by Westminster in an open carriage with the king and queen of Thailand.

But this carefully maintained image was a thin veneer over resentments built up through time. Jane's mother was frustrated by the sacrifices she had made for love and a family. She met J. Boyd later in life—he already had two children from a previous marriage, and she was teaching at a college in California, with a PhD in history. Suddenly, she was a stay-at-home mom with two children to raise. Ruth channeled her unfulfilled ambitions into becoming the model of a suburban executive housewife. Their father, who was mostly away on business trips, left the parenting to Ruth. The few times he reprimanded his children, Boyd remembered, "It was never, *You disappointed me*. It was, 'You disappointed your mother.'"

The perfection Ruth demanded from herself extended to her children. Anything less was not an option. Boyd skipped a grade and was sent to Roxbury Latin, an all-boys prep school. They expected him to dress up and schmooze at cocktail parties, when all he wanted to do was be like the neighborhood boys who could set muskrat traps and wrestle in their backyards. Boyd hated the pressure: "We were singled out too early for being too special. For being more special than we really were."

Ruth wasn't shy about letting her children know when they were falling short of her standards. She was always fussing about their posture and weight. "Those moles on your face, we'll have to take them off someday," she would muse to Boyd. His parents sent him to fat camp. Ruth didn't discourage Jane from trying diet pills. She even paid a neighborhood boy to play catch with Boyd.

Jane responded to the pressure by throwing herself into her studies. In high school, she was class vice president and voted "most intelligent," "most likely to succeed," and "class wit." She was the only one in her grade to get into Radcliffe, and this was *before* her father started working for the college. According to Elisabeth, growing up in that household made Jane determined never to be just somebody's wife.

Boyd, on the other hand, engaged in a campaign of failure. It was his way of taking back control: *I will not allow their plan to be completed*, he thought. Though he could read at college freshman level by eighth grade, he barely got passing marks in high school, and he left college three times.

Talking about the cost of this pressure was off limits. The Brittons were a family characterized by their remove and their silence. Karen John, Jane's childhood best friend, remembers: "I only had dinner with her family once, that I recall, and nobody talked at the dining table."

When Boyd was fourteen, he realized his mother had a drinking problem. He had long suspected something. Sometimes she'd sing "Cats with the Syphilis / Cats with the piles / Cats with their assholes wreathed in smiles" when he had his Boy Scout friends over to the house. At dinner parties, after the second or third cocktail, she would say things to deliberately embarrass Boyd in front of the guests. But theirs was the cocktail-party generation, so it was hard to tell. It was only when he caught her slugging it out of a bottle in the kitchen that he realized she needed it.

Boyd's father never admitted she had a problem, and the town abetted this silence. When she was stopped for driving erratically, the cops, realizing who she was, would just wave her on.

Boyd disappeared into the silence. When friends would ask Ruth what her son did, which by that point was DJing for the local radio station, Ruth would say, "He's working in communications."

"Tell them who I am," he'd beg.

———

Boyd didn't have many personal things to pack—mostly military stuff, his shaving kit, some socks. It all fit in his small briefcase.

When he stepped out of the barracks, his sergeant was there with the Jeep, ready to take him to Bien Hoa airfield. By noon, Boyd was on a United charter DC-8. The plane was filled with GIs who'd just completed their tours. As the wheels lifted off the ground, the other guys cheered and yelled. Boyd sat quietly, watching the country become a quilt, and thought: *Oh god, I'll have to come back here.*

The plane made a fuel stop on an island in the Pacific and Boyd picked up a copy of *Stars and Stripes*. There was a syndicated UPI story, about a third of a column, about Jane: She had been beaten to death in her apartment. *That bastard, Edward*, Boyd thought immediately. Jane's lover Ed Franquemont had always seemed like bad news to Boyd.

In San Francisco, army men took Boyd's jungle fatigues and outfitted him in a standard green army uniform—he thought he looked like a bus driver—and ushered him onto another plane. All of a sudden he was in Boston and it was Thursday, the day before his sister's funeral, and he was greeted by the mother of a friend. She drove Boyd home where there was an enormous gathering. A wake by name, it was more like a well-catered cocktail reception: tons of food and people standing around trying to act normally despite the occasion and the fact that there was a cop in plain-clothes in the living room. It was stiff and odd and surreal. Boyd remembers eating lots of lobster sandwiches but doesn't recall much else. It wasn't until six months later when he got drunk at his half brother's place in Attleboro that he finally cried about Janie. "It takes a while for me. Mostly I was just trying to deal with it."

———

Over the next few days, the press got more and more desperate. The New York papers were still in town, but their diet was getting increasingly meager. The medical examiner, Arthur McGovern, had also been barred from speaking to reporters. "Any information has to come from the chief," McGovern demurred. Reporters for TV stations and newspapers called Jane's family and came to their door. When they found out that Boyd worked in radio, they would cajole, "Come on, man, you're in this business. You know we gotta get our story." Boyd wouldn't budge.

And yet Mike McGovern of the *Daily News* was still churning out articles. He wrote about the booming narcotics business in Harvard Square, which played into the fear that even sweet college towns were turning into crazed underworlds. It included a photo of a bearded hippie wearing a sign that said POT IS FUN. The caption read: "This is a poster which hangs on [the] wall of [the] Cambridge police station. It was seized with narcotics during recent Harvard Square dope arrests."

The picture was of Allen Ginsberg and, according to Joe Modzelewski, his *Daily News* colleague, Mike had his photographer snap it in the poster section of the Harvard Coop store.

Joe had had enough of Mike's stretching news scraps into stories. He was ready to go home. But Mike refused.

The next day, Mike had another article in the paper. A cover story, appearing under the headline SLAIN COED HAD AN ABORTION.

"It's just not true!" Jane's mother sobbed, reading the headline.

"Detectives investigating the cult murder of 23-year-old Jane Britton have learned that the Harvard graduate student submitted herself to a secret operation some months before her death," the article began.

"It is, Mom. It is," Boyd said.

ED FRANQUEMONT

THE BABY, THE MITCHELLS AND Ingrid Kirsch knew and would later tell police, was Ed Franquemont's.

"Nobody nobody *nobody* could get what she liked about him," Elisabeth remembered. "He just seemed like such a mean lump." He was on the wrestling team at Harvard. Compact and practically bald even as an undergraduate, he was the kind of guy "who'd fart at a cocktail party" and would ask people if they liked seafood and then would take a bite, chew for a while, and stick out his tongue. "You didn't want to be in the same room as him," Elisabeth would later say.

Jane and Ed Franquemont at their college graduation in 1967.

Jane started dating Ed her senior year at Radcliffe, and it seemed to Elisabeth that their affair was purely physical. That wasn't unusual for Jane, who was "perfectly capable of grabbing a man and throwing him on the bed," as Sarah Lee Irwin later told police. She might even sleep with a guy to get rid of him. So a physical relationship without any kind of emotional baggage was fine by Jane. "Or at least that's how she portrayed it. Maybe that's how she *wanted* it to feel," Elisabeth said.

But by the fall of 1967, the passion had turned volatile. Ed had started dropping acid regularly. He'd act strangely and wouldn't talk to her for days at a time. And according to Jane, he hit her.

Jane had had enough. That winter, they started their drawn-out, tumultuous breakup. Sarah Lee remembered Jane being the most distraught she'd ever seen her. She told the cops, "If she had, in fact, committed suicide, I think I would not have been surprised."

———

Not long after they had finally broken up, Jane received a terrifying call. "I don't know if he said kill, but it was obvious from what he said," Jill would later tell police. Jane assumed it was someone Ed had put up to the job, maybe one of the boys at the school for troubled kids where he worked part-time. She called him out on it over the phone. Ed denied her accusation and came over to assure her that he'd had nothing to do with it. She found him sweet and concerned. He was the Ed that Jane had first met, and what had started as confrontation ended in comfort. Some friends would later speculate that this was the night Jane got pregnant.

Jane knew she didn't want to have Ed's baby. Through the Anthropology department grapevine, she learned that a former graduate student named Sally Bates might know someone who could handle it. Sally and Jane didn't know each other very well—Sally had dropped out more than a year before—but as soon as Sally learned that Jane "got the trouble," she wanted to help. Sally had almost lost her college roommate to a kitchen table abortion. "When you're young, and not in medicine, you don't know how much blood a person can lose." Sally didn't ask Jane whose baby it was. She just gave her a phone number.

"Try my mom," she said.

Sally's mother, Nancy Bates—a granddaughter of Alexander Graham Bell—was one of the founders of Planned Parenthood in Michigan, and it was an open secret that she helped University of Michigan co-eds gain access to safe abortions, which, until 1967, were illegal in all fifty states. Typically Nancy sent patients of means to a doctor in Mexico City who performed abortions on American women. But that was too complicated in the middle of the semester. So, the last weekend of spring break, Jane flew to Michigan. She drove along the tree-lined freeway to Sally's child-hood home.

The procedure was routine enough that Sally knew what happened to Jane that day. First, her mother told Sally's younger siblings to get out, and she ushered Jane into the master bedroom. Jane got undressed in the bathroom, while Nancy and the female doctor she had hired prepared the bed, lining it with material that was absorbent on one side and imperme-able on the other. Jane was told to lie down and to open her legs, so the doctor could perform a dilation and curettage—essentially, a uterus scraping.

Sally and Jane didn't interact again after the abortion—she didn't even know that it cost Jane $500 and that her graduate student friends had started a collection to repay the loan that Jane got from Harvard. To Sally, helping

Jane wasn't a big deal. "When somebody has a problem like that, and you have a possible solution, it's an easy thing to pass along."

———

When the police learned of Ed, he was no longer in the Boston area. After he and Jane had broken up, he had moved off campus with a few other anthropology students to a farm in Bolton, Massachusetts, a small town twenty-five miles west of Cambridge. Sometime in 1968, he dropped out of Harvard. Rumor had it that he had since moved to Peru, but there was also a report that someone had seen him in Cambridge in December. Ed ticked so many boxes.

But over the next few weeks, the more police looked into the Ed Franquemont angle, the more problematic it became—just not for the reasons they expected.

Police pretty quickly had to admit that no matter how much they would have liked Ed to be their solution, his alibi was airtight. Multiple friends stepped forward to prove to authorities that he was innocent. A student who lived on the farm in Bolton came to police with a postcard Ed had sent from Peru just days before Jane's death. Debbie Waroff, the best friend of Ed Franquemont's current girlfriend, confirmed that Ed had been out of the country since mid-December. She had spent more than two weeks with him and his girlfriend in Peru, and he had seen her off on a British Overseas Airways Corporation flight from Lima back to the United States on January 5, 1969. It took twenty-four hours to get back to Boston from Lima, so Ed couldn't have been in town unless he left on Sunday night, and she knew the only flight out that night was already full. Plus, she said, he didn't have the money. "He only had $90, and airfare one way would be over $200." Her information checked out.

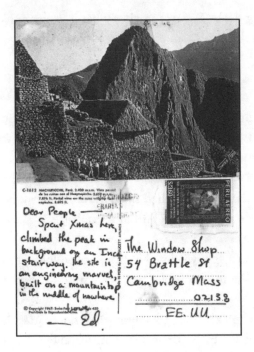

Postcard from Ed Franquemont, turned over to the Cambridge Police.

The trouble with Ed Franquemont was that police couldn't corroborate Jane's stories about him being a mean, violent bastard. Unlike Elisabeth, Jill said she had liked Ed. And Ingrid Kirsch had found that he was "sort of your standard straight guy. I mean, he drank a lot of milk…and he was clean and kind of an upstanding American type…A rather gentle fellow." In fact, Ingrid had been surprised that Jane was attracted to him; compared with the brooding guys she normally went for, Ed was "colorless psychologically."

It raised the possibility for police that Jane's stories about herself might not be reliable, a suspicion that some of Jane's friends already privately harbored. Brenda Bass, Jane's roommate from boarding school, remembered Jane's tendency to exaggerate. Jane, who struck Brenda as a "babe in the woods" when it came to dating men, insisted, for example on "maintaining the fiction" that a boy she had met on spring break with Brenda reciprocated her intense feelings for him. Jane called him her great high school romance and continued telling this story at Radcliffe: She told Ingrid he was her "high school sweetheart," and that she'd lost her virginity to him; to Don, she referred to this guy as her boyfriend from the South.

Tess Beemer, another close friend of Jane's from Dana Hall, confessed that she, too, had come to consider the possibility that Jane "was making everything up as she was talking to me."

John Terrell, the former anthropology graduate student to whom Jane had casually told that she had dreams of waking up dead in her apartment, got the impression that Jane always "seemed to be in some ways posing." But he thought her behavior came from a place of vulnerability, rather than of disingenuousness.

Even Elisabeth Handler had to admit that Jane "may not have been completely truthful in some of her horror stories."

And when cops pressed Jane's friends on the apparent physical abuse, no one could come up with any stories of actually seeing Ed strike Jane or seeing bruises on her. Jill had heard about the abuse from Jane herself, as had Boyd, though they had both been away for part of that time—Jill doing research for her dissertation, Boyd in college and the army. If Elisabeth had been interrogated by police, she would have said the same. In fact, the only time anyone had observed physical violence in Jane and Ed's relationship, Jane had been the one who hit Ed.

It was the spring of 1967, their senior year. The Anthropology department had thrown a party at the faculty club for its graduating class, and everyone got wildly drunk on Drambuie before heading to Ingrid's place. The party was noisy so no one paid particular attention to Jane and Ed in the living room until a sharp, loud SLAP! rang out over the music. Ingrid looked over and there was Jane storming off to the bathroom and Ed with tears running down his face. "My god," he said, "it's the first time any woman has ever slapped me."

"Why do you take it?" Ingrid asked.

"Because I'm afraid I'm in love with her."

Ingrid told police that this wasn't the only time that Jane resorted to violence. In the version of the Jerry Roth story that Ingrid had heard, Jane read the diary entry and, furious, grabbed Jerry by the neck and started to strangle him. "She tried to kill him," Ingrid told the cops, in no uncertain terms.

As one of Ed's friends said, "If there was a darkness around anyone, it was Jane."

CULTURAL AMNESIA

IN EARLY MARCH, STILL REELING from the conversation with Boyd, I went to the Harvard Club of New York when it hosted a "Radcliffe Night." Jay, who understood how emotionally fraught the project had become, agreed to keep me company.

The event was meant to inspire people to donate to the Radcliffe Institute for Advanced Study, the research center that Radcliffe had dissolved into when it merged with Harvard, but it turned into a loaded discussion about the gaps in a community's memory of itself. The dean of Radcliffe gave a talk about how we choose to forget aspects of the past in order to forge a collective identity. She called this cultural amnesia.

"There are many kinds of memory," another speaker said, just as there are many kinds of forgetting. "But the ghosts of alternative histories always surface."

The night ended with a question-and-answer session. A woman got up. She said that her relative, class of 1905, was one of the first Black graduates of Radcliffe. *Where is her memory at Radcliffe, when it doesn't seem like memories of Radcliffe have a place at Harvard?* The mike cut off halfway through her question. It never turned back on. People laughed nervously.

———

Jay and I had barely put our bags down at his place in Mystic, Connecticut, en route to Boston to do some research in the *Crimson* archives, when I took a call from Jane's friend Ingrid, now a practicing attorney. It was the second time we were speaking that month. The first was when I cold-called her during a lunch break at my café. A part of me knew that I had falsely assumed that the constraint of calling her at work would also limit the complexity of what I had yet to learn about Jane.

"Holy smokes!" Ingrid had said when I told her what I was writing about. During our first chat, she'd told me that the Cambridge Police had interrogated her about Jane's "history of involvement with certain men, at least one professor whose name also escapes me. But I can see his face—"

"Lamberg-Karlovsky?" I'd asked, still unable to let go of the early myth.

"No." He was *spooky*, Ingrid had said, but not him. Someone else. Ingrid had remembered that she was "disturbed" by the nature of Jane's relationship with the person whose name she couldn't remember. "He was married and that troubled me. Because not only could it be very hurtful to his family, but also because it could be so destructive to Jane."

She'd offered to search her memory and invited me to call her back.

Our second conversation turned out to be on her sixty-ninth birthday. On the call, as I wandered the backyard of Jay's Connecticut home, Ingrid said she'd remembered only two things since our first chat. The first was that Jane had a cape, a voluminous red one that she sometimes wore instead of an overcoat. "It was the sort of thing that most people wearing it would look like hell and she looked wonderful," she said. "The other thing is that the professor that I said that she had a brief affair with? I swear, the last name was Roth."

My heart jumped. But it was a fact without context. Except for the feeling that Jane shouldn't be playing "kissy face and huggy bear with married men and assume nothing bad is going to happen," Ingrid didn't remember anything more about the Roth affair.

We transitioned to talking about Jane's sex life more generally. Sex may not have been a big deal to Jane, Ingrid said, but she wasn't promiscuous. She was genuinely looking for love.

That duality, Ingrid explained, was common. "You want to remember that we were, in those days, crawling out—and I mean this literally—crawling out from the pre–*Feminine Mystique* days where if you graduated from college in 1960, you were still going to show up in the kitchen in an apron and heels and a skirt and you were going to stay home and you weren't going to work." When *The Feminine Mystique* came out, "at least in my case, [I] said 'Oh my god, of course. Of course!' And there was a great deal of anger."

The anger manifested, in part, as a decoupling of desire and domestication. Sex as empowerment! But this new attitude toward sex didn't immediately change the primacy of age-old stories about love. In Jane's version of empowerment, she did not need a man to feel complete, but she could still long to be loved. It was a fragile stance that put independence at odds with itself.

I thought about Jay, waiting patiently in the kitchen of the house behind me. I thought about how, in the weeks leading up to this moment, I'd go off into my own head, unable to be fully engaged with him, because I could see, despite how badly I wanted to have finally found my person, that I remained unconvinced. He would quote me lyrics sometimes: "I don't mind you disappearing / 'Cause I know you can be found." We'd be lying next to each other, as physically close as two people could be, but he knew I was slipping away from him.

We had come a long way from the pre–*Feminine Mystique* days, but the model I'd inherited of being a strong, independent woman left no space for needing to be loved. And as I tried to own this power, I discovered, as perhaps Jane did, that this trailblazing did nothing to supplant the need for companionship. In fact, it only made the search harder, and the need greater.

There had to be ways to celebrate love without relying on dated and limiting fairy tales. There had to be new stories we could tell ourselves. In Jane's duality, I felt like my version of femininity finally had room to breathe.

But I also knew the toll it must have taken on her. The image of Jane as a crystalline structure, with complicated interlocking facets each at odds with the other, made me sad. "I think that ability to participate and also be alone, and to have all of these different aspects of her personality—it doesn't necessarily make for a happy person," I said, talking about myself as much as I was talking about Jane.

"I don't think she was happy," Ingrid said. "Like everyone else in the universe, she wanted to be. I don't think she was."

She thought for a second, and added, "This is a puzzle that's never going to be solved: the puzzle of who is Jane Britton is never going to be solved. Ever."

FACE THE NIGHT

THE BUSINESS MANAGER OF THE *Crimson* had pulled the bound volumes of old *Crimson*s for me. And there it was, in the January 8, 1969, edition of the paper—Vol. CXXXXVIII, no. 74, Weather: Sunny, high in the 30s—the top left article by Anne de Saint Phalle. It was exactly the same as the one published online. Later, a former classmate of Anne's would put an end to the rumor of a *Crimson* cover-up for good. It was no wonder she couldn't remember writing the article, he said. After college Anne "joined a major cult and blew her brains out on acid."

I was too distracted by another article in the same issue to feel dismayed by the dead end. The author, Jesse Kornbluth (class of '68), had written about the necessity to "admit a loneliness which is perhaps central to the phenomenon of having a good brain." It felt like a hang-in-there pat on the shoulder. Jesse reassured, "But it may not be too late to find the ones with whom we will face the night."

———

Jay, as he had been all trip, was elsewhere. At Dana Hall, Jane's high school, he had stayed in the parking lot. When I left for the *Crimson* that morning, hoping he would spelunk in the archives with me, he said he had to meet an old friend. I missed the boy who wrapped my fingers around the knife, who kept me company at the Radcliffe event, who gifted me Palantir software access for my birthday.

I didn't begrudge him not wanting to be so intimately involved with my obsession. It was just that outside of the spell of Jane's story, I could see how frayed the threads that held us together had become. I'd had a nightmare that he told me he loved me because I knew I couldn't say it back.

I thought about Jane and Jim's relationship. Sometimes I couldn't tell if I liked their relationship because it reminded me of ours, or if I was with Jay because its central premise—holding off the dark—was reminiscent of my understanding of theirs. I wondered if I should stay. If this would eventually be enough. But their story hadn't lasted long enough to give me an answer.

Jay and I didn't talk about what I had begun to feel in Boston for a few months. I didn't want what I was feeling to be true. For all its flaws, this was by far the best relationship I'd been in. I trusted him. He supported me. In the intervening time, we'd even begun saying "I love you," contorting it for my sake with the qualifier: "in whatever weird way we mean it." But eventually, the conversation became unavoidable.

I can't do this anymore, I told Jay.

I didn't explain that I wanted an active love: loving someone *for* something rather than for the removal of a fear—of never being known, of never being able to get the timing right. I didn't say that taking shelter in someone else's loneliness was no longer enough. And I certainly didn't admit—to myself, never mind to him—that Jane had taken his place in keeping me company.

WEBSLEUTHS

THE NEXT MAJOR DEVELOPMENT CAME from an unexpected source: a site called Websleuths. It was a forum for amateur detectives, built around the idea that crowdsourced investigative work might find something that police had missed the first time through. Or at least that the attention would push police to reopen cold cases. Someone with the username "macoldcase" started the thread in November 2012, and I had been monitoring it for years, having tripped over it while Googling Jane's name. Some of the information was good. People with usernames like "Pink Panther," "Ausgirl," and "Robin Hood" posted hard-to-find newspaper articles about the crime and the 1969 map of Harvard's campus and Jane's official death certificate. These strangers must have devoted a great deal of time to her case.

But the thread had the tendency to eddy in wild speculation.

The conversation went in phases. Sometimes it focused on the historical dimension of the red ochre ritual; other times it went deep into possible connections with the unsolved Ada Bean murder that happened in Cambridge a month after Jane's. A number of posts latched onto the idea that Jane was caught in the middle of an antiquities smuggling ring, and much was made of a missing table leg that Jane's neighbors, the Pressers, had reported to the cops about a week after Jane's murder. The Pressers had stored a table in the back hall of the University Road building in June 1968, and when the management company asked residents to remove debris following Jane's death, they noticed that it only had three legs. Could the fourth have been the murder weapon?

A moderator snipped out the most salacious and defamatory of the comments, but it didn't stop the thread from posting revealing information about people associated with Jane—the name of Jim Humphries's wife, for instance—or from heavily insinuating Karl's identity. The focus on Karl had begun a year after the thread's start. "Justice4Jane," who first heard about the case from an anthropology professor in college, reposted gossip from another website saying that a Harvard professor, "a descendent of the Habsburg family (Austrian Royalty)," allegedly murdered a student and covered the body with red ochre. Ausgirl replied: "I am pretty sure they mean Professor Carl (sometimes 'Karl') C. Lamberg-Karlovsky." A number of other users chimed in after that.

I'd watched, silently, sickened by the conversation—a complicated mix of possessiveness and revulsion. I felt protective of Jane's story, and of the people involved. Yet I recognized that I, too, was an amateur detective who thought I could do better than the cops. I, too, was forcing Jane's friends to relive their pain, and I was dragging persons of interest through the public square. I thought that by never posting publicly and by refusing to add to the dance of fact and rumor masquerading as each other, I could be above it. But my conceit was tenuous at best.

And then, on June 16, 2014, Don Mitchell posted for the first time.

I was shocked to see his name. When I reached out a few months earlier, he had said he didn't have any interest in speaking about Jane because he was working on his own book about her. But now here he was, spilling to everyone.

"I'm Don Mitchell, the person who found Jane's body," his post began. "I ran into this thread last night, using Google to see if there were any new reviews of my book. I'm glad to see that there's interest in the case. I'm really busy right now, but here are some unadorned comments. I'm not going to be able to comment very much for a week or so, maybe a little longer."

His post ran on for about a page. And, despite what he said, he continued posting. Three the next day, and six the one after that. Users pounced, eagerly showering him with questions. I could respect his decision not to want to speak to me, but to share everything publicly with a group of faceless strangers felt funny. He seemed intoxicated by the attention.

"I have always believed that it was someone she knew, and let into her apartment without question," Don wrote. His theory—based on the red ochre, the lack of noise, the relatively undisturbed bedroom—was that Jane had let her killer in, and that they had had an argument.

He added a few new details—the cops had apparently asked Don to photograph a fingerprint in Jane's apartment—and dispelled a number of the forum's favorite avenues of speculation. The drug angle he said was utter nonsense. He remembered almost nothing about Ravi Rikhye. He was also certain that Jessie Gill was a dead end. "Nobody took Jessie seriously," he wrote definitively.

He didn't think the press blackout was part of a larger conspiracy involving Cambridge Police and Harvard. "Much of what may seem now like coverup was simple incompetence," he wrote. Lieutenant Frank Joyce, a state police investigator on the case, with whom Don stayed in touch for a decade after Jane's death, hinted to Don that he, too, thought the Cambridge cops had botched the job.

A few things in Don's posts struck me as odd. He said there was a knock on Jane's door the morning of the exam, and he heard the person walk back downstairs when Jane didn't answer. He also said that the night after her body was found, he and his wife heard someone in the hallway. It sounded like the person was trying to get into Jane's apartment. *He's come to get us*, Don remembered thinking at the time. How did Don hear both of those hallway noises so precisely, yet not the person who came into Jane's apartment the night of her murder? Why didn't he hear any screams?

Strangest of all, Don admitted that he and his wife—ex-wife, he clarified—had saved the bloody rugs that had covered Jane. He kept them for nearly forty-five years, until last year when he moved from upstate New York back to his childhood home in Hawaii. (I later learned that he destroyed them—and any possible hint of blood or trace of ochre that remained—in what he described as a "ceremonial bonfire.")

Don wrote that he was resigned to the idea that Jane's story would never get solved. "I put all my trust in Lt. Joyce. He was the investigator with all the tools at his disposal, and as we know, he got nowhere."

Besides, Don was convinced that even if the case were solved, it would be hard for justice to be served. His main suspect—whom he was not prepared to name—was dead. But Don dangled a few clues, as if leaving it a mystery was less out of deference and more to feed the forum's desire to piece it together itself. His suspect was on the faculty of the Harvard Anthropology department, though not a tenure-track professor. He wasn't involved with Tepe Yahya. Jane's dynamic with this professor wasn't "something longishterm and secret, where 'relationship' would be the right term." It was more like "an event or encounter," Don wrote, adding that this man went on to two other institutions after Harvard. His suspect died in 1999.

I liked Don's theory not least because if he was right, it meant that history had only gotten the story slightly wrong. Over the decades, Don's suspect and Karl Lamberg-Karlovsky had become one person: the tenured professor *and* the one with whom Jane had had an affair. The fact that there were *two* professors with whom Jane was close had simply gotten polished off in the telling and retelling. It was elegant in its simplicity.

Don wrote that years after Jane's death, his suspect reportedly confessed while drunk: "I killed someone." The person to whom this person confessed told someone who told someone who told Don, who relayed the lead to Lieutenant Joyce. But before Joyce could work down the chain, the guy to whom the suspect first confessed was struck dead by lightning.

A MYSTERY MAN

ON JANUARY 15, REPORTERS CAUGHT wind of a fifth lie detector test being scheduled for a mystery man. It had been over a week since Jane's death, and six days since Chief Reagan issued the press blackout. This was the first major development in days. The rumor was that it was someone close to Jane who had been previously interviewed by the cops, but whose name hadn't yet figured prominently in the case. The lengths that authorities went to conceal his identity made reporters hopeful that a break in the case was imminent.

Peabody people speculated as to whether this mystery man was the same person as the "Harvard faculty member who was rejected by Jane as a suitor after several dates." The *Daily News*'s Mike McGovern had written about him in the same article where he broke the story about Jane's abortion: a rejected faculty member who now "figure[d] prominently in the investigation."

Reporters staked out Cambridge Police and state police headquarters and kept the buildings under constant surveillance. They caught glimpses of Jane's friends being called in for another round of questioning. But the mystery man never appeared. Reporters later learned he had been whisked off to an undisclosed location.

District Attorney John Droney cautioned the press not to jump to conclusions about this unprecedented level of secrecy. "You have to assume it's a sex case," he said, due to the fact that her nightgown was "disarranged." But, he cautioned, that could still mean many things. "We have not eliminated the possibility that a woman was involved in this crime," he told the press. He refused to go into specifics but he did note that the first blow to Jane's forehead had not been strong enough to break the skin.

Jane's father was similarly tight-lipped when he was questioned by detectives again. They wanted to know more about Karl Lamberg-Karlovsky. "Most people we talked with said that that professor was a bastard," Detective Lieutenant Burns baited.

"All professors are bad—" Jane's father said cryptically before the police tape cut off.

REUNION

By August, the Websleuths thread was back in the realm of speculation, and even Don Mitchell got swept up in it. I tried my best to ignore the specter of the website and made plans instead for how to assess the accuracy of Don's theory. The best place to start would have been by asking Lieutenant Joyce, the detective who had earned Don's trust as he worked the case for years. But he died in the '90s.

The next best step, then, was to identify Don's suspect. I figured it shouldn't be too hard to check in the Harvard archives. There couldn't have been that many Harvard Anthropology faculty members at the time who died in 1999. I timed my archives visit with the forty-fifth reunion of the class of '69 in late September.

———

Welcome drinks for the reunion were on the first night, then club and organization get-togethers, panel discussions, and a formal dinner over the subsequent three days. There was only one event dedicated to Radcliffe. The history of an entire institution and the memories of its returning class had been compressed into a single session. It reminded me of the last question at Radcliffe Night, when the mike cut off. How many people's lived experiences were erased by the desire to simplify the past for the purposes of the present?

Thursday night was the opening reception, which was held in a tent in Harvard Yard. There was a guy there I knew vaguely from the Signet Society, an intergenerational arts and humanities group on campus. His ruddy face always reminded me of an off-duty Santa, and he was the type of person to breathe too close to your face as he told you about his latest "squeeze." But he was a member of the class of '69, I needed an in, and he was happy to show me around.

"This is Becky," he said to his old college buddies. "She's my wife." I giggled awkwardly; it felt necessary to play along if I wanted him to make introductions. When he wasn't looking I shook my head silently as people looked to me for confirmation. I met some classmates who knew the Harvard footballers who "beat Yale" 29–29, and a few of them told me that if you went to Radcliffe, it meant you were really something special, but I didn't get much else that night besides uncomfortable.

Over the next few days, I attended more reunion events. Some people talked longingly about how they had been too young to have a sense of the fragility of institutions. Some talked about how the focus was on everything but academics in those final years—the struggle to establish an African American Studies department, the increasing discontent with ROTC's presence on campus, the agitations of SDS and the Weathermen.

Against that background, for many in the class of '69, the merger of Radcliffe and Harvard that officially started the spring of their senior year was just an administrative technicality. (The *Crimson* headline, however, went for an awkward metaphor about marriage: 'CLIFFE FINALLY PROPOSES MARRIAGE TO TEN THOUSAND MEN OF HARVARD.) Many already identified as Harvard students more than Radcliffe women, and a few enjoyed the 1:4 ratio. But that didn't mean they were pleased to see Radcliffe disappear entirely. One woman told me that Radcliffe and Harvard diplomas were different until 2000. *I know*, I started to say, but she continued.

"It was just horrible," she said. After more than a hundred years, Radcliffe was just erased. It wouldn't have been hard for someone to address it, to ask the head of the Radcliffe Institute to make some mention of the college that meant so much to so many. Instead, the signature disappeared off the diplomas, and, along with it, Radcliffe's place in the memory of Harvard.

———

I fit in as many archive trips as I could around reunion events. The Harvard University archives were located in the basement of Pusey Library. It was a pleasure doing research on an institution so in love with itself—Harvard saved everything, down to the ephemera of student clubs that dissolved four decades ago.

The Jerry Roth part was easy to rule out. In none of the Courses of Instruction or the Directories of Officers and Students from 1964 through 1969 was there any Jerry Roth, or any name close. And there was no Roth, period, in anything remotely related to Anthropology.

Identifying Don's suspect took longer. The only way to net *all* the Anthropology teachers—the lecturers, instructors, teaching fellows, in addition to the tenured faculty members—was to go through every page of the 1968–69 directory. It took hours to reconstruct the faculty lists, cross-check and merge them, and then Google each person's death date.

When I finally finished, of the more than fifty people who were associated with the Anthropology department in the fall of 1968, only two had died in 1999: Professor John Campbell Pelzel and John Whiting, a professor of social anthropology. Neither fit the profile. Though Whiting was interesting because he was known to have worked for the US government, both men were full faculty members. Don had been very specific about his suspect not having had tenure.

My other research leads—Jane's undergrad thesis, her father's files from his time at Radcliffe—turned into more dead ends. Then I pulled the dissertation of Richard Meadow, the roommate of Jim Humphries who had gone to Tepe Yahya with Jane and had stayed at Harvard all these years.

The introduction began with a quote from a Julian Barnes novel:

How do we seize the past? Can we ever do so? When I was a medical student some pranksters at an end-of-term dance released into the hall a piglet which had been smeared with grease. It squirmed between legs, evaded capture, squealed a lot. People fell over trying to grasp it, and were made to look ridiculous in the process. The past often seems to behave like that piglet.

As with Ingrid, I was struck by the fact that despite the nearly fifty years between our eras I was struggling with the same basic problems. This time: Can we ever know the past? Can the historian or archaeologist be separated from his or her findings?

I wasn't yet sure where I fell on these questions, but Richard, at least, concluded:

> It is clear that I have not caught the piglet, and I can only hope that I have not been made to look too ridiculous in the process of trying.

———

The last archive visit I scheduled for that trip was to see the records of the Peabody Museum, which were housed in its basement. As I walked to Divinity Avenue, I passed by a group of older men who had gathered to fish coins out of their pocket to give to a woman who needed to park her car. "Remember us," they shouted down the street after her. "Class of '69. We're the good guys."

The archivist was ready for me. There was a metal cart with gray archive boxes, each stuffed with meticulously labeled manila folders. I had explained I was working on a research project about Harvard-led expeditions in the 1960s. I was too afraid to ask for files that would indicate the true nature of my project—I still worried about alerting the department—so instead I asked for the boxes of Hallam Movius and Hugh Hencken, two tenured professors, whose content summaries indicated correspondence with Karl. The archives were in a windowless room, where the archivist could peer over her computer to monitor what I was doing.

The boxes were filled with letters from the field and names I didn't recognize and jokes I didn't get. Everything felt simultaneously salient and irrelevant, and I couldn't decide which size sift would shake out the dust.

In Hallam Movius's papers, I found Jane Britton's student profile, a typewritten summary of her application to dig at his site in Les Eyzies, France.

Female
Aged 19
Finances: She seems to have a lot of money.
Character: Very eager to do work at the Abri Pataud. Serious, reliable, stubborn.

Someone had underlined, by hand, "a lot of money."

The last line of the sheet was: "I think that she should be highly considered."

The files indicated a more nuanced version of history. Though Movius was a notoriously difficult adviser, he came across as a champion of Jane's. In one letter from Karl, Movius had underlined Jane's name, and replied to Karl that he was delighted to see Jane's name in the mix.

Stephen Williams, the chair of the department and the head of the museum, must have known how much Movius cared about Jane, because after her death, Steve wrote two letters to him in Les Eyzies. The first was the day after Jane's body was found.

Dear Hal:

The enclosed clippings tell the terrible story in more detail than I could possibly want to give you. We are of course stunned by this tragedy, and I knew that you would want to have the information as soon as possible. I thought of cabling last night but knew the information would be too cryptic to be anything other than a cruel introduction to the subject.

Police work continues, and I certainly will keep you abreast of any further developments. She was scheduled to take the first of the three written General Examinations yesterday and her failure to show up at the exam lead [sic] to this terrible discovery.

At this first moment of impact, I am unable to bring the slightest wisdom or explanation to this event.

As ever,
Steve

The second was dated January 20, 1969—the same day that Nixon was inaugurated into office. Tucked within a letter about the visiting lecturers in an anthropology course, Steve included the following paragraphs:

Investigation and speculation continue in the murder case, and it is a great strain for everyone. There seems to have been very good cooperation with the police, and there have been many moments when we have thought that we were getting somewhere. However, there is still no news.

Lee Parsons is due to leave for Guatemala on the 24th, and of course Carl is in the midst of his preparations too, so Peabody is nothing if not busy with comings and goings.

The letters were strikingly urbane in the face of such turmoil, and if Harvard had taught me anything, it was that academics never say anything in a straightforward way. I could feel the temptation to read more into the second paragraph. I didn't know who Lee Parsons was, but I was alert to the possibility that Stephen's writing could be coded language for the whereabouts of the two main suspects, without alerting anyone who might intercept the letter of his suspicions.

I could feel the clock nearing 4 p.m., when I knew the archives closed, so I raced through the rest of the material, taking pictures of everything. I'd read it later, I told myself.

————

My final day in Cambridge, I dragged my suitcase to the Quad library, since I would be heading directly from there to South Station. The Radcliffe meeting was at 3 p.m. I had to promise that I wouldn't talk about what was said at that meeting in order to be allowed to be a fly on the wall. But I can say that it was one large room where a circle of 150 women sat on chairs and introduced themselves—both who they were and who they had become. It took hours to go around the room. The women talked about the struggles to balance family and career. Their concern that my generation's complacency was eroding their advances—namely *Roe v. Wade*. Their feeling of failure because we were failing them: We cared more about making money than about art and history and human rights.

I wanted to speak up. I was in that room because I do care! *We* do care! But I didn't say anything. They had made a cartoon version of my generation in the same way I had made one out of theirs. It took an ambassador in the form of a dead girl to get me in that room, to get me to understand that their feminism wasn't all bra burning, that the merger of Radcliffe into Harvard was as much a submersion of a vital institution as it was a landmark of women's equality. I felt dizzy, dislocated in time—suspended somewhere between my college days four years ago, their college days forty-five years ago, and my own fifth and forty-fifth reunions, still somewhere ahead in the fuzzy future.

On the train home, I opened my laptop and started clicking through the photos from the Peabody archives. Brown page after brown page, onionskin, typewriter, *click click click*.

And then I found what I didn't know that I was looking for. A letter from Professor Hugh Hencken to Department Chairman Stephen Williams regarding Professor Lamberg-Karlovsky's pending tenure application. I was certain that the letter had to have been written before Jane's death because I knew that Karl had had tenure when Jane died. But when I checked the letter, I realized I'd been wrong. Karl was not yet invincible at the time of her death:

The letter was dated January 7, 1969. The day that Jane Britton was murdered.

Part Three

THE RUMOR

2018: FIVE DAYS

YOUR EXPERIENCE CHANGES WHEN YOU know the end is near. *Five days*, Don said, *until we know*.

I feel like I'm glowing radioactively, trying to process things three times as fast, keeping myself ready to spring if my phone rings. Only at the crosswalks do I let myself process how hard my heart is thumping. The evening of Don's call, when I go downstairs to make some toast, I instinctively flick on the hallway lights and wait ten seconds. *I'm coming*, I imagine the lights say. I hold my metal baton out in front of me, my fingers wrapped underneath it, ready to lunge and jut, in case there's an intruder. It's crazy, I know, but eight years ago, it seemed crazy that, after so many decades of silence, the sheer force of my interest would bend reality enough to yield an answer. So who's to say what's rational?

It's no surprise that I can't sleep. I feel powerless—helpless to change the outcome, helpless to know it—and overwhelmed. I desperately want to call Boyd, but I promised Don I would keep the news between us. I run through the scenarios in my head. If it's someone who's alive, maybe this gives police enough time to make the arrest. Then again, if it's someone who's alive, why would they risk the leak and not just wait until the person was arrested to let Don know? What if it's not someone I've considered? What if after I learn the name of the killer, I still don't know why she was killed?

Five days.

I look back at where I started. How quickly everything became a giant puzzle, a world of secrets, where every fact had a double meaning and everyone seemed to have a secret life. The speculative quicksand on which my story was based seemed so limitless that sometimes I had to remind myself that Jane did die and someone did kill her.

I can't get over the timing. That morning, I had been struggling with the question of how to write this book without an answer. Could there be resolution when I didn't have a solution? And here, in the most *deus ex machina* of moves, reality was interceding to provide one.

Five days to live in a world where it could still be anyone.

ARTHUR BANKOFF

I KNOCKED ON THE BLUE door of Room 0213, which was thick with decades of paint. I was on CUNY Brooklyn's campus, in the basement of Ingersoll Hall, about to meet with one of the school's archaeology professors.

Two years had passed since I had found Hugh Hencken's letter supporting Karl's tenure in the archives at Harvard. Since then, I'd discovered a second letter in support of Karl's candidacy, written on the day of her murder. This one was from Professor Gordon Willey, who expressed his delight to Stephen Williams that Karl was being considered; Willey thought the department would benefit greatly from a man like Karl. A cablegram confirmed that Karl's tenure went through on March 13, 1969, when the *ad hoc* committee—the part of the tenure process that Harvard keeps the most shrouded in mystery—voted his application through. After Karl received word, he wrote to Steve to thank him.

I also learned that in January 1969, Stephen Williams had been in a powerful but impermanent position. He was only the *acting* director of the museum. Then, within three weeks of Jane's murder, he was promoted to full director. Even though I'd heard from multiple people that Professor Williams was not a great scholar—former assistant professor Tom Patterson put a fine point on it: "A number of people have described him as the dumbest person in American archaeology"—for a few months after Jane's death, Williams was suddenly both the head of the museum and the chairman of the department. The double appointment was nearly unprecedented in the history of Harvard's Anthropology department.

Aside from the devotion of his small cohort, Williams's success in the department was, likely, the result of his ability to fundraise. He had a good track record: In November 1968, he had secured an anonymous million-dollar donation. But the university was in the middle of its $48.7 million fundraising drive. If Williams wanted the permanent position as director, it was probably crucial to show administrators that he could help them meet that goal. The pressure to keep any scandals at bay must have been enormous.

A disturbing line of thinking occurred to me. If Karl hadn't had tenure at the time of Jane's death, was it possible that he had silenced her to protect his tenure bid? And since the department may have been particularly incentivized to keep unfavorable stories buried during the fundraising drive, had Stephen helped shield Karl in order to spare the department the embarrassment and to safeguard his own promotion?

This was purely an exercise in speculation, and I hardly had the raw material to prove anything. Only Jane's brother, Boyd, had mentioned any antagonism between Jane and Karl. That was barely enough to build a theory on, never mind a case. But I had to admit that at least in the archive, the fates of Stephen Williams and Karl Lamberg-Karlovsky seemed intertwined. When Steve stepped down as the department's chairman that summer, he wrote to Karl to reassure him: "Having gained your professorship during my term of office, there was nothing important left to do." It felt like the archives were begging me to pay attention.

For months after that trip to Cambridge, though, my progress on the book stalled. I took a full-time job at The New Yorker and my days were suddenly busy organizing my boss's schedule, helping with early edits, researching story ideas, and picking up the occasional coffee. I could only work on Jane's story around the edges of my job. But I never second-guessed the trade-off. It felt like I had been plucked from the faceless mass of every barista in Brooklyn who dreamed of becoming a writer. Plus, at the magazine I finally had resources and support for my investigation. I learned how to use Nexis, an online database of public records, to find contact information; how to organize mountains of research and tapes; how to file public records requests; and how to appeal when those requests were inevitably denied. Of all the agencies I queried, the Cambridge Police was the only one to acknowledge that it once had files related to Jane Britton. But, they said, the material may have been lost in a flood. (A source later laughed at me when he heard I had been trying to pry files from Boston authorities: Good luck doing that if your name isn't O'Sullivan.)

My work on Jane's story was limited to what I could do remotely—emails, phone calls on mornings and weekends, and lots of reading—and on vacation time. I used my first days off to head back up to Harvard to poke around the Peabody archives again. Professor Jeffrey Quilter, the then director of the Peabody Museum, heard about my sudden interest in the Anthropology department and asked to meet while I was in town. The request was exactly what I had feared: a signal that I finally had tripped a wire. We met in his office, and I tried to be as vague as possible without lying. I told Professor Quilter I was writing about systems of power and who gets to tell stories of their past. After listening for a while, he gave me a strange smile—an expression I later realized was slight disbelief of what he was about to say. "I'm just going to tell you because I like you," he began. If I wanted to "stir up a hornet's nest," I should look into Jane Britton's death. "The sense that this murder goes unsolved is a cry for justice to me."

But it wasn't until late 2016 that I found myself in front of the blue door on CUNY Brooklyn's campus. My boss had given me the afternoon off because he knew how big a deal this was. For the first time, I was about to meet a friend of Jane's in person.

The door opened, and Arthur Bankoff—Jane's neighbor, confidant, and colleague on the 1968 Tepe Yahya season—stepped out to meet me.

Arthur was shorter than I expected, dressed in khakis with a checked button-down shirt, a vest, and a yarmulke. The long tassels of his tzitzit dangled out of both of his pant pockets. He had lost much of his hair, but his warm, mischievous eyes made him appear much younger than his seventy-one years.

On the phone to coordinate the meeting, he had told me that he suspected Karl as the murderer though he, like Boyd, dismissed the affair angle. There was an animosity between Karl and Jane, Arthur remembered. It started in Iran—Karl questioned her fieldwork and wasn't hesitant about putting her down—and the tension was exacerbated when his wife arrived. But, Arthur reminded me, he had stayed abroad after Iran, and anything could have happened between Jane and Karl once they returned to Cambridge.

I asked why Arthur suspected Karl all these years, then. "Because I hated him," he said.

Now Arthur welcomed me in, and I looked around the office. It was dark and industrial, filled with three computer monitors, a giant metal standing fan, and books about Eastern European archaeology and metallurgy. His Harvard diploma hung on the wall.

Around the perimeter of the room was a slim bit of molding he used as a

shelf to prop up some framed pictures—of his children, of his expeditions in
Eastern Europe, and of the 1968 dig in Iran. It was the picture of everyone
in front of the Land Rover that I had studied years ago. His was nearly
poster-size. He said he'd hung it, despite his hatred of Karl, because it had
Jim and Jane in it. "In with all the kind of painful memories, it also brought
back very good memories."

We walked up to it, and he asked if I could pick out everyone. "Andrea.
Karl. Martha. James," I said. "Jim," he corrected, and added: "It's funny, I
just spoke to him this morning."

Arthur said he'd called to ask if it was okay to speak with me. It was the
first time he had mentioned Jane to Jim in nearly fifty years. "You just don't
talk about certain things. You sit and grunt at each other like you're in a
club." To Arthur's surprise, Jim had said it was fine, and then went on to
mention that he had been reading something in the Harvard alumni magazine about police having caught a serial criminal who had flown under the
radar for years. "Maybe he's the one who was responsible for this," Jim had
said. Arthur doubted it but added that he was here to talk if Jim wanted. Jim
didn't bite. "We went on to discuss our health like old people all do." Still,
the story was enough to give me hope that I might one day speak to Jim.

I edged closer to the expedition photo. As I did, I was startled by
how different Jane's face was in his print than in the smaller version I
had studied. In the monograph, Jane's pose had always seemed rebellious
and her expression—eyes looking down and big grin—had made her seem
almost cocky, as if she knew the performance she was putting on and was
very pleased with herself. But in Arthur's photo—taken, I realized, just a
fraction of a moment before or after the other—her expression was radically
different. Her grin was more of an indecipherable line, and instead of looking away from the group as it originally seemed, Jane was staring upward, at
the camera, and into me. There was a vulnerability in her gaze; beseeching,
almost. No one else's face had changed like Jane's. But the difference was
startling. Jane's eyes felt like they were tracking me.

Jane close-up from the Tepe Yahya monograph photo (top). (Crop of Fig F.6 on page XXXI, from D. T. Potts, Excavations at Tepe Yahya, Iran, 1967–1975: The Third Millennium, American School of Prehistoric Research, Bulletin 45. Copyright 2001 by the President and Fellows of Harvard College, courtesy of the Peabody Museum of Archaeology and Ethnology, Harvard University, by permission from Richard Meadow.)

Jane in Arthur Bankoff's print (bottom).

TEPE YAHYA

THERE'S A SPECIAL KIND OF insanity that descends on a dig. Out in the middle of nowhere, when the only people who speak your language are the same seven people you see every day. When the afternoon is violently hot and at night you shiver with the cold and dysentery. When there isn't enough food and you can't trust the water, and when gin becomes a coveted reward for good behavior. When what you dig is based purely on the luck of what trench you're assigned, but you're judged on what you're pulling up. When you're covered in dust and you have to shower in the cast-off stream filled with camel dung, and you try to sleep despite the fear that those camels will step on your head, and you can't because you learn very early that it's a lie that roosters only crow at dawn. Tensions develop. Hatred develops. And yet, hungry for English, hungry for interaction, you have no choice but to turn to those same seven people.

Jane once wrote about the simmering explosiveness on digs: "Small-group situation tends to create downright psychotic atmosphere. i.e., it's okay for me, I'm used to it, but wouldn't wish it on my worst enemy."

At least this one had started off well.

In mid-June, the crew had arrived in Tehran. It was the final decade before the Iranian Revolution; the shah was still in power, and alcohol still flowed freely. The crew, in fact, had almost exactly traded places with Iran's leader, who had been at Harvard that week, giving one of the graduation speeches and getting an honorary degree. (The other speaker that year was Coretta Scott King, who accepted the invitation in her late husband's place.)

The crew had spent a few days at the British Institute of Persian Studies, which doubled as a plush hotel of sorts, run by David Stronach and Sir Max Mallowan, the archaeologist and husband of Agatha Christie. They whiled away the week picking up odds and ends they would need for the expedition—food from the US embassy commissary, pickaxes, and plastic bags—and waited for Karl to get the final permit for excavation from the government's antiquities representative.

The crew spent the sultry afternoons cooling off poolside or wandering through the bazaar. Jane loved the bazaar itself but hated the crowds. Strangers used the congestion as an excuse to get too close to her. A few pinched her butt. And the traffic in Tehran in general made Jane swear she would never complain about the cars in Rome again—little orange taxis zoomed around, making U-turns and backing up in the middle of the street. But it was good to be back with Jim. Jane found herself catching the odd angle of light on his face and feeling the bottom drop out of her.

On their way to Iran, they had spent a few days together in London, and it was there that Jim had told Jane that he loved her for the first time. He left for Tehran slightly before her, and Jane found she couldn't concentrate on anything in his absence. She went to the opera by herself but kept wanting to turn around to tell him something or to hold his hand before remembering that he wasn't there. She had almost missed her flight to Iran because she couldn't sleep, too consumed by the overwhelming desire to go out and chalk every sidewalk in London with their initials and a giant heart.

She wrote in a letter to him: "There is something different about your chemistry that brings me a great deal of peace, as opposed to the rampant unease I usually have."

But the lack of privacy that awaited the couple in Tehran was getting to Jane. She and Jim didn't want the others on the crew to know they were together, and they attracted too much attention in town—Jim because of how tall he was, and Jane clearly American in her round sunglasses. They spent the whole day waiting for the moment when even the late-hour talkers went to sleep and they could be alone, finally, over a gin and tonic. Otherwise, it was just a peck on the cheek after breakfast if they could find a quiet corner. Jim kept trying to make elaborate plans for them to find a time and place to sleep together for the first time, but the planning made Jane self-conscious. She wished he would just be brave enough to sneak down to her room in the middle of the night and longed for when they'd be peacefully settled in the desert.

The crew set off for Yahya in two separate cars, with Jim and Jane and the Persian antiquities representative in the Land Rover, named Bucephalus after Alexander the Great's horse. When the car stalled ten miles into their drive the first day, they fixed the engine with masking tape and chewing gum. Jim and Jane sang dirty French songs and recited the poems of Robert W. Service, "the Bard of the Yukon," while the antiquities man rode along, patiently. Jane felt more in love with Jim than ever.

By the time they arrived at Yahya, it was too late to properly see anything. She and Jim shared a tent, and they moved their cots outside where it was cooler, not realizing how dramatically the night stripped heat from the desert. They woke up freezing.

It was hard to exaggerate the remoteness of Tepe Yahya, and how much more rugged it was than what Karl had prepared them for. Baghin, the tiny village where they slept, was a few minutes' walk from the majestic seventy-five-hundred-year-old mound. It had no running water, and there was no electricity in the whole of the valley. Some of the local workers, nomadic sheep and goat herders when the expedition wasn't in session, camped in tents close by. The mail came in—*when* it came in—with a man on his bicycle. Drinking water was carried in from over a mile away by a driver on a donkey.

Jane had been used to her dig in France with Professor Movius, where she stayed in a little pension with a bidet in the bathroom. A gourmet restaurant could be found at the foot of the street. At Yahya, the latrines hadn't even been dug yet, and there were so many "animalcules" in the drinking water that it wouldn't have surprised Jane if she could suddenly start seeing them dance. And when Karl told workers where to dig the latrines, Jane complained that he hadn't bothered checking which direction was downwind from camp.

The same lack of concern for detail was on display again that night when Phil Kohl, an undergrad from Columbia, arrived unceremoniously on the back of the truck that belonged to the local chromite miners. Phil, twenty-one years old, had hitchhiked his way to the site by himself because Karl had apparently forgotten—or hadn't taken seriously—his promise to wait for Phil in Kerman.

Karl had warned the crew that he would be difficult to get along with in the field. As a first-time director of a full-scale dig—last year's expedition was only a survey of the area—he was concerned about making a good impression on officials, on whom he felt the success of and continued access to Tepe Yahya depended. This anxiety about projecting the right image made Karl quick to injure and quick to anger, especially if his "no debate with the chief" policy was challenged. Being embarrassed in front of government representatives was a particular sore point. On the trip down to Tepe Yahya, Karl worried the Iranian government representative had misconstrued some laughter among the crew as being directed at the representative himself, and he volubly lectured Arthur and Andrea Bankoff on how to act in front of people who were their hosts.

Digging started on day two, and the work was hard. People came back from the mound looking like they had stuck their faces in flour. The food didn't help matters. Hussein, the cook, did the best with what he had, but the local goats were stringy no matter how long or well you cooked them. The latrine, when it was finally built, was so vile that the crew ended up just using the bushes and ditches. It was no wonder many got very sick very quickly.

But at the beginning, the shared experience of the site's challenges brought the crew closer together. Jane was even surprised by how much she liked Karl. She wasn't attracted to him—she told Andrea "legs too short and has a droopy ass"—but he had a tendency to behave as if he were still at Dartmouth, which meant that he was fun, if a little immature.

She also grew to admire the valley where the mound was located. Though poor and remote, it was beautiful. Near the site was a sacred shrine, an immense gnarled cedar tree growing through a round stone wall. It was surrounded by an enclosure so narrow that a viewer could see nothing but skyward, which made the ancient tree even more majestic. It was said that the tree was where Zacharias, the father of Yahya—John the Baptist in Muslim tradition—was buried. The area was also crossed with a network of qanats, or water wells. Only children could fit in the slim passages, so maintenance and repair were handled by young boys lowered slowly into the qanats. The valley was often filled with the sound of their haunting voices rising up from the tunnel entrances.

But for Jane, the best parts of the summer were Jim and the night sky. Jim "has been spectacular," she wrote to her high school roommate on one of those blue airmail sheets. "He's the first person in a long time that takes care of me." Sick with dysentery at dawn one morning, Jane had come back from her tenth trip to the bushes. She lay on her cot shivering, trying not to wake Jim up, when he moved his bed next to hers. He piled all their blankets on top of her and held her until she stopped shivering and fell asleep. All this when he had to get up at 5:30 a.m. to start excavating and was as exhausted as everyone else.

She and Jim slept together for the first time that summer. Still not wanting to flaunt their relationship, they had discreetly removed the bed railings from their cots and drew them together. One night she felt so full of love she had to get up in the middle of the night to write him a bad poem. She watched him sleep for a while before she drifted off. It felt like watching the stars.

Jim at Tepe Yahya.

When Jim sank into one of his depressive funks, Jane could talk him out of it. One morning when she noticed Jim was particularly withdrawn, Jane made sure that she walked alone with him to the site. "Hey, if you're not doing anything next week, let's have a kid?" she asked. It yanked him from his reverie. "What do you want to call it—Ali?" "No, I had more in mind something like Sherman," she said. They were back in rhythm again.

Jane had a dream where she and Jim were married, but no one could find him. It wasn't urgent, though. Even though she didn't know where he was, there was a feeling that he was right there all the time.

Over the weeks, as sickness and the lack of sanitation lowered the threshold for irritation, even the smallest slights lost all sense of proportion. The pressure that everyone felt to perform well didn't help matters any. Jim, as the oldest student on the dig, was the site supervisor, and he felt bad that Arthur Bankoff had been passed over despite a longer tenure in the department. Jim worked extra hard to live up to the appointment. Jane's impression was that while Karl was busy "playing professional Central European barbarian-aristocrat," walking around and criticizing other people's trenches and archaeological conclusions, Jim ended up doing nine-tenths of the work. Jim was the one who ran the medical clinic on the site. It was meant for the workers, but locals got word of it, and Jim became the one who patiently and skillfully cared for local children burned by cooking fires and suffering from diarrhea and toothaches. Jane found herself wishing that she could tie him down and force him to rest. "I've never seen you stagger before, even from fatigue," she wrote in her journal.

Jane felt a similar pressure because she knew that Karl had been unsure about her when he selected her for the dig. If she was going to complete her PhD, in addition to passing Generals, she needed field opportunities for dissertation research. After Movius's departure, Karl had become Jane's lifeline in the department. "She felt everything academically depended on her doing well and impressing Karl," Andrea Bankoff later explained to police.

But, despite Jane's best efforts, she was completely lost in her trench. While other crew members were pulling up interesting pottery sherds, all Jane was finding were bricks and rodent holes. She was terrified Karl knew she was making a mess of the excavation. More than once, Karl told Andrea Bankoff that he was pleased with everyone's progress except one person. Andrea, who was concerned that Karl was referring to her husband, Arthur, didn't dare ask him to specify.

In the afternoons, after he finished his work for the day, Jim would climb into Jane's trench. Together, they'd try to make sense of it until the light grew too dim to see anything.

———

By late July, goodwill and patience were being gnawed away by the dust storms and the sand flies. Airmail stationery, their only connection to the outside world, was rationed, as was their food: A can of tuna was to be split among three people for lunch. A jar of peanut butter was supposed to last for two weeks. People hallucinated visions of gingerbread and whipped cream and Hershey bars and steaks and green vegetables. They longed for the cold. Jane had so many fly bites it looked like she had a rash. When she was stuck in bed, too sick to supervise her trench, a chicken walked into her tent, crapped, and walked out. Another time, a centipede crawled into her underwear.

Almost everyone—other than Karl and Richard Meadow ("bless his little antiseptic heart")—was sick. Jane had been violently ill on and off since week one. Jim had pink eye and the runs and a case of hemorrhoids so severe that he couldn't sit down. The rest had grumbling, dysenteric stomachs. "We are so frail, all of us, and without the faith or fatalism to meet this place on its own terms," Jane wrote. Coping with it, she said, required either masochism or hyper-attention to duty, which, she suspected, only Jim was capable of. Eventually, even Richard got sick.

Sometimes Jane could no longer talk Jim out of his moods. She told him about the dream she had about their marriage—when she knew where he was even though she couldn't find him—and the next night, he moved his cot away from hers without saying anything. His "I love you" in London changed to "Yes, I probably do." Jane found herself thinking, *It's going to be just like the past, after all.*

"I probably should have waited until I was sure before shooting off my mouth about Humph. I mean everything's OK + all but I doubt me if there's a future in it. In spite of his being a nice guy and all. Which he is. What the hell," she wrote to her parents.

There was still more than a month left on the expedition, and she was already emptied out. Jane wrote to herself: "I think maybe I'd like to be dead so I wouldn't have to see it end, wouldn't have to keep reading between lines to maintain my precarious hold on what's real."

THE LOOP

"IF THIS WERE A MYSTERY novel, I don't see any really good suspects other than Karl," Arthur said, still on the swivel chair in his office. I asked if he had any concrete reason to suspect him. He didn't. It was all speculation. "It looked to me like Harvard was kind of closing up behind its threatened professor. I always connected his getting tenure with Jane's being murdered."

The timing of Karl's tenure had felt too significant to be random to me, too. And a few other mysteries dangled in close proximity: Jane and Karl's relationship had started out well enough, but, if Boyd and Arthur were right, it soured, and I didn't know why.

Also, if Jane's killer was someone in the department, I found it hard to believe that her murder on the morning of Generals, a pivotal moment in her academic career, was simply a coincidence.

And, finally, I was intrigued not just by the timing of Karl's promotion, but also by the fact of it. Until 2005, when Harvard made all junior professor offers automatically tenure-track, it was rare for a junior professor to get tenure at the school. Instead, the university brought in outside scholars who had already made names for themselves elsewhere. Karl was the last junior professor of archaeology to be tenured from within for the next forty-three years. A few former members of the department told me that 1969 had been an exceptional time. (David Maybury-Lewis, then an assistant professor of anthropology, was also given tenure that year.) For some reason that they couldn't explain, a window apparently opened up that year that allowed junior professors into the castle, creating a mad urgency to get tenure before the window shut.

Even so, for Karl to get the promotion, he had to have been exceptional. Karl credited his rapid ascension to his field experience, the recommendation letters his UPenn mentors wrote, and his publication record before coming to Harvard. And Tepe Yahya was a landmark discovery. But would the 1968 season and the survey of the site from the year before have been enough? It certainly wasn't Carmania, as Karl had come back contending. But the tenure committee may not have known that the site's connection with Carmania had been misjudged—or even if it had, that it might not have cared. (Less than two years later, in 1970, the Tepe Yahya progress report made no mention of Carmania.)

Carmania was a good story, and the newspapers had already done their work of amplifying it. In November 1968, the *Boston Globe* celebrated Karl as the man who had unearthed Alexander the Great's lost citadel: "For centuries, scholars have been aware that Carmania once existed. Yet they have never been able to find the fabled fortress. [...] But this past Summer, the

Harvard team headed by C. C. Lamberg-Karlovsky [. . .] dug out the ancient fort." The evidence was scant: supposed elephant teeth found at the top of the mound, and the fact that Tepe Yahya, like Carmania, according to an ancient Greek historian, was located a "five days' march from the sea." But that didn't stop Karl from confidently declaring to the *Globe*: "I am positive we have discovered Carmania."

I was starting to believe that there were two kinds of archaeologists: the scholars like Jim Humphries and Richard Meadow, who were meticulous and bound by data, and, as I'd seen sitting in his class, the storytellers like Karl. I was also starting to believe that the storytellers always won. We seemed to value memorability more than accuracy as long as no one forced us to look too closely. As Arthur had said on the call before we met, "If you can tell a real good story about what your site was and what it was doing and why it was there, and so on, that's what the truth is. The best story? That's the truth. Whether or not it actually happened." Perhaps the only people who could have forced the tenure committee to examine the truth behind Karl's claims were some of the people who had been on the dig that summer.

But proximity, I scolded myself, didn't equal causation.

"I don't know how to close that loop," I told Arthur.

He said he didn't know how to close the loop, either, and added, "Yeah, well, look. If he did it, it's been a long time, but it would be good just to clear it up. As I said, I wish he did, but wishes don't necessarily reflect reality."

GENERAL EXAMS

As POLICE CONTINUED QUESTIONING JANE'S friends, the timing of Jane's death emerged as something salient.

Don Mitchell told the cops that the last time he saw Jane—when she dropped by for a glass of sherry—she had talked about "this Lamberg-Karlovsky person, and whether he was going to pull a fast one on her about the exam." Jane had been sure that Karl didn't like her, but she didn't know why.

Talking to police, Jim recounted similar conversations with Jane about her worries that she would not be graded fairly on this exam. She felt the same thing had happened to her the year before. Jim prefaced his comments by saying that he didn't know the full story because he hadn't been taking Generals that year, "but from what I understand...she should have passed, but it was thought that the people marking the exam had refused to pass her."

Ingrid Kirsch said she knew more, and she didn't hold back. She explained to police that Jane had been failed on all three sections of her general exams, even though she'd technically passed the archaeology section of the test. According to Ingrid, Jane somehow knew that Karl, one of three people grading her exam, had suggested to the grading committee that they should just fail her across the board. Apparently Karl had added that if Jane continued performing so poorly, he would see to it himself that she'd have no future in the department. Karl would later deny this allegation: "That one person could decide to pass or fail a person is absurd. It's a lie."

Stephen Williams tried to assure police that it was impossible to grade the Generals unfairly. He said the marking procedures had been designed precisely to avoid bias. The exam was always graded by a committee of three so that two professors read the response to each question. And each exam was attributed to a number—not a person—ensuring that the graders wouldn't know whose exams they were marking. "We take the precaution of making darn sure that we don't know."

He was adamant with Detective Davenport that he couldn't recognize any of the students' handwriting.

But Stephen Williams's assurances felt thin in light of the fact that Jane wasn't the only one who thought she had been graded unfairly. Students blamed Williams himself for failing another woman the year before: Kitty Caruthers.

The day that Jane had tracked Jim down to his room and asked how it felt to be chased by Sarah Lee Irwin, they'd been gathered in the student commons because they were upset by how unfair Kitty's situation was.

One student wrote a complaint to Karl. On the basis of Kitty's grades—A's and B's—the author of the letter didn't understand why Kitty hadn't been given a second chance to pass generals, especially since two other students had been allowed to make up for failing marks. It was the author's belief that Stephen Williams, who had been consistently rude to Kitty, hadn't given her a fair shot. Williams, the letter alleged, may even have been out to get her. The author appealed to Karl's empathetic side: He, like Kitty—who was in a terrible state, needing to hold herself together with sedatives—should understand what it feels like to have so little recourse.

Kitty didn't deny that she failed her exams; she just wanted the chance to try again.

Kitty was never given that second chance. She left Harvard with a terminal master's in the spring of 1968.

Contrary to Stephen Williams's protestations, students felt that the structure of general exam grading left a lot of room for personal biases to prejudice the outcome. Generals, as much as they were a test, were also a subjective checkpoint: After grading the exam, the faculty discussed whether the student's performance in the department merited continuing on. According to one student in Jane's cohort, the amount of power a professor's opinion had in those deliberations depended on that professor's standing in the department, as well as on how closely that professor worked with the student.

Karl would later call this a "fundamental misunderstanding of the rules and regulations that guide the general exam." Though he acknowledged the faculty-meeting phase of grading, he reiterated that one person did not have the power to sink a student, citing a thwarted attempt by Stephen Williams to fail a different female student. In his entire fifty-one years of teaching, Karl remembered only one person failing Generals, and that was Kitty.

But the student insisted: While the withdrawal of support from a professor who played a negligible role in a student's academic life might or might not be damning, a no vote from a principal adviser could be enough to torpedo the student's intended career.

Ever since Movius had abandoned her for Les Eyzies, Karl had been Jane's principal adviser. And just like the previous year, he was one of three people on the grading committee. Jane might have believed that it wouldn't matter how well she actually performed on the test. Her destiny was in Karl's hands.

INGRID KIRSCH POLICE

INTERROGATION

Detective Lieutenant Davenport: And what is your name, young lady?

Ms. Kirsch: Ingrid Kirsch.

Detective Lieutenant Davenport: I'm going to ask you some questions, and

I'm just asking them for the sake of getting an answer, regardless of what the answer is. We are investigating the staff also because we're thinking along the lines of these tests, and she was definitely scared to death of one test.

Ms. Kirsch: She was.

Detective Lieutenant Davenport: And we have a feeling that it's this Karlovsky's.

Ms. Kirsch: Yes, it was. I'll tell you what I know about that. When she took her examinations last year, she flunked them, and I talked to her after that. She was extremely despondent. She was despondent before she took them and despondent afterwards. And afterwards she said, "Look, I've been screwed. I have been given the end of the stick." And I said, "Well, look, who?" And she said, "Karlovsky has really screwed me." And I said, "Well, not Movius?" And she said, "Eh, Movius."

Movius thought she was an excellent student. Apparently, the recommendation he wrote for her graduate entry was terrific, and the reason she knows this is because she opened it up once. I don't think Movius lost faith in Janie's ability as an archaeologist. She was bloody good. There's no question about that.

But there was something about Lamberg. I don't think that he was tolerant, for example, of the fact that emotions, emotional contingencies, made a difference in her work, a tremendous difference. If she was upset about something, she blew it. Now, around Christmastime, which is about the same time that she took Generals last year, she was breaking up with Franquemont, and boy, this just blew it for her.

So on the examinations, her board sat down and said, "Look, on social anthropology, she has not passed. On physical anthropology, she has not passed. We could pass her on archaeology." And Karlovsky said, "Forget it." He said, "Look, if she continues working this way, I'm going to see that she gets kicked out of the department."

[...] But Karl also, you know, had this argument with her one night. They were over at a party at Karl's and they apparently were both pretty loaded. And Karl lit into her about something, and she lit into him back. And he said to her, "Look, you're just a student in this department, on my grace. And you know, if I can keep you from going on the dig, I would."

Unidentified Male: How long ago was that?

Ms. Kirsch: That was last spring. And what she said was he presented the case to her this way: "Jane, if you do well on this dig and work your ass off, maybe I'll let you stay in the department. If not, I'll see that you get your head chopped off." Well, no wonder she was scared about her exams. She was terrified.

Detective Lieutenant Davenport: So this was prior to the dig.

Ms. Kirsch: This is prior to the dig, but I think that her attitude on the dig towards Lamberg-Karlovsky was colored a great deal by his antagonism towards her. She did not like him, and I think he loathed her, and I don't know why.

SUCH A TOAD

I PHONED DOZENS OF PEOPLE who worked in and around the Peabody Museum—custodial staff, assistant directors, secretaries, registrars, publishers, conservators—as well as graduate students, teaching fellows, and assistant professors, and I quickly learned that there was no unbiased opinion about Karl.

Through my conversations, Karl emerged as a complicated, mercurial man: brilliant, imposing, hot-tempered, ambitious, inspiring, flamboyant, charismatic, exploitative, even paranoid. Some knew to stay away from him, some admired his charisma. But one way or another, he inspired intense reactions, like from Barbara Westman, the museum's in-house artist. Barbara, eighty-eight years old when I spoke with her, kept her comments about the museum anodyne. "Everyone was so nice," she said. "We used to drink coffee on the street." But that changed when Karl's name was mentioned. "He and his wife were so pompous. P-O-M-P-O-U-S, pompous." She laughed, pleased with herself. "He was such a toad."

Ed Wade, the museum's assistant director under both Stephen Williams and Karl, explained that Karl started as the golden boy in the department, but he quickly developed a reputation for being impossible. Ed remembered Karl as a very angry man who tried to maintain his power through intimidation rather than respect. He would explode at people. Stephen Williams often caught the worst of it. By the mid-'70s, a few years after both Stephen and Karl had achieved their promotions, their relationship had tectonically shifted. Karl's was so far from the professional behavior Ed expected from his colleagues, he said he lost his taste for Harvard.

Father Carney Gavin, the former head of the Semitic Museum, which was across the street from the Peabody, said that even when Karl had been firmly established as a powerhouse at Harvard, he would get jealous of anybody he understood to be trespassing into his domain. As someone in charge of a museum associated with the department of Near Eastern Languages and Civilizations, Father Gavin's work overlapped with Karl's, and it hadn't taken long for competition to build to resentment. "Karl would be pretending he was reading scientific magazines in the foreroom to my little office and listening to my phone calls," he said, still incredulous. "He was mean to people. He was horrible to longtime employees. He was an ambitious, very political administrator. And he was hard on his students," Gavin added. "He really was a thug." (Karl would later respond that he thought they'd had a fairly good relationship. "I had no feelings of competition with the rather smaller operations of Carney Gavin.")

Gavin, who had grown up in Harvard's ecosystem—his uncle had been dean of one of the graduate schools—had a nonheroic view of how power worked in the institution: Whoever secured funding secured power. Karl, who traded on his charm, was a better fundraiser than Stephen Williams. "It takes energy and martinis to raise that money," Karl quipped. His success was reason enough, according to Gavin, for Harvard to overlook any flaws.

Several people I spoke to described Karl as a lazy scholar. John Terrell, who started out as Karl's graduate student, remembered one class where he, with utter confidence, accidentally taught an important archaeological sequence upside down. Terrell, unsurprisingly, came to distrust his scholarship and decided not to put his future in Karl's hands. To Terrell, Karl's storytelling seemed like more than just disinterest in the details. "We all tell stories about ourselves. But some people seem to be, well—living them out more." He couldn't tell if Karl wanted others to believe the stories he told about himself, or if Karl believed them, too.

Another former graduate student told me that even the professors who had helped tenure him saw through the charade eventually. As the student remembered, one of them "would laugh about him and kind of admit that, 'Yeah, at the time it all seemed very exciting and very wonderful, but he did turn out to be more of a bullshit artist than otherwise.'"

Not everyone was so critical. Peter Dane, who had also dug at Tepe Yahya with Jane, recognized the role that luck played in Karl's career, but also credited Karl's success to his intelligence and leadership. He could see that Karl had his own quirks—"I mean like all of us"—but he thought that Karl exemplified the kind of person he wished all tenured professors would be: a good guy and an extraordinarily open-minded academic who always wanted all of his students to do well.

To Peter, Karl's sweeping narratives demonstrated a commendable willingness to share the glamour of archaeology with the masses. "It never occurred to him that he was diminishing what he was doing in any way by talking to anybody at all. He would go and talk to a Rotary club." Phil Kohl, another member of the 1968 expedition, also valued Karl's ability to tell a story: "He would paint big, exotic pictures that would fire up your imagination, and even if they were proven wrong, it nonetheless was a stimulus."

From this perspective, Karl's penchant for sexy-sounding ideas and interesting hypotheses wasn't the mark of a glib attitude toward scholarship, but a boldness of imagination: Karl may have initially misjudged Yahya's Carmania connection, but he had the courage both to hazard a guess and then to admit that he was wrong. And this enthusiasm and charisma had a huge impact on generations of archaeology students; even as recently as a few years ago, when Karl would sit behind his desk and hold court, people would come just to listen. As Ajita Patel, a research assistant in the department, told me, "Karl is a dying breed. You need the captivating teachers. The ones to sell the big story. The ones to draw in the students."

But some students put forth much more serious allegations. A few told me he had a history of changing his mind and leaving people in a bind. Bruce Bourque recalled that Karl had once promised him a teaching scholarship and then turned around and offered it to another graduate student even though Bruce was on full financial aid with a kid, while the other one was well off.

Another student, Elizabeth Stone, had a similar story. When Elizabeth was a senior at UPenn, the Assyriology department approached her and said that they had one fellowship, good for four or five years, that they would love to offer her if she was definitely going to accept. (If they offered it to her, and she declined, then the department would have lost that fellowship funding.) Elizabeth responded that she was likely going to Harvard, provided they offered her a similar scholarship. UPenn called to check, and Karl gave his assurances that she would get the Harvard offer with funding. This was all communicated verbally; still, Elizabeth would later explain, "I thought at the time people were honorable and kept their word," so she turned down the opportunity from

UPenn. But when Harvard's official admissions offer came through, Elizabeth was shocked to find that it was only for one year of funding. When she later confronted Karl about it, he told her he had gone back on his word because he knew that after forfeiting UPenn's offer, she'd be left with no alternative.

"He was unabashed about this?" I asked.

"He was," she said.

(Karl later denied having the power to make these financial decisions. "I have nothing to do with how much money the university offers or what kind of a fellowship or scholarship." He added that the decision about Bruce Bourque was made by committee.)

Elizabeth said that it wasn't her first troubling interaction with Karl. She had still been an undergraduate at UPenn when she met him. He and a few other Harvard scholars had come to UPenn for a visit, and she had gone to a party with them. Elizabeth had danced with Karl "a fair amount," but she had meant nothing by it. "I didn't really think that much of it, but other people obviously did," she told me. When the UPenn scholars visited Harvard a little while later, Elizabeth went, too. Martie, Karl's wife, walked up to her at a party. She took Elizabeth by the chin and examined her. "You are lovely, aren't you," Martie said.

But Elizabeth grew to respect Martie. She remembered watching Martie convince a drunk, angry Karl to punch the wall instead of punching a graduate student. (As Elizabeth remembered it, Karl broke his hand.) Besides, Martie might have had reason to be suspicious. Karl had indeed ended up at Elizabeth's place one of those nights at UPenn—just not with her. According to Elizabeth, he had been with her friend.

RUTH TRINGHAM

RUTH TRINGHAM HAD BEEN AN assistant professor in Old World archaeology at Harvard in the 1970s. Karl had, in large part, been responsible for bringing her there. In 1971, he helped her beat out twenty-six other candidates for the position by writing a hearty letter of support to the permanent members of the Anthropology department. According to Karl, after a six-month search process, there was no question that Ruth was the best of the potential new hires. When we first spoke on Skype, Ruth, now a tenured professor at Berkeley, said that she'd largely had a good experience at Harvard and with Karl—until the final six months she was there. But she didn't want to talk about that over the phone.

A few months later, I met her in a café near her home. She had biked over to me, and her cropped hair was mussed from pulling off her helmet.

Ruth had never been one to bother with glamour or pretense. In 1978, when Harvard didn't give her tenure, she wrote a letter to Henry Rosovsky, the dean of the Faculty of Arts and Sciences, that said she would not be coming back to Harvard even when she became a superstar. Her British accent gave her refusal to be proper an extra glint of mischievousness.

I came armed with three letters I had found in Karl's archive and showed them to her, hoping it would coax out whatever she hadn't wanted to say to me on the phone.

The first was that 1971 letter of support from Karl.

The second was a 1975 letter from her to him. She read it out loud.

"Dear Karl," it began. "This really is going to be only a very short letter. I am just at the climax (?!) of preparing my paper for Santa Fe."

She laughed, a little embarrassed. "I'm very, very personal, aren't I? A very intimate conversation."

She continued reading. In this part of the letter, she narrated an imaginary story between Karl and Gordon Willey, one of the older archaeology professors: "Karl's attention begins to wander, he thinks of the Great Heights he's about to attain."

She was taken aback by her directness. "I can't believe I'm writing this to Karl. We must've had a very good relationship at that time, where I felt like I could be doing it." She checked the date of the letter. "This is when he was still promising things." Karl had assured Ruth that they would try to find a way to turn her appointment into a tenure-track position.

Then I slid the third letter across the table. I was pretty sure she had never seen it before. Ruth leaned back in her chair to read.

"The snake," she said. "I never should have trusted him."

It was a 1976 letter from Stephen Williams to Karl in which Stephen reprimanded Karl for his remarks about Ruth to the Permanent Members of the Anthropology department. Apparently Karl's statements about Ruth's excavation project and her involvement in it had been so negative that Stephen felt compelled to ask Karl to present a correction.

"Why would he—" I began to ask.

"Why would he do that?" she finished my sentence. Because she was coming up to the time when they were going to have to decide about her tenure, she explained.

"And he was threatened by the idea that you might become tenured?" I still felt like I was missing something. "There was no precipitating moment where your good relationship switched—"

"Like did he make an advance and I rejected it?" she asked.

I nodded.

"It's possible he did and I didn't know. I've always been so naive to those things." I could almost see her mind moving, making little leaps from one consideration to the next. "Why would he get jealous? He had tenure. He had nothing to lose."

She thought more, until she eventually said: "He's a snake. You know. That's what he is. Maybe all that opening up to me was all a play or a ploy. I mean in the end, he, um"—her phrasing became staccato, but her voice maintained its volume—"that was suddenly after the evening when our relationship went sour."

The 180 from just moments before was jarring. Perhaps she had needed to keep it tightly compartmentalized all these years. Even that day in the café, she was conflicted and careful to qualify that it was only in retrospect that she wondered if she had miscategorized benign behavior in the first place.

In the fall of 1977, more than a year after Stephen Williams had chastised Karl for his negative statements, Ruth had done Karl a favor by letting an archaeologist colleague of his stay at her apartment. The colleague had a reputation of being difficult—abrasive and insulting when it suited him— and Ruth hadn't found that to be an exaggeration. The sweat marks on her bedsheets weren't the worst of the stains he had left behind. Ruth had complained to Karl, and Karl, one night, had come over to say sorry.

At this point in the story, Ruth's memory got a little hazy. She wondered whether she had consciously blocked it out. She remembered Karl apologizing for his colleague and then "there was suddenly a moment when that changed, in which he was speaking about my personal life and my future career in ways that seemed overfamiliar and which made me feel uncomfortable, upset, uneasy. I can't remember anything specific that was said. We were not sitting down, we were standing face-to-face, quite close; he had his back to the window, where it was beginning to get dark, so that he was kind of silhouetted. There was no physical contact, I'm sure of that, but I do remember wanting him out of my apartment."

I asked if he had made his support of her promotion seem contingent on her responding a certain way that evening.

"No," she said. "There was nothing explicit. No, nothing."

Eventually Ruth said it was time for Karl to go. When he left, she still felt she had his support. But after that night, Ruth remembered, "it all went downhill." Karl "kind of became no longer my friend."

A few months later, it was announced that Ruth would not get tenure.

(Decades later, Karl, too, would remember that evening and a conversation about the tenure process that she may have found anxiety-ridden. But he believed they were still on good terms after it. As for her tenure, "There's a difference between friendship and the professional responsibilities one has when it comes to that friend." Plus, her denial was a departmental decision; they voted not to advance her even to the *ad hoc* committee stage.)

Ruth could have stayed another academic year, but she left Harvard as quickly as she could. She wrote that letter to Dean Rosovsky but didn't explain why she was leaving. She never confronted Karl about that evening or about her disappointment in not getting tenure.

"That's not what women did then. You move on, find something else," she said.

Ruth looked at me as if she had just traveled back from forty years ago and remembered we were there in that café because of Jane. She agreed that Jane's story was likely a way to warn students and colleagues about Karl. "It doesn't really help you with understanding what he might have done to Jane but there is a pattern that he'll suddenly drop you . . . You know that even if he isn't the one responsible, it could so easily have been. That's the kind of person he is."

RICHARD MEADOW

When detectives asked Richard Meadow, who had been to Tepe Yahya with Jim and Jane, about the possibility of tension on the dig in Iran, Richard refused to grant that line of inquiry an inch.

Detective Davenport asked whether there was any jealousy as a result of finds on the expedition.

"There certainly was not," Richard said. He also denied any "woman trouble."

"No jealousy existing between—" Davenport began to ask, but Richard answered before he could finish.

"Absolutely not."

"Right," Davenport said. "Now do you know of any bad feelings which have come up among this group since they returned to Harvard, including yourself?"

"No."

Later, Davenport asked Richard why his hands and legs were shaking.

"I'm physically nervous," he said.

DAN POTTS

THE PERSON I MOST DREADED speaking to was Karl's former student Dan Potts. (It was his son Morgan who first told me Jane's story.) Though I always operated as if everything I said was going to end up straight in Karl's ear, talking to his most loyal protégé felt particularly dangerous. Dan had put together Karl's festschrift—a collection of essays and remembrances by colleagues, friends, and students, assembled toward the end of a professor's illustrious career—in honor of his sixty-fifth birthday. Festschrifts were a strange academic tradition, sycophantic and awkward by nature, and Karl's was no exception. Titled "Ingenious Man, Inquisitive Soul," it both dripped with adulation and was stuffed with academic publications that doubled as homages.

Dan Potts's own essay—"In Praise of Karl"—lauded the professor for fostering an atmosphere "charged with energy, anticipation, and the unabashed enjoyment of intellectual endeavor" and for drawing one into his "vortex of creativity." Dan chose as the opening image a photograph of Karl, handsome and smiling, his hair lightly mussed, his pants cuffed. He's holding up a scale bar against the backdrop of a sandy dune; his sleeves are rolled up past his elbow. The consummate archaeologist at work.

I emailed Dan under the pretense of speaking about Tepe Yahya since he, too, had spent many years digging there, and I had heard from his son that he was as meticulous about data as Richard Meadow. Morgan wasn't wrong. Dan was happy to reminisce, and his details were so vivid that I felt like I was right there with him. He told me it was so humid in Bandar Abbas, the closest coastal town, that people would literally wring sweat out of their pants.

After about half an hour, I eased into talking about Karl by asking what Dan thought about my taxonomy of archaeologists—dividing them into Storytellers like Karl, and Scholars like Richard Meadow, Jim Humphries, and himself. Potts added "Boy Scout" to my categories, but he agreed with my general classification. He also emphatically agreed that Karl was the exemplar Storyteller: "He's almost the kind of person who would say he's not going to let a few facts stand in the way of a good story."

The conversation broke open almost immediately. Suddenly, this man—who his son had warned me was so put off by gossip that he had never said more than a few words about the Jane Britton story—let fly decades of pent-up anger.

"When I think about some of the really great scholars who were at Harvard, with whom I could have studied had I not fallen in with him, it just sort of kills me."

Dan brought up the festschrift he had compiled for Karl without my needing to ask about it. He said he had volunteered for the job because he felt that if he didn't do it, no one else would. Even Karl deserved one, he thought. But "I don't know if I'd do it today," he said.

"Because it was so much work, or because it's Karl?" I asked.

"Because it's Karl," he said. "I have the dubious privilege of being deeply embarrassed when somebody says to me, 'And who did you study with?'"

Over the years, Dan Potts had grown disillusioned by the grandeur of Karl's claims and the laziness of his scholarship. "He certainly convinced a lot of people at Harvard that he was a wunderkind and this sort of genius for having discovered Tepe Yahya." That had been a good place to start, but that was kind of all Karl ended up doing. He got "seduced by his own success."

But it was clear that Dan had spent a long time believing in Karl, too, and the betrayal he felt after those years of loyalty was palpable.

Dan added, "I mean you know he's been accused of plagiarism, too. He has plagiarized me. He has also plagiarized another scholar's grant application, which he was then stupid enough to stick some paragraphs into an article. Students would get kicked out for less than that."

It was an enormous accusation, but I would later find traces of it in Karl's archive. The scholar's name was Jim Shaffer, and it was his 1973 National Science Foundation grant proposal. There was a letter from the NSF chastising Karl for allegedly plagiarizing Jim's proposal in a talk called the Reckitt lecture, which was later published in a journal. I also found Karl's apology letter to Jim. In it, Karl explained that he was under the impression that he *had* cited Jim's work in the lecture. It had been an honest mistake. "Please accept my sincerest apologies. I simply do not abuse students, colleagues, anyone in fact," Karl had written. Shaffer accepted his apology. In explaining this incident years later, Karl would add, "There is a difference between convergence and plagiarism," and if the NSF had found evidence of plagiarism, they never would have supported his future grant applications.

Dan, on the other hand, never came forward with his allegation of plagiarism. I didn't understand why, if he felt so certain that his ideas had been stolen, he didn't report it.

Dan tried to explain the power dynamics at play. He said that when he realized that Karl had plagiarized part of his dissertation in an afterword for an anthology, he confronted the professor. Karl was furious at first, and then eventually apologized by letter, telling his former student that he got so worked up because he cared about Dan as a scholar, friend, and academic son.

That's where Dan felt like he had to leave it. He asked me what else he could have done in that situation. If he had gone public, the consequences for an early-stage academic would have been worse than the slap on the wrist Karl might have received. Besides, Karl had been his adviser; Dan had just graduated and needed Karl to write his recommendation letters. If he had asked someone else, it would have looked very suspicious that his main adviser wasn't the one writing them. Dan couldn't afford to speak up.

But that wasn't the only time that Karl tried to get away with piggybacking on Dan's ideas, he alleged. Decades after the dissertation incident, Dan had told Karl about a site in Saudi Arabia regarding which he had been in touch with the country's antiquities council. Six months later, as Dan was still putting plans in place, Karl emailed to announce he would be undertaking an excavation at exactly that site. Dan was furious. "You know, I'm not just any student of yours. I'm the idiot that edited your festschrift for god's sake."

Karl would later claim that Dan had been denied permission for the site because of a dispute with the former director general of archaeology in Saudi Arabia, which Dan refuted on both counts. They agreed, though, that Karl replied to Dan's angry emails with something to the effect of, "It's not what you know, but who you know."

Years later, Dan Potts ultimately forgave him for that, too. "I don't want him to go to his grave or me to go to my grave having this feud, this stupid thing." But, it seemed, I was catching Dan after one too many moments of forgiveness. Magnanimity had an upper limit. "You see that photograph of him," he asked me, meaning the one that opened his festschrift, "where he's holding what looks like a survey pole and it looks like there's sand behind him?"

I was looking at it. It looked like he was in Iran.

The opening image of Karl Lamberg-Karlovsky's festschrift. (Courtesy of the Harvard University Archives © President and Fellows of Harvard College, Peabody Museum of Archaeology and Ethnology, PM 2004.24.28512A)

"That was taken at a construction site opposite the Peabody Museum."

I laughed.

"I was there when that happened. And you see how he's rolled up his sleeves? I mean it's a complete sham."

It was the perfect encapsulation of Karl's games. Even knowing that it wasn't in the desert, I had trouble unseeing the dune. I had to admire the charade.

THE DAY OF JANE'S DEATH:
KARL'S POINT OF VIEW

WHEN KARL WENT DOWN TO the police station on the evening of January 7, 1969, it was entirely of his own volition. He had heard about Jane on the six o'clock news. She had been murdered, the reporter said. Karl already knew that Jane was dead—around four that afternoon, Stephen Williams had told him—but the fact that she had been killed was new information. Williams hadn't known if it was an accidental death, or suicide, or the result of foul play.

"I immediately yanked myself down here because for the first time I got more news than we had heard in the Peabody. There are many rumors that were flying around, and once it became as clear as it apparently is that there's some aspect of foul play in this, then I just popped myself into the car and came down here, simply because also the news said that Jim Humphries was here; and I know their close attachment." He was sitting with Sergeant Petersen, Detective Amaroso, and Detective Tully.

The cops asked him the standard questions: How long have you known the deceased, when was the last time you saw her, did she have any problems you were aware of? Karl said she graduated *magna cum laude* and "Jane really, in terms of her work has—has continued the promise which she showed."

The last time he saw Jane was on Friday when Jane came to his office to tell him what she hoped to do over the summer in Iran. "She was trying to detail what kinds of problems she wanted to attack, what she wanted to write her thesis on, as well as, clearly, to try and get some understanding of the kind of exam which would be coming up...the first part of which was taken today."

As far as he was aware, he said, Jane didn't have difficulties with anyone.

PUZZLE PIECES

I CONTINUED CALLING PEOPLE IN and around the Peabody at the time of Jane's death, inching ever closer to the center of the story, and one thing became clear: Jane's position in the department was very vulnerable in the months leading up to her death.

A graduate student in Jane's year recalled that the semester before her death, Karl had been vocal about Jane not being a very good student, and that he was really unsure about whether or not she was going to pass the exams. I wondered if it was possible that Karl had already decided to fail her out of the program and was just laying the groundwork—a line of thinking Karl would later refute: "The rumors that I was going to sink Jane are simply false...I did not take animosity to a graduate student."

But another student from the time, who didn't want to be named for fear of destroying a valuable professional relationship with Karl, remembered hearing that Jane wasn't going to be allowed back to Tepe Yahya for a second season. It was the first time I had heard that, and it seemed like news too major for only one person to remember. It didn't help that the student could recall neither exactly who relayed the rumor nor Karl's supposed reasons for not allowing Jane back.

The student, however, was adamant: "I'm absolutely sure that I knew that she wasn't going to be allowed back because otherwise why would I believe some rumor about Karl?" As an explanation for why the student had held on to suspicion about Karl all these years, the student said, "It just fit perfectly."

That's when the student provided the final puzzle piece of the theory connecting Karl's tenure and Jane's death: blackmail.

The student walked me through it: Jane might have suspected that Karl was going to fail her on the Generals or refuse to take her back to Tepe Yahya in order to force her out of the anthropology program. To prevent him from doing so, Jane might have threatened Karl that she would "go to the Harvard Corporation and tell all the stories about his wild behavior and that would ruin his chances of getting tenure." Karl might have felt that he had no alternative but to silence her permanently.

The student wasn't alone in this theory. A biological anthropology student named Peter Rodman remembered a similar story of blackmail. Rodman said he didn't know Jane that well despite them being two of only three people to enter the PhD program straight from undergrad at Harvard, but he remembered very clearly the main rumor that circulated in the wake of Jane's death: Jane had threatened one member of her Generals committee that she would expose the affair they had been having if she didn't pass. Karl Lamberg-Karlovsky was the professor at the heart of this rumor.

I didn't have to look too deep to find that this theory hardly withstood examination: I already sincerely doubted that Jane and Karl had had an affair, and I couldn't imagine that even if it were true, it would have been sufficiently damning to his tenure bid. Harvard didn't put a rule on the books about professors having relationships with undergraduates until 2015. There was still no blanket rule about graduate students. Besides, even if Karl did feel threatened by Jane, it was an impossible jump from that to accepting that Karl might have believed the best way to handle the situation was to kill her.

I once again trawled through the alternative theories. Perhaps Karl had been getting jealous of all the time that Jane was spending with Jim, his star student. As Karl had told the press, Jim was the person to whom he entrusted Tepe Yahya when he was away from the site, and as Karl would later tell me, "I've had several other expeditions, and I never had another Jim."

Or maybe it was that Jane really had threatened to expose Karl's exaggerations about the possibility of Tepe Yahya being Carmania. According to the former registrar of the Semitic Museum, Lynne Rosansky, this was one of the leading theories in the Harvard community five years after Jane's death. "There was some speculation that she had something on him about the validity of what he was claiming that would have put his whole stance— what he published—at risk."

Or maybe it was enough that Jane simply drove Karl crazy. She didn't respect his authority or take his directions well, and few things bothered him more than being disrespected.

I ran my thinking past David Freidel, who knew Jane from his undergrad years at Harvard. Karl had been his senior thesis adviser.

Jane wasn't just any student, he reminded me. She was the daughter of a Radcliffe vice president. Maybe whatever Jane had on Karl wasn't that big a deal, he said, but her word carried more weight than most. "Academic politics are deep, nasty, and personal. And also very unforgiving."

When I later raised the issue with Karl, he insisted that he never cared about getting tenure in the first place. As an assistant professor at Harvard, he knew he would get a good job offer somewhere; he'd already gotten one from the University of Pittsburgh. Plus, he said, he never had "Harvarditis—a bad case of necessary attachment to the institution."

I shared this with David Freidel. Though David agreed that junior professorships at Harvard often launched careers at other prestigious universities, he laughed at Karl's gall to say that he didn't care about tenure. "He's lying to you. He's just lying. Oh no...you need to know that."

INGRID KIRSCH, POLICE
INTERROGATION, CONTINUED

Detective Lieutenant Davenport: Do you think that Karlovsky himself is interested in Jane as a woman?

Ms. Kirsch: You know. It's hard for me to say. I've known just a multitude of guys who thought Janie was incredibly sexy, and I know that Lamberg-Karlovsky's marriage is one of those European kinds where he considers his wife's place in the home and his place outside of the home is fairly loose. I think it's entirely possible, you know, that he was attracted to Janie and was repulsed. That's entirely possible.

Detective Lieutenant Davenport: Do you know of her dating a French professor who is a friend of Lamberg-Karlovsky's?

Ms. Kirsch: A professor of French or a Frenchman?

Detective Lieutenant Davenport: A Frenchman.

Ms. Kirsch: Unh-unh (negative).

Detective Lieutenant Davenport: Do you know of anyone in the class?

Ms. Kirsch: Oh. Wait a minute. Was this Frenchman a former classmate of—

Detective Lieutenant Davenport: Yes.

Ms. Kirsch: —Lamberg-Karlovsky's? Jesus-God, I remember a conversation with her that disturbed me very much. She said she thought Karl was a liar, and I said, "Why did you think that?" And she said, "Well, one night, Lamberg invited me over to go out with this guy who was a classmate of his," and she said, "Boy, was he weird." I said, "What do you mean, he was weird?" "Well," she said, "Lamberg and his wife disappeared upstairs after dinner and left me with this cat, and this guy kept going on about what a shit Lamberg was, and he was a liar in college, that he was absolutely pathological about the untruths that he told, that he was unscrupulous in his relationships with females and so forth." I can't remember when she said this went on, but it frightened her terribly.

Detective Lieutenant Davenport: It would have been sometime in the first week of December if I remember rightly.

Ms. Kirsch: I wish I could remember when she told me that. Boy, it upset her because I think she felt that—that Lamberg was not entirely sincere. As a matter of fact, I think she thought he was a liar. He would make promises and rescind on them, or he would make statements and then contradict them talking to someone else, that sort of thing.

Detective Lieutenant Davenport: Do you know anybody that really hated her guts?

Ms. Kirsch: Janie was not universally beloved; I'll just put it that way. I think an awful lot of people were scared of Jane—that more so than disliking her. It was hard to dislike anybody that fascinating, but it's easy to be scared of her. I think that if you wanted to pursue something like that, you'd have to see who felt that competitively they would have been hurt by Jane, because in her work, as in her love affairs, she was not going to take any crap from anybody. She was going to plow right through, and if she had to ruin somebody else's career on the way, she would have done it.

Detective Lieutenant Davenport: Did Karlovsky feel that way about her?

Ms. Kirsch: Could be. I think Karlovsky is very insecure in his own position at Harvard. I don't think his appointment for tenure has come through, and I think he feels very resentful about that.

Detective Lieutenant Davenport: I think he has two more years in his contract.

Ms. Kirsch: As an assistant professor.

CHRISTINE LESNIAK

I HAD ACCUMULATED A PILE of circumstantial evidence—instances of alleged bad behavior, ancient grudges, stories of overpromises and intimidation. But these, even in the aggregate, didn't prove Karl's guilt. And when I tried to corroborate these stories, just to know how firm my foundation was, I ran up against the limitations of memory, of perspective, and of evidence.

Some people were dead, unwilling to speak, or hard to find. Some of the stories never had any witnesses and were always going to be someone's word against Karl's. Some were missing crucial context: Ed Wade, I later learned, had been fired by Karl after a year as his assistant director. (In contrast, Garth Bowden, who succeeded Ed, remembered Karl as "a very good professional, and a good friend.") Others were clear exaggerations or misunderstandings—the products, perhaps, of the distortions of perspective in academia. For example, a number of people had described the intense competition between Karl and Assistant Professor Tom Patterson, with both in the running for a single tenure position in the Anthropology department. But when I spoke to Tom, he said he didn't remember anything of the sort; he left for Yale the year before Karl was tenured.

And even when I did have paperwork, things were slippery. Looking at Dan Potts's dissertation and Karl's afterword, I could see that Karl discussed the same cylinder seal that Dan wrote about. Karl used the same quotes from the same scholars. He reached the same conclusion about the deities pictured. But it wasn't a wholesale copy-paste job. And Karl had, in fact, included a footnote reference to Dan's dissertation. Yes, it was buried in the endnotes rather than acknowledged in the body of the text, and it didn't convey what exactly Karl derived from the dissertation, and how much of it was exactly the same, but Karl had acknowledged it. Couldn't it be said that since they worked on Tepe Yahya together, it was no wonder they would quote from the same source material and reach similar conclusions? Even with all the hard evidence I could hope to find, I still couldn't be certain about intention or malice.

But some of the gaps were particularly tantalizing. I tried to track down the woman whom Elizabeth Stone said had spent the night with Karl. Her name was Christine Lesniak, and she and Elizabeth had both been on the 1971 Tepe Yahya season, two years after Jane's death. Someone else from that year also strongly suspected that there had been an entanglement between Karl and Christine. That person sent me copies of journal entries from that summer, including a description of a mealtime during which Martie tried to dump a pitcher of water on Christine. But I needed to hear it from Christine herself. With her first and last name and the fact that she was interested in epigraphy and had gone to UPenn, I thought she would be easy enough to locate. But there was no trace of her.

I eventually found her entry in the online Harvard directory. It listed a PO box under a different name. I wrote a postcard to that address and gave my number. A week later, I got a call.

"You wanted to talk to Christine Lesniak?" a woman asked. She gave me the third degree: Who was this person who said to contact Christine? How had I reached that person? Does that person have an email address?

When my answers had satisfied her, she softened. "I will fill you in," she said. "I'm her younger sister, and forty years ago she disappeared."

Goosebumps prickled my neck.

Christine, her sister said, had gone to three schools—UPenn, Harvard, and the University of Chicago—"and then something went very, very wrong with her." It was the late 1970s, and Christine was living in Chicago when she vanished. Her sister said she recently spoke to the Cook County medical examiner in Chicago, and he said that as of six years ago, her body hadn't shown up at the morgue. She might still be alive. He couldn't tell her anything more.

The temptation to read into her disappearance was hard to resist. But there was no evidence whatsoever that Karl had anything to do with it; her sister couldn't even recall hearing the name Karl Lamberg-Karlovsky. Karl would later say, "That I had an affair with her is outrageous," and pointed out that another academic had stayed over that night at Elizabeth's, too. Looking back, her sister felt pretty sure that Christine had suffered a schizophrenic break. "The last time I saw her she started having dental problems. Teeth that were rotting," she said. It was unlike Christine, who had always been "very, very meticulous and preppy."

The rational part of me understood, then, that the search for significance in the sheer coincidence of Karl being connected to this missing woman was almost certainly more revealing of *my* ability to retrofit guilt into a narrative than it was of anything else. Besides, I could probably find skeletons like this in anyone's closet if I looked hard enough. I was no exception. If someone wanted to paint me as a murderer using similarly specious logic, they wouldn't have to look very far to find that I was related to a few: My grandfather's brother had allegedly been a hit man for the Chinese Mafia. My great-grandfather on the other side had accidentally killed a man for harassing his pregnant wife. I'm named after that woman.

But even knowing all that, I found it hard to simply file away and accept the fact that two silenced women could be found in the shadow of the same professor.

A SECOND CIPHER

THE NIGHT AFTER JANE'S FUNERAL, Karl was scheduled to give a talk at the St. James Church in Watertown on Route 16, just past Mount Auburn Cemetery, in the part of town known as Little Armenia. Phil Kohl, who was staying with the Lamberg-Karlovskys, accompanied him. Karl spoke with his usual gravitas, and the effectiveness of his talk was aided by the pictures he had brought of life at the dig. He clicked through the images and paused on one. Jane was in the photo.

Karl stopped talking. He looked at the crowd. Phil was startled: Karl was tearing up.

Karl continued on with his talk as if nothing was wrong. But Phil could tell he was still choking up. How do you interpret a guy crying, he would ask himself, still, years later. Do you see that as genuine? Is it because he's guilty of some nefarious act? Was it a performance?

That moment would remain for Phil an encapsulation of something— like the red ochre—that was perfectly ambiguous. A symbol that could be read a dozen different ways.

"You could give a negative interpretation of that if you so desired, I suppose," Phil would later reflect, but "I think that the most likely explanation is the overt explanation: that he genuinely felt sorry. That they were genuine tears. It was a genuine feeling of regret."

PHYSICAL EVIDENCE

My phone lit up while I was at work. I grabbed my notebook and braced myself.

"Hi, this is Becky Cooper," I said, as softly as I could because I was still at my desk.

"Hi, this is Boyd Britton, returning your recent call," he said. His voice was as resonant as ever. "How long has it been now? I remember you, but it's been a while."

"About a year and a half," I said.

I called Boyd because I needed to know if anyone had been actively assigned to Jane's case in recent years.

I was at the beginning of a two-year public records battle with the Middlesex County District Attorney's Office. In Massachusetts, homicides are technically under the jurisdiction of the district attorney where the crime occurred. When I learned this fact, I immediately wrote a public records request to the Middlesex DA; I hoped that even though the Cambridge Police no longer had Jane's records, Middlesex might.

They did, in fact. But they refused to release anything: "Unfortunately, at this time, this Office is unable to provide you with copies of records as the records you are seeking directly relate to an active and open criminal investigation." They cited something called exemption (f) as the grounds for their refusal.

That was it; a one-page rejection. I had ninety days to appeal their decision, the letter informed me.

If I could prove that Jane's investigation was not active, then maybe my appeal stood a shot. Surely the nearly fifty years between Jane's murder and my appeal should be a factor, even if there was no statute of limitations on murder.

After patiently wading through Boyd's discursive conversational openers,

I finally told Boyd the main point of the call, and he said he was happy to help. He looked through his email correspondence to see if there was anything of interest and narrated as he scrolled through his inbox. He eventually came across what he'd been looking for: "Sergeant Peter Sennott," he said. "I don't know if you know his name."

I didn't.

"He's Massachusetts State Police, and they now have the case. It's no longer in Cambridge's hands." According to Boyd, Sennott had said that "physical evidence was retained and could be examined, but the presence of DNA is unlikely. They have it as a cold case, but they have not dropped the ball on it."

Physical evidence. I was too distracted by that new fact to have the "cold case" coup register. If physical evidence existed, it was a game-changer. The case no longer relied on confession. It was no longer victim to the vagaries of memory, and of silencing and erasure and fear. This case might truly be solvable.

I wondered what the physical evidence was, and how well preserved it might be. Saliva on a cigarette butt? Fingerprints on that ashtray? Something from the fingerprint that Don said he had been asked to photograph? I also doubted there was DNA. DNA testing in criminal cases didn't start until the late '80s, and widespread use didn't occur until later, so even if by some miracle the authorities had saved something with DNA on it, the chances it would have been stored well enough to successfully test half a century later were next to zero. But still, it was something.

I asked him if he would feel comfortable forwarding anything he had about it.

My phone buzzed as the email came through. I scanned it as quickly as I could while we were on the phone: From what Boyd could glean, Cambridge PD had been ordered to hand over the files to the Mass State Police. Not much detail on it, but there was a suggestion that the DA was involved. Sergeant Sennott spoke well of a diligent medical examiner who saved things from the initial autopsy. Two Cambridge cops had been enthusiastic about reopening the case in the '90s, Brian Branley and John Fulkerson.

I tracked down all three of the cops. Sergeant Sennott gave me nothing, and I left a voicemail for John Fulkerson. I had a bit more luck with Brian Branley, who confirmed what I needed for my public records appeal: that nobody was directly assigned to the case. I was in the middle of including this detail in my appeal letter when John Fulkerson called me back.

"I remember it very well," Fulkerson said, without hesitation. His Boston accent was so thick I couldn't help but love it. "I don't have all the notes in front of me but she was murdered on University Road in the '60s."

"How do you remember it was University Road?"

"I did the detective work for quite some time. And I kind of don't forget the cases I've worked on." He said he had worked on over forty murders in his career, but "they never leave your mind, you know? They never leave your memory."

He and Brian Branley were both assigned to the homicide unit in the mid-'90s. They were cleaning and reorganizing the old boxes of material in the homicide room of the old Cambridge Police precinct house when he saw Jane's case. It stuck out because there weren't a lot of unsolved murders in Cambridge. Going through the file, Fulkerson and Branley realized there were a few people—"some people that were close to her"—that they wanted to track down and interview. "You know, 80 percent of the people really want to confess to what they did. And sometimes when time goes by they want to talk about it."

Without naming names, Fulkerson said, "I feel that I interviewed someone that was a prime suspect."

"A prime suspect of yours, or a prime suspect then?"

"Prime suspect of mine," he clarified. "This person wasn't really looked at, back then. He was mentioned in the file."

Around the same period, Fulkerson said, the district attorney's office had been making a big push to look at old cases that might be solved by reexamining DNA evidence. In Jane's case, "there was some DNA evidence that they tried to reexamine but it wasn't successful."

The physical evidence was DNA! I wanted to shout. But I resisted. I didn't want to call attention to the enormity of his revelation and have him clam up. Instead, I tiptoed around Harvard's relationship to the Jane Britton case. I said I hadn't been able to shake the story after hearing it, and part of what I found so striking was how alive it still was in the archaeology community. "I find it difficult speaking to, uh, the people at Harvard University," he said in a segue I took to mean that he understood that the department was wrapped up in the case in some way. "It seems like they kind of want things to go away sometimes, you know?"

He addressed the Harvard connection indirectly through the Mary Joe Frug case, a 1991 unsolved murder of the wife of a Harvard Law School professor. He and Branley also reopened that one. "I found it very difficult dealing with Harvard University. The professors. Not the school itself." They were "proud to sit and talk with you, but they may not answer your questions the way you want them to?"

I said that I thought being a Harvard professor lent some a sense of invincibility.

"I think they think they can outsmart you."

In the end, though, with the Jane Britton case, he and Branley had to admit they couldn't solve it. "It just didn't work out for us, you know? Didn't work out for her." In 2005, Fulkerson was asked to pack up the case files. Some years later, Fulkerson got moved off homicide and into traffic.

"I miss it," he said repeatedly. "I feel that I'm really not the same person— the same police officer anymore because I'm not helping people anymore the way I used to."

Fulkerson's whole career had been dedicated to not giving up. His first job had been in a task force on fugitive apprehension at the Department of Correction, and his boss's motto was "He escapes who is not pursued." To Fulkerson, that meant that "if someone's not chasing someone down about something, they're going to get away with it." Fulkerson had had the motto tattooed on his arm.

He told me he still couldn't shake the feeling that Jane's case was solvable: "I'm not accusing anybody, I never accused anybody, but there's something there." I cautiously let myself believe that I'd finally found someone on the law enforcement side who was as haunted by this case as I was.

At the very end of the call, I tried to push my luck by asking him to confirm that there was red ochre at the crime scene.

"I really can't explain that to you because it's an open case. People are going to know where that came from if I talked to you about that."

I said I understood.

"I got a couple more years before I retire. So..." He trailed off. "Hold on to my number. If you need anything, give me a call."

KARL AT POLICE HEADQUARTERS

EIGHT DAYS AFTER JANE'S BODY was found, Karl returned to Cambridge Police headquarters. This time they had asked him to come.

Detective Lieutenant Leo Davenport served as interrogator. Davenport had a quiet way of currying favor and trust with his interview subjects. At the outset, Davenport called Karl an associate professor. *"Assistant* professor," Karl corrected. Davenport apologized. "Wouldn't mind being an associate," Karl replied.

Davenport asked if Karl had ever been to Jane's apartment without his wife present. Absolutely not. He asked if Karl had ever acted as Jane's escort. "Never. Positively, absolutely never." Karl added that he had never been with Jane in any situation which could be considered a date—"absolutely, 100 percent not."

They tried the jealousy angle: that Karl was angry that Jane was distracting Jim. No, he said. Jim was studying as diligently as ever.

"I'll say one thing about you, Professor," Davenport said. "You cover every field. Every avenue we approach, you're right there to block it with an answer."

Davenport asked Karl when he had last been in Jane's apartment building. Two months ago, he said.

"If somebody that we talked to said that you had been over to 6 University Road since January 1 of this year, they were wrong?" another man in the room asked.

"Dead wrong," Karl said.

"Dead wrong," Davenport repeated. "And I hope not the expression. Dead, dead, dead wrong."

PAUL DE MAN

KARL'S FOREWORD TO DAN POTTS'S Tepe Yahya monograph began with a quote from Paul de Man. "What is at stake is not only the distance that shelters the author of autobiography from his experience but the possible convergence of aesthetics and of history."

I had been looking in the Tepe Yahya monographs for the photograph of Jane lying down in front of the Land Rover to see if it was really as different from Arthur Bankoff's print as I remembered when I was struck by that opening quote and the section that followed. It seemed to me that Karl was highlighting exactly what others had accused him of: that people can cushion themselves from the reality of their experience by living inside narrative.

Karl made the case that the value of a story lay in its durability as much as its accuracy. He brought up Heinrich Schliemann, who became world-famous for his excavation of Troy. Few cared about his site report or about the reports that came from later archaeologists excavating the area. Instead, what people remembered was Schliemann's *idea* that he excavated Troy.

Karl did not mention that Schliemann's Troy was likely not Troy at all, and that his method of excavation destroyed any chances for future archaeologists to reinvestigate. Schliemann has been described as a "relentlessly self-promoting amateur archaeologist." However, I got the sense that these details only further proved Karl's point: Schliemann's narrative mattered more than the disappointing truth of facts.

Karl contended that it was impossible to separate archaeology and storytelling. Yes, artifacts existed and data could be recovered, but the archaeologist's job was to give those artifacts meaning—to tell their story. "Artifacts recovered by archaeologists are situated in three dimensions. They are produced within the context of a long past world, recovered as objects within our present world, and offered an interpretation, or a 'meaning,' which may, or may not belong to either world." In short, Karl wrote, "All archaeology is the re-enactment of past thoughts in the archaeologist's own mind."

I later recounted this all to my friend Ben. Ben, the son of a literature professor, stopped me when I said the opening quote was by Paul de Man. "You know who that is, right?" he asked. I didn't. De Man, he told me, had been one of the most important figures in literary theory, but a few years after his death, a graduate student discovered that de Man had written a weekly column for a pro-Nazi paper in Belgium. That finding led to the unraveling of de Man's carefully constructed identity, and his name had become synonymous with duplicity. As *Harper's* Christine Smallwood put it, de Man was "a slippery Mr. Ripley, a confidence man, and a hustler who embezzled, lied, forged, and arreared his way to intellectual acclaim." De Man's double life was discovered in 1987; Karl quoted him in 2001.

Karl, it occurred to me, was too smart for this parallel not to mean anything. It seemed like he was purposefully dropping crumbs and had just been waiting for someone like me to find these quotes and arrange the ellipses. I felt left with three possibilities: Karl really was guilty and brazenly taunted people with his invincibility. He was innocent and both courted and crafted his reputation as a suspected villain. Or, of course, the third possibility: I was the one trapped in a game of symbols of my own invention, finding meaning where there was none to be found.

CLIFFORD A. ROCKEFELLER

"YOU'VE REALLY GOT A COLLECTION in the raw here," the librarian of the university archives in the basement of Pusey Library said, smiling, when he rolled a cart carrying Karl's papers next to me. "It really hasn't been processed," he said.

In May 2016, fifty-one years after he began at Harvard, Karl Lamberg-Karlovsky retired. When he left, the papers in his office were sent to the archives. I'd found out in the summer, and in October 2016, my date at the library had finally arrived.

The archivist said some of the documents in Karl's file had been removed because they contained university and student records that were too recent, but this was everything else. He showed me how to turn the delicate papers without damaging them—from the middle, not the corners—and then left me to my own devices.

At the top of the boxes was a sheet that described where the materials had been found in Karl's office. Box 1: Large cabinets on right side of room. Box 2: Loose on large table in study. Box 10: Letterboxes on shelves above desk. I wondered briefly if Karl had left in a rush, but I thought it more likely that he had just left everything for some archivist to deal with.

I spent the next four days in the archives reading through every single paper. Old lectures he gave, blue aerogram letters from Iran, typewritten museum correspondence, his calendars, book reviews, notebooks, and syllabi from his undergraduate and graduate years. In one undated photo, I saw, unmistakably, the seductive Count Dracula who had captivated the graduate students. In the dead center of that photo was the same pinkie signet ring whose emblem I hadn't been able to make out in class. It was still hard to believe that Karl's reign in the department was over—that legends have ends.

Photo of Lamberg-Karlovsky looking similarly debonair in 1983, next to his wife, Martha, and former graduate student David Freidel. (Gift of the Estate of Gordon R. Willey, 2003. Courtesy of the Peabody Museum of Archaeology and Ethnology, Harvard University, PM 2003.14.28, by permission from Alexandra Guralnick.)

In the files, there, again, was the Karl quick to injure, easy to anger, hot-tempered, even a touch paranoid. The funniest letter was from Victor Mair, a professor at UPenn, who, in reply to Karl's "petulant diatribe," wrote facetiously: "A copy of a strange letter attacking me and appearing over your signature was anonymously sent to my Department by fax. [...] Since the charges in the letter are so fallacious and illogical, the language so intemperate and semiliterate, my first thought is that it must have been forged by someone else who wanted to tarnish your reputation."

But there, too, were glimpses of a Karl who was a supportive mentor, a daring academic, a dedicated professor. In 1970, he came to the defense of students in the Organization for Black Unity who were facing disciplinary action for occupying University Hall. Karl had been in the building at the beginning of the takeover, and he wrote in support of the students' good behavior. In '73, he penned a recommendation letter for Richard Meadow that praised Meadow as the rarest of academic finds: a great teacher, scholar, and person. And the span of Karl's impact was hard to miss—from the "ecstatic appreciation" of two students on the 1967 Yahya survey expedition, to the undergraduate in 1999 who thanked Karl for supporting her interests to an extent no other professor had.

There was also a draft of the textbook he co-wrote with Jerry Sabloff, a former graduate student who was several years older than Jane. In the text, Karl explained that Sumerian and Akkadian, the languages of ancient Mesopotamia, lacked the word for "history." But this absence, Karl wrote, "does not indicate a disinterest in history or in the past, for numerous inscribed clay tablets indicate the contrary to be true. The absence of the word *history* signifies a wholly different approach to the past, or to that which we call history." If we insisted on our conception of history in analyzing their attitudes, we would miss the importance they placed on the past. It was a similar point he had made in that first class I sat in on, and the main thesis of that foreword to the Tepe Yahya monograph that troubled me: The historical gaze is inextricable from the biases of the historian. Even if we think we're uncovering the past, what we are really doing is reconstructing it, adding our own flesh to old bones.

By the end of my time in the university archives, I had one group of materials left to go through. I had purposefully saved Karl's college and graduate school notebooks for last. Karl was a doodler—the margins of his notes were filled with crossbones, skulls, skeletons. A few cartoonish self-portraits were instantly recognizable because of an exaggerated bouffant. One was a man with almost a demonically pointed tongue and sharp teeth, about to lick a set of breasts, drawn on a headless torso.

Doodles in Lamberg-Karlovsky's notebook from graduate school, 1959. (Courtesy of the Harvard University Archives)

But Karl's margins were also often filled with his signature and the years and institutions of his schooling, as if rehearsing his biography. Over and over, he would write his name. Sometimes it was just his initials, sometimes Cliff, but most often it was his name: Clifford Lamberg Karlovsky, both with and without a hyphen.

Karl also tried on different names. Once it was Karl von Lamberg, and then for a series of pages, it was nothing but: Clifford A. Rockefeller. Over and over and over. As if he were not only rehearsing his story, but adopting a new identity.

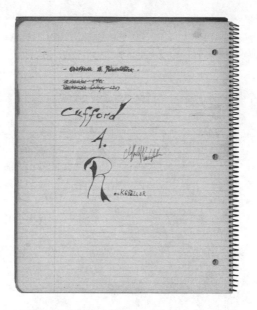

Lamberg-Karlovsky's signatures in the same graduate school notebook. (Courtesy of the Harvard University Archives)

———

At night, I'd go home to Eliot House, where I was staying with friends from college. It was my first time living back in the dorms since graduation. I was even able to sneak in to eat in the dining halls. I felt like no time had elapsed since college until I would catch a reflection of myself in a store window and do a double take, startled by the passage of time reflected back at me.

———

"Pencils only," the Peabody Museum archivist reminded me.

For my last day of research, I moved from the university archives to the museum's to look for Jane's expedition notebook. My suspicion was right: There was a whole cache of Tepe Yahya material that hadn't appeared on Harvard's library website. I had requested the expedition notebooks from 1967, 1968, and 1969, and now the cart in front of me was full of flip-top boxes.

I opened the first carton. It was neatly organized with dividers, each one containing a field notebook from a different trench. One jumped out at me: "Field notebook: Site E, J.S.B." Jane Sanders Britton.

I pulled the notebook out from the divider. It was moss green, fabric-covered, and discolored around the edges.

I opened it to the first page: "Tepe Yahya 1969 Site E Field Notebook. By: JSB / [ ]." The second name had been taped over with a piece of paper.

Nineteen sixty-nine? By the summer of 1969 Jane was dead. Why was her name on a field notebook six months after her death? I knew some poor archivist had had to put that piece of paper there before the file reached me because it pertained to a student who was still alive. I rifled through my Tepe Yahya research to see if I knew who dug Site E in 1969. "J.H." a note said. Jim Humphries.

Going on a hunch, I quickly opened the other boxes until I found what I was looking for: the 1968 Site E notebook. Just as I'd guessed. Site E had been Jane's trench.

That meant Jim had been put in charge of Jane's trench the summer after her death. And when it came to writing up his expedition notes, he had given her credit. It was so different from the tales of hyper-competitiveness in academia I had grown used to. It was a gesture that felt all the more beautiful for how silent it was. No fanfare, no celebration, no calling attention to himself. In a field where everyone was fighting to get their names on things, he'd added hers. First.

I skimmed Jane's notebook. It chronicled her day-to-day, just as I had hoped. Her handwriting was neat and in all caps like an architect's, but it lacked any personal dimension. Instead, it was filled with dozens of to-scale drawings, and tiny handwritten recordings of the features and finds from her trench. The entries were detailed descriptions of where and what she dug on any given day. For example, on the first day of excavation that summer: "30 June 1968: Removed surface sherds; wash + dust cover entire area of trench. Large number of sherds in sandy brown soil." On August 21, Jane wrote that she found "traces of red ochre" in the hearth she was unearthing. It was startling to see "red ochre" in her handwriting.

I looked through the rest of the notebooks. Phil's was the least neat. Arthur Bankoff's included a note to self: "First day of digging. My technique is a bit rocky. I don't think I would know a wall if it bit me."

Richard Meadow's was meticulous. I scrutinized every page. There on blue millimeter graph paper was Richard's to-scale drawing of where he'd found a Neolithic figurine, which was to remain the find of the season. It was made of green soapstone. Along with it were numerous flint chips and worked-stone tools, three soapstone shaft straighteners, and two bone razors and a bone spatula. The figure had a belly button and a round dot for its mouth, which left it in a permanent state of surprise.

At the bottom of the page, Richard had written "Red ochre under and around bone." It was possible that the bone tools near the figurine might have been what Karl was referring to when he told reporters that "there are relics which show that the bones of decomposed bodies were coated with a red material." But I was surprised to see, as I read on in the Tepe Yahya reports, that a human burial with red ochre had in fact been found at Tepe Yahya: In 1970, a body was discovered lying on its left side, its skull crushed, with red ochre on the ulna of one of the arms. Even though this body was only unearthed after Jane's death, it was an eerie coincidence; Karl had been quoted as saying that a composed corpse with any type of powder spread over it had never been found in Iran. Yet, just six months later, there it was, at his very site. And far from a fluke, that burial turned out to be characteristic of those in the oldest layer of the mound. Thomas Beale, a graduate student who had joined the Iranian expedition the year after Jane died, wrote in his monograph on the Tepe Yahya expedition: "In Period VII, Yahya inhabitants painted the bodies of their dead with red ochre."

I pulled my hands away from the notebooks and realized my fingertips were coated in the fine sand from the Tepe Yahya desert, and for an instant the years collapsed.

THRESHOLDS OF IRRITATION

"TODAY'S THE DAY RICHARD FOUND the statue. Jealous! You wouldn't *believe* it. I feel so inferior it's amazing—I mean, I don't begrudge him the discovery but it makes me wonder if I've missed even more than I think I already have," Jane wrote in her journal.

Richard's discovery really was remarkable. A ten-inch soapstone figurine, thousands of years old yet almost completely undamaged. It had been carved from a single piece of chlorite, and it was striking: long and thin, with punctured eyes and a linear nose, no breasts but female genitalia. It looked like a hybrid of the sexes: a woman carved onto a phallus. Karl would later refer to it as a fertility goddess and predicted in five years, it will be a "prize example of primitive sculpture." There hadn't been anything else like it found in any Iranian or Mesopotamian site.

Neolithic figurine discovered by Richard Meadow. (Fig 7.25 on page 200 from Thomas Wight Beale, "Excavations at Tepe Yahya, Iran 1967-1975: The Early Periods," American School of Prehistoric Research, Bulletin 38. © 1986 by the President and Fellows of Harvard College, courtesy of the Peabody Museum of Archaeology and Ethnology, Harvard University)

The discovery couldn't have come at a better time. It was Martie Lamberg-Karlovsky's second day on the site. The crew had been looking forward to her arrival. By that point, supplies were getting low and people were eager for Martie to bring "food, news, and a new face." Even Jane had been excited for Martie—as much for Preparation H for Jim's hemorrhoids as for anything else. Jane's optimism was also fueled by the fact that she and Jim had figured out that Jane's trench was the center of a five-meter wall—possibly the city wall. It was no soapstone figurine, but it would be enough for a dissertation topic.

When Jane sat down to draw the figurine, she was too exhausted to eke it out. She opened her journal instead and started to describe the discovery below that morning's entry where she had written: "Madame L-K, much as I like her, is not exactly a breath of fresh air on this scene, altho am sure CCL-K must be rather glad. One month and some left. Then I have to face the fall all alone."

———

It's never easy to step into an already-formed group dynamic, and Martie irritated the crew almost immediately. She insisted on dressing to the nines and changing her outfit multiple times a day, despite the fact that they were in the middle of the desert. Jane and Andrea Bankoff, who felt particularly grubby in their sweat-stained clothes, took her new wardrobe as an affront, but they recognized that in cooler climates, their grievances would seem petty. "I like her well enough but her awesome enthusiasm for the place leaves one drained," Jane wrote to her parents.

Andrea was quick to suffer the punctilious side to Martie. She recounted the scene to police when they asked about "hostilities" at the dig in Iran. It was Martie's first week at the site, and Andrea discovered that her and Arthur's pet sparrow had made a giant mess over their sleeping bags. She let out a single curse, which displeased Martie who was standing nearby with the antiquities representative. She told Andrea to be quiet and walked away:

> only to return a few minutes later and rather violently bawl me out. She said Karl told her I had embarrassed him at the British Institute by cursing and I must think myself "a cool little chick" but if she ever caught me using foul language, she'd punish me as my mother should have.

It never occurred to Andrea to correct Martie. The first cursing incident at the British Institute wasn't Andrea at all. It had been Jane.

When Andrea recounted the incident to Jane, Jane thought she must have been exaggerating. Indeed, when Martie found out it hadn't been Andrea who had cursed at the British Institute, Martie apologized profusely.

Jane felt a small burst of generosity toward Martie, but it soon wore off. "Everyone in heartily bad mood," Jane wrote in her journal.

Before, even if the food was terrible, it was bearable because everyone was treated equally. But when Martie arrived, she blithely blew through her two-Coke ration that everyone else had regarded as sacrosanct. She also decided—without consulting Andrea, who, as registrar, was also the pantry manager—that people should eat more. Only Richard and Peter, she clarified, because she thought they were getting too thin.

Martie seemed to treat archaeology as a cute hobby. *What a nice game, can I play, too?* she would imply, antagonizing the crew. But she was very serious in thinking that her husband could do no wrong, and the Bankoffs felt she expected his authority to extend to her as well.

Jane was particularly irritated by Martie's constant references to her relationship with Jim. They had fought hard to maintain their privacy and dignity in such close quarters, and now Martie was constantly referring to Jim as "her boy."

And then Jane experienced what Andrea had been talking about firsthand. Per Andrea:

One morning Jane woke up late for breakfast, was more grouchy than usual, drank a cup of coffee quickly and stubbed her foot on her way out and shouted a four-letter word. Martie quickly started to tell Jane ladies shouldn't curse, but Jane didn't even turn around and walked right out. This double standard about men can and ladies can't really annoyed Jane.

The momentary reprieve of the discovery, the new face, and the resupply of peanut butter ("thank Christ") had ended. Tension resurfaced. And now, with less recourse to cursing and crude jokes as relief, there was no outlet for the pressure. The atmosphere—frayed nerves, latent aggressions, bitterness, edginess, interactions brittle enough to snap—became claustrophobic.

One day, the son of the local khan came around and insisted on charging Karl a land tax for digging on "his" mound. Karl knew all archaeological sites in Iran were considered the property of the government and recognized the tax for what it was: extortion. The dig's government representative advised Karl not to pay anything.

In retaliation, the son of the khan called a local workers' strike. The situation grew heated, and Karl eventually flew into a "towering rage," as Arthur Bankoff would later say.

Karl grabbed a pickax. If the khan's son refused to leave without collecting his money, then Karl refused to leave any of his property standing, starting with this mud-brick house right here. He pounded the pickax through its facade. In a "couple of hours [he] could have reduced any of these little houses to rubble," Peter Dane recounted. Eventually the khan's son—likely because the government representative had called in the local gendarmes and threatened to take him to jail—acquiesced.

By that point, the unease had become almost unbearable. Phil Kohl and Peter Dane left early. (Phil's mother didn't recognize her son when she met him at the airport; down with dysentery, he'd lost more than thirty pounds that summer.) And the arrival of the visiting archaeologist Benno Rothenberg made things even worse as Karl, eager to impress him, became harder to bear. Alcohol was suddenly reserved for "adults only"—Benno, Martie, and Karl. Arthur recalled that people were to consider themselves lucky if they were invited to sit on the rug and drink booze with the adults.

Arthur and Andrea became so paranoid by the end of the season—everything a "we-thought-they-thought mental construction"—that they only felt comfortable talking to Jim and Jane. "Defamation was by innuendo, as it always is in academic pursuits, and not a clear word of hate was spoken by anyone," they later wrote to police. Any remaining hope that the Bankoffs had exaggerated the Lamberg-Karlovskys' distaste for them evaporated when Karl told Arthur he wouldn't in fact be invited back for next year's dig. The Bankoffs had planned to spend the year abroad and to work in Tepe Yahya the following season, to earn their return trip home. But now they were stuck in Iran without the funds to get home, which was why they eventually found themselves in Italy when Jane died. "It wasn't a very human thing to do," Arthur would later say.

Even the unrufflable Jim had reached his limit. Per Arthur and Andrea's joint police statement, he confided in Arthur that he thought Martie was a "stupid, vicious, jealous bitch." And he couldn't always bite his tongue when it came to Karl, though he would always go back to "Yes, Boss"-ing him as soon as the tiff was over. The night of Benno's arrival, in the middle of the cocktail party to celebrate the scholar, Karl found out that Jim had arranged for Arthur to take a sick baby, the child of a local, to the doctor at the neighboring mining camp and that Jim had given him $2.26 from his own pocket to pay for the treatment. There was no shouting—Karl didn't want to do it in front of Benno—but his fury was unmistakable. Jim responded that it was "after all, a baby, and his money, and not really Karl's business," but Karl wasn't having any of it. It was reminiscent of a tussle they'd had earlier that summer about Karl threatening to unfairly fire a worker: Jim expected humane treatment of locals; Karl demanded obedience from his crew. "There was some shouting, but nothing violent like physical blows," Arthur remembered, but for Jim, who would sooner walk away than argue his case, it was striking. Karl himself said he did not remember this incident.

The night that it all came to a head, though, was perhaps the quietest fight of all, leaving everyone involved exposed like live wires, ready to spark at any moment. Karl had bought an entire sheep and wanted to roast it whole. He asked Jane for advice since he knew that she'd spent a summer digging in Greece and had some experience roasting sheep.

At dinner that evening, Martie, having just eaten her first bite of the animal, turned to Jane and thrust a declarative sentence across the table like a dagger: "I thought you said you could cook."

KARL'S POLICE INTERROGATION

Detective Lieutenant Davenport: Professor, who would have the authority to decide the members of the expedition?

Professor Lamberg-Karlovsky: This was my decision, which was taken up and discussed by other members in the department. I might say that for each individual that, you know, I am able to take, there are probably two or three other candidates who are wanting to go out with me.

Detective Lieutenant Davenport: Well, bearing in mind, Doctor—I'm going to promote you to a different profession, Professor—bearing in mind the fact that you knew that there was a romantic attachment prior to setting the list, and I think of the remote, possibly remote, problem that might arise in the field with a romantic attachment, and you had so many others to choose from. I was wondering why you settled on this particular girl. I know Mr. Humphries from the previous dig, but the girl herself.

Professor Lamberg-Karlovsky: She already had experience in the field. She came to me well recommended from Professor Movius. I was one of the three faculty members on her committee to read her undergraduate honors thesis. It seemed as if she had both the necessary qualifications and the academic ability to be able to do the job.

I wasn't particularly fearful of the kind of difficulties that might take place given the fact of a romance simply because I knew the way in which Jim operates. He's a very conscientious individual.

This year, I asked Jim for the first time just exactly how serious that relationship is because as I began constructing the list for the people to come next year, I wondered whether or not Jane, in fact, would come again. I asked Jim what his feelings would be. Jim had been very fundamental for two years in terms of the successes of the project. I didn't want to lose Jim on the expedition if I decided not to take Jane. I didn't clearly state to him that I was thinking not to take Jane, but I intimated that possibility, that perhaps this year I would not.

Jim at that time told me "Look, I'm a single person. Don't take that into consideration. Your judgment in terms of who will be going out is entirely your own."

As it happens, however, all of these earlier considerations became irrelevant because I did in effect make that decision that I would take Jane. Jane, as the course of the semester developed, became very interested in a specific aspect of the project, the fortifications system of the early village community, which she was primarily responsible last semester for excavating. She began doing research on it. She wanted to perhaps develop this into a PhD thesis. I thought it only fair, once again, to allow her the opportunity to come out. Although, there was that period of time in which I was considering whether or not I would.

I had discussed my ambivalence with Jane and with the chairman of our department. If I didn't take her, she would have no place to go. She would have no project on which to write her PhD thesis. She would in effect become an individual disenfranchised from the opportunity to do a research project which would result in her PhD. I asked him whether or not there would be—how his feelings were, what the—whether or not he could provide any measure of further judgment as to which way I should go.

Detective Lieutenant Davenport: You're a glutton for punishment. You know that, Professor? You really heap yourself with problems.

Professor Lamberg-Karlovsky: Well, it's—it's a major project. This year, in fact, it's going to become a larger one, and in effect, you see, the director of any excavation and the results of that excavation simply are in a way the sum total of the individuals who are on that project. The better people I have, the better the project.

Detective Lieutenant Davenport: You had the utmost cooperation from them in the last dig.

Professor Lamberg-Karlovsky: Absolutely.

Detective Lieutenant Davenport: Each and every one of them.

Professor Lamberg-Karlovsky: There were some major problems with Arthur and Andie Bankoff. I had cooperation from every single other individual—and I, in fact, had considerable cooperation from Arthur and Andie.

Unidentified Male: Yeah. Well, anyone we talked to said they were doubtful that you were going to take Jane but according to you now, in your own mind you were, but you are the only one that—

Professor Lamberg-Karlovsky: That's right. That's right. I think that it was apparent to many of the individuals that I was doubtful in taking Jane, but I had never said to any individual that she's not going or that she's definitely going.

Detective Lieutenant Davenport: Professor, it has come to our attention, but we don't know if there's any basis on this or not, but there was a feeling between Jane Britton and yourself that there was a dislike present.

Professor Lamberg-Karlovsky: I—I don't know whether or not there was or there wasn't. I don't know whether Jane liked me or disliked me. It's very difficult to know how students feel about you. There were a lot of things about Jane which—over which we had words. One of these was that she tended very often to speak in foul language.

Unidentified Male: Did you dislike her, Professor?

Professor Lamberg-Karlovsky: No, I didn't dislike her. I clearly couldn't have really disliked her very much. I was bothered about some aspects of, you know, the way she behaved, but I didn't dislike her to the extent that, you know, I wouldn't—I didn't allow her to continue on the project. It was her due academically, but I liked Jim a great deal more. He's more responsible. He's—he's—he's a much more—he's a much more sort of responsible, level-headed individual than Jane was.

Unidentified Male: Of the ones that went in your dig—you liked her the least of any of them?

Professor Lamberg-Karlovsky: No, no, I didn't—I—I—because, you see, the—that kind of phrasing suggested that I really disliked her.

Unidentified Male: How did your wife seem towards her?

Professor Lamberg-Karlovsky: Well, my wife didn't particularly like the way she carried herself and the kinds of things she said either.

Unidentified Male: I may be wrong, but I thought I heard from somebody that she had told them that you didn't like her.

Professor Lamberg-Karlovsky: —well, you know, it's her impression perhaps that I didn't—as, you know, it's my impression that perhaps she really didn't have very much love for me.

Unidentified Male: Yeah. It wasn't that you told her but just the way you acted towards her.

Professor Lamberg-Karlovsky: Right. She clearly knew that I didn't like her language. She would make snide comments to another individual, which I would overhear and perhaps she said it so that I would overhear it, about the way I would react to this and the same with my wife.

Unidentified Male: Well, she was tantalizing you.

Professor Lamberg-Karlovsky: Yes, in some ways I suppose that might be fair enough to say. She was tantalizing.

Unidentified Male: Was there anything else you had to speak to her about other than the language?

Professor Lamberg-Karlovsky: I thought that in one area in which she was carrying out her work, she was moving a little bit too slowly, and I advised her to do something else. Jane had worked in France with an archaeologist. She considered herself a good technician. She was one who didn't take correction of the technical aspects of the excavations very well. This was another aspect in terms of perhaps why Jane didn't like me.

Detective Lieutenant Davenport: Could it also be as a result of some of your previous markings of her papers?

Professor Lamberg-Karlovsky: No, no. I doubt it very much because I think the record would show that in terms of her markings, she had always received a B minus or above, which is a passing grade in the department.

Detective Lieutenant Davenport: My understanding is that she was going to take a test on the morning of her death.

Professor Lamberg-Karlovsky: That's right.

Detective Lieutenant Davenport: Which of the three exams would be the hardest part? Do you know, sir?

Professor Lamberg-Karlovsky: Archaeology would—should be the easiest, and archaeology was the one on which last year she did the best. I suppose it might be social anthropology.

Detective Lieutenant Davenport: That would not be your test.

Professor Lamberg-Karlovsky: No, no. No, not at all.

Detective Lieutenant Davenport: And she'd no fear of your test apparently after being on the digs and all—

Professor Lamberg-Karlovsky: Well—

Detective Lieutenant Davenport: —and the research she'd done.

Professor Lamberg-Karlovsky: —all I could say is I would hope not. I would hope not.

Detective Lieutenant Davenport: Would you have been in a position to correct the exams then?

Professor Lamberg-Karlovsky: Yes, oh, yes, indeed. Oh, yes.

Detective Lieutenant Davenport: Well, that's what I was curious about.

Professor Lamberg-Karlovsky: I have, in fact, corrected them last night.

Detective Lieutenant Davenport: How did Jim do?

Professor Lamberg-Karlovsky: Jim did—I was second in line of correcting the exams. Three professors have to correct the exam, and the sum total of the three grades is representative of the composite picture. He did— he did, as I had hoped: well.

Unidentified Male: This day Tuesday that she did not show up for the exam, did anybody else not show up?

Professor Lamberg-Karlovsky: Not to my knowledge. Not to my knowledge.

Unidentified Male: Who would give us that information?

Professor Lamberg-Karlovsky: I suppose Steve Williams because Steve Williams and the secretary were the ones who were involved in proctoring and checking off the names with the numbers. You see, we correct the exams with numbers. We don't know who—whose exam we're correcting. Although, clearly, you know, in some instances this is—this is pretentious because I can tell—I can tell—I can tell the handwriting of those students who are working most closely with me.

FRANKLIN FORD

IN THE DAYS FOLLOWING JANE'S death, Karl got a call from Franklin Ford, dean of Harvard's Faculty of Arts and Sciences. Dean Ford offered Harvard's full support without reservation.

Half a century later, Karl would recount the story to me at our first official interview, grinning over the plateful of chicken liver he'd just ordered: "He didn't even ask me if I did it!"

Part Four

THE MYTH

2018: MIAMI

MONTHS BEFORE—IN THE LONG-ago when Sennott hadn't yet called to say that he would be announcing a break in the case, and Don hadn't texted, and I didn't know how long five days could feel—I committed to going to a bachelorette party that weekend in Miami. Now, as I pack my computer and my reporting notebooks next to my bikinis, I can't imagine anything I would want to be doing less. I email Don from the airport:

Could you sleep last night? I woke up at 3 in the morning with a feeling that's a cross between Christmas morning and a bad dream. How indescribable it is to be excited for an unknown.

In Miami, I get fingerprinted for keyless access to the apartment of a friend of the bride. I try to be a good guest, but carrying the weight of these suspenseful five days pulls me out of the group. I pour myself a glass of wine and pretend to sip it. I can hear their heels clacking on the marble floor in one of the bathrooms, the whir of the blow dryer. I'm on the couch in the living room, my flats kicked off to one side, studying the evolution of forensic DNA technology, creating elaborate if/then charts for what to do depending on the outcome of Monday's call.

I become the watcher I had been in middle school again—the one on the outside of the party, stone-cold sober, unable to lose myself in the fun. We have Moët and lobster on the beach and take Ubers for four blocks, and they talk about DUIs and Ambien addictions, and ramming a Vespa into a Bentley in a parking lot and getting away with it. The reckless hedonism they're able to pull off makes me sad that the universe wasn't as lenient with Jane.

In the afternoons, I escape to my room and try Sergeant John Fulkerson, hoping he'll have gotten word, too, and will let something slip. But as has been the case for the last three months—since April, when he told me he was finally retiring from Cambridge PD and that I should try again in a few weeks—he doesn't pick up. Instead, I draft my next public records request in anticipation that the case might soon be closed.

On Sunday night, the girls and I have our final dinner at Joe's, an old-school steak house on Miami Beach where the waiters are all men who wear tuxedos and whirl trays of stone crabs and tie you with a bib. My mind is preoccupied with how the humidity must be making all the wood in the place decay. I apologize to the bride that I'll be leaving for the airport at 6:30 a.m.; I changed my flight to the earliest one out, assuming that if there's a press conference and I haven't heard about it yet, I'll at least get to hear Don's reaction as close to live as I can get.

The crabs come, and I jam the tiny fork into the stone crab claw. It refuses to break loose and turns to pulp, and with the metal of the fork hitting against the hard shell, creating a cavity, I imagine all too easily that it's a skull, and I've just turned its gray matter to soup. I feel nauseated and stop eating.

We go home, and I head upstairs before midnight, saying goodbye to the girls who are dancing to the Backstreet Boys. I try to make myself realize that this may be the last night I go to sleep not knowing who Jane saw just before she died.

IVA HOUSTON

"I THINK IF YOU WERE to have called me a couple years ago, I would have been more coy. I'm less reticent now, because I think in the field of archaeology, it's important to talk about these kinds of stories, especially with other ladies," Iva Houston said.

Iva and I hadn't seen each other since that day in 2010 when she and James Ronan had set everything in motion. Now she was sitting across from me at Le Pain Quotidien in Midtown Manhattan. I had reached out because, knowing so much more about Jane's case and about Karl, I wanted to talk with her again.

But when I asked her to retell the Jane Britton story, she needed me to clarify which one I was referring to. I didn't understand why she needed more prompting. How many murders could I be talking about? I gave her a few more details—the red ochre, the rumors about Karl—and she caught on, but she could see I was still disoriented by her not remembering in the first place.

"When I say, 'What story are we talking about,' I don't say it in a joking way. I say it seriously," Iva said. "There are so many stories. And what's sad about it is it always ends the same way. It always ends with: We never hear from the girl again."

She continued: "People will talk about female students leaving academia, going into some specialization"—plants, bones, museum work—which means they don't go out in the field anymore. And even if it feels like their choice, that isn't always the entire truth. "There is often a traumatic situation that precipitates her departure."

At Harvard, when Iva started going on expeditions, she was told, "Don't go into the field with so-and-so, because he has grabby hands"; "Don't go into the field with X, because he doesn't pay you." Iva, whose scholarship has shifted to cultural studies, said she didn't switch out of fieldwork because of the high rates of harassment and discrimination, but "I won't lie to you. It's a great benefit to not have to deal with that."

Iva finished her train of thought: "People will say it in conversation, but not always out loud. There is an antagonism. There is a pressure in the field. There is a looming danger. Sometimes it's unsaid. Sometimes it's made very explicit."

I knew exactly what Iva meant. Even in high school I had teachers whom the girls warned each other about. "Don't close the door with him," we would say casually to each other. Or we'd whisper to a friend that a certain teacher could change her schedule if she dropped by his office, *but know he's a creep*, we would add. I never thought twice about the state of awareness I had to get used to as a fourteen-year-old.

While at Harvard, Iva heard Jane's story three times. The details hardly changed. It was usually about a girl who had an affair with her professor, and he killed her when she threatened to tell his wife. Iva never knew her name.

The first time was her sophomore year. A female graduate, striking up a conversation, asked what classes she was taking. Iva said she was in Karl's class and found him charming, engaging, charismatic. He made archaeology very approachable.

"I want to tell you something," Iva remembered the graduate student saying. "It's kind of a weird story, and I don't know how much of it is true, but I want to tell you because I feel like, with girl code—"

Iva's perception of Karl flipped on its head. What she had thought of as charming became too slick. That he was well dressed began to signal that he was hiding something. She moved from the front row of class to the back for the rest of the semester. "You did not want him to single you out. You did not want to be memorable to him. Any idea of going to office hours? Gone. Any ideas of taking other classes? Gone." Karl still seemed like a god in the department—untouchable, invincible—but now that power felt ominous.

The second time was a year later. Iva was telling the story of Jane to a friend who was working in the Middle East. They were in the Peabody student lounge, and though Iva was speaking very quietly, another student interrupted her when she qualified that the story might not be true. "Oh, no. It's a real story," the student said.

And then the third time she heard it was in a group setting. One girl was working in the Middle East and people asked her how she was going to operate in that place, by which Iva understood that the students were asking, *How are you going to deal with Karl?* The student said that her work was going to have nothing to do with him. Iva was struck by her maturity: "She was just like, 'I get it, and I'm just not going to be a part of it.'"

Listening to Iva, I saw that Jane's story, one about a girl disappeared by her adviser, was still so alive in the community because it was an exaggerated, horror-movie version of a narrative that was all too common.

"I have something like eight friends who left academia because of some gossip or something political," Iva said. She told me about one person who had to leave his postdoctoral program for another solely because he went to a conference and interacted with someone his adviser didn't like. When the student escalated the problem to the department's administration, he was told that the professor was too high up for them to do anything, so the student had to make a decision: He had to make it work with this person or leave. He ended up being forced out.

"That happened to be a male," Iva told me, but most of the people disenfranchised in these stories are women. The stories almost always go something like this: "This person made me feel uncomfortable; this person wasn't cool with me when I got married, when I had a baby."

Archaeology, she said, hasn't done a good job of confronting the inequities that have always existed in academia. There's a subfield of the discipline called Gender Archaeology, dedicated to studying the ways in which our implicit gender bias colors the way we reconstruct the past. (For example, is it true that the men did the hunting and the women did the gathering?

Probably not according to the latest evidence.) Also studied are the ways in which gender dynamics shape the experience of the archaeologists themselves. But Gender Archaeology is still not considered mainstream.

Instead, the field prides itself on a masculine tough-it-out mentality. Richard Meadow, she said, was one of the only people in the department who provided a sympathetic ear for students, particularly the female ones. Though he seemed standoffish, in reality he was the complete opposite. "He was basically our Oprah. We'd go to him and cry." She said I should do everything I could to speak with Richard for the story. He wouldn't be forthcoming, but he would know everything.

Iva thought about it all once more. "It's horrible what happened to this particular person," she said, again not quite remembering Jane's name. "But, you know, I hate to say it. I think I was shocked and now, after being in this field for going on a decade, I'm not surprised. If I had heard this story tomorrow, I would have just shook my head and said, yeah. I think it's symptomatic of a much more horrific disease that we don't want to realize that we have."

———

And just like that, Iva, as she had done all those years ago, upended my thinking about Jane's story. As definitively as she had once moved it from lore to truth, this time she elevated it to the status of myth.

If Iva was right and Jane's story functioned as a kind of cautionary tale, then perhaps it was less about the literal truth of what happened to Jane than it was an allegory about the dangers that faced women in academia. The idea reminded me of what Karl had said in that first class: that the past is often appropriated to suit the demands of the modern era. In this case, reporting abuses of power rarely results in meaningful change, and often causes problems for the person bringing the complaint. Jane's story existed, perhaps, to voice injustices that otherwise couldn't be easily raised.

It followed, then, that the elements of Jane's story might just be symbols. Jane stood for every woman in the department. Her killing represented a kind of academic silencing. And the professor who killed her, a symbol of the abuse of power and the institutional oppression of women in academia.

Viewed from this angle, Karl wasn't the murderer at all. He was an imperfect man ensnared in a living myth, but no criminal. We had cast him in a role that he did not deserve, both because—in the absence of answers as to what happened to Jane—we needed it filled, and because with his edginess, charisma, and flair, he could play it so well. Is it ever justifiable, I wondered, to trap someone in a story that robs them of their truth, but voices someone else's?

The idea dovetailed with something else I was slowly beginning to admit. For all the avenues of conjecture I'd unearthed about Karl, nothing had led anywhere concrete. Everything was circumstantial, much of it was gossip, and none of it pointed more than elliptically at a motivation for murder. I had dismissed the affair angle long ago. And the academic blackmail one had less and less steam the more I looked into it. For example, the idea that there was an urgency for Karl to get tenure in 1969 because there was something exceptional about that year didn't withstand examination. I spoke to David Mitten, an art historian who had been tenured as a junior professor that same year. He remembered absolutely nothing about some window threatening to close for junior faculty.

But if Karl didn't kill Jane, then who did?

SHE'D HAVE TO NOT BE A WOMAN

In 2014, MIT PROFESSOR OF biology Nancy Hopkins delivered a speech for the occasion of her fiftieth Radcliffe reunion. She began: "Women who came to Radcliffe in 1960 arrived at the start of a gender revolution." Then Radcliffe president Mary Bunting had filled the students with the expectation that they would surpass the professional achievements of all the women who had come before. And it seemed to be coming true for Nancy: She graduated from Radcliffe in 1964, went to graduate school, and accepted a faculty position at MIT in 1973.

If you had told me then, in 1973, that there was such a thing as gender discrimination, I wouldn't have known what you were talking about. It didn't occur to me that a profession in which half the people on the planet could not participate equally and also have children is discriminatory.

Plus, I assumed the only reason there were no women professors was because all other women chose to be mothers. I would have been shocked to learn that as recently as 1960, women could take classes at Harvard, but essentially, we could not get faculty jobs in America's great research universities.

The 1964 Civil Rights Act made such discrimination illegal. And then, when universities still dragged their feet, Affirmative Action laws and regulations in the early 1970s required them to hire women or lose their federal funding. By 1973, when I was offered faculty jobs, I assumed that gender discrimination was a thing of the past.

But slowly—despite neither looking for it nor expecting it—Nancy began to see that she had been mistaken. "Gender discrimination did exist—even for women who didn't have children. It took such a surprising form that it took me 20 years to recognize it. [...] By then I was 50 years old."

———

When Cora Du Bois arrived at Harvard in the fall of 1954, she was only the second woman to receive tenure at the institution. She had to take the side door to the all-male faculty club and eat in a separate area so she didn't contaminate the atmosphere of the dining room. And when she retired in 1969, she left Harvard's Faculty of Arts and Sciences without a single female professor, at either the tenured or the associate level.

WOMEN IN SELECTED CORPORATION APPOINTMENTS

UNDER THE FACULTY OF ARTS AND SCIENCES*

1969-70

Title	Total	Women	Percent Women
Regular Faculty			
Full Professors	444	0	0.0
Associate Professors	39	0	0.0
Assistant Professors	194	9	4.6
Instructors	18	3	16.7
Teaching Fellows	1104	226	20.5

An excerpt from the March 9, 1970 "Preliminary Report on the Status of Women at Harvard."

Later, Alison Brooks, who had been Jane's roommate at Les Eyzies, confronted Irven DeVore, a tenured professor of biological anthropology, about the lack of women in the department. DeVore replied, "For a woman to be good enough for Harvard, she'd have to not be a woman."

———

When Sally Bates, the woman who would eventually help arrange Jane's abortion, arrived at Harvard in the fall of 1965, the semester began with a mandatory meeting with Professor Douglas Oliver, the chair of the department. Sally knew that Professor Oliver had given each of the men a version of the same pep talk. "We have invested a lot in you. We expect you to get a PhD."

But when Sally walked into the professor's office and casually mentioned how pleasantly surprised she had been about the number of women in her incoming class—about half her cohort—Professor Oliver replied, "You're all looking for MRS, aren'tcha. The Mrs. degree."

Sally dropped out before the end of her spring semester. Eventually, only two or three of the original women in her cohort remained at Harvard, including Alison Brooks, whose adviser told her: "I've never given the PhD to a woman, and I'm not going to start now."

———

It didn't take long for Mary Pohl, who started her PhD in 1967, to become aware of the discrimination at Harvard—the "imbalance," she called it. Her adviser Gordon Willey inducted his students as doctoral advisees by inviting them to lunch at his social club. The club only allowed men.

But when we spoke, she was adamant that I understand that her experience at Harvard wasn't all bad—Jerry Sabloff, a junior faculty member who took over for Willey as her adviser, was a great champion of hers. And she also needed me to know that the discrimination at Harvard was far from anomalous; it was "only a warm-up" for what she would face in her career. For example, at Florida State, where she is now an emerita professor, one of the senior males in her department took exception to her and "would throw angry fits" about her in the front office. When that professor became the department chair, he bestowed overt favoritism on her male colleagues, such as giving only them salary raises. Mary filed a grievance and requested a review of her salary (one of several she would file over the years). A female university faculty member, selected by the administration, reviewed her case and denied her grievance. When Mary went to her office to discuss the findings, she was told, "Your salary is unfair, but life is unfair."

———

When Elizabeth Stone, the student who felt misled into forfeiting the promise of UPenn funding, arrived in the department in 1971, she was appalled by the atmosphere. Years later, she'd call Harvard "the most sexist place I've ever been." The other women in the department dressed "sexlessly" in order to de-emphasize their gender. Elizabeth refused, and as a result, she was the only person in class who professors didn't call by her first name. Instead, she was *"Miss* Stone." When Elizabeth arranged with the University of Chicago to get out of Harvard as quickly as she could, she went to say goodbye to the secretaries, who were all women. One congratulated her: "One of you is getting out of here!"

———

When Sally Falk Moore was tenured in Anthropology at Harvard in 1981, she was the only tenured woman in the department and one of only sixteen tenured women in the entirety of Harvard's Faculty of Arts and Sciences. Professor Moore felt like she was standing alone in the wind, accepted in the department as a friend, but not as a weighty instrument in policy making. She felt used by the administration who promoted her to dean of the graduate school and faculty dean of Mather House, one of the undergraduate dorms. The administration's idea was to elevate the position of women in the university by making them as visible as possible. But those administrative jobs consumed her time and gave her even less voice in the direction of the Anthropology department.

Moore quickly understood that it was going to be a "waste of time and emotion" to struggle against the prevailing culture, and she focused instead on her teaching, research, and writing. She found that there was enough to satisfy her in her professional life without needing to win the departmental battles. She was not unhappy.

Years later, the ninety-three-year-old Professor Moore would say, "I never found being a woman to be completely an impediment. It was a great asset in many ways. I got an awful lot of attention because very little was expected, and instead they got a full human being."

———

When Alison Brooks visited her daughter at Harvard in the mid-'90s—she was an undergraduate, class of '97—she attended a meeting where Harvard was very proud to announce what they were doing to combat sexual harassment, including trainings with freshman men about inappropriate behavior. Alison interrupted to ask what the administration's plan was for harassment by the faculty.

———

Winding to the end of her talk at that 2014 Radcliffe reunion, Nancy Hopkins told her audience that the pattern of gender discrimination in academia eventually became undeniable in 1994 when she discovered that only 8 percent of the MIT science faculty were women. At Harvard, it was 5 percent. The discrimination was finally quantitative. When she told her colleagues at MIT what she had discovered, she realized "the women faculty at MIT had figured it out, but we had each been afraid to say so. In a meritocracy, if you say you're discriminated against, people will think you aren't good enough."

In 2005, Nancy Hopkins walked out of the room when then Harvard president Larry Summers said, at a conference about diversity and the sciences, that men do better than women in math and science careers because of innate biological differences. While Summers recognized the role of socialization, he downplayed its significance. Even after furor erupted over his speech, he defended his position to the Boston Globe: "Research in behavioral genetics is showing that things people previously attributed to socialization weren't due to socialization after all." According to the Guardian, during the first three and a half years of Larry Summers's presidency, the number of tenured jobs offered to women fell from 36 to 13 percent. Summers stepped down in June 2006; I arrived at Harvard the following semester.

Nancy concluded her reunion speech: "Progress for women in our lifetimes was amazing—thanks to visionaries like Mary Bunting. But equality, at the top? Not yet."

SADIE WEBER

IVA HOUSTON WASN'T ALONE. SADIE Weber, the girl with the braid who had been in Karl's class with me all those years ago, had also received Jane's story as a warning. A lecturer of hers at Stanford, a former student of Richard Meadow, had told her as a way to say, *Watch out for Karl*. And Sadie, like Iva, had also come to see Jane's story as part of a bigger picture about gender dynamics in the department. She told me so without prompting at a café in Harvard Square. Her take was that "it's almost this trope of…slightly predatory older professors taking advantage of their academic [advisee who] can't say no but also maybe wants the thrill."

I asked Sadie about her experience in the department. She searched for the right words. She wanted me to understand that she's not the kind of person who goes out looking for examples of mistreatment. But, over the years, the accumulation of slights had made it hard to ignore. Professors commented on how she looked. She found that she and the other female students had to work twice as hard to get noticed.

It was university policy, she told me, to have each department evaluated by a committee of academics outside of Harvard every five years or so, and a few months ago this visiting committee "reamed" Harvard's archaeology program for not having any female faculty. She said Harvard has *never* had a tenured woman in archaeology.

I quickly ran through the list in my head. Cora Du Bois was social anthropology, not archaeology. Cynthia Irwin-Williams, who co-led the expedition in Hell Gap, Wyoming, that trained many of Harvard's best archaeologists, was never given tenure. Neither was Ruth Tringham. Tatiana Proskouriakoff, the Maya scholar with the motorized ashtray, didn't even have an official department position.

Sadie qualified her statement. Never, except once, briefly. Professor Noreen

Tuross had been in the department for five years before she moved to Human Evolutionary Biology when it split from the Anthro department in 2009. Sadie was under the impression that Noreen had been kicked out. (When I spoke to Noreen, she said it was her choice to join Human Evolutionary Biology, but in her ideal world, she would have also stayed a part of Anthro. "I did ask for a joint appointment when this split happened, and it was denied by Anthropology. Why that is you'd have to ask them. I have no idea.")

I asked Sadie if she saw any way for it to get better.

"No? I think this is just the disease of academia... It won't get better until the idea of tenure is reviewed... Richard, I will say, is never like this."

I told her how much I would like to speak with him. Five years after our first encounter, it finally felt like time. She said the best way was probably just to corner him in his lab, and she gave me directions: "The Zooarchaeology Lab is on the third floor of the Peabody Museum. Next to the decapitator god."

We both laughed.

"Seriously."

RICHARD MEADOW

I LOOKED FOR THE "DECAPITATOR GOD" mural. I turned and walked and turned and walked until, in a corner of the archaeology of the Americas section, I saw it: a giant red monster against a mustard-yellow background, with a knife in one hand and a severed head in the other. "You'd think gods would have neater ways of offing someone," my friend responded when I texted him a picture from the bench in front of the mural.

My meeting with Richard did not go as planned.

It wasn't that Richard was unwilling to speak with me. He *was* willing, for the most part, despite caveating his memories with turns of phrase that would make a fact checker's heart sing, like "I can't give you a verified account because I just don't remember." He disclosed that he tried pot for the first and last time at a party at Karl's house. And he admitted that it was "disgusting" that it took almost fifty years for another person to be tenured from within the program after Karl. Though Richard unequivocally denied telling police that Jane and Karl had had an affair, and he refuted the alleged decades-long rift between the two of them, he added, "Karl was no angel."

It was then that my conversation with this man, about whose reticence everyone had warned me, flowed freely for the next hour. The bulk of our conversation, once again unprompted by me, was not directly about Jane at all, but about the experience of women in archaeology. The two seemed as tied for him as they had become for me.

The future of archaeology, he believed, was as a female-dominated field, and the department recognized that it had a long way to go to reflect that in its faculty. When I asked him whether the visiting committee really took the archaeology program to task for not having female professors, he said, "That's been in every visiting committee report for I don't know how long."

I knew that Harvard's program suffered from a perfect storm of problems. It was in a small, fractious department, so there were few tenured positions to begin with and very little big-picture planning. The fact that Harvard's assistant professorships were not, by default, tenure track until 2005 meant that it let go of a lot of candidates who would have diversified its faculty. And the federal law banning mandatory retirement age since 1994 compounded the problem by slowing turnover. The department also felt "burned," Richard said, after Professor Tuross, the first and only female professor tenured within Harvard's archaeology program, left the department. "When it comes to the next person, who are you going to hire?"

But understanding it as a Harvard-specific or even archaeology-specific problem would be shortsighted. Based on the statistics I had been reading, the low number of tenured women wasn't due to a lack of female undergraduates or graduate students. Instead, as women climbed higher in the academic echelons, more and more of them silently dropped out. By the time you got to full tenured professors, the numbers were grim.

A recent report produced by a junior member of Harvard's Anthropology department offered quantitative insight into this silent attrition. Women were disproportionately selected as head teaching fellows, which required significantly more "invisible labor" than a standard TF position. Women also had lower publication rates than their male counterparts in archaeology. (Other studies conducted nationally suggest that women spend more time on teaching, administration, and committee responsibilities, and take more time preparing their manuscripts.) In addition, it found that female graduate students consistently took longer to complete their degrees, suggesting that they received less effective mentorship than the male students. The cumulative effect was clear: Of the withdrawals in the program over the past three decades, 87 percent were female.

Experiences of sexual harassment and assault might also be a significant contributing factor. According to the first systematic study of sexual harassment and assault on field sites, published in 2014, 70 percent of the five hundred women and 40 percent of the 140 men surveyed reported having experienced sexual harassment. More than a quarter of the women experienced sexual assault. But while the majority of the men had been harassed or assaulted by their peers, the majority of women's experiences were at the hands of their superiors. Other research has shown that sexual assault and harassment by a supervisor resulted in significantly greater psychological distress and job dissatisfaction than harassment by a peer.

It was a classic chicken-and-egg problem. Statistically, the most effective way to decrease sexual harassment and assault in the workplace is to promote more women. But if women are leaving the field in part because of this toxic aggression, how then do you diversify it?

I asked Richard how we were going to get there.

"I think everyone's united on the fact that we need women colleagues," Richard said. "But it's not going to be easy." The women—and single men with children, and people of underrepresented communities, he added—who succeed in this system are very tough, very strong, really special people. "I don't know how they do it. It really takes a toughness of spirit."

Richard was right. The old boys' network was a mechanism of social reproduction along class and racial lines as well. The most micro example: The first African American graduate student to complete his PhD at Harvard in Anthropology graduated in 1961.

But Richard's insight left me all the more surprised, then, by his apparent blind spots. "We've had any number of very good Black social anthropologists. They've always gone elsewhere because they're very, very rare commodities." The brazenness of the word *commodity* caught me off guard, but I didn't want to interrupt his thought. "It's their decision in the end what they're going to do. But there are very, very few of them, because they just don't go into the field. It's not that we're discriminating against Black people at all. The reason we don't have them is because they don't stay in many cases. And I don't think it's necessarily because of Harvard. Although it could be, in the sense that because there's not a lot of Black people, they don't have a community, and therefore they go someplace they think they might have more community. Which is fine. But you can't blame the university for that."

I wondered if Richard's word choice was deliberate—a sign of resignation to the current dynamics in academia, in which students are seen as clients, and universities, corporations. Or perhaps Richard, who was so close to seeing through these mechanisms of social reproduction, stopped just short of seeing the full picture. The latter possibility reminded me of Professor Sally Falk Moore who had found a way to navigate her isolation at Harvard that sidestepped the larger structural problems at issue. As she told me, "[If] one has the wit to avoid quarrels...it can be very benign."

On one hand, I was sympathetic to how long it takes to develop systems-level thinking about a problem. I was only beginning to see what I hadn't had the capacity to recognize as an undergraduate: that even if the members of a system were good people, the system to which they belonged could still be destructive. It was only because I was talking to all these women in the department, studying this amorphous pattern of unhappiness, that I was beginning to realize how corrosive institutional habits could be. On the other hand, Richard and Sally were professors in the *Anthropology* department. It struck me that anthropologists, despite focusing their professional lives on observing the patterns of human behavior, might be no better than the rest of us at applying that lens to themselves. As Iva Houston once told me, "It's hard to admit you belong to the world you're studying."

PROFESSOR KARKOV

THE PERSON WHO HELPED ME connect with the most women in the department was a medical anthropologist named Mel Konner who had been a graduate student at Harvard at the same time as Jane. He had written a book called *Women After All: Sex, Evolution, and the End of Male Supremacy*, and he spoke at length about the complicated legacy of his adviser Professor Irven

DeVore. DeVore had been a champion of his female students, but some also saw a misogynistic side; Don and Jill Mitchell, I later learned, called him "Irv the Perv."

(Some of DeVore's students would also dispute the notion that their careers were facilitated by him. Sarah Hrdy, DeVore's first female graduate student, went on to be elected to the National Academy of Sciences and to win a Guggenheim, but she felt that it was despite DeVore's mentorship, rather than because of it. DeVore had once told a committee that she should not be hired for a position because she was married. It was no surprise, she said, that DeVore's main field of study was patterns of male dominance in primate societies. Kathryn Clancy, who published that 2014 study of sexual harassment on field expeditions, credited DeVore, with whom she studied as an undergraduate, as the reason she became an anthropologist—but she stopped short of saying that DeVore championed her.)

But when we got on the phone, Mel surprised me with something else he'd written. In 1981, he said, he published a fictional story inspired by Jane's murder. In his story, a Jane-like character named Evelyn—a student in the Classics department at Ulster College—has been bludgeoned, and her professor, an invented character named Gregory Karkov, comes under suspicion.

Inspired by the atmosphere of mistrust following Jane's murder, Mel's fiction reflects the rampant speculation in the wake of Evelyn's:

> What animated their 'vague,' if not exactly 'smutty' minds, was not an authoritative original source for the rumor, nor a series of logical inferences from fact, nor even a clumsily linked together chain of circumstance, but a simple, animal dislike. The students detested Professor Karkov with a vividness and clarity of feeling that, in the young, is rarely reasonable, and yet not always wrong. Their arrogant tribunal of the spirit pronounced him unattractive, cowardly, dishonorable, disloyal, callous, self-elevating, hypocritical, calculating—guilty in general of conduct unbecoming a young professor, whose age-old role, precious in tradition, was to intercede for the students with the senior faculty. The rumor, then, in which he was depicted as a murderer, was not so much an allegation of crime as it was the punishment they meted out to him for the subtler crime of being what he was, or what, at any rate, they thought he was: a severe, frenetic, icy, driving man.

The rumors, in other words, about Karkov being involved with Evelyn's death were more of a smear campaign than an actual articulation of suspicion. Exactly what I had come to suspect about Karl after talking with Iva.

Mel agreed with my line of thinking, at least as far as his made-up character was concerned. "In a way the only person who takes the rumors seriously is Karkov himself. He's guilty of arrogance, he's guilty of self-absorption, he's guilty of having a temper...he's guilty of basically [being] a jerk," Mel told me. "But he's not guilty of murder."

As I thought more about Mel's assertion that the rumors were a form of punishment, I found myself reading scholarly work on the social functions of gossip. I eventually worked my way to Chris Boehm, a former classmate of Jane's who studied how gossip works in small-scale societies. He had, in fact, used Jane's murder as an example in his paper about gossip as a form of social control.

According to Boehm, social groups necessarily have a certain amount of "leakiness" built in. These are the whisper networks; these are the stories that get swapped in the field and passed quietly between graduate students. Their job is to limit outlier behavior and to keep members of the community safe when what can be said out loud is constrained. Gossip, in other words, is punishment for people who move outside the norm.

Juxtaposing Boehm's theory of the social function of gossip with Karl's larger-than-life persona and the bigger picture of systemic inequality in academia, one thing became abundantly clear: Karl's apparent role as a suspect was both product and reflection of the Harvard bubble.

———

It takes until the end of Mel Konner's short story for Karkov to realize that he couldn't have possibly been the killer, because he was giving a talk at the Bolton Public Library at the time of the murder. It was the police who needed to remind Karkov of his alibi, who responds, stunned:

"But you don't understand, Sergeant. I've spent the last twenty-four hours agonizing over whether l would be going on trial for murder. And the perfect alibi, which I had all along, never even entered my mind. Why didn't I think of it? Why?"

"I don't know, Professor. Guilty conscience, maybe?"

THE GRAND JURY

THE GRAND JURY CONVENED FOR Jane's case almost exactly one month after her murder. Richard Conti, a twenty-nine-year-old MIT graduate and the jury's foreman, sat at a desk directly in front of DA John Droney, and near Droney's first assistant, John Irwin Jr., who ran the proceedings. Conti had been randomly selected like the other twenty-two people on the jury. But Conti, who normally worked for the government contractor Raytheon designing "weapons of limited destruction," had a secret. Some of his closest friends were in the Harvard Anthropology department. He went on vacations with them. His wife's sister had been college roommates with Sally Bates, who helped arrange Jane's abortion. And though he had never met Jane, he and his friends had talked so much about her, he felt like he knew her.

When he finally confessed his connection to the DA's first assistant, Conti was relieved and a little surprised that Irwin didn't care at all. Conti reasoned that perhaps Irwin believed having an insider in the department would be an asset to the investigation, because as the weeks wore on, he had the distinct sense that the grand jury was being used as a "sharpened saber" against the Anthropology department—to get testimony on the record, and to put these professors through the rigor of a grand jury performance, but to do so *out of the public view*.

Conti took pleasure in watching the stars of the department be paraded into the proceedings, vacuumed of their power and privilege. The suffocating academic politics, the incestuous intradepartment relationships, and the decades of grudges and slights revealed by the interrogations lent the whole thing a strange, "cloistered, gothic" feel. Everyone, he said, seemed to have something to hide.

Most of the questions were handled by the assistant DA, but some of Conti's favorite moments were when one of the old ladies would look up from her knitting and ask something totally out of left field. Conti, enjoying the moment, would say, "Please answer." The person would stammer, "No,

I've never knitted a sweater for my granddaughter." What was great was how unnerving it was for witnesses. Afterward, sometimes they'd stumble.

When Karl Lamberg-Karlovsky took the stand, he struck Conti as "the closest equivalent Harvard had to a British twit." He sweated profusely, behavior the DA interpreted as "a consciousness of guilt."

But Karl eventually satisfied the jury of his innocence. What had made the DA suspicious, the jury came to find, had no bearing on actual guilt.

————

While the proceedings continued on for the next six months, the formerly cocooned world of Harvard exploded at nauseating speed.

The extremes of 1969—it was the year of both the moon landing and the Manson family murders—were so opposite that they pulled the world apart at the seams, and that intensity had firmly lodged itself in the campus psyche. In February, discussions for the Radcliffe-Harvard merger began, as did talks about co-ed living arrangements. Later that semester, Harvard finally relented and approved the establishment of a degree-granting program in Afro-American Studies. Anti–Vietnam War protests, which had been escalating all year, came to a head in early April. A group of student activists pinned a list of six demands on the door of the Harvard president's house. Their primary petition? The abolition of Harvard's ROTC program—military-funded scholarships for students in exchange for years served. More than anything, it was a symbol of Harvard's complicity in the war. As Carol Sternhell, class of '71, explained, "We felt that we would be the equivalent of the good Germans in the Nazi era if we didn't stop this war…We felt that we were the *bad* guys."

Jane's death is mentioned in the fifth demand on that list: "University Road apartments should not be torn down for construction of Kennedy Memorial Library. The building where Radcliffe graduate student Jane Britton was murdered last Fall is adjacent to the library site and expected to be demolished." But Jane's murder was about to be sidelined by history.

The following day, at noon on April 9, 1969, about seventy students occupied University Hall, the administrative building in the heart of the Yard. They kicked out deans and administration officials and rifled through files as busts of old white men looked on.

The next morning, at dawn, at Harvard president Nathan Pusey's request,

Cambridge cops and state troopers stormed University Hall. The troopers wore visored helmets and wielded batons. The image of riot cops throwing protesters down the stairs and holding clubs above bloodied heads seared itself into the public consciousness. What had been the concern of a small, radical minority was suddenly transformed into a campus-wide cause.

April 9 quickly became enshrined as a dividing line between the before and the shattered after. A campus-wide strike was called, and ten thousand galvanized people gathered in Harvard's stadium the following week to discuss how to move forward. At the height of the strike, which pitted faculty against teaching fellows against students, class attendance was less than 25 percent. Some conservative members of the faculty appointed themselves protectors of Widener Library and stationed themselves inside the building, ready to thwart any would-be arsonists. Dean Franklin Ford, the man who had a month earlier informed Karl that his bid for tenure was finalized, suffered a minor stroke. The feeling on campus was a genuine uncertainty about whether the institution was going to survive the unrest.

By the summer, Stephen Williams had steered his department through the investigation unscathed, but he still looked back on the year like a man staring out the window of his ivory tower, terrified to come down. He published his reflections in that year's Peabody Museum newsletter: "In Winter I hoped for Spring, and now in Summer I am apprehensive of the Fall. [...] A confident 'Never at Harvard!', may be replaced by a bemused and questioning 'What again at Harvard?' I am not taking any bets this time."

————

More than six months after the first hearing, the grand jury members had to admit that despite their investment, all avenues of investigation had fizzled. The jury never came to a vote about anyone. Conti understood it as only an engineer could: "The response was strong but the signal from all this noise was somewhat meager." The newspapers, which had been so obsessed with Jane, didn't even bother to report on the fact that the jury dissolved without an indictment.

But decades later, Richard Conti dusted off a faded memory. Though Lamberg-Karlovsky's testimony had stuck out to him most all these years, there was someone else about whose innocence Conti was less sure.

Someone shy, hesitant. "He came out of the blue and he seemed to be hiding something," Conti remembered. "Who the hell was he? I don't know."

SPOTLIGHT

THERE WAS NO WAY I could have known, when I gave eight months' notice at the magazine in August 2016, how fortuitous my timing would be. On April 4, 2017, ten days before leaving to work on Jane's story full-time, I got an email from someone at the *Boston Globe:*

> *Becky:*

> *Hope you are well.*
>   *I'm interested in talking to you about a story I am working on. What is the best way to contact you?*

> *Todd*

Todd Wallack was a reporter on the *Globe*'s Spotlight team, and he was writing an article about Jane. He quickly put my surge of jealousy to rest— possessiveness initially blinding my excitement that people were finally paying attention to Jane's story—with reassurances that he wasn't interested in poaching the case. He just wanted to help people like me who were trying to solve it.

Wallack had made his career on exposing Massachusetts's frequent failures to comply with public records law. The state, which likes to think of itself as the cradle of liberty, ranks near the bottom in terms of government transparency. It takes longer to reply to requests; it holds more records exempt from disclosure; it doesn't fine agencies for noncompliance; and, in the cases where it does release files, it charges fees for reproduction so exorbitant that they are their own form of discouragement. Massachusetts is the only state that maintains that all three of its branches of government are exempt from public records laws. As Wallack quoted Thomas Fiedler, once the editor of the *Miami Herald* before becoming dean of Boston University's College of Communication, in a 2015 *Globe* article: "In Florida, the default position is that government belongs to the public [. . .] Here in Massachusetts, I got the sense that the burden is exactly the opposite."

Todd Wallack told me that I wasn't the only one trying to get access to Jane's records. A colleague of his, as well as Mike Widmer, a nearly eighty-year-old man who had spent most of his life in and around Massachusetts politics, had also had their public records requests refused by the state. In Jane's case, Wallack saw an opportunity to ask the question: Is a murder case ever so old that the records holder can no longer justify the withholding of material?

This dusty old story that had lived privately with me for years and years was about to be blown back open on the national stage.

THE NEW SUSPECT

THE EVENING AFTER WALLACK'S EMAIL, I waited until my boss had left for the day and picked up the phone. I called Don Mitchell for the first time in three years.

After his flurry of posts on Websleuths in the summer of 2014, Don, who had seemed so enamored with the thread, had largely taken a break from the site. People kept "bumping for Jane"—posting to keep the thread at the top of people's minds. But other than a momentary spike when Boyd posted for the first time in January 2016—"I feel obliged as a priest and Christian to attempt forgiveness. I am not certain how I would meet such a challenge. This does not mean I am indifferent to finding the truth"—nothing much happened on the thread for months. "Unsolved crime threads on WS never die, they just take extended coffee breaks while waiting for the next good theory or bit of news," Ausgirl wrote on the thread. I stopped checking.

It wasn't until I went back to the site as part of my preparations to leave the magazine that I realized I had missed a crucial new post from Don. His suspect—the unnamed non-tenured professor—had died in 1996, not in 1999, he corrected. "This all happened a very long time ago, so I'm not going to beat myself up for having either compressed or expanded memory-time."

Now it made sense that I hadn't been able to find anyone in the archives who matched Don's description. And, in that same thought, I remembered the letter in Hallam Movius's file—the one from Stephen Williams that felt like a coded update of the movements of the department's two primary suspects. I knew one person Williams described to Movius was Karl. But the other?

I went back through my photos to find it. There it was, on Peabody letterhead, in a letter dated January 20, 1969:

Lee Parsons is due to leave for Guatemala on the 24th, and of course Carl is in the midst of his preparations too, so Peabody is nothing if not busy with comings and goings.

Lee Parsons.

His name had appeared nowhere else in anything connected with Jane. No newspaper articles. No stories from friends or classmates. I Googled "Lee Parsons obituary archaeologist," and pulled up a page called "Miscellaneous Obituaries of Anthropologists." Written by Michael Coe, a famous Maya scholar, Parsons's obituary was long and revealing. It described him as a leading Meso-American archaeologist, but "his life—both intellectual and personal—was often troubled and unhappy." The details checked out with Don's description. He was affiliated with the department, but not tenured; and the years matched up: "With the promise of a position as assistant director, Parsons moved to Harvard's Peabody Museum in 1968. Due to lack of funds, this position failed to materialize, and he spent two personally distressing years there as Curator of Collections, leaving in 1970 by mutual consent."

And, like Don's suspect, Lee Parsons died in 1996. The vacuum that Karl had left behind was suddenly filled.

On the phone, Don sounded confused and impatient. I explained who I was and paused, waiting for him to say something, but he just said "um," so I catapulted myself over the silence by babbling.

He chuckled. "Your name is familiar to me," he said, finally, maybe to make me stop.

I asked if I could meet him for five minutes to explain what I was working on.

"You mean you want to fly to Hilo?" he asked. I knew how ridiculous it sounded. I tried to downplay the absurdity of a trip to Hawaii for just a few minutes of his time by saying I was going to "the West Coast" anyway.

"*That* West Coast." He chuckled again, this time at my euphemism. "Okay," he said. "Yes, I'll meet you."

We planned to meet the second week in May, and I got off the phone and leapt around the office in circles, out of my little alcove and down the hall, thrilled about the prospect of finally meeting someone who had seen the crime scene firsthand. I wanted to celebrate, but there was no one left in the office. I leapt until I was out of breath.

THE INCENSE NIGHT

As some in the Peabody Museum speculated about Karl Lamberg-Karlovsky, Don and Jill Mitchell had another suspect in mind. It wasn't that they had much fondness for Karl. He had always reminded Don of a black walnut tree, which sends off chemicals that poison everything growing near it. But as easy as it was to dislike Karl, and as enjoyable as it was to imagine a moral universe neat enough to align a horrible thing with someone who seemed Machiavellian, Lee Parsons appeared the more likely culprit.

Lee had joined the museum in the fall of 1968, but he hadn't registered on most students' radars. He was more easily described by what he was not. Handsome, but not overly so. Older than Don, but not old. His hair was somewhere between blond and brown. Not fat, not thin, not loud. And the few who did know him, like graduate student Bruce Bourque, thought of him as "marginal somehow. Just off." Another said, "You're afraid if he smiled, his face would fall [off]." His only move was to invite people to his place to listen to records on his hi-fi set.

Don had seen Lee at a few parties, but he didn't know Lee too well. Except for two incidents that were seared in his memory, Don never had much to do with him.

The first incident happened in November 1968. While Jim was still away for the semester in Canada, Jane had invited Don and Jill over for dinner. As they were finishing up their meal, the buzzer rang. It was Lee Parsons, who was teaching one of Jane's classes that fall. Jane let him upstairs, and the four of them hung out for a while until Lee invited everyone over to his place to listen to records. He lived up by the Radcliffe Quad, a fifteen-minute walk, so Don drove everyone over.

Lee's apartment was on the upper floor. The living room had wall-to-wall white shag carpeting. Everyone sat on the floor, drinking. They got tipsy, but no one more so than Lee. He was "drunk as hell," Don remembered. It all felt a little strange, but not dangerously so.

After a while, Lee went into one of the other rooms, and came back with something rolled up in a corn husk. It was big—about the size of five or six cigarettes bunched together and tied up with string. "This is thousand-year-old Mayan incense," Lee slurred.

He lay it on its side on an aluminum ashtray and lit it like a giant cigar. It was about the length of two or three votive candles. Inside the corn husk, Don could see a white substance—a waxy cylinder, like a lipstick without its case. Lee placed the ashtray directly on his carpet.

Everyone stayed on the floor and watched the Mayan incense burn. It smelled earthy and organic. Eventually the ashtray got so hot, it burned a hole in his white rug.

"As Richard Pryor would say, 'That's when I reached for my knife,'" Don remembered.

Jill and Don passed some glances that signaled, *This is too heavy*. They told Jane that they were going to drive home. "Wanna come back with us?" Jane surprised them by saying she wanted to stay.

That night, Don worried about having left Jane alone at Lee's place. He didn't think that she would cheat on Jim, but then again, if she wasn't planning to spend the night, wouldn't she have ridden with Don and Jill to avoid the 3 a.m. walk home? He worried that Jane had realized, too late, *I'm stuck here*.

THE DELUGE

MY PHONE CALL WITH DON unleashed a deluge of emails. He wrote to me with the same frequency and intensity as his stream of Websleuths posts in 2014. He told me I could count on full cooperation from him. He offered to pick me up from the airport when I arrived on the Big Island, even if I flew into the one that was two hours away. He asked what else I would like to see while I was on the island. "We can take you to 14,000' if you like, or anywhere in between. The volcano, of course. Four hundred-foot waterfalls."

The complete reversal was dizzying. There was an overeagerness there, a compensation perhaps for how shy he said he was. But some things he said made me uneasy. "It might cross your mind to call or email Jill [Nash]," he wrote of his now ex-wife. "I wouldn't bother." Why would he dissuade me from talking to the one person who could best corroborate his story?

Old suspicions resurfaced, too. How could this man hear a knock on Jane's door in the morning, but no screams the night she was killed? Why did he save her bloody rugs? Why was he so hungry to talk on Websleuths?

The prospect of being five thousand miles away from anyone I knew, in the presence of someone I couldn't fully dismiss as a suspect, made me feel acutely vulnerable. When I Google-mapped his home to figure out where I should rent an Airbnb, I saw that he had "boiling pots"—falls where the water was so turbulent it looked like it was boiling—practically in his backyard. It was too easy to imagine taking a walk with him in the middle of the interview, asking one question too many, and then him smiling as he knew my fall was so plausibly *just an accident.*

SLEUTHS

IN ONE OF HIS EMAILS, Don suggested I reach out to Alyssa Bertetto, who helped moderate a subreddit dedicated to the world's unsolved mysteries. I felt reluctant—the culture of murder fan-girling made me deeply uncomfortable. I, obviously, was obsessed with Jane's story, but I told myself that it was different. The culture of true-crime fandom felt like it flattened crime into entertainment, using other people's fear and trauma to deal with a sense of bodily vulnerability. I understood the power that comes from bringing yourself to the edge of what you're most afraid of, but I worried that inhaling stories about death at that clip required a detachment from the people who were killed and the families that were grieving. There's a responsibility to the dead as well as the living.

But Don said he'd been in touch with Alyssa Bertetto in recent weeks, and she had impressed him with her Lee Parsons research.

———

Alyssa's voice was warm, and she was quick to laugh. She spoke to me from her home in Colorado. She wasn't at all how I imagined her. She was young and articulate and, well—not crazy.

Alyssa found out about Jane's case when someone mentioned it offhandedly in the comments section of her unsolved mysteries subreddit. "And I thought, *Gosh, that's strange, because I've never heard of that.*" As a moderator of the page, she thought she had come across all the major unsolved murders before.

Alyssa found herself strangely barbed by Jane's case. Though she'd always been attracted to mysteries, Jane's was the first she felt compelled to take on herself. She became a scholar of the case and was even inspired to study for a private investigator's license. I knew exactly how Alyssa felt. I found myself unexpectedly moved by the feeling of talking to someone else who, while otherwise seemingly sane, also bent her life around solving the murder of a stranger.

Alyssa started by trying to get police records. When that went nowhere, she turned to Websleuths and got in touch with Don Mitchell. In private messages, Don shared his suspicion about Lee Parsons. Alyssa, moved to dig up as much as she could about Don's suspect, found that the more she learned about Lee—particularly the descent of his career after Jane's murder—the more he emerged for her as the most intriguing candidate as well.

Backed with diligent public records reporting, Alyssa filled in some blanks on what happened to Lee after he abruptly left Harvard in 1970. He moved to St. Louis, Missouri. His ex-wife and children didn't come with him. (Lee and his wife had divorced the year before.) Instead, he lived there with a man for a while, until eventually ending up in Florida, where he passed away in 1996. Alyssa had tracked down his last will and testament. It seemed like "just basic talk," until "the part where it said that he wanted his body to be cremated and sprinkled over the grave of the man that he was sharing the house with in St. Louis. This was kind of a strange revelation."

It squared, Don had told her, with whispers from the time that Lee was gay or bisexual. He reminded her that in those years—even in progressive Cambridge—many still saw homosexuality as a disease. It would make sense that Lee had kept the truth about himself quiet.

"Would you mind sharing the name of the man he wanted his ashes sprinkled over?" I asked.

"Yes, absolutely. I've had trouble finding this individual. And what's interesting is, well, his name is Stephen . . . it's ph . . . Edward . . . DeFilippo." The name meant nothing to me.

But what's interesting, she continued, is that "he is even younger than Jane." He was born in 1950. He would have been seventeen, eighteen, nineteen in the years that Lee was at Harvard. And, she said, he died mysteriously in September 1979. Stephen was buried in Woburn, Massachusetts.

I asked her if she truly suspected Lee or if she just found him a tantalizing possible suspect.

"The more and more I found out about him, the more and more the possibility of it being him came to seem true to me."

Alyssa offered to share all of the court documents she had pulled up on Lee. I was touched by her lack of competitiveness or possessiveness. Instead, she told me, "It's reassuring that I'm not the only person who was lying awake thinking about this and hoping that someone was going to do something."

THE SECOND INCIDENT

THE SECOND INCIDENT THAT DON remembered with Lee Parsons happened a few weeks after the Incense Night, as he had come to think of it. Jim was in Cambridge, visiting, and Jane had wanted him to see the artifacts that Don had brought back from New Guinea. They hung out at the Mitchells' place for a while, so it was pretty late in the evening when Jane's buzzer rang. Jane, Jill, and Don all knew there was only one person it could be.

Lee had already tried to come over to Jane's place once more after the Incense Night. It was late in the evening; he rang the buzzer and came up the stairs and knocked on her door, to no avail. Jane was in Needham. He then walked across the hall to the Mitchells', who talked to him through the door. He sounded drunk, asking them to let him see Jane and refusing to believe that she wasn't home.

This time, when the buzzer rang, Don noticed that Jane's face hardened into a quiet panic. *What happened the night of the incense party*, Don wondered, *that she so desperately doesn't want to see him now?* Don had tried talking to her the day after when he heard her coming up the stairs. "I don't want to talk about it," Jane had said and walked into her apartment. She didn't come out again for a long time. But it was less what she had refused to say and more the look on her face that had alarmed Don. Her eyes had been too bright for a simple hangover. There had been a rigidity to her face. It looked like she was channeling all her energy to keep herself from dissolving into a heap. Her look had been one of fear.

Lee buzzed again and identified himself by yelling up the stairwell.

"I'll take care of it," Jane said, finally. She descended the first flight of stairs to meet Lee on his way up.

In the meantime, Jill and Don kept Jim company. They tried to play down what was happening. *Oh, you know Lee, he's just a strange guy—very lonely.*

They heard Jane shout up the stairwell. "Don, could you turn off my type-writer?" Jane, trying to make Lee believe he had caught her in the middle of studying, was going to the trouble to pretend she had left her machine running. *She is putting on quite a show for Lee*, Jill thought.

Jill peered out of her doorway and caught a glimpse of Lee and Jane in the hallway. She couldn't hear what they were saying, but she noticed that Lee was all dressed up.

Eventually, Jane came back to the Mitchells' place. Alone. She had managed to convince Lee to go away, but Jill wanted to look out the window to be sure.

"Don't do that," Don said. "He'll see you looking out." Jill stepped away.

THE CAPE LIFTS

My bags were packed. I had finished my last week at *The New Yorker*, and the next day, I'd be five thousand miles away, on the start of my big West Coast trip. In the safety of that knowledge, I did something that up until that point I'd only dreamed about. I called Karl.

Though Karl had stepped out of Jane's story as little more than a symbol of a villain, he was still an important person in her narrative. And, I had to admit, now that I was satisfied that he was innocent, I was even more intrigued by him as a character. What kind of man can survive this kind of rumor?

I had run through this moment so many times before in my mind. In some versions, we talked for hours about Tepe Yahya, and I waited to see if he brought up Jane. In others, I would tell him the rumors I had heard about him and he'd exclaim, *I've just been waiting for someone to ask!* And then he would give me that last clue that I needed to solve it. In most versions, he hung up on me immediately. But now that the moment was finally here, I felt like there was only one way to begin. If I wanted Karl to be as up front with me as possible, I needed him to feel like I was being direct with him, too.

I told him in the first minute that I was writing about Jane Britton, and I began to explain, "who was found murdered in her off-campus apart—"

"Oh I know," he said, his voice now gravelly. But it wasn't the *I know* of someone wishing I'd shut up or go away. It was the weary *I know* of someone who had carried this story for decades. "And you're doing a story on her?"

Exactly.

"Oh," he sighed, and let out a puff of air as he readied his next thought. "You know, many, many years ago I got a call from Truman Capote's agent." Karl told me that Capote was intrigued by the murder, the mystery, the excavations, the university setting, and wanted to write about Jane. As I listened, I felt the tug of the storyteller who pulls you into his orbit. I wanted to believe him, but I couldn't tell if he was just feeding me what I wanted to hear, letting me cast myself in my fantasy.

We spoke for the next two and a half hours. Though I was the one asking questions, I let Karl direct the conversation, assuming that he would talk his way into revealing himself. He described Jane as "very vivacious" and a "very able young lady." He was open, candid. He portrayed himself as someone hurt, confused, left in the dark about the investigation. He said he'd had a hard time distinguishing how much of what the police told him was real. They said that there was blood in the ashtray, and that the person who killed Jane must have put the cigarette out in the blood. They said there was a bloody fingerprint on the kitchen window. They said that it must have been somebody she knew because the stacks of books on the floor next to her were undisturbed. They said that Jane, in her diaries, fantasized about having sex with him. It all felt so exaggerated, he wasn't even sure how much of what he'd heard about how she died was true. "I mean, I frankly didn't believe some of it until they showed me photographs of Jane."

The closest we got to talking about the fact that people suspected Karl was that he said he understood why people scrutinized the Tepe Yahya group. "It really is a kind of an Agatha Christie construct." But he wanted me to understand that they had all gotten along. He highlighted the fact that he had been essentially the same age as everyone else on the dig; there wasn't a hierarchical divide to precipitate a rift.

We took that off-ramp into a discussion of what brought him to archaeology in the first place. He hadn't studied it in college. Karl's uncle, who oversaw his education, had made it very clear that the pre-medical track was the only acceptable course. And even when Karl chose to follow his own path by entering graduate school, not medical school, it was for biological anthropology, not archaeology. It was only by chance that Karl found his way into the field: Robert Dyson, a professor in his department at

UPenn, realized Karl didn't have any plans for the summer after his second year and invited him on excavation.

The news was received by his uncle "with absolute horror." *What's the point of school*, his uncle wanted to know. "Certainly the point of it is not to spend all of this time, effort, and money to do something quite as useless as archaeology."

But Karl was immediately impressed by the scientific rigor of the excavation and analysis. And he was even more enthralled by the fact that the data were only as good as the context he gave it. "I realized that the analysis of material things is meaningless unless" you can articulate the science in "a believable, meaningful story."

"Do you find that the storytelling aspect of it comes naturally to you?" I asked.

"In a certain way, yes."

It felt like the right time to bring up a theory that I had heard from one of Jane's undergraduate mentors. That person had said that people became archaeologists for one of two reasons: either, as a child, they lost something and spent their whole lives trying to find it again, or, as a child, they found something, and spent their lives looking for more. "Does that ring true for you?" I asked.

"Yes, I think so," Karl said. He said the former categorization—the kid who lost something—was more "instructive" for him.

When I asked if he knew what he was trying to recover, he said slowly, as if weighing each word: "I could probably say that I had a not-the-most-pleasant childhood."

Carefully, we waded into the story of his youth. His voice wavered. "My upbringing was very, very nomadic." When the war "broke everything up" in Europe, Karl was two years old. He moved to the States with his grandmother. Karl's father, still in Austria, became a political dissident. He published opposition essays in the *London Times* and took a public stance against the acquiescence of the regime to the Nazis. "I am not myself Jewish," Karl told me, "but my father was killed in Auschwitz."

After the war, Karl and his grandmother returned to Europe, and his family tried to establish new roots "somehow, somewhere. Not always with great success." Karl started to say he moved back to the States in 1952, but he corrected himself: "*I* didn't move. I was moved by the powers that be." He was given no choice but to live with his uncle and aunt in Connecticut who, until that point, might as well have been strangers. His mother, who by then had moved to New York, lived in Scarsdale with her new husband and remained in the background.

Karl continued to feel like he had very little control over his life—"Dependency requires you to do things that you don't necessarily want to do"—which instilled in him two fierce desires. One, the hunger for something stable to ground his liminal existence. And the other, the need to master his own destiny.

In Martha Veale, whom he married a few months after his college graduation, Karl found the answer to the former. Together, they could set their own path. "My wife and I worked hard to achieve what and where we were going." Karl told me that he's stayed with the same woman for fifty-six years. In the background of the call I heard the murmur of a woman's voice. "Fifty-seven years, she corrects me," Karl said. "Fifty-seven years." I hadn't realized I was having a conversation with them both.

His archaeological career was the answer to the second. But none of Karl's accolades seemed to matter to his uncle, except one: "The first time he said anything pleasant was when I told him that I was invited to become an assistant professor at Harvard." But that was it.

"I guess it might have been difficult for him to accept the fact that I made my own way," Karl continued. "I don't know. I don't know. But I can tell you that it was not exactly the most thrilling sort of experience for me."

I watched as the vampire's cape of legend lifted. He was just a man wearing a nice suit. Yes, Karl was a descendant of the Austrian elite, but here was also a boy who never got the support he needed. A boy who felt like he was moved around by powers out of his control. And a college student, perhaps, who signed and re-signed his name because he was filled with the senses of doubt and insecurity we all have at that age. Was his flash and tempestuousness simply him casting about for affirmation and identity? None of this excused his alleged behavior, but it humanized him.

"You know," he segued, "I'll tell you one of the things that I think might be true. The person who experienced in many ways the worst of the element of Jane's death is Jim Humphries."

After Jim's visit to Karl's house on the night of the murder, they never discussed Jane's death again—and their relationship permanently changed. "Not that it was a negative relationship. Not that it was a positive relationship. It was neutral. There was no time for banter." Karl said that Jim came back to Tepe Yahya for a few more seasons but "I don't think that his heart was in it."

"Because he was still grieving?" I asked.

"I don't know," Karl said. "I don't know the privacy of his grief."

And then, because we were near the end of the conversation, and because we had come so far, I had to ask. "It wasn't because he had somehow gotten some suspicion that you were involved?"

"No. No, never. Never. Not that I know of."

THE DEAD. THE NEAR-DEAD.
THE JUST-DEAD.

IN THE EARLY-MORNING HOURS of Tuesday, January 7, 1969, Jill Mitchell woke up suddenly. She felt like she was in a foreign hotel room. "It was like the furniture was rearranged. Some feeling that things weren't right," she later told police. Don woke up, too—whether because of Jill or because of whatever had woken her up, he never knew—and looked at the luminous face of his watch. It was three o'clock.

Jill got out of bed. *I just had to go to the bathroom, that's all*, she told herself. She felt all right again. But as she moved around the apartment, the funny feeling came back.

There was a strange, greenish light in the hallway. She had never noticed it before. It was a steady light that didn't flicker, and it seemed to be coming from the bathroom. She followed it to the window, where she saw that the lights of the Boston public transit station were on. Jill reasoned with herself that the window shade in the bathroom was white and the walls were green, so the light probably always looked that color—she had just never noticed.

Jill heard no noise from outside the building, or from inside her apartment. *This is probably completely crazy*, she told herself. She'd just been having bad dreams.

———

Don was woken for good that morning by a phone call. It was just before 9 a.m., when Jane's exams were scheduled to start. Don picked up as quickly as he could, hoping that the ring hadn't stirred Jill, who had finally fallen back asleep. It was a friend of Don's in the department, who was having trouble with his photo equipment and wanted Don's advice. After the call, as Don walked to the bathroom, he heard footsteps in the hall, followed by the unmistakable sound of someone knocking on Jane's door.

Well, Jane's done it again, Don thought to himself. *She's overslept this exam.* He didn't hear her door open before he went into the bathroom and got into the shower. He hoped that it would work out all right.

———

Later that day, Jill heard footsteps in the apartment stairwell. It was about 12:30 p.m., and she had been listening out, waiting for Jane to come home after her exams. But as those footsteps reached the landing and got closer to her door, Jill knew that it wasn't Jane. The tread was too masculine. She thought maybe it was the electrician coming to see the Pressers, the only other fourth-floor residents, or perhaps it was Jim Humphries, and Jill had just missed hearing Jane coming home.

The stranger knocked on Jane's door. It didn't open. Then she heard the muffled noises of two men talking.

Don had come home from his errands shortly before noon and had started packing for their upcoming expedition to the Solomon Islands. As he rustled around the room, putting stuff in boxes, a large mounting board kept falling off the wall. He was lugging it out into the hall when he saw Jim in the corridor. Don walked past him and set the heavy board down.

"Have you seen Jane?" Jim asked.

No, Don said.

"Well, she didn't take her quiz." Don was struck by the phrasing. He'd never call it a quiz. Maybe it was a Canadian thing.

Don waited outside as Jim and then Jill walked into Jane's apartment. As she retreated to her bedroom to recover from the shock, Jill told Don to call the health service because "there's something terribly wrong."

Don took over from this point. He told Jim to call the police, but no one could remember the Cambridge Police's number (9-1-1 didn't yet exist in Cambridge). They fumbled around the Mitchells' apartment looking for the phone book, and when they finally located it, Jim was too flustered to find the listing. Don took the book from him, thumbed to the right page, and dialed the police.

While they were waiting for cops to arrive, Don tried to reach Jane's family. The Radcliffe line was busy. Nobody answered at their home in Needham. He tried the Radcliffe line again, and this time got Mr. Britton's secretary. Don asked the secretary to tell him to come to his daughter's apartment. Jill assumed the secretary must have given Don a hard time, because after a while, he finally resorted to saying, "She's dead."

Jim kept repeating, "You should call the health service. Call the health service." Jill agreed with him: "Maybe we should take her pulse. Maybe she's not dead." Don began to doubt himself since he hadn't in fact touched Jane to be sure, so he went back into her apartment. He couldn't see her arm, so he felt the back of her knee. There was no pulse. It was completely cold. There was no uncertainty after that.

And so the three of them waited in the Mitchells' apartment in a state of shock. They walked around, and looked out the window, wondering when the police were going to show up. It was a quiet panic. Don thought about how alive Jane had been the last time he saw her. He thought about the stupid errands he had run a few hours ago, how normal and banal they were, and now his friend was dead. He struggled to come to grips with the reality that this thing had happened, but then he struggled to know exactly what *thing* he meant.

Don's memory of Jim Humphries dropped out after this point. In fact, other than crossing paths at the funeral and the grand jury hearing, he didn't remember talking to him again until a chance encounter with a mutual friend in 1984.

The police arrived, and Don pointed to Jane's apartment. A few minutes later, Don heard noises in the stairwell. Two sets of footsteps. They belonged to Jane's parents. Don would later write a prose poem about this moment—immortalizing the kind of weeping that is so total, they were literally loosed with sorrow.

I heard groans and heaves from grief, shock, and not my own. I heard gaspings, breath-catchings, eructations.

I called them forth, I the messenger, called her mother from her pleasant lunch, called her father from his office, saying only, come quickly, something bad has happened. I made them climb four flights of stairs, I made them listen to my tale, telling, tolling: she's dead in there. You can't go in. They belched, they farted, they wept.

The dead are still but the near-dead aren't nor are the just-dead nor those who loudly grieve.

———

That night, after a long interrogation session with the police, Don and Jill lay in bed. There were no racking sobs. No yelling. No loud eruptions of grief. Instead, the silent struggle that had consumed them that afternoon while waiting for the police returned: a disquieting inability to reconcile a reality that no longer made sense. Don turned to Jill. For the first, and he thinks, only time, he told his wife that he loved her.

HAWAII

DON MITCHELL AND I SAT on opposite corners of the couch in the living room of the house that he grew up in. Blue jade and orchid sprays and fragrant hibiscus and grass so green it looked like it was colored with a neon highlighter pressed in on us from the windows. Don's black-and-white prints of people from the island of Malaita, taken during one of his South Pacific expeditions, hung on the walls. I put my tape recorder on the coffee table and hoped that I would be able to hear him above the trilling birds.

The animal soundtrack reminded me of trying to fall asleep amid the swell of coquí frogs the night before. Just before 8 p.m., my plane had taxied into Hilo airport. It was less than twenty-four hours after I had gotten off the phone with Karl. I was the last one off the plane. The humidity on the tarmac hit me instantly. Don had asked if he and his partner, Ruth, could greet me at the airport—Hawaiian hospitality, they had told me. It would feel weird not to, he'd said. He had sent me a recent picture of himself in front of his house so I'd know how to pick him out, like on a blind date.

I stepped onto the escalators, and, just as Don had said, there were people waiting at the mouth of the stairs. I scanned the crowd. Near the banner that said WELCOME HOME, there was Don in a burgundy Hawaiian shirt—I recognized the gleaming bald head and white beard first—and Ruth standing next to him. They were each holding a lei.

Don adjusted his glasses, as if theatrically miming the act of recognizing me. I waved and walked over, my steps skimming the floor. We were all smiling, giddy almost. Ruth, one hand in a cast, reached over my head to put on her lei—a green-and-white one, with what looked like spiky pineapple tops. I stooped to help her. Then Don lifted his lei, a string of purple orchids, over my head. Ruth hugged me and Don kissed me on the cheek. It felt, strangely, like a homecoming, even as a part of me tried to hold on to my reservations. "We knew what you looked like, but we didn't know how tall you were going to be" was the first thing that Don said to me.

They drove me to my Airbnb, the top floor of a small house. Don brought up my suitcase and Ruth handed me a bag of groceries. She told me she had packed me a sandwich and some coffee. Don added, "I brought you a papaya and a soursop." The contrast of Don in person and Don over email was striking. Written Don was exacting and exhausting while in-person Don was sweet, kind, and almost shy. They felt like protective parents who had just dropped me off at college.

The next morning, with the tape recorder now running between us, Don told me he wanted to be as helpful as he could. In advance of my visit, he had spent hours going through the carbons of his old letter stash. He'd changed his mind and thought that it would be worth contacting Jill and wrote down all the angles I might take to optimize my chances of convincing her to be interviewed. He had pulled out great big plastic Tupperware containers filled with letters and negatives and slides that he hadn't yet unpacked since his move from upstate New York. They were sitting in his dining room. We decided to go through them together after we talked. With five days in front of us, it felt like we had the luxury of time.

We started with how he got to know Jane. He said he met her when he moved to Harvard for grad school in the fall of 1964, when she was a sophomore at Radcliffe. "She was warm, open, congenial." He remembered she invited him and Jill over for dinner her senior year, but they weren't close until she moved into the University Road apartment in the late summer of 1967.

After that, he and Jill would see Jane three, four, five times a week. They would go to the movies in the Square. They would run out to the Coop to get the latest Beatles record and would sit in Don's apartment listening. Once, they drew on each other's arms and hands with markers. He found her "attractive in so many ways."

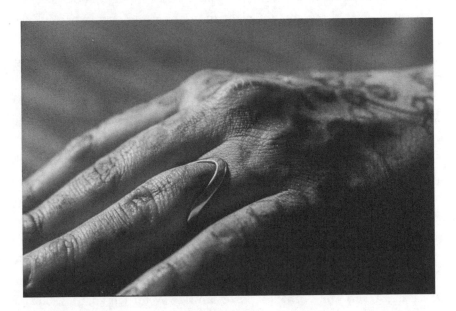

Jane's hand from the marker evening.

Jill, who never saw the point in being anything but blunt—according to Don, she liked to say "the thing I'm best at is being insightful about other people's shortcomings"—once said to her husband, "If I die, you should marry Jane because Jane has always been in love with you."

Early in our interviews, Don handed me an artifact. It was a feline face, barely bigger than the size of my hand, made of glued-together shards of what looked like terra-cotta. Don had taken it from Jane's apartment, he explained, after she died. It was one of the few mementos he still had of her. I understood what the Peabody curators had meant when they told me that touching an artifact was a powerful experience. It wasn't that this object was particularly valuable. There was a magic in holding something I knew she'd held—a material connection to the past.

We eased into a rhythm quickly. I would curl up on the couch, knees to my chest, notebook in hand, tape recorder running, and he would sit at the far end. We would stay like that for four- or five-hour sessions, from late morning after he finished his daily walk until dinner, rarely breaking for lunch. I'd sneak off to the bathroom and scarf down the bag of almonds I had stuffed in my pocket because I didn't want to break the spell.

The normal limits of too much information didn't apply, even when it didn't work in his favor. Don confessed he had thought about sleeping with Jane. He told me about a night that Jane came over, when Jill was in New Mexico, and she was on his couch, drinking, cigarette in hand. The air was charged. "Nothing happened, but it was intense," he told me. He noticed me writing something in my notebook and, clearly looking to establish the boundaries of his attraction to her, added, "Will saying 'I never imagined what might have happened that night and masturbated' help you understand?"

He had been terrified about the prospect of answering the lie detector's questions about whether anything sexual had happened between him and Jane. He worried the lie detector test couldn't tell the difference between *we did* and *I would have*. It didn't seem to occur to him that the latter might be even more damning.

Don's transparency made me feel comfortable bringing up the bloody rugs early on. I asked him how they came into his possession. He said the police had taken some of Jane's possessions away for lab analysis, but for a long time after the murder, the rugs still weren't among those items. "I think Jill and I said, 'We might as well take these rugs.' So we did." They took her cat, too.

I knew from Websleuths that they had saved the rugs for decades. "Did you keep them in a ziplock bag?"

"Oh, we used them!" Don said, unreservedly.

"Even though they had blood on them?"

"We cut the blood off," he said, and laughed, hearing maybe for the first time how grotesque it sounded. "Only one of them had a big bloodstain, and yes, we took scissors and cut it out." The bloodstain, he explained, was about the width of two hands.

I tried to contain my face.

"Yeah, I guess it sounds weird, but to me it was sort of comforting. Like, you know, these are Jane's rugs."

I asked if he thought of them as a memento of her, as I tried not to judge what Karl had called, in reference to Jim, "the privacy of his grief."

Don nodded. He said that when he and Jill divorced, she didn't want them, so he took them and kept them for years until, when he was getting ready to move back to Hawaii, he threw them into a bonfire in his backyard. (Jill, I would later find out through a friend of hers, disagreed and said she kept one until recently.)

Over the ensuing days, keeping the rugs started to fit into a larger pattern of who Don was: a sentimental archivist. He and Ruth had dated as undergrads at Stanford, but they lost touch after graduation in 1964; decades later, Don set their reunion in motion with an email, and the day he sent that message became a holiday they celebrated together each year. "The Annual Reading of the Email," they called it. On his birthday, he always walked the same number of kilometers as he was years old, meditating on the corresponding milestones of his life with every step. He'd think about finding Ruth at the age of twenty—the twenty-kilometer mark—and the fact that it'd take him a marathon of walking before he found her again. The same impulse that made Don a dream interview subject—someone who rehearsed the past and saved its mementos—was the drive that led to the bizarre rug-keeping.

Don also confessed that he worried sometimes that he uses the past to glorify himself, by offering up something that had happened to him as proof that he was exceptional. "Sometimes I will trot out almost being killed by a tidal wave because people will say, 'What?' And sometimes, although much more rarely, I will say, 'You know I was involved in a murder once. I found a body, and it was really bad, and I know what it's like to be sweated by the police.' And I shouldn't do that. But I do it from time to time. And I don't like it."

At night, Ruth would join us, and we'd have dinner together—either in their house, or at a neighborhood favorite like Ken's House of Pancakes, where the special was the Kalua Moco, salted cured pork with two fried eggs over rice. At these times, I was struck by the small moments of tenderness between Don and Ruth. Because of the cast Ruth wore on her hand, Don helped her with her seat belt. She didn't have to ask. At the restaurant, unprompted, he opened her straw. When Ruth told me that her first marriage was to someone who had proposed to her after their first date, Don said, "You're easy to fall in love with. I know. I did twice."

LIEUTENANT JOYCE'S LETTER

DEPARTMENT OF PUBLIC SAFETY
DIVISION OF STATE POLICE

FRANK J. JOYCE
ATE POLICE DETECTIVE LIEUTENANT

District Attorney's Office
72 Belmont St.
Brockton, Mass.

Office ▓▓▓
Residence ▓▓▓

rmonwealth of Massachusetts
Department of Public Safety

CPAC Unit - Mass. State Police
Middleboro, Massachusetts
January 8,1979

Dear Jill and Don,

It does not seem possible that ten years have gone by since Jane Britton was brutally murdered. As you can see I am still a member of the state police although now assigned to the Office of the District Attorney, Plymouth County. However, I am still ready to pursue any information relative to the Britton homicide. I recently received a telephone call from Delda White of Mattapan, Mass. who rekindled my interest. During our conversation she mentioned that both of you either told her or Sarah McNnulty that Lee Parsons admitted that he killed Jane but you chose to discount it because he was mentally unstable. I am still of the opinion that he could have been involved. Therefore, I would appreciate hearing from you as to what he actually said relative to this matter. I understand that he is now located in St. Louis, Missouri. I would appreciate hearing from you as soon as possible. During the week I can be reached at ▓▓▓▓▓▓ Or ▓▓▓▓▓▓. Nights or weekends I can be reached at ▓▓▓▓▓▓. As you can see I have not abandoned hope of solving this case. Looking forward to hearing from you soon. Stay in good health.

Sincerely,

Frank J Joyce
Detective Lieutenant
Massachusetts State Police

THE CAMBRIDGE POLICE

AFTER LIEUTENANT JOYCE WROTE TO the Mitchells in 1979, hoping to follow up on Lee Parsons's alleged confession, Don wasted very little time getting back to him. Apart from a letter in December 1969, they hadn't been in touch in the ten years since Jane's death, but Lieutenant Joyce's discretion and thoroughness had long ago earned Don's trust. The difference between Joyce and the Cambridge cops whom the Mitchells dealt with during those initial heady days of the investigation couldn't have been more stark. Don still remembered some of those moments with the kind of flashbulb clarity that trauma induces.

After the relative calm of the first day of interrogations with the Cambridge Police, the subsequent sessions had been relentless. One time, officers came over to their University Road building and separated Don and Jill to interrogate them simultaneously. They questioned Jill in Jane's room, close enough to the still-bloody bed that she immediately felt lightheaded. "You killed her, you killed her. C'mon, you're going to tell us," one officer baited.

Meanwhile, in Don's room, an officer shouted at him, "You were fucking her, you were fucking her! We *know* you were fucking her! That's why you killed her."

Jill cried.

"It lasted forever but it was probably like fifteen or twenty minutes, maybe not even," Don would later remember. "When Jill came back in she said, 'I almost told them, "Yeah I killed her." Anything to make them stop.'"

Another time, when Don was alone with interrogators at headquarters, an officer opened up a manila folder. Inside were eight-by-ten prints. The officer fanned them out on the table and slid them over, forcing Don to look. "Here is your friend. Is this her skull?" Don didn't want to see. "Look at these! Look at these! Did you do this?" Jane's scalp had been flayed to expose the cracks in the back of her skull from the attack. The whole region behind where Jane's left ear would have been was busted in and deformed. "It was shocking and disgusting and beyond saddening."

The Mitchells felt their vulnerability acutely. "Harvard may not quite have thrown me and my wife under the bus but they didn't back us up," Don would later remember. Stephen Williams "was busy trying to deflect any suspicion from anybody connected with the museum," but the Mitchells, as lowly graduate students, didn't seem to count as worthy of protection. Only Professor Bill Howells, Don's former adviser, stuck his neck out for them. He called to ask if there was anything he could do and offered to put them up in a hotel at his own expense if they needed. He said reassuringly, "We'll get through it."

The relentlessness of the scrutiny felt all the more unbearable in juxtaposition with what seemed to the Mitchells to be police incompetence. Jane's apartment hadn't been secured in the weeks after her murder, which meant Don and Jill could go in and out as they pleased.

One of those times—perhaps the same day they had gone into Jane's place to pick out the outfit she was to be buried in at her parents' request—Don noticed something on the wall of Jane's apartment. Red powder, as if someone had stood at the foot of her bed, with a handful of dust, and winged it at the wall. There was a center portion that was slightly more dense, and a spray that climbed up the wall. He hadn't noticed it the day that he found Jane because tunnel vision had kicked in. Now he couldn't unsee it, and he was certain that it wasn't an accident. He immediately called the police and left a message to say what he had seen, in case they, too, had missed it the first day. He didn't know if it was just a coincidence that news broke about the red ochre the next day.

During another visit, they noticed that the gravestone in Jane's room—a relic, some later speculated, from an undergraduate class that studied the colonial headstones at Plimoth Plantation—had been moved. Jane normally kept it by her coffee table, not by the bed where they now saw it. It looked, Don thought, like the killer had taken the stone and placed it by the bed to make it a burial.

And during yet another visit—this time when they had gone in to feed Jane's turtle Sargon—Jill saw at the bottom of the murky tank, soupy with algae, a teardrop-shaped Acheulean hand ax, completely free of vegetation. It looked like it had just been cleaned. It was about six inches long, and made of flint, and was the sort of tool that was common across Africa and Europe during the Old Stone Age. The Mitchells were certain they had not gifted this ax to Jane, if this was the same archaeological tool that had been reported missing after her murder.

Don looked down at the carpet in front of the turtle tank. It was beige and there was a "lunate" bloodstain on it, the curve of which exactly matched the line of the hand ax. He flashed back to the autopsy photographs the police had forced him to look at. In one of them, she'd had a superficial gash on her forehead, which authorities told Don hadn't killed her, but probably knocked her out.

A reconstruction of what happened to Jane that night suddenly seemed so obvious to Don that it felt like a "bad joke." Jane knew her killer and had let him in. Some argument erupted and the killer struck her across the forehead with the curved part of the hand ax and ripped a flap of skin. She fell, face-first, unconscious on the rug. The fatal blows to the back of her head were struck with another, sharper instrument, and at some point her body was moved to the bed where the killer covered her up, moved the gravestone, threw ochre around, cleaned the hand ax, and left.

Don was outraged by how elementary the solution seemed. It reinforced his suspicion that the Cambridge cops were either dumb or incompetent. "This is third-grade stuff! It's so third grade, I can't help thinking that they must have known that, and maybe it was the kind of thing that they keep quiet so only the killer would know. But if they're going to do that, then don't leave the apartment open. Take the rugs."

The Mitchells shared all this with Lieutenant Joyce—the worries about the lack of crime scene security, Don's sense that the Cambridge PD was leaky and sloppy, his hand ax theory, his suspicion about Lee Parsons—because they felt like he was on their team. Though Lieutenant Joyce never came straight out and said that the Cambridge Police were incompetent, he certainly gave the Mitchells the impression that he knew where they were coming from.

That sympathy gave Don the courage to share one more detail about the investigation that had always given him pause. One day, not long after Jane's funeral, a police officer returned, by himself, to the Mitchells' place. Don couldn't remember his name—but he was a youngish guy. Perhaps it was Detective Giacoppo, who had dusted the apartment for fingerprints the first day. According to the *Boston Globe*, Giacoppo had found matches for all the prints in Jane's apartment, except one set.

The officer asked Don if he could go next door with him to photograph a fingerprint in Jane's apartment. Don thought to himself, *Don't they have people to do this stuff?* But he said nothing and picked up his camera and close-up lens and walked into Jane's apartment with the officer. They went to the kitchen, and the officer pointed to the fingerprint in question. It looked like a bloody stamp, large enough that Don thought a thumb might have left it. The print was on the glass of the window in Jane's kitchen, by the fire escape that led out into the courtyard.

Don took a number of photos and then the cop asked Don to develop the negatives for him. *I'll have to go with you*, the cop said. Don agreed, thinking maybe it was a chain of custody, police procedure kind of thing.

Don's darkroom was in the basement of Professor Irven DeVore's house. The setup was no bigger than where he had been interrogated by police. As Don pulled the roll out of his camera and prepared the developing solution and the fixer, the officer nosed around the place. Around his studio, Don had clipped some of the photos he was most proud of. In the red light of the developing bulb, everything looked a little bit dead and monochromatic.

"Is that Jane?" the officer asked, pointing to a high-contrast, grainy portrait. "Yeah," Don said. He had asked Jane to pose for a series a few years ago, when she was a junior at Radcliffe. Jane normally hated having her picture taken, but she could be very photogenic when she wanted. There was an intimacy in the picture. Her hair dusted her shoulders, and her gaze had the same beseeching quality as in Arthur Bankoff's version of the Tepe Yahya photo.

February 1966 photo of Jane, from the same series as the one hanging in Don's darkroom.

"And there's my wife over there," Don said, pointing to another photo he had hung up, so the officer wouldn't get the wrong idea.

Don handed the officer the prints, the negatives, and the whole roll of Ektachrome slide film. "We'll have this developed," the officer said.

Weeks went by and Don didn't hear anything. "I just assumed they wanted to see my darkroom," Don justified to himself. And when curiosity got the better of him, Don finally followed up with police. "Whose fingerprint was it?" he asked. *Jane's*, the cops said. *Don't worry about it.*

———

After Don had received Lieutenant Joyce's letter, written just after the tenth anniversary of Jane's death, Don telephoned his friend Gene Ogan to try to pin down the rumor that Lee Parsons had confessed. Gene still hadn't gotten back to him by the time Don replied to Lieutenant Joyce:

About a year or perhaps even two years ago, a friend of ours [Gene] told us on the telephone that he had heard from a colleague of his (in the same anthropology department) that that second anthropologist had heard that Lee Parsons had told yet a third person something to the effect that he had killed someone. That's a long chain. Our friend was going to try to get something more on it, but he never progressed very far. The chain involved someone who he regarded as hard to get next to, someone who he was reluctant to ask about it.

Only later did Don find out that the first person in the confession chain was an archaeologist named Dennis Puleston. He had died on expedition six months before Lieutenant Joyce even caught wind of the rumor. Puleston had been standing on a pyramid at the ancient site of Chichen Itza in Mexico when he was struck by lightning.

FINAL DAYS IN HAWAII

BACK ON DON'S COUCH, WE ran through some of the other topics I wanted to cover—his grand jury testimony, his hand-drawn blueprint of Jane's apartment—but, even though our remaining time together had dwindled, I didn't feel rushed. I was certain that our conversations would continue long after I left the Big Island. The only thing I still needed to do was listen to the piece that Jane had played at his and Jill's wedding: Bach's Toccata in F Major. Don had told me that after Jane's death, when he and Jill got home from Bougainville, he would get drunk and put on that record. He still put it on when he was thinking of her. I wanted to watch him listening to it.

We tried it on his laptop, but the bass wasn't powerful enough to replicate the experience. "You lose everything without the low note." So we walked into his office and stood as it played on his speakers. It was an impressive piece—baroque, eerie, powerful—an accomplishment simply to play. For almost eight minutes, we were held, spellbound. I thought I could see Don's eyes tearing up, but I didn't know if I just imagined it. I wanted to be able to dissolve into the scene, but I couldn't picture where Jane was.

"If this is where the minister is, then the organ is up there," he said, pointing above and behind us.

I turned around as if she were actually behind me. "Oh, so you couldn't see Jane. No one could see Jane."

"No one could see Jane unless they turned around to look at her, no. She's just sitting on top of everyone else."

"Do you picture her playing it when you hear—" I began to ask.

"I don't picture anything," Don said. It was more that he felt her life and death. Listening to it, Don said—especially the descending notes at the end— "That's when I come closest to screaming: *Why the fuck did this happen?*"

ERASURE AND ARTIFACTS

AFTER I LEFT DON MITCHELL, I met a friend in Phoenix so we could drive to Santa Fe, where former Peabody director Stephen Williams now lived. I knew Stephen was suffering from dementia—an erasure of a different kind—but I just wanted to be in the same room as him. As we drove through the rusty, Martian landscape of the American Southwest, it was impossible to ignore that we were surrounded by mountains of red ochre.

From the parking lot outside our hotel at the Grand Canyon, I found enough cell reception to talk to Michael Coe, the Maya scholar who had written Lee Parsons's obituary. It was the day after his eighty-eighth birthday; he had been out celebrating till 1 a.m. in Chinatown the night before. I told him that I was writing about Jane Britton and—delicately—added that I had heard Lee and Jane were acquaintances. "I knew Lee very well," he told me. "He was a good friend of mine. And he got sort of accused by some of his contemporaries of having perpetrated that."

Michael and Lee met as Harvard anthropology graduate students in the late '50s. Though Lee was already married, Michael said he might have always known that Lee was bisexual. Lee was a "wonderful guy" and a "very good archaeologist" but it always seemed like something was "bothering him or tearing him."

Michael volunteered that Lee and Jane Britton had dated, but he was certain that Lee had nothing to do with Jane's death. The dynamics of the department made it all too easy to suspect him. He was awkward, shy, Midwest-earnest in a department defined by the trappings of the New England elite. And though there had been at least one openly gay professor in the department, Harvard's atmosphere was far from tolerant. (Andrew Tobias, class of '68, described the experience of being homosexual at Harvard at the time: "We simply repressed it or faked it or lived in terror until some time after graduation.")

Plus, he was already on rocky footing when Jane died. The position he had been hired for never materialized, largely because Lee and Stephen never got along. It was a "grim time" when Stephen was head of the department, Michael said. "He's still alive so I don't want to say anything libelous here. But he was not our favorite person by a long, long, long shot. He was a perfectly awful director." And since Lee was already out of favor with the leadership of the department when the crime happened, and there were murmurs that he and Jane had been seeing each other, it was easy to scapegoat the lonely, awkward man. "You know he was the number one suspect at one point." Only toward the end of Lee's life did Michael ever see Lee somewhat settled in himself. Lee and his partner—"a very smart young Black man" whose name Michael could no longer recall—had come to visit him and his wife. "I think he was happy."

Michael had to get off the phone to take some medication, and when we reached each other again, my reception was swallowed up by the Grand Canyon. We never talked about the alleged confession. Or what happened to Stephen Edward DeFilippo, Lee's partner in St. Louis. As with Jane, the more I learned about Lee, the less I felt like I knew him. If Karl was a master storyteller, Lee was a master at disappearing. Despite how well they knew each other, Michael had told me, he had no pictures of Lee.

———

The road trip continued through the millennia-old great houses and petroglyphs of Chaco Canyon and the ruins of Pecos Pueblo. When my friend and I finally got to Santa Fe, we drove up the gravel roads to Stephen Williams's house. The Williamses weren't expecting me. I walked onto his property, looking for a front doorbell. I crossed the driveway, went through their backyard, and passed what seemed like a guesthouse. This felt like much more of an invasion than I had hoped.

Finally, I got to what might be the front door and rang the buzzer. An older woman, dressed in the manner I'd become familiar with at Harvard—elegant, but casual; her hair blond and bobbed—answered the door. It was Stephen's wife of fifty-five years, Eunice Williams. She invited me in and made an appointment for me to come back and meet him the next day. But in a moment of impromptu generosity, she added that he was eating his supper in the next room, and that I was welcome to say a quick hello. I was tempted, but I didn't want to disturb him. I told her I would see them both tomorrow.

But she called the next morning. It wasn't a good time. The next day wasn't good, either. It was never the right time. My flight to California took off before I got any closer to him than I had been that first day. I would never get the chance. Dan Potts emailed me two weeks later with the news that he had died.

————

I got off the train in San Jose where Elisabeth Handler, Jane's best friend at Radcliffe, tall and thin with perfectly manicured nails, stood waiting for me outside her parked car. I liked to imagine that Jane would have been similarly stubborn about aging.

Elisabeth, who handled public relations for the city, suggested lunch at a downtown crêperie. She said she didn't know anything about Lee Parsons, but found it plausible that Jane and Lee had dated. "I wouldn't be surprised at all if Jane had figured out that there were advantages to her to being sexually available, like—*who gets into what seminar, who goes on digs?* You know? That was currency. It still is. But it was much more understood that that's part of being a successful woman—using sex to lift you up."

Elisabeth told me that her section leader, Karl Heider, had made a pass at her during his office hours. He sat next to her on the couch and extended his arm on the back of the seat, leaving it to rest around her shoulders. It wasn't that Elisabeth didn't like him. She found him attractive, but acting on it felt too dangerous. She left his office. Over the years, Elisabeth would replay that moment many times. The scene still made her cringe, but sometimes she blamed herself for not knowing how to "carry it off."

"I think women really had the sense that somehow no matter what the outcome of an advance, that we were at fault. That somehow we either brought it on ourselves or we didn't handle it right or it was bad of us not to want to accommodate it or bad of us to want to. You know? No matter what the outcome was, there was always the sense that it was kind of a moral failing on the woman's part."

She invited me back to her house after lunch and showed me pictures of her family. The middle name of her eldest daughter was Jane. As she stood in the kitchen, and I sat by the counter, we talked about Jane's secret-keeping, and Elisabeth's creeping suspicion that Jane was also a storyteller, an embroiderer. Her life had always seemed so much more dramatic than anyone else's. Jane made it seem like she had fourteen boyfriends at once. Elisabeth never felt like it was her place to question the stories. She got the sense that Jane needed them. Elisabeth told me that Jane would disappear for days on end in college. She would close the blinds, exclude the world. "I have the sense that she was battling demons."

Before I left, Elisabeth handed me the contact sheet of her wedding photographs where Jane was her maid of honor, and the blue aerogram paper of a letter Jane sent her from Iran. "It's literally the happiest I ever heard her to be," Elisabeth said. "You can have this."

I looked at her hesitatingly, unwilling to take the original of the last letter from her best friend.

"It's the record. You should have the record," she insisted. "I know what artifacts mean to you, and to this story."

JANE'S LETTER TO ELISABETH

Saturday 27 July 1968

Dear [Ensign +] Mrs. Ozawa—you can show it to him if you want

I understand you're making a splash amongst the social set of gay exotic greater Needham. Fine stuff but isn't it a bit heady? Don't parades really grab you? I'm in off the site this afternoon, having strategically blown lunch + been grepsing (belch if you don't speak Yiddish) all aft. PEW. All the khan's wives, sisters + aunts are staring in the door of our chic thatch hut because Mrs. H. Arthur Bankoff just fainted. They all think she's pregnant, ha-ha-ha. (She ain't.) Did you get my first letter, E? The one with the NEWS—or maybe my parents told you. Essentially, I will repeat; you remember the large Canadian?

  HE LOVES ME

  Fancy that. That + the night sky are about the only two saving graces about this place. September-December are going to be hell (Jim's going off to

Baluchistan) and I'd stay drunk the entire time if I didn't have to study for
generals. I am getting very skinny since meals around here are a real ratfuck.
Also malnourishing. When I think that a month and a half ago I was having
tournedos at the Savoy my tum rebels even further. [. . .] Known him well 5
months + he does stuff like, walks to Covent Garden 530AM + wakes me at 7
with an armload of flowers. [. . .] There's only one fly in the ointment:

> *James is 26*
> *James' father is 80*
> *James' father's father was 62 when James' father was born.*

Bodes ill—like I told parents, I'll probably waste my youth on this chap
only to have him run off with some sweet young thing because I'll be too old to
have kids. SIGH. Maybe he'll break precedent, though (hope, hope.) NB—do
not ever buy a small camp bed. They are DANGEROUS and bend at a weight
of precisely 320 pounds. UGH. I smell onions frying BLEUGHH, 3 others sick,
in here + farting up a storm. Pleasant, no.

Nothing else to say except hang loose + have a pastrami sandwich, ginger-
bread with whipped cream, a Hershey bar, chocolate malt, cheeseburger, steak
+ baked potato with sour cream, Brigham's sundae, quart of milk, + a cup of
real coffee for me.

Best + cheers,
J
> *P.S. I should be home about 20 Sept—you be around?*

BOYD IN PERSON

THE DOORBELL OF MY COUSINS' house in Los Angeles rang before I was
expecting it to. I ran out of the side gate, and there Boyd was—short and a
little heavyset, his gray hair combed back—facing the main entrance.

"Hello!" I said, louder than I normally would, to draw his attention.

He turned toward me, and I was caught off guard by the intensity of
seeing Jane's face in his. I didn't think I knew Jane's face that well, but the

familiarity of Boyd's could only be explained by the fact that I knew hers in some fundamental way—the roundness, the button tip of the nose, the impish grin. He was wearing a black button-down and a clerical collar.

"It's nice to meet you!" he said, more cheerfully than I'd expected. "I got here a little early—can't trust the 405."

He climbed into his silver-gray Nissan and reached over to unlock my door. "This is the cheapest car you can buy with air-conditioning," he said, still a little out of breath from the exertion, "and one of the ways you can keep the cost down is one keyhole." I took my seat and tried to ignore the mysterious itch on my legs that started the second I got into the car. *No-see-ums*, I later learned—biting flies so small they're nearly invisible.

His life was radically different from the comfortable one he had grown up in, where they stayed in the Plaza on every trip to New York. A wooden cross hung from his rearview mirror. "Forgive the costume," he said. "I would not have dressed this way but for the fact that I have to work tonight."

The plan was to drive up to Santa Barbara, where he was the vicar for the Anglican Church of Our Savior. It was a midweek service for Ascensiontide, Boyd explained, to mark forty days after Easter—the second of three Christian miracles, when Jesus ascended after his resurrection.

It was a two-hour ride, and we settled into the rhythm I had become familiar with from our phone calls. I would ask a question, and he'd monologue for minutes at a time. It was both of our most natural states. He reminded me of a character in an S. J. Perelman story: formal and wry and belonging to a different time. "Burying the needle," he'd say about testing how fast his father's Chrysler would go. The wit, the vocabulary, the references to famous people and plays and books I'd never heard of but felt too ashamed to admit. "Let all the poisons that lurk in the mud hatch out," he bellowed. I nodded. It kept me off balance. I had the impression that some of it was for my benefit—a kind of performance to impress me with his cleverness—and some of it was just to keep him entertained, since maybe my timid questions weren't doing the trick. Most of all, though, it left little space for vulnerability and reflection. Boyd was never going to let himself play the role of the grieving brother that was expected of him.

"You'll find me, if I live long enough, out in Barstow in the state veterans' home, a cranky old man who can't feel his feet. Now I wake up every morning, a bit annoyed that God hasn't done it overnight."

We talked sometimes about Jane, but mostly about everything else.

Trump. LA's war on homelessness. His childhood. "None of these people were bad. But people can wind up being bad for one another." His poor track record with women. There was the married stripper, the spokesmodel, and the quart-a-day alcoholic. The "Bipolar Bear." The one who woke up from a coma and thought she was "Almighty God." The Mormon. The one with the dog that was half coyote. Maybe the last two were the same. His favorite story was about bringing home his stripper girlfriend to meet his parents. Boyd's mother took him aside and said, trying to be encouraging, "We think Judith is very nice. Do you want my diamonds?" "No," Boyd said. "Her husband thinks she's very nice, too."

We talked about his addiction history—at the height of his DJ years he drank, did coke and meth—and getting sober. His return to faith. He was forthcoming, but not sentimental. I felt I needed to ask him three questions about anything else to earn myself one question about Jane. And when he did speak about her, there was sometimes a fondness, but little softness. I asked if Jane reminded him of Dorothy Parker, as Elisabeth had said. "There were the out-of-place romances and the out-of-place intellectual, but Dottie Parker had a productive talent. My sister really did not."

The closest Boyd got to admitting how much her death affected him was when he relayed a dream he'd had after she died. He was with his parents when Jane showed up. "I was trying to say in the dream, 'Why is she here?' and everybody said, 'We don't talk about that.' We didn't talk about what happened between us, and we didn't talk about why she was back to life."

We drove toward the ocean and then along it, two hours up the coast to Ventura and beyond.

———

"Here we are, La Colina." We were in the parking lot of a Catholic high school.

He got out of the car and walked around to my side to open the door. Then he grabbed his binder of sermons from the backseat and brushed his hair with a pocket comb. For the past few years, he'd suffered from neuropathy, which made the tips of his fingers and toes tingle, so he walked carefully. He pulled out the key to the chapel, and we entered a room with wall-to-wall mauve carpeting and mauve chairs for pews and mauve kneeling blocks.

The altar was made of rose-colored marble. The room smelled vaguely like incense. We walked past the pews to a hallway beyond.

"Am I allowed to come in here?" I asked.

He said yes. It was a small room, about the size of a pantry. He pulled out a loose-fitting white robe from the closet. It's called a cotta, he said. "Since I was known as The Leakin' Deacon by the amount I perspire, I talked the bishop into letting me wear this somewhat lighter garment."

He unwrapped a large gold cup. The chalice. "This is called the purificator," he said, pointing to a small white linen cloth, which he folded carefully in thirds. "This is the paten"—a shallow plate—"and then we put on top of it, the pall." He demonstrated by covering the plate with the stiff cover.

It struck me how much Jane would have liked all this. All the vocabulary, the symbols, the hidden meanings. She wasn't religious, but on the ride up Boyd had told me that Jane loved Roman Catholic mass because it was so full of ritual.

In another world, where Jane was still alive, she would have just gone through her own ritual: her fiftieth reunion for Radcliffe. Instead of the cotta, Jane would have worn her own robe—the crimson-and-black stripes of a doctorate. She would be processing through Harvard Yard with the rest of the class of 1967. The thirtieth reunion students would join behind them, the twenty-fifth reunion behind that, and so on, until finally, the students of the class of 2017 rounded out the line. Then the bells would chime in the distance, and as the procession snaked around, the fiftieth reunion would end up parallel to the 2017 part of the line, and future and past would be standing next to each other. (Or, if we're being more realistic, Jane would have been in a rented convertible with Elisabeth Handler, blowing off the reunion entirely, heading to Revere Beach.)

———

We took the coastal highway back to LA, avoiding the back roads and agricultural lands of Ventura County.

Boyd described the pattern of his romantic life like this: "In my head, there was a bell, which basically was the bullshit alarm, and once it started ringing, you ignored it at your peril, and you couldn't shut it off. So that spoiled some relationships. And of course the other was the invisible sign, but I'm convinced it was there—flashing on and off like bright neon—it was very visible both to good and bad women. The good were prone to avoid it, the bad were raring to go. Because it says in *giant* letters, CHUMP. CHUMP. CHUMP." He could see the situation from the third person and yet was helpless to change it. Maybe part of him didn't want to. With the wrong women, at least there was always "the escape clause," as he called it. He could always say it had been doomed from the start.

And then, Boyd's facade cracked for a moment: "The one thing I miss, or never got enough of, is a rare and precious quality in a relationship, and that's tenderness. A trust, a feeling that nothing is a threat. The feeling that no demands are being made. There are no expectations. You like it the way it is."

My heart dropped a bit. I knew that quiet feeling of happiness he was describing because I so longed for it. I had felt a version of it with Jay. He had seen all the shards of myself that I usually only let people see a fraction of at any given moment—and he held them. But it made me ache all the more with the desire to be loved by someone whom I loved in turn.

"And the real heartbreaking part of the story, well I mean it's all heartbreaking, but the part that just adds an extra edge of horror to it is that she had really found a good guy," I heard Elisabeth saying to me. Jane had found tenderness. The flowers at 5:30 a.m. in London. Their cots pulled next to each other in the Iranian desert. *"She was really happy for the first time."*

Finally, after more than seven hours together, Boyd voluntarily turned the conversation to Jane's murder.

"As I think about it now, my two questions are always the same: Who did it?...And, would she have been happy? Perhaps because my own deal with happiness is that it's overrated—I find it in little pieces, in little moments, not in the grand plan—I don't think she would have been...People did not satisfy her expectations very well."

He turned on his headlights as we headed into the hills of LA to my cousins' house. I asked if he would be willing to see me again before I left the city. He was unwilling to pin down a date but also didn't say no.

"It'd be nice to look at any family photos or letters you still had, if you wouldn't mind sharing," I added.

"If I can find them," he said. "I might have been in a to-hell-with-my-past mood and ditched a bunch of it." All he had now, he said, was probably one letter from Jane in Iran, and his mother's travel journal from their 1960 European tour.

He parked in my cousins' driveway. "We'll figure something out," he said, softening a bit. He let me out of the car, and I thanked him for the day. The car door failed to shut tightly behind me.

"Slam it hard," Boyd said, and the moment was over.

FAMILY SILENCE

AFTER JANE DIED, BOYD TRIED to settle back into life in Needham. It had always been a quiet, stiff house, but now it was insufferably so. Nobody talked about what had happened. His father went back to work at Radcliffe and fielded parents' concerns about their daughters' safety. He would not mention his own daughter in his replies to them. His mother was consumed with grief. "Everything was gloomy. Everything was involved with her pain, and everything was involved with her still feeling that nothing was ever right." Boyd felt completely suffocated. There was no room to move.

Though Jane's parents were high-profile enough to make sure their daughter's murder was fully investigated, their carefully tended status in that elite society depended on upholding those institutions. Whatever their private beliefs may have been, they let their silence speak for them instead: The police would get it solved; Harvard was innocent.

Jane's father, J. Boyd, had gotten the job at Radcliffe in the first place because the Cabots of Cabot Corporation were on the board of Harvard. When they heard that J. Boyd had gotten a hernia shoveling snow, and was going to have to retire from Cabot Corp., they told him not to worry. J. Boyd, who had no experience in academia, was suddenly the vice president of one of the best colleges in the country.

Boyd knew the rich took care of their own. He also knew that *as long as you don't embarrass them* was the unspoken second half of that sentence.

Jane's father may have been well connected to the upper crust of Boston, but he wasn't *of* that class. He had been *invited* in. J. Boyd had grown up in St. Louis, Missouri, and for a time he played the banjo in dance bands on the riverboats. He had worked his way up Cabot Corporation, first in sales, then management. He married a woman in Springfield, Illinois, and had two children, Charlie and Susan. Susan was born with cerebral palsy. He had just divorced Charlie and Susan's mother when he met Ruth Reinert on a business trip to California. She was from a wealthier family in Wisconsin and was teaching at Scripps. They soon married, and she moved with him to Massachusetts.

The social self-consciousness of the Brittons couldn't be exaggerated. After Boyd embarrassed them by leaving Princeton for the second time and announced that he was going to head to California to work in radio, they told him to call up a guy in Watertown. The next thing Boyd knew, he was taking a physical exam for the army. While other parents were doing everything they could to keep their children out of Vietnam, the Brittons had cleared all the paperwork for him.

Boyd's deployment was scheduled for late November 1968. His parents took him to the airport. J. Boyd shook his hand. "I hope they send you to the peace talks," he said. His mother burst into tears. Boyd couldn't remember if Jane came to the airport. The goodbye that made the biggest impression on Boyd was a hug from Jane's Dana Hall friend Tess Beemer, whom he happened to run into in the Square just before setting off. Tess would remember the hug fifty years later, too. "Oh my goodness, I haven't had a hug like that..." Tess remembered Boyd had said. She trailed off.

Boyd stayed with friends in San Francisco waiting for his flight number to come up. The morning he left Oakland for Vietnam, the Byrds' "You Ain't Goin' Nowhere" kept playing on the radio.

Then, just three months later, Boyd was back in Needham. His family had called in some favors and gotten him compassionate reassignment. But Boyd had had no say in that decision; it was made because sending him back to war would further devastate his mother. Once again, Boyd felt like a puppet.

Now, not only was their daughter dead, but if they pushed for investigation, there was the indignity of her reputation being besmirched in death and the risk of being thrown out by the elite circles that formed their community. As Elisabeth said, "I had the feeling they would almost have preferred not to know what happened."

———

The silence became its own kind of poison.

Boyd got the "one job I never wanted," handing out posthumous medals to the families of soldiers killed in Vietnam. One woman lived in a brick basement apartment in Southie. He had to tell her that her only son was gone. She never stopped weeping. Another family up in Andover had so many kids, it seemed like they barely noticed the loss.

Boyd was so eager to get out of town he even put in some long-distance calls to Saigon to reserve a slot for himself on Armed Forces Network radio. Going back to war was preferable to staying in Needham. One night, the suffocation finally became too much. "Nothing's ever going to be right," he screamed. "I have no purpose in being here because I can't make it right." Boyd stormed away from the dinner table, and he left for the West Coast as soon as he could. "If anything I regret having done in my life, it was having had no other way to deal with my mother than to get the hell away from her," Boyd reflected.

A couple of years after Jane's death, Ruth developed cancer. "Her end was deeply sad," Boyd would remember. She had been a lifelong smoker, but Boyd was absolutely certain that heartbreak was to blame. Doctors operated to take out the lung tumor, but they botched the surgery and left her in permanent pain. It was unrelievable except with strong opiates. The cancer came back as a metastasized tumor on her brain, the "size and shape of a small pancake," which caused dementia.

"She continued to decline physically, medically, mentally for the next eight years and I stayed away. I didn't want any part of it. 'I'm sorry you're dying. I'm sorry you're unhappy. But you never were happy that I remember much about. Sorry I disappointed you.'"

Boyd's father, in contrast, rarely left her hospital bedside. He did needlepoint and waited for the end. Ruth's one request was that he never put her in a nursing home, and J. Boyd had gone through a great deal of trouble to make sure she had hospital care for her final days. But one day, the community hospital where Ruth was being taken care of told J. Boyd that she would have to be moved. They'd lose their Medicare accreditation if they kept taking care of a terminal patient. He reluctantly drove her to the nicest nursing home he could find. It was in Wellesley. He checked her in and then briefly went back to the hospital to get her sweater and other belongings. By the time he returned, she was dead.

FOR BOYD R. BRITTON FROM JBB

BOYD CALLED ME THE MORNING of our second scheduled meeting. I thought he was going to cancel, and my heart dropped. But it was just to say that he couldn't find his mother's journal.

I arrived at the café first, and from my table, a few minutes later, I saw Boyd struggling up the sidewalk. He was trying to balance a giant file box, a bursting manila envelope, and a picture frame. I rushed over to him. "I've got some goodies," he said, mischievously, knowing he had dramatically undersold the treasure he was about to show me.

We sat down, and I noted the manila folder said in big black Sharpie: "Jane Britton Murder Files. Other Family Papers." He filled the table with the contents of the file box, which was torn and retaped at the seams; "For Boyd R. Britton From JBB," it read on the spine—J. Boyd Britton. His parents had compiled this archive of Jane: her Radcliffe commencement program, the picture books she used to draw, all the letters she wrote back home from her digs. Childhood photos. Her funeral book.

I tried multiple ways of asking if it was hard for him to look at this stuff. He deflected by addressing his writing we found in the file. "Some of the things I'd forgotten I'd done."

I took pictures of everything as he pulled them out of the file, not wanting to lose these artifacts that only minutes before I thought had long since been erased. He looked at me funny. "I'm turning the box over to you," Boyd said. I didn't know if I understood him correctly. "There's no time like the present, and there's no time at the present to see all this." He told me to make a copy and give it back to him one day. The only thing he asked was for me to replace the ratty box that the files had lived in for the last fifty years.

I wanted to cry at the generosity of his gesture. Nothing could have meant more in that moment. He even opened the picture frame to give me a picture that Jim Humphries had taken of Jane in Iran so I could make a proper scan.

We walked to the parking lot after lunch, and I thanked him for trusting me with Jane's story and her letters. "Well, you have impressed people that you're trustworthy. Mitchell especially. Elisabeth said words to the effect: 'She's charming, so I hope she's trustworthy.' Well, not quite those words. Her implication was that she enjoyed talking with you. As have I."

He emptied a large garbage bag that had been sitting in the back of his car and handed it to me to keep the file box safe, a rare hint of sentimentality. I thanked him again. "That's okay. I'm not exactly busy first of all. And second of all, this means a lot."

JANE BRITTON FAMILY FILES

I UNDID THE CRUMBLING RUBBER bands holding together the bundles of Jane's letters as soon as I got back to New York. Many of them were written in ink, double-sided on onionskin. It would take me ages to decipher, but there she was. More of her than I ever dreamed still existed.

She was bold, witty, warm. "Can't say I mind contemplating getting married. But then I also don't mind contemplating the pizza I'm going to have when I get home," she wrote to her parents from Movius's excavation. There was so much of her, it overflowed to the back of the envelopes: she'd draw herself as a guinea pig holding the French flag, or she'd complain about licking the letter closed. "Pew! Peppermint-flavored envelopes." Other times, she'd scrawl: "Greetings to the postman from Gay, Exotic Les Eyzies."

There it all was. Jane, the summer after her sophomore year at college, congratulating her father on getting the job at Radcliffe. Report cards dating back to junior high school. A cartoon of Karl Heider, Elisabeth's section leader, as a bird whose main attribute was "deceptive mating habits."

Jane's caption reads: "The Greater Fuzzy-Thinking Heider. Deceptive + not very benevolent. Peculiar mating habits. Call: uh, uh, well, uh."

There was her parents' collection of files on Jane's murder: The UPI and the New York tabloid articles that I had come to know so well. The telegram that Boyd's parents had sent him in Vietnam. His orders for emergency leave. The *Needham Times* funeral announcement. The signatures of the attendees at her funeral. Karl. Martie. Stephen and Eunice Williams. Jim Humphries. The Mitchells.

There were also the things I didn't know to expect, like the package of Tepe Yahya articles that Karl had sent to Jane's father just before Christmas 1979. And his cover letter that read: "Jane would have been pleased to see the importance of the work emerge; the more so as she would have become a major contributor to its success." There were no hints as to how that exchange came to be. "If there is more I can do please call upon me. Warmest regards in this Christmas season," Karl ended his letter. He had underlined her name in one of the articles he sent over.

I saved Jane's letters for last. I wanted to study them in preparation for the meeting that Karl had promised me when I got back east.

I typed her letters as I read them. I loved the feeling of her words coming through my fingers. The letters had doubled as her diary entries—she told her parents to save them for her for that reason—and whatever her relationship to her parents may have been, she poured herself onto those pages. Perhaps the hunger for human contact on the digs had grown stronger than her worry about what she was revealing. It took me almost a week to type them all up, and it induced a somewhat hallucinatory state. I laughed out loud at her fifty-year-old jokes. I started writing my own emails like her. It felt a lot like love—a confusing mix of admiring her, devouring her, inhabiting her, emulating her, channeling her, and thinking I was her.

Dearest Muddah, Dahlink Faddah, here I am at—Verroia animal farm and how the Hell do I stop people calling me "Fangface"?

I wouldn't want to do anything if I wasn't going to do it very close to superbly.

Did I ever tell you after that amazing dinner Jim carried me across Russell Square . . .

Had a letter from Bwad (pre-Cal) who was going stir-crazy + helping me plot revenge on Franquemont (*which whole story may no one ever know, InshAllah) and I guess he has us both pegged, having said, "We may not be famous for running our lives very well, but nobody is gonna F___ WITH THE BRITTONS (wurf-wurf!)" The way I figure it, some people are natural predators + others are natural victims + we fall some-where in between, not having the guts to be the first nor the humility of the second.

And then, in the middle of one of her 1965 letters, there was a reference to Jerry Roth, that mystery person whose untraceability had planted the seed for me that Jane might be an unreliable narrator. "In case my last letter missed you," Jane wrote to her parents, "Jerry Roth is a geology major from Maine, son of Henry Roth who wrote 'Call it Sleep.'"

The son of *Henry* Roth, not Philip Roth as Elisabeth and Boyd had remembered. Jane hadn't been lying after all. It was just another detail lost in a game of telephone.

The feelings hit me in waves. At first, I was relieved that even if I could never know everything about her, some of her mysteries might have ends. I wrote to Boyd and Elisabeth. I knew they wondered, like I did, that if Jane had been lying about this, then what else wasn't true? This fact put a stop to that erosion for me, and I hoped it might offer them the same peace.

But then relief turned into tremendous guilt. I had doubted Jane. We had all doubted Jane. We were quicker to blame her than to open ourselves up to the faultiness of our memory, and I realized that this wasn't the only way that we had shifted the blame onto her. Even in the stories we told about what happened to her that night, in so many of the versions, *Jane* was the one at fault. *She* had an affair with Karl. *She* blackmailed someone. *She* angered someone.

Perhaps Jane's story was a morality tale in more ways than I had realized. Not only did it serve as a narrative check on someone with power, like Karl, who was seen as transgressing, it was also a way of cautioning against promiscuous, assertive behavior from someone in Jane's position: a female graduate student. Assigning guilt to the victim helped distance us from what happened to her; it wouldn't happen to us, as long as we stayed in check. But in so doing, we had unconsciously been perpetuating a story whose moral derived from the very patriarchal system we thought we were surmounting by telling the story in the first place.

I'm sorry.

LIE DETECTOR TEST

THE LIE DETECTOR MACHINE WAS the size of an old electric typewriter, and the output looked like an EKG. One line recorded Karl's breathing. The line below that registered sweat-gland activity. The bottom tracing was a record of his heart movements—the shunting of his aortic valve, the whooshing of his blood after each squeeze.

"What was fun about the lie detector test," he would remember decades later, is that "you can only answer yes or no. You can't tell a story."

Where were you the night of Jane's death, Lieutenant Joyce asked Karl. *Did you ever have a date with her? Did you have sexual intercourse with her?* "All these wonderful questions," Karl would say, remembering.

Karl could see the needle of the lie detector machine from where he was sitting. "What I suspected was the needle must have some kind of asymmetrical relationship to truth and lies. So the asymmetry would come out with the needle going like this"—he violently jerked his finger up and down, demonstrating decades later.

Karl kept a careful eye on the needle's movement as he answered the questions. None of the "telltale" ones about Jane threw the machine. "I would have really been through the roof." Instead, the needle stormed up and down in response to a question about Karl's own story. He had just answered "Yes" to the question "Were you born in Prague, Czechoslovakia?" when the needle started shaking. "Wait a minute!" Karl blurted out.

Karl's complicated relationship to his identity, it seemed, had made the truth register as a lie.

KARL IN PERSON

I RAN ACROSS HARVARD YARD to Church Street, but slowed to a walk a block short, so I wouldn't be out of breath by the time I reached Toscano where, under the brick arch of the restaurant, I saw Karl standing, waiting for me. It was the first time I had seen him since I sat in on his class five years before.

We sat down. We made small talk for a little bit, and he asked, coyly, "Have you found the killer?" I looked him straight in the eye and nodded. He looked at me searchingly—not ceding the power he had in the conversation, but recognizing that I might be playing my own cards. I admitted I was kidding.

"You do know that people talk about you having been involved," I said.

"Oh, sure," he said, as if I'd just asked him if he enjoys vacations.

The waiter came around and asked if we were ready. We hadn't even opened our menus. But Karl said yes, "I'm getting what I always have," and ordered—off menu—a plate of chicken livers and a beer. I scrambled.

We—he—talked for five hours. He was nearly eighty years old by that point, and still enviably lucid, but he dribbled occasionally when he got so involved in what he was saying that he forgot to close his mouth. It was especially disconcerting that his mouth was filled with organ meat when he did it. I had come into our meeting remorseful about my part in imprisoning him in a myth that he didn't deserve, but I could feel a part of me slip, against my better judgment, into the old suspicions as we spoke.

I asked if it was true that when police asked if he had been having an affair with Jane he said, "Why go out for a hamburger when you have steak at home?"

He chuckled. "It sounds like it could be me. I don't remember saying that, but it sounds as if it could be me."

When he spoke of the mystery of Jane's death, he said: "I must say long after the event, and even not long after the event, I was never captivated by it."

He brought up skiing. He talked about how he would go on trails where he knew that if one thing went wrong, he would die. I asked him if he had always felt invincible. He corrected me. Invincibility, he said, is the feeling someone has when they don't believe something could happen to them. He, on the other hand, fully knew that he *could* catch an edge and die—he just knew it *wouldn't* happen. "I was not invincible but I also knew that I wasn't vincible. I was arrogant."

Skiing, he said, was the one art he had truly mastered. "If you're an academic, you can go up on the podium and tell them anything. Right, wrong, indifferent, controversy, no controversy, this theory, that approach, this data, that data, et cetera et cetera. Big deal. You have to master skiing."

It felt like he was teasing me with the notion that any set of facts could conform to any narrative, if you chose to arrange it a certain way.

I realized how long I hadn't moved, pinned under his presence, so I got up to go to the bathroom. When I came back, he had a question for me.

"Becky, are you married?"

I was taken aback. Was he purposefully playing so squarely into his stereotype? I said I was not.

"If you're smart, you don't marry today," he said. Now that men and women think they're equal, marriage is all conflict and calculated compromise.

"Knowing what you know, would you have gotten married?" I asked.

"Sure," he said, "because I was lucky. I found the right girl." Martie went on all his digs and was his right-hand person at the Peabody Museum.

For a period in the '70s, he said, that wasn't enough for her. "I got tired of listening to her say, 'I'm a person in my own right.'"

"What happened?" I asked.

He didn't answer the question and instead praised her work overseeing the commissary and organizing the house staff on his digs and how gifted she was as his administrator. I felt up to the challenge of guiding this part of the conversation. "But when she was saying that she was a person in her own right, did she want to do something else with her life?"

"No, no. She was very happy to be a home-mom," he responded.

We talked about his father. Though Karl knew that some referred to his father as the "Conscience of Austria," he struggled to celebrate his father's moral stand. I wondered if a child could ever completely disentangle a parent's heroism from the resultant abandonment. Even so, Karl's indignance about his father's inviting death was striking: *Why couldn't he just trust that his family had been in power for thousands of years, and they'd be in power again? Why couldn't he just keep his mouth shut?*

We talked more about his childhood. I pressed him on Clifford A. Rockefeller, the seeming obsession with the name. He gave me two answers. He told me that his father's family name, Lamberg, had been kept off his passport to escape Austria. Then he said that one does not speak ill of one's mother. I said, okay, but why Rockefeller? He paused. "When you have a childhood like mine, identity is a little more fluid than it is for most." He added, "We all create ourselves. It doesn't make any difference who we are. We all create the person we think we are, pretend to be."

Someone had once told me that Karl knew what people said about him and played into it, wagering, perhaps, that he couldn't be buried under a rumor if he was its master narrator. Karl would later say, "The murder of Jane Britton...certainly was not something that gave me any machismo aspect at all." But in our meeting that day—as Karl oscillated between man and symbol before me—it felt like he wanted to show me that he could inhabit the role of villain better than anyone could write it for him.

WRESTLING

IT WAS WARM OUT. ABOUT half a dozen graduate students and Karl Lamberg-Karlovsky took their seats at Boston Garden, the arena next to North Station, for a professional wrestling match. They nearly filled a row. Boston wrestling fans were notoriously quick to erupt in violence, and the place simmered. It smelled like popcorn and pizza and alcohol. The match was scripted, everyone knew, but that was part of the fun.

Peter Timms, a graduate student and a friend of Jim Humphries, had organized the outing. His idea was to go to a prizefight, like in the Roaring '20s, but wrestling was the closest thing that Boston had.

When the lights came down for the match, John Yellen, another graduate student, was grateful. It got so dark in the arena—and the haze of the smoke made it even darker—that the crowd could hardly see that Peter had requested that they all dress in black tie. The lone woman in the group, in an evening gown, sported a gorilla mask. Karl wore a tuxedo and carried a cane with an ivory head.

They descended into the crowd like Cambridge lords, coming down among the common folk. Karl found it funny, as did Peter, but for John, who had grown up in deep Brooklyn, it was one of the most embarrassing nights of his life.

The match began. It was less sport than theater. Passionate. Grotesque. Performance. Pantomime. The wrestlers, for the minutes they were in the ring, were no longer mortals. They became avatars of human experience: anguish, triumph, justice. As literary theorist Roland Barthes wrote, "Wrestling presents human suffering with all the amplification of the tragic masks." The wrestlers played out our morality. And at Boston Garden, it was the same ancient myth enacted every time: The good defeated the bad.

At the end of the match, Karl walked down the stairs. He looked immense. He could feel the excitement of the crowd—there were still thousands in their seats—and waited for his moment like a magician. The promoter introduced him as Count Karlovsky, and Karl strutted around—a god, for that moment, flooded in light. He whacked his cane hard enough that the ivory head came tumbling off.

Part Five

THE ECHO

2018: LAND IN BOSTON

THE SUNRISE IN MIAMI DEVELOPS like a Polaroid—slowly and out of nothing. I scan the morning's *Boston Globe* headlines. There isn't anything, and I worry I've just imagined that they've cracked the case. What if Sennott is merely planning to announce that they were able to develop a profile? Or even less than that?

I'm in the last row of the plane, and we're on the tarmac. A loud sound, like an engine falling off, rattles everyone. The flight attendants behind me, despite their training, or maybe because they think no one can hear them, don't conceal their reaction. "Jesus Christ. What was that?" one says. "Thunder," another answers. The cabin gets bright from some unseen lightning bolt. *That would be fitting, wouldn't it,* I think morbidly.

———

The second my plane lands in Boston, just before noon, I check my phone. My hands are freezing again, and I haven't had an appetite in days. But there are still no headlines or texts or alerts. Only an email from Don saying he hasn't heard anything.

I make my way back to my little tree-house bedroom in Harvard Square, knowing that at this rate, barring an unannounced press conference, I won't hear anything until 4 p.m., when Sennott knows that Don will be back from the doctor. But beyond setting Twitter alerts for the Middlesex District Attorney's Office, I struggle to do anything productive. I force myself to eat lunch. I unpack, make some coffee. I try to write, but how can I when I don't yet know the ending? Three hours is nothing in the grand scheme of my years of waiting, but it's an incredible amount of time to watch tick by.

At my desk, I'm surrounded by my cork boards of index cards and pictures, all pinned up with dissection needles. There's a picture of one of the young men who accompanied Lee Parsons in Guatemala in January 1970. He's sliding down the canyon—lithe, with his shirt unbuttoned. There's Lee himself hunched over some mushroom stones in a museum, studying the artifacts, unaware of the camera. A few wisps of his dirty-blond bangs tumble over his glasses. Is that what his hair looked like as he lurched at Jane? Did his glasses stay on after the first blow? I can't make it work in my head.

Lee Parsons. (Courtesy of the Peabody Museum of Archaeology and Ethnology, Harvard University, PM969-48-00/2.3)

"What is a *good* story?" one index card says, *good* underlined to emphasize the moral connotation of the word as much as its strict traditional sense. "Who controls the past?" another one asks.

My phone lights up. DONALD MITCHELL, it says, a relic from when I put his name in my phone before I knew him, when he wanted nothing to do with me. I pick up.

BELIEF VERTIGO

As promised, Todd Wallack's *GLOBE* article—the lead story of the June 18, 2017, Sunday *Globe*, with a big picture of Jane over the fold—placed the Middlesex DA's refusal to release Jane's records within the larger context of Massachusetts's history of restricting public access to documents. Wallack cited a case in Worcester in which the district attorney refused to release records on a sixty-six-year-old murder despite the state police acknowledging that the prime suspect was dead. He contrasted that denial with instances in other states in which releasing information about cold cases generated exactly the information needed to crack them.

"We can't know what is going to be the piece of evidence that matters," District Attorney Marian Ryan countered. "That is the dilemma for us."

Wallack's article also publicly confirmed that the last round of DNA testing in the Jane Britton case was in 2006, and that there was still some DNA that remained that authorities could test.

Afterward, the emails started coming in. Karl wrote to say that he disagreed with the authorities' decision not to release records. Don Mitchell was rattled by readers' comments; they'd found his taking the bloody rugs repulsive and a sure sign that he was the killer. But that was outweighed by his gratefulness for the attention to Jane's case and the chance to tell himself a new version of the story. A lawyer reached out to offer pro bono legal counsel to me and Mike Widmer, the nearly eighty-year-old who had been trying to get the files. The lawyer's plan was to threaten escalating the matter to the attorney general's office for enforcement. We gladly accepted his help.

Mike Widmer, it turned out, had been the first reporter on the scene back in 1969. It was from his UPI article, syndicated in *Stars and Stripes*, that Boyd first learned that Jane had been murdered. Mike and I met for the first time shortly before Wallack's article came out at Flour Bakery in Harvard Square, around the corner from Jane's University Road building. This used to be Cronin's Bar, where Mike had called in the original story. Mike was sprightly, his eyes quick to delight. He swam to Alcatraz for his seventy-fifth birthday. I realized he had been almost exactly my age when he first covered Jane's story, and the number of years that separated us were almost exactly the number of years between Jane's death and our quest for the files.

It had only been his second day on the job at UPI when the Boston bureau chief, Stan Berens, called him into his office, motioning with his pointer finger. "We've got a classy murder for you," Berens said.

Mike got on the Red Line and headed into Harvard Square. It felt like going home—he was just finishing his graduate studies at Harvard; his best friend lived across the street from the University Road apartments—but that familiarity only underlined the surrealness of the moment. Mike walked into Jane's building, and talked to the cops, and called in the story as quickly as he could to the rewrite guy manning the desk that afternoon.

His story hit the A wire, which immediately sent it to the UPI bureaus around the world. It was printed in some of the evening papers and was syndicated by dozens more the next morning. Mike still has the sheet where the New York bureau chief congratulated him for having beaten AP's version of the story with a tally of twenty-four reprints to two. "It literally made my career," Mike Widmer told me.

We left Flour Bakery and sneaked into Jane's building. A postal worker was exiting, and we slid in and ran onto the elevator. As soon as the door closed, we giggled, and I saw the years dissolve off him. Suddenly we were the same age, pursuing this story. The building had been extensively renovated over the years, and he found it hard to recognize the layout. But we tried to locate the old stairwell on the fourth floor to let his body remember what he did that day all those years ago.

When we left the building, we still weren't ready to say goodbye, so we made our way to a nearby park. As he tried to recall what time Jane's body had been taken out of the building, I remembered I had an old newspaper photo of the stretcher being carried out. Mike took my phone, zoomed in. He turned it back to me and pointed to a young man with a mustache and a light-colored trench. "That's me," he said, seeing himself in a picture that he hadn't known existed.

Mike Widmer, in light trench and black tie.

I realized we were sitting in the same park where I had heard about Jane for the first time. I felt the echo and wondered if this story was particularly laced with coincidences, or if I desired them so much I made them.

RICHARD MICHAEL GRAMLY

BY FAR, THOUGH, THE BIGGEST thing that shook loose after Wallack's article was that someone named Richard Michael Gramly, a graduate student in Harvard's Anthropology department at the time of Jane Britton's death, moved from the periphery of her story to somewhere much closer to its dead center.

I had first come across Gramly's name on Websleuths the summer of 2014, around the same time that Don Mitchell had first started posting on the site. Richard Michael Gramly, who went by many names—Mickey, Dick, RMG, or, most often, Mike—hadn't been questioned in connection with Jane's murder at the time of her death. People only began suspecting him after 1976 when a young archaeologist named Anne Abraham disappeared during their two-person expedition in Ramah Bay, a remote part of Labrador, Canada. Gramly had been the last person to see Anne alive.

The Websleuths thread had devolved into gossip about Gramly and his alleged hair-trigger temper, and it was this ugly speculation about Gramly that pushed me to ignore the website for years. It had seemed like guilt being thrown retroactively on someone who had the misfortune to be associated with another tragedy. No one was sure if Gramly had known Jane Britton, never mind if he was even in Cambridge at the time of the murder.

None of Jane's close friends thought Gramly a likely candidate, but that didn't stop his name from surfacing periodically over the years in private conversations. In 2016, Boyd mentioned that he had spoken with the family of Anne Abraham. He said that though he had tried to offer some encouragement since he sympathized with the pain of living with a gaping, unanswered question, Boyd felt that he had nothing concrete to offer. Anne Abraham's disappearance was, to Boyd, "a separate matter entirely." In Hawaii, Don Mitchell told me he had heard about the ill-fated Labrador expedition and had written to Lieutenant Joyce about it, but he also didn't see much substance to the suspicion.

But by 2017, Gramly's name had come up enough that I felt compelled to do a little sleuthing, just in case.

I spoke with Bill Fitzhugh, who ran the Labrador expedition during which Anne Abraham disappeared. Fitzhugh, who was now the director of the Arctic Studies Center at the Smithsonian, said that Gramly was a "very complicated" person. But he assured me that the Smithsonian had done a thorough investigation after Anne's disappearance, and the institution had been satisfied by the explanation that her death was a horrible accident. As for Jane's death: Though Fitzhugh had also been a graduate student at Harvard in 1969 and knew Jane casually, he didn't know if the same had been true for Mike. "Whether he's involved in Jane's is just something I can't—I don't know enough to talk about," Fitzhugh said.

In the spring, around the time of my West Coast trip, I had even called Gramly himself. I'd been nervous about intruding on someone's life with baseless speculation and had no desire to test the truth of the tales of his temper. But it felt remiss not to attempt contact.

Over the phone, Gramly—his voice swinging from a clear tenor to a raspy growl often in the same sentence—told me that he knew people talked about his being involved in Jane's murder. He said he thought it was "a fine how-do-you-do" because all this time he had just been trying to help solve the case. He had contacted the Cambridge Police more than once about the investigation, irritated by their lack of progress. "The problem is that no good deed goes unpunished in our society," he said and reminded me that Massachusetts was where the Salem witch trials took place.

"Now dig this," Gramly said and launched into a story.

In the mid-1970s, Gramly was the keeper of the Peabody Museum's Putnam Lab, and he took it upon himself to do a deep clean of it, which hadn't been done since it opened in the late '60s. In the very back of the bottom shelf of a cabinet, he said, he found an opened box of red ochre, out of which it looked like a handful had been scooped. Gramly thought immediately of Jane's death, and felt compelled to report his discovery, believing it some kind of evidence.

Gramly brought the box to Stephen Williams, who was still the director of the museum. When Williams recognized the contents of the box, a flash of horror came across his face. That was the last Gramly heard of it.

"Why didn't you go to the police?" I asked him.

He says he had trusted Stephen, his beloved adviser, to take care of it.

But after decades of silence, Gramly felt he had no choice but to tell the police himself. Because, he believed, that box of red ochre belonged to the person who had been caretaker of the lab at the time of Jane's murder: Lee Parsons.

———

By the time Todd Wallack's *Boston Globe* article came out, I felt comfortable dismissing Gramly as nothing more than a minor character in Jane's story. Lee Parsons had become my main focus. And then I read the piece.

Tucked in a tiny, seemingly inconsequential paragraph, was an innocuous quote from Gramly: "Jane never got justice." For a reader who hadn't spent years studying Jane's story, the quote wouldn't register at all. But for me, it felt enormous. Wallack's decision to include a quote from Gramly—even one in which he appeared as an advocate for Jane—read like an official declaration that Gramly was more than just a peripheral figure. His mere presence lent credibility to an avenue of investigation that I had relegated to the realm of speculation. It also prompted Anne Abraham's family to get in touch with me.

I'd been holding off contacting the Abrahams, because I had heard that the peace that they had found in the decades following Anne's disappearance was fragile. I also worried about overpromising—I was working on Jane's case, not their sister's. But at Newark airport, waiting for a flight, I got an email from Todd Wallack with the phone number of Anne's brother Ted. With Ted's permission, Todd let me know that he had something to share about Gramly.

The flight was to Rome, the first leg of my travel to Bulgaria, where I was about to dig a Copper Age site for the next four weeks. Tell Yunatsite, a mounded city, where the present was literally layered on top of the past, was as close as I could get to what Jane dug at Tepe Yahya. Arthur Bankoff had supported my decision. I had been looking forward to the excavation for months—I'd wanted to feel the insanity as much as I'd wanted to understand the way dirt feels on a trowel—but suddenly it was the last thing I wanted to be doing.

I made the call just as my flight started boarding.

Ted's voice was thin and somber. He was speaking to me from Oklahoma, where for the past ten years he worked as a radiation oncologist treating members of the Cherokee and Osage nations. I had to cup the phone to hear him over the PA system at Newark.

Ted said he had found Gramly's behavior "quite suspicious" as it pertained to his sister's disappearance. The summer of their expedition, Mike had failed to set up radio communication in Labrador as he was supposed to. It was only after Anne vanished that he finally posted a signal.

Ted said he wasn't the only one to think Mike capable of the unspeakable. Two women had been so alarmed by him, they had spent a good portion of their lives keeping an eye on Gramly. "One of them has documented all of the murders that have occurred in the vicinity of where he has been over his entire career." Of particular note was the unsolved murder of the daughter of one of Gramly's bosses.

Ted explained that it had taken him decades to connect the murder of Jane with the disappearance of his sister. He had been an undergraduate at Harvard at the time of Jane's death—he mispronounced her last name with an emphasis on the second syllable—and her death "sort of thinly registered." But by the late '90s, the connection in his mind had become firm enough that he'd contacted the police repeatedly, begging them to investigate Gramly in connection with Jane.

Ted's letter to the Cambridge Police never received a response, but now, finally, the news that there was DNA evidence in Jane's case felt like hope. Ted saw the possibility of solving Jane's as an avenue to get closure for Anne's. "My focus is on just trying to find one case that can implicate him. That would be enough to satisfy me."

Ted and I returned to talking about Anne, and as he explained that his parents had fought unsuccessfully to sue the Smithsonian for negligence, his voice broke. "The goal was basically to make sure that this sort of thing—" He stopped. It was hard to tell if he was coughing or sobbing: "—didn't happen in the future."

It was the sound of grief that I had expected from Boyd. Whatever certainty or excitement I had had about Lee Parsons as a suspect shattered. The speed with which my suspicion switched felt like something akin to whiplash. I promised Ted I would do what I could.

He thanked me. "I feel a little bit like Hamlet in terms of not being able to take action. I don't want to wrongly do anything to somebody that might be innocent, but I think Gramly has to be investigated seriously."

———

Just before takeoff, I got an email from Ted saying that he'd connect me with his younger sister Alice as well as with the two women who had spent decades amassing information on Gramly. He also sent along two attachments. I downloaded them to read on the flight, and I wanted to scream as I did because in my canister in the sky—unable to tell anyone or do anything about it—I saw, in the *Smithsonian* article by Bill Fitzhugh, the leader of those expeditions in Labrador, a photo of Anne, her face covered in red ochre.

Fitzhugh had written:

The most important find in 1975 was an Indian cemetery at Rattlers Bight. Anne excavated a grave that contained a bundled human skeleton buried with walrus tusk axes, harpoons, finely made tools of polished slate and a huge sheet of mica which may have been used as a mirror—all smothered in thick ceremonial red ochre. I remember her trembling with excitement, brushing the ochre away and seeing herself as the first reflection thrown back by the mica in 4,000 years; she paused, wondering at the previous image so long darkened, and then dipped her hands into the ochre, impishly smearing some on her face to break the spell.

Anne kneeling in a grave she excavated. Her face is dusted in red ochre.

My stomach felt like it was filled with acid. I pounded the snack mix the flight attendant handed out, thinking that food would help. It didn't.

Because what no one knew, but I did, was that on the same phone call that Gramly had so animatedly recounted the story about the red ochre in the Putnam Lab where Lee Parsons had allegedly worked, Gramly had also told me that he did, in fact, know Jane Britton.

MICKEY

IT WAS GRAMLY'S FIRST SEMESTER at Harvard. Though he was six foot one with strawberry-blond hair, he passed unnoticed by many of the upper-classmen. But Jane, who made a point to know everyone and had a gift for befriending people who felt out of place, chatted with him on the steps outside the Peabody Museum, where people would congregate when the weather was warm. Jane carried herself like she owned the place, and Mike was impressed. "She was a socially gifted, outgoing person who had a friendship network, male and female, which was unbelievably wide."

Their casual conversations were companionship during a lonely time in his life. He and a serious girlfriend had just broken up over the long distance. But he knew better than to mistake Jane's warmth for something more. As he would later recall, "I'm just some kid from upstate New York, for crying out loud. Here I am at a prestigious Anthropology department; I'm a hardworking person and all that, I know my archaeology, but I'm not a you know, a New England blue blood."

A year younger than Jane, Richard Michael Gramly grew up in Elmira, New York. After his parents divorced when he was ten—the certificate listed "violence" as the reason for the divorce—Gramly lived during the school year with his father, a machinist, and his grandmother, a chambermaid.

As a child, Mickey, as he was known, was mischievous and entrepreneurial, with a touch of the mad scientist. The rockets he set off had the tendency to land on neighbors' roofs. Mickey always seemed like he was up to something, and many of the younger kids in the neighborhood were intimidated by him. When he grew older, he showed a friend how the marines could kill someone in minutes by pressing on the carotid artery.

In high school, he was something of a mystery. He was known as Dick, and he was in the science club and the German club, president of the numismatic club, and a member of the yearbook literary staff, but he didn't have the kind of social presence you'd expect from someone involved in so many activities. At graduation in 1964, he was one of seventeen first-honor-roll students in a class of four hundred, but few people would remember him years later. One honor-roll student, Carrie Besanceney, said, "All I recall was sitting next to him in Mrs. Houlihan's social studies class. He was good-natured, but I don't have a clue when it comes to whom he socialized with or what he did outside of school."

What Carrie didn't know was that Dick loved the outdoors—hunting, fishing, walking along the railroad tracks. Dick's favorite pastime was wandering the plowed fields and the Big Flats near Elmira and scouring for arrowheads. He started his own dig off the Chemung River in high school, and his big break came when William Ritchie, the archaeologist for the State of New York, responded to a letter from Gramly and became his unofficial mentor. Gramly spent his college summers working for him, and though Ritchie never went to Harvard himself, it put Gramly on the fast track for its PhD program. Ritchie sent a cohort of young men there—Bruce Bourque, Harvey Bricker, Mike Moseley. They saw themselves as an "informal club." Bruce Bourque would later reflect that the information about red ochre's usage in North American burials probably came with them. "This red ochre ritual business" was something that fascinated Bill Ritchie and his whole crowd.

Gramly followed Bruce to Harvard after college. According to Gramly, he met Jane early in his first semester, the fall of 1968; they were in the same class, one taught by the anthropologist Carleton Coon, who was trying out the material that would later form his book *The Hunting Peoples*. Gramly remembered talking with Jane about how shocking it was that Coon was unapologetic that, during his fieldwork, he wouldn't ask for permission before chopping off a lock of someone's hair for physical samples.

Jane invited Gramly over to her place for tea after class a couple of times. It was evening by the time they walked over to University Road; the street-lights had already switched on. "It was nice and cozy," he remembered, and described the desk next to her bed on which she rested the artifacts that she was drawing for Coon.

Gramly reminded himself that her invitation wasn't anything more than friendly. They were there to drink tea and talk; Mike was thinking about working in Iran, and Jane could offer him some advice about it. He couldn't help but notice, though, how easily her behavior might have been misconstrued. Jane was sweet on a lot of people, he had heard—not that she necessarily went to bed with them. But, he told himself, *you know, who knows.*

A SCHOLAR OF REMAINS

IT WAS A TWO-HOUR drive from Sofia to Pazardzhik. My site, run by a Bulgarian university, was in the middle of the middle of the country. I had hoped for a ten-person crew, but the only other digger was in the car with me, a man in his sixties named Daniel. His pant hems were ripped from where he repeatedly stepped on them, and he was still short of breath from just getting in the car. I worried about how he would fare in the hundred-degree heat that was heading our way.

Instead of camping under the stars, we were put up in a hotel in downtown Pazardzhik, fifteen minutes from the site, which was too cushy to complain about. I had a room of my own with a desk and air-conditioning, a municipal pool nearby that stayed open until 9 p.m., and twin beds that I pushed together.

I didn't see the site, Tell Yunatsite, for the first few days. The directors, a father-and-son team, wanted to cover the methodological and theoretical groundwork first and gave lectures to the two of us in the breakfast nook of the hotel. They informed us that there had been a massacre at Yunatsite six thousand years ago. Daniel asked: "What does it feel like to come across the remains of someone you know was murdered?" The younger director said, "On the one hand you understand it as a tragedy. But, as an archaeologist, strange as it may seem, it's your good luck. It's your only chance to see a human story."

During the afternoon breaks, I drew the long, red curtains, which lent a dream-like *Twin Peaks* feeling to the whole affair, and pored back through the Websleuths thread. I looked for Alice Abraham's posts since I'd learned from her brother that she was one of the contributors, but I was surprised to find that her first post wasn't until 2016. The most condemning entries about Gramly were earlier, from someone with the handle "Scrutin-eyes."

Scrutin-eyes laid out a damning case against Gramly, painting him as a pariah in the field, with a combustible temper and a history of ethical transgression, such as the "macabre handling of human remains." S-E said Gramly had gone rogue from the professional archaeological community. He had been forbidden from digging at Native American burial sites in New York after being sued for grave desecration. According to S-E, Gramly was known to his students at Stony Brook as "Mad Mike," because he "often flew off the handle, verbally attacking colleagues who disagreed with his interpretations, causing at least one to contact me worry[ing] about safety."

I was able to corroborate some of S-E's allegations. Gramly had in fact let his membership in the Society for American Archaeology lapse in 1982. While on the stand to defend an artifact collector accused of looting and trespassing, Gramly explained that he did not renew his membership because "it says quite clearly in the By-Laws of the Society of American Archaeology that transacting artifacts is not permitted." Instead, he founded the American Society for Amateur Archaeology in the early '90s and published his excavations' findings with his own press. One of the first pieces his press put out was a compilation of questionnaires about each of the fifty states' individual historical preservation laws. Gramly was specifically interested in the local law on human remains. The first few questions were: "1) Does your state/territory have a law that applies to exhuming Human burials? 2) If you answered 'yes': Is a distinction made between marked and unmarked graves?"

Gramly—and Canisius College, where he was working at the time—had indeed been sued by the New York attorney general and by the local Native American communities. The charges were for grave desecration and for the mishandling of cultural artifacts and human remains at a seventeenth-century Iroquoian village on the Niagara frontier. It marked the first time any state had sued under NAGPRA, the 1990 federal law to protect and repatriate Native American cultural artifacts. For more than a year, Gramly had had a funerary object in his office and some human bones in cardboard boxes in the hallway of his artifact repository, without the proper conditions for preservation. Eliot Spitzer, the then attorney general, accused Gramly not only of breaking the law, but also of using these artifacts for personal gain in a manner that "violated common decency." Gramly argued that the cardboard storage was only temporary; he was in the process of building a crypt with a granite monument for the exhumed bodies when legal action was filed. The settlement in 2000 demanded that Gramly repatriate all human remains and other cultural artifacts from that site. It also forbade him from ever digging a Native American site in New York again without permission from the tribe or nation in question. Later that year, he moved to Massachusetts.

While I didn't speak to anyone who knew about the "Mad Mike" moniker from his students, I did find other people who described his instability and their physical fear of him. A thread on the now defunct "Arrowheadology" website described an incident of Gramly's temper. Jason Neralich was an amateur archaeologist who, in 2003, paid to work at Gramly's Olive Branch excavation, where the agreement was that whatever a volunteer found after-hours could be kept. During one of those post-shift digs, Neralich discovered two flint blades, one of which he called the "holy grail of the Olive Branch site." Gramly, allegedly, was not happy when he heard about the discovery: he "flew out of the vehicle in a complete psychotic rampage, that of a lunatic, making a complete fool of himself and shell-shocking the entire crew. It was about at this moment that he directed his drunken state of rage towards me. He got within inches of my face, screaming at the top of his lungs. I could smell the alcohol on his breath and I got hit by spit overspray as he continued his vulgar, drunken, incomprehensible jargon. Time seemed to have stood still that evening around me at that moment and the only thing I remember Gramly screaming was, and I quote: 'And you call yourself an archaeologist!!!!!' "

Gramly said that this was a mischaracterization of site protocol. While people could keep whatever they found in a specific part of the site called the railroad cut, the blades were discovered right *next* to the cut, and, crucially, they were still in their original context. Artifacts like those belonged to Dr. Douglas Sirkin, on whose property the dig was located. Even so, Gramly said, Sirkin paid Jason an honorarium, and the cache was named after him. "I don't know what you've got to do [when you tell people what site protocols are]. Make people sign in blood?"

Other people told me similar stories. One young academic who asked to remain anonymous out of fear of retaliation spoke of his interactions with Gramly. "From, *geez*, my earliest years as a grad student I had very established archaeologists…pull me aside out of the conference and say,

'Hey, I heard that you might have some interaction with Gramly. Just a word of advice, don't ever be alone with him.'" This academic described a "pattern of intimidation" wherein Gramly, slighted by what he felt had been inadequate citation, would call people at various universities "telling everyone what a terrible person I was, to never work with me. Trying to basically kind of blackball me."

For the most part, the people Gramly called didn't take him seriously. As the aggrieved academic explained, "Everyone knows that this guy has a long history of unethical things in various capacities." Instead, they contacted the academic and joked, "Oh, you've pissed off Gramly again. He's back on the warpath."

I also learned that Jane's Websleuths thread had been started by someone with firsthand experience of Gramly's rage. The user, macoldcase, feared for their family's safety but spoke to me on the condition of anonymity. MCC said that they had infuriated Gramly by failing to cite him in a small article they had published in a "rinky-dink little journal that only Paleoindian archaeologists read." Out of the blue, MCC received an angry email from Gramly saying that they were a disgrace to the archaeological community, that they should be dropped from their PhD program, and that they would have trouble finding work. "I could just envision him screaming at his computer as he's pounding on the keyboard," they said.

Gramly contacted MCC's graduate advisers and also where they worked. MCC explained the situation to their supervisors, who were understanding. "At the end of this sit-down meeting, one of my bosses said, 'I think he went to grad school at Harvard in the '60s, and I always heard this rumor about this ochre murder up there.'" The boss added in a joking tone, "I wonder if he did it."

It was the first that MCC had heard of Jane Britton's murder, but "the more I started asking around about this guy, everybody who has either worked in the Northeast who was at Harvard at the time, or does Paleoindian archaeology, has at least one story about his explosive temper, how he's really sketchy, and so at that point I posted that thing anonymously on Websleuths." In MCC's post that started the Jane Britton thread, they said nothing about possible suspects; they only asked if anyone knew any more about the case. MCC was astonished when the thread turned, without their insistence, to Gramly as its suspect.

On the thread, Scrutin-eyes summed up the case against Gramly:

We have two young female archaeologists dead, and RMG seems to have been
at Harvard at the time and definitely was the last to see Ann [sic] Abraham
alive in Labrador. He has been and still is a loose canon [sic], [...] and
other archaeologists have expressed a concern for their safety around him.
Someone in law enforcement needs to get off their ass and explore the links
between Jane Britton's death and the disappearance of Ann Abraham!

THE THREE SUSPECTS

I GOT A CALL FROM an unknown number. It was Stephen Loring, an Arctic
archaeologist whom I'd contacted a while ago at Bill Fitzhugh's suggestion.
Loring had been a part of Fitzhugh's Labrador expedition in 1976, the
summer that Anne disappeared. "His mind is very retentive about a lot
of details," Bill told me, but warned that Loring might not want to talk
about Anne, since he was in a fragile state. His wife had died less than
a year ago.

I had been vague in my initial email, so when Loring called, he
thought I wanted to interview him about Arctic cuisine. When I told him
I was writing about Jane Britton, his voice descended like a slide whistle:
"Weeelllll, it's a long story." He laughed as if he had waited fifty years for
this phone call.

I held the phone tightly to my ear because the connection was weak.

"You know, it could go any way you want. The three suspects are all
interesting and twisted characters."

The *three* caught me off guard.

"There are different camps of who murdered Jane Britton. Lee's kind of
a minor character. But then there's a Lamberg-Karlovsky group, and Mike
Gramly of course is the third contender."

It was the first time I'd heard anyone else talk about the—well, *my*—three
suspects like that.

Though Loring did not go to Harvard and had never met Jane Britton,
his life kept intersecting with the world she had left behind, as if they were

yoked. Loring explained that in 1969, during his first year of college at Goddard in Vermont, he had a winter term job at the Peabody. His first day on the job was the Monday after Jane Britton was murdered, and one of his first memories of the place was of Stephen Williams showing a detective around the bowels of the museum.

From his basement desk, Loring also came into Lamberg-Karlovsky's orbit, though Karl never bothered to interact much with the temporary museum staff. To Loring, Lamberg-Karlovsky was only ever "a character stalking around the corridors" of the Peabody.

Mike Gramly? "That's a live wire." Loring had been Anne Abraham's boyfriend when she disappeared, he revealed, and he remained very close to the Abraham family. He had recently spoken to one of the two women whom Ted Abraham described as having dedicated their lives of late to investigating Gramly. Loring described her reasons for suspicion, entirely disconnected from Anne Abraham, interesting enough to "sort of move him up in the queue."

But, Loring said, he knew Lee Parsons best of all. He spent a lot of time with Lee after he accepted his invitation to go on expedition in Guatemala. And—

Static started to take over the call.

I called him back. "Hi. It's Stephen's answering machine on his cell phone."

I tried him again. He picked up. But I still couldn't hear him. I tried once more, not wanting to lose him at this pivotal moment, and this time it just rang and rang.

ON THE DIG

I SPENT MY DAYS ON the dig in Bulgaria crouched inside a seven-thousand-year-old clay pit whose sides I could not touch without them crumbling. It felt like I was dusting dust off dust. But I loved it. The feeling of learning how to see more, knowing that a change of color in the soil was the footprint of an ancient posthole. I never quite got over the idea that we could recover the negatives of the past.

Daniel, the other digger, drove me crazy. He called soda "carbonated water," and it pained me to see him slather inches worth of the cook's homemade honey on white bread, when he refused to eat the vegetables. But there was a kind of meta joy in the insanity. *Small-group atmosphere tends to create downright psychotic atmosphere*, indeed. It made me feel closer to Jane. I similarly relished learning how to draw sherds with a profile gauge, because I knew that was her specialty. And I enjoyed the tension of attraction as I watched the dig director use the edge of his knife to flick dirt off a profile I was trying to expose. The juxtaposition of danger and delicacy was tantalizing.

Becky at Tell Yunasite.

We dug from 6 in the morning until 1 p.m., and broke at the height of the afternoon heat, only to go back to the site to wash sherds and sort for three hours. The field director told me he wished for days when he didn't have to see both the sunrise and the sunset. Between the heady flush from the plum rakia and the bells of the goats returning home for the evening, I could have been anywhere in time.

I slept greedily at night and set my alarm for the last possible moment before running to the car that took Daniel and me to the dig site. So when, one morning, I woke to a text from Don Mitchell, I only had a few minutes to process what he was saying before I had to rush to the mound:

> *Becky—Peter Sennott from the Mass State Police just called me, to talk. Ma[d]e sure he knew where I was—says they're going to do more DNA and would I give a swab. I said sure, of course. He said that he might have to fly out to take it. Anyway...trees shaken, shit's falling down. He didn't reveal too much beyond saying "new testing methods."*

"What a time to be in the middle of nowhere," I replied, my glasses still sitting on the bedside table.

Don sent me a link to a segment on public television: a panel discussion with DA Marian Ryan, *Globe* reporter Todd Wallack, and Mike Widmer, my partner in pushing for Jane's records, which had aired the night before. I watched it as I brushed my teeth.

Marian Ryan argued that her job was not to disclose files; it was to give families resolution and to find evidence enough to sustain prosecution beyond a reasonable doubt. She hoped that she would be able to do so with the remaining DNA.

"You haven't done DNA testing since 2006!" Mike Widmer countered. "And now suddenly after all of this fury you're—"

Everyone started talking over each other.

I texted Don in the middle of watching the segment:

> *i have to head to the site in 2 minutes*
>   *i mean, honestly, i'm glad they're swabbing*

I had been concerned that even if the authorities were doing DNA testing, they were only going to run the profile through the national database known as CODIS (the Combined DNA Index System) that was started in 1990. I worried that whoever killed Jane wasn't going to be in the database, and that the killer would slip through the cracks.

The moderator asked the group, "By the way, is anybody getting anywhere?...Is Cooper getting anywhere?"

Mike replied, "I don't know. I talk to Becky now and again."

My absence in the room, on that screen, felt like those ancient postholes, where the negative was all that remained. They were telling Jane's story—my story, our story—and I couldn't answer.

After a few more minutes of this back-and-forth, the moderator said, "We're running out of time," but it wasn't too late to end the segment with a firm commitment.

The district attorney said, "Where I am right now is I expect to know whether we can develop a DNA profile within four to six weeks."

The moderator followed up, pinning her to a promise: "At the end of which you will make a decision about sharing the information?"

She nodded. "Yes."

MARY MCCUTCHEON

I MOVED UP MY FLIGHT home to two weeks earlier than originally planned, but I still had a few more days in Bulgaria. I tried my best to stay connected to the story in the meantime. From my hotel bed after I got back from sherd processing, I called Mary McCutcheon, who taught anthropology at George Mason University until 2007. She was one of the two women who had spent decades pursuing the possibility of Gramly's guilt in both Jane's death and Anne's disappearance.

On the phone, Mary told me she met Gramly when she was a junior in college, in the spring of '68. Mary had been surveying the bayous of Houston with her professor when he introduced her to an acquaintance of his, Richard Michael Gramly. Gramly was working for an oil company as a geologist after graduating from Rensselaer Polytechnic Institute. He was handsome, with reddish hair, strong arms, and broad shoulders, and he offered her a ride home in his Mustang convertible. "I was smitten," she remembered. He asked her to call him Mick because that's what his half sisters called him. It made them feel like old friends, instantly. He invited her to his "Clovis Club," and on the membership card he handed her, he signed his name with an extra e: Gramley. They started dating. It was a "whirlwind" courtship, and, before long, Mary found herself impulsively agreeing to go on a road trip with him to Mexico.

Mary McCutcheon's Clovis Club membership card that Gramly signed with an extra e.

THE ROAD TRIP

MICK PARKED, AND WITHOUT THE wind, the broiling heat of the summer day in East Texas was unbearable. Mary knew that Mick had been spending his weekends excavating a burial site near the Harris County Boys' School—a former home for dependent and delinquent boys—and she was excited when he suggested they stop by on their way to Mexico. They spent the afternoon with their trowels and dental picks and brushes, and Mary found herself wishing she were sipping iced tea instead. But Mick seemed enthralled, talking constantly of his hope that the next trowel of dirt might yield some red ochre. He taught her the principles of how to use a proton magnetometer to detect the iron-laden substance, a technique he had learned from Bill Ritchie in New York. Mary knew that interest in red ochre wasn't rare, but she had never seen someone with quite such a passion. He was even writing a paper about it.

They didn't find any, but Mick was thrilled by what his scraper did hit: human remains. They worked until they exhumed the whole skeleton, and shortly after, Mick packed the bones in the trunk of the car.

By the time they got to the border, they had all but forgotten the bones in the back, until a border agent asked them to pop the trunk. Mick— a handsome, white American and a great storyteller—talked them out of trouble just in time to catch their train to Mexico City.

"I was just waltzing through life and tripping over everything and causing hurt and damage in an unconscious way, too," Mary would later reflect. "I look back at myself in those days and I think, ugh."

From Mexico City, they traveled by third-class bus across Chiapas and the Yucatán, visiting ancient archaeological ruins and cenotes—mineral pools hidden beneath the cities. It was hard to stray very far from the topic of rituals and death. Some of the cenotes had been sacred places for the ancient Maya; their milky water, the site of human sacrifices.

In Palenque, an ancient Mayan city with giant stone pyramids, Mary and Mick carried their packs up and down the structures. A fer-de-lance, a vicious poisonous snake, crossed their path but scooted past them, more of an omen than a threat. When they noticed an oncoming thunderstorm, they raced to the highest point they could find, eager to watch it violently break through the sky. They perched on top of the pyramid, watching the lightning strike the trees, knowing full well that a bolt could easily strike them dead, but feeling protected by their youth and enthusiasm. As the rain pelted, Mary watched Mick slip into a state of rapture. He chanted to the Mayan gods and went on and on about the spread-eagle position that he believed sacrificial virgins took before they were killed and thrown into the cenotes. Mary was equal parts frightened and transfixed.

At the end of the trip, Mary went home to Illinois and Mick headed to the border where his car was still parked with the skeleton in the trunk. They spent the rest of the summer of '68 apart, except for a quick visit Mick paid to Mary at her family home. Mary's mother instantly disliked him, with a forcefulness that seemed born of gut instinct more than anything Mick had actually done wrong. She pulled Mary aside while he was still there to tell her as much. It reminded

Mary of an eerie time a stranger in Mexico had watched her and Mick on a bus and whispered to her in Spanish, "Get rid of this guy. He's no good."

In the end, Mary reflected, "They were probably very right."

Mary was done with the relationship, but she didn't want to "make waves" with Gramly during the summer, so she continued corresponding with him, sending tepid replies and hoping Mick would get the hint. She started seeing a guy at her field school, and she chose not to think too much about a necklace that Mick had sent her, which he called a "Guatemalan wedding necklace." She didn't know that it was a Guatemalan tradition to tie a piece of jewelry around bride and groom to symbolize their being bound together forever.

But that fall, when Mick started at Harvard, he wrote to her with renewed ardor. He asked her to marry him. Mary felt blindsided. Sure, they had been impulsive to go to Mexico together after only a few dates, but to propose to someone after knowing her less than a summer? "I always thought, *Why would a guy from an unhappy marriage want to get married to someone after only six weeks of being with them? That's insane.*" She suddenly saw the Guatemalan necklace in a new light.

Mary responded to Mick's letter. *I'm sorry I misled you or gave you reason to believe I was more serious than I am but I'm not.* She packaged the necklace with the letter and sent both away.

Mick didn't take kindly to the news. His reply was a "vitriolic condemnation of me and a bitter rebuke for returning the necklace," she remembered. "Chillingly angry."

Soon after, her sister, who was studying at Harvard to be an architect, called to tell her that Mick had shown up at her doorstep on her birthday. Mary had no idea how Mick knew where her sister lived, or that October 15 was her sister's birthday. Her sister said Mick had introduced himself as her sister's ex-boyfriend and had presented her with a chocolate cake.

"Don't eat it!" Mary advised her sister.

In January, less than three months later, Mary was reading the newspaper in Houston. A story about a bludgeoning in Cambridge caught her eye. The description of the victim reminded her of herself: an outgoing, flirtatious anthropologist with a touch of insouciance. "As soon as I got to the part about the red ochre, I said, 'Huh. I think I know who did that.'"

But Mary didn't tell anyone about her suspicions. "Partly I was scared. Partly I figured, *Oh, the police will solve this in five minutes.*" She told herself she had nothing to go on except a gut feeling. So Mary went on with her life. Other than a postcard Mick sent her in 1972 to say that he was getting married, the two lost contact. And for the next fifteen years or so, she would think, incorrectly, that she was alone in linking Gramly to Jane Britton.

THE GOLDEN GIRLS

THROUGH THE YEARS, MARY FELT like Gramly was haunting her. When she worked at the Smithsonian, she was startled to see cartons with Gramly's name in the hallway, and to learn about Anne Abraham's disappearance.

Mary had been careful to keep her number unlisted because she didn't want Mick to find her. But he did once, in the early '90s, to congratulate her on a piece she had published. Other than "Where did you get my number?" Mary didn't ask any questions.

It wasn't until years later, when Mary started Googling, that she realized the Jane Britton story had already found its way back to her. The articles about Jane's case mentioned Don and Jill Mitchell. She knew them, Mary realized, and had for years. They had been going to the same annual meeting for Pacific Island anthropologists for as long as she could remember. Jill Mitchell—who once again went by her maiden name, Nash—spoke openly with Mary about her suspicions (she, like Don, favored Lee Parsons), while Mary shared her gut feelings about Gramly.

A year or so later, another woman, Patricia,[3] contacted Jill with similar concerns about Gramly. Patricia explained that she had known Gramly before graduate school, and that she, too, had had dubious enough interactions with him that news of Jane Britton's murder had instantly turned her

---

3 Pseudonym.

mind to Gramly. Decades later, still unable to shake this suspicion, Patricia had taken it upon herself to do her own investigation into Jane's murder, which was how she ended up on the phone with Jill. Jill told Patricia she had a "twin" in Mary and soon put the two in touch.

In some ways, Mary and Patricia made the perfect odd couple. "She's very, very persevering, and I'm sort of a flibbertigibbet," Mary told me. Whereas Mary had the connections to the anthropology world and loved to do the talking, Patricia was the organized one, who drove hundreds of miles across the country for archives of obscure local papers. In the past decade, Patricia had given over a den in her house to Gramly material: maps, files upon files of research, bookshelves covered in volumes, both academic and popular, about getting inside the mind of a serial killer. Her family made fun of her for what she called her "strange hobby."

"Her work is striking," Mary said. Patricia had exhaustively documented all the unsolved murders that took place within a plausible radius of Gramly's whereabouts. She had compiled a document with those murders, cross-referenced with his digs, his conferences, the American Society for Amateur Archaeology meetings, and the major highways he took to get to his excavations. It represented years of meticulous work. There were a dozen dead bodies on that list.

But Mary and Patricia's similarities were more fundamental than their superficial differences, and, over emails and phone calls, they found companionship in their decades of private suspicion. When Mary and Patricia met with the DA's office and Sergeant Sennott in 2012, both women were in their sixties. In internal communication, the Mass State Police office referred to them as the "Golden Girls."

At the same time, both women were aware of how easily and dangerously guilt can be retrofitted onto someone. "Everybody can be spun," Mary told me. "You can tell a story and the person listening to the story can be so easily manipulated . . . that they're going to jump to the conclusion that he's guilty even if he might not be." Mary said that as strong as her gut feeling about Gramly was, "the other part of my personality is very, very, very wedded to an American system of justice. And for the rights of the defendant to a really, really good defense."

Mary knew that she had nothing concrete against Gramly. She told me her sister didn't even remember the birthday cake incident. "If I were a defense attorney in this case, I'd knock all of this stuff out of the park."

She continued: "He may just be an innocent person who's made a few enemies along the way. Or he may be a true psychopath."

ANNE ABRAHAM

As Anne Abraham prepared to fly in to Ramah Bay in the Torngat Mountains, the northernmost part of Labrador, which was already itself in the far north of Canada, she copied into her journal a passage from a Forbes travel guide about the area:

> *Stretching away into the interior as far as the eye can see, rise innumerable peaks. [. . .] In almost any properly illustrated storybook may be seen just such fantastic mountains as these. Invariably they harbor the castles of ogres and giants and other bad characters.*

The landscape carried within it the promise of magic. The name Torngat came from the Inuktitut word *Tongait*, or "place of spirits." The name, she wrote in her journal that night, "is an evil spirit, and how excited I am."

Though this was going to be her first time in Ramah Bay, it was Anne's sixth season in Labrador on Bill Fitzhugh's expedition. She had grown close to the Fitzhughs over the years. Her first time had been five years before in the summer of 1971, the Fitzhughs' first expedition up in Labrador. Her brother Ted, who had Bill as a teaching assistant in a course at Harvard, had been invited, and her older sister Dorothy and Anne, fourteen, were also allowed to come along.

Anne impressed everyone on that first expedition with her unique combination of fearlessness and sensitivity. Lynne Fitzhugh, Bill's wife and the camp manager, remembered: "She was the first person when we had a storm at night...to go rushing out, jump into the freezing cold water, to get the speedboat that had dragged its anchor and was floating away. Everybody else just kind of stood there. She didn't hesitate for anything. She just went."

Life on the expedition was hard—they traveled by trap boat and got rolled around in the rough seas, avoiding icebergs that peeled off the coastline like scabs—but Anne thrived. Lynne, who was taking care of her two young kids in addition to the archaeologists, recalled, "I was washing diapers in the stream and the wind's blowing and storms [are threatening], and Ben would fall and cut his head, and we would have to call the small emergency plane to come." But Anne was always there to swoop in. "It was very hard and I loved it, but I probably wouldn't have loved it as much if it hadn't been for Anne." On the rare occasion when neither of them had to watch the kids, Anne was the one who Lynne asked to go on adventures, like finding a rhubarb patch rumored to be growing in the next valley over. And at night, as the neighboring settlers and Inuit families gathered to play the harmonicas and recorders the crew had brought, Anne would pull out her fiddle. Somehow, under the Arctic skies, it worked.

———

On one of her last mornings with the rest of the team before heading up to Ramah, Anne went on a long walk before breakfast. She came across an old campsite and, just beyond it, a beach. Anne shrank back in horror when she realized the sand was strewn with dog carcasses. There were five of them, all teeming with maggots. She was sure they had been shot by the Mounties. Anne continued on and saw a woman in a 1950s dress looking seaward and singing. When Anne approached, the woman stopped, and when Anne asked what she had been singing, she turned to Anne and howled.

The beauty of Labrador was inseparable from its violence. It was as much "the land God gave to Cain," as Jacques Cartier once called it, as it was Eden, "pure, grandiose country, stark and elemental and wild, softened by wildflowers and lingering golden twilights, with clumps of dwarf birch and willow, scattered spruce, myriad birds and animals, spectacular views and pulsating northern lights," Bill Fitzhugh wrote.

Lynne captured it best in her oral history of the place, a book dedicated to Anne: "Labrador's is among the most lethal climates on the continent not because it is the most harsh, but because it is so utterly disarming. The balmy southwest breeze that glorifies a summer morning can slam around in a heartbeat—dark shadows racing across the limpid sea like chills, stripping the skin from the flattened water and hurling it against the land so hard it makes the ledges flute and scream."

Back on the plane, Anne knew the coming 1976 season was going to be a challenge. The mission was to find the mythic Ramah chert quarries— the source of a very special kind of stone that flaked so well, it was prized for toolmaking by the native communities. Chert, a kind of quartz, was normally gray and dull like flint, but Ramah chert was semi-translucent. It looked like milky ice. But finding the quarry would mean hiking up and down the unforgiving slopes of Ramah. Anne had taken rock climbing and geology courses in preparation for the trip, and she hoped that her co-leader, Mike Gramly, an assistant professor of geology at Stony Brook, was as good as he seemed on paper. They had met only once before, at a seminar in the Peabody Museum in February of that year. Fitzhugh had hired Gramly as an expert on lithic sources for the quarry mission, and Anne volunteered to accompany him. The others would be 175 miles away at base camp in September Harbor, and in the cliffs of Ramah it was only going to be the two of them.

Stephen Loring, whom Anne had been dating since they met on last summer's expedition, arrived before nightfall. They held each other until the morning, when it was time to load the plane.

The last time Lynne Fitzhugh saw Anne was when she walked inside the fisherman's shack that had been repurposed as that season's headquarters. Lynne had been laid up with a headache, and Anne walked up to the bed and kissed her right on the mouth. Lynne would remember that moment years later: "It was like she was really saying a final goodbye."

———

The flight to Ramah Bay was uneventful. From Thalia Point where Anne loaded in, the pilot picked up Mike from Mugford before dropping them off at the remote site.

They set up a camp in the footsteps of an old Moravian mission. The landscape was marshier than the guidebooks had made it out to be. Sure, there were the majestic fjords and cliffs, but there were also brooks where trout swam and thick moss that made the ground spongy underfoot, and even a little beach area where the pebbles kicked into the ocean.

In Ramah, there was no equivalent to Dog's Nose, a big basalt cliff overlooking the ocean, where, in years past, Anne and Lynne and the Fitzhugh children bathed in the rain pools while humpback whales swam up beside them, their mouths open, scooping up capelin. But the landscape was not without its promised magic. On clear days, in some areas of the range, sound traveled so clearly you could almost sing a duet with your own echo across the valley. From the tent, Anne could hear the waterfall near base camp gurgle like boiling water. She wrote in her journal, "The surf unrhythmically plays on the shore."

They spent their first few days hiking around the area looking for the quarry. Anne didn't like that Mike had the tendency to go on ahead without her, and she found his constant talk tiring. "My ears are tired of his voice, though it is all interesting, I don't care for the deep, back of the throat attempt-to-be mature tone [...] and his mustache—another subject all together," she wrote in her journal. At night, sleeping in the same tent, Mike would tell Anne about his time in Africa—fantastic tales of giant snakes called mambas—which he defended as true stories.

But they got along well enough, and the days quickly blended together; Anne's journal entries lost their time pegs. One morning, Mike hiked so far ahead, Anne could no longer see him. "I went up a chimney and the shale is so crummy that I had a close call with the rock crumbling as I tried for a hand hold, important. Mike finally waited after I yelled my gut out."

They hiked together along the ridge above the valley where the stream flowed. Their goal was to climb down into the valley and follow the stream to its mouth. Mike took the quickest, steepest route down the talus slope, but Anne took her time, climbing down a more diagonal route. Anne was just above the stream when she looked down and saw a boulder that gleamed with that milky translucence of Ramah chert. Anne picked up a flake and pitched it to Mike. It fell short, and he teased her about her throwing arm, but they both knew what it meant. Anne had found a Ramah chert quarry.

Anne in the Ramah chert quarry. Mike Gramly captured this moment—one of the last photos of her ever taken.

The quarry was enormous—one-quarter of a mile long—and made of solid chert. Anne and Mike spent the rest of the day walking up and down it, picking up flakes. The hike back was tiring—there was no quick way back to camp except by going all the way around again—but Mike surprised Anne by making dinner for her while she rested in the tent. She realized that she must have lost her gray cap the day before, and Mike said, "'Twas a sacrifice to the mountains."

They returned the next day, and the excitement had not diminished. "Time went unrecognized," Anne wrote. She noted that a lot of the chert was naturally iron-stained. "Perhaps this was an inspiration for red ochre."

Later that day, Mike signaled to Anne that he was heading to camp. Again, Anne was left to scramble the crumbling rock alone. As much as she wanted to catch up to him, she resisted rushing because she didn't trust the ground beneath her. The rock in Ramah Bay fractured in clean, large sheets, and it was all too easy to imagine a whole section breaking clear from under her. Anne was relieved to find that Mike had been waiting for her at the steepest part of the slope, but afterward, he left her again. Anne took her time downclimbing and entered into another world alone. Grasshoppers, asters, dandelions, so many butterflies. A white-breasted bird circled as if examining her. A few black bears had been spotted in the distance in recent days, but there were none that evening to spoil her renewed good humor. Anne returned to camp, singing.

The following day was overcast and rainy, and the weather the one after wasn't much better—windy and cold—so it wasn't until Thursday that Anne put on her waders and tried to make her way along the shore to see if there was a quicker way to get to the quarry. She tried four different routes up the cliff from the shore, but the wind was still too strong, and she didn't trust the "nasty, fracturing shale" to hold both her and the load she was carrying, so she walked back to camp to help Mike roast the goose he had shot the previous afternoon. After their feast, they talked and talked, and this time it was Anne who found herself providing the majority of the conversation. She talked about how she was doing at George Washington, and how much she loved her family while nevertheless desiring to get away from home. Anne was grateful for a break from the chat when she left camp to watch the sunset by herself. She wrote by candlelight that evening, enjoying the smell of woodsmoke on her clothes, until the wick had nearly run out: "I feel good and bad for telling him so much," she reflected, and went on a bit before ending on, "I love Stephen."

The next morning was so still it felt strange. The air was heavy and overcast, and there wasn't a breath of wind. Because of the stillness, she and Mike decided to try again to find a shortcut around the shore to the quarry. As they prepared for the day's hike, she noticed Mike was hacking at a caribou antler he had picked up, sharpening it into a back scratcher. In her journal, Anne also noted that Mike had set up the radio.

About twenty-four hours later, the morning of August 7, 1976, Mike would reach Bill Fitzhugh at base camp by radio for the first time. Anne, he said, had vanished.

THE SECOND CALL

"WHEN YOU'RE IN A REMOTE tent camp and you know your friend is probably dead, you like to forget it if you can."

I was on the phone with Gramly for the second time. Over an hour into the call, I finally found the courage to ask him about Anne Abraham.

"Well, you know, they're quite different, those two things," he replied. Whereas he barely had more than a passing acquaintance with Jane, he had gotten to know Anne quite well over that week in Ramah. But, as with Jane, Gramly said he knew that people suspected him of being involved in Anne's death. "I get focused upon by people who want to disparage me or discredit me because they fear me."

People, he said, were afraid of him because he threatened their professional identity. Despite his lack of institutional affiliation, he had recently finished excavating the first set of mastodon remains with any proof of human contact in Orange County, New York. His findings were now part of the collection at Harvard's Museum of Comparative Zoology. "I do archaeology because I love it. And I don't need to get paid to do it all the time." He said their suspicion saddened him, but "not to the point where I'd argue with anyone."

When he was later confronted with the various allegations of his temper and people's fear of him, he met the news with composure and resignation. In response to his alleged "Mad Mike" moniker and that people at Stony Brook had been worried about their safety: "I don't even know what they're talking about." And, of course, he told me that he did not murder Anne, Jane, or anybody else, despite the suspicions that had fallen upon him. He added, "I don't care about what people say. I've never been false to myself."

His defense was an interesting counterpoint to the criticisms I had heard from the professional archaeology community. Professionals accused Gramly of digging so quickly that not only were his sites destroyed forever, but his data were unusable. Gramly accused them in turn of being selfish with their data, as they obsessed over measurements that might never be useful—slow to the point, sometimes, of never publishing. Whereas professionals argued that being an archaeologist carried with it legal obligations and methodological and moral standards, Gramly argued that the only difference between an amateur and a professional archaeologist was whether they get paid to do the work. Gramly, after all, had a PhD in the subject. What professionals saw as encouraging looters and trespassers, he depicted as "preservation" archaeology—saving artifacts from destruction by either nature or man.

Gramly wasn't alone in this stance. Bruce Bourque—a professor at Bates for more than forty years and a friend of Gramly's since their William Ritchie days—said that the whole Ritchie group is now seen by some as unorthodox or unconventional. But Bourque attributed this view to "a sea-change in how archaeology is being done. There is a great aversion to doing field work. It's been replaced by 'public archaeology' and 'cultural resource management.'"

Still, Gramly's position felt like a magnificent, calculated dance: He expertly skirted the spirit if not the letter of the law. While Gramly was obviously an extremely intelligent man, it was possible he thrived off living on the edge of normative ethics.

He summarized his approach. "I won't suck up to the government and the party line. I'm the real thing. You're talking to a real archaeologist here, a scientist. I've done archaeology since I've been ten years old. And I published my first works when I was thirteen and a half. Okay? And I'll do it till I can no longer physically do it."

Given all I had heard about his temper, I was surprised by how openly and undefensively Gramly spoke about Anne and their trip to Labrador.

"I was in tent camp the night I knew she was gone. I just knew it. We had a bottle of whiskey, an Imperial quart. You know how much whiskey's an Imperial quart?" he asked me. I didn't. It's over a liter. "I drank three-quarters of an Imperial quart of whiskey, and I couldn't even get a buzz. Because I was so jacked up about that. I couldn't even forget it, do you understand? That's what it means to lose someone like that. You want to forget it for just a few hours. I wasn't even able to forget it. And I never have forgotten it."

He described Anne as outgoing and gung-ho. He told me she was a good field person and could keep up with him, but he did his best not to hike too far ahead of her. Or when he did, he always looked back for her. He emphasized how remote Ramah was. "Danger is everywhere. And it comes in waves you don't even know sometimes."

He accused her of taking risks he would never take. "One day we're up on top of this three-thousand-foot mountain. And I could see the cliff end, so I go up to it. Of course no one's ever walked up there and you don't know how safe the rock is...So I got on my belly and spread my weight out, and I crawled up to the edge and looked over. Oh my god. Oh my god. A three-thousand-foot fall right into the fjord. Windy as hell, too, up there. And I looked to my side and there's Anne standing on the edge, right next to me with the wind buffeting her. You know, if she had been blown off right there I would've been blamed for that, you hear me?"

As when I talked to him about Jane, class came up in the conversation. He remarked that Anne had gone to a "wealthy day school for wealthy people in Washington DC, where they call their teachers by their first name." He would never do that, Gramly told me.

We got back to the day she disappeared. "She must've fallen off a 275-foot-high point into 2,000 feet of water," he said. "She was carrying our lunch and the rock hammer on the way out on this one day we were walking along the fjord. It's too much weight. She must've just gone down right into the water and that's where she stayed all these many years. It's a tragedy. A terrible tragedy."

Gramly had told the Royal Canadian Mounted Police that on Anne's final morning, they had been looking for a shortcut to the quarry. The route they had been following—up a stream, across knife-edge ridges, and steeply down along another stream—took three hours each way. They believed there might be an alternative route along the shore if they could figure out how to get around a talus point—a slope of rock that spilled from the cliffs onto the beach. One option was to go around the point by climbing the rocks at its base, and the other was to go up a steep cut in the slope itself. The staircase, they called it.

That morning, Gramly and Anne waited for low tide. Around 11 a.m., Gramly attempted to go around the point, but he found the rocks too slippery. He fell several times and got thoroughly wet and returned to where Anne was on the beach. Gramly tried the staircase route but didn't get very far before he jumped back onto the beach to avoid a fall. Anne tried, too, and got about thirty feet up. "I don't like the risk so I decide to give the sea route one more try," he wrote in his statement. He went around the point again, leaving Anne up the cliff and out of sight. When he returned about fifteen minutes later, he said he couldn't see her anywhere. She wasn't on the cliff. She wasn't on the beach. He yelled to her but got no answer.

He told me he did everything he could to look for her. "In fact, I climbed that goddamn mountain so many times up and down that I ruined my hip." He said he used his left leg as his brake, sliding down the mountain. "I was semi-crippled for a while after that, and of course eventually my hip had to be replaced."

When he got back to camp that night, "I knew she was gone. I just knew it." He drank the whiskey and read her diary. "I'm not proud of the fact that I read someone's diary, but I knew that I had to." He said the lack of implicating material in the entries, and Anne's own admissions of her treacherous climbs, were a great asset to him legally. "That's how we stopped it all from the dad who wanted to sue every-one's ass for that little thing up there," he said, referring to Anne's likely death.

He continued: "The father got me fired from my job at Stony Brook, okay? He made sure of that. He was vengeful." (Ted Abraham, Anne's brother, had no knowledge of their father having anything to do with Gramly being fired from Stony Brook. "No, I think Gramly got fired based on his own bad behavior.")

In the months following Anne's disappearance, Gramly named a creek in Ramah Bay Hilda's Creek in honor of both Anne's mother and Anne herself, whose middle name was Hilda. He also told me he sent the last photographs ever taken of Anne to her family and to Stephen Loring. But when I checked with Stephen and with Anne's siblings, they said that they never received those photos.

The Smithsonian conducted an internal review, but, from the outset, Gramly felt confident he would be cleared. "I had already gone through the interview with the Royal Canadian Mounted Police and the lie detector test," he told me. "Passed that all fine and everything. You know, they knew that I didn't commit the murder, but they all—" He stopped and chuckled at his gaffe. "*A* murder," he corrected. "I mean, I hadn't."

THE ANNE ABRAHAM RESCUE

OPERATION

FROM EXPEDITIONS IN YEARS PAST, Anne knew how important radio communication was; Bill Fitzhugh had been very clear that protocol for the Ramah team was to radio in once a day at 7 a.m. Yet four days had gone by since Anne and Gramly were dropped off, and Fitzhugh still hadn't heard a word from them.

Fitzhugh was worried enough about the lack of communication that he planned to evacuate them early, but everything that could have gone wrong did: He tried to arrange a boat rescue for the Ramah team, but the vessel's engine had broken down. He then tried to arrange a charter flight with Labrador Airways, and when that didn't work, he tried to convince a private pilot to pick them up, but the pilot already had plans to fly south that night. Fitzhugh assured himself it was probably just atmospheric conditions in Labrador interfering with radio frequencies; he had experienced periods of up to a week when no communication was possible. But when he still hadn't heard from Mike and Anne by August 6—a full week had elapsed since their drop-off—Fitzhugh was determined to make a trip to Ramah the next day. Before he could, on August 7, 1976, Fitzhugh got the call from Gramly.

————

On August 8, Ted Abraham's phone rang. It was his mother calling to say that Anne was missing and had last been seen on an iceberg floating out to the bay. The information was garbled, but the message was clear: Ted needed to go up to help find her.

The journey felt endless. Ted drove up to Montreal with his friend Michael Maloney, and they hopped on the first flight to Goose Bay. At 6:45 a.m., a search-and-rescue helicopter transported them up to Nain, where

Stephen Loring had been waiting. From there, the three men, accompanied by a Canadian police officer, flew a couple of hours farther north. The diesel fumes that wafted through the helicopter carriage were nauseating.

Ted was confused when they landed. He thought they'd finally be in Ramah Bay, but instead, it was an old military base with bunkers and lots of cement. They were on Saglek, he learned, but it still wasn't clear why they had stopped there.

The officer led him to a room where there was a guy sitting at a desk. Ted didn't recognize him, and the guy didn't look up from the task at hand: He was making detailed drawings of rocks on a piece of paper. It wasn't until the helicopter had been refueled, and Stephen told the man it was time to get in, and the man said, "No, I'm not going with you guys back there," that Ted realized who this stranger was.

It was the first and only time Ted ever met Gramly. "I was in no position to say, *You've got to come along.* But I was shocked." Their meeting was all of five or ten minutes. They never made eye contact.

———

As the helicopter flew over Ramah Bay, the sight was disheartening. As spectacular as the cliffs were, they were largely barren. A person would have been hard to miss on the naked slopes, and the only movement they saw was a herd of caribou.

The chopper dropped the three men off, leaving them without boat or plane charter for the search-and-rescue mission. The men set up camp where Gramly and Anne had slept. Ted crawled into Anne's old tent, where he saw her journal. The entries were filled with observations about the natural world, some stories about hiking with Gramly, and a few sketches. He couldn't tell if any pages had been torn out.

There was only one mention of the radio in her journal—that last entry about Mike setting it up.

———

Ted, Stephen, and Michael spent five days on Ramah Bay and had no trouble reaching the Fitzhughs by radio. Stephen, who was the only one familiar with the area, served as guide. Ted kept imagining he'd see Anne around the corner, waiting for him, and she'd greet him by saying, *Gee, you shouldn't have come all the way up here, I was just lost for a while.*

They tried to retrace Anne's final hours, walking to the point along the shore where Gramly said they had tried to find a shortcut. The beach was about thirty feet wide, and as Ted walked along the shore, a cliff rose up sharply to his left. To get to the quarry, Anne would have had to climb up the cliff, and then either carefully let herself down the other side or edge along a high ridge. As Ted examined the slope and tried to scale it himself—it was made of large chunks of shale that got more crumbly the higher he went—Ted believed Gramly's story less and less. Ted was certain that Anne would not have attempted it. She may have been intrepid, but she was a careful climber. Besides, if she had fallen halfway through the attempt, she would have fallen onto the beach where Gramly would have found her. And in a landscape where sound traveled crisply, it was hard to believe he hadn't heard anything. (When Gramly's police interrogator asked him if he would have heard Anne yell if she had fallen at this point, he said that the water was too noisy and he was concentrating hard on his footing.) Though Bill Fitzhugh entirely believed Gramly's account of Anne's final hours—and told Canadian cops, the RCMP, as much—Ted was sure Gramly's story was bogus.

Some time after, Ted thought he saw someone—or something—floating in the water. It was orange—a piece of plastic, maybe, or a poncho. It was hard to tell since it was half a mile away. He waded as far as he could into the icy water, but he was helpless to examine it more closely. When Ted finally managed to flag down a boat, the couple sailing it was German, and they couldn't understand his pleas.

Meanwhile, rough weather and disagreements between Fitzhugh and the RCMP slowed progress. Fitzhugh was angry that the search party he had organized comprising rock climbers and local Inuit wasn't going to be allowed to examine the area because the authorities argued that an aerial search would be more effective. Harsh winds also grounded the RCMP team and their search dog. By the time they were able to land in Ramah, the ground held no scent of Anne, if there had been any to begin with.

Ted, struggling not to feel disheartened, would later say as he looked back at that moment: "There is no proper grief and there is no proper response in a situation like that...[We were in the middle of] something bigger than we could really master."

———

By the end of the first week, they had to admit the chances of finding Anne alive were close to zero. Ted, Stephen, and Michael Maloney held a small ceremony for her, and watched as the candles they lit floated out to the sea.

On the search party's final day in Ramah, Fitzhugh flew in with some RCMP officers. One of the officers told Ted, "Time's up. You gotta get out." The police had already done a lie detector test, which Gramly had passed "with flying colors," and they didn't want to have three amateurs wandering around. They allowed Stephen Loring to do a final search of the sea caves, but by that night, everyone had returned to Nain. Fitzhugh had the task of calling Anne's father to let him know that the search had been terminated, unsuccessfully.

The RCMP said they would continue looking for Anne's body, but they called off the active search, because, according to members of the local Inuit population, the sea was swarming with sea lice. If Anne had fallen into the water, which everyone now assumed that she had, her body would have been completely devoured within three days.

Two months later, in October 1976, the Newfoundland Department of Justice announced that it "has been definitely established" that Richard Michael Gramly "bears no criminal responsibility for whatever misadventure befell her."

The Smithsonian also began its own internal review, and it had no choice but to complete its report without access to the Canadian police files, since authorities refused the institution's multiple requests. In March 1977, the Smithsonian found that negligence could be ruled out as a cause of Anne's disappearance and that it was understandable that Gramly, under such stressful circumstances, had been reluctant to volunteer for the search parties. (On the day he was evacuated from Ramah, a nurse needed to give him a sedative.) However, on the question of what happened to Anne Abraham, the report concluded: "We are frankly unable to say with any certainty what happened to her."

———

Among the files that the Smithsonian had been denied access to was the fifteen-page partial transcript of Gramly's interrogation by the RCMP. He was questioned by Officer MacDonald on August 11, 1976, five days after Anne was last seen.

Gramly told the officer that the moment he noticed she was missing, "I had a feeling right then, man, that something was wrong...A very, very strong feeling." He tried to "submerge that feeling" by reassuring himself that she must have just gone on to the quarry. So instead of contacting Fitzhugh immediately, he went back to base camp and packed enough supplies to accomplish a solid day's work at the quarry, and a sleeping bag to spend the night there. He raced over the long mountain route to try to head her off, and imagined telling her, *Anne, you beat me, you showed me up*.

But when he got to the quarry around 2:30 p.m., there was no trace of her. "See nothing, yell and yell her name with no answer received." He scanned the hillsides, searched along the stream, and called frequently for her. He also spent about an hour collecting rock specimens and taking photos. Gramly eventually returned to camp, arriving around 10 p.m. Too late, he said, to reach the Fitzhughs by radio (though the frequency was available for emergency calls at all hours). A part of him still believed that she would make her way back at low tide. He said he hardly slept at all that night, feeling low and worried, a word he underlined in his statement.

Officer MacDonald wanted to know about the nature of his relationship with Anne, and Gramly knew what he was getting at. He swore that he and Anne were not intimately involved. Stephen Loring was his friend, and "I got a wife and twin[s]. I'm not into that kind of thing, playing with her," though he admitted, "She's [a] very attractive girl. As I say, very good to rest my eyes on."

He said he admired Anne, but she was too strong-willed for his taste. Sometimes she would listen to him, and sometimes she'd call him on his exaggerations. He admitted he had felt insecure when he saw Anne writing in her journal. He worried that she didn't believe his stories.

Gramly kept talking. He said how hurt he had been the night that she was missing when he read her diary and came across an entry where she thought his story about seeing a seal in the water was bullshit. "It stung me to the quick, man...I was too shy to read any more in the journal. Because I didn't want to—what the hell am I going to see in the journal?...Maybe the clothes I wear or something like that or the way I talk or who knows. It's heavy reading."

By the end of his interrogation, Gramly's manner of speech had taken on almost a performative quality: "I don't like being the only person around when this woman is not—shows up missing. It reflects bad to me. Do you know what I mean? People is going to say, well, look, alright me killing a person. Okay. I shoved her off the cliff. That's precisely it. And I know that you have to ask about that. It's an important point."

DON MITCHELL AND
SERGEANT SENNOTT

AROUND THE SAME TIME AS I packed up my bags and said goodbye to everyone in Bulgaria, Don Mitchell walked into police headquarters in Hilo where Sergeant Peter Sennott had been waiting for him. "All you got to do is brush your gums, your jaw, your gums, your jaw, and then the roof of your mouth and stuff," Sergeant Sennott instructed Don Mitchell in one of the small interrogation rooms.

Sennott, six feet tall and husky, was much more jolly than Don expected. He was quick to laugh, and when the conversation loosened a bit, he didn't hesitate to throw in a casual *fuck*. He had a thick Boston accent, so when he said Don, it sounded more like *dawn*, and ochre was *okra*.

Sennott looked a little uncomfortable, but it wasn't just because the Hilo cops had given him a tough time on the way in. Sennott had instantly recognized that mistrust of outsiders and reflexive protecting of their own. *It's like Southie here*, he told Don. Sennott stuck out because he was far too warmly dressed for the Hawaiian weather. He told Don he planned to buy some shorts after they finished.

Don did as directed and handed the Q-tip back to the sergeant, who tucked it away with the rest of the lab materials.

"I always worry it isn't enough so I give them back the lollipop," Sennott said and laughed. "This goes to our lab and it doesn't get used anywhere else except in this case. It doesn't go into that CODIS database or any of that."

Peter had brought with him a backpack full of folders and files, but before Don let Peter get to any of it, he said, "I want to talk a little bit about why you are here and what's going on." It was what Don called his don't-fuck-with-me feeling. After having been extremely nervous before Sennott flew over—*What if they're going to pin the murder on me after all this time? What if they're only going through the motions of investigation to justify withholding the police files?*—Don relished it. "I'm having a hard time believing that this investigation is really active again...I don't think it's a coincidence that you called me not long after the *Globe* article."

Peter was patient and understanding. He was also up front. He said a lot of what he was able to do depended on the resources at his disposal. "Right now the budget must look pretty good; I'm in Hawaii," he said light-heartedly, but the message was clear: It hadn't been easy to divert resources to a fifty-year-old murder.

"I get all that," Don said. "But there are still some things that are troubling to me." He wanted proof that Massachusetts was actually working on Jane's case.

"There is stuff," Peter said. "That's the reason behind that." He gestured toward the DNA sample that Don had just handed over. "There has been a round of testing before, and there is—*something* exists. It's not astronomical numbers." He didn't reveal what the "something" was, but he told Don it wasn't the cigarette butt that many people had speculated about. "Now, were cigarette butts in the apartment? Absolutely. My god, that ashtray was filled." But they didn't exist in the lab report. Or in the evidence box.

"All I want to understand is that there is at least one object that could be tested if it worked out," Don said.

Peter nodded. "Whether it's viable? Whether it's a knock-out-of-the-park home run? Who knows." He explained, "Our lab won't test DNA unless you have something to test it against. But they'll bring it to a point and go, 'Okay, there's something here, but we're not going to go there if you don't have something to compare it to.'" Plus, they needed Boyd's DNA because they didn't have anything from Jane. "When they say there's two people here—well, which one's the victim?"

But, he explained, they did not have infinite amounts of DNA to test. "I'm sure you know this from archaeology," Peter said. After each test, the sample gets "smaller and smaller and smaller." Authorities had lifted DNA from the mystery object almost as many times as it could be lifted. This was, he was certain, their last chance.

Peter looped back to Don's earlier question about commitment. "I can look you in the eye and tell you right now that at two o'clock in the morning Boston time, Adrienne"—the assistant district attorney in charge of homicide—"was talking to me about this. Adrienne is consumed with this right now. And she's a pit bull." To prove how dedicated they were to getting this solved, he told Don they'd tracked down a reel-to-reel tape player. Not even the Cambridge cops who reopened the case in the '90s had been able to listen to the 1960s interviews, because no one could track down a machine to play them on.

"We found it from a schoolteacher that collected them…And then transferred it to this and transferred it to that. It isn't easy, okay, but people are committed to working on it. They're paying to get it done as opposed to sitting in line for ten months. They're committed to it. Sure, absolutely, newspaper things spark and push and do things…Look where I am. So help me with ancient history. You're an archaeologist. Here I am. I want to dig."

BIRTHDAY CAKE

WHEN I GOT HOME FROM Bulgaria, someone at the Harvard archives wrote me to say it had no evidence that the class where Gramly claimed he and Jane had met was ever taught. Where did the truth end: the class, knowing Jane, or both—or neither?

I turned to the notes I took during my two phone calls with Gramly, hoping to find a version of events that would feel like it held together for at least a moment. And that's when I saw it: It was during the second call, when he had been describing his difficult breakup with Mary McCutcheon—who became one of the Golden Girls.

"In fact," he had told me, "her sister was a student in the master's program at the university somewhere. I even baked her a birthday cake."

COME OUT OF THE DARK EARTH

THE "FOUR TO SIX WEEKS" that District Attorney Marian Ryan said the DNA testing would take came and went. Mike Widmer and I were still waiting for a response from our June appeals. The lawyer who had offered pro bono help stopped responding to emails. The supervisor of public records, Rebecca Murray, had ordered an *in camera* inspection of a sample of the records, so that she could personally assess the DA's claims, but she hadn't yet announced whether the DA's office had provided sufficient evidence that the case was indeed active and ongoing.

As August threatened to turn to September, I got ready for a permanent move back to Harvard. I wanted to be as close as possible to the archives and to the institution at the heart of the story. I had finagled that "Elf" position in Adams House, which would grant me room and board and, most important, time as I tried to make sense of all these stories and all my notes. It hadn't occurred to me how physically vulnerable I would feel writing about Jane's story on Harvard's campus. Instead, I dreamed of what I called immersive insanity. I wanted to focus on nothing but Jane, but I didn't realize the extent to which I'd get my wish.

When I arrived and unpacked, I was caught off guard by how much my body remembered the standard-issue furniture. I had forgotten how well I knew the wooden desk chair that was built to tip back; I hadn't realized my foot still remembered how high to kick to close the bottom dresser drawer.

The intensity of my bodily recognition made it harder to reconcile the unfamiliarity of the faces. Sometimes the undergraduates cleared a space around me when I sat at a table in the dining hall. Other times, I was so invisible that people actually walked into me. Surrounded by the shadows of my friends, I felt like I belonged to a world of before.

———

In mid-September, Alice Abraham, Anne's sister, wrote me. It was the first time we had been directly in touch. She was back from her summer travels and invited me to meet her in person at her wife's office in Brookline.

Alice was a big woman, tall, with caribou-shaped earrings and a braid that reached her mid-back. But as she spoke about her sister's death, pulling out photos and maps, I realized she was more like glass than anyone I'd ever met. She said that when she read Gramly's "Jane never got justice" quote in the *Boston Globe* article, "it triggered insomnia for twenty days and a lot of ugly things in me. I was basically screaming inside about the arrogance of Gramly." I was grateful that her wife, Chris, stayed in the room with us—an anchor, and a professional therapist—so I didn't have to take all the emotional responsibility, not that I even would have known how.

Alice's voice quivered as she spoke. She said Anne's death had haunted her family. In high school, Alice was the person teachers sent students to after the passing of a relative or a friend. Her mother, like Jane's, passed away from cancer within a few years of the tragedy. Alice functionally lost her sister, Dorothy, to religion. That left her brother Ted, but they didn't discuss Anne until recently. "He has his own problems, and he handles it very differently," Alice told me. He felt responsible for Anne having gone up there, for having introduced her to Bill Fitzhugh in the first place.

In the silence, the wound festered. Alice still lived inside the grief.

I asked her what she wished people would have asked her all these years.

"I guess wanting validation. Being believed. Heard at least. Because it's been a knot, you know, honestly. There's no way to explain to most people. There's nothing they can relate to, to grasp this. Do I call what it is a disappearance? Do I call it a death? Do I call it a murder? A cold case? These labels, what do they mean?"

She told me how much of a godsend Stephen Loring had been to her, sending her eclectic postcards for years. She described him as a kind of "imaginary character" trying to keep up her spirits. She surmised that the poetry he saw in the world was a way of distancing himself from the reality of it. I hadn't realized that Stephen and his wife, who had passed not long before I spoke to him for the first time, had been married for thirty-five years. (I also hadn't realized his wife was Joan Gero, one of the founders of Gender Archaeology—the subfield that Iva Houston had told me about at the coffee shop.)

Chris left, and Alice and I discussed the trip to Labrador for the thirtieth anniversary of Anne's disappearance that Stephen had helped her with. Alice didn't expect to find Anne's remains. She wanted to touch the rocks that Anne had loved so much and to see the place that she had had nightmares about since her sister's disappearance.

At the end of the trip, Alice, Chris, Stephen, and a childhood friend of Anne's held a small memorial service for her. Alice made a short speech: "Well, Anne, we came up here to say hello. It's been a long time. Thirty years. And we're leaving a picture of you, and a poem by May Sarton. And a tiny little gold frog off one of your bookmarks because the trauma of losing you"—her voice broke—"was a major bookmark in all of our lives."

Stephen read the Sarton poem called "Invocation," whose haunting lines were, appropriately, part farewell, part incantation. It began:

> Come out of the dark earth
> Here where the minerals
> Glow in their stone cells
> Deeper than seed or birth.

Now Alice told me, "I didn't know if actually I was ever coming back to work. Or if I was gonna—Chris doesn't know this. I didn't know if my heart was going to just break, and I was going to want to die there."

At the end of the interview, Alice handed me a piece of the milky Ramah chert she'd brought home from her visit to Labrador. It was exactly what I had imagined from reading about it—almost a sugar crystal. She wanted me to keep it, so I tucked it in my bag, along with a few other items she had given me.

One of these was a copy of a paper Anne wrote in high school: "Most people react to death with sorrow," the paper began. "I hope that my death-state will not be emphasized by a marked grave. If I must have a tomb, then let me be buried in the ocean."

I couldn't shake how troubled I was that Anne, like Jane, seemed to predict her own death. I felt lightheaded as I walked back into the sunlight. It was as if I'd spent all my energy holding it together for the two-hour conversation, and when it was done, my body finally let all the tension go. My toe caught on the metal tracks of the Green Line, and I went horizontal and spread like a flying squirrel. That was the night that Lulu asked me if it was true that when you turn thirty your body falls apart and all your friends leave you because they get married, and I nodded as I hugged my bandaged knees.

THE INVESTIGATION

IN 1995, THE YEAR AFTER Gramly founded the American Society for Amateur Archaeology, Cambridge Police officer John Fulkerson met with a writer named Susan Kelly. Susan had gotten to know some of the Cambridge officers doing research for her crime novels, and she had stumbled across Jane Britton's murder while working on her book about the Boston Strangler. She looked into the red ochre mystery, and the deeper she got in it, the more she came to suspect a man who lived in North Andover. She had come to report her suspicions to Fulkerson.

Fulkerson listened to what Susan had to say and was startled when later that day a letter arrived from a Dr. Richard M. Gramly, on "Great Lakes Artifact Repository" letterhead.

It was addressed to the Keeper of the Records of the Cambridge Police Department:

Dear Sir/Madam:

Several months ago I contacted your office by telephone and asked about records relating to the murder of Miss Jane Britton. She (and another person, as I recall) had died under bizarre circumstances in 1968 (October?).

Jane was a fellow student in the same academic department at Harvard University. To this day her death disturbs me.

Now that over 25 years have elapsed and certain persons have retired from the University, I intend to look into this sorry matter with the hopes of getting to the bottom of it (in my own mind).

Therefore, I request permission to access the Britton file and the file of the other victim who was murdered at the same time (?) and under similar circumstances (?). I learned about the other victim from the newspaper stories at the time of the events.

I am planning to come to Cambridge on the 25th or 26th of October. Kindly tell me what procedures I must follow.

Thank you for your assistance.

Sincerely,
R. M. Gramly, PhD
Curator

The second murder Gramly was referring to was likely Ada Bean's, which had happened less than a month after Jane's on Linnaean Street. Fulkerson highlighted Jane Britton and Richard Gramly's names. If Gramly had called months before, the message had missed him. Fulkerson scrawled at the bottom of the page: "Same name as one given today!" The coincidence alone seemed enough to reopen the investigation.

Jane's case file—about four boxes, each four by two feet—was in shambles. Reports were scattered at the bottom of the boxes; an ashtray was tossed in; there was evidence that had never been logged. As Fulkerson and his partner Brian Branley put it back together, they realized that the boxes seemed incomplete. There were no crime scene photographs. No polygraphs. No medical examiner report. No record of what additional physical evidence might have been preserved. He knew the standard for police work was different in the '60s, but it still felt strange.

When Fulkerson got Gramly on the phone, Gramly asked how far the police had gotten with their investigation. The officer felt like he was digging for information.

They made plans for Gramly to come by the station when he was next in town. But shortly before the scheduled meeting, he changed his mind and sent a package to Fulkerson instead. The package contained a cover letter; a hand-drawn map of the Peabody Museum, indicating the location of the Putnam Lab; and a letter about his suspicions, which he titled: "WHAT I RECALL ABOUT THE JANE BRITTON MURDER AND AFTERWARD." His story was a little different than the one he would tell me two decades later. Gramly admitted to knowing Jane—he wrote that she had invited him over for tea—and finding the opened container of red ochre in the Putnam Lab was the central scene here, too. But in this version, the person it pointed to was not Lee Parsons, but Carleton Coon. (Gramly would later say that he never saw a roster of the Putnam Lab caretakers, so he couldn't be sure who came before him.) Coon was the professor of the class where Gramly would later say he got to know Jane—the one Harvard had no record of.

> *I formed an idea that Carleton Coon may have committed the murder as he had 1) an irascible temperament, 2) had reason to go to J. Britton's apartment [she was drawing artifacts for him], 3) had an office right across the hall from my lab where the ochre had been found, and 4) knew the significance of the ochre.*

Fulkerson contacted Susan Kelly after Gramly's letter came in, and he let her read it. She saw that Gramly also tried to throw suspicion at a second person: a woman named Martha Prickett, a graduate student of Lamberg-Karlovsky's, who by all accounts was shy, nervous, and studious. Gramly explained that in 1978, Martha Prickett was helping him move items from the fifth floor to the Peabody's attic storage when Jane's murder came up.

> *IMAGINE MY SHOCK when she mentioned that one of the 'suspects' was the person who found the box of red ochre in the Putnam Lab!!!!!!! She did not even realize it was I! Clearly she had heard this lie from someone wishing to cover their tracks or she had concocted it herself! And why not? I got to thinking that 1) Martha was certainly strong enough to commit battery, 2) she had no boyfriends and perhaps, therefore, Jane was a possible love of hers, 3) Martha was very protective (in my mind) of Lamberg-Karlovsky and she may have acted defensively if Jane had entangled Karl in some web of romance, 4) she had been to Iran and knew about red ochre.*

Gramly ended his letter: "Coon has gone to his grave but Prickett is still 'out there.'"

The accusations, the anger, and the avoidance of direct questioning all pointed in the same direction. Fulkerson felt sure they had their guy. He and Branley just needed to get the evidence to confirm it.

Over the course of the year that followed, Fulkerson obtained a set of

Gramly's fingerprints from the FBI, who had them from Gramly's Peace Corps days, and he escalated the case through the department. By November 1996, Cambridge PD's commander of detectives Thomas O'Connor described Gramly as "a primary suspect in this case." O'Connor asked for assistance in tracking down any and all physical evidence, since the only items they had a record of were "an ashtray with a latent fingerprint on it, and the butts of several cigarettes. Also found was a piece of granite with blood on it," which he didn't feel was the murder weapon. The medical examiner report had still not been located, "thus we are unsure if the victim may have been raped." O'Connor had no particular reason to suspect that other physical evidence existed but was hoping that an unaccounted stash of serological evidence might be found and could be tested all these years later.

In January 1997, Massachusetts State Police got involved again. Trooper Peter Sennott met with John Fulkerson, Assistant DA John McEvoy (Adrienne Lynch's predecessor), and Cambridge Police officer Patrick Nagle. Sennott agreed to help with the reinvestigation. The day after the meeting, Sennott contacted the Massachusetts State Police Crime Lab, looking for any and all evidence related to the Britton case. And he contacted the RCMP about Anne Abraham's disappearance. Sennott wrote down the names of Corporal Jon Langille and Corporal Dexter Gillar of Nain, and he jotted notes while on the call with the RCMP:

> Polygraph transcript. "Past tense" ie → dead
> Statement analysis → he is lying (Gramly) [. . .] Very suspicious
> Polygraph in 76 passed. Re exam now think he did it

Despite this renewed suspicion of Gramly, Corporal Langille told Sennott there was no plan to reopen the Anne Abraham case, but he agreed to look for her file and pass it along.

In the meantime, Sennott got the news he had been hoping for. Dr. George Katsas, the man who had performed Jane's autopsy, had in fact saved physical evidence. On February 20, 1998, Dr. Katsas turned over the thirteen slides he had saved from Jane's autopsy. Among those slides was a vaginal smear, which contained trace amounts of semen. If Jim Humphries was telling the truth, and he and Jane really hadn't had sex that night, then that sperm belonged to an unaccounted-for man, who, at the very least, was among the last to see Jane alive. Police needed to know who that man was, and in order to do so, they needed to develop a DNA profile from the vaginal smear. The chance of developing something usable from forty-plus-year-old DNA was slim, but not zero. Sennott sent the slides to the crime laboratory.

While Sennott was waiting to hear back, Corporal Langille got in touch. It was now June, and he faxed Sennott to say he had finally located a copy of the case report for Anne Abraham. A week later, it arrived in the mail. Langille's cover letter stated: "We believe that Dr. Gramly knows a lot more about this young lady's disappearance than he told the investigators at that time." Sennott forwarded the case report to the assistant DA and summarized the contents that had lived inside a manila folder labeled "DO NOT DESTROY (body not located)." "In short," Sennott wrote, revealing his take on the incident, "Anne Abraham disappeared off the face of the earth in 10 minutes, she was not reported missing for 20 hours."

In September of the same year, Cellmark Diagnostics, a lab in German-town, Maryland, announced it had developed a profile from the DNA found on the vaginal smear slide. The lab had been able to differentiate the sperm fraction and the non-sperm fraction of the vaginal smear slide—meaning that it contained, as suspected, both male and female DNA—and the test had yielded information about three locations on the male's genome. Three loci were enough to narrow down the range of suspects, but hardly enough to get it down to a single person. (In comparison, CODIS searches today require at least eight loci.) About half of the sample had been consumed in the process.

Labs across the country ran the limited DNA profile through their CODIS databases. There were a number of hits for people in Alabama and Florida, but those leads went nowhere. One of the people had been five years old at the time of the murder.

By 2004, the technology had advanced enough that authorities were hope-ful they might be able to get a more informative profile from the vaginal smear. Again, they used a differential extraction procedure to try to isolate the sperm fraction from the other cellular matter. They tested the material at nine different loci, plus the sex indicator. But this time, there wasn't a result that could help identify a suspect at any of the locations. There just wasn't enough DNA.

Undeterred, Cambridge Police and Massachusetts State Police, working in tandem, pushed on with their investigation. MSP found Gramly's license details, including his ID photo. He was no longer the lithe man that Mary McCutcheon had fallen so quickly for. The years had thickened his face and added jowls. A heavy mustache lidded his upper lip. They pulled details about his family members, the books he had written, and his archaeological sites. On a printout of the residential property record card for his house, someone had added a handwritten note that trash was picked up on Tuesday mornings.

It was all building to the day in November 2005, when Sennott showed up at Gramly's house in North Andover. He asked Gramly for a saliva sample. Gramly agreed and signed the consent form. Sennott sent the sample to Bode Technology Group in Virginia for testing and comparison. There may not have been enough DNA in the 2004 testing to produce a profile, but if Gramly matched on the three loci of the 1998 profile, they might finally be somewhere.

On February 6, 2006, Bode sent its Forensic Case Report to ADA John McEvoy. It had been more than ten years since Fulkerson received that eerily timed letter from Gramly, setting off the decade of patient detective work that led to this moment. McEvoy had to flip to the second page for the result:

Richard Gramly can be excluded as a potential contributor to the profile obtained from the vaginal smear slide (A-69-8-V).

Part Six

THE LEGACY

2018: SOMETHING HAS BEEN SETTLED

"Hello?" I say.

"Hello," Don replies in a strange, resigned singsong. I scrutinize his voice for any hint of what he knows, and his tone makes me doubt that there's finally an answer, a name. But then again, Don doesn't always have the most straightforward reactions.

He chuckles. "I just got off the phone with Peter, and the news is that—" He searches for the right words. "There isn't all that much news except that something has been settled. It's going to be another two weeks before they make a public announcement. But they *will* make a public announcement."

I try to modulate my disappointment into something that sounds closer to curiosity, but it comes out as "Huh." All I'm thinking is, *We waited for five days, only to learn we have to wait for two more weeks?*

"Here are my notes," Don says, and he reads off his bullet points:

- *We've ID'd somebody.*
- *He said this person came across our screens a few years ago but we couldn't do anything. Or we couldn't get anything done.*
- *Nobody who's alive.*

From the original three, that leaves only Lee Parsons.

Don tells me that Sennott was jovial on the phone. A little jokey, even. But when it came to confirming that they've got someone as a suspect in this case, Peter "didn't waffle at all." He said, "We've got this. This is done."

They are going to try to get Boyd to go to the press conference, but Boyd doesn't want to be a part of the circus. He says he has some "commitments." Don doesn't mention whether or not he would want to attend. But he tells me he has another idea for how to mark the occasion. When important people visit or important milestones are reached, Don and Ruth plant something in their backyard to memorialize the moment. There was one for each of their grandchildren, and one, even, for me. Don says that he wants to plant a tree for Jane on the day we find out who killed her.

He also said that Sennott gave a little teaser for the denouement ahead: "'You know, it's a pretty amazing story. You'll love it when it comes out.'"

"He didn't offer anything else?" I ask.

"Nope. Not a damn thing."

I guess we'll wait for two weeks, we lamely say, unsure how to say good-bye. We want to stay on the phone, two of the only people in the world with the information, linked in the limbo of knowing without knowing anything.

After we hang up, my body goes limp like it did when I was little, and my mother came home from the hospital after three days away for tonsillitis. My father passed me to her, and she hugged me tightly, expecting me to hold her back, but instead my body just collapsed into hers, my muscles finally letting go after days of tension.

I consciously don't put the metal baton that Harvard police gave me on my bedside table that evening. It's the first night I go to sleep without a bogeyman in almost a decade.

STEPHEN LORING

WHEN I REACHED STEPHEN LORING again, I expected to hear another account of Gramly's suspicious behavior. Yes, Stephen was disappointed—disgusted, even—by Gramly's behavior after Anne disappeared, but mostly he was just very, very saddened by the devastation Gramly left behind.

Loring said he never suspected Gramly in Anne's death. He had long ago accepted that it just was an accident. "I went and climbed the cliff that she was reportedly climbing and fell off of it. It was a hard place that nobody should be on."

But Stephen understood that the Abraham family never achieved a similar peace. "It's so easy to mistrust Mike" that, for some, thinking he was behind Anne's death was "almost the easiest solution." So he found himself telling them Jane Britton's story as a kind of comfort, because in his version of

Jane's murder, Gramly was not the suspect. "This other wild card," he told me, was. Loring hoped that by convincing Anne's family that someone else killed Jane, he might be able to convince them that her death was a tragedy, not a murder, and that the thought would offer some solace.

"I'm very comfortable with Lee Parsons as the culprit," Stephen told me and began to elaborate.

MONTE ALTO

STEPHEN LORING HAD DONE WELL enough during his winter and summer jobs at the Peabody Museum in 1969 that Lee Parsons, whom he had been helping to move the African art from the gallery space to storage, invited him to join the second season of his National Geographic–sponsored expedition in Monte Alto, Guatemala. Lee explained that he needed someone to drive his project vehicle down from Milwaukee, and if Stephen did that, he was welcome to stay and help. Stephen couldn't imagine anything better.

A few months later, in January 1970, Stephen flew to Milwaukee and met Noah Savett, an Antioch student, whom Lee had also invited on the expedition. While they were getting ready to set off, Lee got in touch with a strange request. He explained a few months prior, his mentor, Stephan de Borhegyi, had died, and that in order to fulfill his promise to his mentor, Lee needed to scatter his ashes in Lake Amatitlán in Guatemala. Could Stephen and Noah pick up de Borhegyi's ashes from a funeral home in Milwaukee before heading south?

Stephen and Noah loaded the ashes in the back of the ocean-blue International Travelall alongside the digging equipment. They were ready to drive down to meet Lee in Guatemala when all of a sudden Lee showed up in Milwaukee. He was visibly distraught and disheveled. Lee announced that he wanted to go with them. Stephen and Noah knew they couldn't say no. *You're the boss*, they said.

They drove all night. As soon as they crossed the Texas-Mexico border, Lee directed them to the first bodega. He drank beer after beer, until he got "blind, stumbling drunk." He would tie another one on as soon as the bender showed signs of wearing off, and he stayed like that for three or four days, until they were south of Oaxaca.

For the next week, Lee stayed sober during the day while they visited with research colleagues at a number of important archaeological sites. At night, they'd camp, and Lee would get drunk again. He would proposition Stephen and Noah, but he was so drunk, he was easy to handle. "Leave us alone," Stephen would say, and he'd roll Lee off without a fight. Stephen wrote most of it off as the side effects of intense grief for his mentor.

Stephen Loring at one of the archaeological sites during the roadtrip to Monte Alto in January 1970. (Courtesy of the Peabody Museum of Archaeology and Ethnology, Harvard University, PM969-48-00/ 2.1)

They kept driving until they reached south-central Guatemala, where the volcanoes are up so high that before they came to the passes between them, they went through a cloud forest thick enough that they couldn't see beyond. On the other side, they descended into a world separate from everything else, with miles and miles of lakes and pastureland, the Pacific down below, and the Volcán Pacaya off in the distance, glowing red in the middle of the sky.

When they finally reached the site, Stephen was thrilled by the work—clearing the jungle brush off the mounds with a machete, watching out for poisonous snakes, wandering around looking for any rock that seemed to stir on the surface because it might have been a sculpture. Monte Alto had been part of the early development of the Mayan civilization. Colossal stone potbelly figures were being unearthed after having lain dormant for a millennium and a half. The sculptures were enormously fat, with low-relief arms carved and wrapped around the circumference of the belly like a body painted on a Christmas ornament. Some had jowls, some had defined nostrils, some were just heads, but they all seemed like serene sleeping gods watching over the land.

A Monte Alto worker kneels next to a recently uncovered potbelly sculpture for scale.

Lee's benders continued once they reached the site, but they were innocent enough. "Come on, you're supposed to be back in camp tonight," Noah and Stephen would say, dragging Lee out of the bodegas in town.

But one night, Stephen Loring was driving Lee Parsons back to Escuintla from Antigua, where they had gone to pick up money to pay the workers down at Monte Alto. Noah hadn't come along, and Stephen was alone with Lee who had been drinking all day. By the time they were ready to start back over the mountain to Escuintla, he'd had quite a lot.

Stephen made his way down the road very carefully. Much of the two hours back from Antigua was unpaved—soft volcanic ash. The fine dust the car kicked up was enough to cause a chronic runny nose. The conversation had been relatively unremarkable, but somewhere in those steep switch-backs, with the elevation constantly dropping, Lee decided it was time to bring up something that had obviously been weighing on his mind. He told Stephen that he had been accused of murder.

Lee said that he and the girl who was killed had had an affair, and that he was devastated when she cut it off. There had been some party, an end-of-year student gathering, and an accident had happened, and a rug had been burned. Lee stopped by her place sometime after this party—not long before the girl was murdered—hoping to talk to her. He came to her apartment late at night. He knocked on the door and asked to come in, but she wouldn't let him in. He pounded again. Eventually Lee left, but he came back not long after, and tried to speak to her through her door. The girl's neighbors later told police about Lee's banging on the door and shouting that night. At this point in the story, Lee turned to Stephen and said, getting increasingly heated: "You know me, Stephen. You know me. I wouldn't get angry. I don't get angry. I didn't...I don't get angry, do I?"

Stephen, never having seen Lee like this before, tried to soothe him by agreeing: "No, no. You wouldn't do that. You couldn't do that. You're a nice guy. You don't get angry. You don't get mad. You're a calm guy."

Lee was yelling now: "I'm not—I would never shout at anyone!"

The edge of the mountain road dropped off on one side of the car. Lee's sense of panic and anger was escalating, and Stephen feared that he was going to grab the steering wheel and drag them over the mountain.

He continued to try to soothe Lee. "No, no, Lee. No, you're a nice guy. You don't get angry. You don't get mad. You're a calm guy."

"Why would the neighbors say I did this? Why would they do it?"

STEPHEN LORING, CONTINUED

"I MEAN HE DIDN'T SAY he did it, but that whole conversation in the car going down over the mountains was pretty damn close to it, you know?" Stephen said, still on the call with me. "If it hadn't been for that wild night's drive through the mountains, I wouldn't have thought twice about anything."

I was struck by how much Stephen's story matched, beat for beat, Don Mitchell's. None of it—the incense, the rug, the yelling—had ever appeared in any newspaper articles. And to the best of my knowledge, Don Mitchell and Stephen Loring had never spoken.

Stephen also told me that Lee had been called back to Cambridge from Monte Alto in 1969 in order to take a lie detector test. Lee had told Stephen that he'd failed it "spectacularly," but police explained away his poor performance as an unreliable reading on a jittery drunk. Loring imagined how that might have happened: "His heartbeat must be going a million miles an hour. They can't establish the baseline. 'What's your name?' Bleep. Lie. 'What color is the room?' 'Blue.' A lie." Lee had also told Stephen that Harvard had him "lawyered up to the gills." If true, this would mean that Lee was someone worth protecting even if he was a misfit of the department.

———

A few months later, I went down to DC to meet Stephen in person for the first time. We sat on mesh chairs outside the café in the National Gallery's sculpture garden, down the street from the Smithsonian museum where he still worked for Bill Fitzhugh. He made sure I got the chair that hadn't been soaked in that morning's rain. He was in a trench coat and had a face like Tom Brokaw's that made you trust him instantly.

We talked outside for over three hours together. The sky was metal gray and kept threatening to crack open again, but for late October, it was unseasonably warm.

Our conversation kept getting interrupted by Stephen standing up to help passersby. A woman in a wheelchair struggled to open the café's door. Stephen was up, pulling the door, and extending his arm to keep it open. Leaving enough space for the chair meant shoving himself against the glass of the revolving door. "You're so nice!" the woman's friend said.

Another time, he noticed that someone had dropped her clutch in the revolving door. He picked it up and went inside the restaurant. I watched the scene through the glass. He tapped a little girl on the shoulder, and he held out a white-clasped purse with flowers. She was so startled that, for a moment, she didn't recognize it as hers. He came back through the push door. "I'm not usually this much of a good Samaritan," he said.

"I don't believe you for a second."

He joked that he had slipped them all five bucks before I arrived.

We talked about Anne. I told him that I had met with Alice, to make him feel more at ease talking about her. We discussed how fragile Alice was, and how their mother had been the same way. "After Annie disappeared, I went over a couple of times. To console them, I guess. I think it meant a lot to them. But I couldn't take it. Her mother was just—you listen to Alice talk about her mother after Anne, and it just sounds like she couldn't go on."

"What was Anne like temperamentally compared to them?"

"You're like Anne," he said.

It was the first time anyone had told me what I secretly so wanted to be true. After all these years of researching Jane, I had long ago accepted that our boundaries had dissolved, at least in my mind. But when Anne had started to creep in the edges, too—hadn't I, long before hearing Anne's name, dreamed of running off to Yellowknife; or imagined rafting to Alaska, eating salmon and frozen cranberries for breakfast?—I discounted the uniqueness of the experience. I was attracted to writing about characters like Jane and Anne precisely because I also was drawn to remote landscapes and romantic adventures. That we all happened to be about the same age and brunette and predisposed to writing in our diaries seemed insufficient evidence of what felt fundamental. I attributed the depth of my feelings to the natural process for a biographer. Breathing life into someone on the page was an act of both resurrection and transubstantiation: I wrote them by learning about them, then by holding them inside me, then by feeling for them. By the end, I'd become their host, so of course I would forget where they ended, and I started.

But for Stephen to feel the same thing was an entirely different matter.

"No, really," he said, seeing that I was reluctant to let myself believe him. He said that Alice must have seen it, too, which was why she opened up to me. "You have an Annie aspect both physically and I think..." He trailed off and changed the subject slightly.

CHATTER IN CAMBRIDGE

"I'VE BEEN CONCERNED ABOUT SOMETHING that Jane told me or asked me about, about a month ago, and I didn't know if it was relevant to this case or not, but I had a feeling it might be," Jane Chermayeff, who had been in Lee Parsons's Primitive Art class with Jane Britton that fall, told the Cambridge cops. "One day just before the class she took me aside in the smoker, and she said, 'The strangest thing happened. At twelve thirty last night, the doorbell rang.' And she said, 'I was a little surprised because most people who know me just walk up, don't bother to ring.' And it was him." After that, Jane Britton missed a couple of Lee's lectures.

Jane Chermayeff wasn't the only person in the Anthropology department talking about Lee Parsons to the Cambridge police. After all, everyone in the Peabody had seen the newspaper articles. Though Lee's name was never mentioned, many felt that only one person fit the description. On January 9, two days after Jane's body was found, the *Boston Globe* ran a cover story that included the line, "Also questioned was a faculty member who admitted dating Miss Britton once and attending several parties at which the murdered girl was present in the company of others." On January 13, the *Daily News* reported that the "Harvard faculty member who was rejected by Jane as a suitor after several dates now figures prominently in the investigation." Though some—like graduate student Frances Nitzberg—were certain that Lee was incapable of injuring someone, others wondered if Lee, whom many had seen wandering the streets of Cambridge drunk, might just have been strange enough to be the killer.

Karl Lamberg-Karlovsky said that he had been struck by how disturbed and upset Lee had seemed after Jane's death.

Even the gossip-avoidant Richard Meadow told police when he was pressed, "It has come to my attention…that Dr. Lee Parsons dated her on one occasion."

Lee's alibi for the night Jane was killed was, according to some gossip, Pippa Shaplin, the Peabody registrar. Jill's sister wrote about her in a letter to the Mitchells: "[One of the Peabody secretaries] told me that she was driving to work and when she drove past Shaplin's house, she saw her and Lee Parsons coming out. She said that she then inquired around and found out that Miss Shaplin is about 10 years older than Lee and was Lee's alibi for the night Jane was murdered. That is supposed to account for the scratches on Lee's arms. Quite interesting, I thought."

When police called Pippa into headquarters, she got so angry with the line of questioning about her romantic relationship with Lee, she shook in her chair. Detective Davenport had to ask her to stop because she was rocking the door.

ANNE MOREAU

When I got back to Cambridge from DC, I set about corroborating Stephen's story in as many ways as I could. Noah Savett, the other student who had been at Monte Alto with Loring, was nowhere to be found, and I couldn't track down any details about Stephen Edward DeFilippo, the young man on whose Woburn grave Lee had asked that his own ashes be scattered. But almost everything I *could* pin down checked out. The details about the dead mentor. The road trip down to Guatemala. That Lee had been contacted by the Cambridge Police when he was at Monte Alto. The gaps in his attendance on the site made it possible that he had returned home for the grand jury hearing. A long effort to track down a copy of Lee's lie detector test via its likely administrator ultimately came up empty, and I could find no record of Lee having been lawyered up by Harvard. But Richard Conti, the foreman of the grand jury, said he remembered Lee Parsons's name from the trial proceedings.

With confidence that I had exhausted my ability to find out about Lee through more indirect means, I finally mustered the courage to call Lee's ex-wife, Anne Moreau. All I knew was that she was born in 1932, was the daughter of Karl Jansky, who had discovered cosmic radio waves, and she lived in Ohio. I caught her as she was putting away groceries. She was so immediately open with me, I worried I was taking advantage of her disinhibition. I made it clear to her that I was calling because I was writing about Jane Britton, and that people thought that Lee might have been involved with her death.

"Oh, but it couldn't have been him," she said. "He was out of town skiing that weekend." I didn't remind her that Jane died on a Monday night. "He was not a violent person by any stretch of the imagination," she went on.

We talked for another hour, and she spoke about Lee without a trace of acrimony. Anne and Lee had met in college. They were assigned the same pit house to excavate in New Mexico—a structure dating to AD 800–1000, made by basket-maker Native Americans. She could still picture the sewing needles set vertically in graduated sizes inside the wall of the structure that she excavated. She hadn't had much experience with men until she met Lee. Anne and Lee spent eight hours in the pit house together every day that summer of '53, and by 1956, they were married.

The newlywed Lee had just finished his second year in Harvard's Anthropology department. To support him through graduate school, Anne became a teacher at a local private school. "It was a case of what we used to call PHT. Putting Hubby Through." At Harvard, Lee was a good student, but he was painfully shy and never understood how to trade in social cachet, like you had to. He found that drinking allowed him the freedom to express himself.

Later, while he was still working on his PhD, they moved to Milwaukee where Lee got a job as curator at the public museum. Lee felt at home in the intellectual climate of the Midwest—it was more inclusive and more intimate. They never had an abundant social life, but they had close friends and a community. Picnics and lake swims. Even Lee's dry sense of humor made public appearances. But when the offer came from the Peabody in 1968 to return as the museum's assistant director, Lee couldn't refuse.

This time, Anne did not go back to Cambridge with Lee. Their marriage had already become fraught—not because of his sexuality, she said, but because of his drinking problem. As the years went by, it had gotten worse. She didn't want their two girls to grow up thinking it was normal. She filed for a divorce.

Anne asked me to remind her when Jane Britton was killed.

January 1969, I said.

"Yes, our divorce was final that month."

They kept in touch a little bit through the years, for their daughters' sake. "From everything I've heard, his life at Harvard...They made it so difficult for him to be..." She stumbled to find the right words. "His difficulty in social situations really caught up with him there." Lee told her that he wished he'd never left Milwaukee.

Anne knew that after Cambridge, Lee had eventually moved to St. Louis, and she knew about Stephen DeFilippo. They'd met in Cambridge, she said, and Lee was very happy with him.

"Stephen passed away very young," I said, trying to confirm my research.

"You don't know how he died?"

I didn't.

"He drowned in a swimming pool," she said. "I don't know whether Lee had unwisely led him into a situation in a pool where maybe it was too deep for a person who had only recently learned how to swim."

When Lee died in 1996, Anne was not at his bedside. She said she'd had the chance—shortly before his death, she was told Lee was dying of AIDS—but she had decided not to go. "I'm not good with death anyway. I'd just like to go off into air or something. Spare everybody on earth anything to do with what's left of me."

I pointed out that it was interesting for someone who had worked on an archaeological site to feel that way.

She saw the irony, but maybe knowing what people can spin from your material traces made her want to erase herself all the more. "I want no part in being listed on any kind of grave memorial." No fuss. No ceremony. No grieving.

Lee's will had asked for the same thing. He wanted his ashes scattered over Stephen's grave, and he specified that there be no marker left behind. Lee just wanted to disappear.

LAST WILL AND TESTAMENT
OF LEE ALLEN PARSONS

LAST WILL AND TESTAMENT
OF
LEE ALLEN PARSONS

D2-5205

I, **LEE ALLEN PARSONS**, of the City of Fort Lauderdale, Broward County, State of Florida, being of sound mind and body do hereby declare and publish this instrument to be my Last Will and Testament, hereby revoking and canceling all former Wills and Codicils I may heretofore made and I request that my Estate be disposed of as follows:

FIRST

I hereby direct that the payment and expenses of my last illness and my specific directions contained herein for my funeral be paid as soon as practical after my death. In that regard, I wish to be cremated with no unnecessary ceremony or expense, including any grave or marker. I direct my Personal Representative, hereafter named, to take whatever token ashes exist after the cremation and have them spread over the grave of Steven De Filippo, in the Woodbrook Cemetery in Woburn, Massachusetts. I hereby instruct my friend, ████████████ of St. Louis to carry out this unorthodox last request, and the expenses of same be considered part of the last illness and funeral of my Estate.

CONFESSION CHAIN

ALL INVESTIGATIONS REQUIRE LUCK AS much as skill. I had written Jill Nash in an effort to get her to share her recollections with me directly, but as Don suspected, she proved unwilling. Nevertheless, in the final email she sent me, buried at the bottom of her response, she offered one glimmer of hope that I might be able to get farther than either Don or Lieutenant Joyce had in chasing down the alleged Lee Parsons confession chain. She wrote:

> I don't know why I react so strongly after all these years; my feelings about the case seem to get worse. Maybe it's because in the last part of my life, I see more clearly all the things that Jane was denied. [. . .] You speak of rumor and misinformation as though these can be corrected—I do not share your optimism. I even find my ex-husband revealing details that I don't believe are accurate. The "truth" about Jane's murder, how and why it happened, is not knowable. This is why I don't want to talk to you about it. I have talked myself blue in the face about it, and it has all amounted to nothing, except giving me a great fear of law enforcement.
>
> I will give you a little tidbit, though, which might add to your story: there is a woman named Olga Stavrakis, the widow of the archaeologist Dennis Puleston, who told my late friend Eugene Ogan (also a Harvard anthropologist) that she had been on a dig with Lee Parsons, and that he confessed to all [that] he had killed Jane. She lives in Minneapolis and is in her 70's. As far as I know, none of the many Jane-ites have cited her account. Perhaps you can contact her.

Once I emailed Olga, we were on the phone together within the hour.

Olga described herself as a retired anthropologist who lectured on cruise ships on the subject. It had been a kind of renaissance for her after a number of decades out of the field. On her website, she wrote that "in 1978 my Anthropological career came to an abrupt end with the unexpected death of my husband. [. . .] The academic world was unrelenting to women who had children in those days."

We turned directly to the subject of Jane Britton, and Olga said she and her husband didn't know Lee Parsons all that well. "I think I met him once or twice at professional meetings, but I can't say that I knew him at all." They worked in different parts of Guatemala, which for archaeologists was enough to be a different world.

"I understand," I said, but explained that I was trying to track down a rumor that Lee had confessed to either Dennis or to her that he had killed Jane Britton.

"Oh no, that rumor came from Joyce Marcus," she said. "She told us."

"Joyce Marcus?"

"Yes, uh-huh, at Michigan—Ann Arbor. She was at Harvard, in the department."

"And what did she tell you?"

"It was in a bar at night, and she said he had gotten drunk and said that he was somehow connected with it. I don't know. I don't even remember if I was there or if Dennis told me, so *hearsay hearsay*, you know?" But Olga was sure Joyce would have told Dennis in either 1971 or 1972, because they were in frequent touch with Joyce during those years.

Returning to Joyce's memory of hearing the confession, Olga said: "She wasn't sure if he was just drunk and talking, or if it was really real. 'We were all sitting around. We were young. We were drinking. We were partying. And it was one of those things that was just thrown out.'"

I contacted Joyce Marcus immediately after I got off the phone with Olga. Marcus, who graduated from Harvard with a PhD in 1974, was now an archaeologist at the University of Michigan. Professor Marcus was in and out of meetings all day, so she asked me to email her my questions. We exchanged a few messages and finally, without naming Lee, she allowed that she had heard "rumors and even weird drunken confessions from a few people." But, she said, "I never knew how much of that was alcohol or a need for attention." The implication that the aforementioned "few people" were involved in the crime had always struck her as "unlikely."

I asked again if she'd speak on the phone, but I never heard back.

HOW ODD AND STRANGE

WHEN JILL SAW JANE THE afternoon after the Incense Night, she noticed Jane's eyes sparkling, but she assumed it was because of her diet pills, not because she was spooked as Don thought. Jane had developed somewhat of a habit of taking uppers after she had gotten back from Iran and didn't want to gain back all the weight she'd lost.

Jane told Jill that after she and Don had left, Lee had taken out pictures of his kids. He had confided in her about how distraught he was about being cut off from them. Jane had been feeling lonely herself. Jim had been away for most of the semester—recuperating and studying in Toronto—and his visit in October seemed like ages ago.

But Jill was confused when Jane kept going on and on about "how odd and strange and everything he was." That he missed his children hardly seemed surprising. For the entire fall semester of 1968, Lee had made no secret of how upset he was about his impending divorce. She and Don both knew that when Lee visited a married couple he knew from the department, he gazed lovingly at their six-month-old daughter and asked to hold her. "I have two little girls," he said. They handed her to him, and he cuddled her, and tears started running down his face.

It seemed to Jill that something else had happened that night that Jane didn't feel ready to talk about.

WHO IS THE GHOST HERE

I FELT MYSELF AT A loss for what to believe. On the one hand, I worried I was just trying to fit suspicion onto Lee because it was easy to scapegoat the outsider and because it was hard not to love the rush of clues accumulating around a new suspect. Even Stephen Loring had said, "I don't think of Lee as an evil person. I think of him as incredibly tortured." On the other hand, perhaps my reluctance to consider him as capable of murder was replicating a pattern of disbelief. Was I excusing him like the cops had allegedly excused his lie detector test results, and Joyce Marcus had dismissed the supposed drunken confession?

Everything felt like quicksand.

I'd been back at Harvard for a few weeks, and my grip on the present had already begun to erode. There really wasn't anyone around to see me. I desperately did not want to be the "creepy" Elf, so I aimed instead for "mystery" Elf, by drinking iced coffee in my kimono in the courtyard. Needless to say, I overshot the mark.

In the dining hall, I had my own force field, and ate most meals alone. When one boy asked if the seat in front of me was taken, I looked up at him too eagerly, I'm sure. "Nope!" I said with a smile.

"Thanks," he said and pulled the chair across the way.

I had left a city I loved and an apartment I loved and a job I loved. A blossoming relationship wasn't wearing the long distance well, and I resented that I felt like I had been asked to choose between work and romance. Would the same have been true if he was the one who had to move?

But a secret part of me was also relieved. I believed—without daring to let the thought become fully conscious—that if I was happily in love, I would forget the visceral experience of longing for it, and I would lose access to Jane.

In order to make the sacrifices worth it, I threw myself even further into Jane's story. I signed up for the Harvard University Police Department self-defense course. They gave me that metal baton that looked like a ribbed shiv, and they warned me not to try to take it on airplanes. "It's legal, for now," one of the officers said. Walking around the Square, I practiced sliding away the fifty years. Bank of America was once again Elsie's, JFK Street was home to the Wursthaus, the *wurst of all possible houses*. The punk kids by the T stop were Jane's "ankle biters."

But it wasn't just Jane's life that imposed itself on me.

Adrienne Rich describes her experience of feminism as a kind of *re-vision* in her 1972 essay "When We Dead Awaken." "The sleepwalkers are coming awake," she wrote. "It's exhilarating to be alive in a time of awakening consciousness; it can also be confusing, disorienting, and painful." Her words registered in me like a shiver.

Because this strange second chance at college was insisting I also re-see *my* time at Harvard.

The undergraduates, thank goodness, were just as remarkable as I remembered my classmates being—but little else was spared.

Academia no longer felt like an idealized kingdom of learning; it was nasty and political.

The graduate students who had seemed creepy and sad were now my peers. And I realized that many were downtrodden not because that was the *type* attracted to academia, but because of the system they were locking into. Treated as interchangeable and disposable.

I saw some undergraduates—the *chosen* few, I knew—wearing heels and tuxes and rushing down the street. I knew they were headed to a "punch" event, where hopefuls would try to impress the final club members enough to give them a spot in the new class. The clubs hadn't been my entire life at Harvard, but they had been a bigger part than I cared to admit. I knew the clubs were elitist, I knew they created a problematic power dynamic, and I knew that many of my best friends had never stepped inside, and yet, I was never so critical of them that I stopped going. I had even joined one of the few all-women ones, telling myself that there was no damage done if its very existence helped mitigate the power imbalance. I saw now that it was a privilege not to be forced to examine the issue more critically, and that no matter how much I thought I stood apart from them, my hands were not clean of having perpetuated the structural problems they reinforced.

There was the Vonnegut quote that Jane had loved: "Peculiar travel suggestions are dancing lessons from God." And as I thought of it, I smiled, realizing that she'd done it again. I thought I was in Boston to retrace her steps, when in fact I was also retracing my own. And in trying to track Jane's ghost, I had become a ghost myself.

TORONTO

FOR YEARS, EVERY TIME I took a flight, I'd route the layover through Toronto, so I could contact Jim Humphries and say I'd be in town. The first time I tried, his wife replied to my email saying that my request was reasonable, but that Jim was going through a rough time. She wasn't going to pass along the message to Jim, she said, but she asked me to try again later. I never again got a reply to my messages, but the initial response had opened the door just enough for hope. This time I had sent a hand-written letter. As long as she didn't write back with a definitive no, I told myself, I could show up at his front door. I knew that Jim probably wouldn't talk about Jane, but I just needed to know that someone had actually asked.

On the day I landed in Toronto, still not having heard from either Jim or his wife, I considered how little I still knew about this man, despite my years of research. All I knew was that after four more seasons at Tepe Yahya, he suddenly withdrew from the Anthropology department. He never completed his PhD. Instead, he took over the family business on the farm he had grown up on, got married, and all but disappeared from the lives of his archaeology cohort.

The next morning, I wrote down Jim's name, and the phone number of my mother in case I didn't return home that night, and handed it to the friend of a friend who had agreed to host me for a few nights. He flashed me a look that meant, *What have I signed up for?*

I put on the most wholesome thing I owned, an ankle-length yellow sundress that made me look like a character in *Little House on the Prairie*, and took an Uber to Jim's place, which had been described to me as the last remaining farm in Mississauga. The address I put in turned out to be the side of a two-lane road. Even the driver was concerned: "Are you sure you're in the right place?" *Uh-huh*, I said unconvincingly.

I walked down a long driveway surrounded by woods on both sides. It would take me at least five minutes to run back to the main road, I realized. Toronto's Pearson Airport was less than a mile away, so planes were screaming in the sky. No one would hear me if I yelled.

In the silence between planes, I heard a woman's voice in the distance. I started toward it and came upon a house. I walked up to the front door and knocked. Nothing. I took pictures and kept moving down the small road, deeper into the woods. I scared a flock of birds into a sudden, flapping movement, and the surprise made me shake. I came upon another house, this one with a tennis court and a giant gate protecting the driveway. It seemed too fancy to match the description I'd heard from Arthur Bankoff, who had kept in touch with Jim over the years.

I continued even farther. I saw a smaller house to the right and a barn off in the distance. It hadn't occurred to me how hard it would be to show up unannounced at a farm—there were doors everywhere. I approached a greenhouse with broken windows and three canoes out back. I knocked. No one. There were papers pinned up against the windows inside. One sheet was a calendar from 1997.

I continued on, letting my imagination wander. There was rusting farm machinery everywhere: car parts, metal pipes, wooden pallets. So many dark spots where heavy equipment could fall on me, and it would look like an accident.

What if he were watching me from one of the windows? "MR. HUMPHRIES," I called. I didn't want to scare him. "MR. HUMPHRIES!" Nothing. I walked past the hay storage barn and the tanks of diesel. It felt like a high-stakes game of hide-and-seek, but I wasn't sure if anyone else was actually playing. I crossed the high grass field to a brick house crammed with unused furniture. I knocked, reluctantly. Again, no answer.

I promised myself that I wouldn't leave until I had searched everywhere I could. I had waited too long. I'd come this far.

The path ended by opening into two final fields. Mississauga's new highway ringed the edges of his farm. Cars glinted in the space between the trees. I was standing in a bubble of the decaying past, surrounded on all sides by the encroaching present.

I turned back up the driveway and passed by the smaller brick house I had walked by earlier. Walking down its tributary driveway, I finally saw the white paper sign taped to the door. On it, handwritten, was the number of the house I had been looking for. It was so straightforward that it made me laugh. I walked until I could see my reflection in the glass pane of the outer door. I reached for my phone to take a picture of the sign, but before I could, I noticed through the door's mesh screen, silhouetted by the windows at the end of the hallway, a shape in an armchair—head tilted back, glasses on head. I didn't know if the person was looking at me, but I knew whoever it was was facing me. I put away my phone. The buzzer was an actual bell, and I pulled the string to sound it, trying not to lose my courage with each tug.

NOVEMBER 1968

JANE HAD TO YANK HARD to open her door. She had shut and locked it while she was with her family in Needham for the Thanksgiving break. The wood had swollen and warped so much in that time that she couldn't be bothered to lock it again for the rest of that winter of 1968. Her apartment was cold, and she made a mental note to get the landlord to fix her heat. Not long after, she found a letter from Jim Humphries waiting for her in her mailbox.

Over the summer in Tepe Yahya, imagining Jim's semester away, she had worried about getting letters signed *Sincerely Yours*. Addressing him in her journal, she mused, "Maybe you could compromise + put Dearest Jane instead of Dear or something?"

Dear Jane, Jim's letter began.

Look, I know I'm not terribly encouraging on phone calls but don't beg for comfort and affection and sentiment. It's degrading for you and it's no compliment to me. I know you've had and have more than your share of troubles but not to throw them at me. The Humph's slanted and probably threadbare shoulder is always available with pleasure if it helps anyone, but don't make it a basis of a relationship.

Less than six months before, Jim had literally been sweeping her off the street in London, where they shared a few days before continuing to Iran. He had bought her flowers at 5:30 in the morning. Now this letter was her reality. Even before she'd left Cambridge for the summer, she warned herself not to let her guard down: "Should have been my old wary self and known there's gotta be a catch somewhere." But there had been one day in particular when she'd let herself think it was going to be different with Jim.

While in London, they had taken a day trip to Oxford. They lounged by the river and allowed themselves to imagine the peaceful rural life they could have if they stepped away from academia. They were so happy they half joked that it'd be a good idea to cable Fearless Leader—what they called Karl—to say they were retiring to raise ducks and the hell with archaeology.

On the train back, Jane and Jim ran into an old friend from Jim's college years, who had insisted on treating the two of them to a round in the Paddington Station bar. They made friends with a few locals, each of whom also insisted on treating them to a round, so Jim and Jane were tipsy and tired by the time they poured themselves onto the Underground to head back to the hotel.

At 9:30 p.m., they still hadn't had dinner.

"What about food?" Jane had asked.

Jim walked over to the phone. She couldn't hear who he was speaking to.

"Get dressed, we're going to eat," he'd called over to her.

Once he had finished putting on a new shirt, he walked back to her and saw what she'd picked out. "No, you better put on something dressy," he said. "It's kind of a swish place."

"Where are we going?" Jane asked. Jim didn't answer. He shaved in her sink and changed his shirt again.

It wasn't until their taxi pulled into the driveway off the Strand that Jane understood: They were at the Savoy, the fanciest hotel in the city. After dinner, Jim took to the dance floor. "Have you ever danced with anyone 6'7" in altitude?" Jane would later write.

It was almost 3 a.m. by the time they started making their way back to the hotel. They bought a bottle of milk off a milkman and drank it down and sang Irish songs, and Jim picked her up and carried her across Russell Square, with Jane playfully yelling, "PUT ME DOWN!" A cop smiled at them.

Jane woke up early the next morning to rearrange the bedding before housekeeping came so it would look as if Jim had just come in to pack up his gear. When Jim left to do some errands, Jane started a letter to her parents: "Ah to be in London + in love. He is, you know. With me, I mean. [. . .] Said so, too. Funny, I think, all things being equal, this might be the real thing. Time will tell."

It was the first time he had said it. She couldn't stop smiling. She wrote that she felt like a piece of tarnished silver that had just gotten polished.

"The thing about this one is that he's *real*. And does insane and un-anthropological things like *cares*. And likes doing things for people (like me, for example) and doesn't have any kind of macho complex or take drugs + loves horses + let's just see what happens. He's the only person I've EVER met who can snap me out of a Mood + also tells me I'm beautiful which is horseshit but what an incredible feeling."

Jane realized how much she was spilling to her parents—"God, this drivel I'm pouring out!"—so she turned to her journal. "And all this time I thought you were just making the last days of the marmot a little (hell, infinitely) more blissful. Oh, I love you too, big Canuck. It's been a long time since I really loved someone, pure + simple + no questions asked, instead of playing at being in love." Jane tried to suppress the sense that it might all come tumbling down. She prayed he wouldn't turn back on his words. "It would tear me apart," she had written.

But now here was this letter. He spent the next third of it explaining that he couldn't help guarantee her a spot on the next season of Tepe Yahya. "If you are wanting to continue at Yahya, either for proximity to me or for putting in time, it would be much better if you knocked it off."

He had said he didn't want to be alone anymore. He had said he really loved her. That day in London, she had felt like the girl bunny in *Pogo*, her favorite comic strip, with whom a fish fell in love and the girl replied: "And me only a week old." That's how Jane had felt. Different. Softer, somehow. Numb, even.

Jim ended the letter:

I enjoy and cultivated your company because Jane Britton is capable, intelligent and has diverse and imaginative interests, not because she is one bedraggled, bewildered marmot with a potential for scratching backs, affection, comfort and other silly things. I'm not moving around for crumbs of cookies but for a whole big cake with chocolate icing as well. In other words, there is no question of Dogsbody wanting a fur coat but this man wouldn't mind escorting a queen, otherwise forget it entirely.

Above not intended as a broadside but as a warning of a state of mind.

Looking at his letter, dashed off on loose-leaf paper, her fears about *Sincerely Yours* seemed silly in comparison, because was there anything more horrifyingly indifferent than "Health + luck, Jim"?

JIM HUMPHRIES

THE FIGURE SILHOUETTED BY THE window of that Toronto farmhouse did not move. Another emerged, however, and as this second figure got closer, it took the shape of a woman. She had short-cropped white hair and was maybe five foot three. She opened the door, and when I saw the brightness of her blue eyes, I instantly felt apologetic. There was no hint of wariness. She had no idea who I was.

"Hello?" she said.

"I just wanted to introduce myself," I said, and her eyes narrowed a bit. She knew what I was about to say. "My name is Becky Cooper—I had written you a couple of emails and letters—"

"We've been trying to tell you. Jim doesn't want to see you."

"I just—" I stammered. I wasn't welcome there. The insanity of having just trespassed on his property registered all at once. "I'm just trying to do my best to celebrate Jane's life, and I'm talking to as many people as possible who knew her. If I could just ask Jim in person if he—"

"I'll ask," she said reluctantly. "But he did tell me that if this happened, he just didn't want to talk."

She shut the door and walked to the figure in the armchair. The figure uncurled his body from his seat and became bigger as he approached the door. He opened the screen and then the glass—the removal of each one like lifting a filter off himself. When he appeared in the doorframe, with nothing mediating the space between me and him, it was like color rushing into a black-and-white film.

He propped his hand on top of the door and leaned his hip into it to keep it open. "So you've finally tracked down Jim," he said, knowing he was already a character in my story.

He was wearing a dark chambray shirt, and the front pocket was loaded with pens. He was much more handsome than I expected him to be. And much more mischievous. His hair was gray, but he had a full shock of it, and he tilted his head boyishly. I almost didn't know if it was really him. He seemed too young, too playful. I wanted to shake his hand—to bridge the gap—but I didn't.

"Now we know what the other looks like," he said. I had entered into his life as a character as well. He continued: "But look, two things." He told me that he had to deliver hay somewhere right now and that he should get going soon. "And, second thing: I don't want to talk about Jane."

"Can I ask why?"

"It's a long time ago," he said. "And I just don't think it's anyone's business."

I had expected this. I had my own version of this complaint, which I offered to him, as a kind of entreaty: "What bothers me is that people talk about what happened to Jane, but no one knows anything about her."

"Oh, that's okay. People will talk," he said. "Even in farming we have our stories."

I let the moment linger. That was all I had needed to know. It felt like the world's quietest victory just to have finally been able to ask and to hear his answer. I promised him I would no longer bother him. And then I took the long walk back to the main road.

On the car ride home, I reflected on the irony of all these archaeologists telling me that something was too far in the past. They claimed that there was no point in unearthing a truth from so long ago, but of course this claim stood in direct opposition to the central premise of their work. Sure, any story told about Jane was bound to be contaminated and flawed—a narrative used in service of a current purpose. But there was value in the truth preserved, and value in studying the distortions introduced and the nature of the details lost.

Nevertheless, I wondered whether Jim's silence might be the most honorable approach to Jane's story. By not talking about it, he refused to wield it in service to himself. It stood in stark contrast with the reappropriation and molding of Jane's story by so many of the others I had spoken to. For female graduate students, it had become a kind of cautionary tale about the systemic imbalances they faced. Karl sometimes seemed to have his own strategic relationship with the myth. I wasn't innocent, either: Jane had become something to keep me company. A way to structure my life. Something to give it meaning.

I began to wonder if there was something inherently American about this repurposing of the past, versus Humphries's refusal to cling on. This certainly seemed to ring true at Harvard where ceremony and tradition were passed down as an invitation into something much larger than just school. It was an initiation into a different life. I had wanted that velvet and sherry, and it was only in coming back to it—because of Jane—that I had stopped to ask what else I was accepting in order to take in all of the lushness.

What would a culture look like, I wondered, that, recognizing the limitations of memory and rejecting the half-truths of reconstructions, discouraged nostalgia? What would the consequences be of a collective shedding of history? I tried to imagine how the future would change if we really allowed ourselves to let go.

JANE'S LAST DAY

On January 6, 1969, the day before exams, things were going much better with Jim. He had been back since just after Christmas, and the chilliness that she'd felt from his Thanksgiving letter had dissipated. In fact, Bill Rathje, who had been with Jim just before he had written her the letter, was sure that what had come out as frostiness was just Jim's reluctance to dive into something headlong. Jim needed Generals out of the way before he could have the clarity of mind to fully commit. But Bill was sure that Jim liked Jane very much.

Other people noticed, too. In early January, when Jane dropped by her friend Ingrid's place to congratulate her and her husband on their recent marriage, Ingrid couldn't remember Jane ever looking so good. Jane unloaded the armful of books she had been carrying, plopped down on Ingrid's bed, and talked happily about how she was going to go over to Richard and Jim's place that night because they were going to cook her dinner. Even Sarah Lee Irwin, who tried to date Jim in the spring, had to admit that things seemed to be going well between the two of them. Later, she would tell the police, "There has been a great change in Ms. Britton in the last two months, and for the first time I think she has achieved a measure of security, or peace."

The evening of the sixth, Jim arranged dinner at the Acropolis on Mass Avenue for Jane and himself and three friends—Richard Meadow, Kent Day, and Bill Rathje—because all five of them were going to be taking Generals, and a little distraction would be good to calm the nerves. Jim, who was in a coat and tie and the maroon rugby sweater he wore when he skated, showed up early with Richard. Jim left his skates by the cigarette machine at the front of the restaurant, and they reserved a table in the back while they waited for the rest of the crew to arrive.

Rathje had agreed to pick up Kent and Jane. Kent had to ring her buzzer repeatedly to summon Jane from her room, and she eventually yelled down at him from the stairwell to knock it off. She had been napping—Don felt bad when he had woken her up earlier that afternoon to get some London broil from her freezer for dinner—and she hated that buzzer.

Don heard the commotion and went out of his apartment to talk to Jane.

"Are you going out?" he asked. She said yes. He could tell she was in a bad mood. He asked if she'd be back at eight because she always came over on Monday nights to watch TV. She said no and didn't offer any more details.

"Here I am. Let's go," Jane said when she opened the door to Rathje's car. She was wearing a skirt and her auburn fur coat. Her mood eased over the course of dinner—she and Jim and Rathje split a bottle of retsina, and they all made it a point to avoid talking about Generals—but Jane looked happiest, Rathje noticed, when they split off at 7:30 p.m.: Richard to his girl-friend's place, Rathje and Kent home to watch TV, and Jim and Jane to walk by themselves down Mass Avenue back to the Square.

Jim checked to make sure Jane still felt like skating, which she did, so they went back to her place so she could change out of her skirt and grab her skates. Jim waited in the kitchen while she got changed. He smoked a few cigarettes and was relieved that her apartment was warm. He knew she had been having trouble with her heat the weekend before. He thought to himself, *At least she'll be okay for tomorrow.* She left her fur coat at home and wore her blue ski parka instead.

The sky was still mostly clear when they reached Cambridge Common. It wasn't a cold night, but it was cold enough for solid ice. They only skated for twenty minutes before they were both tired. A pint of beer sounded like a better idea. They walked the ten minutes back to the Square and had a pint at Charlie's Kitchen down the block from Jane's apartment. By the time Jim walked Jane home, around 10:30 p.m., a little sleet was coming down.

At Jane's, they took off their coats, and she made hot cocoa while Jim kept her company in the kitchen. Then they sat on her bed, over her fur throw spread like a coverlet. Books were scattered around them. They cupped their metal enamel mugs while they talked. He stayed for long enough to smoke four cigarettes. The lightness of Jane's mood from earlier in the evening had clouded back over. She was in one of those states that her friend Ingrid knew well: "She would get very depressed about work. The thing about Jane was you would try to tell her she was a great girl. You know, you try to mention all these talents of hers and her accomplishments and so forth, and she'd just sit there and stare at you, you know. If she was depressed, you could not get through to her. And she let herself get completely inundated by negative thinking." Jim tried his best, reassuring her about the exams and about Iran.

It was nearly midnight when Jim stood up to put his coat on. Jane said she would drive him home. She didn't normally—Jim liked the cold air after an evening spent inside smoking—but it had started raining heavily while they were talking. He said no. Jane said she wanted to start her car anyway; it had been a while since she'd driven it. He still didn't let her. There was no point in dragging her all the way out. He didn't want her to get cold. He kissed Jane good night and started the fifteen-minute walk home, lugging his skates in the pouring rain.

After Jim left, Jane, still in her slacks and sweater, knocked on the Mitchells' door. "Have you got my cat?"

"Sure," Don said, and invited her in.

Jane sat on the floor, and Don poured her a small glass of sherry.

At about the same time, Richard Meadow heard Jim walk in. Richard noticed the time because, true to character, he had been planning to go to bed *exactly* at midnight to get *exactly* eight and a half hours of sleep. He was hoping that Jim would be back by that time, so he could turn off the light and not be disturbed by Jim fumbling around in the dark. Their mattresses were in the same bedroom, about eight inches apart, and Jim slept on the one near the window, farther from the door.

Jim took off his coat and hung it in the closet.

"Is it raining out?" Richard called to Jim, who walked into the bedroom where Meadow was in bed reading. Looking up, he saw Jim was soaked.

"Where have you been?" Richard asked.

"Over cheering up Jane," he said. "It's very difficult sometimes calming people down and making them feel better about something that's coming up."

"It is a rather thankless task, isn't it?" Richard said, but Jim didn't answer. He dried himself off and changed into his pajamas and walked to the bathroom.

At the Mitchells', Jane didn't appear to be in a hurry to get to sleep, though she was vague about who she'd been out with, and Don didn't press. When she finished her glass, Don offered her another. She declined. It was already after midnight. "I think I'll go to bed," she said.

Jane took her cat, and Don saw her to the door. Jill wished her good luck and said she'd see her tomorrow.

Fifteen minutes away, Jim crawled into the far bed, set the alarm, and turned off the lights.

"If I don't remember tomorrow, best of luck on the exam," he said to Richard.

"The same to you," Richard said, and he slept soundly until the morning's alarm.

RICHARD ROSE

THE THING ABOUT CHASING A story like Jane's was that, as Jim Humphries had said, everyone had their versions. For every thread that appeared, I only had time to follow a few, and it was only in retrospect that any of them gained shape.

One of the threads I had put to the side was from 2014, when someone named Parker Donham—the Harvard student who had been the reporter for the original *Boston Globe* story about Jane's murder—suggested I track down two people: "a guy whose last name was Rose" and a woman named "Mary" whose last name was "Shift or Swick." He said I should talk to them about Ed Franquemont, Jane's ex-boyfriend, because they were Harvard anthropology students who had lived with him on a farm in Bolton. It wasn't suspicion of Franquemont that made me feel bad for not following up on the suggestion. It was guilt. Parker had written me a heartfelt thank-you email two years after we had first spoken, and I didn't want to respond until I could tell him how following up on his leads had gone. I let his message linger in my inbox for almost six months.

But embarrassment was a stupid reason for stasis, so, finally, in May 2017, when I had been out in LA waiting around for Boyd, I'd called Merri Swid. It turned out Parker's ex-wife had alerted her that I would be reaching out, and she had been expecting me for years. Merri told me about her experience at the farm when, about four months after Jane's death, a detective had come out to speak with her. He had said he wanted to hear everything about the dynamics on archaeological digs and in the Anthropology department—even if it was just rumor or gossip. She couldn't remember much else about that afternoon other than that she had hoped the detective couldn't tell she was tripping on acid. Another anthropology student who was questioned alongside her might remember better, she said. *Richard* Rose. But she had lost touch with Richard after they moved out of the farm when the old man who owned the place died in the mid-'70s. "I don't know if Richard's still alive. He was the oldest of all of us. Richard would be about eighty now."

Richard, indeed, was alive and living out in Gloucester, a seaside town north of Boston. I gave him a call, and we chatted for a while about Ed. Richard, like Merri who spoke at length about Ed's lightness and gentleness, remembered him with great fondness. He said that Ed was a wonderful guy—extremely fair and kind. When I ran out of things to ask about him, we tossed out names of other people in the department. The usual suspects had come up—Lamberg-Karlovsky, Professor Gordon Willey—and then Richard mentioned Lee Parsons. No one usually remembered Lee.

It turned out that Richard, like Stephen Loring, had worked at Monte Alto with Lee in the 1970 season, though Loring had left just before Richard got there, so they never overlapped. "Lee and I became very close," he told me. Richard had been with Lee when they scattered de Borhegyi's ashes in Lake Amatitlán.

"I think he needed me. And Jane, my wife," who accompanied him to Guatemala. Richard was the first to admit that Lee was a troubled person. We talked about Lee's drinking problem, his benders, his days-long disappearances, as well as his struggles with his sexual identity. In Jane and Richard, Lee had found nonjudgmental support. "We just became family, you know? We would shake our head at his behavior, but he needed our help, I think. I think he needed someone to talk to." He thought about it some more. "Maybe we were the only people who were close to him."

"Did he ever talk with you about Jane Britton?"

"Not really. That I can recall." He remembered hearing that the police had suspected Lee at one point, but it was hard for Richard to imagine Lee ever doing anything like that. Lee was a tortured man, but he was gentle. Richard reminded me: "There were other things happening at the time, too. It wasn't all about Jane Britton."

But if I was interested, Richard said he had pictures of Ed, Merri, and Lee at the farm—"they're all jumbled; they're slides"—and I would be welcome to come over and see when I moved to Boston in the fall.

———

When I first arrived at the Roses' house, it was tense. I felt guilty for being welcomed into their home when the only reason I was there was to put a face to my suspicions of their friend. Jane Rose poured Richard some chaga tea—mushroom tea for cancer—and then for me, too. She leaned against the fridge, as far from me as possible. Richard told me he had been diagnosed with cancer a few months ago. He had just finished chemo. When we had spoken in May, he said, he was in the middle of treatment, so he wasn't sure how accurate his memories had been.

The three of us went for a walk. His wife walked in front with me, Richard behind. He was wearing a blue button-down and glasses that were so strong on the right side, it made his eye look like it was bulging. He used a gnarled wooden cane. He and Jane Rose had been married for nearly forty-seven years. As we walked the Sunset Loop, down to the old granite quarry wall, we started to talk about archaeology and the expeditions. By the time we were at a colonial cemetery, we'd gotten in a groove, and it felt like everyone knew the role they were expected to play.

Back at the house, Richard and his wife set to work on dinner. Beets and string beans and swordfish marinated in soy sauce and sesame oil. Jane Rose started pouring alcohol. It didn't stop flowing for the rest of the night, and I was going with it, trying desperately to take mental notes and also to keep up.

Because it was then that everything started to come out.

We talked about cigarettes. Lee was a chain smoker. "I always picture him with a cigarette," Jane said. "He was a dirty smoker; he'd turn any place into an ashtray." I had chills. They had no reason to know that I was picturing Jane's room as Sergeant Sennott described it, with *dozens* of cigarette butts.

What kind of cigarettes, I wanted to know, because all I knew was that supposedly there had been cigarette butts from a brand that neither Jane nor Jim smoked. According to Elisabeth Handler, Jane loved her Gauloises. Richard couldn't remember. "Come on," his wife urged, moving closer to put her arm on his shoulder. He was sitting across from me at the kitchen table. "Remember, he'd take out his pack of cigarettes, and we'd all sit around and pass them, it was a social thing to do," Jane Rose said. "*Remember*...Camels? Unfiltered Marlboros?"

"Gauloises?" Richard said.

"No," Jane Rose said, dismissively.

"How do you know?" Richard said.

"Because I never smoked a Gauloises in my life," his wife said, and bless her.

She turned her back to me to prepare the vegetables, but she continued talking. "We would drink beer every afternoon in the *tienda* in that awful town. And he'd talk about Jane," she confided, referring to Lee.

Richard told me how isolated Lee had been at Harvard. "Other than us, and Pippa," he said.

My ears perked up. I remembered, with a flash, the letter from Sally Nash to the Mitchells about the Peabody registrar, Pippa Shaplin. Don had sent me a scan of it just after Hawaii:

Miss Shaplin is about 10 years older than Lee and was Lee's alibi the night Jane was murdered. That is supposed to account for the scratches on Lee's arms.

No one until then had been able to verify for me that Lee and Pippa were even friends.

They were "very close," Richard said.

"*How* close?" I asked, trying to insinuate something sexual with my tone of voice.

"Were they romantically involved, are you asking? I don't know. I don't think so."

I told him I had heard that she was his alibi that night.

Richard considered the information. He found it plausible.

Jane Rose jumped in, "But they were close enough that she would have given him an alibi."

"If it's not provable one way or another," I said, "I could probably see myself saying, 'You're my best friend. I believe you. I'll give you an alibi.'"

"Now what about the cat," Richard said, softly. "The cat scratch."

I looked at him searchingly. He was holding both hands pressed together. Rubbing his thumbs. No one else had brought up the scratches. The scratches on Lee that supposedly occurred when he stayed at Pippa's house that night. I had never talked to *anyone* about the scratches.

"What about the cat scratch? How do you know about that?" I asked.

From the stove, his wife watched him remember.

"Lee was out at our farm"—it must have been between the murder and when he left for the dig—"and Lee's arm was scratched up like he had done battle, as he said, with Merri's cat at our farm." It had struck Richard as odd even at the time. Merri's cat wasn't the nicest, he explained, but it also wasn't evil, and Lee wasn't the kind of guy to play with a cat.

"Do you even remember Lee being at the farm before Jane's death?" Jane Rose asked. It was possible she was also hearing these details for the first time.

"I...I don't know."

She put her hand on his shoulder again to encourage him to remember. "I wish I had known you then," she said.

I thought of Jane Britton's cat Fuzzwort. Of that *Newsweek* magazine article that called her cat the "one mute witness." Maybe Jane didn't have time to struggle, maybe there was no skin under her fingernails—but what about her cat? Did they even check?

"Did you see the scratches?" I asked him.

He nodded. "It was a scratch on the arm that a cat would make—

or a girl's fingernails. Not my fingernails. Somebody," he surmised, "who manicured their nails and was distraught enough to be protecting herself."

My heart felt like it was breaking.

Lee had talked with Jane Rose about Jane Britton's death in the afternoons at the bar while they were at Monte Alto. She didn't think much of it back then, "but now that we're discussing it from our perspective, looking back, it does seem like he was very nervous that whole time. He was always drinking. He was always smoking. He was always shaking." But things had clouded over "in the haze of time," Jane Rose hedged. The only thing she was certain of was that "I never suspected him of being involved in her death. Never."

"I can't say the same," Richard confessed. All these years, the scratches had continued to give him pause. It was the one thing he couldn't square.

———

The next day we clicked through slides, projecting the past onto the wall. Of the hundreds of photos, Lee was only in a handful, and in each one, his head was always turned. In the only playful photo of him, taken at the farm in Bolton, Lee was facing away from the camera, standing in the crop field, forming a line with Merri Swid and another visitor to the farm, imitating the scarecrow in their midst. His head was turned to the side, and I could see the heavy black frames of his glasses, but absolutely nothing of his expression. Later I took the slide out of the carousel and stared at him through the smallest lens of the magnifying glass, moving it farther and closer to my eye to get him in focus.

"He wasn't necessarily happy with the way he was," Richard told me. Though Lee was a brilliant scholar, for some at Harvard, that might not have been enough. "I think people were bothered by Lee's sexuality. People weren't as comfortable then as now, perhaps. Although even now, sometimes, I doubt how comfortable people are about it."

Richard said Lee never seemed to know who he should be.

Lee Parsons, Merri Swid, and Bob Gage at the farm in Bolton.

———

Richard drove me down to the commuter rail. It was a monochromatic New England day, and raining heavily. We were early, so we sat in his car, which felt like a confession booth. He said he had started thinking of his life like the Beethoven string quartets, which were classified as early, middle, and late. "Now it's the late years. And I'm trying to learn how to be happy and function well."

He thanked me for bringing him flashes of his past life. Helping put together this period for me had helped him make sense of those years. "I like being part of that," he said, and he invited me to visit again whenever I wanted. I thanked him.

"Yeah, well, you're a member of the family now, you know, whether you want to be or not."

CITY ISLAND

A FEW MONTHS EARLIER, THERE was one thing I had wanted to do before I left New York for Boston. I wanted to go to an island off the coast of the Bronx called City Island. Oliver Sacks used to swim around it regularly for exercise.

For absolutely no good reason other than that it seemed magical to have a hidden seaside town in New York City, and that it was the sort of place you'd have to take a train to a train to a bus to, City Island had settled itself in my mind as a kind of mythic place. It was one of the first things I mentioned in relationships as a place I'd like to go, and it became a sort of symbolic landmark to aim for.

I still had never been. My relationships always seemed to end just before the trip.

I didn't want to wait any longer. I treated myself to the express bus and when I got out to switch for the local, it was there that I met up with Iva Houston. I had invited her along when I found out she was in town for research.

The sun beamed on us as we walked along the main street and ate fried fish and steamed snapper and watched the seagulls swoop over Hart Island in the distance. We talked about what I had learned about Jane, and Iva apologized to me. She said hearing about Jane as a real person made her realize how much she had unconsciously blamed Jane all these years. The moral of the story she had understood had equally been: *This is what happens to a woman when you act like Jane. Don't get involved with your professor, and certainly don't open your mouth about it if you do.*

We all need to be self-critical, Iva told me. Ruth Benedict, one of the pioneering women in anthropology, is thought to have said that the main point of the field was "to make the world safe for human differences."

"We forget that," Iva said.

JANUARY 14, 1969: LEE PARSONS POLICE

INTERROGATION

Detective Lieutenant Davenport: Might I request, sir, Mr. Parsons, that you keep your voice up. You notice I speak quite loud, but yours doesn't seem to carry too well into that microphone. Your name is Lee Parsons, sir?

Dr. Parsons: That's right.

Detective Lieutenant Davenport: You have a title before your name, sir. What is it?

Dr. Parsons: Doctor.

Detective Lieutenant Davenport: As a result of being a Doctor of Philosophy, are you currently employed at Harvard University?

Dr. Parsons: I presume it has some relation to it.

Detective Lieutenant Davenport: Are you residing with your wife, sir?

Dr. Parsons: No. I'm going through divorce proceedings.

Detective Lieutenant Davenport: Do you at the present time have a girl-friend?

Dr. Parsons: Yes. Mrs. Shaplin.

Detective Lieutenant Davenport: Shaplin? Is she a student?

Dr. Parsons: No. She works at the museum.

Detective Lieutenant Davenport: I would like to inform you before I go any further: At this time, you are not a suspect in the crime. If at any time—

Dr. Parsons: I feel as though I am.

Detective Lieutenant Davenport: No. You're not, sir. If at any time during this investigation or during this interview it comes out that you may have placed yourself in the category of a suspect, this interview will come to a halt, at which time we'll inform you of all your Massachusetts state rights and your constitutional rights. If after being informed of these rights you wish to continue, we will do so. Is this agreeable with you, sir?

Dr. Parsons: Yes.

Detective Lieutenant Davenport: Have you ever been out with Jane?

Dr. Parsons: Yes, once.

Detective Lieutenant Davenport: Just once. Have you been to her apartment?

Dr. Parsons: Yes.

Detective Lieutenant Davenport: When was that?

Dr. Parsons: I don't remember precisely, but it must have been late in November. She had invited me over, just an open invitation to come over for supper sometime, and I went over on a Saturday evening. And I spent the early evening there. The Mitchells were with her. They were drinking, and about midnight I suggested coming over to my apartment, which we did. We stayed there until the early morning, maybe around four o'clock. And that evening the rug got burned.

    A couple weeks later I went over to her apartment again, but she wasn't there. I think it was a Saturday night. I saw Don Mitchell, and he said she was at home [in Needham]. And the third time I went over there was just before Christmas vacation. I rang her buzzer, and she met me halfway down the stairs; and I just chatted with her for a moment. She said she was studying and busy, and I only talked to her for a few minutes.

Sergeant Peterson: And at this time your sobriety was what?

Dr. Parsons: I may have had six bottles of beer or so.

Detective Lieutenant Davenport: Are you a heavy drinker, Doctor? This doesn't go beyond here, Doctor, in case you're thinking along the lines of Harvard.

Dr. Parsons: Well, these things are relative.

Detective Lieutenant Davenport: Of course they are.

Dr. Parsons: I drink.

Detective Lieutenant Davenport: Do you drink to excess, Doctor?

Dr. Parsons: I have in the past.

Detective Lieutenant Davenport: Dr. Parsons, getting back to that evening at your apartment with the Mitchells and Jane, did you at that time progress your friendship any further than what it had been prior to arriving at the apartment house?

Dr. Parsons: Well—

Detective Lieutenant Davenport: That's a nice way of saying it.

Dr. Parsons: We only talked, and when she said she was going to leave, I did ask her if she wanted to stay longer. She said no. She left. So that's as far as it got.

Sergeant Peterson: All right. How did she get back? Did you walk her back?

Dr. Parsons: I didn't. I offered to, and she went home alone.

Detective Lieutenant Davenport: Doctor, have you, on occasion, had different moments of depression?

Dr. Parsons: Yes. I've been depressed this fall, especially.

Detective Lieutenant Davenport: So much so that you would call upon others to discuss the situation?

Dr. Parsons: Yes.

Detective Lieutenant Davenport: Would Jane Britton have been one of these persons?

Dr. Parsons: That's probably why I wanted to talk to her, just to talk to someone.

Detective Lieutenant Davenport: When was the last time you saw her?

Dr. Parsons: New Year's Eve.

Detective Lieutenant Davenport: Where were you last Monday night?

Dr. Parsons: Home in my apartment.

Detective Lieutenant Davenport: What time did you get home?

Dr. Parsons: Let's see. About 5:30, I guess, from the museum.

Detective Lieutenant Davenport: Stayed in all night?

Dr. Parsons: As a matter of fact, I went to bed very early. I'd been skiing this weekend up in Maine, and we got back Sunday night. I was very tired so I went to bed right after supper on Monday.

Detective Lieutenant Davenport: Right after supper. Had you been drinking that day, Doctor?

Dr. Parsons: No.

Detective Lieutenant Davenport: Do you recall what time you woke up Tuesday morning?

Dr. Parsons: Usual time. It must have been about 7:30.

Detective Lieutenant Davenport: Then you're a good sleeper. Thirteen hours sleep?

Dr. Parsons: I was tired.

Detective Lieutenant Davenport: I imagine you must have been really upset when you found out that Ms. Britton had been killed in the manner that she was killed. Didn't that upset you? Your emotional state must have been really something to behold immediately after you learned.

Dr. Parsons: I don't know.

Detective Lieutenant Davenport: You don't know?

Dr. Parsons: I was upset. Yeah.

Unidentified Male: Do you have an injury on your right hand?

Dr. Parsons: Uh-huh (affirmative).

Unidentified Male: How recent is it?

Dr. Parsons: This weekend skiing.

Unidentified Male: Who were you skiing with?

Dr. Parsons: Mrs. Shaplin.

Detective Lieutenant Davenport: How about your arm, Doctor?

Dr. Parsons: The cat.

Detective Lieutenant Davenport: Cat?

Dr. Parsons: I think it was—

Detective Lieutenant Davenport: That you don't have anymore?

Dr. Parsons: No. It was someone else's cat.

Detective Lieutenant Davenport: Would you mind telling us whose cat, if you don't mind? You don't have to tell us if you don't wish to. But what's one cat among friends?

Dr. Parsons: It's cats that belong to the Richard Roses.

Detective Lieutenant Davenport: Richard Rose?

Dr. Parsons: Uh-huh (affirmative).

Detective Lieutenant Davenport: The boy that lives out in Bolton?

Dr. Parsons: Uh-huh (affirmative).

Detective Lieutenant Davenport: Doctor, would you be agreeable for our expert here taking a look at the remainder of your arm, sir?

Dr. Parsons: No, not at all.

Detective Lieutenant Agnes: Would you roll up your sleeve? The cat grab you?

Dr. Parsons: Actually, it must have happened when I was sleeping because the cats were in the same room.

Detective Lieutenant Davenport: Professor, how many other scratches do you have on your body right now?

Dr. Parsons: I don't think I have any other scratches.

Detective Lieutenant Davenport: You don't believe you have, sir? You don't have any up near your shoulder, do you?

Dr. Parsons: I may have some marks, but they're not scratches.

Detective Lieutenant Davenport: What kind of marks would they be, sir?

Dr. Parsons: Bites.

WILL YOU ACCEPT THIS

A FEW DAYS AFTER COMING back from seeing the Roses in Gloucester, I got an email from Alice Kehoe, an anthropologist and an old friend of Lee's, whom Stephen Loring had suggested I reach out to. She's a delight, he'd said, and one of Lee Parsons's greatest defenders.

Alice had missed my email because she had been away from her computer for six weeks in the Rockies, but she would be happy to talk. "I certainly am the most knowledgeable person now, remembering Lee Parsons." On the phone, she asked why I wanted to talk about Lee since he "was a person who could easily be forgotten." I told her I was writing about Jane Britton. She didn't know who that was. I didn't elaborate.

Alice's husband Tom had known Lee since college, where they'd been in the same fraternity, but Alice had gotten to know Lee when the three of them had been anthropology grad students at Harvard in the '50s. The discrimination against minorities and female students at the time was profound, she reminded me, and Alice had her own firsthand experiences with the latter, such as when her adviser told her to write an ethnography for her dissertation rather than one in archaeology. Otherwise everyone would think her husband had done it for her.

She described blatant discrimination along class lines as well. The department "was ruled by those who were either independently wealthy like Philip Phillips or else they married wealth like Gordon Willey." But J. O. Brew, whom everyone called Joe, was the exception. He had gotten the job because Harvard needed someone to teach Southwest archaeology since many wealthy Bostonians had winter homes out there and were invested in the archaeological history of the area. As a result, "he got all the shit work"—like the river basin archaeology that no one thought was important at the time, and advising the students that the faculty who came from socially prominent families weren't interested in. She, Tom, and Lee all studied with J. O. Brew. "He cared about us. He was our kind. Us against them."

Lee Parsons found himself in an interesting position at Harvard. On the one hand, he came from an Anglo-Protestant family. He had blue eyes and classically handsome features. But he was from Wausau, Wisconsin, a small city in the northern part of the state, where being a leading citizen didn't make you one of the Harvard elite.

When Stephen Williams promised to make Lee the Peabody Museum's assistant director, Lee's wife, Anne, begged him to get a contract. Lee said that wasn't how things worked at Harvard. He believed Williams and left his good job at the Milwaukee Public Museum while Anne stayed behind with their daughters for what he thought "was going to be his real dream job. And there was nothing." Williams treated Lee terribly, and Alice never forgave him.

I said that it was amazing to me that a group of anthropologists wouldn't recognize the biases that they were perpetuating themselves.

She laughed at me: "Of course they recognize them! But they wanted to perpetuate them."

"Why?"

"Because it solidified their positions of power."

Alice gave me several leads on issues related to sexual harassment in the field and urged me to look into them. But she was hopeful that things were changing.

"It's going to be like at the top of the mountain. There's the spring, and the water from the spring is a little trickle. And as it goes down the mountains, it gets to be more than a trickle. It gets to the creek, and it finally ends up a river." It'll take a long time, but it's happening.

Eventually, she brought us back to Lee.

She wanted me to understand that three things had happened when Lee was at Harvard. The first was his divorce. In 1969, the first Christmas after the divorce was finalized, Lee had stayed at Alice's house. She lived two blocks away from Lee's wife and daughters. One night, well past midnight, Alice was wrapping presents for her kids on the dining room table and "Lee was sitting in the chair there, and he was crying. And what could I do? All I could say was, 'It's very sad. But Lee, you've just got to accept the situation. You understand it. It's for your daughters' welfare.' And he knew it. That was part of why he was crying." Alice told me that Lee's family had a genetic predisposition toward alcoholism. She didn't want to go into further detail, and I didn't push.

The second was that two people—Pippa and Stephen DeFilippo—were both in love with Lee and started fighting over him. Pippa wanted him to move in. But Steve, who was "aggressively jealous of anybody encroaching on his relationship with Lee," didn't allow it. Years later, when Lee and Steve had moved to St. Louis together, Pippa would write to him and Steve would refuse to give Lee her letters.

The third was that—it's almost unbelievable, she told me—he became friends with a group of anthropology graduate students. One was wealthy enough to have her own apartment (*oh my god, was this Jane coming at me the other way?*), and he went over to her room and they listened to records (*yeah yeah, a garbled version of the Incense Night*), and then he left around midnight. And the next morning, she was found dead. Killed with a stone maul. No one saw Lee leave.

My hands were cold.

He said he was in her apartment the night she was killed, I repeated back to her, just to be sure.

She assumed so. "He even told us the records he was listening to," though she couldn't recall now. But Lee was also adamant that he had done nothing to hurt the young woman.

Alice said a detective came out to Milwaukee to interview her about Lee. "Oh my god, it was so surreal." She described her friend to the detective. How gentle he was. Passive. That he drank himself into a stupor. She told the detective: "I have known him for many, many years in various situations, and I am absolutely sure he could not have harmed anybody."

Could it have been Pippa or Steve, I wondered, jealous of Lee paying attention to Jane? But I didn't know if Steve even knew Lee yet. Had Lee just convinced himself through the months of the investigation that he really might have been there that night? Or could Alice herself be misremembering? His ex-wife, I knew, didn't recall Lee ever saying anything about visiting Jane the night before her murder. (She said that when they were still married, and younger, they once asked each other, "What is the worst thing that you can imagine ever happening to you?" They both agreed that it would be being accused of something one hadn't done.)

But what about the scratches, I reminded myself.

And "stone maul" felt oddly specific. Never, anywhere—not in any of the news reports, not in any of the gossip, not even talking to any anthropologist about possible stone tools that would effect that kind of injury—had anyone referred to it as a stone maul. From the kind of impact on Jane's head—small, deep skull punctures—and the description of other tools that could have caused that injury (ball peen hammers, a pickax), it seemed to most likely have been a small stone tool affixed to a stick. I quickly Googled for images of stone mauls. And there it was. A small, sharp stone or pointed metal shimmied onto a stick, often bound with twine.

"Was this over the phone?" I asked, needing to situate this memory back in its context.

"No. He talked about it right here. Right where I'm actually sitting right now in our home." Alice could still see it very clearly. She, Anne, and her late husband were sitting across from Lee, and Lee was leaning forward, saying, "I am telling you this. This is the truth. Will you accept this? This is the truth."

JANUARY 14, 1969: LEE PARSONS POLICE

INTERROGATION, CONTINUED

Detective Lieutenant Agnes: The night that Jane was killed, you were at home that night?

Dr. Parsons: Yes.

Detective Lieutenant Agnes: You sure of it?

Dr. Parsons: Yes.

Detective Lieutenant Agnes: You don't stay—

Dr. Parsons: I wish—I wish that I hadn't—I wish that someone were with me that night, but—

Detective Lieutenant Agnes: You wish there was somebody with you that night?

Dr. Parsons: Well, sure. Why not?

Detective Lieutenant Agnes: Who for instance?

Dr. Parsons: Anyone.

Detective Lieutenant Agnes: An alibi?

Dr. Parsons: Sure. It appears to me that much of what happened must sound suspicious, but I certainly want to tell you the truth and that's it.

Detective Lieutenant Davenport: Do you know the truth, Doctor? That's what I want to know. Do you actually know the truth?

Part Seven

THE RESOLUTION

JULY 31, 2018: STOP THE FAIRY LAND

THE MORNING AFTER DON'S NO-news call, I wake up early and scan my phone for updates. There's an email from him. Again, it's strange—stiff and formal. He says he's going to call me around 11:30 a.m. my time.

I wait for hours, and then, a few minutes after the appointed time, I text him, because my impatience is turning the suspense into a kind of purgatory.

He calls right away. His voice sounds full, like he's barely containing a smile. "I have some news, and I thought I would call you. I'll just tell you what it is, and then you can react. Boyd called last night."

"Uh-huh."

"He knows what we want to know, and here it is."

It takes me a second to comprehend the enormity of what I'm about to find out.

"It was a rape-murder—by a stalker." He says it flat and pauses to let it sink in. Her murderer was "just some random killer."

The word *random* feels heavy and dangerous, like a pinball. I watch it dart around, shattering the scaffolding of suspicion that had built up around Karl. Gramly. Poor Lee, who might have died wondering if people thought it was him.

There was semen at the scene. That's how they matched it. And the assailant died in prison in 2001.

"Oh my god," I say, unable to find any other words.

"I know. I told Ruth, and she started to cry. It's so different and awful. You'll come to terms with it however you come to terms with it, but I'm still sort of chewing on it. Apparently the guy—I mean they don't know, of course, 'cause he's dead—but they have placed him in Cambridge at the time, so they seem quite certain. But it would seem he waited until Jim left, or Jane went home from our apartment, because that was the last thing. And then just went in. Probably the whole sequence of actions that we all thought happened, happened, except for the rape part."

I wanted there to be more of a story so that it wasn't so awful. "It seems just even more senseless than I—" I trail off, lost in the eddy of, *It was random? It was senseless? It could have been anyone?*

He had been following her. He waited until Jim left. He let himself in. He beat her. He raped her. I never wanted to imagine her scared or tortured or in pain. I had let myself believe that she was knocked unconscious before she was beaten, and maybe she didn't even see her killer. That she maybe only felt the sharp surprise of the first hit before she passed out. The randomness forces me to confront the awful fact that she might have suffered.

Look, it says.

I can't. I don't want to. I feel awful in the absence of mystery, of narrative echo, of symmetry or rhyme or sense.

Don fills the silence.

He tells me he doesn't know the culprit's name. He says that he, like Boyd, will not be at the press conference in Boston. The authorities are going to put on a show, and Don doesn't want to be their "trained monkey" for another performance of this story.

Unlike Boyd, though, who said that as a minister, it was his job to pray for both Jane's and the assailant's souls, Don is far from there yet. He is still grappling with how much he had depended on the mystery to shield himself from the horror of what happened. "All of my elaborate structures have collapsed. Just as if an earthquake had knocked them all down," he says. "I was invested in a puzzle that involved a lot of people, and archaeology, and departmental dynamics, and people hiding their sexuality...And now I find out no, it was some son-of-a-bitch who walked in off the street, broke her door, raped her, killed her." He feels brutalized by the ugly, unadorned facts and by the realization that he had betrayed himself, seduced by a story he *preferred* to believe.

"Stop the fairy land," he scolds himself.

AUGUST 16, 2018:

BOYD'S BIRTHDAY EVE

The press conference, Don tells me, is supposed to happen in two weeks. And then two weeks gets pushed to three. We speculate that part of the delay is the police trying to firm up evidence connecting Jane's case to Ada Bean's, the unsolved murder in Harvard Square that happened a month later. But Sennott doesn't reveal anything.

In the absence of information, all I can do is watch as my feelings about this conclusion warp with all the waiting. After the initial shock, I'm left with a bodily fear, a sense of vulnerability more acute than at any other point in investigating Jane's story. The single bogeyman is replaced by a pervasive, expansive evil—one capable of killing without reason or motive. There had never been any puzzle to be solved; no code to decipher. And because of that, I can no longer believe that I have any power to protect myself. The fear oozes like a hot caramel that has seconds to be poured before it hardens; I have to will myself to go outside.

Then, like Don, I grow angry at myself. I had been reassuring myself that I was doing the right thing by telling Jane's story, but I, too, had been propagating the things we *preferred* to believe. I was wrong—we were wrong.

I hear Gramly's gravelly voice saying that Massachusetts is the same state that started the Salem witch trials. And Karl reminding his readers that "All archaeology is the re-enactment of past thoughts in the archaeologist's own mind." Narratives are seductive. These stories are dangerous.

Jane's favorite quote, pinned to my wall—"I was a victim of a series of accidents, as are we all"—might have prepared me for this conclusion long ago, but this is exactly the kind of retrospective pattern-matching that demands mistrust. People are more than symbols. Not everything has thematic heft. The tools of storytelling can blind us from the truth. How then do you tell a responsible story about the past after all?

And then, finally, Sennott gives Don a date: Monday, August 20, 2018.

Four days before the conference, I notice a missed call from Boyd. He and I haven't talked in half a year, and he doesn't know that I know anything, because I promised I wouldn't betray Don's confidence.

I call Boyd back as soon as I can. It's the night before his birthday, and I expect he's just going to thank me for the slightly lewd birthday card I sent. But when he picks up, he booms, "I have an interesting story to tell you."

He lays it all out. The random intruder. The rape. The DNA results.

And then he says that he and Peter Sennott had spoken to each other again a few days ago. After nearly fifty years, Boyd finally learned the name of the man who killed his sister: Michael Sumpter.

The name means absolutely nothing to me. I've never come across it before.

Sennott, who told Boyd he had been on vacation in Nantucket the previous two weeks (*is that what we've been waiting for?*, I wonder), described Sumpter as "an African American career criminal."

My heart sinks. I hate that he's Black. I realize that of all the suspects that had been considered over the years, no one's ever suspected someone Black, which in retrospect is a small, strange comfort. But, I remind myself, that's also because the anthropology community was so white. The lack of Black suspects wasn't a lack of racism, but a product of yet another systemic bias.

"How are you feeling about all of it?" I ask.

"Well, fine. They've got the answer they wanted. I had the answer I wanted a long time ago."

"Which was...?"

"Which is, she got killed."

He takes a beat and offers a more expansive response. As always with Boyd, it feels like vulnerability is doled out like a gift: "I'm relieved, you know? I don't have to sit around wondering anymore."

Fifty years ago tomorrow, he reminds me, he was celebrating his birthday, getting his first legal drink with a sergeant and a corporal from Fort Worth, Texas. Forty-nine years ago tomorrow, I remind myself, he was back from Vietnam and his sister was dead.

I ask if he's told Elisabeth Handler. Yes, he says, two hours ago, which I realize is the same time I missed his first call. I'm warmed by the realization that he had contacted me at the same time as Jane's best friend.

We chat a little while longer, until he grows tired of either me or being on the phone. "I suggest you prepare to find out where that thing is on Monday and attend it," he says. He gives me permission to call the DA's office and get the details; Sennott didn't swear him to secrecy. "Take care and enjoy the show Monday. You have the script now."

AUGUST 16, 2018: LATE

MICHAEL SUMPTER IS NOT WHO I would have wanted cast in this role. He is a caricature of a villain, the star of a different myth: the faceless, nameless, shadowy Black figure who abducts white women and has his way with them. A brute. A savage. A beast. This ancient trope is racist and tired. *Birth of a Nation. King Kong.* Willie Horton. The Central Park Five. An echo of the worst of Boston. And it masks the truth: A woman is much more likely to be killed by a loved one than by a stranger. In recent years, nearly half of all murdered women in the US were killed by their partner while "stranger danger" could be blamed for less than 10 percent. But my reluctance to embrace this ending changes nothing.

I'm stretched out on my stomach, and my elbows press into the floor as I awkwardly type, because I don't want to waste time changing position. I know the drill so well by now. Google. Newspaper archives. Nexis search. This may be the last rabbit hole I will ever go down for this story.

The first article I click on is a 2010 piece in the *Boston Globe*: DNA LINKS CONVICT TO '72 KILLING OF WOMAN. There were other victims. I stare at the picture at the top of the page. A twenty-three-year-old brunette, with fair skin and an inviting smile. She could have been Jane.

One of the last photos taken of Ellen Rutchick. (Photo courtesy the Rutchick family)

Her name is Ellen Rutchick. She was from St. Paul, Minnesota, and the second oldest of four. She had recently graduated from the University of Minnesota. On January 6, 1972—one day shy of the three-year anniversary of Jane's murder—Ellen failed to show up at work at the Colonnade Hotel in Boston. Police entered her tenth-floor apartment and found her lying on her back on the living room floor—beaten, raped, and strangled with the hi-fi cord from her stereo set. Authorities think that Sumpter attacked her so quickly, she didn't have time to take off her coat.

She wasn't the only one.

On December 12, 1973, Mary McClain—also brunette, and fair, and twenty-four—had gone to her room for the night in her Beacon Hill apartment. Like Jane and Ellen, Mary lived on the top floor of her building. Her roommates were home at the time. They heard her whimpering in her room and assumed she had broken up with her boyfriend. The soft cries stopped. The next day, she was found in her bed, raped and strangled, and covered with bedding.

Mary McClain. (Photo courtesy the McClain family)

Both murders remained unsolved for decades.

In 2005, Ellen Rutchick's siblings asked Boston Police to reopen her case. They knew that there were some forensics from the crime scene. Investigators with Boston Police's Unsolved Homicides Squad agreed to take on the Rutchick case. As Sergeant Bill Doogan, who became the supervisor of the squad in 2010, explained: "It's not a case of how much is it going to cost if we do it. It's a case of *what's it going to cost if we don't.*"

But investigators soon came across a stumbling block: There was indeed biological evidence from the crime scene, but in the 1970s, evidence was affixed to the lab slides with a kind of glue that was almost impossible to separate without destroying the cells in the process. BPD sent the slides to an independent lab specializing in DNA analysis to see if they could work some magic.

It took four years, but in September 2009, the lab told investigators that it had successfully extracted a genetic profile from the slides. Five months later, BPD, in conjunction with Suffolk County prosecutors, announced that it finally had the answer that the Rutchick family had waited nearly four decades for. There had been a hit in CODIS, and his name was Michael Sumpter.

Sumpter had been dead for almost nine years. When he passed away in 2001 from a heart attack and prostate cancer, he was serving time for a 1975 rape. He was fifty-three years old, which, I quickly calculated, meant that he was only twenty-one when he killed Jane.

In 2010, BPD's cold case squad turned to Mary McClain. This time, the CODIS hit took less than two years. "It's been 40 years, and it's just haunted me my whole life, wondering who did this to her," Kathy McClain, Mary's only surviving relative, told the *Boston Herald*.

Suffolk County DA Daniel Conley made the news public at a press conference in October 2012. But the announcement was shadowed by the portrait of Sumpter that, only in death, was becoming clear. Sumpter killed Rutchick while on parole. He killed McClain just three weeks after he escaped from the first furlough he had been granted. The rape he committed in 1975, for which he was serving time when he developed cancer, was during a work release program. A decade later, Sumpter escaped on the first day of another work release program. He remained on the lam for a year and a half, with a seemingly clean record; it was only after his death that authorities discovered he had raped a woman in Back Bay during his escape. Sumpter lived his whole life with the secrets of some of his most heinous crimes safe.

Sergeant Doogan tempered the sense of accomplishment: "Do you think that's all he's ever done? I don't think so."

RECKONINGS

IT HAD BEEN A LONG fall and spring in Cambridge. Nearly a year separated my talk with Alice Kehoe about Lee Parsons and Don's news of a break in the case.

Just a few days after I'd talked with Alice, the *New York Times* and *The New Yorker* published their stories about Harvey Weinstein's decades of sexual predation, harassment, and intimidation. The distance between my world and Jane's had already become hallucinatorily thin in spots, but the

#MeToo movement felt like 1969 had come crashing fully and completely into the present day. What had, for years, felt like a secret confined to the halls of archaeology was suddenly what everyone was talking about: whisper networks, the need for rumor to tell stories with no other outlet, the corrupting influence of power, the silencing, the erasure. It felt inevitable that the conversation would wend its way to academia.

In February 2018, *The Chronicle of Higher Education* published a long article about Jorge Domínguez, a tenured professor in Harvard's Government department. The arc of the story was deeply familiar. Terry Karl alleged that Domínguez made unwanted sexual advances on her when she was an assistant professor in the same department. She said he made it clear to her that, as a full professor in her discipline, he controlled her fate in the institution. He allegedly said one night, as he tried to kiss her and slide his hand up her skirt, that he would be the next department chairman and would decide her promotion. And according to Terry Karl, he also stalked her and made her feel physically threatened.

For two years, she reported this behavior to Harvard, but nothing changed. Though the then dean of the Faculty of Arts and Sciences adjudicated in her favor, he allegedly indicated that she would be the one to have to leave. Karl felt that she had no choice but to file a formal complaint with the Equal Employment Opportunity Commission.

Even at the time, the assistant professor knew that she wasn't alone in her experiences with Domínguez. She claimed that he had already harassed at least two students and one other assistant professor, including an under- graduate whose senior thesis he graded unfairly when she rejected his advances. (Her grade was later changed after review by an outside party.) Karl warned the university that he was a "repeater."

Harvard took some action. It found Domínguez guilty of "serious misconduct," stripped him of his administrative responsibilities for three years, and removed him from a position of reviewing Terry Karl's work. (In a comment to the *Chronicle*, Domínguez denied allegations and stated he "sought to behave honorably in all my relationships.") Karl was given three semesters of paid leave, and her tenure clock was put on hold for two years.

But when the *Crimson* and the *Boston Globe* published their stories in the fall of 1983 about the disciplinary action against Domínguez, they didn't have access to this information. Harvard had refused to disclose the precise nature of the assistant professor's "grievance" and the measures taken against Domínguez. "There are a lot of us who feel that in some ways, the University is more concerned with its reputation than with the proper adjudication of a very serious matter," a Harvard professor told the *Crimson*.

Terry Karl also felt that the university was not taking the matter seriously enough. There was still no clear grievance procedure for faculty members, and no guarantee of protection against retaliation. The administrative sanctions also did not keep her insulated from Domínguez. Her lawyer wrote to the dean of the Faculty of Arts and Sciences, who replied that additional restrictions wouldn't be appropriate: "It was specifically not our intention to lock Domínguez away."

Eventually the assistant professor felt like she had run out of recourse. Filing a complaint, she would later write, "pits a person against an institution that is predisposed to defend the accused." Terry Karl felt she had no choice but to leave. It was the same pattern that Iva Houston had identified all those years ago: The women disappear, and the men get to stay.

Karl went on to get tenure from Stanford, and she tried her best to keep this period of sexual harassment from defining her.

In the meantime, Domínguez kept getting promoted at Harvard. In 1995, he was selected as the director of the Weatherhead Center for International Affairs. In 2006, he became a Harvard vice provost. In 2014, he traveled to Mexico with Drew Gilpin Faust, then president of Harvard, as part of the university's outreach efforts. In 2016, a dissertation prize was set up in his honor after the opportunity had been refused by the Latin American Studies Association, which knew of his disciplinary history. (The Harvard plan was later changed when some raised similar concerns.)

Then, in November 2017, Professor Karl got a call from a number she didn't recognize; two women were on the line, each had allegedly experienced sexual harassment by Domínguez, and they were ready to come forward. Eventually fifteen other women would join the three of them, with accusations that spanned forty years.

The *Chronicle* story roiled the campus, prompting student groups such as Our Harvard Can Do Better and the Women's Cabinet to host meetings and town halls. Cover stories splashed across the *Crimson*. Alan Garber, the university's provost, emailed the Harvard community to say that it was "heartbreaking" to read the victims' accounts in the *Chronicle* story, and underscored: "To those who are thinking about coming forward, please know Harvard will support you." Harvard president Faust also reaffirmed the university's commitment to combatting sexual harassment in a faculty meeting. "It remains the case that very clearly there is more to be done."

Harvard placed Domínguez on administrative leave, and, two days later, Domínguez announced his decision to retire at the end of the semester. At the conclusion of the Title IX investigation, which substantiated the claims, Harvard stripped Domínguez of his emeritus status and banned him from campus.

Nonetheless, Professor Karl told me, she does not see this moment as a reckoning. She maintains that Harvard has still refused to talk to any of the women in this case, apologize to anyone, or take any action to "make whole" the women who suffered. Looking back, she feels that Harvard's complicity through inaction had allowed for even more victims. By repeatedly promoting Domínguez, despite warnings about his behavior, the university sent the signal that speaking up does nothing but harm the accuser.

As Professor Karl told the *Chronicle*, she calls Harvard's encouragement of a culture of silence "the great enabling."

AUGUST 17, 2018: TELL NO MAN

THE MORNING AFTER I LEARN Sumpter's name, I call the DA's office, but they don't pick up or return my call. I check in with the *Boston Globe*'s Todd Wallack, but he hasn't even heard the rumblings about a development in the case. And when Wallack tries his own luck with the DA's office, the press office denies any upcoming press conference. Instead, they want to know who's spreading this misinformation. He doesn't give my name.

I tell Boyd that I can't get a straight answer about Monday. He says he doesn't know the story, either, but he can't stay on the phone to speculate. He has to race off to prepare for the weekend's sermon. By an absolute coincidence of the Anglican liturgical calendar, he'll be delivering a sermon called "Tell No Man," about the episode in the Gospel where Jesus facilitates miracles and demands that witnesses *don't tell anybody*.

"Things have changed since the Resurrection," Boyd says. "There are obligations to tell everybody."

SEPTEMBER, OCTOBER 2018:

WAITING AND WAITING AND WAITING

THE PRESS CONFERENCE DOESN'T HAPPEN on Monday. Or that week. Or that month. There are no further updates from Sennott or from the DA's office.

In the meantime, the students come back to school, and the dining hall comes back to life.

Don, who was diagnosed with prostate cancer in the spring, is in his final weeks of radiation treatment.

Richard Conti, who had served as foreman of the grand jury, passes away. He dies never knowing that the case was solved.

Don, Boyd, Elisabeth, and I wait and wait and wait and wait. We've gone from the maddening silence of not knowing to the stifled silence of knowing but being able to tell no one.

———

In mid-September, Elisabeth gets in touch with me. She says she would have accepted law enforcement's story unquestioningly—that she would have been happy to think that investigators finally did what they had promised all those years ago—if only they had announced their results weeks ago. But in the pause that followed, questions began festering again, like: Hadn't the cops been sure that Jane wasn't raped? She wants to know if I have any insight into what's taking so long.

I give her my best guess: that detective work takes time and that maybe they're trying to coordinate the announcement with DA Marian Ryan's re-election campaign. But I admit that I, too, can feel the vines of speculation climbing again. Isn't it a little too convenient that the suspect is dead and Black and can't defend himself? But I don't know if I can trust that feeling.

Still burned from my years-long investment in stories that turned out to be untrue, I worry my reluctance to believe is less an indication that something is amiss than it is the return of my desire to construct a story to hide behind.

But unlike Don and me, Elisabeth says she actually finds the police's version somewhat comforting. It transforms the red ochre from a sadistic clue to the vestige of Jane kicking the shit out of a stranger. She even finds a bit of dark humor: "It's like a Hercule Poirot story with a postmodern ending," she says, where Poirot combs through suspect after suspect only to discover on the last page: "It was a brick. Sorry guys."

And more than anything, Elisabeth finds solace in knowing that Jane, who had had such bad luck with men throughout her life, didn't have to look into the eyes of her killer and feel betrayal as her last waking feeling.

KIMBERLY THEIDON

In the midst of the apparent reckoning that was happening in the fall of 2017, a number of friends had confided in me about their experiences with harassment by faculty at Harvard. I couldn't tell whether I was stumbling across all these stories because of what I was writing about, or because the floorboards were finally being lifted.

And then a *Crimson* story caught my eye. A former anthropology associate professor had sued Harvard for failing to give her tenure on the basis of her gender and her outspoken advocacy for victims of sexual assault. Her name was Kimberly Theidon. It took me a second to realize why her name sounded so familiar. I had seen her present at the Social Anthropology Day all those years ago, talking about the mute woman repeatedly raped inside her own home, and the community, hearing her gurgled screams, that did nothing.

Professor Theidon, a scholar of structured silences, had made no secret of speaking out against sex discrimination and of defending victims of sexual assault. In 2010, she had complained about the disparate treatment of women in Harvard's Anthropology department to the university's senior vice provost for faculty development and diversity, Judith Singer. In 2004, Theidon relayed, when she started at Harvard, there was only one tenured woman in her department. That professor had warned Theidon that, as a woman, she would be expected to do more administrative tasks and advising, and that she would be held to a higher standard than her male counterparts. If Theidon wanted to succeed at Harvard, she shouldn't complain about the extra workload. Be a "dutiful daughter," the professor had advised Theidon.

Theidon didn't exactly heed the advice. She blogged and tweeted about sexual assault and wrote letters in support of student victims, complaining about Harvard's lack of adequate protections for them. In 2012, Theidon allowed a student to distribute leaflets after class on behalf of Our Harvard Can Do Better, a student group dedicated to "dismantling the rape culture on campus."

Even so, until spring 2013, as Theidon later told a *Crimson* reporter, "There was never a moment when I was given anything other than positive indications about where I was headed at Harvard." She had been promoted to associate professor in four years, and then appointed to an endowed position reserved for tenure-track faculty, which the dean of the Faculty of Arts and Sciences called an "honor richly deserved." In February 2013, the Anthropology department voted in favor of offering Theidon tenure.

Then, less than two weeks later, with the final steps of Theidon's tenure bid still pending, the *Crimson* published an article about Harvard's lagging sexual assault policy and the working group established to assess the sexual assault resources on campus. The comments section of the article had become a hotbed for fears of false accusation. A Men's Rights Activist (MRA), not affiliated with the university, vehemently questioned the claims of one of the accusers in the story, "Julie." Theidon knew that "Julie" had read the comments and that they made her feel violated all over again, so she stepped in and launched a volley that went on for pages.

In the wake of the *Crimson* article, a former graduate student who now worked for the department confided in Theidon about inappropriate behavior by a senior male Anthropology professor named Theodore Bestor. Theidon advised her to speak with two senior members of the department—the woman who had given Theidon the advice to be a "dutiful daughter," and the then head of the department, Gary Urton—because they were the formal channels to file a report. Professor Urton told the former student not to involve Theidon any further because she had "enough on her plate" with her tenure review, and assured her, "I can take care of this."

In late May 2013, Harvard convened Theidon's *ad hoc* committee—nine people, including Judith Singer, the person Theidon had warned about the gender bias in the Anthropology department. The final stages of getting tenure at Harvard are, famously, some of the most shrouded proceedings on campus. The *ad hoc* committee's deliberation—the seventh step of Harvard's elaborate eight-step process—takes place behind closed doors, no notes are typically taken, the identities of the experts are concealed, and the candidate receives no report or explanation besides the binary outcome: yes or no. The tenure decision-making process "is an invitation to abuse," Howard Georgi, a Harvard physicist who has served on tenure committees told *Science* magazine in 1999. "There's no question this has affected women."

In Theidon's case, however, Judith Singer did take notes. She felt compelled to when Professor Urton—the first of four departmental witnesses called on behalf of Theidon—provided the opening statements. Singer was surprised by the "unenthusiastic tenor" of Urton's comments, particularly in contrast with the letter he had submitted to the tenure review committee earlier that year.

After hearing from the departmental witnesses, the committee members considered Theidon's materials, including the statement prepared by the Anthropology department, which reflected letters solicited from external reviewers. Even the most positive of these letters came with commentary about her productivity, but they had been prepared by scholars who had not been sent copies of Theidon's articles about Colombia, which were to form the basis of her third book.

A Harvard dean, who had read previous drafts of the statement, realized this omission and admonished the Anthropology department for failing to include the Colombia articles for consideration. The omission constituted, in the dean's words, a "major mistake," and he advised Professor Urton to revise the statement. (According to one member of the department, this omission was simply the result of "miscommunication.") They revised the statement twice, but for some reason, still unknown, the less favorable penultimate draft of her statement made its way to the *ad hoc* committee rather than the more glowing final one.

The *ad hoc* committee recommended against giving Theidon tenure, and, in late May, President Drew Faust agreed with that recommendation. (At Harvard, all tenure decisions rest with the president.)

In response, Theidon set up a meeting with Judith Singer, who, according to Theidon's notes from the time, explained that the committee concluded Theidon's "unusual career" did not align with the work being done within Harvard's Faculty of Arts and Sciences. Also, according to Theidon, Singer described her "activities" as the "sort of activities scholars postpone until they have tenure."

Theidon appealed her tenure decision, and then filed a complaint and eventually a lawsuit. Contending that her tenure denial was retaliation for refusing to stay quiet, Theidon told the *Crimson*, "This is about silencing a problem on this campus." The school responded through its spokesperson: "The University would never consider a faculty member's advocacy for students who have experienced sexual assault when making a tenure decision. Instead, tenure decisions are based on the quality of a faculty member's research, teaching, and University citizenship."

Theidon left Harvard when her contract expired in 2014 and was granted tenure at Tufts in 2015. On March 26, 2018, in the article that caught my eye, the *Crimson* announced that Theidon had lost her suit.

When I tried to reach Professor Theidon for comment, I was met only with silence. But on the day it was publicly announced that she lost her appeal, Theidon issued a statement that urged readers to see her struggle in its larger context:

> *On college campuses nation-wide, senior professors—frequently male—wield tremendous power over their students and junior colleagues...These gatekeepers operate with virtual impunity, administering silences, humiliation, and career-ending decisions. The black box of tenure, lacking transparency, is precisely how silencing and impunity work to the disadvantage of those who would speak up and unsettle the status quo.*

Though her specific battle was over, the fight, she argued, must continue on behalf of what she called the "missing women" of academia—those driven out of their careers of choice because "they [had] been ground down, groped, sexually harassed."

Four months later, in May 2020, the *Crimson* published an explosive article with allegations of sexual misconduct by three tenured anthropology professors at Harvard: John Comaroff, Theodore Bestor, and Gary Urton, who allegedly was having an affair with a former student at the time that Theidon directed the complaint about Bestor. According to a sealed affidavit in the Theidon case, the affair allegedly began when he pressured the student into "unwanted sex" in exchange for a recommendation letter. Other than one incident in 2017 for which Bestor takes full responsibility, all three men deny the allegations.

As Theidon had noted at the end of her January statement: "My journey illustrates why women do not come forward; and, this is why we must."

SEPTEMBER 9, 2018: THE TREE

THE DAY AFTER I SPEAK with Elisabeth, Don tells me that he's decided he can't wait any longer. During the weeks of silence, Jane's tree—the plant that he bought the day after Sennott first called him—was getting root-bound waiting to go into the ground. He had chosen an ʻōhiʻa, a flowering tree that figures prominently in Hawaiian mythology and popular culture—the same kind he had planted for me after my visit. Ruth had wanted a stately white one, but Don opted for one with limbs rebelliously shooting out all over. To Don, this plant said, *I don't give a shit about anything*. Seeing Jane's defiant plant stuck in its pot made him sad.

He tells me a hurricane is coming for the Big Island, and Jane's plant will be safer in the ground than top-heavy in its pot. After years of living in limbo, waiting for others to give him closure, Don thinks of this act as a reclamation of power.

The next day, he records the ceremony and sends the video to me so I can be a part of the ritual.

He scrapes the topsoil away, revealing a tongue of hardened lava to the air for the first time in thousands of years. Over time, exposed to the elements, it will deepen to black, but for the moment, it is a beautiful red. He fills the hole with layers of volcanic cinders and compost and potting soil and hoses it down to make sure the mixture is moist.

He kneels to drive the plant into the ground, pushing the root ball into the dirt, and then pours potting soil to level the hole. Before the very last stage—patting down the cinders around Jane's tree to stabilize and secure it—he takes off his gloves. The gesture, he says, feels pure: "It doesn't have anything to do with the politics of the Massachusetts DA. It doesn't really have anything to do with that bastard who killed her. Or Peter Sennott. Or anything. It's just about Jane and her tree, and you and me, and the rest of us."

He says he's purposefully turned the main axis of Jane's tree toward my 'ōhi'a so that our trees point toward each other. He likes the idea of Jane's tree growing between old flows of lava, and the image of our roots stretching to each other through those hard places, and eventually intertwining.

When the announcement from the DA's office comes—*if it comes*, he corrects—he'll put a lei on her tree. And that, he suspects, will feel like a funerary ritual. But this gesture, for the moment, isn't a sorrowful act.

It had never occurred to me until just then how the very same act of burial could be the start of something new.

A still from Don Mitchell's video of planting Jane's 'ōhi'a.

OCTOBER 28, 2018: HE ESCAPES WHO IS

NOT PURSUED

I CALLED JOHN FULKERSON, ONE of the Cambridge cops who reopened Jane's case in the '90s, nearly every two weeks for almost a year. I left pretty much the same message each time. "Hi Sergeant Fulkerson, it's Becky Cooper. I was wondering when might be a good time to get coffee."

I met him once in 2017 when, in the middle of a Boston winter, I trekked to police headquarters in Kendall Square and waited in the lobby for him. He said that he had been warned not to talk to the press. *But a coffee?* I asked. *That might be okay*, he said. So I kept calling and kept leaving messages.

In February 2018, for the first time in months, he picked up. He told me he was retiring from the Cambridge police soon. *Just keep trying me*, he said. I did, but it was another months-long stretch of unanswered calls.

Now it's October, and as I pick up the phone to call him, I realize it's probably my fiftieth attempt. As usual, I get his answering machine and leave the same message.

A few minutes later, he calls me back.

He tells me he's finally retired from the Cambridge Police. He's a Harvard Police officer now, and he would be happy to meet me for coffee next week. Before we hang up, he underscores: *If you need anything else while you're at Harvard, I'm here now.*

————

We meet at a café where Mount Auburn Street and Mass Avenue converge; our seats point almost directly at the Harvard Police station. Fulkerson has a stern face and steely blue eyes and a buzz cut that looks like it would pass muster in the military. He sits awkwardly on his stool, leaning a little forward, like a man perched on a child's play set. I thank him for meeting me, and he says it's the least he could do after blowing me off so many times. His seriousness melts when he smiles.

I jump into talking about how long I've been waiting for the press conference, but his blank stare makes me realize that he has no idea that there's even been a break in the case. He hadn't heard anything about it since last year, when they told him not to talk to the press.

I watch Fulkerson process the information—relief and disbelief and excitement mixed with sadness. He swirls his coffee as he thinks. "I really wanted to be the guy that solved the Jane Britton case. I really did," he says.

His investment reminds me of the story he told me about his tattoo. I ask him about it, and he takes off his HUPD jacket with the sergeant pin and rolls up his sleeve to show me, but the sleeve doesn't push up enough to reveal more than an inch of the design.

Without hesitating, he takes off his black clip-on tie. He considers for a second lifting his shirt in the middle of the café before glancing back and seeing how many patrons are around. Instead, we walk through the bakery area and into a small hallway by the bathroom. He hands me his jacket and tie, and he slips the bottom of his shirt over his right arm and neck. I look away as he bares his stomach before he holds his shirt in front of him like a camera-shy model between takes—except with his shirt off, I can see that this model has chest hair and a gun in his right pocket holster.

The tattoo extends from elbow to shoulder. It's the Angel of Freedom, accompanied by two doves, some roses, and a police badge, standing on a ribbon that says in all caps HE ESCAPES WHO IS NOT PURSUED. He designed it himself.

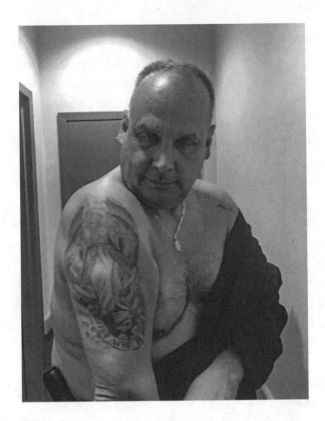

Sergeant Fulkerson shows his tattoo.

We walk back to our seats past a girl in line for the women's restroom, mouth agape at the stripping cop. We're both a bit out of breath and flustered, less by the physical exertion and more by the delayed realization of how intimate the innocent gesture was.

Back at our stools, with trust firmly established, I tell him everything I know, careful to flag the fact that I know none of this directly from Peter Sennott himself, and that Peter doesn't know I know any of this. "I don't think he likes me," I say.

"He doesn't like anybody really," Fulkerson says and laughs. They know each other well. It was to Sennott that Fulkerson gave the Jane Britton files in 2005 when Cambridge PD handed the case to Mass State Police. Fulkerson calls him Pete.

When I get to the identity of the suspect, he asks me to repeat it so he's sure he understood correctly. "You know that it's someone completely random?" he asks.

I nod.

"Wow. I'm struggling," he says. It doesn't make sense to him. The crime scene had seemed staged. He said it wasn't clear from the case file that she had been raped. He also thought it had to have been someone she knew. I hear him trying to reason with himself: *It has been a long time since I saw the police files.*

I ask if there was anything about either the Jane Britton case or the files that stuck out to him.

Fulkerson swirls his coffee again. "Things are being hidden, and I don't know why."

He felt that way even when he worked on Jane's case in the '90s. With all the other cold cases John and his partner Brian Branley investigated, his supervisors never gave them any trouble. For the unsolved murder of Mary Joe Frug, for example, CPD flew them to California without hesitation. But with Jane's case, he was met with reluctance and skepticism: *You really want to work on that? How about these new cases?* Reinvestigating the case felt like opening a wound.

"They could have been more supportive. Created less administrative roadblocks," he says.

"Who's 'they'?" I ask.

Cambridge PD administration and the district attorney's office, he says.

We get pulled into a side conversation about internal Cambridge PD politics, how ugly it got toward the end of his time there, and how much better it is for him now as a Harvard officer. He's happy to once again be working for the guy who had been his boss during the happy years of his career at Cambridge PD. A man named Mike Giacoppo.

Mike Giacoppo, I knew, was the son of the fingerprint expert on Jane's case back in 1969. Of the original investigators, there were, at most, two left: Fred Centrella, who hadn't wanted to speak about an open case, and Mike's father, for whom I hadn't been able to find an obituary. But when I spoke to the younger Giacoppo about Jane's case in early 2018, he made no mention of his father still being alive. "My father was not one to bring his work home with him and never much talked about his job," he said in the past tense. It seemed rude to insist.

I check with Fulkerson just to be sure.

"No, Mike's father's still around," Fulkerson says. He's eighty-seven, but he's very active. In fact, they had seen each other on Saturday. Fulkerson, who calls the elder Giacoppo a good guy and a great cop, thinks he would be willing to talk to me. "He's got nothing to hide."

As we get ready to leave the café, Fulkerson promises to call the guys he knows in the DA's office to see what's up with the silence. If he were the DA and he had solved a cold case like this, he would want the world to know as soon as all the *i*'s were dotted and the *t*'s crossed.

I walk him back to headquarters. He shakes my hand. I want to hug him. "We'll be in touch," he says.

––––––

Instead of contacting the elder Giacoppo directly, I email the son for advice. He had been so forthcoming when we had spoken, saying, for example, how disappointingly thin old police records often are—"I've seen lost dog reports that had more information than a missing person [report]"—that I trust him.

Mike replies the next day:

Unfortunately he is dealing with health & memory issues. Like most people his age and condition he is up one day and down others. My sister, with whom he lives, has told me that she would prefer that he not be subjected to any interviews. Realistically I'm not sure his recall would be that reliable. If you had a specific question/s I could ask him if the timing was good for him, but he is memory challenged.

I send Mike four questions about the case, focusing on the red ochre, the press blackout, and the fingerprint on Jane's kitchen window.

I never hear back.

NOVEMBER 2018: SHIFTS

OCTOBER PUSHES INTO NOVEMBER AND the dining hall is already getting ready for Thanksgiving break, giving up and serving corn four different ways.

Fulkerson isn't able to shake anything out from his friends in the DA's office, and after so many months suspended in this limbo, I almost get used to the idea that the answer will forever be an unknown known. Besides, with a dead suspect, having an answer sometimes felt arbitrary—it doesn't make Jane any less of an enigma for me, and other than knowing that the person who killed Jane could no longer hurt anyone else, it doesn't give me any greater sense of peace.

I head home to New York the week before Thanksgiving. And, just as it's always been with this story, the second I step away, everything shifts.

I get an email from the DA's communications director, Meghan Kelly, asking if I'd be around the next day for a phone call.

I don't even bother feigning surprise when we speak. She says there will be a press conference about the case on Tuesday afternoon. A press advisory will go out on Monday to invite everyone.

"I'll be there," I say.

REACTIONS

I TAKE A BUS BACK to Cambridge early the next morning, relishing the remaining moments of quiet. I only have one chance to get this ending right.

I quickly gather all the things I'll need—an extra phone battery, a list of questions for the DA, a recording device, my notebook, and an updated public records request for the police files. I'm eager to clear the mundane items off my to-do list to have time for what I really want to be doing: calling everyone close to the story. I don't want them to be caught off guard by the news.

Arthur Bankoff, who was with Jane at Tepe Yahya, says that he's relieved it's none of his friends.

There's a catch in Dan Potts's throat after he hears that it was someone random. "What about the rug and the ochre?" his wife, Hildy, who had been an archaeological illustrator at the Harvard Semitic Museum, asks. They have me on speakerphone in their car. "And the hand ax thing," Dan adds. Hildy pulls herself back from the brink of skepticism—"I mean I suppose you can't quibble with DNA"—and wonders out loud, with the same kind of half seriousness of the rumors that plagued Karl in the days after the murder, whether there might be a part of Karl that will be disappointed in being stripped of his mythology.

Stephen Loring, back from his weeks-long archaeological expedition up north, answers the phone cheerfully, "Well, *hellooo!*"

The news hits him in waves. At first, he finds it comforting that it's none of our three "characters." Then he hovers over the story, as if it's no longer events he lived, but a narrative whose structure he can admire: "I like this ending." He finds a beauty in the way it forces a reassessment of old thought patterns, and in doing so, makes obvious the blinders that experience and desire put on us.

Each of us had our own reasons for being seduced by a particular version, he says. The Abraham family, for instance, would have liked for Gramly to be a villain because then Anne's death is no longer just "an accidental twist of fate. It was a malevolent human action." For some, it is easier to believe in an evil person than an uncaring God.

He writes a gentle email to Alice Abraham and her wife, Chris, to break the news. "I am sorry to be the bearer of these tidings not that they make our loss any less painful nor bring any closure to the sad days in '76, or absolve Mr. Gramly of his poor behavior and judgment, but they do close down one avenue of speculation which—I suppose—is a good thing."

Alice writes instantly to Patricia, one of the two "Golden Girls" who had pegged her suspicions on Gramly. Patricia says she thinks it's wonderful that it's solved, but it will take her a while to process her own relationship to the news. Where do you go from here, I ask her. She doesn't yet know. On the one hand, it's also an ending for her, and yet: Do you throw *everything* away?

I also get an email from Mary McCutcheon, the other half of the Golden Girls. At first, she's as bubbly as ever. "WOW," she writes in all caps. "I hope he feels exonerated and vindicated." But over time, her enthusiasm settles into deep remorse. She writes me again: "The overactive pattern-recognition part of my brain came to, what I now know, was a false conclusion. For any pain I caused, I am so very sorry."

Ted Abraham, Anne's brother, writes with a greater sense of peace than I feared might be the case. "It was an unexpected outcome but at least there is some closure to one haunting mystery."

Richard Meadow, still a lecturer at Harvard, is the only one who knows the news already when I call. Jim Humphries had told him weeks ago. I'm happy to hear that Jim already knows—I didn't want to bother him, but I also didn't want him to find out from a newspaper article.

Jill Nash, unlike everyone else, wishes that she never heard the news. I learn this from Don, who, in his final effort to get her to talk, argued that I helped pressure the police into finding a solution. *Isn't speaking with me the least she could do to show her gratitude?* Jill, still angry about everything—the way she had been interrogated by the cops, how long the resolution took, that she was now forced to alter her narrative of this horrific event to include an even more horrific ending—doesn't budge.

The parade continues, and time insists on itself. Peter Panchy is recovering from surgery; Richard Rose's new cancer treatment is helping him manage the disease.

James Ronan says it's fitting that this story, which has tracked archaeological methods and theories in thematic ways, would end with DNA, in much the same way that the field itself has turned to genetic analysis for studying human origins and migration patterns. Perhaps this is the answer to how archaeology found its way out of the mire of post-processual nothing-means-anything: by turning away from digging and storytelling, and toward science.

He also tells me that Harvard's archaeology program has made its first female hire in years: a tenure-track professor named Christina Warinner, who specializes in biomolecular archaeology.

The conversations feel like a reunion of a strange and beautiful community, bolstering me for whatever will come tomorrow. Jane—who had always been the one to approach the person standing alone at the party; the one who, for better or worse, had decided to stay after Lee burned the carpet; the friend who had made Radcliffe less isolating for Elisabeth—had once again brought a band of outsiders together.

I call Jay. We haven't spoken in years. But we were clear to each other that if we ever needed the other, we would be there. He picks up immediately, even though he's late running off to a meeting. His voice sounds exactly the same. He's grateful for the call, and we slip right back into a rhythm, but the familiarity is precisely the danger. We both know that this momentary reprieve changes nothing in the scheme of our frozen friendship—we're still waiting for the one day *maybe*, it will be okay—so I relish our connection for the moments it lasts. It feels like paying honor to the relationship that founded this story.

Before the day is done, I call Karl.

A man answers the phone. The voice sounds American, with no hint of drama or bellow. A son, perhaps?

"I was hoping to speak with Karl," I say.

"Speaking."

I scramble. "Hi, this is Becky Cooper. We were in touch about the Jane Britton—" story? Murder? Case?

"Oooooooh," he says, lyrically descending, and there is that flair again. He asks me how it's going.

"I was calling to let you know—it hasn't been officially announced yet—but there will be a press conference on Tuesday at 1 p.m., announcing a break in the case."

"Do you know—" He hesitates. "Do you know what the break is?" His tone is flat again.

"I think they've solved it."

Three seconds of silence.

"You think they. You think they. You think they—what?" I've never heard him at a loss for words like that.

I pronounce *solved* as slowly as I can.

He breathes deeply again.

"Oh, I see," he says. "Well, that is good news." His voice dips despite the cheeriness of the remark.

I ask if we might meet for one more interview after it breaks. After Thanksgiving, he agrees. I thank him.

"Yep, bye-bye."

I'm disoriented by the lack of bravado. Was he just caught off guard? Distracted? Nervous?

And then, slowly, it occurs to me that it might have been something else entirely: sadness.

NOVEMBER 20, 2018:

PRESS CONFERENCE

ON TUESDAY MORNING, WITH FOUR hours to go until the press conference, I head downstairs, still in my pajamas. The faculty deans of Adams House are at the dining room table, settling things up before they head off to the Cape for Thanksgiving.

"I was going to write you a note for today," one of the deans says, "but I didn't know what it should say! 'Good luck'? 'Hope it's satisfying? Interesting? Ghoulish?'"

I say that I hope it feels like an ending.

———

Mike Widmer texts to let me know that, as always, he's early. He's in a maroon Honda, parked in front of Harvard Hillel. He pops his trunk so I can throw in my suitcase—my plan is to head straight back to my family in New York whenever it's over.

I slide into the passenger seat, and he reaches over to give me a hug. It makes me feel worse about keeping such a big secret from him: Mike doesn't know what's about to happen. I hadn't been able to bring myself to tell him. I wanted to preserve the purity of his reaction to the press conference.

"Don't you think they're going to tell us they cracked the case?" he asks as he turns left to follow the Charles River. "They're not going to get us all together just to say they narrowed it down to thirty-four people."

I turn toward him. I can't lie to him.

He says his wife told him to expect the unexpected today.

It would probably be a better scene if I keep quiet, but being honest with him means more than the story does. I know what they're going to say, I tell him. I ask if he would rather find out from me or from the press conference.

"I would like to know," he says.

"From me?" I clarify.

"We're in this together," he says.

I tell him everything.

"Oh my god," Mike says, refusing to take his eyes off the road. Everything is gray—the sky, the leafless trees, even the mist that the cars kick up behind them. "There was never any point to the murder."

He knows from experience that one of life's hard lessons is its arbitrariness. So many people die randomly. And none of this matters to Jane because she's dead. But somehow it still matters. It matters how she died. And why she did. He, like all of us, wanted there to be an explanation. "Now there's nothing."

As we make our way to Woburn and try to shed ourselves of old theories, landmarks of the past keep insisting on themselves. Boston Garden—now TD Garden—where Karl had attended the black-tie wrestling match. The Raytheon building, where the foreman of the grand jury worked. Even Woburn itself is bound up in the past. It's where Stephen DeFilippo's grave is and where Lee Parsons's ashes are scattered. It's hard to let go of old stories.

———

The Middlesex DA's office is an ode to brutalist architecture: a box in the middle of a parking lot. Mike pulls in and turns off the car, and I notice I have a voicemail from Boyd. He says that Sennott's asked him to take the "DNA match" out of the statement he released to the press. It's too late, Boyd says, the statement's already been released. It reads:

> A half century of mystery and speculation has clouded the brutal crime that shattered Jane's promising young life and our family. As the surviving Britton, I wish to thank all those—friends, public officials and press—who persevered in keeping this investigation active, most especially State police Sergeant Peter Sennott. The DNA evidence match may be all we ever have as a conclusion. Learning to understand and forgive remains a challenge.

The request for retraction feels like an ominous beginning to the press conference.

The rain's turned to snow by the time we enter the room on the fourth floor of the building. Other than office staff who are milling around, we're the first ones there. Mike says hi to Meghan Kelly while I gawk in disbelief. On giant foam-core boards are high-resolution prints of things that I had long ago accepted I would never see: a blueprint of Jane's apartment that the historical commission said no longer existed. A photograph of the fire escape that led from Jane's kitchen to the courtyard; another of her living room. The wicker of her seats, the angle of her kitchen chair, the upholstery of her curtains. These are the details—like the feathers and flesh in an archaeological site—I thought had been lost forever.

Cambridge Police photo of the fire escape leading out from Jane's apartment.

Mike and I take two seats in the front row. Over the course of the next hour, an armada of news cameras set up behind us. The radio people plug into the sound system and try not to trip over their own wires. The seats fill up with reporters. "I'm at the Harvard murder press conference," one reporter enunciates into her phone.

My heart is pounding. I put my hand on Mike's cheek to show him how cold it is. He puts his hand on mine, too. It's also freezing.

Someone shouts, "Everybody ready to roll?"

And then, just past 1 p.m., it starts.

District Attorney Marian Ryan walks in and lays a manila folder on the lectern. People file in after her: Adrienne Lynch, her chief of homicide, Peter Sennott, and three other state police officers. They stand with their hands clasped in front of them. There is no representative from the Cambridge Police. Ryan speaks slowly, prioritizing clarity over affect:

> For the past 50 years, the murder of Jane Britton has intrigued members of the public and has posed a number of investigatory challenges for law enforcement. Multiple teams of investigators have looked into tips from the public, followed up on all available leads, and ruled out multiple suspects.
>
> As a direct result of their perseverance and the utilization of the latest advances in forensic technology by the Massachusetts State Police crime laboratory, I am today confident that we are able to say that the mystery of who killed Jane Britton has finally been solved.
>
> This is the oldest case that the Middlesex District Attorney's office has been able to bring to a resolution. This year, as a result of numerous forensic tests on DNA samples collected, both those collected at the time of Jane's murder and those collected more recently, we were able to positively identify Michael Sumpter as the person responsible for Jane's murder.

Photographers crawl around the front row like snipers. The woman to my left is Periscoping the conference on Twitter. I've emailed the link to Boyd, Elisabeth, and Don so they can follow along.

Ryan explains that Sumpter had ties to Cambridge. He lived there as a young child and attended first grade in the area. He had run-ins with the Cambridge cops as a juvenile, and his girlfriend in the late '60s lived in the neighborhood. In 1967, Sumpter worked at an establishment on Arrow Street in Harvard Square, less than a mile from Jane's apartment. And several years later, he was arrested and convicted of assaulting a woman in her Boston home, whom he had met earlier that evening at the Harvard Square T stop.

Ryan mentions the transit worker who, on the night of Jane's murder, saw a man fleeing her building around 1:30 a.m.—170 pounds, six feet. When Sumpter was arrested in 1970, he was 170 pounds, six foot one. She also says that authorities think that Sumpter entered Jane's apartment via the fire escape, and that police learned of a resident who heard noise on the escape. She does not mention that the witness was seven years old, and that Don Mitchell had entered Jane's apartment after the apparent noise and saw nothing amiss.

Ryan thanks Sergeant Peter Sennott and Adrienne Lynch for their tireless dedication. Sennott, she says, has been assigned to the case for over twenty years. The four cops don't change their facial expressions. But Lynch's, as it had throughout Ryan's speech, can't help but emote— mostly a frown of intense emotion. There is a sweetness to her face that reminds me of my beloved elementary school music teacher, so it makes sense to me when, later that afternoon, she writes to the Abraham family with her apologies that this conclusion doesn't provide answers to their family.

The district attorney speaks for ten minutes. She does not make any mention of Ada Bean. She confirms that they used the last of the DNA sample in the testing. And, she concludes: "It is my hope today, especially as we enter into Thanksgiving week and to the holiday season, that finally knowing who is responsible for Jane's brutal murder will provide some consolation to Jane's surviving family and friends." Then she takes questions.

But what about the ochre, one journalist asks. Ryan says it may have just been a "red herring" all along.

———

Mike Widmer answers reporters' questions after the press conference.

As soon as it's over, reporters start swarming around Mike like fish being fed. I move out of the fray because Kelly promised me some time alone with Marian Ryan, Adrienne Lynch, and Peter Sennott, and I don't want her to forget. I catch her eye, and she escorts me to an office to meet with the investigators. She waits in the room with me. When the door opens again, it's just Marian Ryan. I can feel how short the time I have with the district attorney will be, so I have no choice but to say okay and begin. I race nervously down my list of questions.

I ask about the headstone. Like the ochre, she says, it "took on a life of its own. And it doesn't appear that it had anything significant to do with anything."

Was there any evidence of a struggle? Only one laceration on her arm.

Has the murder weapon been identified? No.

Has the ax in the turtle tank been ruled out? It wasn't in the evidence box.

Do you have any indication that the crime was premeditated? Don had very specifically said that Sennott called him a random *stalker*. Ryan says they have no idea.

The only solid new piece of information I'm able to draw from the DA is that it was my and Widmer and Wallack's public records push that helped drive the investigation to this conclusion. Forensic tests on the crime scene sample had stalled in 2004, when there wasn't enough DNA to yield a result. Authorities' hope was that technology would advance even further so that the minute amount of DNA that remained might one day be sufficient to yield a robust profile.

And then, twelve years later, our public records requests came through. If Middlesex County wanted to withhold the files because they held out hope for solving the case and prosecuting someone, they had to make good on their claim that the investigation was active, which meant testing the remaining genetic material. Waiting for some hypothetical date when the technology *might* advance enough was no longer an option. Ryan said, "We decided to do one last sweep of the file. Is there *anything* else that maybe the lab could look at, maybe they could do?"

We were obviously living the end of that story.

"And will the files now be—"

"Yes," Ryan says.

"Can I submit my public records request?" I lay an envelope down on the table.

"We can give it to you," Ryan and Kelly say in near tandem.

"If you want to come with me, I can get you a copy of it," Kelly says.

———

By the time I'm done with the district attorney and the press office, the conference room has been entirely cleared out. Mike has been moved to a waiting room on the third floor.

"I have an early Christmas present for you," I say and hand him a CD in a flimsy paper jacket.

"Is this today?" he asks, thinking it's the information packet from the press conference.

"It's the file," I say.

He pauses in disbelief. He looks at this tiny CD in his hand, wondering if it really could be what we've been fighting for years for. "—What?"

"Four thousand pages of files," I say.

He doesn't say anything for a long time. And then, finally: "Now I know what I'll be doing with the rest of my life."

Mike holds the CD containing the Jane Britton police file.

We wind back through Woburn and Belmont. Mike feels satisfied. With the solution. With the investigation. With the fact that he played a big role—and a *good* role—in this. Even the brutality of the randomness has faded. The certainty of today's conference, he says, trumped the randomness.

He reflects that there had been some solace in this quest even before today's answer: The journey created a community around this case, which was healing in itself. It brought things out in people that they didn't know they needed to share.

I can see the post office up ahead, and I know what's about to come. On the right-hand side is Jane's apartment. We take one lap around it—the parking lot, her living room window that faced the river—before continuing onward.

It occurs to us that a cousin of randomness is serendipity.

THE FILES

ON A DARKENED, CROWDED CHINATOWN bus, I'm on my computer, having just popped in the disk of files. I can hardly believe that no one else on this bus knows how monumental this moment is. That the woman in front of me is watching a Korean binge-eating YouTube channel while I'm sitting on the edge of Tutankhamun's sarcophagus, crowbar in hand, about to pry it open.

There they all are. The autopsy. The letter that Gramly wrote to the cops. Photos of the crime scene. The original Cambridge cops' notes, Lieutenant Joyce's investigation, the chemist's report, the trail of renewed interest in the case. The pictures from the funeral that the cops took under Don Mitchell's direction. The RCMP report on Anne Abraham's disappearance. The Bankoffs' statements from Rome. A letter Jane sent to her high school friend Irene duPont so close to her death that it arrived posthumously.

I want to inhale the files so quickly that it's hard to discipline myself to go through them methodically, but I try my best. They're organized by the agency that collected them. The Cambridge Police. The Massachusetts State Police. The Middlesex District Attorney's Office.

In the Massachusetts State Police files are Sennott's notes taken when he collected DNA from Don, Boyd, Jim Humphries, Karl Lamberg-Karlovsky, and Boyd's suspect Peter Ganick. In the folder, too, are the results from when they all were—like Gramly had been in 2006—excluded as possible sources of the DNA from the crime scene. (Lee Parsons could not be excluded because he was already deceased and cremated. ADA Lynch had considered collecting DNA from a relative of his, but later learned that the lab could not perform the comparative analysis required.)

Among the district attorney's files is documentation of the various stages of the forensics, from the medical examiner handing over the original autopsy slides in 1998, to the CODIS link with Michael Sumpter in July 2018. (This is when Sennott first called Don and Boyd.) And, finally, the confirmation that it was, indeed, Sumpter at the crime scene, when his brother was eliminated as a possible source of the DNA that September.

I'm intrigued that most of the DNA testing reports starting in 2017 are signed by a Mass State Police analyst named Cailin Drugan. She was the one who, in July 2017, did the first DNA tests on the crime scene sample since 2006. She was the one who, when that test didn't have enough DNA to yield results suitable for comparison, indicated her desire to continue being assigned to Jane's case. She was also the one who found more genetic material to test. It feels almost miraculous: Unwilling to give up on Jane's case, she discovered some skin cells on the test tube that held the vaginal smear swab. Drugan was the one whose idea it was to do a Y chromosome test on the skin cells. Since only men have Y chromosomes, the idea was that it would isolate the suspect's DNA from Jane's and might produce clearer results. Drugan was also the one who developed the DNA profile in October 2017, and she was the one who, when the investigators had dead-ended with the usual suspects, helped bring ADA Lynch's attention to a "soft hit" to Michael Sumpter in 2004 buried deep in Jane's file.

There's very little documentation about this "soft hit" other than the fact that someone had done a keyboard search of the 1998 three-loci profile in the Massachusetts CODIS database, and that state police had been verbally informed of a link with Michael Sumpter's DNA. There are a few requests for police records on Sumpter from shortly thereafter, and a note that authorities had tried, unsuccessfully, to locate Michael's brother. But that's it. Sumpter's name doesn't appear again until Drugan and a colleague bring him up to ADA Lynch fourteen years later.

In a summary of the case, Lynch admits: "What was done in 2017 could arguably have been done [...] when Sumpter's name first is mentioned in our file."

About a quarter of the four thousand pages on the disk are about Michael Sumpter. Sumpter was in and out of jail for so much of his life that, stitched together, his police records read like a biography.

Sumpter was born in Boston, the middle child of three. His parents divorced when he was six, and his mother was in and out of mental institutions for the rest of her life. The Sumpter children were raised by their maternal grandparents in the Old Harbor Housing Project in South Boston, the same public housing where Whitey Bulger grew up.

Sumpter's first arrest was at the age of fifteen in 1963 for larceny, and his late adolescence was littered with arrest reports of crimes with escalating severity—vehicle larceny, pickpocketing, assault and battery with a dangerous weapon. When he served his first state sentence two months after his eighteenth birthday, an officer conducted a psychological evaluation. "He appears [to be] quite impulse-ridden and reveals characteristics of a typical character disorder. [. . .] Asked why he had appeared in Court, which no one [else] in the family had done [. . .], he replied, rather close to tears, that he guessed that he was the 'rotten egg in the bunch.'"

In 1966, Sumpter was paroled, and it was during his release that he worked in Harvard Square. But his freedom didn't last long. Sumpter was back in prison six months later for using a stolen credit card. During another psychological evaluation, the young man said he was certain that he was crazy, and he feared that once he started opening up, he would lose control. The evaluator warned that Sumpter had been passive during his first institutionalization, but "things will be different this time; he will fight back."

Less than a year later, in July 1968, Sumpter was released again to live with his brother in Boston. Six months later, Jane Britton was dead.

The rest of Sumpter's history is a frightening carousel of arrests, paroles, violations, recommitments, and escapes. Sumpter caught the brief moment in American history when there was a strong belief in inmate rehabilitation, and Massachusetts law went further than most. Even prisoners who had been sentenced to life without the possibility of parole were eligible for furloughs—a set number of unsupervised hours away from prison. Sumpter comported himself well while he was incarcerated, impressing supervisors with his work ethic and conduct—one called him "beyond reproach" and another commended him as "always a gentleman." But as soon as he would get outside, he'd commit another crime.

There is a possibility that Sumpter feared this about himself. In December 1971, he refused to continue doing his assigned prison work. When the corrections officer reminded him that he was going home soon, and not to do anything to jeopardize it, Sumpter replied that the officer "should lock him up." No one took his comment seriously. Two weeks later, Sumpter was released as scheduled. Less than a month later, Ellen Rutchick was dead. And three weeks after that, Sumpter attacked the woman he had met at the Harvard Square subway station. He had walked her home, insisted on coming upstairs, and put a knife to her throat when she resisted his advances. The victim survived, but Sumpter had cut her throat so deeply she needed a tracheotomy.

The same thing happened in 1973: Sumpter behaved well in prison, was granted a twelve-hour furlough, and escaped by simply walking away. Three weeks later, he raped and killed Mary McClain.

And again in 1975: Sumpter, who, a week after Mary's murder, had been caught and returned to jail for robbery and attempted assault of a police officer, was granted work release. On August 2, instead of showing up to work, he went to the fourth-floor apartment of a woman in Boston. He had been in her hallway, and she let him in for some refreshment after he introduced himself as her new neighbor. Sumpter emerged from her bathroom wearing surgical gloves. He tied her up, gagged her, assaulted her, and raped her. Sumpter was caught for this rape—the only one that he was convicted of during his lifetime—and it was for this crime he was serving time when he died. It is chilling to think that were it not for this conviction, his DNA would never have been preserved.

And yet he was let out again. In 1985, he walked away from his first day of work release and raped a woman in Back Bay.

Sergeant Doogan of the Unsolved Homicides Squad would later characterize Sumpter's behavior this way: "You mean that lion that's crouched down in the tall grass watching the gazelles isn't usually that short? Same thing. He's a predator. He'll do what it takes to succeed. He's goal-oriented, and his goal is to rape women."

But I refuse to let Sumpter's shadow eclipse the materials I'm most eager to get to: the ones that belonged to Jane. They're in the Cambridge Police files, alongside notes from the original investigators. I plow through them as though they could disappear at any moment. Her driver's license. The Christmas cards she received a month before her death. The letter Boyd sent her from Vietnam.

Answers to questions I thought I would never resolve had been there all along, waiting in the files.

The married professor whose name Ingrid Kirsch couldn't remember— the one she told police Jane had had an affair with—was Hal Ross, Jane's tutor sophomore year.

The red powder at the crime scene was, it seems, spread in a discernible pattern—at least according to Cambridge Police detective Halliday.

Detective Halliday, examining the crime scene photos, described the powder as a "circle line...which is run...just across her back, onto the pillow, and up to the wall." (I can't describe it for myself because the photos that might include the powder are redacted.)

And, after years of wondering if authorities had actually analyzed the powder, I find a note in the state police's lab report that a chemical analysis of the mystery substance had, in fact, been conducted. "Mixture of black and red iron salts," the April 1969 report says. And later, the chemist concludes, "consistent with ochre."

The problem, though, is that ochre is an *oxide*, not a salt; the powder can't be both types of molecules. Perhaps the chemist was just using the word *salt* loosely, but that is conjecture. The most that can be said, then, is that the chemist determined that the powder's main metal was iron—which would be true for red ochre, as well as for many kinds of commercially available red pigments. In other words: the substance may have been ochre after all, but there is still uncertainty.

I also don't know what exactly happened during the Incense Night after the Mitchells left and Jane was alone with Lee Parsons. According to Lee, they never even kissed. Jane left his place around 4:30 in the morning and walked home by herself, only to return the next afternoon to help Lee repair his carpet. While she was there, she handed him a bag—a present, she explained. She knew that Lee was heading home in a few weeks to see his family for Christmas. He looked inside; it was a child's construction set.

I'm as close to the white-hot center of the knowable as I'll come, but that just makes the absences in the record that much more glaring. There is never any explanation for why the chemists found blood on Jim's skates and sweater, and no further explanation for why Jill Nash tested "strong positive" for blood on her hands. No one ever comes forward as the person who knocked on Jane's door at nine o'clock the morning of Generals. There are no copies of the lie detector tests, and nothing to substantiate the story that Lee had failed his. There's no record that authorities ever analyzed the red ochre sample that Karl provided, never mind a comparison with the powder found at the crime scene.

The semen stains in the crotch of the women's underwear found in Jane's bathroom might be Michael Sumpter's, but the underwear was lost before forensic DNA testing became even a distant dream. No one admits to having had sex with Jane other than Jim Humphries, but that was before he left for Christmas break, three weeks before she died.

There's never any clarity on who made that threatening phone call to Jane just after she and Ed Franquemont broke up. And no record in the files that the fingerprint that Don had taken a picture of was, in fact, Jane's, as the cops had told him, nor any explanation of why authorities had asked him to take the photo in the first place.

Instead, there's a transcript from Sergeant Sennott's conversation with Don when he went out to Hawaii to collect DNA. In it, Don says, "God, it was so funny. I mean, I was just—I was kind of thinking, *Why—don't they have people to do this stuff?*" And Sennott responds, "Trust me, that's what we're thinking, too."

Most unsettling are Jane's fears, threaded throughout the files—in journal entries, in letters, in interviews with Jane's friends—that she was very sick and might not have long to live. I had never come across those concerns before. In June 1968, before heading off to Iran, she wrote to Jim, who was soon to leave for London: "It's very difficult to get caught in the middle of two sets of time—focusing all your attention on the beauties of the minute, planning for the future, and then kicking yourself back to the moment because one way or another there isn't going to be any future." The letter continued: "I'll know in October, maybe a little earlier if this stuff achieves complete remission (you may have to cover for me towards the end of the summer, September or so, because if it doesn't I may begin to get a little tireder more easily.)" She described the illness as the "Sword of Damocles" hanging over her head.

But there are no doctor's records in the file. No evidence of Jane's parents mentioning an illness to the cops. When I ask Boyd and Elisabeth Handler, they say Jane gave no indication that she was sick. Don says it "rings some distant bell," but he's sure it was just an annoying bug she had caught on expedition. The closest I get to a diagnosis is from Ingrid Kirsch, who relayed to police that Jane had told her she'd been having some trouble with her blood for about a year. According to Jane, doctors had said it was "some queer form of anemia," but Ingrid reminded police that Jane was always inclined to the morbid and may have exaggerated the drama.

I have no idea what to make of this story line. I want to believe Jane, but I can't make the details add up. (A momentary epiphany that the "black and red iron salts" of the mystery red powder might have been iron supplements for her anemia is quickly quelled by Robert Skenderian, a compounding pharmacist at Skenderian pharmacy in Cambridge, which has been in the area for three generations. Iron powder was not a common form of supplement, even in 1969, he says. "Iron powder—*very* dangerous.") I try, instead, to admire the fact that every time I start to think I've pinned down my heroine, she wriggles past the outlines I've drawn for her. This admiration, however, is tinged by the guilt I feel for writing a biography of someone who will always be a mystery to me.

My computer is about to run out of battery on the bus, but not before I find, tucked within the state police folder, the greatest gold of all: the original interviews I thought I would never get to hear, transcribed from the reel-to-reel tapes. Jill. Jane's father. Pippa Shaplin. And even Lee Parsons. In the dark of the bus, they feel like voices from beyond the grave.

JANUARY 14, 1969: LEE PARSONS

INTERROGATION

Dr. Parsons: There is something that I think you should be aware of. That first evening that she was at my apartment, she made a very cryptic remark, which now bothers me. I don't remember precisely what we were talking about, except that the subject was longevity and terminal illnesses. She started to make a statement...but she cut herself off immediately and said she didn't want to talk about it. It was really a very obtuse and cryptic remark. She didn't seem frightened or—it was something that she'd accepted. Well, now—now it just makes me wonder what really was on her mind.

UNSATISFIED

A NUMBER OF MY SOURCES reach out to me, cautioning me to interrogate the DA's story before accepting it wholesale. Iva Houston questions the timing of the conference: Why, after all these years, did they hold it two days before Thanksgiving when people were unlikely to be paying attention?

Mike Gramly contacts me, unprompted, to insist on his doubt about the DA's version of events. He writes, "I heard that the 'killer' of Jane Britton had been 'found.' I don't believe it. The police are always trying to pin murders on notorious criminals. Look what they did with DeSalvo."

I call him, and we speak for over an hour. "I just think there's something strange here," he says. "There's more to the story than this guy Sumpter."

Gramly is disappointed by the inconclusiveness of the evidence, and he's "pissed off" that no justice had been served. He wants me to notice how convenient it is to pin Jane's murder on a dead suspect. "All we know for sure is Michael Sumpter had sex with her," he says. "That still doesn't prove who did the murder."

The pigment specialist I consult also expresses some reservations. Narayan Khandekar, a senior conservation scientist at Harvard and curator of the Forbes Pigment Collection, is troubled by the suggestion that the powder might have been kicked over accidentally. "You don't just have piles of powder. It's not a spice market."

He is not a forensic specialist, but he knows pigments well. Pigment powder, including ground ochre, is extremely fine; synthetic pigment particles are a fiftieth the width of a human hair. When you handle these powders carefully, the particles still get everywhere, so he finds it hard to believe that Jane would have left her container open. Besides, even if an open container of it were tipped over during a scuffle, it would billow into a cloud and make a smudgy mess before it would leave a discernible pattern.

I read him the detective's description of the powder's distribution: "Circle line which is run just across her back—"

"Circle line," he repeats.

Ochre, or any kind of paint pigment, he explains, "is pretty unmanageable when it's a powder. So to actually draw a circle, you have to be wanting to." He encourages me to try it for myself by going to an art supply store, and then adds, "That means something. I don't know what it means, but it means something."

Even John Fulkerson joins the chorus of doubt.

"Let's just say I have a lot of questions," he says on a call a week after the press conference. "It doesn't compute. It doesn't match up...There's not going to be a trial to prove any of this stuff, you know? So they can kind of say whatever they want to say."

Fulkerson says that he's seen people get off on more solid evidence. He tells me about an unsolved murder he worked on in Newton where a suspect had been in the area at the time, and the headboard of the passenger side of his car had gun powder residue. Yet the DA wouldn't even let Fulkerson bring it to the grand jury for indictment.

The evidence in Jane's case, on the other hand, was even more circumstantial, yet it was deemed sufficient to close the case. "Does the DNA match? Yes. Is he a bad guy? Yes. But it doesn't answer the question, 'Who murdered Jane Britton?' in my opinion."

I am also haunted by a small note on the October 2017 lab report by Cailin Drugan: "Profile is a mixture consistent with two male contributors. A major and a minor contributor were observed." Nowhere in any of the press about the solution to the case is there any mention of this minor contributor. Sumpter's profile was linked to the major contributor—but the minor? Karl, Gramly, Boyd, Don, Jim, and Peter Ganick were all excluded as possibilities. To date, the minor contributor remains unidentified. And because it's a Y-chromosome profile, it can't simply be run through CODIS.

According to the Middlesex district attorney's office, the minor contributor is likely contamination, perhaps from the medical examiner who collected the slides in 1969. Standards were different then, ADA Lynch reminds me. Samples were collected to test for the presence of sperm cells or blood type, not DNA. The examiner might not have been wearing gloves, or he might have been shedding. It's also possible that the minor contributor is just an artifact of analysis—the kind of fuzziness that comes from amplifying such small amounts of degraded DNA at such high levels.

A forensic analyst I speak to, though, assures me that the location of the peaks for the minor contributor isn't where you'd expect them if they were just stutter. And, of course, there's the possibility that it was from someone else Jane was in contact with before she died—an acquaintance or, perhaps, a second suspect. (Sgt. Doogan confirms that in neither McClain's nor Rutchick's case was there DNA from a second male.) The Massachusetts State Police deny my request to see the original forensic lab files for Jane's case, and when I ask for an interview with analyst Drugan, I'm told that I would not be allowed to speak with her—or to anyone else in the MSP crime lab for that matter. None of the forensic scientists I consult is able to tell me the significance—or the lack thereof—of the minor contributor. "You've come to the end of the line of the knowable," one says.

I don't want to pay attention to this persisting doubt. The story, for a moment, had felt so neat and final—and I have not seen any evidence to convince me that Sumpter wasn't the murderer—but the things I tamped down in order to feel that closure resurface with these reminders to stay vigilant. Like the fact that Sumpter—a Black serial killer, who escapes from work release to rape and kill white women in their homes—sounds like the poster child for "tough on crime" politics. Or what Boyd had told me on the call when I first learned Sumpter's name: Sennott had told him "there was a problem with one of the officers' conduct during the initial investigation that would have warranted Internal Affairs." Boyd said Sennott hadn't gone into detail and didn't think he ever would. But that was before I got the police files.

GIACOPPO

ON MAY 27, 1969, LIEUTENANT Frank Joyce of the Massachusetts State Police pulled District Attorney Droney aside. He had major news to share about the Jane Britton case.

For the past month, the Cambridge and Massachusetts State Police had been investigating a new suspect in the Britton case, a veterinarian in

Dover named Frank Powers. His name first came to their attention when, in late April, Cambridge Police received an anonymous tip implicating someone named Dr. Paul Rhudick in her murder. But when detectives followed up with Dr. Rhudick, they learned that the tip was part of a string of harassing incidents that had started when Rhudick's current girlfriend left another man to be with him. The other man was Frank Powers.

When Cambridge detectives met with Frank, they questioned him about Jane, and he admitted to knowing her. His daughter had gone to school with her, and his sister ran both the horse stables where Jane had learned to ride and the horse camp that Jane attended as a kid, Camp Roanna. But, Frank said, he hadn't seen her in over a decade.

A few days later, Dover police received a call from Cecelia Powers, Frank's wife. She was calling from a neighbor's house where she and the kids were sheltering. Frank had assaulted her and the children. Cecelia told the officer that this wasn't the first time he had been violent with her, and she feared what Frank was capable of. She was going to ask for a divorce.

Four days later, Cecilia called the Dover Police again. Frank had left her a letter stating that she "could find him in the woods off Powisset Street in Dover." On a quiet street half a mile from the main road, a Dover Police officer found the body of Dr. Powers, dead from a self-inflicted gunshot wound to the head.

Cambridge Police got permission to fingerprint the late Dr. Powers as a suspect in the murder of Jane Britton. Three days later, on May 15, Massachusetts State Police confirmed that a previously unidentified print on an ashtray recovered from Jane's room matched the left thumbprint of the late veterinarian.

Cambridge Police photo of the ashtray in question.

However, the day that Lieutenant Joyce approached the district attorney to tell him about major news in the Britton case, he had come to say that there was no way that Dr. Powers had killed Jane. Frank hadn't been in the country. Moreover, Joyce had an idea about how Powers's fingerprint had gotten on that ashtray: Joyce "strongly suspected" that Detective Giacoppo, the Cambridge Police officer who had worked on Jane's case since day one, had "planted" it.

———

Lieutenant Joyce had begun to suspect that something was strange when he interviewed Cecelia Powers at her home on May 16, six days after her husband's body was discovered. Officers had obtained a search warrant for their home after the fingerprint match. While other officers looked around, Lieutenant Joyce spoke with Cecelia. She told the lieutenant that she and her late husband were in the British West Indies the night Jane was killed. She provided Lieutenant Joyce with a copy of the check she had paid to Travel Services Bureau in the amount of $382 for their vacation, and a copy of her late husband's passport, including a stamp at JFK Airport, where they had an evening connecting flight to Boston, dated January 7, 1969. Dr. Powers hadn't yet landed in Logan Airport when Jane's body was discovered.

Though Jane had received the "ashtray" in question as a trophy from Camp Roanna, which was run by Frank Powers's sister, Joyce ruled out the possibility that Powers's fingerprint was there from that original summer. Jane's mother assured Joyce that she had scrubbed and polished the trophy multiple times in the intervening years, including with steel wool.

Joyce began toying with a different theory. He knew that it was Cambridge officer Giacoppo who had informed his superiors that there was an unidentified fingerprint on the ashtray, and he knew that Giacoppo did so only *after* Frank Powers had died, even though the ashtray had been in police possession since the week after Jane's body was discovered. Joyce also knew that Giacoppo was the Cambridge police officer who had fingerprinted Powers for comparison by going to the Needham funeral home where the late veterinarian's body lay. It wasn't too hard to deduce the rest.

The district attorney said that he couldn't bring himself to believe Lieutenant Joyce's theory, but he promised that he would look into it.

On Wednesday afternoon, the day after raising his concerns, Lieutenant Joyce accompanied Giacoppo to state police headquarters, across the river from the stretch of land between Harvard and MIT. Joyce had arranged for Giacoppo to meet with the state lab's police photography expert. As requested, Giacoppo turned over the silver ashtray, a photograph of the alleged latent fingerprint, and the fingerprint card with inked impressions of Frank Powers's left hand. Giacoppo stayed in the room as the MSP officer examined the items, so he was there when the expert failed to find Powers's fingerprints on the ashtray. When the expert asked why, despite how obvious the fingerprint had been in the photograph, it was nowhere to be found, Giacoppo said that in the days since finding the fingerprint, a lot of people had handled the ashtray.

The expert dug deeper: *Isn't it unusual in a capital case, for anyone to be able to handle the evidence, especially since fingerprint evidence is so delicate?*

Giacoppo replied: "When the higher-ups want to see something I'm not going to stop them."

After the meeting, Lieutenant Joyce once again laid out his suspicions, this time to the DA, the ADA, and Giacoppo himself. Giacoppo denied the allegations, but he admitted that he had photographed the latent print on the ashtray two days *after* he had fingerprinted Frank Powers, and he acknowledged that it was poor practice to have waited to take that picture, when atmospheric conditions could cause a print to disappear at any time.

All he offered by way of justification was that he had been "tied up in other matters."

When the district attorney asked the detective to take a lie detector test, Giacoppo requested to speak to the DA alone. Lieutenant Joyce stepped out of the room. The DA later told Joyce that though Giacoppo continued to deny planting the fingerprint, he was now convinced by Joyce's suspicions.

The next day, Giacoppo asked the DA if he could be allowed to face the Cambridge police chief alone to "tell the truth." The DA agreed, but by the end of the workday, Giacoppo still hadn't been able to reach the chief. Droney insisted that Giacoppo find him, even if that meant going to Chief Reagan's home after work.

It is unclear if Giacoppo ever spoke to Reagan that night.

Early Friday morning, Lieutenant Joyce got a call from DA Droney, who had just spoken to Giacoppo's wife. The detective had attempted suicide the night before. He survived, but she had arranged for him to be committed to Bournewood Hospital, a private psychiatric facility in Brookline.

Later that day, a report from a state police examiner was delivered to Lieutenant Joyce, relaying the results of his chemical analysis of the ashtray: "CONCLUSION: The blackish impression on the submitted ash tray is consistent with having been made with a carbon tetrachloride-soluble ink."

The fingerprint on the ashtray was, in other words, not made by normal skin oils, but by ink—perhaps the same ink that Giacoppo had made those fingerprint cards with moments prior. The inky fingerprint might have been left long enough to take the photograph, but rubbed off before he turned the evidence over to the MSP analyst for examination.

Chief Reagan told Joyce that he suspended Detective Giacoppo, and he impounded all the evidence in Jane Britton's case for security. Reagan also said that he planned to conduct a review of all cases in which Giacoppo's testimony played a part to ensure that no miscarriage of justice had taken place. Later, the city solicitor advised Reagan that Giacoppo's resignation would be appropriate given the circumstances.

Within a month, Lieutenant Joyce went to Cecelia Powers's home to tell her, in person, that he was convinced beyond a shadow of a doubt that her husband had nothing to do with Jane Britton's death.

CRUMBS

In 2005—THIRTY-SIX YEARS after Lieutenant Joyce issued his report about the Frank Powers phase of the Jane Britton investigation—Cambridge PD was recused from the case due to "an unwaiverable conflict of interest." The announcement came in the form of a letter from then DA Martha Coakley, and it was this letter that sent John Fulkerson packing Jane's files to hand over to Peter Sennott. (Fulkerson, who says he was kept in the dark about the nature of the conflict, had felt blindsided.)

Six weeks after that letter, Sennott and the head of the Middlesex DA's internal detective unit, Detective Lieutenant James Connolly, questioned the elder Giacoppo in his home in connection with the case.

Connolly's notes are difficult to decipher, with no differentiation between quote and fact. The only note in the margin says, *Wasn't stupid, it was crazy*, but without quotation marks, it's impossible to tell if that's Connolly's feelings or Giacoppo's words. The rest of the notes read like a cryptic poem:

> *12-13 years on Camb*
>> *Remembers fingerprinting Dr. in casket in Needham*
>> *Doesn't recall taking pics*
>> *Dom Scalese was his partner / I only told Dom that there was a match /*
> *Dom told everyone then they did search warrants*
>> *Did speak to Droney—he was wrong*
>> *I made a mistake. The print was never on the ashtray*

One thing is clear, though: Giacoppo told investigators that he "did not resign" from Cambridge PD.

———

All of this had been staring me in the face for years. Four years ago, Boyd told me about Frank Powers and the alleged fingerprint plant. Two years ago, after my talk with Fulkerson, I began wondering why Cambridge PD had had to hand over the files to state police. Now I see that Adrienne Lynch herself spelled out that the "conflict of interest" was, in fact, Cambridge police misconduct related to the investigation.

I still do not believe that this alleged misconduct is the reason that Jane's case went unsolved for so long. Nor do I believe there was any intergenerational cover-up, even though the younger Giacoppo did not admit to me that he knew anything more about the Jane Britton case on our 2018 phone call—though, I realize now, he had been responsible for overseeing the investigations and records units of the department at the time of Cambridge's recusal. If anything, I believe it firmed up the younger Giacoppo's drive to solve the case: Mary McCutcheon, one of the two Golden Girls, told me that Mike had once referred to solving Jane's case as a "two-generation commitment."

But it is still an important part of the story. And despite how astonishingly transparent the Jane Britton file is about this misconduct, my hope of reconstructing the why, and not just the what and when, dissipates quickly. There are so many things missing from the file: Whether Reagan ever actually carried out that review of cases that Giacoppo played a role in. Any evidence that Giacoppo was even suspended. Any note about when or how Sergeant Sennott first became aware of the police misconduct. Any reasoning as to why, after decades of the misconduct being an open secret within the DA's office and the Cambridge PD, Martha Coakley would suddenly decide in 2005 that Cambridge PD could no longer handle the case. And certainly, there was no answer to the main question all of this posed: why the elder Giacoppo would have tampered with evidence. Did he want the glory of solving the case, and he assumed that everyone would be relieved enough to have a dead, philandering abuser to blame that people would stop looking for the truth? Had someone pressured him?

Dom Scalese, Giacoppo's partner, is dead. As are the two Cambridge Police officers who accompanied him to the funeral home that day. As are the DA, his assistant, the police chief, and, of course, Lieutenant Joyce himself.

Neither Giacoppo, father nor son, respond to my repeated requests for comment.

The elder Giacoppo is still a celebrated member of the Massachusetts police community: He was president of the Massachusetts Association of

Italian American Police Officers for thirty-five years, and he's spent over three decades in the leadership of the Middlesex County Deputy Sheriff's Association. In 2009, he was invited to teach a fingerprinting course at the Middlesex Sheriff's Youth Public Safety Academy. And in December 2018, less than a month after I received the police files, the elder Giacoppo was given the lifetime achievement award by the Association of Italian American Police Officers.

MYTHMAKING

Less than two weeks after that call from Don announcing the break in the case, I got an email from Brian Wood, the husband of the late Stine Rossel, the last keeper of the fabled graduate student file of the Jane Britton case, passed down through generations. His timing was uncanny, though, at that point, Brian had no way of knowing. As if on cue that after fifty years of waiting, reality was finally rushing in on this myth.

He wrote: "The retelling of this story was like a folkloric experience in itself among the graduate students in archaeology, and this dossier was passed around through many hands." He attached the elusive "file" as the least mythic parcel of all: an email attachment.

As I already suspected, the file didn't contain anything groundbreaking. A number of old *Boston Globe* articles and clippings from the *New York Times* and the *Crimson*. But the feeling of disappointment of peeking behind the curtain of the Wizard of Oz never came. Instead, I felt astonished that this mythic file was real, and that I was now in possession of it. I was also touched by the fact that the file comprised photocopies of original articles, compiled before the internet made such things easy. Someone had had to go to the library, and to the offices of these newspapers, to find these artifacts. These graduate students believed in the myth enough that they had created a talisman—this file—to ward off the villain they perceived in their fairy tale.

I tried to hold the idea of the file still in my mind. But it shimmered—an object real and mythic. After a decade of trying to separate fact and rumor,

I had finally found the point where it felt meaningless to disentangle one from the other.

DECEMBER 2018: KARL

KARL AND I WALK GINGERLY from the Peabody Museum to a restaurant on Massachusetts Avenue. This is the interview he promised me when I broke the news to him. He uses two hands on the railing to ease himself down the Peabody stairs, heavily favoring his left leg.

It's early December 2018, and Karl went skiing recently, he tells me. I'm surprised to hear it because he had made such a big show out of his retirement from the sport when we last met. Skiing was the one art he had mastered, not teaching, he had said. He seemed to miss it more than academia.

The day he decided to return to skiing, he'd had such a great time, he tried his luck again that same week. On the second run, he went into a turn, slightly lost his balance, and knew immediately what he had done. He felt his right knee pop and found himself on the ground. "I should not have done it. I'm eighty-one years old. C'mon!"

Karl had always known the dangers, he had told me when we last sat down. But he always felt safe: not that it couldn't happen to him, but that it wouldn't.

It happened to him three weeks ago, right when I called him about a break in the case. I'm about to press him on whether there was any cause-and-effect connection between the two events when he changes the subject entirely at the crosswalk by Annenberg, the freshman dining hall.

"I've given some thought to the solution," Karl says, about Sumpter I suppose. I search his face, but it gives nothing away. "You know. I have an argument with David Reich," he continues.

I have no idea where he's going with this. "I don't know who that is," I say.

Karl explains that David Reich is a Harvard geneticist who analyzes ancient DNA to map out the migration patterns of humans thousands of years ago.

"Here's the crux," Karl says. "The DNA studies are in many ways in direct conflict with the archaeological record."

Reich's work, I later learn, is controversial. Critics fault him for drawing broad conclusions that overhaul our sense of the ancient world, based on apparently paltry evidence, like the DNA from just four skulls. They accuse his attempts to remodel our understanding of the world with science of falling prey to the same problems that oversimplified previous historical narratives. In our eagerness to find answers and simple through-lines, we overlook complexity, ignoring facts that don't fit. The danger is that we are even more ignorant of our blindness when the narratives come with the gloss of science.

Karl and I pause to give his knee a rest.

"How do you reconcile this?" he asks. He doesn't think David Reich's analysis of the genetic material is wrong. "All I know is that the archaeological record doesn't conform to the DNA, and the DNA is supporting a narrative that archaeology finds difficult to support."

"And you draw the parallel in Jane's case," I say.

Karl doesn't answer.

We start walking again, and when we get to the restaurant, I hold the door open for him.

"I'm not an invalid yet," he says.

As always with Karl, we luxuriate in time. Three hours go by at lunch. His eyebrows look like tumbleweeds trying to roll toward his ears. We reminisce about other people on the Tepe Yahya digs. He shoots me a glare when I ask him about Christine Lesniak, the woman who disappeared. "Christine?" He pauses, then says he doesn't think Christine was ever particularly interested in becoming an archaeologist. "She dropped out of school, and I don't know what happened to her. I have no idea." We don't get into it.

He says he didn't talk to Jim again after Jane died. Didn't Jim go to Tepe Yahya with you a few more seasons? *Oh yes oh yes*, he says, and seamlessly changes the story to we never talked *about Jane* again. He insists that you couldn't fail out of Harvard by failing your Generals. That Jane had only been scheduled to take her exams once.

I know that these statements are false, and I wonder if he's told the story like this so many times that he doesn't remember the way it really was. But then I realize this conclusion might speak more to the limitations of my own perspective: If I'm the one who's rehearsed the details of

Jane's life with the regularity that obsession demands, is it his fault for not remembering?

Toward the end, we order espressos and as he holds the tiny cup, his signet ring on his pinkie catches my eye. I had wondered about it since that first class of his I sat in on.

"What's the iconography on your family crest?"

"A coat of arms," he says first, and then, "Dogs. Hunting dogs."

"Why?"

"Hunting in Europe is a status aspect. And you display the horns of your—" He pauses, perhaps to weigh whether he wants to say the next word or to emphasize it. "—kill."

One of the Habsburg emperors had decided he wanted a keeper of the hounds, and he chose a relative of Karl's. Karl's family crest has had a hunting dog on it ever since. The signet ring, I later find out, was his father's.

"But we came to talk about Jane," Karl says. He seems uncomfortable talking about his family history and taps on the table, searching for words. "It's—I don't—" He keeps stopping himself mid-sentence, until finally he says: "I'm not quite sure why I've been so lucky."

I press him on what made him think of luck, and he dodges the question.

"Right place at the right time. Meeting the right person at the right time. Selecting the exact appropriate wife. God, we've been married fifty-eight years. It's a long time. A long time."

"What made you think of luck there?"

"No two have ever had a better time than I've...we've had a wonderful time. We surely did."

"What made you think of luck?"

"Oh, luck. Luck that I got the education that I was able to get. Luck that I married the right person. Luck that I stayed out of jail my whole life. I always believed that luck comes to the well-prepared person, and I mean that only in the sense of scholarship. I worked hard to master—*to pretend to master* the field," he corrects. "It sure as hell was worth it."

RECONSTRUCTION

WHEN BOYD LEARNED MICHAEL SUMPTER'S name and emailed Sennott a draft of his press statement, he appended a private note to the detective: "If the identity of the suspect was a 'very bad man who died in prison and had no connection to Jane or her associates' the DNA match does exhaust the investigative measures and evidence available. It does not, for many, 'close the case.'"

I would like to be able to tell you exactly what happened the night Jane was killed. I want to know what to make of the allegations of police misconduct, or of the fact that Gramly can't let go of the story. I wish I could tell you that the red ochre was an accident—a red herring—revenge—hubris—remorse. I wish I could tell you whether or not it was even red ochre.

But I can't. Some days, I don't even know what to tell you about Jane. I know even less about whether telling a responsible story of the past is possible, having learned all too well how the act of interpretation molds the facts in service of the storyteller. I have been burned enough times to know: There are no true stories; there are only facts, and the stories we tell ourselves about those facts.

I have tried to be honest about the way in which telling Jane's story blurred into a vehicle for telling my own. I've tried to be honest about the way in which I am a part of the world I'm studying. About the biases I had going into the story that shaped the woman I understood Jane to have been. About the limitations of my imagination as I tried to reconstruct the crime that befell her. I tried to disentangle myth from fact, and to study the iterations of these myths for what they revealed about the storytellers. I have tried to listen to the stories to hear what they weren't saying. And I have tried to get to know the people who loved Jane, who shaped her.

But for what it's worth, after having chastised us all enough for the act of speculation, I bare my bias and offer you my best guess of what happened to Jane the night she was killed:

I don't think Sumpter entered Jane's apartment through the fire escape. I think he entered her building through the unlocked cellar door that was still unlocked days later. I think he waited for Jim to leave and for her apartment lights to turn off. She had changed into her nightgown, and maybe she lit the candles by her bed, to ease herself to sleep. The chemist noted that the candles in Jane's candelabrum had been left to melt for so long they had bent over. Perhaps Sumpter climbed the back stairwell (which explains why he escaped being heard by the Mitchells), and pulled a leg off her neighbors' table in the hallway. As described in a police report from the time, the dimension of the table leg, and its attributes—both the blunt wood and the sharp metal where it adhered to the tabletop—possibly fit the description of the murder weapon. Sumpter would likely have passed that table before he entered Jane's apartment through the rear door.

That door opened into Jane's kitchen. Perhaps Jane heard a noise, went to her kitchen, and found Sumpter. As Elisabeth, Don, Jill, and Ingrid were all sure, Jane probably tried to kick the shit out of the intruder—perhaps she picked up the greasy frying pan in the kitchen to wield it as a weapon, leaving a trace of grease on her right hand, and tried to hold him back with her left, which explains the twist of wool in that hand. As in the time she was attacked sophomore year, she was probably too scared to scream. Perhaps Sumpter hit her for the first time in the kitchen—maybe causing the contusion on her right arm, which was wielding the pan, and leaving trace bloodstains in both the greasy frying pan and the kitchen sink. Then he continued his assault on her in the bedroom. I find it believable that he fled through the kitchen window, taking the table leg with him, to the fire escape and the courtyard, leaving the window open in the process. Perhaps he was the one who had left the fingerprint on the glass.

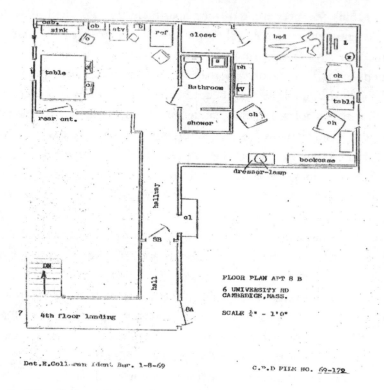

Detective Colleran's to-scale diagram of Jane's apartment.

Even so, with all the clues lining up just right, I still find it hard to believe that the ochre was an accident. I struggle not to see meaning in the coincidences.

JANE SANDERS BRITTON

In the midst of my research, months before we had any resolution to Jane's death, I had tried to find my own by visiting her grave.

I went on what would have been Jane's seventy-third birthday. I had asked Don, Elisabeth, and Boyd if there was anything they wanted me to bring or do or say for them. Boyd asked for a picture of the grave. Don asked me to read a note to her. He said that he didn't believe in the afterworld, but if he was wrong, the statement would probably make Jane happy. Regardless, it pleased Don to know that something would be said on his behalf. I hadn't heard back from Elisabeth by the time I took the 9:53 a.m. commuter rail from South Station into Needham Junction.

I tried writing my own letter to Jane, but I kept starting and stopping. Should I update Jane on what was going on in the world? Should I write what I would have wanted to say if I met her? *Thank you for guiding my life this past decade*—It felt ridiculous. I was talking to myself.

I tried again: *Hi Jane. This is Becky. I'd like to think you already know that and that you don't mind me telling your story. It feels like you're helping me do it.*

It still felt self-involved. And to believe I wasn't writing to myself was to believe, more firmly, in the existence of the supernatural.

I didn't have much time to ruminate. In less than an hour, the train delivered me to her neighborhood. I stepped out into the overcast day that was deceptively humid and warm. The lilacs had just finished blooming.

I wandered around Needham, walking down her childhood street, peering over the azaleas at her childhood home, wandering down to Farley Pond where Jane and Karen John had gone ice skating—the outer limits of their Big Woods world. I recognized parts of her neighborhood from photos, but I felt a bodily familiarity incongruous with a past that didn't belong to me. It struck me that I was approaching this trip like a conjuring; Jane had yet to come to me in a dream.

On almost every resident's front yard was a copy of the *Needham Times*, with a single headline visible over the fold: VIGIL HOPES TO HEAL.

I continued wandering around her old neighborhood, waiting for the caretaker of Jane's grave to call me back. I had tried visiting her grave two years prior, and I walked up and down the hills of Needham Cemetery, searching for the headstone. When I finally admitted defeat, the friend who had driven me said reassuringly, "You'll find her eventually." So this time, I'd called the cemetery caretaker in advance, and he promised to take me to the grave himself. But he had made this promise days ago, and now he was nowhere to be found.

I checked my phone again and noticed that Elisabeth had emailed and asked, if it wasn't too late, to get a package of Gauloises for Jane. The gas station attendants just looked confused when I asked if they carried the brand, so I headed to Kinko's to print a picture of the blue cigarette carton. It was then that the caretaker called and offered to pick me up.

He was already in the parking lot when I exited the store with the cigarette printout, and I climbed into his pickup truck filled with power tools. His name was Tom, and he must have been in his fifties, balding but trim, with a kind face and blue eyes. He laughed at me for putting on my seat belt.

We pulled in past the old tomb where, he told me, they used to store bodies in caskets in the winter, piled up, waiting for the ground to thaw. Now it's the cemetery office.

He parked the truck in Jane's section of the cemetery. The grass was thick and freshly mown. We were at the top of a hill, looking down at what must be a hundred gravestones, all gray, some decorated with American flags. He said he might need to consult his book to find her grave, but we decided to give it a once-over first.

"There should be three of them together," I called over to him. I was about ten feet behind him, scanning in parallel a few rows down. It couldn't have been more than a few minutes before Tom shouted, "Right here." He stopped walking, and I raced to catch up to him.

He read the rectangular stone plaques sunk flush to the ground. "J. Boyd." "Ruth Reinert." I knew who the third would be. He kicked the plot with his work boot to clear out the grass that was crowding it and obscuring her name. "And Jane." He kicked it again. The sound of his sole on the stone made me flinch. It was like he was kicking her, and I felt it in my body. "Jane *somebody*."

The family headstone was about eight feet in front of us, toward the top of the hill.

"Hold on a sec. Let me see if I got—" he said and headed to his truck before he finished his sentence. He walked back with a metal scraper in his hand, and he kneeled down and took the flat of the blade to the stone to shave off the years. Green lichen had flaked and scaled over the Britton name. Tom kept scraping. "Is he here? J. Boyd." Jane's father died in the early 2000s, but no one had come back to give him a death year.

My thought that I might encounter someone doing the same pilgrimage today, or some flowers left behind anonymously for Jane, was met by the very different and very believable alternative that nobody had come here in decades. It was a comfort to know that Tom, at least, took good care of the land.

Tom made his way around the headstone to the markers again, and, like an archaeologist spotting a shadow, he looked at the ground and saw what was missing. His tool scraped grass and then dirt. He got down on his knees and edged the lawn, hammering his scraper down into the ground to break the roots and lift up the sod. It made the high sharp sound of metal hitting stone. "I think it's a four-grave lot." He cleared it to a recognizable shape. The stone was blank. Tom had found Boyd's plot.

He asked me if I wanted a ride back, but I said I wanted to stay a while. I watched him pull off, and I set my stuff down so that her marker was at my knees. I was at her feet.

The *J* of her first name was buried in dirt and the *DERS* of *SANDERS* faded into the ground. Grass hung over the top of her plaque and dirt encroached on her last name from the bottom. I began to clear the dirt and the grass that had grown thick after fifty years. I hadn't thought to bring any tools, so I just did it with my hands. I took off my jacket—the sun had come out for the first time all day—and I rose to my knees to get more leverage. It took both hands to yank hard enough to rip the roots of the grass, revealing small curled-up earthworms.

I had amassed a small mountain of dirt and grass and roots, but there was still more to lift. I used the last of my water to wipe away the dust I'd created. As the water was drying, I recited what Don asked me to say: "Don has never forgotten you and never will, and you remain alive in his memories."

Her marker still wasn't clear enough for the picture I wanted to take for Boyd. Some mud had caked in the letters, and roots still clung to the final *s* of her middle name. I looked around for a twig sturdy enough to dig it out. The first one wasn't thin enough, and the second was too brittle. I tried my fingers, but, already caked in dirt, they didn't do much better than the twigs. And then I saw my pen that had become buried in the dirt and roots and grass. Of course. I picked it up and, drawing my pen tip around the curves, I etched out her name, letter by letter.

And there, finally, after years of wondering if her grave had any epitaph, was my answer. In a stately serif font, surrounded by an etched double-line border, her stone said nothing more than was absolutely necessary:

JANE SANDERS
BRITTON
1945–1969

I knew what I wanted to write her. I used the same pen, now weak because it was still clotted in the dirt that had covered her, and my hands, coated with the same soil, stained the paper.

Dear Jane, I hope I'm telling the story you want me to tell.

I folded my letter inside the picture of the Gauloises, as if it was a cigarette that Jane could light and look at me with a wry smile and say, *Whyyyyy darling.*

———

When I had spoken to Iva Houston in advance of the press conference, she told me not to think of it as anything other than another iteration of Jane's story. Like Karl's version, or Gramly's, or Lee's, it was a story in service of an end. A revelation of the interests of the storytellers. The DA's version made the ending seem neat and definitive, but the story was too big at this point for any clear resolution. "There isn't a right version. It isn't a wrong version. But it's their version," Iva said. "It's just the most recent iteration of the same damn story." It also won't be the last one, she underscored.

I asked her, "The question is, how do you restore the story to her? How does she get to tell it?" We had come this far, and I still felt like I had no idea how to tell a responsible story about the past.

"You can't," she says. "The only way to do it truly is to have her come back and do it herself."

Iva thinks more. "There's an idea of this that's becoming increasingly common in anthropology, which is this idea of restorative justice, restorative methodology. You know, things that attempt to establish some semblance of what's right, what's just, what's equitable."

In practice, Iva says, I start by giving Jane her name back. And then the best I can do is write: "She was flawed. She had ambition. We'll never know what might have happened to this person. What she might have done. Just give her her name and explain how this woman was complicated. She wasn't this dumb young girl, and she wasn't this vixen. She was like any of us. She was something in between."

————

Now, more than a year later, I've read almost every line on every page of the four thousand pages of police notes. I'm still in Boston, still in Apthorp House, still looking out the window at my sophomore-year fire escape, still reaching for some resolution to tell me I'm done even if her story will never be. And, as from the beginning, I'm still dancing to her choreography, guided through her history, and my own. Only this time, it's not just Jay and me clinging to each other in a room of ghosts. Don's there, too. Elisabeth. Boyd. Stephen Loring. Mike Widmer. And we're encircled by the past versions of ourselves, waltzing between what was and is and will be—seamlessly sliding from Cronin's to Flour Bakery, and back again—joined across time by the woman whose short life has structured our own.

I'm down to my very last MSP file in the stack. And to my own incredulity, I see that there's a note handwritten in black ink in the top left corner of the first page: "*Book 1 1968*. J.S. Britton. British Inst of Persian Studies Box 2167. Tehran IRAN."

Jane's journal. The diary she kept the summer in Iran. On unlined paper, about the size of a Moleskine notebook, are her to-do lists and packing reminders for rolls of film and underwear and insect repellent and special delivery stamps and dextrose tablets and the address of Phil Kohl's family in Tehran. And—there they are. The entries.

The first is dated June 6, 1968. *"Jim,"* it begins. Each entry is written as a letter to Jim Humphries. *"This book,"* she writes, *"is a hell of a thing to do to anyone—if you get it it'll be under circumstances where you can't answer back."*

It feels prescient. Celestial.

"In a way maybe you are two-timing me—with time. I often wonder about that—what kind of person you could have loved, why it stopped. If only I had the time. If if. Miserable word. Almost as bad as time itself." I can feel—despite knowing that it's meant for Jim, despite how awfully hokey it is—the blurring again. *"You know more about what makes me tick than anyone else, oddly enough."* For just a moment, I let myself believe that she's speaking to me, that this is her answer to the letter I left on her grave. In it, she bids me: *"Be my chronicler, so the tale of the Brit is told throughout the land, or at least that one person remembers me the way I am instead of the way they see me."*

Be my chronicler, so the tale of the Brit is told Throughout the land, or at least that one person remembers me The way I am instead of The way they see me.

ACKNOWLEDGMENTS

When I started, I didn't know Jane's name. I didn't know where the research would take me. And I certainly didn't know who killed her. But what I did know is how much luck and how much generosity it would take to get anywhere close to the end of this journey. I was gifted with both, in spades, for this book. So, after more than ten years of reaping the kindness of friends, family, colleagues, mentors, and strangers, it's nice—if very daunting—to finally be able to say thank you to the people without whom *We Keep the Dead Close* would not have been possible.

First and foremost, I have to thank everyone who agreed to be interviewed, many of whose names don't even appear in the text but whose insight was invaluable for giving me a solid understanding of the time and material. I wanted to give a special mention to a few people, though, starting, of course, with Boyd Britton. Thank you for your time, your candor, and, most of all, your trust. As I told you in California, I promised to do my very best for Jane's story. I hope you feel like I have lived up to that promise.

To Jane's friends from childhood through college—Karen John, Emily Woodbury, Irene Light, Tess Beemer, Brenda Bass, Jennifer Fowler, Cathy Ravinski, Jean Hendry, Lucy DuPertuis, Ingrid Kirsch, Karen Black, and Peter Panchy—as well as to Charlie Britton, I also hope you feel like I have done right by Jane. Elisabeth Handler, I could not imagine this book without you.

Don Mitchell and Ruth Thompson, I am so grateful for your friendship, your hospitality, your mochi care packages, and your unending belief in me and in this project. Don, thank you also for your photographs, not least the cover image of Jane, which sent shivers in me when I first saw it.

Mike Widmer, you are a true friend and kindred spirit.

Morgan Potts and Lily Erlinger. You are where this story began. It feels only appropriate—and very fortunate—that you also took my author photo, Lily.

Dan and Hildy Potts, Ruth Tringham, Elizabeth Stone, Mary Pohl, Sally Falk Moore, Alison Brooks, Sarah Hrdy, Sadie Weber, Bruce Bourque, and Sally Shankman, thank you for your courage and for trusting me with your stories. Dan, thank you also for your willingness to track down the answer to any Yahya question I had, no matter how detailed.

To the Abraham family, Stephen Loring, and the Fitzhughs, thank you for everything that helped me bring Anne to life in these pages. She was an extraordinary woman, and it was an honor to live so closely with her. Stephen, talking with you is always a particular joy. Thank you for my own set of eclectic postcards, which never ceased to buoy my spirits. Alice and Ted, I'm sorry this book doesn't offer more answers, but I hope it closes more wounds than it opens.

Richard and Jane Rose, I enormously appreciate your hospitality and your trust in me. Your slides from Bolton and Monte Alto sit proudly on my shelf of treasured possessions; thank you for letting me reprint some of the images in the book.

Mel Konner, what a journey, and I'm thrilled with where we ended up. That's one hell of a piece of writing.

Mary McCutcheon, thank you for your warmth and hospitality.

Arthur Bankoff and Richard Meadow, thank you for reminiscing with me and for your permission to reprint the 1968 Tepe Yahya photos.

Anne Moreau and Alice Kehoe, thank you for your candor.

Karl Lamberg-Karlovsky and Mike Gramly, I am very grateful not only that you agreed to speak with me, but also that you were so generous with your time. I know the conversations were difficult, and that it is not easy to be the focus of a book, in part, about the dangers of pattern-matching. I am thankful that I was able to incorporate your perspective.

Jim Humphries, Jill Nash, and Andrea Bankoff, I respect your decision not to speak with me for this book. I hope I have not caused you unnecessary pain.

And to the people who asked to remain unnamed because of fear of retaliation: I admire you, and I am grateful for your honesty.

Now for the people who brought this book into being:

Marya Spence, my agent at Janklow & Nesbit—how did I get so lucky? You understood this book—and what it could become—even before I took my reporting trip out west. You're fearless, brilliant (a little psychic even?), and the best champion I could imagine. Thank you also to Rebecca Carter, Clare Mao, and Natalie Edwards, as well as to Jason Richman at UTA, for seeing this story's creative potential.

Maddie Caldwell, you had me at "ritual." I've loved our mind meld since the first time we met. Thank you for trusting me to tell Jane's story in all its complexity (and length), for fighting to get me all the time I needed, for deciphering my brain dump when I needed to know how the chapter outlines were shaping up, for knowing when to let me loose and to rein me in, for editing and re-editing, and for loving Jane as much as I do. This book found its perfect home with you. A huge thank you, as well, to the rest of the team at Hachette and Grand Central Publishing, for all the in-house love and patience and for giving me this opportunity: Michael Pietsch, Ben Sevier, Karen Kosztolnyik, Brian McLendon, Matthew Ballast, Bob Castillo, and Jacqueline Young, as well as Albert Tang and Alex Merto, for the cover of my dreams.

I am also very grateful to Jason Arthur and the team at William Heinemann, my UK publisher, for taking a chance on me and for being a big supporter of the book.

Carrie Frye, thank you for your delicate, wise touch and for untangling the knots.

Jack Browning, for soothing my nerves with your calm and expertise.

My dear Sameen Gauhar. You came in at exactly the moment I needed you most and dedicated yourself with a ferocity that rivaled my own. Your brain astonishes me. (Who else would query "evening" when I meant "night," or catch that Jane wrote "BLEUGHH" with two *H*'s instead of three?) This book was a Herculean amount of work to check to the level of a *New Yorker* print piece—about a hundred people to call, in addition to meticulously examining every source—and you did it all with your signature humanity, grace, and intelligence. Needless to say, any errors that remain are my own.

This book would not have been possible without the time and space afforded by elving in Adams House. Judy and Sean Palfrey, who embody and fight for the best of Harvard, thank you for giving me a home, both then and now. To my fellow elves: Larissa Zhou, Andrés Ballesteros, Nick Seymour, Brendan Eappen, and Lulu Masclans, your goofiness and support was a perfect antidote to the solitude of book writing. My deep gratitude to the

Adams House community, in general, for welcoming me back in. And thank you to the undergrads who kept me happy and (relatively) sane, especially Catie Barr, Matt Hoisch, Maria Splaine, Kieren Kresevic, Francesco Rolando, and Tori Tong.

To my friends who read and reread every page of this giant book and heard it in all its iterations before anything existed on the page: Every writer should be so lucky to have readers like you. Gideon Wald and Miju Han. Ben and Lianna Burns. Svetlana Dotsenko. Patrick Chesnut. Cat Emil. Leila Mulloy. Elsa Paparemborde. Ben Naddaff-Hafrey. Charlie Damga. I look forward to finally being able to return the favor.

Todd Wallack, you are a gentleman and a remarkable reporter. Your work was integral to Jane's case being solved, and your thoughtfulness in connecting me with Jane's grave caretaker and in forwarding me messages that came in after your story was published is a model for the journalist I hope to be.

Thank you also to Alyssa Bertetto for your generosity in sharing your Lee Parsons research, and to Mechthild Prinz and Greg Hampikian for walking me through the forensic reports and the nitty-gritty of DNA analysis.

Ron Chernow, I owe so much of this book to you. Your early encouragement and mentorship, when I still knew you better as "Spinach Salad Ron," was what motivated me to dive back into the research wholeheartedly. And thank you to Ted & Honey—the magical cafe in Brooklyn that no longer is—which fostered that serendipitous meeting and so many others.

David Remnick, I'm not sure what I said during my interview that convinced you to hire me (all I remember is blurting out that *Batman: The Animated Series* was my favorite TV show), but thank you for believing in me. You are as deeply kind and good as you are brilliant, and I can only imagine how much energy that asks of you.

To the community at *The New Yorker*, who made me look forward to going to work every day and who has stayed family even though I've been away now for as long as I was there: I miss you. A thank-you especially to Bruce Diones, for keeping the lights on and the candy drawer filled. Brenda Phipps, for the wisdom and the laughs. The brilliant Pam McCarthy. Adam Gopnik and Martha Parker, for taking me under your wing way back when. Fabio Bertoni, for your tireless help. Nick Trautwein, for the straight-shooting and the shit-shooting. For teaching me how to file FOIA requests and appeals: Mattathias Schwartz and Raffi Khatchadourian. For the advice and the inspiration: Patrick Radden Keefe, Ariel Levy, Paige Williams, David Grann, Sarah Stillman, John McPhee, Jill Lepore, Henry Finder, Deborah Treisman, Peter Canby. I am so grateful for your friendship Carolyn Kormann, Liana Finck, Mina Kaneko, McKenna Stayner, Sara Nics, Antonia Hitchens, Ben Taub, Nick Niarchos, Colin Stokes, Natalie Raabe, Eric Lach, Stanley Ledbetter, Anakwa Dwamena, Neima Jahromi, Jess Henderson, Emily Greenhouse...I would go on but Maddie would KEEL me.

I am also enormously grateful to law enforcement for its dedication to Jane's case in recent years: Sergeant Peter Sennott, ADA Adrienne Lynch, DA Marian Ryan, the MSP Crime Lab, Sgt. John Fulkerson, and Sgt. Bill Doogan. Thank you also to Meghan Kelly for facilitating interviews and communication, and for handing me the files in 2018, without which this book would have looked very different.

To your support through the years, and for your understanding when I disappeared for months on end, a big thank-you to: Liz Livingstone; Anna Ondaatje; my beloved senior thesis adviser, the late Sally Livingston; Sandra Naddaff; Ama Francis; Jay Troop; Lugh O'Neill; Martin Mulloy; Zach Frankel; Dan Bear; Michelle Lee; Sol Krause; Monica Lindsay-Perez; Alex Terrien; Charlie Custeau; Ruby Awburn; Arjun Gupta (sorry for giving you that fright in Toronto); Tom Wiltzius; Nikki Donen; Grace Sun; Adam Hunt; Abe Lishansky; Meg Thompson; Sean Lavery; and Jack Pickering, whose calls felt like a lifeline.

For your help with archival research and permissions, thank you to Katherine Satriano and Patricia Kervick at the Peabody Museum archives; Jeffrey Quilter and Jane Pickering, directors of the Peabody Museum, for permission to access and publish from a closed archive; Kate O'Donnell and Bridget Manzella with Peabody Publications; Timothy Driscoll and Juliana Kuipers at the Harvard University archives; Michael Dabin for the *Daily News* photos and Kevin Corrado for the *Boston Record-American* ones; and Charles Sullivan at the Cambridge Historical Commission.

I am deeply appreciative of the Howard G. Buffett Fund for Women Journalists and the Fund for Investigative Journalism, without whose support I would have struggled to make reporting trips to Hawaii and Bulgaria. Thank you also to Peggy Engel, who went above and beyond to matchmake this project with opportunities. The Schuster Institute at Brandeis was a wonderful welcome into the Boston community. Thank you to Florence Graves and

Lisa Button for believing in the importance of Jane's story, and to Yael Jaffe for your hard work.

My darling Colin Turnbull, thank you for the design advice and the photo assistance, of course, but more importantly, for the lasting tenderness that I worried would never be mine to know.

And, most of all, thank you to my family, especially my parents, to whom this book is dedicated. To my father, thank you for your steady stream of calls, texts, dad jokes, trivia, and song recommendations that let me know I was always deeply loved. And to my mother, who listened to every chapter after I finished, who proofread every source note, who lived with me through every moment of this, and who understood before I did that this was a risk I needed to take—I love you.

NOTES

ABBREVIATED SOURCES

People and Agencies

CCLK: Clifford Charles (Karl) Lamberg-Karlovsky
CPD: Cambridge Police Department
DOC: Department of Corrections
MDAO: Middlesex District Attorney's Office
MSP: Massachusetts State Police
RCMP: Royal Canadian Mounted Police
RMG: Richard Michael (Mike) Gramly

CPD-SLI: Sarah Lee Irwin interview transcript, Jan. 13, 1969, 3:14–4:12 p.m.
CPD-SW: Stephen Williams interview transcript, Jan. 9, 1969, 11:37 a.m.–unspecified end time.
CPD-WR: William Rathje interview transcript, Jan. 14, 1969, 4:05 p.m.–unspecified end time.
CPD-WR & KD: William Rathje and Kent Day interview transcript, Jan. 7, 1969, 6:15 p.m.–unspecified end time.

Cambridge Police Transcripts

CPD-BB: Boyd Britton interview transcript, Jan. 16, 1969, time unclear (start listed as 4:37 p.m., end as 1:15 p.m.).
CPD-CCLK 1: Karl Lamberg-Karlovsky interview transcript, Jan. 7, 1969, unspecified time.
CPD-CCLK 2: Karl Lamberg-Karlovsky interview transcript, Jan. 15, 1969, 11:58 a.m.–1:05 p.m.
CPD-DM: Donald Mitchell interview transcript, Jan. 8, 1969, unspecified time.
CPD-IK: Ingrid Kirsch interview transcript, Jan. 16, 1969, 4:50–6:15 p.m.
CPD-JBB: J. Boyd Britton interview transcript, time and date not specified.
CPD-JC: Jane Chermayoff interview transcript, Jan. 14, 1969, unspecified time.
CPD-JH: James Humphries interview transcript, Jan. 7, 1969, 1:45 p.m.–unspecified end time.
CPD-JM 1: Jill Mitchell interview transcript, Jan. 8, 1969, unspecified start time–12:35 p.m.
CPD-JM 2: Jill Mitchell interview transcript, Jan. 15, 1969, 3:55–4:37 p.m.
CPD-LP 1: Lee Parsons interview transcript, Jan. 14, 1969, unspecified time.
CPD-LP 2: Lee Parsons interview transcript, Jan. 14, 1969, 2:37–3:38 p.m.
CPD-RM: Richard Meadow interview transcript, Jan. 14, 1969, unspecified start time–2:25 p.m.

Documents

Arthur Bankoff statement: Letter from Arthur Bankoff to Don and Jill Mitchell, Jan. 16, 1969; sent from Rome (CPD file); Arthur gave permission for it to double as his signed police statement. Andrea and Arthur wrote their letters separately "without discussion or cooperation to give as many separate points of view as we can" (p. 2).
Andrea Bankoff statement: Letter from Andrea Bankoff to Don and Jill Mitchell, Jan. 16, 1969 (CPD file).
Joint statement: Letter from Arthur and Andrea Bankoff to Don and Jill Mitchell, Jan. 19, 1969.
Dan Potts Yahya monograph: Dan Potts, *Excavations at Tepe Yahya, Iran 1967–1975: The Third Millennium*, American School of Prehistoric Research, Bulletin 45, Peabody Museum of Archaeology and Ethnology, Harvard University (2001).
CCLK foreword: C. C. Lamberg-Karlovsky, "Excavations at Tepe Yahya: The Biography of a Project," pp. XIX–XLI in Dan Potts, *Excavations at Tepe Yahya, Iran 1967–1975: The Third Millennium*, American School of Prehistoric Research, Bulletin 45, Peabody Museum of Archaeology and Ethnology, Harvard University (2001).
Smithsonian Report: "Report to the Secretary: Abraham Internal Review Panel," Smithsonian Institution, Mar. 8, 1977.

MORNING OF GENERALS

3 Gale warnings along the coast: "Weather: Heavy Rain—High Winds," *Boston Globe*, Jan. 7, 1969.

3 black-and-white picture of a girl: Uncredited photo on p. 1 of *Harvard Crimson*, Jan. 7, 1969.

3 second day of reading period: *Courses of Instruction Harvard and Radcliffe, Faculty of Arts and Sciences 1968–1969*, Official Register of Harvard University, 65, no. 18 (1968): 7.

3 By 9 a.m.: Stephen Williams, "Written General Examinations" Memorandum to Harvard Anthropology graduate students, Dec. 6, 1968.

3 "terminal" master's: "Temporary Supplement to the General Announcement," regulations by the Department of Anthropology, Harvard University, May 1967, p. 2.

3 smelled like the mummies: Interviews with Stephen Loring and Bruce Bourque in 2017.

JAMES AND IVA

9 its own amnesty policy: "College Issues New Alcohol Amnesty Policy," *Harvard Magazine*, Apr. 2, 2012.

10 Lothrop, a former Peabody Museum curator: Gordon R. Willey, *Samuel Kirkland Lothrop 1892–1965* (Washington: National Academy of Sciences, 1976), p. 256.

10 convenient covers for espionage: "The Spies Who Came in from the Dig," *The Guardian*, Sept. 3, 2003—an edited extract of David Price's article which first appeared in *Archaeology Magazine* 56, no. 5 (2003).

THE BODY

10 The general exams finished just after noon: CPD-WR & KD, p. 12.

10 "Christ, the only reason": CPD-IK, p. 36.

11 "The rumors of my death": Interview with Bruce Bourque in 2017.

11 called her twice: CPD-JH, p. 14.

11 reserved to the point of brooding: CPD-SLI, p. 23.

11 face wasn't expressive even at the best of times: Arthur Bankoff statement, p. 17.

11 The Gentleman: CPD-IK, p. 64.

11 helping girls with their coats: CPD-IK, p. 65.

11 writing thank-you notes: CPD-SLI, p. 49.

11 met in the spring of 1968: CPD-JH, p. 22.

11 a seminar to prepare: Interview with Richard Meadow in 2017.

11 Count Dracula: Interview with Francesco Pellizzi in 2017.

11 *Boston Globe* hailed Lamberg-Karlovsky: "Harvard Team Unearths Alexander's Lost Citadel," *Boston Globe*, Nov. 10, 1968.

11 "They had a chance": "Find Ritual Clue in Co-Ed's Papers," *New York Post*, Jan. 11, 1969.

11 Church of the Unwarranted Assumption: Undated handwritten story by Jane about her imaginary marriage to Jim (CPD file).

11 Jane hadn't answered either call: CPD-JH, p. 95.

12 students headed for lunch: CPD-WR & KD, p. 13.

12 across the road to call Jane: CPD-JH, p. 91.

12 The Craigie: Cambridge Architectural Inventory for 2-4-6 University Road, Summer 1967.

12 commissioned by Harvard: Chapman Arms pamphlet by the Homeowners Rehab Inc. & Cambridge Neighborhood Apartment Housing Services, Inc., Nov. 20, 2014, back page.

12 less expensive housing option: "The Craigie Dormitory," *Cambridge Chronicle*, Oct. 2, 1897.

12 natural wood trim: Letter from Lawrence J. Sparrow, Project Manager, to Cynthia MacLeod of the National Park Service, Nov. 5, 1986.

12 fallen into disrepair: Bob Kuehn, "Craigie Arms" Memorandum to Interested Parties, Nov. 11, 1983.

12 parking lots...and an alley: Mo Lotman, *Harvard Square: An Illustrated History since 1950* (New York: Stewart, Tabori, & Chang, 2009), p. 41.

12 Cronin's, a watering hole with a small TV screen: Lotman, *Harvard Square*, pp. 40, 83; TV screen detail from interview with Mike Widmer in 2017.

12 $75 a month: Letter from Kenneth Babb, Property Manager for R. M. Bradley & Co., Inc, to Jane Britton, May 13, 1968 (CPD file).

12 Jane had secured her apartment: Interview with Don Mitchell in 2017.

12 Mitchells always used their dead bolt: Interview with Don Mitchell in 2017.

12 Jane almost never locked her door: Multiple, including CPD-JM 2, p. 5.

12 around 12:30 p.m.: CPD-JH, p. 91.

12 pushed in the front door...skylight: "Building 'Looks like Slum'; Still No Lock on Front Door," *Boston Globe*, Jan. 9, 1969; "Harvard Coed,

22, Found Brutally Slain," *Boston Record-American*, Jan. 8, 1969.

13 *"Maybe," said Mrs. Kylie*: "Harvard Coed, 22, Found Brutally Slain," *Boston Record-American*, Jan. 8, 1969.

13 heat made the wood swell and the lock finicky: CPD-JM 2, p. 4.

13 Don and Jill Mitchell heard the noise: CPD-JM 1, p. 4; CPD-DM, p. 7.

13 walked into the hallway: Jim and Don's memories differ slightly here. This is Jim's recollection per his police transcript (CPD-JH, p. 8). Don remembers already being in the hallway, carrying out a piece of cardboard when he met Humphries (CPD-DM, p. 6).

13 "Is Jane home?" "I guess so.": CPD-JH, p. 8.

13 "Well, she didn't take her quiz": CPD-DM, p. 7. Don told police he distinctly recalled Jim's phrasing because the generals were too big an examination to be called a quiz.

13 Don's face changed: CPD-JH, p. 64.

13 He encouraged Jim to go in and check: CPD-DM, p. 7.

13 Jim knocked... "Can I come in?": CPD-JH, p. 65.

13 Don waited by the door: CPD-DM, p. 8.

13 Jim felt a cold gust of air coming from the kitchen: CPD-JH, p. 33.

13 the window was wide open: CPD-JH, p. 32.

13 certain it hadn't been open the night before: CPD-JH, p. 31.

13 Jim reached his head back: CPD-DM, p. 66.

13 she thought there was a gas leak in her kitchen: CPD-JM 1, p. 23.

13 screen had long ago rotted off: CPD-JM 1, p. 23.

13 room was its usual homey mess: CPD crime scene photos; interview with Don Mitchell in 2017.

13 A turtle tank: Interview with Don Mitchell in 2017.

13 brandy bottles: Photo by Don Mitchell.

13 Ceramic owls: CPD-IK, p. 48.

13 painted cats, giraffes, and owls: "Cambridge Murder Victim Is Recalled as Intelligent and Witty," *New York Times*, Jan. 19, 1969.

14 not until he fully walked into the apartment: CPD-JH, p. 69.

14 right leg: CPD-JH, p. 70 (at least one foot on the ground); CPD-DM, p. 9 (Don remembers right leg).

14 directly on the floor: "The Case of the Unlocked Door to Death," *Pictorial Living Coloroto Magazine*, Apr. 13, 1969.

14 blue flannel nightgown: Susan Kelly, the author of *The Boston Stranglers* (New York: Pinnacle Books, 2002), researched, for a time, the Jane Britton case. In the late '90s, she interviewed a number of people close to Jane. Some of her notes and letters became part of Jane's police file. This detail is from Susan Kelly's letter to John Fulkerson, July 25, 1996.

14 pulled up to her waist: CPD-JH, p. 70.

14 He didn't try to shake her: CPD-JH, p. 9.

14 "a woman's job": CPD-JH, p. 93.

14 She needed to lie on her bed. She felt sick: CPD-JM 1, p. 11.

14 bolt of guilt: Interview with Don Mitchell in 2017.

14 Above her waist: CPD-JH, p. 93; p. 36.

14 sheepskin rugs: Interview with Don Mitchell in 2017; Elisabeth Handler confirmed that Jane had sheepskin rugs in a 2017 interview.

14 until he could see the back of her head: CPD-DM, p. 10.

14 He didn't turn her over: CPD-DM, p. 10.

14 no question: CPD-DM, p. 11.

IT BEGINS

15 mention of a cigarette butt: "Police Examine Ochre Found Near Slaying Victim," *Boston Globe*, Jan. 10, 1969.

15 vice president of administration at Radcliffe College: "Cambridge Murder Victim Is Recalled as Intelligent and Witty," *New York Times*, Jan. 19, 1969; cross-checked in the Schlesinger Library Archives.

15 single mention of a grand jury hearing: "Grand Jury to Hear Britton Case," *Boston Globe*, Jan. 29, 1969.

15 "I came here to be of whatever assistance": "Harvard Girl Brutally Slain in Apartment," *Boston Globe*, Jan. 8, 1969.

15 in the *New York Times*: Professor Lamberg-Karlovsky pacing: "Cambridge Murder Victim Is Recalled as Intelligent and Witty," *New York Times*,

Jan. 19, 1969. The lover of Bach detail is from this article, as well.

15 accomplished horseback rider: Here through "excelled at Dana Hall," "Jane's Home Town Not Used to This Kind of Thing," *Daily News*, Jan. 11, 1969.

16 "Peculiar travel suggestions are like": "Portrait of Jane Britton," *New York Post*, Jan. 9, 1969, quoting Kurt Vonnegut, *Cat's Cradle* (New York: Dial Press Trade Paperback, 2010), p. 63.

16 favorite was from *The Sirens of Titan*: "Cambridge Murder Victim Is Recalled as Intelligent and Witty," *New York Times*, Jan. 19, 1969.

16 "had a kind of insight": "Cambridge Murder Victim Is Recalled as Intelligent and Witty," *New York Times*, Jan. 19, 1969.

16 "If justice be cruel": "Portrait of Jane Britton," *New York Post*, Jan. 9, 1969.

16 "vulnerable person"..."hangers-on and acid heads": "Cambridge Murder Victim Is Recalled as Intelligent and Witty," *New York Times*, Jan. 19, 1969.

16 talk of a secret abortion: "Murder Quiz Finds Jane Had Abortion," *Daily News*, Jan. 13, 1969.

16 "It is not possible to characterize": "Cambridge Murder Victim Is Recalled as Intelligent and Witty," *New York Times*, Jan. 19, 1969.

16 one of the Iranian expedition monographs: CCLK foreword, p. XXXI.

THE COPS ARRIVE

19 Detectives William Durette, Michael Giacoppo, and Fred Centrella: "Harvard Coed Viciously Slain in Cambridge," *Boston Record-American*, Jan. 8, 1969. Detective Michael Giacoppo's full name is Matthew Michael Giacoppo. I refer to him as M. Michael Giacoppo in these source notes to differentiate him from his son, Michael D. Giacoppo.

19 cat skittered out: "Harvard Coed, 23, Beaten to Death," *Daily News*, Jan. 8, 1969.

19 Valuables...lay untouched: "Harvard Girl Brutally Slain in Apartment: Radcliffe Vice President's Daughter," *Boston Globe*, Jan. 8, 1969.

19 no signs of a struggle: "Police Seek Coed's Killer," *Bridgeport Post*, Jan. 8, 1969.

19 Two of Jane's windows were open: "Harvard Coed, 23, Beaten to Death," *Daily News*, Jan. 8, 1969.

19 eighteen-man Bureau of Criminal Investigations: "Harvard Coed, 23, Beaten to Death," *Daily News*, Jan. 8, 1969.

19 acting chief of the homicide division: "Harvard Graduate Student Bludgeoned to Death," *Boston Herald Traveler*, Jan. 8, 1969.

19 publicly dismiss the significance of these open windows: "Harvard Coed, 22, Found Slain: Daughter of Radcliffe Exec Beaten on Head," *Boston Record-American*, Jan. 8, 1969.

20 [Photo]: Mel Finkelstein/*New York Daily News*.

20 "class of brass": David Degou, *Cambridge Police Department* (Mount Pleasant: Arcadia Publishing, 2009), p. 84.

20 survived a hammer attack in her home...curlers that saved her: "Coed's Friend Nixes Lie Test," *Daily News*, Jan. 9, 1969.

20 Davenport himself had been assigned: "Harvard Coed, 22, Found Slain: Daughter of Radcliffe Exec Beaten on Head," *Boston Record-American*, Jan. 8, 1969.

20 The case remains open: Kelly, *The Boston Stranglers*; interview with Sergeant William Doogan in 2020.

20 shortly after the detectives: "Harvard Girl Brutally Slain in Apartment," *Boston Globe*, Jan. 8, 1969.

20 sitting in the Mitchells' apartment: Interview with Don Mitchell in 2017.

20 surveyed the room at the police's request..."She was a good girl": "Harvard Girl Brutally Slain in Apartment," *Boston Globe*, Jan. 8, 1969.

21 Detective Giacoppo...dusted the apartment for fingerprints: Report to Daniel I. Murphy, Captain of Detectives by Det. Lt. Joyce of MSP, June 2, 1969; and Report of Lt. David Desmond re: Thumb Print on Ashtray May 29, 1969 (MSP file).

21 lying about his age to fight in World War II: Interview with Michael D. Giacoppo in 2018.

21 processing and crime scene photographing the next day: Report of Asst. Chemist Joseph Lanzetta, Apr. 1, 1969 (MSP file).

21 He did not find a weapon: Report of Asst. Chemist Joseph Lanzetta, Apr. 1, 1969 (MSP file). The list of items collected as evidence does not include a weapon.

21 superintendent's seven-year-old daughter: Report by Det. Centrella (Priscilla Joyce interview), Jan. 7, 1969 (CPD file).

21 beer from her fridge: Report of Statement by Donald Mitchell, Jan. 7, 1969 (CPD file).

21 home at 12:15 a.m.: "Police Seeking Massachusetts Axe Murderer," *Pittsburgh Press*, Jan. 8, 1969.

21 party with her on Saturday: "Neighbors Heard Nothing, Cat Upset," *Boston Herald Traveler*, Jan. 8, 1969.

21 Stephen, a Harvard law school: "Harvard Coed Is Found Slain," *Kansas City Times*, Jan. 8, 1969.

21 awake until two in the morning...ran a test: "Neighbors Heard Nothing, Cat Upset," *Boston Herald Traveler*, Jan. 8, 1969.

21 built specifically to be soundproof: "The Cambridge Dormitory," *Cambridge Chronicle*, Oct. 2, 1897.

21 "he was acting wild": "Neighbors Heard Nothing, Cat Upset," *Boston Herald Traveler*, Jan. 8, 1969.

21 between 1 a.m. and 7 a.m.: Report to Lt. Davenport by Officer James Lyons (overnight patrol car 6), Jan. 7, 1969; Report to Lt. Davenport by Officer Dennis McCarthy (night patrol car 6), Jan. 7, 1969 (CPD files).

21 A transit worker said he saw a man: Officer

Richard Lyon Police Report re: Patrick Joyce, Jan. 8, 1969 (CPD file).

22 Ravi Rikhye, twenty-two: Rikhye details from "Police Seek Coed's Killer," *Bridgeport Post*, Jan. 8, 1969, and "Harvard Girl Brutally Slain in Apartment: Radcliffe Vice President's Daughter," *Boston Globe*, Jan. 8, 1969. When I spoke to Rikhye in 2018, he no longer remembered the night with the same detail.

22 Capello stood outside: *Boston Record-American* photo, uncredited, Jan. 8, 1969, p. 29.

22 art deco headquarters: Degou, *Cambridge Police*, p. 91.

22 Jane's parents were among the first interviewed: "Harvard Graduate Student Bludgeoned to Death," *Boston Herald Traveler*, Jan. 8, 1969.

22 J. Boyd Britton held his hat in one hand:

"Harvard Coed, 22, Found Brutally Slain," *Boston Record-American*, Jan. 8, 1969.

23 [Photo]: Dennis Brearley / *Boston Record-American*. Image courtesy *Boston Herald*.

23 examiner tested Don's and Jill's hands: Report of Asst. Chemist Joseph Lanzetta, Apr. 1, 1969 (MSP file).

23 "I—I was cutting up some meat": Interview with Don Mitchell in 2017.

23 furrowed into two dark streaks: As shown in the photo on page 24. Leo Tierney / *Boston Record-American*. Image courtesy *Boston Herald*.

24 [Photo]: Leo Tierney / *Boston Record-American*. Image courtesy *Boston Herald*.

DEPARTURES

25 anthropology professors at Buffalo State: Buffalo State website; interview with Don Mitchell in 2017.

25 had withdrawn from Harvard: "The Case of the Ocher-Covered Corpse," *Boston Magazine*, Sept. 1982.

25 Anthropology 1065: *2012–2013 Courses of Instruction*, "Previous Course Offerings," Registrar's Office website, Harvard University's Faculty of Arts and Sciences.

INITIAL QUESTIONING

26 No caution tape, no barriers: Interview with Don Mitchell in 2017.

26 inside the University Road apartment: Here through "What good will an investigation do now?" from "Girls Afraid to Stay Alone," *Boston Herald-Traveler*, Jan. 8, 1969.

27 [Photo]: Stan Forman / *Boston Record-American*. Image courtesy *Boston Herald*.

27 anxious to assist authorities: "Girl Slaying Gets National Attention," *Boston Record-American*, Jan. 9, 1969.

27 "I suppose you'd say I was her boyfriend": This section (until break) from CPD-JH police transcript.

28 Shortly before midnight: "Harvard Girl Brutally Slain in the Apartment," *Boston Globe*, Jan. 8, 1969.

29 no visible blood except on the mattress and pillows: Notice of Death form completed by Officer Lyons, Jan. 7, 1969 (CPD file).

29 the coroner, Dr. Arthur McGovern: "Harvard Graduate Student Bludgeoned to Death," *Boston Herald Traveler*, Jan. 8, 1969.

29 contusions and lacerations of the brain: Autopsy Report, Drs. George Katsas and Arthur McGovern, undated, but the autopsy was performed at 6:45 p.m. on Jan. 7, 1969 (MSP file).

29 a four-inch slash across her hairline and an inch-long wound: "Police Probe Vicious Slaying of College Official's Daughter," UPI, Jan. 9, 1969.

29 fatal hit: "Harvard Graduate Student Bludgeoned to Death," *Boston Herald Traveler*, Jan. 8, 1969.

29 crack her skull: Interview with Don Mitchell in 2017.

29 "She had been hit from" . . . blunt and sharp: "Hammer Sought in Coed Slaying," *Baltimore Sun*, Jan. 9, 1969.

29 sharp rock, a hatchet or a cleaver . . . ball peen hammer: "Harvard Girl Brutally Slain in Apartment," *Boston Globe*, Jan. 8, 1969.

29 not found any clear evidence of sexual assault: "Pretty Graduate Student Found Slain in Apartment," *The Day*, Jan. 8, 1969.

29 pending a more in-depth autopsy: "Harvard Girl Brutally Slain in Apartment," *Boston Globe*, Jan. 8, 1969.

29 compulsively thorough: "Dr. George G. Katsas, 79; Leading Forensic Pathologist," *Boston Globe*, June 21, 2001.

29 for at least a week: "New Medical Tests on Slain Coed Fail," *Boston Record-American*, Jan. 15, 1969.

29 "We have no firm suspects at this time":

"Harvard Graduate Student Bludgeoned to Death," *Boston Herald Traveler*, Jan. 8, 1969.

29 Humphries had come voluntarily: "Harvard Graduate Student Bludgeoned to Death," *Boston Herald Traveler*, Jan. 8, 1969.

29 "It was someone she knew": "Quiz Harvard Men in Coed Slaying," *New York Post*, Jan. 8, 1969.

KARL

31 at Harvard since 1965: CCLK curriculum vitae, available on CCLK's page on Harvard's Department of Anthropology website.

31 early newspaper reports: "Harvard Team Unearths Alexander's Lost Citadel," *Boston Globe*, Nov. 10, 1968; "Archaeological Unit From Harvard Unearths Lost Fortress in Persia," *Harvard Crimson*, Nov. 12, 1968.

31 key trading stop…Proto-Elamite texts: Interview with Dan Potts in 2019; interview with CCLK in 2020.

31 directing archaeological surveys in Saudi Arabia…thirteen years: CCLK curriculum vitae.

31 nothing ever surpassed Yahya: CCLK did not dispute this on a 2020 phone call, but he said that he was most proud of having fostered the careers of his graduate students.

31 while Karl couldn't dictate the use of funds, he had a major say: Phone call with CCLK in 2020.

33 the *Crimson* article: "On Hike, a Life Is Cut Short," *Harvard Crimson*, Oct. 24, 2007.

RED OCHRE

33 Sirhan Sirhan's trial: "Quiz Harvard Men in Coed Slaying," *New York Post*, Jan. 8, 1969.

33 even *Newsweek* magazine: "The Riddle of the Red Dust," *Newsweek*, Jan. 20, 1969, p. 17.

33 at home in Colorado…"every day across the country?": Interview with Brenda Bass in 2016.

34 [Photo]: *Boston Record-American*, Jan. 8, 1969, p. 1. Image courtesy *Boston Herald*.

34 four reporters: Interviews with Joe Modzelewski (2014) and Mike McGovern (2016). "Four" includes the photographer in the count.

34 private plane: "Girl Slaying Gets National Headlines," *Boston Record-American*, Jan. 9, 1969.

34 second-floor corridor: "The Cambridge Rambler: The Scene is Changed," *Boston Record-American*, Jan. 11, 1969.

34 two men were being sought: "Police Seek Peru Hippie in Coed Slaying," *Fresno Bee*, Jan. 8, 1969.

35 this man was a faculty member: "Murder Quiz Finds Jane Had Abortion," *Daily News*, Jan. 13, 1969.

35 a gift from Don and Jill Mitchell: "'Gift' Rock May Be Cambridge Death Weapon," *Boston Globe*, Jan. 9, 1969.

35 sent men to look: "Police Seek 2 for Quiz in Girl's Brutal Killing," *Boston Record-American*, Jan. 9, 1969.

35 "minor inconsistencies": "'Gift' Rock May Be Cambridge Death Weapon," *Boston Globe*, Jan. 9, 1969.

35 "peculiar and sinister": Interview with Laurie Godfrey in 2018.

35 "swirling horror of interest and speculation": Interview with Mel Konner in 2017.

35 what the department secretaries found: Interview with Liz Gude in 2017.

36 [Photo]: Photograph by Don Mitchell.

36 "There was a considerable amount of crime": Interview with Francesco Pellizzi in 2017.

36 "I think everyone had a heightened sense": Interview with Mel Konner in 2017.

36 Speaking at the time, Ingrid: "'Gift' Rock May Be Cambridge Death Weapon," *Boston Globe*, Jan. 9, 1969.

36 Galligan, a square-faced man with a button nose: Degou, *Cambridge Police*, p. 27.

36 "we are leaving no stone": "Girl Slaying Gets National Headlines," *Boston Record-American*, Jan. 9, 1969.

37 Twenty-three people: "3 to Get Lie Test in Slaying," *Akron Beacon Journal*, Jan. 8, 1969.

37 scheduled lie detector tests: "'Gift' Rock May Be Cambridge Death Weapon," *Boston Globe*, Jan. 9, 1969.

37 whom he refused to name: "Police Seek Slayer of Harvard Coed," *Bennington Banner*, Jan. 9, 1969.

37 What some know as iron oxide: For extensive reading on red ochre, see Kate Helwig, "Iron Oxide Pigments" chapter in *Artists' Pigments: A Handbook of their History and Characteristics Volume 4*, edited by Barbara Berrie (New York: Archetype Publications, 2007), pp. 39–109.

37 ceiling and the wall where a headboard might have been: "Coed's Slayer Went through Ancient Ritual," *Boston Record-American*, Jan. 9, 1969; interview with Don Mitchell in 2017; CPD-SW p. 3.

37 "It was described to me": Here until the end of this chapter is from "'Gift' Rock May Be Cambridge Death Weapon," *Boston Globe*, Jan. 9, 1969.

THE RITUAL

41 friendship with the Taylors: Interview with Boyd Britton in 2016.

42 [Photo]: *New York Daily News*.

42 "the fact that apparently": "Harvard Coed: Mystery Surrounds Slaying," *The Tech* (MIT), Jan. 14, 1969.

42 Francesco Pellizzi later recalled: Interview with Francesco Pellizzi in 2017.

42 "I mean, who knows": Interview with Paul Shankman in 2017.

43 liquid daubed: "Girl Slayer Performed Burial Rite," *Boston Herald Traveler*, Jan. 9, 1969.

43 powder that had been strewn: "Coed's Slayer Went through Ancient Ritual," *Boston Record-American* (evening edition), Jan. 9, 1969.

43 It was red: "Coed's Killer Held Weird Rite: Threw Red Powder over Body," *Daily News*, Jan. 10, 1969.

43 mahogany or cocoa-colored: "'Gift' Rock May Be Cambridge Death Weapon," *Boston Globe*, Jan. 9, 1969.

43 some articles called it ochre: "Coed's Slayer Went through Ancient Ritual," *Boston Record-American* (evening edition), Jan. 9, 1969.

43 others called it iodine oxide: "Girl Slayer Performed Burial Rite," *Boston Herald Traveler*, Jan. 9, 1969.

43 according to the *Boston Globe*: "'Gift' Rock May Be Cambridge Death Weapon," *Boston Globe*, Jan. 9, 1969.

43 only stable oxide of iodine: Interview with Narayan Khandekar in 2020.

43 was in Italy: Arthur Bankoff statement.

43 "People who said so": Interview with Arthur Bankoff in 2016.

43 portion of a colonial gravestone: CPD-SW p. 3; colonial detail from source below; also interview with Don Mitchell in 2017.

43 winged skull: Susan Kelly notes from interview with Paul Shankman, July 31, 1996 (police file).

43 Cambridge Police's source: Stephen Williams never publicly admitted being the police's source on the matter. This conclusion is drawn from multiple sources. Many newspaper reports cite a Harvard Anthropology professor as the source of the information about red ochre (e.g., "'Gift' Rock May Be Cambridge Death Weapon," *Boston Globe*, Jan. 9, 1969). In a few, Williams is named as the police source/consultant: "Slain Harvard Student Buried—Police Film All at Service," *Boston Globe*, Jan. 11, 1969; "Coed's Killer Held Weird Rite," *Daily News*, Jan. 10, 1969; "Harvard Coed: Mystery Surrounds Slaying," *The Tech* (MIT), Jan. 14, 1969." This reporting is corroborated by CPD-SW, in which Williams discusses the ritual element of red ochre and mentions that the police had already called him to discuss red ochre on the evening of Jan. 8, 1969, before the news broke.

STEPHEN WILLIAMS AND DETECTIVE HALLIDAY

43 This chapter is an excerpt of CPD-SW. This police transcript, as well as the others that appear later in the book, has been edited for concision and clarity. In places, I have made decisions about rearranging the sequencing within the interviews to reflect the way in which I discovered and pieced together the story from the investigatory materials. However, in all cases, these editing decisions were guided by the intent to keep the spirit and sense of the original preserved.

KEEP THE DEAD CLOSE

46 buried the dead under their houses: For more on burial customs at Ain Mallaha: François Valla, et al., "Eynan (Ain Mallaha)," in *Quaternary of the Levant: Environments, Climate Change, and Humans*, edited by Yehouda Enzel and Ofer Bar-Yosef (Cambridge: Cambridge University Press, 2017), pp. 295–296.

THE PEABODY

47 Karl's first day...PhD at UPenn: CCLK curriculum vitae; interview with CCLK in 2020.

47 hair down to his shoulders: This description from interviews with CCLK in 2017 and 2020. He also said, "I used to go into my class and take my helmet off, and the kids would cheer."

47 ninety-ninth birthday: Peabody founded in 1866 per "Museum History," Peabody Museum at Harvard University website.

47 Castle was only ten years old: Completed and opened to the public in Feb. 1855 per "Great Hall of Smithsonian Castle Opens to Public," engraving, Feb. 8, 1855, W. W. Turner to J. R. Bartlett, Jan. 31, 1866, J. C. Brown Library, Brown University.

47 founded for another four years: AMNH founded in 1869, per "Museum History: A Timeline," AMNH's website.

47 codified program of teaching: Peabody became incorporated into Harvard University in 1897, Gérald Gaillard, *The Routledge Dictionary of Anthropologists* (London: Routledge, 2004), p. 56.

47 all fields of anthropology, including archaeology: The fact that archaeology is categorized as a subfield of anthropology is a quirk of American archaeology—the legacy of Franz Boas's Four-Field approach. In Europe, archaeology is often a discipline in its own right, or it is taught under the umbrella of history or classics or Oriental studies. For more on this, and the tension it creates within the discipline in the US, see Bernard Wood, "Four-Field Anthropology: A Perfect Union or a Failed State?" *Society* 50, no. 2 (2013): 152–155.

47 "were made to hold powerful magic": Interview with Barbara Allen in 2017.

47 Mexico's sacred cenotes: "Envoy: From Deep to Dark," *Harvard Advocate*, Commencement Issue, 2011.

47 feathers and spirit masks and saliva samples: Interview with Barbara Allen in 2017.

48 P. T. Barnum's mermaid: Interview with Anne Kern in 2018.

48 network of secret passages: Interview with Alison Brooks in 2017.

48 Joe Johns: Interview with Joe Johns in 2017; interview with Richard Meadow in 2017.

49 Duke of Montrose: "Ian Graham, 93, Intrepid Investigator, Interpreter of Mayan Ruins," *Boston Globe*, Aug. 3, 2017.

49 smoked like a chimney: Interview with Tom Patterson in 2017.

49 tiny one that flipped: Interview with David Freidel in 2017.

49 never gave her an official position: Interview with Michael Coe in 2017; interview with Richard Meadow in 2020.

49 only place to smoke...almost blue: Interview with Bruce Bourque in 2017.

49 academically uninspiring: Many of Williams's students, however, were grateful for his support, like Bruce Bourque, who remembered Williams as a "really decent human being [who] took good care of his students."

49 all-male faculty club: The club didn't open to women until 1968 per "History," Harvard Faculty Club website.

49 West End duck hunting club: Interview with Tom Patterson in 2017.

49 the only tenured woman: "The First Tenured Women Professors at Harvard University," infographic developed by Harvard University's Faculty Development & Diversity, Office of the Senior Vice Provost, 2011.

49 turned away from her: Interview with Alice Kehoe in 2017.

49 hair parted in the middle: Harvey Bricker, *Hallam Leonard Movius Jr. (1907–1987): A Biographical Memoir* (Washington, DC: National Academy of Sciences, 2007), p. 2.

49 lieutenant colonel: Bricker, *Hallam Leonard Movius Jr.*, p. 9.

49 egg timer...twelve-minute break: Interview with Alison Brooks in 2017.

49 one of his female graduate students: Source wishes to be unattributed.

50 "Hamilton, that's a much better name": Interview with Sally Shankman in 2017.

50 "All archaeology is the re-enactment": CCLK foreword, p. XX, paraphrasing R. G. Collingwood by substituting "archaeology" for "history."

50 people made fun: Interview with Liz Gude in 2017.

50 black-tie parties...rarely wore jackets: Interviews with CCLK in 2017 and 2020.

50 big impression on David Freidel: Interview with David Freidel in 2017.

51 spring of 1967: "Culture History of the Old World: Ethnography," Record of Subjects and Grades in Jane Britton's Radcliffe student file; cross-referenced with *Courses of Instruction Harvard and Radcliffe, Faculty of Arts and Sciences 1966–1967*, Official Register of Harvard University, 63, no. 17 (1968): 43.

51 committee for her undergraduate thesis: CPD-CCLK 1, p. 2 and CPD-JH, p. 10.

51 Karl had dangled: Letter from Jane to her parents, June 24, 1966.

51 third straight summer: Letters from Jane to her parents in summers 1965–1967.

51 "a pigheaded old bastard...fur fly": Letter from Jane to her father, June 2, 1965.

51 space opening up in the department: Openings in Harvard department used to be calculated with

something called the Graustein formula. See "Faculty Moves away from Power Politics," *Harvard Crimson*, Nov. 10, 1988.

52 Movius suddenly announced: CPD-IK, p. 17.

52 Decades later, Francesco Pellizzi: Interview with Francesco Pellizzi in 2017.

SPEAKING OF SILENCES

53 Jim Humphries's roommate: CPD-JH and CPD-RM.

53 his dissertation adviser: CCLK curriculum vitae.

53 director of the Peabody's Zooarchaeology Laboratory: Interview with Richard Meadow in 2020.

BLACKOUT

55 deeply upsetting. Infuriating and misinformed—nasty even: Interviews with CCLK in 2017 and 2018.

55 "There were complaints": "Cambridge Murder Victim Is Recalled as Intelligent and Witty," *New York Times*, Jan. 19, 1969.

55 "completely ridiculous...burial ceremony": "Profs, Cops Differ on Slaying," *New York Post*, Jan. 10, 1969.

56 obliged when authorities: Interview with CCLK in 2017.

56 "total fabrication": "Profs, Cops Differ on Slaying," *New York Post*, Jan. 10, 1969.

56 "so-called Harvard": "Indications Jane Knew Her Slayer," *Boston Herald Traveler*, Jan. 11, 1969.

56 "I want to underline": "Police Examine Ochre Found Near Slaying Victim," *Boston Globe*, Jan. 10, 1969.

56 one of her pigments: "Britton Case News Blackout Ordered," *Tuscaloosa News*, Jan. 10, 1969.

56 "If you ever do or say this again": Interview with CCLK in 2018.

56 1010 Commonwealth Avenue: Don Mitchell interview transcript with Sergeant Sennott, July 17, 2017, p. 181 (MSP file).

56 each lasted about an hour: "Coed's Killer Held Weird Rite," *Daily News*, Jan. 10, 1969.

56 Don spoke to reporters: "Strange Clue in Coed Case," *New York Post*, Jan. 9, 1969.

56 starched white button-down: Description from *Daily News* photo by Mel Finkelstein, Jan. 9, 1969.

56 presence of an attorney: "Coed's Friend Nixes Lie Test," *Daily News*, Jan. 9, 1969.

57 [Photo]: Mel Finkelstein/*New York Daily News*.

57 cigarette slowly enough: "Suspect Rite

Performed Co-ed's Killer," *Chicago Tribune*, Jan. 10, 1969.

57 "If it wasn't as serious": "Jane's Killer Enacted Ancient Rite over Her," *Daily News*, Jan. 10, 1969.

57 Late that afternoon: "Police Examine Ochre," *Boston Globe*, Jan. 10, 1969.

57 the first time since: "Cambridge Rambler: The Scene Is Changed," *Boston Record-American*, Jan. 11, 1969.

58 thinning white hair: Uncredited photo in *Daily News*, Jan. 13, 1969.

58 since last summer: "Rapping with the Cambridge Cops," *Harvard Crimson*, Mar. 23, 1970.

58 overseen a handful of murders: "Murder in Cambridge, 1959–1989," compiled by the Cambridge Police Department's Crime Analysis Unit.

58 "There will be no statements": "Police Examine Ochre Found Near Slaying Victim," *Boston Globe*, Jan. 10, 1969.

58 "Suddenly the chief": Interview with Mike McGovern in 2016.

58 blackout felt like a cover-up: Interview with Joe Modzelewski in 2014.

58 "Around here, Harvard is thicker than water": "Covering Harvard—A View from the Outside," *Harvard Crimson*, June 12, 1969.

58 "We couldn't get anybody...pretend like it didn't happen": Interview with Joe Modzelewski in 2014.

58 stone tool...had been located: "Police Examine Ochre," *Boston Globe*, Jan. 10, 1969.

58 any further details: "Cambridge Police Declare Black-out On Britton Case," *Harvard Crimson*, Jan. 10, 1969.

DANCING WITH GHOSTS

59 international drug smuggling: "Officials Jail Alumnus in 1500-lb Hash Bust," *Harvard Crimson*, Feb. 21, 1970.

59 FBI informant: "Jessie Gill's Story: Is It Fact or Fancy?" *Harvard Crimson*, Apr. 12, 1973.

59 another murder occurred: Multiple, including

"Widow 2D Cambridge Victim of Bludgeoning in Month," *Boston Globe*, Feb. 7, 1969.

59 covered with a blanket: Medical Examiner Report of Death by David Dow (CPD file).

59 looked much younger: "2 Murders in Cambridge Seen Similar," *Boston Herald Traveler*, Feb. 7, 1969.

60 dark hair and hazel eyes: Medical Examiner Report of Death by David Dow (CPD file).

60 Of the four murders: "Murder in Cambridge, 1959–1989," compiled by the Cambridge Police Department's Crime Analysis Unit.

60 "Don't do it": Phone call with Alec Klein in 2014.

60 "Only people of a certain disposition": Nick Hornby, *High Fidelity* (New York: Riverhead Books, 1995), p. 30.

60 the Mountain Cabin restaurant: This was our name for the Black Mountain Wine House (415 Union St.).

61 "You've changed": "You've Changed," written by Carl Fischer and Bill Carey, Melody Lane Productions, Inc. Copyright 1942.

2018: WHO WOULD YOU RATHER HAVE IT BE?

65 Conversation with Don Mitchell took place on July 25, 2018.

FUNERAL

66 like they had the plague: "Cambridge Rambler: News Blackout Hit," *Boston Record-American*, Jan. 18, 1969.

66 banged on Ingrid Kirsch's door: Here through "nose over a couple of feet," from CPD-IK.

66 Christ Episcopal Church: "'Gift' Rock May Be Cambridge Death Weapon," *Boston Globe*, Jan. 9, 1969.

66 it had been her church: Interview with Boyd Britton in 2019.

67 Giacoppo clutched his movie camera: Mel Finkelstein photo, "Cops & Cameras Study Crowd at Jane's Rites," *Daily News*, Jan. 11, 1969.

67 250 attendees: There is a slight discrepancy in the newspaper reports for this number. The *Boston Globe*, *Boston Record-American*, and *Daily News* estimated 400 attendees, but I went with the *New York Times*'s 250 because there were only about 200 signatures in Jane's funeral book.

67 tell him who to film: "Cops & Cameras Study Crowd at Jane's Rites," *Daily News*, Jan. 11, 1969; interview with Don Mitchell in 2017.

67 [Photo]: Mel Finkelstein/*New York Daily News*.

67 accompanied by his brother: CPD-RM, p. 50 and Cambridge Police photos from funeral (CPD file).

67 Richard Meadow's father: CPD-RM, p. 25 and interview with Richard Meadow in 2018.

67 dean at Harvard med school: "Henry Coe Meadow: Memorial Minute," *Harvard Gazette*, May 13, 2004.

67 set him up with: "3 Friends of Slain Co-Ed Take Lie Tests," *Boston Herald Traveler*, Jan. 10, 1969.

67 paler and more sleep-deprived: CPD-RM, p. 49.

67 oversize pair of sunglasses: Mel Finkelstein

photo, "Cops & Cameras Study Crowd at Jane's Rites," *Daily News*, Jan. 11, 1969.

67 Jane's mother stooped over: Cambridge Police photos from funeral.

68 [Photo]: Jane Britton police file.

68 made their way from the parking lot: Cambridge Police photos from funeral.

68 shown up to help as a courtesy: Interview with Boyd Britton in 2016.

69 [Photo]: Jane Britton police file.

69 Richard Meadow walked alone: Cambridge Police photos from funeral.

69 donations to be made: "Slayer Performed Ancient Ritual over Victim," *Boston Record-American*, Jan. 9, 1969. The Jane S. Britton Memorial Book Fund was started in her honor ("Britton Memorial Fund," *Peabody Museum Newsletter*, winter 1969, p. 2).

69 Mary Bunting: Bunting does not appear in the Cambridge Police photos, but her signature appears in Jane's funeral book, and her appearance was noted in "Slain Harvard Student Buried—Police Film All at Service," *Boston Globe*, Jan. 11, 1969.

69 not so for J. O. Brew: Cambridge Police photos from funeral.

69 "My god. Has he got balls": CPD-IK, p. 72.

69 Jane's neighbors, the Pressers: Woodward photographed next to the Pressers in the CPD photos from funeral.

69 stained-glass cross glittered: Author visit to Needham Episcopal; confirmed with Boyd Britton in 2019.

70 Jim Humphries sat in front: Don Mitchell Websleuths (WS) post #492, July 1, 2014.

70 White roses: "Slain Harvard Student Buried—

Police Film All at Service," *Boston Globe*, Jan. 11, 1969.

70 Soft organ music: "Jane Britton Laid to Rest," *Boston Herald Traveler*, Jan. 11, 1969.

70 Reverend Harold Chase: "Slain Harvard Student Buried—Police Film All at Service," *Boston Globe*, Jan. 11, 1969.

70 "peace now and forever"…no eulogy: "Jane Britton Laid to Rest," *Boston Herald Traveler*, Jan. 11, 1969.

70 "I remember being there": Interview with Mel Konner in 2017.

70 dabbed their eyes: "Cops & Cameras Study Crowd at Jane's Rites," *Daily News*, Jan. 11, 1969.

70 a single sob: "Cops & Cameras Study Crowd at Jane's Rites," *Daily News*, Jan. 11, 1969. In a 2017 interview, Jane's half brother Charlie Britton told me the sob was likely his.

70 less than thirty minutes: "Slain Harvard Student Buried—Police Film All at Service," *Boston Globe*, Jan. 11, 1969.

70 "Get him": "Cops & Cameras Study Crowd at Jane's Rites," *Daily News*, Jan. 11, 1969.

70 slipped out a side door: "Find Ritual Clue in Coed's Papers," *New York Post*, Jan. 11, 1969.

TRUE CRIMSON

70 forty-thousand-year-old interment: "First Humans in Australia Dated to 50,000 Years Ago," *National Geographic News*, Feb. 24, 2003.

71 Moorehead burial complex in Canada: Interview with Bruce Bourque in 2017.

71 stone coffin burials in southern Russia: Interview with Ruth Tringham in 2017.

71 Shanidar Cave in Iraq: Interview with Ed Wade in 2017.

71 Red Queen of Palenque: "Mystery Queen in the Maya Tomb," *National Geographic*, Feb. 2, 2018. She is covered in a different red powder: cinnabar, otherwise known as the highly toxic mercury sulfide.

71 nineteen-thousand-year-old: "The Red Lady of El Mirón," *Archaeology*, Sept.–Oct. 2015.

71 thirty-three-thousand-year-old: "The 'Red Lady' of Paviland," Oxford Museum of Natural History's website.

71 turned out to be a young man: "The Secrets of Paviland Cave," *The Guardian*, Apr. 25, 2011.

71 earliest example of symbolic thought: "Cave Colours Reveal Mental Leap," *BBC News Online*, Dec. 11, 2003.

71 Archaeologists speculated: Nicola Attard Montalto, "The Characterisation and Provenancing of Ancient Ochres," PhD dissertation, Cranfield Health, Translational Medicine, Cranfield University, 2010, p. 21.

71 Greek for "blood-like": Dictionary.com entry for the origin of "hematite," based on the *Random House Unabridged Dictionary* (New York: Random House, 2020).

71 history of Harvard's school color: See R. Leopoldina Torres, "The Colorful History of Crimson at Harvard," Harvard Art Museums website, Oct. 3, 2013. Reverend Gomes's quote from "Harvard Explained: Why Is Crimson Harvard's Official Color?" *Fifteen Minutes*, Apr. 11, 2002.

71 a couple of Neolithic sites: Sites include Ganj Dareh, Chogha Sefid, and Ali Kosh. See, e.g., Abbas Alizadeh, *Chogha Mish II: The Development of a Prehistoric Regional Center in Lowland Susiana, Southwestern Iran, Final Report on the Last Six Seasons of Excavation, 1972–1978*, Oriental Institute Publications 130 (Chicago: Oriental Institute, University of Chicago, 2008).

71 forbade cremation and burials: For more on Zoroastrian burial practices see Daniel Potts, "Disposal of the Dead in Planquadrat U/V XVIII at Uruk: A Parthian Enigma?" *Baghdader Mitteilungen* 37 (2006): 270.

71 the Freshman Register: *The Freshman Register: Radcliffe 1967*, Radcliffe College, 1967.

71 All three hundred of them: "How to Pick 300 Effective Human Beings," *Radcliffe Quarterly*, June 1969, p. 10.

72 different until 2000: "So Long, Radcliffe," *Harvard Crimson*, Apr. 21, 1999.

72 an all-male college: The end date of Harvard being an all-male college is hard to say since the merger happened in stages (e.g., Radcliffe students started taking classes with Harvard men in 1943, but it isn't until 1975 that a joint Harvard-Radcliffe Office of Admissions started admitting male and female undergraduates). Harvard and Radcliffe's long, drawn-out merger is explored more in a later chapter, but for a detailed history of it, see "Our History," Radcliffe Institute for Advanced Study Harvard University website.

72 "Hello?" she said: The rest of this chapter is from a 2014 interview with Susan Talbot.

73 it was still there: True as of the time of the conversation. In October 2019, after more than sixty years, Out of Town News closed.

JANE

74 chemist's analysis: Details in section from Report of Asst. Chemist Joseph Lanzetta, Apr. 1, 1969 (MSP file), unless otherwise indicated.

74 those sperm cells were intact: Chronology of DNA Investigation, prepared by the MDAO, Oct. 29, 2018, p. 1 (MDAO file).

74 Officer Giacoppo also found: Report to Det. Lt. Davenport by Det. Ed Colleran re: crime scene, Jan. 8, 1969.

74 Dr. Katsas's in-depth autopsy did not comment: Autopsy Report, Drs. George Katsas and Arthur McGovern, Jan. 7, 1969 (MSP file).

74 on her right arm: Autopsy Report, Drs. George Katsas and Arthur McGovern, Jan. 7, 1969 (MSP file).

74 Detective Lieutenant Davenport joked: CPD-JC, p. 17.

75 got the names and addresses: "Notes re: contact for James Humphries, Donald Mitchell, Lee Parsons, and Boyd Britton," unsigned and undated (CPD file).

75 obtained a directory: Graduate Students Roster, Department of Anthropology, Harvard University, fall term 1967.

75 her recent phone calls: "Notes of Names Linked to Series of Toll Calls," unsigned and undated (CPD file).

75 phone book and diary: "Coed Phone List Fails to Give Clues," *Boston Record-American*, Jan. 19, 1969.

75 three statements: Arthur Bankoff statement, Andrea Bankoff statement, joint statement.

75 US embassy in Rome: Letter to Lt. Davenport from US Vice Consul-Italy (encl. three letters), Jan. 17, 1969 (CPD file).

75 "Jane was not the type": "The Case of the Ocher-Covered Corpse," *Boston Magazine*, Sept. 1982.

75 "I think she'd kick him": CPD-IK, p. 43.

75 Jill Mitchell told cops: This paragraph and the following are from CPD-JM 1, pp. 42–44.

75 "gentleman to the point": CPD-LI, p. 49.

76 "I should think that": CPD-IK, p. 13.

76 the chemist's analysis revealed: This section is from Death Certificate by Dr. Arthur McGovern, Jan. 9, 1969 (MSP file). The maroon rugby sweater detail comes from Report by Sgt. Peter Sennott re: Jim Humphries, Oct. 12, 2017 (MSP file).

76 "What was the attraction?": Exchange is from CPD-IK, p. 63.

DO YOU FOLLOW ME

76 could not be immediately dismissed: This a condensed version of my research that focused on Theodore (Ted) Wertime, the head of a metallurgical annex team, sponsored by the Smithsonian, that visited Tepe Yahya the same season that Jane was there. It is thanks to Wertime that the Yahya expedition secured US commissary privileges; he worked for the Office of Strategic Services during World War II, did further intelligence work for the State Department from 1945 until 1955 (*Washington Post* obituary, Apr. 16, 1982), and was, for a time, the cultural attaché in Iran; but I ultimately found no evidence connecting his work at Yahya with any intelligence collection. For diligent scholarship on the connection between some anthropologists and the CIA, David Price's work is excellent.

76 "I never worked for the US government": Phone call with CCLK in 2020.

77 refused to either confirm or deny: Michael Lavergne, Executive Secretary of the Agency Release Panel, CIA, Mar. 18, 2016.

JANE AND JIM

77 The spring before: Scene based on CPD-IK and CPD-SLI, who both describe this moment—including the dialogue—in their police interviews. Sarah Lee Irwin went by Lee, but I refer to her as Sarah Lee in the book to avoid confusion with another Lee who appears later.

RADCLIFFE MEMORIES

78 original *Harvard Crimson* article: "Grad Student Killed," *Harvard Crimson*, Jan. 8, 1969.
78 French genealogy website: Geneanet.org.
78 *New York Times* obituary: "Paid Notice: Deaths, de Saint Phalle, Virginia," *New York Times*, Nov. 6, 2006.
78 She was eager to help: All following is from interview with Sat Siri Khalsa in 2014.

REAL ESTATE

78 "Does it take a murder": "Tenants Claim Harvard Ignored Building Code," *Harvard Crimson*, Jan. 14, 1969. For more on the scrutiny of Harvard's real estate policies, see "Harvard to Probe No Locks on Doors," *Boston Globe*, Jan. 10, 1969; "Harvard Defends Housing," *Boston Globe*, Jan. 12, 1969; "Harvard Panel Urges Improved Community Ties," *New York Times*, Jan. 14, 1969.
79 bought the place in 1967: "University Wins Fight to Purchase Building," *Harvard Crimson*, May 10, 1967.
79 residents should not expect renovations: "Booming Biz in Narcotics Jars Harvard," *Daily News*, Jan. 12, 1969.
79 "We tried to request": "Tenants Claim Harvard Ignored Building Code," *Harvard Crimson*, Jan. 14, 1969.
79 $48.7 million fundraising drive: According to the *Daily News*, this is a $52 million fundraising drive ("A Shadow of Blight Settles on Hallowed Harvard," Jan. 14, 1969), but this $48.7 million figure is taken from *Peabody Museum Newsletter*, summer 1968, p. 1.
79 young reporter pressed: "Covering Harvard—A View from the Outside," *Harvard Crimson*, June 12, 1969. The reporter was Parker Donham.
79 "With all the problems that Harvard brings":

"Tenants Claim Harvard Ignored Building Code," *Harvard Crimson*, Jan. 14, 1969.
79 real estate company that managed: "University Wins Fight to Purchase Building," William Galeota, May 10, 1967.
79 "Due to the recent happenings": "Front Door Locked at Jane's Building," *Daily News*, Jan. 11, 1969.
79 give residents the keys: "Slay Site Bldg Gets New Locks," *Boston Record-American*, Jan. 11, 1969.
80 "They just wanted it to die down": Interview with Joe Modzelewski in 2014.
80 frozen winter soil: "Slain Student Buried—People Film All at Service," *Boston Globe*, Jan. 11, 1969.
80 A cloudless sky: "Cops & Cameras Study Crowd at Jane's Rites," *Daily News*, Jan. 11, 1969.
80 performed a brief graveside: "Slain Student Buried—People Film All at Service," *Boston Globe*, Jan. 11, 1969.
80 only time Jane's father showed emotion: Interviews with Boyd Britton in 2016 and Charlie Britton in 2017.
80 the sloping hill: "Cops & Cameras Study Crowd at Jane's Rites," *Daily News*, Jan. 11, 1969.
80 two workmen: "Cops & Cameras Study Crowd at Jane's Rites," *Daily News*, Jan. 11, 1969.

ELISABETH

81 At the two-week mark: This chapter is from an interview with Elisabeth in 2014 unless otherwise noted.
81 "three feet on the ground at all times": There was no parietal rule worded as such in the *Redbook*, but this is how students shorthanded it. See also "More as People than Dating Objects," *Harvard Magazine*, Nov.-Dec. 2011.

81 mandatory skirts and stockings: *Redbook: A Guide to Student Living at Radcliffe 1963–1964*, edited by Karen Johnson, Radcliffe Government Association, p. 25.
81 It wasn't until 1973: "'Cliffe to Yard Shuttle Buses Begin," *Harvard Crimson*, Sept. 21, 1973.

JANE AT RADCLIFFE

82 That first week of freshman year: This chapter is from an interview with Elisabeth Handler in 2014 unless otherwise noted.
83 the more difficult of the two: Marcia G. Synnott, "The Changing 'Harvard Student': Ethnicity, Race, and Gender," *Yards and Gates:*

Gender in Harvard and Radcliffe History, edited by Laurel Ulrich (New York: Palgrave Macmillan, 2004), p. 297.
83 green and widely spaced: Susan Kelly notes from interview with Elisabeth Handler, May 24, 1996 (police file).

83 black it was almost blue: Interview with Brenda Bass in 2016.

83 built like a brick shithouse: Interview with Bruce Bourque in 2017.

83 she smoked: Interview with Lucy DuPertuis in 2018.

83 eschewed hair-sprayed updos: Interview with Irene (duPont) Light in 2016.

83 She had a low voice: Interview with Jennifer Fowler in 2016.

83 erupted spontaneously: Email from Cathy Ravinski, Aug. 1, 2017, 10:25 a.m.

83 cock her thin eyebrows: Interview with Jennifer Fowler in 2016.

83 Jane slept on the lower bunk: Details of Jane's freshman-year room from interview with Lucy DuPertuis in 2018.

83 ironing board and iron: Here through "five hours a week of housework," from *Redbook*, p. 19.

84 "be discreet when sunbathing"…"good taste demands": *Redbook*, p. 25.

84 Smoking was allowed everywhere (except in bed): *Redbook*, p. 32.

84 alcohol was forbidden…exceptions were made for sherry: *Redbook*, p. 85.

84 the social rules: *Redbook*, p. 79.

84 needed to be signed in: *Redbook*, pp. 82–83.

84 "Man on!" to alert people: "'Cliffe Parietals Committee Meets for Action on Spring Referendum," *Harvard Crimson*, Sept. 25, 1969.

84 the Harvard Annex in 1879…Harvard classes since 1943: "Radcliffe Timeline," *Harvard Crimson*, Apr. 21, 1999.

84 Professors resented: Nancy Weiss Malkiel, *"Keep the Damned Women Out": The Struggle for Coeducation* (Princeton, NJ: Princeton University Press, 2017), p. 37. This is an excellent book on the history of how elite universities in America and the UK went co-ed.

84 Harvard instructors' experience of teaching co-ed classes: "The 'Cliffe Girl: An Instructor's View," *Harvard Crimson*, Apr. 18, 1953.

85 the June before Jane arrived: Malkiel, *"Keep the Damned Women Out,"* pp. 42–43.

85 second-class citizens: Interview with Ellen Hume in 2014.

85 same scholarship money and financial aid: Marie Hicks, "Integrating Women at Oxford and Harvard Universities, 1964–1977," *Yards and Gates*, p. 363.

85 weren't allowed to enter Lamont: "Lamont Will Open to Cliffies after Twenty Celibate Years," *Harvard Crimson*, Dec. 8, 1966.

85 required to have escorts: *Redbook*, p. 86.

85 nine women's bathrooms: *Redbook*, p. 118.

85 freshman boy could invite: "More as People than Dating Objects," *Harvard Magazine*, Nov.–Dec. 2011.

85 make the women as uncomfortable as possible: "More as People than Dating Objects," *Harvard Magazine*, Nov.–Dec. 2011.

85 classes started a week later: According to *Redbook*, p. 5, freshman orientation lasted eight days that year.

85 met three times a week: *Courses of Instruction Harvard and Radcliffe*, Faculty of Arts and Sciences 1963–1964, Official Register of Harvard University, 60, no. 21 (1963): 37.

85 There was an old joke: Interview with Jonathan Friedlaender in 2018.

85 party at his house: Scene is from interviews with Elisabeth Handler (2014) and Peter Panchy (2017). Red wine with cloves detail from Susan Kelly notes from interview with Elisabeth Handler, May 24, 1996 (police file).

86 an Albanian immigrant: Interview with Peter Panchy in 2017.

86 mandatory abstinence lecture in Cabot Hall: Interview with Susan Talbot in 2014.

86 In October 1963, a scandal hit: "Parietal Rules," *Harvard Crimson*, Oct. 1, 1963.

86 Students had been complaining: "Living Off-Campus," *Harvard Crimson*, Mar. 21, 1963.

86 Two Harvard deans pushed back: "Parietal Rules," *Harvard Crimson*, Oct. 1, 1963.

87 brought a television into…tolled every fifteen minutes: Interview with Lucy DuPertuis in 2018.

87 Sophomore year, Jane and Elisabeth: Jane Britton's Radcliffe student file.

87 an old frame house: Interview with Elisabeth Handler in 2014.

87 1950s living room furniture…Jane was particularly fond: Interview with Karen Black in 2017.

87 *Here we were, smelling like a stable:* Letter from Jane Britton to her parents, June 12, 1964.

87 Drugs hit campus that year: Interview with Susan Talbot in 2014.

87 dodge water balloons: "The Whispers of a Movement," *Harvard Crimson*, May 25, 2015.

87 rarely more than three Black students: Synnott, *Yards and Gates*, p. 301.

87 Susan Talbot only became aware: Interview with Susan Talbot in 2014.

88 remember the electricity of this moment: Interview with Carol Sternhell in 2014.

88 the hunter-gatherers: Interview with Karl Heider in 2017.

88 fasting for seventy-two hours: Susan Kelly notes from interview with Elisabeth Handler, May 24, 1996 (police file).

88 Jane came alive at night: Here through "cockeyed optimist," Susan Kelly notes from interview with Elisabeth Handler, May 24, 1996 (police file).

88 a 1962 white convertible: Elisabeth remembers this as Jane's car, but Boyd (2020) said the car was bought by their father for their mother.

88 Chez Jean, a sweet French bistro: Also appears in Susan Kelly notes from interview with Elisabeth Handler, May 24, 1996 (police file).

BACK WITH ELISABETH

89 In early January 1969: Interviews with Elisabeth Handler (2014) and Peter Panchy (2017).

90 "I felt so guilty just for being alive": Susan Kelly notes from interview with Elisabeth Handler, May 24, 1996 (police file).

90 Ed Franquemont had been a Harvard: Interview with Peter Rodman in 2017.

90 He and Jane dated for less than: Multiple CPD interviews, including CPD-IK, CPD-DM.

91 "cold as a slab of china": CPD-IK, p. 29.

EVERY BAD THING YOU KNOW ABOUT HER

91 "She wasn't murdered because": Don Mitchell WS post #374, June 15, 2014.

92 "Now that I think about it": CPD-JM 2, p. 46.

92 Ingrid echoed the Mitchells' admission: CPD-IK, p. 41.

92 Jim was a total mystery to the Mitchells, too: Paragraph from CPD-DM, p. 61.

92 Bankoffs were in Europe: Arthur Bankoff statement.

92 Boyd had been deployed to Vietnam: Boyd Britton military records, National Personnel Records, Department of Defense.

92 moved to Norfolk, Virginia: Interview with Elisabeth Handler in 2020.

92 Cops pushed Ingrid to remember: Exchange from CPD-IK, pp. 35–36.

93 Growing up in Needham: Details here about Jane's childhood are from interview with Karen John in 2017 unless otherwise noted.

93 [Photo]: Britton family file, courtesy Boyd Britton.

93 Jane's father was often away: Karen and Boyd's memories differ here. Karen doesn't remember Jane's father being away, but Boyd spoke of their father taking frequent business trips. I've gone with Boyd's memory.

94 Emily Woodbury, another childhood friend: Interview with Emily Woodbury in 2017.

94 "Fit hit the Shan": Letter from Jane Britton to her parents, July 7, 1966.

94 Her childhood drawings: Britton family file.

94 [Photo]: Britton family file, courtesy Boyd Britton.

95 spent a summer riding on the Cape: Interview with Boyd Britton in 2020.

95 foxhunt simulations: Per Boyd (2020), there were no foxes left in the region, so Jane's neighbors filled bags with fox urine and dragged them along the trails for the hounds to later follow.

95 Don and Jill were used to seeing Jane every day: CPD-JM 2, p. 47.

95 disappear at eight in the morning: CPD-JM 2, p. 47.

95 Jane left in a rush at 10 p.m.: Here through "If she really had a date" from CPD-JM 2, p. 45.

95 "Do you know of anyone else": Exchange from CPD-SLI, p. 34.

WHAT'RE YOU SO AFRAID OF?

96 Drafts of a letter Jane wrote to Jim: "Collected Correspondence in Britton Apt," various dates 1968, p. 6 (CPD file). The fact that these drafts were intended for Jim is inferred from the marmot reference in the letter. Jane often calls herself a marmot (e.g., Jane's journal entry, June 14/15, 1968: "And all this time I thought you were just making the last days of the marmot a little (hell, infinitely) more blissful").

BOYD

97 Boyd's first response...Boyd's second response: Boyd Britton, as quoted in email from Elisabeth Handler, Feb. 17, 2014, 5:06 p.m.
98 Boyd wrote again: Email from Boyd Britton to Elisabeth Handler and me, Feb. 17, 2014, 6:23 p.m.

98 "Perhaps I watch too many detective shows": Email from Boyd Britton, Feb. 18, 2014, 11:54 a.m.

FRAGMENTS OF JANE

99 A young Boyd dripped water: Interview with Boyd Britton in 2016.
99 In fourth grade, Jane sat uncomfortably: Interview with Emily Woodbury in 2017.
99 Jane and Boyd wandered into their parents' room: Interview with Boyd Britton in 2017.
100 Jane and her roommate knit a scarf: Interview with Brenda Bass in 2016.
100 In the school production of *Oklahoma!*: Interview with Boyd Britton in 2016.
100 Cole Porter on the grand piano: Interview with Brenda Bass in 2016.

100 Jane told her friend Cathy: Email from Cathy Ravinski, July 28, 2017, 10:57 a.m.
100 a kind of electric force controlling people's lives. CPD-JM 2, p. 52.
100 who was born in Prague: Interview with CCLK in 2017.
100 the "Canceled Czech": Letter from Jane to Boyd, approx. June 17, 1968.
100 "Porcelain Ass": CPD-IK, p. 79.
100 "I have dreams of waking up dead": Interview with John Terrell in 2017.

FIRST TALK WITH BOYD

101 All details in this chapter are taken from my 2014 interview with Boyd Britton unless otherwise noted.
101 had been over to her apartment: Boyd was

not aware of this fact when we spoke. This detail comes from Peter Ganick's CPD interview transcript with Detective Lieutenant Davenport, Jan. 8, 1969, 10:25–10:35 a.m.

VIETNAM

105 On the night of January 7: Details in this section are from multiple interviews with Boyd Britton (2014–2020), unless otherwise indicated.
105 Vietnam for only a month: Boyd arrived on Dec. 6, 1968, per his military records, National Personnel Records, Department of Defense.
105 the 16th Public Information Detachment: CPD-BB; also letter from Boyd to Jane, undated (approx. Dec. 1968).
105 "Your sister Jane killed": Telegram from Jane's parents to Boyd, Jan. 8, 1969 (Britton family file).
106 [Photo]: Britton family file, courtesy Boyd Britton.
106 "Visiting her parents": Susan Kelly notes from interview with Elisabeth Handler, May 24, 1996 (police file).
106 "gay exotic Needham": Letter from Jane to Elisabeth Handler, July 27, 1968.
107 on Needham's finance committee: "J. Boyd Britton; Was Chemist, Executive, Radcliffe Officer; 93," *Boston Globe*, Oct. 29, 2002.
107 vice president of Cabot Corporation: "J. Boyd

Britton; Was Chemist, Executive, Radcliffe Officer; 93," *Boston Globe*, Oct. 29, 2002.
107 *The Lowells speak only to Cabots*: "Home of the Bean and the Cod," *The Telegraph*, Dec. 22, 2002.
107 Cordon Bleu–certified cook: Susan Kelly notes from interview with Boyd Britton, Feb. 27, 1996 (police file).
107 the first Boeing 767: "Boeing 767: A Cautious Debut," *New York Times*, Sept. 8, 1982.
107 two children from a previous marriage: Interviews with Boyd and Charlie Britton (2017).
107 PhD in history: Ruth Gertrude Reinert, "Genoese Trade with Provence, Languedoc, Spain, and the Balearics in the Twelfth Century," PhD dissertation, History Department, University of Wisconsin, 1938.
108 Ruth didn't discourage Jane: In a letter home to her parents (July 12, 1966), Jane asked her mother to pick up "some of that prescription; they're really great those pills; keep my appetite down."
108 she was class vice president: Dana Hall Yearbook, 1963.

108 "most intelligent": Superlatives from Dana Hall Yearbook, 1963, p. 103.

108 only one in her grade to get into Radcliffe: "'63 at College," *Dana Hall Bulletin*, Jan. 1963, p. 26.

108 *before* her father: Jane started Radcliffe in 1963. In a letter dated July 20, 1965, she congratulated her father on getting the job.

108 just somebody's wife: Susan Kelly notes from interview with Elisabeth Handler, May 24, 1996 (police file).

108 left college three times: Boyd was asked to leave Princeton the first time because, he said, he flunked everything. After that, he went to Emerson, where he was on the dean's list, but left on his own accord. Then he returned to Princeton and eventually dropped out.

108 "I only had dinner with her family once": Interview with Karen John in 2017.

108 "Cats with the Syphilis": There are a number of versions of this song, which is sung to the tune of "D'ye Ken John Peel?"

109 By noon: Boyd Britton military records, National Personnel Records, Department of Defense.

109 a syndicated UPI story: "Girl 22 Beaten to Death," *Pacific Stars and Stripes*, Jan. 9, 1969.

109 The New York papers were still in town: Interviews with Joe Modzelewski (2014) and Mike McGovern (2016).

109 "Any information has to come from the chief": "D.A. Droney Hints Coed Slay 'Repeat,'" *Boston Record-American*, Jan. 14, 1969.

109 called Jane's family and came to their door: Interview with Boyd Britton in 2016.

109 narcotics business in Harvard Square: "Booming Biz in Narcotics Jars Harvard," *Daily News*, Jan. 12, 1969.

110 Mike had his photographer snap it: I could not cross-check this with Mike McGovern. He died before I had the chance.

110 A cover story: *Daily News*, Jan. 13, 1969, p. 1.

110 "It's just not true!": Interview with Boyd Britton in 2014.

110 "It is, Mom. It is": Interview with Boyd Britton in 2014.

ED FRANQUEMONT

110 the Mitchells: CPD-DM, p. 47.

110 and Ingrid Kirsch knew: CPD-IK, p. 34.

110 "Nobody nobody *nobody*": Interview with Elisabeth Handler in 2014.

110 the wrestling team: "Franquemont Wins, Loses in NCAA Wrestling Meet," *Harvard Crimson*, Mar. 30, 1965.

110 Compact and practically bald: Here through "You didn't want to be in the same room," from Susan Kelly notes from interview with Elisabeth Handler, May 24, 1996 (police file).

111 [Photo]: Jane Britton police file.

111 Jane started dating Ed her senior year: CPD-IK, p. 31.

111 "perfectly capable": CPD-SLI, p. 45.

111 sleep with a guy to get rid of him: Susan Kelly notes from interview with Elisabeth Handler, May 24, 1996 (police file).

111 "Or at least that's how she portrayed it": Interview with Elisabeth Handler in 2017.

111 But by the fall of 1967: These two paragraphs from CPD-JM 1 and CPD-IK.

111 he hit her: CPD-JM 1, p. 30.

111 "If she had, in fact": CPD-SLI, p. 10.

111 Jane received a terrifying call: CPD-JM 1, pp. 37–40.

112 at the school for troubled kids: The Charles River School, per "Notes Phone Call with Ed Franquemont," Jan. 9, 1969 (CPD file).

112 found him sweet and concerned: CPD-JM, p. 39.

112 speculate that this was the night that Jane got pregnant: CPD-DM, p. 48.

112 Through the Anthropology department grapevine: Section is from an interview with Sally Bates Shankman in 2017.

112 one of the founders: Email from Bentley Historical Library re: the Planned Parenthood of Mid-Michigan Records, Mar. 2, 2018, 3:05 p.m.

112 the last weekend of spring break: Receipt for her car rental in Michigan in the CPD file dated Apr. 7, 1968. According to Harvard's academic calendar for 1967–1968, spring break ended on Apr. 7 that year.

112 it cost Jane $500: Jane's letter to Brenda Bass, July 4, 1968. Also photo of a check made out to cash for $500, dated Apr. 5, 1968 (CPD file).

112 had started a collection: CPD-DM, p. 47; CPD-JM 2, p. 30.

113 police learned of Ed: CPD first ask about Ed in CPD-CCLK 1, dated Jan. 7, 1969.

113 moved off campus: Interviews with Merri Swid and Richard Rose (2017); CPD-IK, p. 34; CPD-CCLK 1, pp. 8–9.

113 had seen him in Cambridge: "Police Seek Peru Hippie in Coed Slaying," *Fresno Bee*, Jan. 8, 1969.

113 But over the next few weeks: Part of the Jane Britton investigation lore is that cops "chased

Franquemont down to Peru." While this feels like an exaggeration, and there are no travel records or notes from 1969 in the police file from this alleged trip, I found one possible mention of it on p. 1 of "ADA Background Notes 2017" (MDAO file): "Report concerning information received from Lt. Frank Joyce by Billy Powers and/or Jimmy Connolly concerning...the trip to Peru with the polygraph person to interview Frankquemont [*sic*]."

113 came to police with a postcard: Richard Rose interview in 2017; the postcard is part of the CPD file.

113 Debbie Waroff, the best friend: This exchange taken from Deborah Waroff interview transcript with Detective Sergeant Galligan, Jan. 9, 1969, unspecified time (police file).

113 Her information checked out: I also spoke with Dave Browman (2017), a former anthropology graduate student, who said he was with Ed Franquemont in Peru on the night of Jane's death.

114 [Photo]: Jane Britton police file.

114 Jill said she had liked Ed: CPD-JM 1, p. 35.

114 "sort of your standard straight guy": CPD-IK, p. 30.

114 "colorless psychologically": CPD-IK, p. 30.

114 "babe in the woods": Interview with Brenda Bass in 2016.

114 "high school sweetheart": CPD-IK, p. 28.

114 her boyfriend from the South: CPD-DM, pp. 16, 39.

115 "was making everything up": Interview with Tess Beemer in 2016.

115 "seemed to be in some ways posing" Interview with John Terrell in 2017.

115 "may not have been completely truthful": Susan Kelly notes from interview with Elisabeth Handler, May 24, 1996 (police file).

115 Jill doing research for her dissertation: Jill Nash, who did not agree to be interviewed for the book, did participate in the checking process. This detail comes from her response to the checking memo.

115 Jane had been the one who hit Ed: CPD-IK and CPD-SLI.

115 It was the spring of 1967: This scene is from CPD-IK.

115 "If there was a darkness": Interview with Merri Swid in 2017.

CULTURAL AMNESIA

116 "Radcliffe Night": This event happened on Mar. 6, 2014.

116 took a call from Jane's friend Ingrid: The rest of this chapter is from my interview with Ingrid Kirsch in 2014.

118 "I don't mind you disappearing / 'Cause I know you can be found.": "In Reverse," Track #9 on *Lost in the Dream*, The War on Drugs, 2014.

FACE THE NIGHT

119 Jesse Kornbluth (class of '68): "Crimson Compass," Harvard Alumni Database.

119 "admit a loneliness": "Coming Together: Love in Cambridge," *Harvard Crimson*, Jan. 8, 1969.

WEBSLEUTHS

120 started the thread in November 2012: "macoldcase" Websleuths post #1, Nov. 2, 2012.

120 antiquities smuggling ring: E.g., "December" Websleuths post #207, Sept. 15, 2013.

120 much was made of a missing table leg: E.g., "Robin Hood" Websleuths post #106, Jan. 1, 2013.

120 Pressers, had reported to the cops: "Report from M/M Stephen Presser (table leg)," Jan. 14, 1969 (CPD file).

120 noticed that it only had three legs: "Report from M/M Stephen Presser (table leg)," Jan. 14, 1969 (CPD file).

121 "Justice4Jane," who first heard: "Justice4Jane" Websleuths post #160, Aug. 9, 2013.

121 "a descendent of the Habsburg family": "Justice4Jane" Websleuths post #186 quoting from a College Confidential thread, Aug. 15, 2013.

121 "I am pretty sure they mean": "Ausgirl" Websleuths post #188, Aug. 15, 2013.

121 Don Mitchell posted for the first time: Don Mitchell Websleuths post #374, June 16, 2014.

121 Three the next day: Don Mitchell Websleuths posts #377, #381, and #382, June 17, 2014.

121 six the one after that: Don Mitchell Websleuths

posts #392, #393, #395, #396, #397, and #400, June 18, 2014.

121 "I have always believed": Don Mitchell Websleuths post #381, June 17, 2014.

121 asked Don to photograph a fingerprint: Here through "may seem now like coverup" from Don Mitchell Websleuths post #374, June 16, 2014.

122 Cambridge cops had botched the job: Don Mitchell Websleuths post #381, June 17, 2014.

122 knock on Jane's door the morning of: Here through "He's come to get us," from Don Mitchell Websleuths post #400, June 18, 2014.

122 ex-wife, he clarified: Don Mitchell Websleuths post #374, June 16, 2014.

122 saved the bloody rugs: Don Mitchell Websleuths post #381, June 17, 2014.

122 until last year when he moved..."ceremonial bonfire": Don Mitchell interview in 2017.

122 "I put all my trust in Lt. Joyce": Don Mitchell Websleuths post #492, July 1, 2014.

122 His main suspect: Don Mitchell Websleuths posts #396, June 18, 2014 and #453, June 28, 2014.

122 "something longishterm and secret": Don Mitchell Websleuths post #395, June 18, 2014.

122 His suspect died in 1999: Don Mitchell Websleuths post #465, June 29, 2014.

123 reportedly confessed while drunk: Don Mitchell Websleuths post #479, June 30, 2014.

123 "I killed someone"...struck dead by lightning: Don Mitchell Websleuths posts #396, June 18, 2014, and #464, June 29, 2014.

MYSTERY MAN

123 On January 15, reporters caught wind: "Is Table Key to Britton Murder?" *Boston Globe,* Jan. 16, 1969.

123 "Harvard faculty member who was rejected": "Murder Quiz Finds Jane Had Abortion," *Daily News,* Jan. 13, 1969.

123 Reporters staked out: "Coed Case—Mystery Man," *New York Post,* Jan. 16, 1969.

123 to an undisclosed location: "Quiz Mystery Man in Murder of Coed," *Boston Record-American,* Jan. 16, 1969.

124 "You have to assume it's a sex case": "D.A. Droney Hints Coed Slay 'Repeat,'" *Boston Record-American,* Jan. 14, 1969.

124 had not been strong enough to break the skin: "Harvard Faces Criminal Action," *Boston Globe,* Jan. 14, 1969.

124 Jane's father was similarly tight-lipped: Exchange is from CPD-JBB pp. 3–5.

REUNION

124 But he died in the '90s: Public death record for Lt. Frank Joyce.

125 "beat Yale" 29–29: "Harvard Beats Yale," *Harvard Magazine,* Nov. 15, 2018.

125 establish an African American Studies department: "Rosovsky's Report," *Harvard Crimson,* Jan. 29, 1969, and "The Faculty Committee on African and Afro-American Studies Report," Jan. 20, 1969, as reprinted in *Blacks at Harvard: A Documentary History of African-American Experience at Harvard and Radcliffe* (New York: New York University Press, 1993), edited by Werner Sollors, Caldwell Titcomb, and Thomas Underwood, pp. 401–402.

125 discontent with ROTC's presence on campus: "The Strike as History," *Harvard Crimson,* Apr. 23, 1979.

125 agitations of SDS and the Weathermen: "SDS and Weathermen Hold Separate Protests," *Harvard Crimson,* Nov. 26, 1969.

125 'CLIFFE FINALLY PROPOSES: "'Cliffe Finally Proposes Marriage to Ten Thousand Men of Harvard," *Harvard Crimson,* Feb. 23, 1969.

125 identified as Harvard students more than Radcliffe: Multiple interviews, including with Carol Sternhell and Elisabeth Handler.

125 a few enjoyed the 1:4 ratio: Interview with Ellen Hume in 2014.

125 signature disappeared off the diplomas: Laurel Thatcher Ulrich, now an emerita professor in Harvard's History department, wrote a powerful essay on the erasure of women from Harvard's history in 1999, six months before the Radcliffe signature disappeared: "Harvard's Womanless History: Completing the University's Self-Portrait," *Harvard Magazine,* Nov. 1999. She writes: "There is no conspiracy here, just collective complacency and an ignorance compounded by separatism. Writers and publicists at Harvard have never considered Radcliffe their responsibility. Radcliffe has been too busy negotiating its own status to promote its history."

126 none of the Courses of Instruction: *Courses of Instruction Harvard and Radcliffe, Faculty of Arts and Sciences,* Official Register of Harvard University: six volumes consulted, 1964–1969.

126 Directories of Officers and Students: *Directory of Officers and Students*, Harvard University: six volumes consulted, 1964–1969.

126 Professor John Campbell Pelzel: David Browman and Stephen Williams, *Anthropology at Harvard: A Biographical History, 1790–1940* (Cambridge, MA: Peabody Museum Press, 2013), p. 454.

126 John Whiting, a professor of social anthropology: "John Wesley Mayhew Whiting: Memorial Minute," *Harvard Gazette*, June 3, 2004.

126 known to have worked for the US Government: David Price, *Anthropological Intelligence: The Deployment and Neglect of American Anthropology in the Second World War* (Durham, NC: Duke University Press, 2008), p. 92.

126 the dissertation of Richard Meadow: Richard Meadow, "Animal Exploitation in Prehistoric Southeastern Iran: Faunal Remains from Tepe Yahya and Tepe Gaz Tavila-R37, 5500–3000 B.C.," PhD dissertation, Anthropology Department, Harvard University, 1986, p. 1.

126 quote from a Julian Barnes novel: Julian Barnes, *Flaubert's Parrot* (New York: Vintage, 1990), p. 14.

127 *It is clear that I have not caught:* Meadow, "Animal Exploitation," end of introduction.

127 *Female / Aged 19:* 998-27-40/14628.2, Hallam L. Movius Jr. papers, Peabody Museum of Archaeology & Ethnology, Harvard University.

128 *Dear Hal: / The enclosed:* Letter from Stephen Williams to Hallam Movius, Jan. 8, 1969, found in 998-27-40/14628.2, Hallam L. Movius Jr. papers, Peabody Museum of Archaeology & Ethnology, Harvard University.

128 *"Investigation and speculation continue:* Letter from Stephen Williams to Hallam Movius, Jan. 20, 1969, found in 998-27-40/14628.2, Hallam L. Movius Jr. papers, Peabody Museum of Archaeology & Ethnology, Harvard University.

130 A letter from Professor Hugh Hencken: Letter from Hugh Hencken to Stephen Williams, Jan. 7, 1969, 995-18, Hugh O'Neill Hencken papers, Peabody Museum of Archaeology & Ethnology, Harvard University.

2018: FIVE DAYS

133 This scene took place the evening of July 25, 2018.

ARTHUR BANKOFF

134 promoted to full director: "New Director Appointed," *Peabody Museum Newsletter*, winter 1969, p. 1.

134 "A number of people have described him": Interview with Tom Patterson in 2017.

134 for a few months after Jane's death: Feb. 1969 to summer 1969. End date per letter from Stephen Williams to CCLK, July 22, 1969.

134 nearly unprecedented: Donald Scott held both roles from 1947 to 1948, per the plaques at Harvard's Peabody Museum.

134 million-dollar donation: Peabody Annual Report 1968–1969, Official Register of Harvard University, 67, no. 23 (Oct. 30, 1970): 445.

135 "Having gained your professorship during": C. C. Lamberg-Karlovsky Personal Archive, 1957–2014, (Accession Number 2016.113), Box 6: Letterbox, correspondence A–Z 1965–1969, Folder X, Y, Z, Letter from Stephen Williams to CCLK, July 22, 1969. Reprinted with permission from Timothy Williams.

135 the material may have been lost in a flood: Phone call with CPD. Flood also referenced in "Murder in Cambridge, 1959–1989," compiled by CPDs Crime Analysis Unit.

135 *Good luck doing that if your name isn't O'Sullivan:* Interview with Richard Conti in 2017.

136 asked to meet while I was in town: Email from Jeffrey Quilter, Sept. 4, 2014, 1:01 p.m.

136 "I'm just going to tell you because I like you": Interview with Jeffrey Quilter in 2014.

136 The door opened, and Arthur Bankoff: Interview with Arthur Bankoff in 2016.

137 reading something in the Harvard alumni magazine: *Harvard Magazine*, July 2010 capsule review of Jessica Stern's *Denial: A Memoir of Terror* (New York: HarperCollins, 2010), a book about her unsolved rape that was eventually linked to the serial rapist Dennis Meggs.

138 [Bottom photo]: Courtesy Arthur Bankoff, with permission from Richard Meadow.

TEPE YAHYA

139 There's a special kind of insanity: Description of Tepe Yahya is drawn from interviews with crew members during that season's expedition (Phil Kohl, Arthur Bankoff, and Peter Dane), and later ones (including Tom Beale, Dan Potts, and Elizabeth Stone), as well as with David Stronach, who ran the British Institute of Persian Studies. CCLK's foreword also offers an "ethnography" of life on the dig. Dialogue and other details also pulled from Jane's letters home to family and friends, her journal entries, the field notebooks, the CPD interview transcripts, and Arthur and Andrea Bankoff's police statements. (In their statements, the Bankoffs repeatedly ask the police to be aware of the distortions of perspective caused by trying circumstances, e.g., "Most of the annoying things we thought so vital over the summer have become forgotten what with our re-entry into places of good food, bathrooms and hot water.") Where there are conflicting accounts, I've indicated below.

139 "Small-group situation tends to create": Jane's response to the Summer Questionnaire 1966, Jane Britton's Radcliffe student file.

139 mid-June: Letter from Jane to her parents, June 17, 1968.

139 one of the graduation speeches: "Commencement Day Speakers," Harvard University website.

139 honorary degree: "Shah of Iran, Miro, Wirtz, Whitney Young, Brennan, and Finley Get Honorary Degrees," *Harvard Crimson*, June 13, 1968.

139 Coretta Scott King: "Coretta Scott King at Class Day," *Harvard Crimson*, May 21, 2018.

139 which doubled as a plush hotel of sorts: Interview with David Stronach in 2018.

139 food from the US embassy commissary: Letter from Jane to Boyd, approx. June 17, 1968.

139 pickaxes, and plastic bags: Here through "cooling off poolside," letter from Jane to her parents, June 17, 1968.

140 A few pinched her butt: Letter from Jane to Boyd, June 21, 1968.

140 traffic in Tehran in general made Jane swear: Letter from Jane to her parents, June 17, 1968.

140 catching the odd angle of light: Here through "a giant heart" from Jane's journal entry, June 14/15, 1968.

140 She had almost missed her flight to Iran: Letter from Jane to her parents, June 17, 1968.

140 overwhelming desire to go out and chalk every sidewalk: Jane's journal entry, June 14/15, 1968.

140 "There is something different about your chemistry": Letter from Jane to Jim Humphries, June 4, 1968 (CPD file).

140 the lack of privacy: Letter from Jane to Boyd, June 21, 1968.

140 Jim because of how tall he was: Letter from Jane to her parents, June 17, 1968. The round sunglasses detail is also from this letter.

140 alone, finally, over a gin and tonic: Letter from Jane to her parents, June 21, 1968.

140 peck on the cheek after breakfast: Letter from Jane to her parents, June 17, 1968.

140 Jim kept trying to make elaborate plans: Jane's journal entry, June 20, 1968.

140 longed for when they'd be peacefully settled: Letter from Jane to her parents, June 17, 1968.

140 two separate cars: Letter from Jane to her parents, June 29, 1968.

140 the Persian antiquities representative: Letter from Jane to her parents, June 29, 1968.

140 named Bucephalus: Interview with Dan Potts in 2017.

140 When the car stalled: Letter from Jane to her parents, June 29, 1968.

140 Jane felt more in love with Jim than ever: Jane's journal entry, June 26, 1968.

141 it was too late: Here through "They woke up freezing," from letter from Jane to her parents, June 29, 1968.

141 Baghin, the tiny village: Letter from Jane to Brenda Bass, July 4, 1968.

141 seventy-five-hundred-year-old mound: "Tepe Yahya," *Encyclopædia Iranica*.

141 no electricity: CCLK foreword, p. XXIII.

141 camped in tents close by: Dora Jane Hamblin, *The First Cities* (New York: Time-Life, 1973), p. 26.

141 a man on his bicycle: Interview with Peter Dane in 2014.

141 a driver on a donkey: CCLK foreword, p. XXVI.

141 little pension with a bidet: Letters from Jane to her parents, June 26 and July 7, 1966.

141 "animalcules"...hadn't bothered checking: Letter from Jane to her parents, June 29, 1968.

141 arrived unceremoniously on the back of the truck: Interview with Phil Kohl in 2017. A version of this story also appears in CCLK foreword, but in CCLK's version, Kohl arrives on the back of a melon truck.

141 Karl had warned the crew: Andrea Bankoff statement, p. 7.

141 As a first-time director of a full-scale dig: Joint statement, p. 4.

141 on whom he felt the success of and continued access...depended: Phone call with CCLK in 2020.

141 "no debate with the chief" policy: Joint statement, p. 4.

141 had misconstrued some laughter: Arthur Bankoff statement, p. 7.

142 stuck their faces in flour...local goats were stringy: Interview with Dan Potts in 2017.

142 ended up just using the bushes and ditches: Letter from Jane to her parents, July 4, 1968.

142 many got sick very quickly: CPD-CCLK 2, p. 18.

142 brought the crew closer together: Arthur Bankoff statement, p. 8.

142 "legs too short and has a droopy ass": Joint statement, p. 3.

142 behave as if he were still at Dartmouth: Letter from Jane to her parents, June 17, 1968.

142 John the Baptist in Muslim tradition: John Renard, *All the King's Falcons: Rumi on Prophets and Revelation* (Albany: State University of New York Press, 1994), p. 87.

142 qanats, or water wells: Qanat anecdote is from interview with Tom Beale in 2017.

142 Jim and the night sky: Letter from Jane to Elisabeth Handler, July 27, 1968.

142 "has been spectacular": Here and rest of paragraph, letter from Jane to Brenda Bass July 4, 1968.

142 She and Jim slept together: Jane's July 8, 1968 journal entry.

142 discreetly removed the bed railings: Rest of paragraph from Jane's July 5, 1968 journal entry.

143 [Photo]: Jane Britton police file.

143 "Hey, if you're not doing anything": Letter from Jane to her parents, June (unspecified) 1968.

143 Jane had a dream: Jane's journal entry, July 5, 1968.

144 lack of sanitation lowered the threshold: Arthur Bankoff statement, p. 6.

144 Jim, as the oldest student on the dig: Arthur Bankoff statement, pp. 2, 5.

144 "playing professional Central European barbarian": Letter from Jane to her parents, June 29, 1968.

144 Jim ended up doing nine-tenths of the work: Letter from Jane to her parents, June 29, 1968.

144 ran the medical clinic...Jim became the one who patiently: CCLK foreword, p. XXVI.

144 "I've never seen you stagger": Jane's July 5, 1968 journal entry.

144 Jane felt a similar pressure: While Karl did not dispute that this may have been Jane's perception, he wanted to make clear that it was not unheard of for students to switch dissertation topics: "We've had graduate students who started working in the Near East and ended up writing their dissertation on the Maya...Sometimes they would change it in their fourth or fifth year."

144 "She felt everything academically depended": Andrea Bankoff statement, p. 2.

144 bricks: Letter from Jane to parents, July 27, 1968.

144 rodent holes: Letter from Jane to parents, July 4, 1968.

144 Karl told Andrea Bankoff that he was pleased: Andrea Bankoff statement, p. 4.

144 Jim would climb into Jane's trench: Arthur Bankoff statement, pp. 7–8.

144 grew too dim to see anything: Andrea Bankoff statement, p. 4.

144 Airmail stationery, their only connection: Letter from Jane to her parents, July 14, 1968.

144 can of tuna was to be split...peanut butter was supposed to last for two weeks: Arthur Bankoff statement, p. 10.

145 People hallucinated visions of gingerbread: Letter from Jane to her parents, July 27, 1968.

145 many fly bites...chicken walked into her tent, crapped: Letter from Jane to parents, July 4, 1968.

145 centipede crawled into her underwear: Jane's July 5, 1968 journal entry.

145 other than Karl: Phone call with CCLK in 2020; CPD-RM, p. 11.

145 "bless his little antiseptic heart": Letter from Jane to her parents, July 14, 1968.

145 Jim had pink eye: Letter from Jane to her parents, June (unspecified), 1968.

145 a case of hemorrhoids so severe...grumbling, dysenteric stomachs: Arthur Bankoff statement, p. 9.

145 "We are so frail, all of us,": Jane's July 3, 1968 journal entry.

145 even Richard got sick: CPD-RM, p. 10.

145 She told him about the dream: Jane's July 7, 1968 journal entry.

145 *It's going to be just like the past, after all*: Jane's July 8, 1968 journal entry.

145 "I probably should have waited": Letter from Jane to her parents, July 27, 1968.

145 "I think maybe I'd like to be dead": Jane's July 8, 1968 journal entry.

THE LOOP

145 "If this were a mystery novel": Interview with Arthur Bankoff in 2016.

146 Until 2005: This change was formally announced in William C. Kirby's February 2005 annual letter to the faculty. See "The New Tenure Track," *Harvard Magazine*, Sept.–Oct. 2010.

146 Karl was the last junior professor: Interviews with CCLK and Richard Meadow. The next junior professor of archaeology to be tenured was Rowan Flad, in 2012, confirmed with his curriculum vitae. The department's director of administration and operations did not respond to my checker's request to verify this statement.

146 Maybury-Lewis...assistant professor: "David Maybury-Lewis, eminent anthropologist and scholar, 78," *Harvard Gazette*, Dec. 6, 2007.

146 Karl credited his rapid ascension: Phone call with CCLK in 2020.

146 Karl had come back contending: CCLK, "Excavations at Tepe Yahya," 1968, p. 2.

146 in 1970, the Tepe Yahya progress report: CCLK, *Excavations at Tepe Yahya, Iran: 1967–1969 (Progress Report I)*, American School of Prehistoric Research, Bulletin 27, Peabody Museum of Archaeology and Ethnology, Harvard University (1970).

146 the *Boston Globe* celebrated: "Harvard Team Unearths Alexander's Lost Citadel," *Boston Globe*, Jan. 10, 1968.

147 supposed elephant teeth: "Archaeological Unit from Harvard Unearths Lost Fortress in Persia," *Harvard Crimson*, Nov. 12, 1968. On the phone in 2020, Karl did not dispute saying this to the *Crimson*. He did not remember what animal the teeth turned out to have come from: "It could have been horse; it could have been donkey."

147 an ancient Greek historian: "Harvard Team Unearths Alexander's Lost Citadel," *Boston Globe*, Jan. 10, 1968.

GENERAL EXAMS

147 "this Lamberg-Karlovsky person": CPD-DM, p. 28.

147 Jim recounted similar conversations: CPD-JH, p. 17.

148 Ingrid Kirsch said she knew more: CPD-IK, pp. 18–19.

148 "That one person could decide to pass": Phone call with CCLK in 2020.

148 Stephen Williams tried to assure police: CPD-SW, p. 33.

148 The day that Jane had tracked Jim: CPD-SLI, p. 47.

149 terminal master's in the spring of 1968: "Crimson Compass," Harvard Alumni Database.

149 "fundamental misunderstanding": Phone call with CCLK in 2020.

149 he was one of three people on the grading committee: CPD-CCLK 2, p. 32.

INGRID KIRSCH POLICE INTERROGATION

149 This chapter is an excerpt of CPD-IK.

SUCH A TOAD

151 "Everyone was so nice": Interview with Barbara Westman in 2017.

151 Ed Wade, the museum's assistant director: Interview with Ed Wade in 2017.

152 the former head of the Semitic Museum: Interview with Carney Gavin in 2014.

152 "I had no feelings of competition": Phone call with CCLK in 2020.

152 "It takes energy and martinis": Interview with CCLK in 2017.

152 remembered one class where he: Interview with John Terrell in 2017.

152 "We all tell stories about ourselves": Interview with John Terrell in 2017.

152 recognized the role that luck played: Interview with Peter Dane in 2014.

153 "He would paint big, exotic pictures": Interview with Phil Kohl in 2017.

153 people would come just to listen: Interview with Sadie Weber in 2017.

153 "Karl is a dying breed": Interview with Ajita Patel in 2018.

153 Bruce Bourque recalled: Interview with Bruce Bourque in 2017.

153 Elizabeth Stone, had a similar story: Interview with Elizabeth Stone in 2018.

154 "He was," she said: In 2020, CCLK responded that he thought Elizabeth left because she had been unable to do both ancient languages and archaeology at Harvard. And, regardless, funding and scholarship decisions aren't in his hands but under the auspices of the financial aid office—a comment he also offered in response to Bruce Bourque's account. When I took this comment back to Elizabeth, she replied that she had been studying both subjects at Harvard without problem, so it is untrue to say that that motivated her departure. Plus, she may not know exactly how funding works at Harvard, but she knows how it works at other universities where departments get to decide how to allocate their funding and scholarship positions. Therefore, though CCLK did not have sole power, she said, it is likely fair to say he would have had say.

RUTH TRINGHAM

154 This chapter is from interviews with Ruth Tringham in 2017 and 2018.

155 "Dear Karl," it began: C. C. Lamberg-Karlovsky Personal Archive, 1957–2014, Accession Number 2016.113, Box 7: Temp box, Letters 1975/1976, Folder T/U/V, Oct. 16, 1975, Ruth Tringham to CCLK. Reprinted with permission from Ruth Tringham.

157 Decades later, Karl, too, would remember: Phone call with CCLK in 2020.

RICHARD MEADOW

157 This chapter is drawn from CPD-RM.

DAN POTTS

158 Karl's festschrift: "Ingenious Man, Inquisitive Soul: Essays in Iranian and Central Asian Archaeology for C. C. Lamberg-Karlovsky on the Occasion of his 65th Birthday by a Selection of His Students, Colleagues, and Friends," *Iranica Antiqua* 37 (2002).

158 a strange academic tradition: "The Festschrift Is Dead. Long Live the Festschrift!" *Chronicle of Higher Education*, Apr. 13, 2001.

158 Dan Potts's own essay: Dan Potts, "In Praise of Karl," *Iranica Antiqua* 37 (2002): 2–6.

159 Dan was happy to reminisce: The rest of this chapter is from an interview with Dan Potts in 2017.

160 a letter from the NSF chastising Karl: Letter from Eloise Clark (Deputy Asst. Director, Biological and Social Sciences, National Science Foundation) to CCLK, Sept. 30, 1975.

160 later published in a journal: CCLK's Albert Reckitt Archaeological Lecture of 1973 later published in *Proceedings of the British Academy* 59 (1974): 283–319.

160 "Please accept my sincerest apologies": C. C. Lamberg-Karlovsky Personal Archive, 1957–2014, Accession Number 2016.113, Box 7: Temp box, Letters 1975/1976, Folder K/L, Oct. 6, 1975: CCLK to Jim Shaffer. Courtesy of the Harvard University Archives.

160 Shaffer accepted his apology: Email from Jim Shaffer, May 26, 2017, 9:32 p.m.

160 "There is a difference between convergence": Phone call with CCLK in 2020.

160 later claim that Dan had been denied permission: Phone call with CCLK in 2020. Dan's refutation is from a 2020 call with him.

THE DAY OF JANE'S DEATH: KARL'S POINT OF VIEW

162 This chapter is drawn from CPD-CCLK 1.

PUZZLE PIECES

163 The two former graduate students at the beginning of the chapter did not want to be named as sources.

164 Peter Rodman remembered a similar story: Interview with Peter Rodman in 2017.

164 two of only three people: Per Rodman (2017), Ed Franquemont was the third.

164 rule on the books about professors having relationships with undergraduates: The 2015 policy also bans relationships between professors and graduate students, as well as graduate students and undergraduates, if they are teaching, supervising, or evaluating them. See "New Harvard Policy Bans Teacher-Student Relations," *New York Times*, Feb. 5, 2015.

164 "I've had several other expeditions": Interview with CCLK in 2018.

164 Jane wasn't just any student: Interview with David Freidel in 2017.

165 he'd already gotten one from the University of Pittsburgh: Letter from David Landry to CCLK, Nov. 7, 1968.

165 "Harvarditis—a bad case of necessary attachment to the institution": Phone call with CCLK in 2020.

INGRID KIRSCH, POLICE INTERROGATION, CONTINUED

165 This chapter is an excerpt of CPD-IK. It is interesting to note that Don Mitchell also told the CPD about a date Jane had with a French archaeologist, arranged through CCLK: "I don't know his name, but he was an ex-colleague of Lamberg-Karlovsky, who's—I think he was French. I think

he was an archaeologist. And Karlovsky called up one day—actually they called me wondering where Jane was, if I knew. Then they got a hold of her and said well, this friend was in town and they wanted a date, get a date for him just to go out" (CPD-DM, p. 63).

CHRISTINE LESNIAK

167 Ed Wade…had been fired by Karl: Phone call with CCLK and interview with Garth Bowden in 2020.

167 "a very good professional": Interview with Garth Bowden in 2020.

167 intense competition between Karl and Assistant Professor Tom Patterson: Multiple, including interview with David Browman in 2017.

167 didn't remember anything of the sort: Interview with Tom Patterson in 2017.

167 Dan Potts's dissertation: Daniel Potts, "Tradition and Transformation: Tepe Yahya and the Iranian Plateau During the Third Millennium B.C.," PhD dissertation, Anthropology Department, Harvard University, 1980. Pages in question are pp. 539–544.

167 Karl's afterword: Afterword to *The Bronze*

Age Civilization of Central Asia: Recent Soviet Discoveries (Armonk, NY: Sharpe, 1981), edited by Philip Kohl, pp. 386–397.

167 included a footnote reference: *The Bronze Age Civilization of Central Asia: Recent Soviet Discoveries*, edited by Philip Kohl, p. 396 n. 5.

168 both been on the 1971 Tepe Yahya season: Figure F.9, CCLK foreword, p. XXXIV.

168 Someone else from that year: This person asked not to be named.

168 "You wanted to talk to Christine": Interview with Christine Lesniak's sister (name left out for privacy) in 2018.

169 a hit man for the Chinese Mafia: I haven't been able to verify either family legend in newspaper reports.

A SECOND CIPHER

169 This chapter is from an interview with Phil Kohl in 2017.

PHYSICAL EVIDENCE

170 "Hi, this is Becky Cooper": Interview with Boyd Britton in 2016.

170 beginning of a two-year public records battle: My initial request to the MDAO dated July 18, 2016.

170 jurisdiction of the district attorney: "State DAs Decide Who Will Investigate Homicides," *The Enterprise*, Jan. 7, 2016.

170 When I learned this fact: A very big

thank-you to David Grann, who first alerted me to this.

170 though the Cambridge Police no longer had Jane's records: Email from Maeve Ryan, Records Administrator, CPD, May 19, 2015, 3:34 p.m.

170 "Unfortunately, at this time": Letter from Kerry Anne Kilcoyne (MDAO Assistant DA), July 28, 2016.

170 exemption (f): William Francis Galvin, "A Guide to Massachusetts Public Records Law," Division of Public Records, Mar. 2020, p. 21.

171 didn't start until the late '80s: Celia Henry Arnaud, "Thirty Years of DNA Forensics: How DNA Has Revolutionized Criminal Investigations," *Chemical & Engineering News* 95, no. 37 (Sept. 18, 2017): 16–20.

171 the email came through: Email from Boyd, Aug. 3, 2016, 10:51 a.m.

172 Sergeant Sennott gave me nothing: Phone call with Sergeant Sennott in 2016.

172 I had a bit more luck with Brian Branley: Phone call with Brian Branley in 2016.

172 John Fulkerson called me back: The rest of this chapter is from this 2016 interview with John Fulkerson. Note: Fulkerson did not participate in the checking phase of the book. All material concerning him is accurate to the best of my ability.

173 Frug case: E.g., "Mary Joe Frug's Brutal Murder Stunned a Contentious Academic Community," *Boston Sunday Globe*, Aug. 28, 2016.

KARL AT POLICE HEADQUARTERS

174 This chapter is drawn from CPD-CCLK 2.

PAUL DE MAN

175 "What is at stake": CCLK foreword, p. XIX.

175 Schliemann's Troy was likely not Troy: Brian Rose interview on *This American Life* (Episode 689: "Digging Up the Bones"), Dec. 6, 2019.

175 "relentlessly self-promoting amateur archaeologist": Susan Heuck Allen, *Finding the Walls of Troy: Frank Calvert and Heinrich Schliemann at Hisarlik* (Berkeley: University of California Press, 1999), publisher's description.

176 graduate student discovered: "The Case of Paul de Man," *New York Times*, Aug. 28, 1988; see also "The de Man Case," *New Yorker*, Mar. 24, 2014.

176 "a slippery Mr. Ripley": *Harper's*, Feb. 2014 review of Evelyn Barish, *The Double Life of Paul de Man* (New York: Liveright, 2014).

CLIFFORD A. ROCKEFELLER

176 fifty-one years: CCLK curriculum vitae.

176 Karl Lamberg-Karlovsky retired: CCLK became a research professor, which is distinct from being emeritus. See "12. Retired Professors. Description: Professors Emeriti, Research Professor," *FAS Appointment and Promotion Handbook*, Harvard University's Faculty of Arts and Sciences, Office for Faculty Affairs' website.

177 a sheet that described: Chart of box contents in C. C. Lamberg-Karlovsky personal archive, 1957–2014, Harvard University Archives, Accession Number 2016.113.

178 "petulant diatribe": C. C. Lamberg-Karlovsky Personal Archive, 1957–2014, Accession Number 2016.113, Box 1: Letterbox 1996, Folder M, Nov. 28, 1998, Letter Victor Mair to CCLK. Reprinted with permission from Victor Mair.

178 "ecstatic appreciation" of two students: C. C. Lamberg-Karlovsky Personal Archive, 1957–2014, Accession Number 2016.113, Box 6: Letterbox, correspondence A-Z 1965–1969, Folder B, Sept. 26, 1967, J. O. Brew to CCLK. Reprinted with permission from Alan Brew.

178 draft of the textbook he co-wrote: This draft became C. C. Lamberg-Karlovsky and Jeremy Sabloff, *Ancient Civilizations: The Near East and Mesoamerica*, 2nd ed. (Prospect Heights, IL: Waveland Press, 1995).

178 "does not indicate a disinterest in history": C. C. Lamberg-Karlovsky Personal Archive, 1957–2014, Accession Number 2016.113, Box 4, Jerry Sabloff, and CCLK, "Chapter 1: Intellectual Background to the Study of Ancient Civilizations Ancient Views of the Past." Courtesy of the Harvard University Archives.

181 "Field notebook: Site E, J.S.B.": 2015.6.1, C. C. Lamberg-Karlovsky Tepe Yahya expedition records, Peabody Museum of Archaeology & Ethnology, Harvard University.

181 "Tepe Yahya 1969 Site E Field Notebook. By: JSB / []": 2015.6.1, C. C. Lamberg-Karlovsky Tepe Yahya expedition records, Box 3, Folder 3.7.

181 the 1968 Site E notebook: 2015.6.1, C. C. Lamberg-Karlovsky Tepe Yahya expedition records, Box 7, Folder 7.8.

181 "30 June 1968: Removed surface": 2015.6.1, C. C. Lamberg-Karlovsky Tepe Yahya expedition records, Box 7, Folder 7.8, p. 1.

181 "traces of red ochre": 2015.6.1, C. C. Lamberg-Karlovsky Tepe Yahya expedition records, Box 7, Folder 7.8, p. 10.

181 "First day of digging.": 2015.6.1, C. C. Lamberg-Karlovsky Tepe Yahya expedition records, Box 2, Folder 2.6.

182 "Red ochre under and around bone": 2015.6.1, C. C. Lamberg-Karlovsky Tepe Yahya expedition records, Box 7, Folder 7.5.

182 "there are relics which show": "Profs, Cops Differ on Slaying," *New York Post*, Jan. 10, 1969.

182 In 1970, a body was discovered: Thomas Beale, *Excavations at Tepe Yahya, Iran 1967–1975: The Early Periods*, American School of Prehistoric Research, Bulletin 38, Peabody Museum of Archaeology and Ethnology, Harvard University (1986), p. 133.

182 the ulna of one of the arms: Beale, *Excavations at Tepe Yahya*, p. 109.

182 Karl had been quoted as saying: "Profs, Cops Differ on Slaying," *New York Post*, Jan. 10, 1969.

182 "In Period VII, Yahya inhabitants": Beale, *Tepe Yahya: The Early Periods*, p. 263.

THRESHOLDS OF IRRITATION

182 "Today's the day Richard": Jane's journal entry, Aug. 1, 1968.

183 a single piece of chlorite: Beale, *Tepe Yahya: The Early Periods*, p. 109.

183 "prize example of primitive sculpture": "Archaeological Unit from Harvard Unearths Lost Fortress in Persia," *Harvard Crimson*, Nov. 12, 1968.

183 Martie Lamberg-Karlovsky's second day: Letter from Jane to her parents, Aug. 2, 1968.

183 "food, news, and a new face": Martha Lamberg-Karlovsky denied bringing food and medicine with her (2020). However, this version of events taken from three contemporaneous sources: Andrea Bankoff's police statement ("We were all looking forward to Karl's wife coming and bringing food, news, and a new face," p. 4), Jane's journal, and her Aug. 2, 1968, letter home to her parents.

183 Preparation H for Jim's hemorrhoids: Letter from Jane to her parents, Aug. 2, 1968.

183 five-meter wall: Letter from CCLK to Hallam Movius, Sept. 7, 1968.

183 enough for a dissertation topic: Andrea Bankoff statement, p. 4.

184 too exhausted to eke it out: Letter from Jane to her parents, Aug. 2, 1968.

184 "Madame L-K, much as I like her": Jane's journal entry, Aug. 1, 1968.

184 Martie irritated the crew: In response to this section, CCLK said in 2020, "I'm not going to contest the trivial kind of things that they're saying about my wife. That she wore clean clothes, that she did this, that she did that. I mean that is the gossip that takes place on an expedition." In their joint statement, the Bankoffs acknowledged that getting irritated by this behavior was "petty."

184 dressing to the nines: Arthur Bankoff police statement, p. 10; Jane's journal entry, Aug. 5, 1968.

184 "I like her well enough but": Letter from Jane to her parents, Aug. 2, 1968.

184 pet sparrow had made a giant mess: Anecdote from Andrea Bankoff statement, pp. 7–8.

184 Andrea to correct Martie…recounted the incident to Jane: Anecdote from Andrea Bankoff statement, p. 8.

184 "Everyone in heartily bad mood": Jane's journal entry, Aug. 5, 1968.

185 two-Coke ration…archaeology as a cute hobby: Joint statement, p. 8.

185 expected his authority to extend to her as well…*One morning Jane woke up*: Andrea Bankoff statement, p. 8.

185 resupply of peanut butter ("thank Christ"): Jane's journal entry, Aug. 5, 1968.

185 One day, the son of the local khan: There are differing accounts of this story—whether it's the khan (CCLK foreword) or the khan's son (Arthur Bankoff statement; phone call with CCLK in 2020); whether it was a tax on the workers (Arthur Bankoff statement) or a land tax (CCLK foreword and call). I have narrated as closely as possible to CCLK's version. E.g., the detail about the government representative calling in the local gendarmes comes from the CCLK foreword and the phone call. However, CCLK denies the pickax detail, calling it a "fairytale." I have kept this detail in because both Peter Dane (2014 interview) and Arthur Bankoff's statement describe it.

186 Phil Kohl and Peter Dane left early: Phil Kohl told me about getting sick in a 2017 interview. He denied it, however, during the checking process, saying he only got sick on the way home. I have kept this detail in because it appears in Jane's letters home (July 27, 1968, and Aug. 13, 1968), the Andrea Bankoff statement (p. 5), and in the CCLK foreword ("Phil Kohl lost more than thirty pounds in his first field season," p. XXVII).

186 Phil's mother didn't recognize her son: Interview with Phil Kohl in 2017.

186 thirty pounds that summer: CCLK foreword, p. XXVII.

186 the arrival of the visiting archaeologist Benno Rothenberg: Arthur Bankoff statement, p. 11.

186 "we-thought-they-thought mental construction": Andrea Bankoff statement, p. 7.

186 only felt comfortable talking to Jim and Jane: Andrea Bankoff statement, p. 5.

186 "Defamation was by innuendo": Joint statement, p. 10.

186 wouldn't in fact be invited back: Joint statement, p. 9; CPD-CCLK, p. 14.

186 "It wasn't a very human thing to do": Interview with Arthur Bankoff in 2016.

186 "stupid, vicious, jealous bitch": Joint statement, p. 9.

186 "Yes, Boss"-ing him: Interview with CCLK in 2018.

186 Karl found out that Jim had arranged for

Arthur: Anecdote from Arthur Bankoff statement, pp. 3–4.

187 did not remember this incident: Phone call with CCLK in 2020.

187 Karl had bought an entire sheep: This scene is from Andrea Bankoff's police statement (p. 9) and an interview with Arthur Bankoff in 2016. In a 2020 phone call, Martha Lamberg-Karlovsky denied being there for this dinner and CCLK refuted the notion that Jane Britton had anything to do with preparing the meal. Even so, I have used this version of events because the Bankoffs' accounts independently corroborate each other. ("Independent" given the fact that Andrea's statement had been prepared without consultation with Arthur, Arthur had not read the statement in almost fifty years, and they have been divorced for some time.)

KARL'S POLICE INTERROGATION

187 This chapter is an excerpt of CPD-CCLK 2.

FRANKLIN FORD

192 This scene is from interviews with CCLK in 2017 and 2020.

192 "He didn't even ask me": Interview with CCLK in 2017.

2018: MIAMI

195 *Could you sleep last night?*: Email to Don Mitchell, July 26, 2018, 12:43 p.m.

195 since April, when he told me: Interview with John Fulkerson in 2018.

IVA HOUSTON

196 "I think if you were to have called": Interview with Iva Houston in 2016.

198 Gender Archaeology: For foundational texts on the subfield, see *Engendering Archaeology: Women and Prehistory*, edited by Joan Gero and Margaret Conkey (Hoboken, NJ: John Wiley & Sons, 1991), and *Woman, Culture, and Society*, edited by Michelle Rosaldo and Louise

Lamphere (Stanford, CA: Stanford University Press, 1974).

199 Probably not according to the latest evidence: "Early Men and Women Were Equal, Say Scientists," *The Guardian*, May 14, 2015.

200 I spoke to David Mitten: Interview with David Mitten in 2018.

SHE'D HAVE TO NOT BE A WOMAN

200 Nancy Hopkins delivered a speech: Nancy Hopkins, "Mirages of Gender Equality," speech delivered to the fiftieth reunion of the Harvard-Radcliffe Class of 1964.

201 Cora Du Bois arrived: Susan Seymour, *Cora Du Bois: Anthropologist, Diplomat, Agent*

(Lincoln: University of Nebraska Press, 2015), p. 250.

201 only the second woman: "The First Tenured Women Professors at Harvard University," infographic developed by Harvard University's Faculty Development & Diversity, Office of the Senior

Vice Provost, 2011. Professor Helen Maud Cam was the first.

201 take the side door: Seymour, *Cora Du Bois*, p. 264.

201 [Photo]: "Preliminary Report on the Status of Women at Harvard," Women's Faculty Group, Mar. 9, 1970, p. 2.

202 Jane's roommate at Les Eyzies: Alison Brooks interview in 2017; Jane's letters home to her parents in 1966.

202 "For a woman to be good enough for Harvard": Interview with Alison Brooks in 2017.

202 When Sally Bates: Interview with Sally Shankman in 2017.

202 only two or three of the original women: "Two or three" is based on Sally Shankman (2017) and Arthur Bankoff's (2016) memories. None—not even Alison Brooks (2020)—could remember who the other one or two women were in the cohort. It is possible, then, that Alison was the only woman in her cohort who managed to stay through the PhD. This was Paul Shankman's memory (2017). My checker posed this question to Monique Rivera, the Anthropology department's graduate program administrator, but never received a response.

202 "I've never given the PhD to a woman": Interview with Alison Brooks in 2017. Brooks added that Movius eventually did give a PhD to a woman in 1974, but that student was "in a different category because she wasn't really an American as far as Movius was concerned."

202 It didn't take long for Mary Pohl: Paragraphs per interview with Mary Pohl in 2017 and 2019.

203 When Elizabeth Stone: Paragraph per interview with Elizabeth Stone in 2018.

203 When Sally Falk Moore: Paragraphs per interview with Sally Falk Moore (2017) and email from her, Mar. 21, 2020, 6:10 p.m. "Sixteen" is per the 2017 interview, which is consistent with

"Anthropology Moore Is Settling In," *Harvard Crimson*, Dec. 9, 1981.

204 When Alison Brooks visited her daughter: Interview with Alison Brooks in 2017.

204 the pattern of gender discrimination in academia: Hopkins also measured lab space and found that female professors at MIT were given less space than their male counterparts. In 1995, Hopkins led a committee to analyze the status of women faculty in MIT's School of Science, and she also worked on the groundbreaking *Report on Women in Science* in 1999. See *MIT Faculty Newsletter* 11, no. 4 (Mar. 1999). MIT's president Charles Vest endorsed the report, acknowledging the systemic discrimination: "I have always believed that contemporary gender discrimination within universities is part reality and part perception. True, but I now understand that reality is by far the greater part of the balance" ("M.I.T. Admits Discrimination against Female Professors," *New York Times*, Mar. 23, 1999). While MIT's reaction to this report was, in many ways, a model for transformation, the changes were by no means guaranteed to be permanent. In 2019, Hopkins told me that Summers's statements were so enraging because they threatened to undo the still fragile victories just six years after the report was released.

204 Hopkins walked out of the room: "Summers' Remarks on Women Draw Fire," *Boston Globe*, Jan. 17, 2005.

204 a conference about diversity and the sciences: "Diversifying the Science & Engineering Workforce: Women, Under-Represented Minorities, and Their S&E Careers," A Conference of the Science and Engineering Workforce Project (SEWP) at the National Bureau of Economic Research (NBER), Jan. 14–15, 2005.

204 According to the *Guardian*: "Why Women Are Poor at Science, by Harvard President," *The Guardian*, Jan. 18, 2005.

SADIE WEBER

205 This chapter is from an interview with Sadie Weber in 2017, unless otherwise noted.

205 by a committee of academics: A Visiting Committee is appointed to "report on each school, department or administrative unit at the University. Each committee is typically chaired by an Overseer, and includes as members alumni active in the

field and experts from outside Harvard," "Visiting Committee," Harvard Medical School website.

206 split from the Anthro department: "What is HEB?" Department of Human Evolutionary Biology website.

206 When I spoke to Noreen: Interview with Noreen Tuross in 2017.

RICHARD MEADOW

206 This chapter is from interview with Richard Meadow in 2017, unless otherwise noted.

207 tenure track until 2005: William C. Kirby's February 2005 annual letter to the faculty.

207 mandatory retirement age since 1994: The law was passed in 1986, but there was an exemption for tenured professors that expired at the end of 1993: Age Discrimination in Employment Act, 1986, Section 12(d). See also *Ending Mandatory Retirement for Tenured Faculty: The Consequences for Higher Education*, edited by P. Brett Hammond and Harriet Morgan (Washington, DC: National Academy Press, 1991).

207 the numbers were grim: "Though More Women Are on College Campuses, Climbing the Professional Ladder Remains a Challenge," Brown Center Chalkboard of the Brookings Institute, Mar. 29, 2019.

207 A recent report produced by a junior member: Ari Caramanica, "Report from the Gender Imbalance in Academia Conversation Group," Department of Anthropology, Harvard University, May 19, 2019. Caramanica, who produced the report as a College Fellow, said that the Anthropology faculty were very receptive to the suggestions in the report, but she is not sure what they have implemented as official policy. (She has since left Harvard, for reasons unrelated to the report.)

207 Women were disproportionately selected as head teaching fellows: Caramanica, "Gender Imbalance," p. 1.

207 lower publication rates: Caramanica, "Gender Imbalance," p. 2.

207 Other studies conducted nationally: These include Dana Bardolph, "A Critical Evaluation of

Recent Gendered Publishing Trends in American Archaeology," *American Antiquity* 79, no. 3 (2014): 522–540; Scott Hutson, "Institutional and Gender Effects on Academic Hiring Practices," *SAA Bulletin* 16, no. 4 (1998): 19–21, 26; and "Gendered Citation Practices in American Antiquity and Other Archaeological Journals," *American Antiquity* 67 (2002): 331–342.

208 took longer to complete their degrees: Caramanica, "Gender Imbalance," p. 3.

208 first systematic study of sexual harassment and assault: Kathryn Clancy, *et al.*, "Survey of Academic Field Experiences (SAFE): Trainees Report Harassment and Assault," *PLoS One* 9, no. 7.

208 Other research has shown: M. Sandy Hershcovis and Julian Barling, "Towards a Multi-Foci Approach to Workplace Aggression: A Meta-Analytic Review of Outcomes from Different Perpetrators," *Journal of Organizational Behavior* 31 (Dec. 2009): 24–44.

208 Statistically, the most effective way to decrease sexual harassment: Frank Dobbin and Alexandra Kalev, "Training Programs and Reporting Systems Won't End Sexual Harassment. Promoting More Women Will." *Harvard Business Review* 15 (2017): 607–631.

208 first African American graduate student: James Gibbs per Seymour, *Cora Du Bois*, p. 264. Gibbs did not respond to my request for an interview.

209 current dynamics in academia: E.g., "Are We Commodities?" *Chronicle of Higher Education*, Oct. 17, 2010.

209 "It's hard to admit you belong": Interview with Iva Houston in 2017.

PROFESSOR KARKOV

209 *Women After All*: Mel Konner, *Women After All: Sex, Evolution, and the End of Male Supremacy* (New York: W. W. Norton, 2015).

210 "Irv the Perv": Interview with Don Mitchell in 2017; Jill Nash confirmed in 2020.

210 Sarah Hrdy, DeVore's first female graduate student: Interviews with Sarah Hrdy in 2017 and 2020.

210 Kathryn Clancy...credited DeVore: Blog maintained by the Clancy Lab group, Dept. of Anthropology, University of Illinois, Urbana-Champaign, lee-anthro.blogspot.com, Apr. 26, 2010 post.

210 stopped short of saying that DeVore: Interview with Kathryn Clancy in 2020.

210 when we got on the phone: Interview with Mel Konner in 2017.

210 fictional story inspired by Jane's murder: Melvin Konner, "Winter in Bolton," manuscript, edited by John Gardner and L. M. Rosenberg, fall–winter 1981, pp. 1–33.

210 *What animated their 'vague'*: Konner, "Winter in Bolton," p. 9.

211 my way to Chris Boehm: Interview with Chris Boehm in 2017.

211 Jane's murder as an example: Christopher

Boehm, "Gossip and Reputation in Small-Scale Societies: A View from Evolutionary Anthropology," in *The Oxford Handbook of Gossip and Reputation*, edited by Francesca Giardini and Rafael Wittek

(Oxford: Oxford University Press, 2019), pp. 253–275.
211 *"But you don't understand, Sergeant"*: Konner, "Winter in Bolton," p. 30.

THE GRAND JURY

212 grand jury convened for Jane's case: Feb. 3, 1969, per the Grand Jury Summons, Jan. 29, 1969 (CPD file).
212 Conti, a twenty-nine-year-old: This chapter is from interviews with Richard Conti in 2017 unless otherwise noted.
212 His wife's sister had been college roommates: Sally Shankman confirmed this in a 2020 interview.
213 Harvard exploded at nauseating speed: *Harvard Crimson* published an excellent day-by-day summary of 1968–1969 at Harvard: "That Memorable Year, 1968–69...," *Harvard Crimson*, June 12, 1969.
213 In February, discussions for the Radcliffe-Harvard merger began: "That Memorable Year, 1968–69...," see Feb. 22 entry.
213 talks about co-ed living arrangements: "That Memorable Year, 1968–69...," see Feb. 5 entry.
213 degree-granting program in Afro-American Studies: Approved on Apr. 22, 1969, see "African and African American Studies at Harvard: Historical Sources," Harvard Library website.
213 came to a head in early April: See, e.g., "Echoes of 1969," *Harvard Magazine*, Mar.–Apr. 2019.
213 "We felt that we would be the equivalent of the good Germans": Interview with Carol Sternhell in 2014.
213 mentioned in the fifth demand on that list: "Statements on Both Sides at Harvard: Pres. Pusey," *Boston Globe*, Apr. 10, 1969.

213 noon on April 9, 1969: "On Campus," *Radcliffe Quarterly*, June 1969, p. 16.
213 about seventy students: "Echoes of 1969," *Harvard Magazine*, Mar.–Apr. 2019.
213 The next morning, at dawn: "On Campus," *Radcliffe Quarterly*, June 1969, p. 17.
214 wore visored helmets and wielded batons: Jean Bennett, "Echoes of 1969," *Harvard Magazine*, Mar.–Apr.
214 ten thousand galvanized people: Ten thousand is conservative. "Harvard Students Occupy University Hall" page of MassMoments website puts the number between ten thousand and twelve thousand.
214 attendance was less than 25 percent: Ely Kahn, *Harvard: Through Change and Through Storm* (New York: W. W. Norton, 1969), p. 27.
214 appointed themselves protectors of Widener Library: Faculty members included Archibald Cox, Donald Fleming, and Herschel Baker ("Shook the University...," *Harvard Crimson*, June 12, 1969).
214 a month earlier informed Karl: Letter from Franklin Ford to CCLK, Mar. 20, 1969.
214 suffered a minor stroke: "Until the April Crisis...," *Harvard Crimson*, June 12, 1969.
214 "In Winter I hoped for Spring": Stephen Williams, "The Editor's Scrapbasket," *Peabody Museum Newsletter*, summer 1969, p. 5.

SPOTLIGHT

215 email from someone at the *Boston Globe*: Email from Todd Wallack, Apr. 4, 2017, 3:32 p.m.
215 Wallack had made his career on exposing: "Todd Wallack of the *Boston Globe* to Receive NEFAC's 2018 Freedom of Information Award," *New England First Amendment Coalition*, Jan. 25, 2018.
215 bottom in terms of government transparency: "Mass. Agencies Often Limit Access to Records," *Boston Globe*, July 18, 2015.
215 only state that maintains: "Massachusetts

Public Records Law among the Country's Most Restrictive," *MuckRock*, Oct. 18, 2018. This was even after the new public records law (H4333; the first since the state's law was enacted in 1973) went into effect on Jan. 1, 2017.
215 quoted Thomas Fiedler: "Mass. Agencies Often Limit Access to Records," *Boston Globe*, July 18, 2015.
216 Todd Wallack told me: Interview with Todd Wallack in 2017.

THE NEW SUSPECT

216 "bumping for Jane": "Pink Panther" Web-sleuths post #684, Oct. 9, 2014; "Pink Panther" Websleuths post #707; Feb. 18, 2015; etc.
216 "I feel obliged as a priest": Boyd Britton Web-sleuths post #741, Jan. 15, 2016.
216 "Unsolved crime threads on WS never die": "Ausgirl" Websleuths post #701, Nov. 29, 2014.
217 "This all happened a very long time ago": Don Mitchell Websleuths post #799, May 12, 2016.

217 *Lee Parsons is due to leave*: Letter from Stephen Williams to Hallam Movius, Jan. 20, 1969, found in 998-27-40/14628.2, Hallam L. Movius, Jr. papers, Peabody Museum of Archaeology & Ethnology, Harvard University.
217 On the phone, Don sounded: Interview with Don Mitchell in 2017.

THE INCENSE NIGHT

218 reminded Don of a black walnut tree: Inter-view with Don Mitchell in 2017.
218 Lee had joined the museum in the fall of 1968: CPD-LP 1, p. 5.
218 Handsome, but not overly so: Description of Parsons from Don Mitchell (2017) and Richard Rose photos.
218 "marginal somehow. Just off": Interview with Bruce Bourque in 2017.
218 "You're afraid if he smiled, his face would fall [off]": CPD-IK, p. 52.
218 listen to records on his hi-fi set: Interview with Bruce Bourque in 2017.
218 Don had seen Lee at a few parties: Interview with Don Mitchell in 2017.
219 first incident...November 1968: Interview with Don Mitchell in 2017; CPD-DM; CPD-LP 1; CPD-JM 2.
219 finishing up their meal: Interview with Don Mitchell in 2017; CPD-LP 1.
219 teaching one of Jane's classes that fall: Jane Britton's Radcliffe student file; CPD-LP 1.
219 Don drove everyone over: CPD-DM; CPD-LP 1.
219 wall-to-wall white shag: Interview with

Don Mitchell in 2017; Jill Nash response to checking memo (2020); she remembers it as white wool.
219 size of five or six cigarettes bunched together: Don Mitchell interview in 2017, which tracks with what Lee Parsons told police (CPD-LP 2, p. 20): "They're about six or eight cylinders that they wrap up in a cornhusk, and you burn the insides."
219 on an aluminum ashtray: Jill Nash response to checking memo (2020); CPD-LP 2, p. 37.
219 burned a hole: Don Mitchell (2017); Jill Nash response to checking memo (2020); CPD-LP 2, p. 36.
219 "As Richard Pryor would say"...*This is too heavy*: Interview with Don Mitchell in 2017.
219 she wanted to stay: Interview with Don Mitchell in 2017; CPD-LP 1, p. 5.
219 didn't think that she would cheat on Jim: Interview with Don Mitchell in 2017.
219 3 a.m. walk home: CPD-JM 2, p. 48; CPD-LP 1, p. 5. (Don thought they left around 4 or 4:30 in the morning: CPD-DM, p. 63.)
219 worried that Jane had realized, too late: Inter-view with Don Mitchell in 2017.

THE DELUGE

220 a deluge of emails: Emails from Don Mitchell, Apr. 5, 2017, 9:25 p.m.; Apr. 6, 2017, 4:15 p.m.; Apr. 6, 2017, 7:45 p.m.; Apr. 6, 2017, 8:59 p.m.; etc.
220 "We can take you to 14,000'": Email from Don Mitchell, Apr. 8, 2017, 7:30 p.m.

220 "It might cross your mind": Email from Don Mitchell, Apr. 5, 2017, 9:25 p.m.

SLEUTHS

221 helped moderate a subreddit: reddit.com/r/UnsolvedMysteries.
221 Alyssa's voice was warm: Interview with Alyssa Bertetto in 2017.

222 abruptly left Harvard in 1970: Lee Parsons obituary by Michael Coe.
222 moved to St. Louis, Missouri: *Steven DeFillippo & Lee Parsons v. Lowell Nations D/B/A Nations Roof-ing Company*, Cause No. 407153, Petition, Circuit

Court of the County of St. Louis, Missouri, Apr. 10, 1978.

222 Lee and his wife had divorced: Interviews with Anne Moreau in 2017 and 2020.

222 he lived there with a man: *DeFillippo & Parsons v. Lowell Nations.*

222 ending up in Florida: Letter from Charles D. Barnard to Judge Zebedee Wright re: *State of Florida v. Lee Allen Parsons*, Oct. 18, 1991.

222 his last will and testament: Last Will and Testament of Lee Allen Parsons, Broward County Commission 33862, signed Dec. 30, 1992.

222 He was born in 1950: Public birth records.

222 Stephen was buried in Woburn, Massachusetts: Last Will and Testament of Lee Allen Parsons.

THE SECOND INCIDENT

223 a few weeks after the Incense Night: Interview with Don Mitchell in 2017.

223 Jim was in Cambridge, visiting…Jane had wanted him to see the artifacts: CPD-JM 2, p. 37.

223 Jane, Jill, and Don all knew there was only one person it could be: CPD-JM 2, p. 37.

223 once more after the Incense Night: Interview with Don Mitchell in 2017; CPD-JM 2, p. 40; CPD-LP 2, p. 11.

223 talked to him through the door: CPD-JM 2, p. 40.

223 Don noticed that Jane's face hardened into a quiet panic: Interview with Don Mitchell in 2017.

223 *What happened the night of the incense party*, Don wondered: Interview with Don Mitchell in 2017.

223 identified himself by yelling up the stairwell: CPD-JM 2, p. 40.

223 "I'll take care of it," Jane said: Through "turn off my typewriter," CPD-JM 2, pp. 37–39.

224 *She is putting on quite a show for Lee*, Jill thought: CPD-JM 2, p. 20.

224 Jill peered out of her doorway…all dressed up: CPD-JM 2, p. 40.

224 Jill wanted to look out the window to be sure: Exchange from CPD-JM 2, p. 20.

THE CAPE LIFTS

224 I called Karl: This chapter is drawn from my interview with CCLK in 2017.

225 I wanted to believe him: I have not yet been able to corroborate that Truman Capote was interested in Jane Britton's story.

226 one of Jane's undergraduate mentors: Interview with Bill Simmons in 2017.

226 "my father was killed in Auschwitz": Karl Othmar Von Lamberg, Identification Number 62376, Document Number 41205, Arrest Data from the Vienna Gestapo Reports, per the Holocaust Survivors and Victims Database of the United States Holocaust Memorial Museum.

227 the vampire's cape of legend lifted: Recent graduate students were absolutely sure that CCLK used to walk around the Peabody in a cape, but after speaking to dozens of graduate students, whose collective tenure at Harvard spanned decades, I realized that no one ever actually saw him wear one at the museum. (In 2017, CCLK told me he owned one—his father's—but he doesn't remember wearing it to work.)

THE DEAD. THE NEAR-DEAD. THE JUST-DEAD

228 In the early-morning hours: This chapter is from CPD-JM 2, unless otherwise noted. Looking back at what she said in 1969, Jill wrote in 2020, "This is all too much of a muchness. If Jane had not been murdered, I would never think this remarkable. The cops pressed us on stuff, and I really didn't know what they wanted."

229 hoping that the ring hadn't stirred Jill: CPD-DM, p. 4.

229 as Don walked to the bathroom: CPD-DM, p. 4; Interview with Don Mitchell in 2017.

229 *Well, Jane's done it again*, Don thought: CPD-DM, p. 5.

229 He hoped that it would work out all right: CPD-DM, p. 5.

229 Jill heard footsteps: From here to "muffled noises of two men talking," CPD-JM 1, pp. 4–6.

229 a large mounting board kept falling off the wall: CPD-DM, p. 6.

229 Don waited outside: CPD-DM, p. 8.

229 Jill walked into Jane's apartment: CPD-JH, p. 11.

229 call the health service: CPD-JM 1, p. 10.

229 Don took over: CPD-JM 1, p. 11.
229 no one could remember the Cambridge Police's number: CPD-DM, p. 11.
230 9-1-1 didn't yet exist in Cambridge: "Boston, Brookline to Dial 911 in Fall to Speed Police Calls," *Boston Globe*, Sept. 4, 1972; Cambridge not included in list of communities that use 911: "Randolph, Quincy Using Emergency No.," *Boston Globe*, Aug. 16, 1971.
230 Don took the book from him: CPD-DM, p. 11.
230 Don tried to reach Jane's family: CPD-DM, pp. 13–14 and interview with Don Mitchell in 2017.
230 Jim kept repeating, "You should call": CPD-DM, p. 12.
230 "Maybe we should take her pulse": CPD-JM 1, p. 12.

230 Don began to doubt himself: Here to "when the police were going to show up" from CPD-DM, pp. 12–13.
230 Don thought about how alive Jane had been: Interview with Don Mitchell in 2017.
230 Don's memory of Jim Humphries dropped out: Here to "loosed with sorrow," interview with Don Mitchell in 2017.
230 *I heard groans and heaves from grief*: Don Mitchell, "Hill Training in Forest Lawn Cemetery," unpublished.
231 For the first, and he thinks, only time: Interviews with Don Mitchell in 2017 and 2019. In her 2020 response to the checking memo, Jill Nash said she had no recollection of this: "Don was not demonstrative."

HAWAII

231 Don Mitchell and I sat: This chapter is from interviews with Don Mitchell in 2017 unless otherwise noted.
233 movies in the Square: In her response to the checking memo, Jill Nash said she did not remember movies or buying records.
233 [Photo]: Photograph by Don Mitchell.
233 "If I die, you should marry Jane": CPD-DM, p. 17.

235 Jill, I would later find out: Interview with Mary McCutcheon in 2017. In her response to the checking memo, Jill explained that she kept the largest of the three rugs until about three years ago, "when it was so worn in places, I thought it should be recycled."

LIEUTENANT JOYCE'S LETTER

236 [Photo]: Letter from Det. Lt. Joyce to Jill and Don Mitchell, Jan. 8, 1979 (MSP file).

THE CAMBRIDGE POLICE

237 Don wasted very little time: Letter from Don Mitchell to Det. Lt. Joyce, Jan. 22, 1979 (MSP file).
237 letter in December 1969: Letter from Det. Lt. Joyce to Jill and Don Mitchell, Jan. 8, 1979.
237 difference between Joyce and the Cambridge cops: The rest of this chapter is from interviews with Don Mitchell in 2017 unless otherwise noted. Details concerning Jill were cross-checked in her 2020 checking memo. (Jill wrote that the cops also made her look at Jane's autopsy photos.)
238 pick out the outfit she was to be buried in: Jill Nash wrote that she did not remember this.
238 a relic, some later speculated: Class taught by James Deetz, per Susan Kelly notes from interview with Paul Shankman, July 31, 1996 (police file). Jane was in a class taught by Professor Deetz (Anthropology 207) the fall of her junior year (Jane Britton's Radcliffe student file).

238 Jane normally kept it by her coffee table: CPD-BB, p. 32.
239 certainly gave the Mitchells the impression: Don Mitchell Websleuths post #381, June 17, 2014.
239 police officer returned: Sennott also asked Don Mitchell about this on July 17, 2017 (transcript; MSP file).
239 Perhaps it was Detective Giacoppo: I emailed Don Mitchell eight photographs of CPD officers who were involved in Jane's case to see if he could identify the officer who asked him to photograph the fingerprint (Mar. 8, 2020). None of the photos were labeled. Don picked out the photo of former Detective M. Michael Giacoppo as the only possible. (He also correctly identified the photo of Lt. Leo Davenport.)
239 According to the *Boston Globe*: "Mystery Fingerprints at Slaying Scene May Belong to Jane

Britton's Killer, Say Cambridge Police," *Boston Globe*, Jan. 13, 1969.

240 Don took a number of photos: Don Mitchell's Nikon F and tripod setup to try to capture the fingerprint on the window in question is visible on page 4 of "Color Slides of Crime Scene" (CPD file). The windowpane was removed from its frame and propped up in the kitchen to better capture the print. Don emailed me a recent photo of the same tripod, which is still in his possession (Mar. 8, 2020, 2:06 p.m.).

240 [Photo]: Photograph by Don Mitchell.

241 *About a year or perhaps even two:* Letter from Don Mitchell to Det. Lt. Joyce, Jan. 22, 1979 (MSP file).

241 He had died on expedition six months before: Peter Harrison and Phyllis Messenger, "Dennis Edward Puleston, 1940–1978," *American Antiquity* 45, no. 2 (Apr. 1980): 272–276.

FINAL DAYS IN HAWAII

242 Back on Don's couch: This chapter is from interviews with Don Mitchell in 2017 unless otherwise noted.

242 Bach's Toccata in F Major: Particularly Michael Murray's version, Track #2 on *Bach and Franck Organ Works*, 1979.

242 "She's just sitting on top of everyone else": Don later sent me a photo of Jane playing the piece at his wedding. His description tracks; her hair was also covered with a white cloth.

ERASURE AND ARTIFACTS

243 to talk to Michael Coe: Interview with Michael Coe in 2017.

243 "We simply repressed it or faked it": "In and Out of the Closet at Harvard, 1653–1998," *Harvard Magazine*, Jan.–Feb. 1998.

245 emailed me . . . with the news: Email from Dan Potts, June 4, 2017, 1:29 p.m.

245 I got off the train in San Jose: The rest of the chapter is from my interview with Elisabeth Handler in 2017.

JANE'S LETTER TO ELISABETH

246 *Saturday 27 July 1968*: Letter from Jane to Elisabeth Handler, July 27, 1968.

BOYD IN PERSON

247 The doorbell of my cousins' house: This chapter is from an interview with Boyd Britton in 2017 unless otherwise noted.

248 "Let all the poisons": Robert Graves, *I, Claudius* (New York: Harrison Smith and Robert Haas, 1934).

249 getting sober: Boyd has been sober since early 2011.

249 "My sister really did not": In 2020, Boyd added, "Jane never got the opportunity."

250 fiftieth reunion for Radcliffe: The fiftieth reunion was May 21–25, 2017.

250 The thirtieth reunion students would join: The thirty-fifth, fortieth, and forty-fifth reunions were held in the fall that year: "Fall in with Classmates," *Harvard Magazine*, May–June 2014.

FAMILY SILENCE

252 After Jane died, Boyd tried: This chapter is drawn from interviews with Boyd (2014–2020) unless otherwise noted.

252 mention his own daughter in his replies: Records of the Radcliffe College Office of the Administrative Vice-President, 1959–1972 (inclusive),

Radcliffe College, RG IIA, Series 1, Schlesinger Library Archives.

252 J. Boyd had grown up in St. Louis, Missouri: "J. Boyd Britton; Was Chemist, Executive, Radcliffe Officer; 93," *Boston Globe*, Oct. 29, 2002.

252 banjo in dance bands on the river boats: "J.

Boyd Britton; Was Chemist, Executive, Radcliffe Officer; 93," *Boston Globe*, Oct. 29, 2002.

252 first in sales, then management: J. Boyd Britton curriculum vitae, Britton family file.

252 married a woman in Springfield, Illinois: Interview with Charlie Britton in 2017.

253 just three months later: Confirmed with Boyd Britton military records, National Personnel Records, Department of Defense.

253 "I had the feeling they would": Susan Kelly notes from interview with Elisabeth Handler, May 24, 1996 (police file).

FOR BOYD R. BRITTON FROM JBB

255 Boyd called me the morning: This chapter is from an interview with Boyd Britton in 2017 unless otherwise noted.

255 "Jane Britton Murder Files. Other Family Papers": Britton family file.

255 [Photo]: Photograph by Becky Cooper.

JANE BRITTON FAMILY FILES

257 "Can't say I mind contemplating": Letter from Jane to her father, July 20, 1965.

257 a guinea pig holding the French flag: Letter from Jane to her parents, July 20, 1965.

257 "Pew! Peppermint-flavored envelopes": Letter from Jane to her parents, June 25, 1964.

257 "Greetings to the postman from Gay, Exotic Les Eyzies": Letter from Jane to her parents, Aug. 7, 1965.

257, 258 [Photos]: Britton family file, courtesy Boyd Britton.

258 his cover letter that read: Letter from CCLK to J. Boyd Britton, Dec. 21, 1979.

259 save them for her for that reason: Letter from Jane to her parents, July 16, 1965.

259 *Dearest Muddah, Dahlink Faddah*: Letter from Jane to her parents, July 16, 1965.

259 *I wouldn't want to do anything if I*: Letter from Jane to her father, July 22, 1964.

259 *Did I ever tell you after that amazing dinner*: Letter from Jane to her parents, July 14, 1968.

259 *Had a letter from Bwad (pre-Cal)*: Letter from Jane to her parents, July 27, 1968.

259 was a reference to Jerry Roth: Letter from Jane to her parents, Feb. 11, 1965.

LIE DETECTOR TEST

260 The lie detector machine: Description from "The Lie Detector Confirms His Story," *Life Magazine*, May 15, 1964, and cross-checked with "Polygraph with Improved Cardiac Monitoring," Lafayette Instrument Co., Inc, Patent Number 4940059, July 10, 1990. Leonard Harrelson, the expert in the *Life* article, administered the second round of tests in Jane's case ("Grand Jury

Hears Girl's Slaying," *Boston Herald Traveler*, Feb. 4, 1969).

260 "What was fun about the lie detector test": The remainder of this chapter is from an interview with CCLK in 2017. As far as I have been able to determine, no records of the lie detector test questions or results exist.

KARL IN PERSON

261 I ran across Harvard Yard to Church Street: This chapter is from my interview with CCLK in 2017.

WRESTLING

264 It was warm out: Scene from interviews with Peter Timms (2017), John Yellen (2017), and CCLK (2020). The memories differed slightly (over details like whether Karl climbed into the ring, who introduced him to the promoter, etc.). The scene as

written sticks to as many details as possible consistent with all three sources. The key difference is that CCLK does not remember the top of his cane tumbling off.

264 smelled like popcorn and pizza and alcohol: "In

City's Wrestling Prime, No Holds Were Barred," *Boston Globe*, Sept. 26, 2004.

264 "Wrestling presents human suffering": Roland Barthes, *Mythologies: The Complete Edition in a New Translation*, translated by Richard Howard and Annette Lavers (New York: Hill and Wang, 2012), p. 8.

264 The good defeated the bad: "In City's Wrestling Prime, No Holds Were Barred," *Boston Globe*, Sept. 26, 2004.

2018: LAND IN BOSTON

269 The scene took place on July 30, 2018.

BELIEF VERTIGO

271 Todd Wallack's *Globe* article: "A Cold Case, a Cold Reality: Records Are Closed," *Boston Globe*, June 18, 2017.

271 last round of DNA testing…was in 2006: This refers to the last time *any* DNA was tested in relation to Jane's case. The last time the crime scene sample itself was tested was 2004 (MSP Crime Lab report dated Aug. 18, 2004).

271 Karl wrote to say: Email from CCLK, June 18, 2017, 11:21 a.m.

271 Don Mitchell was rattled by readers' comments: Email from Don Mitchell, July 11, 2017, 1:33 p.m.

271 A lawyer reached out to offer: LinkedIn message from Robert Bertsche, June 18, 2017, 3:41 a.m.

271 threaten escalating the matter: Letter from Robert Bertsche to Rebecca Murray, June 20, 2017.

271 Mike Widmer, it turned out: The rest of this chapter is from interviews with Mike Widmer in 2017.

271 UPI article, syndicated in *Stars and Stripes*: "Girl 22 Beaten to Death," *Pacific Stars and Stripes*, Jan. 9, 1969.

272 twenty-four reprints to two: Roger Tatarian (then editor-in-chief at UPI), internal UPI document, Jan. 8, 1969.

RICHARD MICHAEL GRAMLY

274 archaeologist named Anne Abraham: Bill Fitzhugh, "Tribute to Explorer Lost in Labrador," *Smithsonian* 7, no. 9 (Dec. 1976).

274 devolved into gossip about Gramly: See, e.g., Websleuths posts circa late Aug. 2014–Oct. 2014.

274 In 2016, Boyd mentioned: Interview with Boyd Britton in 2016.

274 written to Lieutenant Joyce: Letter from Don Mitchell to Det. Lt. Joyce, Jan. 22, 1979 (MSP file).

274 I spoke with Bill Fitzhugh: Interview with Bill Fitzhugh in 2017.

274 Over the phone, Gramly: Interview with RMG in 2017.

275 "Jane never got justice": "A Cold Case, a Cold Reality: Records Are Closed," *Boston Globe*, June 18, 2017.

276 email from Todd Wallack: Email from Todd Wallack, June 20, 2017, 3:54 p.m.

276 a Copper Age site: The dig, run by Kaman and

Yavor Boyadziev, was part of the Balkan Heritage Field School.

277 Ted's letter to the Cambridge Police: Letter from Ted Abraham to Sgt. Nagle, Aug. 23, 1996 (CPD file).

277 fought unsuccessfully to sue: "In the Matter of George Abraham, Claiming as Father of Anne Abraham, Deceased, and Smithsonian Institution, Washington, D.C.," Docket No. 84–108, Hearing Sept. 14, 1984, Issued Oct. 30, 1984, United States Department of Labor.

277 I got an email from Ted: Email from Ted Abraham, June 20, 2017, 5:34 p.m.

277 in the *Smithsonian* article by Bill Fitzhugh: Fitzhugh, "Tribute to Explorer Lost in Labrador."

278 [Photo]: Courtesy Bill and Lynne Fitzhugh.

278 he did, in fact, know Jane Britton: Interview with RMG in 2017.

MICKEY

279 It was Gramly's first semester: This chapter is from my interviews with RMG in 2017, unless otherwise noted.

279 six foot one: License details for RMG (MDAO file).

279 A year younger than Jane: Public birth records.

279 certificate listed "violence": Aug. 6, 1957, divorce certificate, Jefferson County, Alabama Department of Health, Bureau of Vital Statistics. When I spoke with RMG in 2020, he said he wasn't aware that his father had hit his mother, but he wouldn't be surprised. "My father was a wonderful person," Gramly shared, but his father had hit him, too.

279 As a child, Mickey: This section from interviews with people who knew Gramly from the neighborhood. Names left out by request.

280 Ritchie sent a cohort of young men: Ritchie details from interview with Bruce Bourque in 2017. In 2020, Gramly agreed and added, "Ritchie's idea of heaven was being elbow-deep in red ochre."

280 *The Hunting Peoples*: Carleton Coon, *The Hunting Peoples* (Gretna, LA: Pelican, 1971).

280 she was drawing for Coon: Coon also wrote that Jane drew artifacts for him in his CPD "Report of Statement," Jan. 10, 1969 (CPD file).

A SCHOLAR OF REMAINS

282 Scrutin-eyes laid out a damning case: "Scrutin-eyes" first posted on Aug. 14, 2014 (Websleuths post #598). "Scrutin-eyes" never replied to my request for an interview.

282 "macabre handling of human remains": "Scrutin-eyes" Websleuths post #604, Aug. 15, 2014.

282 Gramly had gone rogue: "Scrutin-eyes" Websleuths post #645, Aug. 20, 2014.

282 He had been forbidden from digging: "Scrutin-eyes" Websleuths post #598, Aug. 14, 2014.

282 "often flew off the handle": "Scrutin-eyes" Websleuths post #604, Aug. 15, 2014.

282 let his membership in the Society for American Archaeology lapse: RMG confirmed in a 2020 interview. He also said he renewed it for a time, but is not currently a member.

282 "it says quite clearly in the By-Laws of the Society": Cheryl Ann Munson, Marjorie Melvin Jones, and Robert Fry, "The GE Mound: An ARPA Case Study," *American Antiquity* 60, no. 1 (Jan. 1995): 138. In an April 12, 2020, letter to me, Gramly wanted to make clear that he "cannot think of any time that [he] sold, exchanged, or 'transacted' artifacts discovered on his digs for personal gain," and he "never paid for labor (my own or anyone else's) by giving away scientific specimens."

282 compilation of questionnaires: "The Amateur Archaeologist," *American Society for Amateur Archaeology* 1, no. 1 (fall 1994): 21.

282 Gramly—and Canisius College . . . had indeed been sued: *State of New York, et al. v. Gramly, et al.*, US District Court, Western District of New York (Buffalo), 1:99-cv-01045-WMS-HKS. Case filed Dec. 28, 1999. Settled July 7, 2000.

282 NAGPRA, the 1990 federal law: Julia Cryne, "NAGPRA Revisited: A Twenty-Year Review of Repatriation Efforts," *American Indian Law Review* 34, no. 1 (2009–2010): 99–122.

282 "violated common decency": "Landmark Settlement Protects Native Burial Site," NY State Office of the AG press release, July 18, 2000.

282 Gramly argued that the cardboard storage: Interview with RMG in 2020.

283 Jason Neralich was an amateur archaeologist: Neralich did not reply to a request to comment.

283 mischaracterization of site protocol: Interview with RMG in 2020; letter from RMG, Apr. 12, 2020. In "Return to Olive Branch: Excavations 2002–2005," *American Society for Amateur Archaeology* 13, nos. 1–2 (Jan. 2008): 61, RMG refers to the bifaces as "The Neralich Cache."

283 One young academic: Interview with "young academic" in 2018.

284 The user, macoldcase, feared: Interview with "MCC" in 2018.

284 Scrutin-eyes summed up the case against Gramly: "Scrutin-eyes" Websleuths post #608, Aug. 16, 2014.

THE THREE SUSPECTS

285 I got a call from an unknown number: This chapter is from an interview with Stephen Loring in 2017.

ON THE DIG

287 a text from Don Mitchell: Text from Don Mitchell, June 28, 2017, 3:55 a.m. (Bulgaria time).

288 segment on public television: "Cold Case: The Murder of Jane Sanders Britton, 48 Years Later," *Greater Boston*, WGBH, June 28, 2017.

288 national database known as CODIS: To be very precise, CODIS is the *software* that searches the database.

288 that was started in 1990: "Combined DNA Index System (CODIS)," Laboratory Services, FBI website.

MARY MCCUTCHEON

289 I called Mary McCutcheon: Interview with Mary McCutcheon in 2017.

289 Mary told me she met Gramly: In 2020, RMG confirmed many of the details in Mary's account. He also sent me a copy of his unpublished *Diary of a Young Man (June 1, 1968–Sept. 1, 1971)*, though the

section he sent me covers only June 1–29, 1968. He wrote that he began "this 'project' 10–12 years ago and dropped it." In the following chapter, I indicate anywhere that RMG's memory differs from McCutcheon's.

290 [Photo]: Courtesy Mary McCutcheon.

THE ROAD TRIP

291 Mick packed the bones in the trunk of the car: RMG wrote that this was his plan more than a week before the trip. "Will give up my sub-lease on the 12th—the day we drive down to Laredo and catch the train to Mexico City.... The trunk and the back seat will have to be crammed with stuff—including the human skeletal remains and artifacts from the Boys School site" (June 2, 1968 entry in *Diary of a Young Man*).

291 agent asked them to pop the trunk: RMG confirmed in a 2020 interview. He did not write about the incident in *Diary*, but noted that when he crossed the border on his return, "One of the US border guards remembered who I was and spoke up for me during the inspection."

291 A fer-de-lance: RMG's *Diary* states that they stayed at Palenque (June 14–16, 1968), but he makes no mention of being perched atop the

temple during the storm. Instead, he writes that "we were comfortable and dry within the temple." He also writes that the fer-de-lance crossed *his* path in the morning, not *theirs*.

291 Mary at her family home: RMG wrote about this visit in his June 27 and 28, 1968, entries in *Diary*.

292 continued corresponding with him: RMG wrote about their summer correspondence in *Diary*, but by his account he had already made peace with the fact that he and McCutcheon were not meant to be: "Such a long-distance relationship could never be practical. But it did not mean we had no deep feelings for each other.... For me no relationship with Mary could just be fun and casual. If it could not be total, then better none at all." His entries, however, do not continue into the fall.

THE GOLDEN GIRLS

293 Through the years: This chapter is from multiple interviews with Mary McCutcheon in 2017.

294 Patricia had given over a den in her house: Author's visit.

294 Mary and Patricia met with the DA's office: Adrienne Lynch, "Additional Notes ADA on Investigation 2017," undated (MDAO file).

294 the "Golden Girls": Adrienne Lynch, "Additional Notes ADA on Investigation 2017," undated (MDAO file).

ANNE ABRAHAM

295 *Stretching away into the interior*: Anne's diary entry from July 21, 1976. (As I wrote in the book, Anne only sporadically dated her entries, and she

tended to write about multiple days in one sitting, so pegging her entries to calendar days was challenging. Based on her changing from present to past tense mid-Aug. 1 entry, I believe she started an entry on Aug. 1, and continued it on Aug. 5, the same evening she wrote about Aug. 2–4. According to this timeline, her last entry is dated Aug. 6, which corresponds to the date of her disappearance in the Smithsonian Report. Where the date of the entry is unclear below, I've pegged it to the beginning of the paragraph instead. Also, if my description or timeline varies from the one set out in the Smithsonian Report, I have indicated why and how in subsequent source notes.)

295 *Tongait*, or "place of spirits": Anne's diary entry from July 21, 1976.

295 it was Anne's sixth season in Labrador: Smithsonian Report, Part 2, p. 23.

295 Bill as a teaching assistant: Interview with Ted Abraham in 2017.

295 Anne impressed everyone: Description of Anne from Lynne Fitzhugh (2017) unless otherwise noted.

296 On one of her last mornings: Anne's diary entry from July 25, 1976.

296 "the land God gave to Cain": As quoted in Fitzhugh, "Tribute to Explorer Lost in Labrador," p. 112.

296 "pure, grandiose country, stark": As quoted in Fitzhugh, "Tribute to Explorer Lost in Labrador," p. 112.

296 "Labrador's…most lethal climates": Lynne Fitzhugh, *The Labradorians: Voices from the Land of Cain* (St. John's, NF: Breakwater, 1999), p. 17.

297 the mythic Ramah chert quarries: Interview with Bill Fitzhugh in 2017.

297 Chert, a kind of quartz: "Quartz, Chert, and Flint," Department of Geology and Planetary Science's website, University of Pittsburgh.

297 Gramly, an assistant professor of geology at Stony Brook: Smithsonian Report, Appendix 3.

297 met only once before: Smithsonian Report, Part 1, p. 2.

297 175 miles away: Smithsonian Report, Part 1, p. 3.

297 held each other until the morning: Anne's diary entry from July 25, 1976.

297 last time Lynne Fitzhugh saw Anne: Interview with Lynne Fitzhugh in 2017.

297 Thalia Point where Anne loaded in: Smithsonian Report, Part 1, p. 3.

297 camp in the footsteps of an old Moravian mission: Smithsonian Report, Part 1, p. 3.

297 landscape was marshier: Anne's diary entry, paragraph starting "West of the mission."

297 Dog's Nose, a big basalt cliff: Interview with Lynne Fitzhugh in 2017.

298 sound traveled so clearly: Interview with Stephen Loring in 2017.

298 Anne could hear the waterfall: Anne's diary entry, paragraph starting "Moist, misty morning."

298 "My ears are tired of his voice": Anne's diary entry, paragraph starting "The next day I got up."

298 tell Anne about his time in Africa: Anne's diary entry, paragraph starting "Mike told me about mambas."

298 "I went up a chimney and the shale": Here through "Anne had found a Ramah chert quarry," Anne's diary entry, paragraph starting "We started for a short hike."

299 [Photo]: Photograph by RMG.

299 one-quarter of a mile long: Fitzhugh, "Tribute to Explorer Lost in Labrador."

299 "'Twas a sacrifice to the mountains": Anne's diary entry, paragraph starting "Mike fixed supper."

299 "Time went unrecognized": Anne's diary entry, paragraph starting "The time went unrecognized." Red ochre detail also appears in "Brother Tells of His Labrador Search for D.C. Woman," *Washington Post*, Aug. 16, 1976.

299 Mike signaled to Anne: Description from Anne's diary entry, paragraph starting "My period started and I felt grubby."

300 The following day was overcast: Anne's diary entry, paragraph starting "The next day (I am confused as to days)."

300 the one after wasn't much better: Anne's diary entry, paragraph starting "The next day I got up."

300 Anne put on her waders and tried: Anne's diary entry, paragraph starting "Today I tried." Anne's attempt to find another route to the quarry this day—as well as the goose detail—also in Smithsonian Report, Part 1, p. 6.

300 so still it felt strange: Anne's diary entry, paragraph starting "The most unusual thing"; Smithsonian Report, Part 1, p. 7.

300 hacking at a caribou antler…the radio: Anne's diary entry, paragraph starting "The most unusual thing."

300 About twenty-four hours later: Smithsonian Report, Part 1, p. 10; Report by Cst. W.W. MacDonald, Corner Brook. Sub-Division of the RCMP, Oct. 18, 1976, p. 2; Transcript of Interview between Cst. W.W. MacDonald & RMG, Nain, Labrador, Aug. 11, 1976, p. 7.

THE SECOND CALL

300 "When you're in a remote tent camp": This chapter is from an interview with RMG in 2017 unless otherwise noted.

301 the first set of mastodon remains: RMG, *Archaeological Recovery of the Bowser Road Mastodon: Orange County, New York* (New York: ASAA/Persimmon Press Monographs in Archaeology, 2017).

301 collection at Harvard's Museum of Comparative Zoology: Interview with RMG in 2020; "MCZ Receives 13,000 Year Old Mastodon," *News,* Museum of Comparative Zoology's website, Nov. 27, 2017.

301 he met the news with composure and resignation: Interview with RMG in 2020.

302 "a sea-change in how archaeology is being done": Interview with Bruce Bourque in 2020.

303 Gramly had told the Royal Canadian Mounted Police: Transcript of Interview between Cst. W. W. MacDonald & RMG, Nain, Labrador, Aug. 11, 1976, pp. 1–4.

303 up a stream, across knife-edge ridges: Smithsonian Report, Part 2, p. 12. "Knife-edge" from interview with RMG in 2020.

303 a slope of rock that spilled: Here through "around 11 a.m." from Smithsonian Report, Part 1, pp. 7–9.

303 Gramly attempted to go around the point: Gramly describes this moment in transcript of interview between Cst. W. W. MacDonald & RMG, Nain, Labrador, Aug. 11, 1976, p. 2.

303 jumped back onto the beach to avoid a fall: Smithsonian Report, Part 1, p. 9.

303 Anne tried, too, and got about thirty feet up: Smithsonian Report, Part 1, p. 9; report notes that Gramly said both ten feet and thirty feet up.

303 "I don't like the risk": RMG statement to RCMP, "Sequence of Events at Ramah, Labrador: July 30–Aug. 8, 1976," Aug. 12, 1976, p. 1.

304 "No, I think Gramly got fired": Interview with Ted Abraham in 2017.

304 Hilda's Creek in honor of: Interviews with RMG and Alice Abraham in 2017.

304 checked with Stephen and with Anne's siblings: Interviews with Stephen Loring in 2019; Ted and Alice Abraham in 2020.

THE ANNE ABRAHAM RESCUE OPERATION

305 radio in once a day at 7 a.m.: Smithsonian Report, Part 2, p. 6.

305 Fitzhugh was worried: "He viewed the silence from Ramah as ominous," Smithsonian Report, Part 2, p. 7.

305 On August 8, Ted Abraham's phone rang: Interview with Ted Abraham in 2017; "Brother Tells of His Labrador Search for D.C. Woman," *Washington Post,* Aug. 16, 1976.

305 6:45 a.m., a search-and-rescue helicopter: Report by F. A. McCully, Happy Valley Goose Bay Detachment of the RCMP, Oct. 8, 1976, p. 3. Fitzhugh thought the helicopter would be able to take his search crew as well, but, loaded with extra fuel, it was already at capacity. Per the Smithsonian Report, Stephen Loring was only allowed on after insisting that the pilot offload two hundred pounds of equipment (Part 2, p. 21).

306 the diesel fumes...were nauseating: Interview with Ted Abraham in 2017.

306 They were on Saglek: The Smithsonian Report leaves this stop in Saglek out of their timeline, but I feel confident that it happened. Ted Abraham first mentioned it to me in 2017, and it's corroborated in the RCMP files: "Arrived Saglek 11:40am and arrived Ramah Bay 12:30pm" (Report by F. A. McCully, Happy Valley Goose Bay Detachment of the RCMP, Oct. 8, 1976, p. 3). RMG did not dispute this encounter.

306 They never made eye contact: In response, RMG said in 2020, "I should have gone back, maybe, but I thought everyone knew where I was and everything. And I just didn't think that—well I just didn't want to—there wasn't anything I could do to bring her back."

306 herd of caribou: Interview with Ted Abraham in 2020. The Smithsonian Report also lists a polar bear sighting from this day, but that was after they dropped off the search party (Smithsonian Report, Part 1, p. 13).

306 dropped the three men off: Report by F. A. McCully, Happy Valley Goose Bay Detachment of the RCMP, Oct. 8, 1976, p. 3.

306 men set up camp: Interview with Ted Abraham in 2017.

306 no trouble reaching the Fitzhughs by radio: Interviews with Ted Abraham in 2017 and Bill Fitzhugh in 2020.

307 *Gee, you shouldn't have come:* "Brother Tells of His Labrador Search for D.C. Woman," *Washington Post,* Aug. 16, 1976.

307 tried to retrace Anne's final hours: Description from Ted Abraham's recollections (2017).

307 water was too noisy...concentrating hard on his footing: Transcript of interview between Cst. W. W. MacDonald & RMG, Nain, Labrador, Aug. 11, 1976, p. 11.

307 Ted thought he saw someone: Anecdote about floating orange object from interviews with Ted Abraham (2017, 2020). Per the Smithsonian Report, Anne's raincoat was orange (Smithsonian Report, Part 1, p. 8).

307 Fitzhugh was angry that the search party: Through "no scent of Anne," Smithsonian Report, Part 1, pp. 12–13.

307 "There is no proper grief": Interview with Ted Abraham in 2017.

308 watched as the candles they lit: Interview with Ted Abraham in 2017; Stephen Loring did not remember this.

308 "Time's up. You gotta get out": Interview with Ted Abraham in 2017; this tracks with Fitzhugh's experience. He felt "under intense pressure from the RCMP" to terminate the search for Anne (Smithsonian Report, Part 2, p. 16).

308 Gramly had passed "with flying colors": Bill Fitzhugh, "A Brief Chronology of Events: Ramah," Appendix 13, Smithsonian Report, p. 3.

308 a final search of the sea caves: Through end of paragraph, Smithsonian Report, Part 1, p. 16.

308 sea was swarming with sea lice: Report by F.A. McCully, Happy Valley Goose Bay Detachment of the RCMP, Oct. 8, 1976, p. 6.

308 Newfoundland Department of Justice announced: Letter from Asst. C.I.B. Officer, A. E. Vaughan to the Deputy Minister of Justice, St. John's, Newfoundland, Oct. 29, 1976.

308 Smithsonian...own internal review: Memorandum from George S. Robinson (Assistant General Counsel of the Smithsonian Institution) to Mr. S. Dillon Ripley (Secretary), Subject: Internal Review Panel relating to the disappearance of Anne Abraham in Labrador, Oct. 21, 1976.

308 without access to the Canadian police files: Letter from John G. Kelly (Director of Public Prosecutions, Government of Newfoundland and Labrador, Department of Justice) to George S. Robinson, Dec. 17, 1976.

308 In March 1977: Memorandum from John Motheral, John Eisenberg, and David Pawson to S. Dillon Ripley (Secretary of the Smithsonian Institution), Subject: Report of the Panel established to review the disappearance of Ms. Anne Abraham, Mar. 8, 1977.

309 fifteen-page partial transcript: RMG statement to RCMP, "Sequence of Events at Ramah, Labrador: July 30–August 8, 1976," Aug. 12, 1976. The rest of this chapter is drawn from this source.

DON MITCHELL AND SERGEANT SENNOTT

310 "All you got to do is brush your gums": This chapter is from an interview with Don Mitchell in 2017 and the Don Mitchell interview transcript with Sergeant Sennott, July 17, 2017 (MSP file).

310 six feet tall: Sgt. Sennott's response to his checking memo.

BIRTHDAY CAKE

312 someone at the Harvard Archives wrote me: Latest email from the Harvard University Archives, Apr. 5, 2019, 1:32 p.m. When I told Gramly that the archives had no record of the class, he assured me that he and Jane had taken the course. He said he had taken it for credit and would try to get his transcript from Harvard to show me. As

of the time of publication, I have not yet seen his transcript.

313 "In fact," he had told me: Interview with RMG in 2017. He reconfirmed in 2020.

COME OUT OF THE DARK EARTH

313 ordered an *in camera* inspection: Letter from Rebecca Murray to Assistant District Attorney Elizabeth May re: SPR17/820, June 30, 2017.

314 Alice Abraham, Anne's sister, wrote me: Email from Alice Abraham, Sept. 9, 2017, 12:22 p.m.

314 Alice was a big woman: The rest of this

chapter is from an interview with Alice in 2017 unless otherwise noted.

314 married for thirty-five years: "Loring, Stephen" entry in *Encyclopedia of Global Archaeology*, edited by Claire Smith (New York: Springer-Verlag, 2014).

315 one of the founders of Gender Archaeology:

See, e.g., her work with Margaret Conkey to organize the "Women and Production in Prehistory" Conference, Apr. 5–9, 1988, Wedge Plantation, South Carolina.

315 Stephen had helped her with: In a 2019 interview with Stephen Loring, he wanted to make clear that Alice should get all the credit for the trip; he had been happy to help the family.

315 touch the rocks that Anne had loved: Description of this trip drawn from recordings that appear in "A Long Journey North to Say Goodbye," *The World*, PRI Radio, Dec. 26, 2006.

315 *Come out of the dark earth*: May Sarton, "Invocation."

315 "Most people react to death with sorrow": Undated. Anne, it seems, got an A on the paper.

THE INVESTIGATION

316 Cambridge Police officer John Fulkerson: Interviews with Fulkerson in 2016 and 2018.

316 Susan had gotten to know: Kelly, *Boston Stranglers*, preface.

316 letter arrived from a Dr. Richard M. Gramly: Letter from RMG to CPD Keeper of the Records, Aug. 31, 1995 (CPD file).

317 Jane's case file—about four boxes: Interview with Fulkerson in 2018.

317 No record of what additional physical evidence: This squares with interoffice correspondence from Deputy Superintendent Thomas F. O'Connor (Commander of Detectives) to Commissioner Watson, Subject: "Cold Case" Homicides, Nov. 4, 1996 (CPD file).

317 The officer felt like he was digging for information: Interview with Fulkerson in 2018.

317 changed his mind and sent a package: Deputy O'Connor, "Cold Case" Homicides, Nov. 4, 1996 (CPD file).

317 a cover letter: Letter from RMG to John Fulkerson, Oct. 26, 1995.

318 never saw a roster of the Putnam Lab caretakers: Interview with RMG in 2020.

318 Fulkerson contacted Susan Kelly: Fax from John Fulkerson to Susan Kelly, Nov. 14, 1995.

318 felt sure they had their guy: Interview with Fulkerson in 2018.

319 fingerprints from the FBI: RMG fingerprints saved alongside FBI, US Department of Justice envelope (undated, no postmark) (CPD file).

319 By November 1996: Deputy O'Connor, "Cold Case" Homicides, Nov. 4, 1996 (CPD file).

319 In January 1997: "Det. Notes by unsigned re. Gramly," Jan. 14, 1997 (MSP file).

319 The day after the meeting, Sennott contacted: Letter from Trooper Peter Sennott to Lt. Kathy Stefani, Crime Lab, Jan. 15, 1997 (MSP file).

319 there was no plan to reopen: "Det. Notes by unsigned re. Gramly," Dec. 30, 1997 (MSP file).

319 On February 20, 1998, Dr. Katsas: Letter from George Katsas to John McEvoy (Office of the District Attorney), Feb. 20, 1988 (MDAO file).

320 Sennott sent the slides to the crime laboratory:

Request for the Examination of Physical Evidence, delivered by Peter Sennott to the State Police Crime Laboratory in Sudbury, MA, Feb. 25, 1998 (MDAO file).

320 Corporal Langille got in touch: Fax from Cpl. Langille to Peter Sennott, June 11, 1998 (MSP file).

320 "In short," Sennott wrote: Letter from Peter Sennott to John McEvoy, July 12, 1998 (MSP file).

320 In September of the same year: Report of Laboratory Examination, Cellmark Diagnostics, Sept. 17, 1998, using the GenePrint STR Multiplex System and the GenePrint Sex Determination System (Amelogenin).

320 Labs across the country: At the time, Massachusetts had neither a DNA unit nor a CODIS database (ADA Lynch's reply to checking memo).

320 people in Alabama: Letter from Sue Rogers (Alabama's CODIS administrator) to Mary McGilvray, Dec. 14, 1998.

320 and Florida: Fax from Mary McGilvray to Peter Sennott, Nov. 24, 1998, which contains letter from Tara Hockenberry at the Palm Beach County Sheriff's Office to Mary McGilvray, Nov. 4, 1998.

320 One of the people had been five years old: Chronology of DNA Investigation, Oct. 29, 2018 (MDAO file).

320 Again, they used a differential extraction procedure: DNA-STR Report, MSP Crime Laboratory (Sudbury, MA), Aug. 18, 2004. Due to the limited sample, only AmpFlSTR Profiler Plus was used to test the sample.

320 a result that could help identify a suspect at any of the locations: The only result above threshold was the Amelogenin consistent with the X chromosome in the non-sperm fraction—to be expected since this was Jane's (female) DNA.

321 MSP found Gramly's license details: Mass RMV re: Richard Gramly, June 8, 2004 (MDAO file).

321 details about his family members: Mass RMV re: Gramly, same address, June 8, 2005 (MDAO file).

321 printout of the residential property record

card: Property Record, same address, June 8, 2006 (MDAO file).

321 the day in November 2005: Consent for Saliva Sample signed by RMG, MSP form, Nov. 9, 2005.

321 sent the sample: Letter from Lynne Sarty (MSP Crime Lab) to Bode Technology Group, Jan. 10, 2006.

321 Bode sent its Forensic Case Report: Forensic Case Report, Bode Technology Group, Inc., Feb. 6, 2006.

2018: SOMETHING HAS BEEN SETTLED

325 Conversation with Don Mitchell took place on July 31, 2018.

STEPHEN LORING

326 When I reached Stephen Loring again: Interview with Stephen Loring in 2017.

MONTE ALTO

327 Stephen Loring had done well enough: This chapter is primarily from interviews with Stephen Loring in 2017, but also the Monte Alto field photos and notebooks (Edwin Shook, the field director, was an astonishingly thorough note taker) in the Peabody Archives and "Archaeological Research in Western Guatemala," *Peabody Museum Newsletter*, p. 4.

327 Stephan de Borhegyi, had died: "Dr. Stephan F. de Borheygi," Milwaukee Public Museum website.

327 the ocean-blue International Travelall: Interview with Gene Paull in 2018.

328 where the volcanoes are up so high: Interview with Gene Paull in 2018.

329 Monte Alto had been part of the early development: Interview with Richard Rose in 2017.

329 [Photo]: Photograph by Lee Parsons, courtesy Richard Rose.

330 Much of the two hours back: Ed Shook's 1969–1970 field notebook, 969-48-00/1, Monte Alto Expedition Records 1969–1971, Peabody Museum of Archaeology & Ethnology, Harvard University.

STEPHEN LORING, CONTINUED

331 "I mean he didn't say he did it": This chapter is from interviews with Stephen Loring in 2017.

331 If true, this would mean: Again, I have not found any evidence that the lie detector test questions or results still exist, so I have not been able to verify this statement.

CHATTER IN CAMBRIDGE

333 "I've been concerned about something": CPD-JC, pp. 3–4.

333 Lee Parsons's Primitive Art class: Tracks with CPD-LP 1 and Jane Britton's Radcliffe student file.

333 *Boston Globe* ran a cover story: "'Gift' Rock May Be Cambridge Death Weapon," *Boston Globe*, Jan. 9, 1969.

333 On January 13, the *Daily News*: "Murder Quiz Finds Jane Had Abortion," *Daily News*, Jan. 13, 1969.

333 like graduate student Frances Nitzberg: Frances Nitzberg interview transcript, Jan. 12, 1969, 3:15–4:25 p.m. (CPD file).

333 wandering the streets of Cambridge drunk: CPD-JC, p. 13.

333 Karl Lamberg-Karlovsky said: CPD-CCLK 2, p. 21.

333 Richard Meadow told police when he was pressed: CPD-RM, p. 41.

334 "[One of the Peabody secretaries] told me": Letter from Sally Nash to Don and Jill Mitchell, Oct. 17, 1969.

334 she shook in her chair: Philippa Shaplin CPD interview transcript, Jan. 14, 1969, 12:47–5:00 p.m., p. 17.

ANNE MOREAU

334 Noah Savett, the other: I have since located Noah Savett, but he hasn't responded to a request for comment.

334 The road trip down to Guatemala: Per Monte Alto photos and field notebooks in the Peabody Archive.

334 Lee had been contacted by the Cambridge Police: Ed Shook wrote that they drove into Guatemala City so Lee could phone the Cambridge police on Mar. 10, 1969 (Ed Shook's 1968–1969 field notebook, p. 83).

334 gaps in his attendance on the site: Ed Shook's 1968–1969 field notebook. Parsons's notebook is not in the Peabody Archive.

334 track down a copy of Lee's lie detector test: The administrator of the second round of lie detector tests, Leonard Harrelson, had passed away, but I tracked down Terry Ball (of Ball & Gillespie

Polygraph) who now owns some of Harrelson's equipment; Ball and Harrelson had been friends. I asked Ball if he had inherited any of Harrelson's old tests, and he replied that it was too expensive for lie detector administrators to keep records beyond the required window, which used to be five years. Now, it's three.

334 Conti...said he remembered Lee Parsons's name: Email from Richard Conti, May 3, 2017, 4:54 p.m.

335 she was born in 1932: Public birth records.

335 discovered cosmic radio waves: "Karl Jansky and the Discovery of Cosmic Radio Waves," National Radio Astronomy Observatory website.

335 I caught her as she: The rest of this chapter is from my interview with Anne Moreau in 2017.

LAST WILL AND TESTAMENT OF LEE ALLEN PARSONS

337 [Photo]: Last Will and Testament of Lee Allen Parsons: Broward County Comm. 33862, signed Dec. 30, 1992.

CONFESSION CHAIN

338 I had written Jill Nash: Letter to Jill Nash, May 26, 2017.

338 in the final email she sent me: Email from Jill Nash, June 2, 2017, 1:11 p.m.

338 Once I emailed Olga: Email to Olga Stavrakis, June 5, 2017, 8:44 a.m.

338 we were on the phone together: The rest of this chapter is from this 2017 interview unless otherwise noted.

339 I contacted Joyce Marcus immediately: Email to Joyce Marcus, June 5, 2017, 11:05 a.m.

339 graduated from Harvard with a PhD in 1974: "Crimson Compass," Harvard Alumni Database.

339 an archaeologist at the University of Michigan:

Joyce Marcus page on the University of Michigan's Department of Anthropology website.

339 "rumors and even weird drunken confessions": Email from Joyce Marcus, June 5, 2017, 6:23 p.m. When my checker reached out to confirm this statement, Professor Marcus sought to clarify her quote. She wrote that "the rumors I heard in the 1970s came from a few people who knew Jane, i.e. they were NOT confessions from a few people." However, Olga Stravrakis was not the only person to tell me that Lee had confessed to Joyce Marcus; David Freidel also told me this in a 2017 interview.

HOW ODD AND STRANGE

340 When Jill saw Jane the afternoon after the Incense Night: In Jill's 2020 response to her checking memo, she wrote, "I didn't know Jane took diet pills." However, in 1969, she had told police, "She'd also had these diet pills that she had gotten so she wouldn't get fat again after she came back from Iran, and I think she had been taking one because she was very, you know, sparkling sort of" (CPD-JM 2, p. 49).

340 Jane told Jill that after she and Don had left: CPD-JM 2, p. 49.

340 Jim had been away for most of the semester: CPD-JH; CPD-RM.

340 "how odd and strange": CPD-JM 2, p. 49.

340 when Lee visited a married couple: CPD-JM 2, p. 42.

340 something else had happened that night that Jane: CPD-JM, p. 50.

WHO IS THE GHOST HERE

341 "I don't think of Lee as an evil person": Interview with Stephen Loring in 2017.

341 Bank of America...Elsie's: "Spicy Variety of Restaurants Flavors Tour," *Wellesley News*, May 4, 1967.

341 the *wurst of all possible houses*...Jane's "ankle biters": Interview with Don Mitchell in 2017.

341 "The sleepwalkers are coming awake": Adrienne Rich, "When We Dead Awaken: Writing as Re-Vision," *College English* 32, no. 1, Women, Writing, and Teaching (Oct. 1972): 18–30.

342 one of the few all-women's ones: In 2017, the Harvard Corporation approved social group sanctions, barring members of single-gender final clubs and Greek organizations from leadership positions, prestigious fellowships, and varsity captaincies. In 2018, the last of the all-female final clubs announced their plan to go co-ed: "Harvard Is without All-Female Social Groups after Last Three Holdouts Agree to Go Co-Ed," *Harvard Crimson*, Aug. 24, 2018. While some of the all-male clubs have voted to go co-ed as well, others filed state and federal lawsuits. On June 29, 2020, following the Supreme Court decision in *Bostock v. Clayton County*, Harvard University president Bacow announced that the university would drop its social group sanctions.

TORONTO

343 The next morning, I wrote down Jim's name: This scene took place on Sept. 14, 2017.

NOVEMBER 1968

345 yank hard to open her door: Per CPD-JM 2, p. 9, Jane locked her door when she went home for Thanksgiving, and per CPD-JM 1, p. 22, closing it required a "monumental effort," so presumably the same applied to opening it.

345 The wood had swollen and warped: CPD-JM 2, p. 9.

345 *Sincerely Yours*: Jane's journal entry, Aug. 1, 1968.

345 "Maybe you could compromise": Jane's journal entry, Aug. 1, 1968.

345 *Dear Jane*, Jim's letter began: Letter from Jim Humphries to Jane, Nov. 27, 1968; date from Bill Rathje's police transcript, when he says that he visited Jim in Toronto the Monday before Thanksgiving, and stayed at his house for two nights (CPD-WR, p. 10).

345 sweeping her off the street: Letter from Jane to her parents, July 14, 1968.

345 He had bought her flowers at 5:30: Letter from Jane to Elisabeth Handler, July 27, 1968.

345 "Should have been my old wary self": Letter from Jane to Jim Humphries, June 4, 1968 (CPD file).

346 taken a day trip to Oxford: Scene from letter from Jane to her parents, June 12, 1968; letter from Jane to Boyd, June 21, 1968; letter from Jane to Brenda Bass, July 4, 1968; letter from Jane to her parents, July 14, 1968; and Jane's journal entries.

346 "Ah to be in London + in love": Letter from Jane to her parents, June 12, 1968.

347 a piece of tarnished silver that had just gotten polished: Jane's journal entry, June 14/15, 1968.

347 "The thing about this one is that he's *real*": Letter from Jane to her parents, June 12, 1968.

347 "God, this drivel I'm pouring out!": Letter from Jane to her parents, June 12, 1968.

347 "And all this time": Here to end of paragraph, Jane's journal entry, June 14/15, 1968.

347 He had said he didn't want to be alone anymore: Letter from Jane to Brenda Bass, July 4, 1968.

347 He had said he really loved her: Letter from Jane to her parents, June 12, 1968.

347 felt like the girl bunny in *Pogo*: Here to end of paragraph, Jane's journal entry, June 14/15, 1968.

JIM HUMPHRIES

348 figure silhouetted by the window: Jim Humphries did not participate in the fact-checking process of the book.

JANE'S LAST DAY

350 since just after Christmas: Jim was back in time to go to a New Year's party with Jane (CPD-JH, p. 44).

350 Bill Rathje, who had been with Jim: Description from CPD-WR, pp. 12–13.

350 when Jane dropped by her friend Ingrid's place: CPD-IK, p. 49.

350 Even Sarah Lee Irwin: CPD-SLI, p. 24.

351 Jim arranged dinner at the Acropolis: CPD-WR & KD, p. 3, p. 6.

351 Richard Meadow, Kent Day, and Bill Rathje: CPD-WR & KD, CPD-RM.

351 in a coat and tie and the maroon rugby sweater: CPD-JH, p. 43.

351 he wore when he skated: CPD-RM, p. 14.

351 Jim left his skates by the cigarette machine: CPD-RM, p. 54.

351 Rathje had agreed to pick up Kent and Jane: CPD-WR & KD, p. 7.

351 yelled down at him from the stairwell: CPD-WR, p. 5; CPD-JM 2, p. 35; CPD-DM p. 24.

351 She had been napping: CPD-DM p. 23.

351 get some London broil: CPD-DM p. 23. London broil detail is from interview with Don Mitchell in 2017.

351 she hated that buzzer: CPD-DM pp. 23–24.

351 went out of his apartment to talk to Jane: Here to "offer any more details" from CPD-DM, p. 24.

351 "Here I am. Let's go," Jane said: CPD-WR, p. 5.

351 wearing a skirt and her auburn fur coat: CPD-WR, p. 8; CPD-JH, p. 43.

351 Her mood eased over the course of dinner: CPD-WR, p. 5; CPD-WR & KD, p. 10.

351 split a bottle of retsina: CPD-JH, p. 75; CPD-WR & KD, p. 3.

351 made a point to avoid talking about Generals: CPD-WR, p. 6.

351 Jane looked happiest, Rathje noticed: CPD-WR & KD, p. 10.

351 when they split off at 7:30 p.m.: CPD-WR & KD, p. 4.

351 Richard to his girlfriend's place: CPD-RM, pp. 47–48.

351 Rathje and Kent home to watch TV: CPD-WR & KD, p. 4.

351 Jim and Jane to walk by themselves: CPD-RM, p. 47.

351 Jim checked to make sure Jane still felt like skating: CPD-JH, p. 42.

351 could change out of her skirt and grab her skates: CPD-JH, p. 43.

351 Jim waited in the kitchen: CPD-JH, p. 44.

351 thought to himself, *At least she'll be okay for tomorrow*: CPD-JH, p. 32.

351 blue ski parka instead: CPD-JH, p. 87.

351 It wasn't a cold night: CPD-JH, p. 43.

351 They only skated for twenty minutes: CPD-JH, p. 18.

351 A pint of beer sounded like a better idea: CPD-JH, p. 85.

352 around 10:30 p.m., a little sleet was coming down: CPD-JH, pp. 18, 57.

352 she made hot cocoa while Jim kept her company in the kitchen: CPD-JH, p. 34.

352 Then they sat on her bed: CPD-JH, p. 35.

352 metal enamel mugs: CPD-JH, p. 31.

352 to smoke four cigarettes: CPD-JH, p. 89.

352 had clouded back over: CPD-JH, p. 85.

352 "She would get very depressed": CPD-IK, p. 53.

352 about the exams and about Iran: CPD-JH, p. 16.

352 Jane said she would drive him home: CPD-JH, p. 24.

352 Jim liked the cold air after: CPD-JH, p. 56.

352 Jane said she wanted to start her car anyway: CPD-JH, pp. 56–57.

352 He kissed Jane good night: CPD-JH, p. 85.

352 lugging his skates in the pouring rain: CPD-JH, pp. 32, 94.

352 still in her slacks and sweater: CPD-DM, p. 26.

352 "Have you got my cat?": CPD-DM, p. 25.

352 Jane sat on the floor, and Don poured her a small glass of sherry: CPD-DM, p. 26.

352 Richard Meadow heard Jim walk in: CPD-RM, p. 20.

352 hoping that Jim would be back by that time: CPD-RM, p 20.

352 about eight inches apart: CPD-RM, p. 22.

352 Jim slept on the one near the window: CPD-RM, p. 22.

352 Jim took off his coat and hung it in the closet: Here to "walked into the bedroom," CPD-RM, p. 31.

353 Meadow was in bed reading: CPD-RM, p. 20.

353 Jim was soaked: CPD-RM, p. 31.

353 "Where have you been?" Richard asked: CPD-JH, p. 90.

353 "Over cheering up Jane": CPD-JH, p. 90.

353 "It is a rather thankless task, isn't it?": CPD-RM, p. 32.

353 Jim didn't answer: CPD-RM, p. 32.

353 He dried himself off and changed into his pajamas: CPD-JH, p. 13.

353 Jane didn't appear to be in a hurry: CPD-DM, p. 31.

353 she was vague about who she'd been out with: CPD-DM, p. 27.

353 Don didn't press: CPD-DM, p. 28.

353 When she finished her glass: Here through "I think I'll go to bed," CPD-DM, p. 31.

353 Jane took her cat, and Don saw her to the door: CPD-DM, p. 28.

353 Jill wished her good luck and said she'd see her tomorrow: CPD-JM 1, p. 20.

353 "If I don't remember tomorrow": Exchange from CPD-RM, p. 22.

RICHARD ROSE

353 "a guy whose last name was Rose": Interview with Parker Donham in 2014.

354 heartfelt thank-you email: Email from Parker Donham, Oct. 29, 2016, 3:17 p.m.

354 I'd called Merri Swid: Interview with Merri Swid in 2017.

354 a detective had come out: "Added Information Re: Jane Britton Murder Case," prepared by Steven A. Obartuck of the MSP is consistent with Merri's memory: Det. Lts. John Burns and Obartuck spoke with Richard Rose and Merri Swid in Bolton on May 21, 1969 (MSP file).

354 Richard, indeed, was alive: Interview with Richard Rose in 2017.

355 When I first arrived at the Roses' house: This scene took place on Sept. 29, 2017.

356 dozens of cigarette butts: Don Mitchell interview transcript with Sgt. Sennott, July 17, 2017, p. 181 (MSP file).

356 According to Elisabeth Handler, Jane loved her Gauloises: Interview with Elisabeth Handler in 2017.

358 The next day we clicked through slides: The last two scenes took place on Sept. 30, 2017.

359: [Photo]: Photograph by Richard Rose.

CITY ISLAND

360 This scene took place on Aug. 9, 2017.

360 "to make the world safe for human differences": It is common, but somewhat controversial, to attribute this quote to Ruth Benedict, as it doesn't turn up in her collected writings. She did, however, write upon the death of her mentor, Franz Boas, that, "He believed the world must be made safe for differences" Charles King, Gods of the Upper Air: How a Circle of Renegade Anthropologists Reinvented Race, Sex, and Gender in the Twentieth Century (New York: Doubleday, 2019).

JANUARY 14, 1969: LEE PARSONS POLICE INTERROGATION

361 This chapter comprises excerpts of CPD-LP 1 and CPD-LP 2, which have been merged in places for clarity and concision. As always, the edits were made with the goal to preserve the spirit of the original.

WILL YOU ACCEPT THIS

365 I got an email from Alice Kehoe: Email from Alice Kehoe, Sept. 22, 2017, 6:30 p.m.

365 She's a delight, he'd said: Interview with Stephen Loring in 2017.

365 On the phone, she asked: The rest of this chapter is from this 2017 interview with Alice Kehoe unless otherwise noted.

366 Anne, begged him to get a contract: In 2020, Anne Moreau said that she did not remember that Lee had not signed a contract. What she remembered more clearly was that the Kehoes had warned Lee Parsons about Stephen Williams: They'd said that he should not be trusted.

JANUARY 14, 1969: LEE PARSONS POLICE INTERROGATION, CONTINUED

368 Excerpt of CPD-LP 2.

JULY 31, 2018: STOP THE FAIRY LAND

371 There's an email from him: Email from Don Mitchell, July 31, 2018, 2:08 a.m.

AUGUST 16, 2018: BOYD'S BIRTHDAY EVE

373 The press conference, Don tells me: Section from a series of phone calls with Don Mitchell in 2018.

374 I call Boyd back as soon as I can: Phone call with Boyd in 2018.

AUGUST 16, 2018: LATE

375 An echo of the worst of Boston: For a thorough examination of racism in Boston, see the *Boston Globe*'s series "Boston. Racism. Image. Reality," Dec. 10, 2017.

375 And it masks the truth: According to the FBI's "Uniform Crime Reports," homicide was least likely to be committed by a stranger (only 18 percent of cases): Arthur Kellerman and James Mercy, "Men, Women, and Murder: Gender-Specific Differences in Rates of Fatal Violence and Victimization," *Journal of Trauma* 33, no. 1 (July 1992): 1–5.

375 nearly half of all murdered women: 44 percent of female murder victims killed by intimate family; 9.6 percent by a stranger. Table 3 of Emma Fridel and James Fox, "Gender Differences in Patterns and Trends in U.S. Homicide, 1976–2017," *Violence and Gender* 6, no. 1 (2019): 32.

375 2010 piece in the *Boston Globe*: "DNA Links Convict to '72 Killing of Woman," *Boston Globe*, Feb. 18, 2010.

376 She was from St. Paul, Minnesota: Details from "Family of Former St. Paul Woman Killed in Boston in 1972 Finally Has Some Answers," *Pioneer Press*, Feb. 18, 2010. All facts cross-checked with Ellen's sister Cori.

376 found her lying on her back on the living room floor: Interview with Sgt. William Doogan in 2020.

376 On December 12, 1973, Mary McClain: "DNA Links Dead Man to Second Cold-Case Murder," Press Release from DA Daniel F. Conley of the Suffolk County District Attorney's Office, Oct. 18, 2012. All details cross-checked with Mary's sister Kathy. The news reports at the time call her Mary Lee McClain; this is an error. Her middle name, according to her sister, was Lea, but she just went by Mary.

376 They heard her whimpering in her room: Interview with Sgt. William Doogan in 2018.

377 In 2005, Ellen Rutchick's siblings: "Family of Former St. Paul Woman," *Pioneer Press*.

377 "It's not a case of how much is it going to cost if we do it": Interview with William Doogan in 2018. Four months after Jane's case was solved, the Middlesex DA announced the formation of a cold case unit. In October, the MSP and Suffolk County followed suit.

377 but in the 1970s, evidence was affixed to the lab slides: "Family of Former St. Paul Woman," *Pioneer Press*.

377 It took four years, but in September 2009: "Family of Former St. Paul Woman."

377 BPD, in conjunction with Suffolk County prosecutors, announced: "Suspect, Now Deceased, Identified in '72 Murder," Press Release from DA Daniel F. Conley of the Suffolk County District Attorney's Office, Feb. 17, 2010.

378 Sumpter had been dead for almost nine years: Michael Sumpter Death Certificate, transmitted June 2, 2005 (MSP file).

378 a heart attack and prostate cancer: Michael Sumpter Death Certificate. Sumpter at the time was in hospice care, on parole.

378 serving time for a 1975 rape: "Family of Former St. Paul Woman," *Pioneer Press*, which tracks with Sumpter's incarceration records.

378 "It's been 40 years": "DA: 1973 Rape, Murder Solved," *Boston Herald*, Oct. 19, 2012.

378 DA Daniel Conley made the news public: "DNA Links Dead Man to Second Cold-Case Murder," Press Release from DA Daniel F. Conley of the Suffolk County District Attorney's Office, Oct. 18, 2012.

378 escaped from the first furlough: Michael

Sumpter DOC file 3 of 4, p. 25. (All four files are from the MDAO.)

378 Sumpter escaped…on the lam for a year and a half: Sumpter DOC 2, p. 72.

378 discovered he had raped a woman in Back Bay: "Family of Former St. Paul Woman," *Pioneer Press*.

378 "Do you think that's all he's ever done?": "DA: 1973 Rape, Murder Solved," *Boston Herald*, Oct. 19, 2012.

RECKONINGS

378 Just a few days after I'd talked with Alice: My interview with Alice Kehoe was on Oct. 4, 2017. The *New York Times* published Jodi Kantor and Megan Twohey's "Harvey Weinstein Paid Off Sexual Harassment Accusers for Decades," on Oct. 5, 2017. The *New Yorker* published Ronan Farrow's "From Aggressive Overtures to Sexual Assault: Harvey Weinstein's Accusers Tell Their Stories," on Oct. 10, 2017.

379 *The Chronicle of Higher Education* published: "She Left Harvard. He Got to Stay," *Chronicle of Higher Education*, Feb. 27, 2018. Details cross-checked with Terry Karl.

379 stalked her and made her feel physically threatened: Here through "she had no choice," from Terry Karl, 2020 response to checking memo.

379 knew that she wasn't alone: Paragraph from "Harvard Cannot Investigate Itself," *Harvard Crimson*, Apr. 9, 2018.

379 Karl was given three semesters of paid leave: "She Left Harvard," *Chronicle*.

379 the *Crimson* and the *Boston Globe*: "Harvard Disciplines Professor for Sexual Harassment," *Harvard Crimson*, Sept. 28, 1983; "Harvard Faculty Council Hears Report on Sexual Harassment," *Boston Globe*, Oct. 27, 1983.

380 "There are a lot of us who feel": "Harvard Disciplines Professor for Sexual Harassment," *Harvard Crimson*, Sept. 28, 1983.

380 university was not taking the matter seriously enough: "She Left Harvard," *Chronicle*.

380 no clear grievance procedure for faculty members: "She Left Harvard," *Chronicle*. While there were some formal procedures being instituted for students to report harassment by faculty, there were none for faculty members being harassed by faculty members.

380 "It was specifically not our intention": "She Left Harvard," *Chronicle*.

380 "pits a person against an institution": "Why Women Stick Around," *Boston Globe*, Oct. 12, 1991.

380 tenure from Stanford: Terry Karl curriculum vitae.

380 to keep this period of sexual harassment from defining her: When she settled with the university in 1985, Professor Karl prioritized two outcomes: She wanted to be a professor when it was done, and she wanted Harvard to adopt grievance procedures for victims of sexual harassment and an ombudsperson's office to handle complaints. As part of the settlement, Harvard agreed to distribute a definition of sexual harassment to all employees and students for five years ("Sexual Harassment: A Victim Advises Others on How to Win," *Stanford University News Service*, Oct. 25, 1991).

380 Domínguez kept getting promoted at Harvard: "She Left Harvard," *Chronicle*; Domínguez's personal website.

380 Professor Karl got a call: "She Left Harvard," *Chronicle*.

380 Eventually fifteen other women: "Harvard Prof. Dominguez Stripped of Emeritus Status Following Conclusion of Title IX Investigation," *Harvard Crimson*, May 9, 2019.

380 Alan Garber…emailed: Email from Alan Garber to members of the Harvard community, Mar. 2, 2018, 4:34 p.m.

381 Harvard president Faust also reaffirmed: Drew Faust, Remarks at FAS Faculty Meeting, Mar. 6, 2018.

381 conclusion of the Title IX investigation: "Harvard Prof. Dominguez Stripped of Emeritus Status Following Conclusion of Title IX Investigation," *Harvard Crimson*, May 9, 2019.

381 banned him from campus: "Harvard Bans Former Scholar, Citing 'Unwelcome Sexual Conduct' over Decades," *Chronicle of Higher Education*, May 9, 2019.

381 she does not see this moment as a reckoning: Terry Karl, 2020 response to checking memo.

AUGUST 17, 2018: TELL NO MAN

381 I check in with the *Boston Globe*'s Todd Wallack: Email to Todd Wallack, Aug. 18, 2018, 10:28 a.m.
381 when Wallack tries his own luck: Email from Todd Wallack, August 18, 2018, 4:42 p.m.

381 I tell Boyd that I can't get a straight answer: Phone call with Boyd in 2018.

SEPTEMBER, OCTOBER 2018: WAITING AND WAITING AND WAITING

382 Don, who was diagnosed: Interview with Don Mitchell in 2018.
382 Richard Conti, who had served as foreman: "Richard Conti, 1940–2018," *Boston Globe*, Sept. 27, 2018.
382 Elisabeth gets in touch with me: Facebook Messenger, Sept. 8, 2018, 9:18 a.m.

382 she would have accepted: The rest of this chapter is from an interview with Elisabeth Handler in 2018.
382 Ryan's reelection campaign: "Middlesex DA Ryan Re-Elected in Close Race," *Lowell Sun*, Sept. 4, 2018.

KIMBERLY THEIDON

383 a *Crimson* story caught my eye: "Court Dismisses Gender Discrimination Lawsuit against Harvard," *Harvard Crimson*, Mar. 26, 2018.
383 complained about the disparate treatment: Most of the details in this chapter are drawn from two documents, the "2018 ruling" (*Theidon v. Harvard University and the President and Fellows of Harvard College*, Redacted Order on Defendant's Motion for Summary Judgment, Civ. A. No. 15-cv-10809-LTS, Feb. 28, 2018) and the "2020 ruling" (*Theidon v. Harvard University and the President and Fellows of Harvard College*, Appeal from the US District Court for the District of Massachusetts, No. 18-1279, Redacted Opinion, Jan. 31, 2020). Unless otherwise noted, the details I used are from the sections of the documents described as the "undisputed facts" (2018 ruling) or the "Factual Bearings" (2020 ruling). This detail is from the 2018 ruling, pp. 6–7.
384 when she started at Harvard, there was only one tenured woman: 2018 ruling, p. 4; 2020 ruling, p. 8.
384 She blogged and tweeted...allowed a student to distribute leaflets: 2018 ruling, p. 10.
384 group dedicated to "dismantling the rape culture on campus": "Our Harvard Can Do Better" website.
384 "There was never a moment when": "Professor Files Charge Alleging University Violated Title IX in Denying Her Tenure," *Harvard Crimson*, Apr. 18, 2014.
384 promoted to associate professor: 2018 ruling, p. 5.
384 an "honor richly deserved": 2020 ruling, p. 7.

384 Anthropology department voted in favor: 2018 ruling, p. 13.
384 *Crimson* published an article: "Sexual Assault at Harvard," *Harvard Crimson*, Mar. 7, 2013.
384 Harvard's lagging sexual assault policy: Per this article, Harvard lags behind peer institutions in its hesitance to adopt an affirmative consent policy and its adjudication of cases on a "sufficiently persuaded" standard vs. "preponderance of evidence" basis, which Princeton and Harvard are alone among the Ivies for insisting on.
384 Theidon knew that "Julie" had read the comments: "Professor Files Charge Alleging University Violated Title IX in Denying Her Tenure," *Harvard Crimson*, Apr. 18, 2014.
384 former graduate student: 2020 ruling, p. 33.
384 who now worked for the department: 2018 ruling, p. 16.
384 inappropriate behavior: 2018 ruling, p. 16.
384 by a senior male Anthropology professor: Here through "I can take care of this," from 2020 ruling, p. 33.
385 Harvard convened Theidon's *ad hoc* committee: 2020 ruling, p. 27. Details of who was on her committee from 2018 ruling, pp. 18–19.
385 Harvard's elaborate eight-step process: 2018 ruling pp. 2–3; 2020 ruling, starting on p. 10.
385 behind closed doors: 2018 ruling, p. 3 notes that the *ad hoc* committee discussion is "strictly confidential."
385 "is an invitation to abuse": "Tenured Women Battle to Make It Less Lonely at the Top," *Science*, n.s., 286, no. 5443 (Nov. 12, 1999): 1272–1278.

385 Singer did take notes: 2020 ruling, p. 27.

385 "unenthusiastic tenor": 2020 ruling, p. 27.

385 letters solicited from external reviewers: For more detail on this, see 2018 ruling, pp. 2–3.

385 Even the most positive of these letters came with commentary: Per 2020 ruling, p. 17, "External scholars described Theidon as a 'first-rate, brilliant and original scholar,' 'whose name came to the top of the list of young scholars who will soon be shaping the field.' Notwith-standing the encomium, even the most positive reviews came with commentary on Theidon's productivity."

385 not been sent copies of Theidon's articles about Colombia: The 2020 ruling notes that though physical copies of the Colombia articles were not included in the material distributed to external scholars, Theidon's website did contain links to PDFs of three of them (p. 17).

385 A Harvard dean, who had read previous drafts of the statement..."major mistake": 2020 ruling, pp. 23–25. Dean Marsden felt that the "reservations about Theidon's scholarly productivity would have been reduced or eliminated if [the external schol-ars] had received copies of Theidon's Colombia related research article.

385 simply the result of "miscommunication": 2020 ruling, p. 24 n. 22.

385 some reason, still unknown: 2018 ruling, p. 18.

385 less favorable penultimate draft: While this is true, it should be noted that the penultimate draft did include text responsive to Marsden's concerns (2018 ruling, p. 15).

385 ad hoc committee recommended against: 2020 ruling, p. 29.

386 President Drew Faust agreed with that recom-mendation: 2018 ruling, p. 21.

386 Theidon set up a meeting with Judith Singer: Note: this paragraph is not taken from the "Factual Bearings" section of the 2020 court ruling. It is in the section assessing Theidon's retaliation claims: p. 66 n. 41.

386 "This is about silencing a problem": "Professor Files Charge Alleging University Violated Title IX in Denying Her Tenure," Harvard Crimson, Apr. 18, 2014.

386 "The University would never": "Professor Files Charge."

386 granted tenure at Tufts in 2015: "Former Pro-fessor Suing University Granted Tenure at Tufts," Harvard Crimson, Apr. 3, 2015.

386 Theidon had lost her suit: In both the 2018 and 2020 rulings, the courts considered evidence of general discrimination against women in the An-thropology department, but concluded that such evidence, even if indicative of general bias, was insufficient to prove discriminatory intent in Thei-don's specific case. The distribution of the wrong draft of her case statement and the omission of her Colombia articles was, at most, an "administrative error" (2020 ruling, p. 46). In terms of retaliation, while a member of Theidon's tenure review com-mittee had been alerted about Theidon's Crimson comments (2018 ruling, p. 16), there was no evi-dence that her "activities" were discussed during the ad hoc committee (2018 ruling, p. 37), or that President Faust was aware of them when she made the final decision (2020 ruling, p. 55). Temporal proximity, they ruled, was not enough to establish motive (2018 ruling, p. 37).

386 When I tried to reach Professor Theidon for comment: Email to Kimberly Theidon, Mar. 26, 2018, 1:32 p.m.

386 On college campuses nation-wide: "Statement: Update on My Title IX Lawsuit," Kimberly Thei-don's website, Jan. 31, 2020.

386 in May 2020, the Crimson published: "Pro-tected by Decades-Old Power Structures, Three Renowned Harvard Anthropologists Face Allega-tions of Sexual Harassment," Harvard Crimson, May 29, 2020.

SEPTEMBER 9, 2018: THE TREE

387 Don tells me that he's decided: This chapter is from phone call with Don Mitchell in 2018.

387 prominently in Hawaiian mythology: "The Cultural Significance of 'Ōhi'a Lehua," Hawai'i Magazine, Apr. 11, 2016.

387 sends the video to me: Email from Don Mitchell, Sept. 10, 2018, 10:36 p.m.

388 [Photo]: Photograph by Don Mitchell.

OCTOBER 28, 2018: HE ESCAPES WHO IS NOT PURSUED

389 In February 2018, for the first time in months: Phone call with Fulkerson, Feb. 13, 2018.

389 he calls me back: Phone call with Fulkerson, Oct. 24, 2018.

389 We meet at a café: The rest of this chapter

is from this 2018 interview with Fulkerson unless otherwise noted.

391 [Photo]: Photograph by Becky Cooper.

392 The crime scene had seemed staged: This tracks with Deputy O'Connor, "Cold Case" Homicides, Nov. 4, 1996 (CPD file): "There were several aspects of the crime scene that appeared to be staged."

392 Fred Centrella, who hadn't wanted to speak: Interview with Fidele Centrella in 2018.

392 when I spoke to the younger Giacoppo: Interview with Michael D. Giacoppo in 2018.

393 I email the son for advice: Email to Michael D. Giacoppo, Oct. 30, 2018, 3:52 p.m.

393 Mike replies the next day: Email from Michael D. Giacoppo, Oct. 31, 2018, 9:26 a.m.

393 I send Mike four questions: Email to Michael D. Giacoppo, Oct. 31, 2018, 10:17 a.m.

NOVEMBER 2018: SHIFTS

394 an email from the DA's communications director: Email from Meghan Kelly, Nov. 15, 2018, 6:33 p.m.

394 bother feigning surprise when we speak: Phone call with Meghan Kelly in 2018.

REACTIONS

394 All phone calls in 2018, unless otherwise noted.

395 He writes a gentle email to Alice: Email from Stephen Loring to Alice Abraham, Nov. 19, 2018, 12:33 p.m.

395 Alice writes instantly to Patricia: Interview with Alice Abraham in 2020.

395 I also get an email from Mary McCutcheon:

Email from Mary McCutcheon, Nov. 19, 2018, 6:01 p.m.

395 "The overactive pattern-recognition part": Email from Mary McCutcheon, Feb. 26, 2020, 9:12 p.m.

395 Ted Abraham, Anne's brother, writes: Email from Ted Abraham, Nov. 20, 2018, 7:31 p.m.

NOVEMBER 20, 2018: PRESS CONFERENCE

399 statement's already been released: "Statement from Boyd Britton, Released by Request on His Behalf by the Middlesex District Attorney's Office," posted on MDAO website Nov. 20, 2018.

400 [Photo]: Jane Britton police file.

401 attended first grade in the area: Per Sumpter DOC 4, p. 113, he also attended kindergarten in the area.

401 He had run-ins with the Cambridge cops as a juvenile: Michael Sumpter CORI, p. 6 (MDAO file).

401 girlfriend in the late '60s lived in the neighborhood: I have not been able to find a document that corroborates this. In a November 2019 interview, ADA Lynch added that it was the same woman whose name he had tattooed on his arm ("Regina" and "R.M.," per Sumpter DOC 4, p. 250). While "Regina" did live in Cambridge, I believe he was dating a different woman at the time (Sumpter DOC 3, p. 108).

401 an establishment on Arrow Street: Matheson Higgins Die-Cutting Company, 12 Arrow Street. In 2018, Don Mitchell said he wasn't familiar with the shop, and wasn't aware that Jane had ever gone there.

402 at the Harvard Square T stop: Sumpter DOC 4, p. 175.

402 he was 170 pounds, six foot one: During the press conference, DA Ryan cited his height and weight from a 1972 arrest report: five foot eleven, 185 pounds. I substituted these measurements for ones closer from a January 12, 1970 arrest report.

402 witness was seven years old: Report by Det. Centrella (Priscilla Joyce interview), Jan. 7, 1969 (CPD file).

402 Don Mitchell had entered: Report of Statement by Donald Mitchell, Jan. 7, 1969 (CPD file).

402 writes to the Abraham family: Email from Adrienne Lynch to Ted and Alice Abraham, Nov. 20, 2018, 5:47 p.m.

403 [Photo]: Photograph by Becky Cooper.

403 helped drive the investigation to this conclusion: Mike Widmer's initial public records request to the MDAO was Nov. 5, 2015; mine was July 18, 2016. In her checking response (2020), ADA Lynch wrote that she became involved in reviewing the Britton file in 2016. That said, of course, ADA Lynch's tireless dedication, as well as Sgt. Sennott's detective work and the MSP Crime Lab's analyses, deserve a huge amount of credit.

405 [Photo]: Photograph by Becky Cooper.

THE FILES

406 The autopsy: Autopsy Report, Drs. George Katsas and Arthur McGovern (MSP file).

406 letter that Gramly wrote: Letter from RMG to CPD Keeper of the Records, Aug. 31, 1995 (CPD file).

406 Photos of the crime scene: "Color Slides of Crime Scene" (CPD file).

406 The original Cambridge cops' notes: E.g., Report to Lt. Davenport by Officer James Lyons, Jan. 7, 1969; and Report to Lt. Davenport by Officer Dennis McCarthy, Jan. 7, 1969 (CPD files).

406 Lieutenant Joyce's investigation: E.g., Report to Daniel I. Murphy, Captain of Detectives by Det. Lt. Joyce of MSP, June 2, 1969.

406 the chemist's report: Report of Asst. Chemist Joseph Lanzetta, Apr. 1, 1969 (MSP file).

406 the trail of renewed interest in the case: E.g., Adrienne Lynch, "Additional Notes ADA on Investigation 2017," undated (MDAO file).

406 The pictures from the funeral: Cambridge Police photos from funeral (CPD file).

406 RCMP report on Anne Abraham's disappearance: E.g., Transcript of Interview between Cst. W.W. MacDonald & RMG, Nain, Labrador, Aug. 11, 1976.

406 sent to her high school friend Irene duPont: Letter from Jane to Irene (duPont) Light, Jan. 4, 1969; forwarded to the Cambridge Police on Jan. 16, 1969 (CPD file); interview with Irene Light in 2016.

406 Don, Boyd, Jim Humphries, Karl Lamberg-Karlovsky, and…Peter Ganick: Respectively, Report to Det. Lt. Sullivan by Sgt. Sennott re: Donald Mitchell, July 18, 2017; Report cover sheet to Det. Lt. Sullivan by Sgt. Sennott re: Boyd Britton, July 18, 2017; Report by Sgt. Sennott re: Jim Humphries, Oct. 12, 2017; Report by Sgt. Sennott re: CCLK, Jan. 8, 2018; Report by Sgt. Sennott re: Peter Ganick, Oct. 3, 2017 (MSP file).

406 excluded as possible sources: Boyd, Don Mitchell, and RMG excluded in Report 4, MSP Crime Lab, Oct. 3, 2017; Peter Ganick, Jim Humphries, and CCLK excluded in Report 5, MSP Crime Lab, Feb. 12, 2018 (MDAO file).

406 Lee Parsons could not be excluded: Here, to end of paragraph, from ADA Lynch response to checking memo (2020). Since all males in a paternal line are expected to have the same Y chromosome DNA, if Parsons had a full male relative, authorities could have tested that relative's Y-DNA and compared it to the profile developed from the crime scene sample. If the relative's Y chromosome did not match, then Parsons could have been

excluded as a contributor. Lee had no sons, however, and his brother was deceased. Another option considered was testing his ex-wife and daughter's autosomal DNA and comparing it to the three-loci profile from 1998, but this would have required comparing DNA tested using different kits/instrumentation, which Bode Labs was unable to do. A specialist familiar with both kits would be needed to perform this kind of "legacy analysis."

406 autopsy slides in 1998: Dr. Katsas: Letter from George Katsas to John McEvoy (Office of the District Attorney), Feb. 20, 1988 (MDAO file).

406 CODIS link with Michael Sumpter in July 2018: Letter to Sgt. Sennott from Dorothea Sidney Collins (MSP Crime Lab), July 16, 2018.

407 brother was eliminated as a possible source of the DNA: The CODIS link to Michael Sumpter in July was the result of a manual comparison between the Y profile from the crime scene and the Y profile of the available CODIS reference sample for Michael Sumpter (2020 checking memo response from Darina Griffin, MSP's legal counsel). But by Massachusetts law (MGL c. 22E), the CODIS sample could only be used for investigatory purposes. For further adjudication, investigators needed to get a non-CODIS sample. Because Michael was already dead and cremated, the only way to get a comparable Y chromosome sample was to test that of a full male relative. Using "a variety of databases including Ancestry.com" (2020 Adrienne Lynch checking response), Sgt. Sennott was able to track down Michael's brother Nathaniel and obtain a DNA sample with his consent. As expected with full brothers, Nathaniel and Michael's Y profiles matched. To disambiguate the brothers, authorities looked at Nathaniel's autosomal DNA and compared it to the 1998 profile with the help of Charlotte Word, who performed the legacy analysis (Report of Dr. Charlotte Word, Sept. 3, 2018 [MSP file]). Unlike Michael's, Nathaniel's did not match the 1998 profile, therefore, Nathaniel could be eliminated as a contributor to the crime scene DNA. (Note: the police files do not include the original electropherograms, so I have been unable to verify this for myself or to get a second opinion from a forensic expert. My public records request was denied on Mar. 25, 2020. I am still pushing.)

407 DNA testing reports starting in 2017: DNA Testing Report 1, July 18, 2017; DNA Testing Report 2, July 31, 2017; DNA Testing Report 3, Oct. 3, 2017; DNA Testing Report 4, Feb. 12, 2018; DNA Testing Report 5, July 23, 2018. All MSP Crime Lab (MDAO file).

407 Mass State Police analyst named Cailin Drugan: Drugan did not receive permission from her supervisors to speak with me. Instead, David Procopio, the MSP press secretary, responded, "We are going to decline to make anyone from our lab available to discuss the Cambridge homicide. The ultimate decision here was in keeping with our position (and that of the scientific community generally) is to let the work speak for itself" (email, Jan. 10, 2020, 3:42 p.m.). The MSP crime lab did, however, participate in the checking phase of the project, responding through Darina Griffin, the MSP's legal counsel.

407 desire to continue being assigned to Jane's case: Per the MSP legal counsel's response, Drugan "did not have a stake in being assigned the case, or in the resulting work." The legal counsel wanted me to understand that it is common for the same analyst to perform multiple rounds of testing. This pushback notwithstanding, I have kept in this detail because I am quoting two emails in the MDAO file: Email from Sharon Convery to Brian Cunningham, July 19, 2017, 6:51 a.m.: "FYI—Cailin said she would be available to take this" and email from Brian Cunningham to Lynn Schneeweis, July 20, 2017, 10:29 a.m.: "I know Cailin was hoping to perform the testing on this case." ADA Lynch also wrote in her checking response: "Cailin (Drugan) wanted to do round 2 testing in this batch."

407 skin cells on the test tube: Nov. 2019 interview with ADA Lynch. The MSP's legal counsel underlined that Drugan's identification of additional testing is "a standard determination that analysts address as part of any case" (2020 checking memo response).

407 the DNA profile in October 2017: DNA Testing Report 3, Oct. 3, 2017 (MDAO file). It should be noted that the result obtained in this lab report was consistent with both a major and a minor contributor. Michael Sumpter's DNA matched the major contributor. Boyd, Don, Jim, Peter Ganick, RMG, and CCLK were all ruled out as contributors—i.e., they were neither the major nor minor contributor. To date, the minor contributor has not been identified. In a November 2019 interview, ADA Lynch stated that it was likely contamination from the medical examiner, since standards were different back then (forensic DNA testing wouldn't become standard for two decades). It is also possible that the minor contributor was an artifact of analysis, or DNA from someone else Jane had been in contact with before she died. Y profiles cannot be searched in CODIS. Even after talking to many DNA experts, I don't have enough information to explain the significance (or the lack thereof) of

the minor contributor. Sgt. William Doogan confirmed that there was no second male contributor in either Rutchick's or McClain's cases.

407 helped bring ADA Lynch's attention: 2020 Lynch checking response; Chronology of DNA collection, Oct. 22, 2018 (MDAO file).

407 keyboard search: This, as well as "verbally informed" from Chronology of DNA Investigation, Oct. 29, 2018 (MDAO file). I asked the MSP Crime Lab if there were other "soft hits" in 2004, since the keyboard search was of the three-loci 1998 profile. The legal counsel responded, "The documentation associated with the case speaks for itself. We cannot comment further other than what is documented in the file."

407 requests for police records: E.g., Fax re: Michael Sumpter history with Brookline PD, Feb. 27, 2004 (MSP file).

407 tried, unsuccessfully, to locate Michael's brother: 2005 Crim. History report re: Nathaniel Sumpter for Tpr Sennott (MSP file). Confirmed in November 2019 interview with ADA Lynch.

407 In a summary of the case, Lynch admits: "Adrienne Lynch, Additional Notes ADA on Investigation 2017," undated (MDAO file). As ADA Lynch elaborated in her 2020 checking response, "Y-STR testing was validated for forensic work by 2003, therefore, it 'arguably' could have been done. That being said the kits used in DNA testing in 200[4] versus 2018 tested less loci and the instrumentation was not as refined as instrumentation used in 2018 when the profile from the vaginal swab extract was obtained. We sometimes forego immediate testing anticipating advances in the science in the future. Doing so here was a benefit."

407 his police records: Sumpter DOC 1 through 4.

407 Sumpter was born in Boston: Michael Sumpter death certificate (MSP file).

407 the middle child of three: MDAO profile on Michael Sumpter, Oct 2, 2018 (MSP file).

407 divorced when he was six: Sumpter DOC 3, p. 116.

407 in and out of mental institutions: Nathaniel Sumpter DOC, p. 5.

407 their maternal grandparents: Sumpter DOC 3, p. 116.

407 Old Harbor Housing Project: Sumpter DOC 4, p. 155.

407 where Whitey Bulger: "Whitey Bulger's Death Marks the End of an Era in South Boston," *Business Insider*, Nov. 1, 2018.

408 age of fifteen in 1963 for larceny: Sumpter DOC 4, p. 114.

408 two months after his eighteenth birthday: Sumpter DOC 4, p. 157.

408 "He appears [to be] quite impulse-ridden": Sumpter DOC 4, p. 162.

408 worked in Harvard Square: Here through "stolen credit card," from Nathaniel Sumpter DOC, p. 30.

408 "things will be different this time": Sumpter DOC 4, p. 114.

408 live with his brother in Boston: Sumpter DOC 4, p. 240.

408 Massachusetts law went further than most: "Most States Allow Furloughs from Prison," *Washington Post*, June 24, 1988. See also "Willie Horton Revisited," *The Marshall Project*, May 13, 2015.

408 "beyond reproach": Sumpter DOC 3, p. 106.

408 "always a gentleman": Sumpter DOC 4, p. 30.

408 "should lock him up": Details and dialogue from Sumpter DOC 4, p. 97.

408 released as scheduled: Sumpter DOC 4, p. 96. Disciplinary report issued Dec. 2, 1971. Sumpter released Dec. 17, 1971.

408 Sumpter attacked the woman: Jan. 24, 1972, per Sumpter DOC 4, p. 175.

409 granted a twelve-hour furlough: Sumpter DOC 3, p. 55.

409 robbery and attempted assault: Sumpter DOC 3, p. 7.

409 On August 2, instead of showing up to work: Sumpter DOC 3, p. 55.

409 In 1985, he walked away from his first day: Sumpter DOC 2, p. 249.

409 Hal Ross, Jane's tutor sophomore year: CPD-IK, p. 26.

410 "circle line...which is run": CPD-SW, p. 3.

410 "Mixture of black and red iron salts": Report of Asst. Chemist Joseph Lanzetta, Apr. 1, 1969 (MSP file).

410 ochre is an *oxide*, not a salt: Helwig chapter in Berrie's *Artists' Pigments*, pp. 39–109; interview with Narayan Khandekar in 2020.

410 According to Lee, they never even kissed: CPD-LK 2, p. 13.

410 it was a child's construction set: CPD-LK 2, pp. 19–20.

410 women's underwear found in Jane's bathroom: Report of Asst. Chemist Joseph Lanzetta, Apr. 1, 1969, pp. 3–4 (MSP file).

410 the underwear was lost: Email from Cailin Drugan to Sharon Convery and Lynn Scheeweis, "Other than the slides, no other items of evidence (ie. pillow, nightgown), exist," July 18, 2017, 2:28 p.m. (MDAO file).

411 three weeks before she died: Dec. 17, 1968 per Adrienne Lynch, "Additional Notes ADA on Investigation 2017," undated (MDAO file).

411 fingerprint that Don had taken a picture of: See earlier note in section 4 re: photo of fingerprint and Don's tripod.

411 transcript from Sergeant Sennott's conversation: Don Mitchell interview transcript with Sergeant Sennott, July 17, 2017, p. 181 (MSP file).

411 threaded throughout the files: CPD-SLI pp. 53–54; CPD-IK, p. 37; CPD-LP 1, p. 14; letter from Jane to Jim Humphries, June 4, 1968 (CPD file); Jane's journal entries from June 6, June 7, June 14/15, and June 28, 1968.

411 "It's very difficult to get caught": Letter from Jane to Jim Humphries, June 4, 1968 (CPD file).

411 Jane's parents mentioning an illness: Jane's parents report that she was not under treatment by a physician (Report to Lt. Davenport by Officer James Lyons, Jan. 7, 1969).

411 When I ask Boyd and Elisabeth Handler: Interviews with Boyd and Elisabeth Handler in 2019.

411 Don says it "rings some distant bell": Interview with Don Mitchell in 2019.

411 Ingrid Kirsch, who relayed to police: CPD-IK, p. 37.

412 Robert Skenderian, a compounding pharmacist: Interview with Robert Skenderian in 2020.

412 has been in the area for three generations: "About Us," Skenderian Apothecary website.

JANUARY 14, 1969: LEE PARSONS INTERROGATION

412 Excerpt of CPD-LP 1.

UNSATISFIED

413 Iva Houston questions the timing: Interview with Iva Houston in 2018.

413 "I heard that the 'killer'": Email from RMG, Jan. 2, 2019, 9:19 a.m.

413 "I just think there's something strange here": Interview with RMG in 2019.

413 "You don't just have piles of powder": Interview with Narayan Khandekar in 2020.

413 a fiftieth the width of a human hair: Dave Kleiman, *The Official CHFI Study Guide (Exam 312-49) for Computer Hacking Forensics Investigators* (Burlington, MA: Syngress Publishing, 2007), p. 67.

413 "Circle line which is run just across her back":
CPD-SW, p. 3.

414 John Fulkerson joins the chorus of doubt:
Interview with Fulkerson in 2018.

414 small note on the October 2017: DNA Testing
Report 3, Oct. 3, 2017 (MDAO file).

414 all excluded as possibilities: RMG, Boyd, and
Don Mitchell excluded in DNA Testing Report
3, Oct. 3, 2017; CCLK, Peter Ganick, and Jim
excluded in DNA Testing Report 4, Feb. 13, 2018
(MDAO files).

414 According to the Middlesex district attorney's
office: Nov. 2019 interview with DA Marian Ryan,
ADA Adrienne Lynch, and Sgt. Sennott.

415 Sgt. Doogan confirms: Interview with Sgt.
William Doogan in 2019.

415 Massachusetts State Police deny my request:
Letter from Darina Griffin of the MSP Crime
Laboratory, March 25, 2020.

415 told that I would not be allowed to speak
with: Email from David Procopio (MSP director
of media communication), January 10, 2020,
3:42 p.m.

415 anyone else in the MSP crime lab: It should
be noted that the MSP crime laboratory did
participate in the checking process for the book,
responding through its legal counsel, Darina
Griffin.

415 Boyd had told me on the call: Interview with
Boyd in 2018.

GIACOPPO

415 On May 27, 1969, Lieutenant Frank Joyce:
All details in this chapter, including dialogue, are
drawn from Report to Daniel I. Murphy, Captain
of Detectives by Det. Lt. Joyce of MSP, June 2, 1969
(MSP file), unless otherwise noted.

416 anonymous tip implicating someone named
Dr. Paul Rhudick: Here through end of follow-
ing paragraph from Report of Det. Lt. Charles
Byrne of MSP re: James Powers, May 23, 1969
(MSP file).

416 Dover police received a call: Paragraph from
Report of Dover Officer George Michel re: Cecelia
Powers call, May 5, 1969 (MSP file).

416 Four days later, Cecelia called: Report of Dover
Officer (unnamed) re: Search for James Powers,
May 11, 1969 (MSP file).

416 Cambridge police got permission to fingerprint: Report of Det. Lt. Charles Byrne of MSP
re: James Powers, May 23, 1969, p. 3 (MSP
file). Permission received from Medical Examiner
Dr. Joseph King.

416 May 15, Massachusetts State Police confirmed:
Report of Det. Lt. Charles Byrne of MSP re: James
Powers, May 23, 1969, p. 3 (MSP file).

416 matched the left thumbprint of the late veterinarian: Report of Lt. David Desmond re: thumb
print on ashtray, May 29, 1969 (MSP file).

417 [Photo]: Jane Britton police file.

417 However, the day that Lieutenant Joyce:
Paragraph, including "strongly suspected" and
"planted" from Report to Daniel I. Murphy, Captain of Detectives by Det. Lt. Joyce of MSP, June 2,
1969 (MSP file).

417 interviewed Cecelia Powers at her home:

Report of Det. Lt. Joyce re: Antigua travel, May 23,
1969 (MSP file).

417 Officers had obtained a search warrant: Report
of Dover Sgt. Carl Sheridan re: Search Powers,
May 16, 1969.

417 check...to Travel Services Bureau: Report of
Det. Lt. Joyce re: Antigua travel, May 23, 1969
(MSP file).

417 evening connecting flight to Boston: Report
of Det. Lt. Joyce re: Antigua travel, May 23, 1969
(MSP file).

418 run by Frank Powers's sister: Report re: silver
plated ashtray by Det. Lt. Joyce, May 23, 1969
(MSP file).

418 including with steel wool: Report re: silver
plated ashtray by Det. Lt. Joyce, May 23, 1969
(MSP file).

418 fingerprinted Powers...Needham funeral
home: Report of Det. Lt. Charles Byrne of MSP
re: James Powers, May 23, 1969 (MSP file).

418 expert failed to find Powers's fingerprints:
Report of Lt. David Desmond re: thumb print on
ashtray, May 29, 1969 (MSP file).

418 a lot of people had handled the ashtray: Exchange from Report of Lt. David Desmond re:
thumb print on ashtray, May 29, 1969 (MSP file).

419 "CONCLUSION: The blackish impression":
Report of Asst. Chemist Melvin Topjian re: ashtray, May 30, 1969 (MSP file).

419 convinced beyond a shadow of a doubt: Letter
from Det. Lt. Joyce to Cecelia Powers, Dec. 3,
1969 (MSP file).

CRUMBS

420 Lieutenant Joyce issued his report: Report to Daniel I. Murphy, Captain of Detectives by Det. Lt. Joyce of MSP, June 2, 1969 (MSP file).

420 "an unwaiverable conflict of interest": Letter from DA Martha Coakley to Commissioner Ronnie Watson (CPD), Aug. 23, 2005 (MDAO file).

420 Fulkerson, who says he was kept in the dark: Interview with Fulkerson in 2018.

420 Connolly's notes: Notes of Det. Lt. Connolly re: M. Michael Giacoppo, Oct. 4, 2005 (MSP file).

420 Four years ago, Boyd told me: Interview with Boyd Britton in 2014.

421 Adrienne Lynch herself spelled out: "Additional Notes ADA on Investigation 2017," undated (MDAO file).

421 our 2018 phone call: Interview with Michael D. Giacoppo in 2018.

421 responsible for overseeing the investigations and records units: CPD Annual Crime Reports for 2004 to 2006 lists Michael D. Giacoppo as the Superintendent of Support Services for all three years; the CPD website breaks down the responsibilities of this superintendent.

421 "two-generation commitment": Interview with Mary McCutcheon in 2017.

421 Any evidence that Giacoppo was even suspended: I spoke to Philip Cronin in 2019, Cambridge city solicitor at the time, who said he was never consulted about the alleged misconduct even though Chief Reagan said as much in Joyce's report. Cronin was more comfortable concluding the report was wrong about Reagan's actions than the possibility that he misremembered fifty years later. Therefore, I do not feel comfortable taking Reagan's word in Joyce's report about Giacoppo's suspension without corroboration.

421 president of the Massachusetts Association of Italian American Police Officers: E.g., "Welcome to the 45th Annual Massachusetts Italian American Police Officers Association Awards Banquet," Oct. 19, 2013, p. 6.

422 leadership of the Middlesex County Deputy Sheriff's Association: *The Guardian: A Publication of the Middlesex Deputy Sheriff's Association*, Jan. 2010, lists M. Michael Giacoppo as president, p. 2.

422 teach a fingerprinting course: *The Guardian: A Publication*, p. 18.

422 lifetime achievement award: "Mass Association of Italian American Police Officers Lifetime Achievement Awarded to Mike Giacoppo," *Somerville News Weekly*, Dec. 8, 2018.

MYTHMAKING

422 I got an email from Brian Wood: Email from Brian Wood, Aug. 3, 2018, 4:23 p.m.

DECEMBER 2018: KARL

423 Karl and I walk gingerly: This chapter is from an interview with CCLK (Dec. 6, 2018) unless otherwise noted.

424 Reich's work…is controversial: "Is Ancient DNA Research Revealing New Truths—or Falling

into Old Traps?" *New York Times Magazine*, Jan. 17, 2019.

RECONSTRUCTION

426 "If the identity of the suspect": Email from Boyd Britton to Peter Sennott, Aug. 13, 2018, 6:59 a.m.

427 cellar door…still unlocked: "Harvard Defends Housing," *Boston Globe*, Jan. 12, 1969. Per article, this door led to the back staircase.

427 the candles in Jane's candelabrum: Report of Asst. Chemist Joseph Lanzetta, Apr. 1, 1969 (MSP file).

427 climbed the back stairwell: Per Arthur Bankoff's statement, p. 19, "Jane surprised me

once…by walking along the fire escape to my window. Anyone could have come in that way, via the back stairs to the fire escape door behind our apartment and thence to Jane's."

427 As described in a police report: "Report from M/M Stephen Presser (table leg)," Jan. 14, 1969 (CPD file).

427 That door opened into Jane's kitchen: Scene scale diagram, Det. Edward Colleran, Jan. 8, 1969 (CPD file).

427 trace of grease on her right hand: This and

"twist of wool" from Report of Asst. Chemist Joseph Lanzetta, Apr. 1, 1969 (MSP file).
427 contusion on her right arm: Autopsy Report, Drs. George Katsas and Arthur McGovern (MSP file).

427 the greasy frying pan and the kitchen sink: Report of Asst. Chemist Joseph Lanzetta, Apr. 1, 1969 (MSP file).
428 [Photo]: Jane Britton police file.

JANE SANDERS BRITTON

428 what would have been Jane's seventy-third birthday: May 17, 2018.
428 Boyd asked for a picture of the grave: Email from Boyd, May 11, 2018, 1:37 p.m.
428 Don asked me to read a note to her: Email from Don Mitchell, May 11, 2018, 2:58 p.m.
429 VIGIL HOPES TO HEAL: "Vigil Hopes to Heal after Hate Incident," *Needham Times*, May 17, 2018.
429 "You'll find her eventually": Dan Bear, in 2017.
429 Elisabeth had emailed: Email from Elisabeth Handler, May 17, 2018, 12:05 p.m.
432 [Photo]: Photograph by Becky Cooper.
432 When I had spoken to Iva Houston: Interview with Iva Houston in 2017.
433 restorative justice, restorative methodology:

For restorative justice from an anthropological perspective, see Ann Kingsolver, "Everyday Reconciliation," *American Anthropologist* 115, no. 4 (Dec. 2013): 663–666.
433 I'm down to my very last MSP file in the stack: This scene took place on Dec. 29, 2018.
433 "*Book 1 1968*. J.S. Britton. British Inst of Persian Studies Box 2167. Tehran IRAN": MSP file.
434 "*Jim*," it begins: From here to end, Jane's journal entry, June 6, 1968.
434 [Photo]: Jane Britton police file.

ABOUT THE AUTHOR

Becky Cooper is a former *New Yorker* editorial staff member and Senior Fellow of Brandeis's Schuster Institute for Investigative Reporting. Her undergraduate thesis, a literary biography of David Foster Wallace, won Harvard's Hoopes Prize, the highest undergraduate award for research and writing. She is also the author of *Mapping Manhattan: A Love (and Sometimes Hate) Story in Maps by 75 New Yorkers* (Abrams, 2013). Research for this book was supported by the Fund for Investigative Journalism and the International Women's Media Foundation's Howard G. Buffett Fund for Women Journalists.